language
skills in
elementary
education

language skills in elementary education

second edition

Paul S. Anderson
Professor of Education
San Diego State College

The Macmillan Company, New York
Collier-Macmillan Limited, London

THE MACMILLAN COMPANY
866 THIRD AVENUE, NEW YORK, NEW YORK 10022
COLLIER-MACMILLAN CANADA, LTD., TORONTO, ONTARIO

Library of Congress catalog card number: 75–151692

First Printing

ACKNOWLEDGMENTS

Grateful acknowledgment is made to the following for permission to use excerpts from the copyrighted works cited.

ABINGDON PRESS From *The Right Play for You* by Bernice Wells Carlson. Copyright © 1960 by Abingdon Press.

ALLYN AND BACON, INC. "Cooperative Poetry—A Creative Project," by S. G. Gilburt in *Language Art News,* Fall 1957.

AMERICAN BOOK COMPANY *Composition Through Literature* by H. T. Fillmer et al., 1967.

APPLETON-CENTURY-CROFTS, INC. *Teaching English Grammar* by Robert C. Pooley. Copyright 1957 by Appleton-Century-Crofts, Inc. Reprinted by permission of the publisher, Appleton-Century-Crofts.

ASSOCIATION FOR CHILDHOOD EDUCATION INTERNATIONAL "Helping Children to Create," by Lois Lenski. From *Childhood Education,* November 1949, Vol. 26, No. 3. Reprinted by permission of Lois Lenski and the Association for Childhood Education International, 3615 Wisconsin Avenue, N.W., Washington, D.C. Copyright © 1949 by the Association.

BAY REGION INSTRUCTIONAL TELEVISION FOR EDUCATION "Program Eleven," *Bill Martin's Language Arts Teachers' Manual,* 1967. Used by permission of the publisher and the author.

BENNETT, JOAN RODNEY "Locomotive" by Rodney Bennett, copyright 1941 by Rodney Bennett, reprinted by permison of the author's estate.

BLACKIE & SON, LIMITED "W-O-O-O-O-W!" by Nancy Hayes, from *Silver Book of Children's Verse.*

BROWNE, SALOME "The First Grade Child Not Quite Ready for Beginning Reading Instruction," *Proceedings of Summer Conference,* Vol. XX, Western Washington State College, Bellingham, Washington, January 1968.

WILLIAM C. BROWN COMPANY *Practical Plans for Teaching English in Elementary Schools* by Ruth Drews et al., 1965. Used by permission of the publisher.

THE BRUCE PUBLISHING COMPANY "List A: 350 Most Useful Spelling Words" from *The Teaching of Spelling* by James A. Fitzgerald, pp. 15–17. Copyright © 1951 by James A. Fitzgerald. Used by permison of the publisher.

BURGESS PUBLISHING COMPANY *Resource Materials for Teachers of Spelling* by Paul S. Anderson. Copyright 1964 by Paul S. Anderson. Reprinted by permison of the publisher.

CCM Professional Magazines, Inc. "Slang 20 Years Ago" by Anna McCormic and Norma Dove. Reprinted from the February, 1969, issue of *Grade Teacher* magazine with permission of the publisher. This article is copyrighted. © 1969 by CCM Professional Magazines, Inc. All rights reserved. "Soft Is the Hush of Falling Snow" by Emily Carey Alleman. Reprinted from the March, 1953, issue of *Grade Teacher* magazine with permission of the publisher. This article is copyrighted. © 1953 by CCM Professional Magazines, Inc. All rights reserved. "Icklenoof? Pommoy? Glipped? My Word! What Words Are These?" by Nell Stevenson. Reprinted from the October, 1967, issue of *Grade Teacher* magazine with permission of the publisher. This article is copyrighted. © 1967 by CCM Professional Magazines, Inc. All rights reserved.

University of Chicago Press "Listening in Grades Four Through Eight" by D. M. Mills, in *Reading and the Language Arts,* edited by H. Alan Robinson (1963), pp. 59–61. © 1963 by the University of Chicago.

The Christian Science Publishing Society "Clouds," by Helen Wing, from *The Christian Science Monitor,* reprinted by permission of the publisher.

Dell Publishing Co. Study guide to *Prairie School* by Lois Lenski from *Releasing Children to Literature* by Charles F. Reasoner. Copyright © 1968 by Charles F. Reasoner. Reprinted by permission of the publisher, Dell Publishing Co., Inc.

Doubleday & Company, Inc. *Wag Tail Bess,* by Marjorie Flack, copyright 1933 by Marjorie Flack Larsson, reprinted by permisison of Doubleday & Company, Inc. "Mice," from *Fifty-one Nursery Rhymes,* by Rose Fyleman, copyright 1932 by Doubleday & Company, Inc., reprinted by permission of Doubleday & Company, Inc., and The Society of Authors, London.

Doubleday & Company, Inc., and World's Work Ltd. "The Wonderful Words" and "Antonyms, Synonyms, Homonyms" from *Words, Words, Words* by Mary Le duc O'Neill. Copyright © 1966 by Mary Le duc O'Neill. Reprinted by permission of Doubleday & Company, Inc., and World's Work Ltd.

E. P. Dutton & Co., Inc. "Presents" by Marchette Chute. Copyright 1932, 1960 by Marchette Chute. From the book *Around and About by* Marchette Chute. Copyright © 1957 by E. P. Dutton & Co., Inc., publishers and used with their permission. "Aeroplane" by Mary McB. Green. From the book *Another Here and Now Story Book* by Lucy Sprague Mitchell. Copyright, 1937 by E. P. Dutton & Co., Inc. Renewal, ©, 1965 by Lucy Sprague Mitchell. Published by E. P. Dutton & Co., Inc., and used with their permission.

E. P. Dutton & Co., Inc., and The Bodley Head From the book *My Side of the Mountain* by Jean George. Illus. by the author. Copyright, © 1959 by Jean George. Published by E. P. Dutton & Co., Inc., and used with their permission and that of The Bodley Head.

Expression Company, Publishers "Red Squirrel" by Grace Rowe from *Choral Speaking Arrangements for the Lower Grades* by Louise Abney and Grace Rowe. Copyright 1953. By permission of Expression Company, Publishers, Magnolia, Mass.

Fisher, Aileen "Coffeepot Face," copyright by Aileen Fisher and reprinted by permission of the author.

Follett Educational Corporation *The World of Language,* Book 4, Muriel Crosby, Ed. D., General Editor. Copyright © 1970 by Follett Educational Corporation. Used by permission of Follett Educational Corporation.

Gale Research Company Handwriting examples from *Date Book Calendar.*

Ginn and Company From the *Manual for Teaching the Reading Readiness Program, Revised Edition,* by David Russell et al., of THE GINN BASIC READERS. © Copyright, 1961, by Ginn and Company. Used with permission.

Ginn and Company Ltd. *Impetus to Integrated Studies,* by Bartlett and Bates, 1969.

Harcourt Brace Jovanovich, Inc. "Little Sounds," from *Something Special,* © 1958, by Beatrice de Regniers. Reprinted by permission of Harcourt Brace Jovanovich, Inc. "Trees," from *The Little Hill,* copyright, 1949, by Harry Behn. Reprinted by permission of Harcourt Brace Jovanovich, Inc. "Counting," from *Windy Morning,* copyright, 1953, by Harry Behn. Reprinted by permisison of Harcourt Brace Jovanovich, Inc. "Good Night," from *Smoke and Steel* by Carl Sandburg, copyright, 1920, by Harcourt Brace Jovanovich, Inc.; copyright, 1948, by Carl Sandburg. Reprinted by permission of the publisher. "The Secret Cavern," from *Little Girl and Boy Land* by Margaret Widdemer, copyright, 1924, by Harcourt Brace Jovanovich, Inc.; copyright, 1952, by Margaret Widdemer Schauffler. Reprinted by permission of the publisher. From *The Roberts English Series, Complete Course* by Paul Roberts, copyright © 1967 by Harcourt Brace Jovanovich, Inc., and reprinted with their permission.

HARPER & ROW, PUBLISHERS "The Meal" from *Alexander Soames: His Poems* by Karla Kuskin. Copyright © 1962 by Karla Kuskin. Reprinted with permisison of Harper & Row, Publishers.

HARPER & ROW, PUBLISHERS and LUTTERWORTH PRESS *Farmer Boy* by Laura Ingalls Wilder. Copyright © 1933 by Harper & Brothers. Renewed 1961 by Roger L. MacBride. Reprinted with permission of Harper & Row, Publishers, and Lutterworth Press.

HARVARD EDUCATIONAL REVIEW "Why Children Fail to Read: A Linguistic Analysis," *Harvard Educational Review,* 25 (Spring 1955), pp. 74–76. Copyright © 1955 by the President and Fellows of Harvard College. Used by permission.

D. C. HEATH AND COMPANY. Reprinted by permission of the publisher from H. L. J. Carter and D. J. McGinnis, *Teaching Individuals to Read* (Lexington, Mass.: D. C. Heath and Company, 1962).

HOLT, RINEHART AND WINSTON, INC. and LAURENCE POLLINGER LTD. "Theme in Yellow" from *Chicago Poems* by Carl Sandburg. Copyright 1916 by Holt, Rinehart and Winston, Inc. Copyright 1944 by Carl Sandburg. Reprinted by permission of Holt, Rinehart and Winston, Inc., and Laurence Pollinger Ltd.

THE HORN BOOK, INC. "One Day When We Went Walking," by Valine Hobbs, copyright 1945 by The Horn Book, Inc., reprinted by permission of the publisher.

HOUGHTON MIFFLIN COMPANY "A Prayer for Little Things" by Eleanor Farjeon, copyright 1943 by Houghton Mifflin Company. *Improving Your Language* by Paul McKee, copyright 1957 by Houghton Mifflin Company. *Come Along* Teacher's Manual by Paul McKee, copyright 1957 by Houghton Mifflin Company. *Bright Peaks,* teacher's edition, by Paul McKee, copyright 1958 by Houghton Mifflin Company. *Student Centered Language Arts Curriculum* by James Moffett, copyright 1968 by Houghton Mifflin Company. Reprinted by permission of the publisher.

THE INSTRUCTOR PUBLICATIONS, INC. "Three Cheers for Peter" by Alice Hartich, © 1961, by the Instructor Publications, Inc. Used by permission. "You Can Teach Handwriting with Only Six Rules," by Max Rosenhaus, © 1957, by the Instructor Publications, Inc. Used by permission. "Phonics Clinic" by Selma A. Herr, copyright 1957 by Selma Herr. Used by permission.

INTERNATIONAL READING ASSOCIATION "How to Find Books Children Can Read," by Eldon Ekwall and Ida Heny, *The Reading Teacher,* December, 1968. Reprinted with permission of the authors and the International Reading Association. "Usefulness of Phonic Generalizations," by Lou E. Burmeister, *The Reading Teacher,* January, 1968, pp. 352–56. Reprinted with permission of Lou E. Burmeister and the International Reading Association.

BERTHA KLAUSNER INTERNATIONAL LITERARY AGENCY, INC. "Funny the Way Different Cars Start" by Dorothy Baruch.

LAIDLAW BROTHERS, PUBLISHERS "Song of the Pop-Corn" by Louise Abney, from *On the Way to Storyland,* 1961. "The American Flag" by Louise Abney, from *From Every Land,* book 6, copyright 1961 by Laidlaw Brothers, reprinted by permission of the publisher.

LE CRON, HELEN COWLES *Little Charlie Chipmunk,* reprinted by permission of the author.

J. B. LIPPINCOTT COMPANY *Poetry Therapy* by J. J. Leedy, 1969. "A Letter Is a Gypsy Elf" and "Indian Children" from the book *For Days and Days,* by Annette Wynne. Copyright, 1919, by J. B. Lippincott Company. Renewal, 1947, by Annette Wynne. Reprinted by permission of J. B. Lippincott Company.

LONGMAN GROUP LTD. "Hints on Pronunciation for Foreigners," cited by Macky and Thompson in *Programme in Linguistics and English Teaching,* Paper No. 3, p. 45.

MCCULLOUGH, CONSTANCE M., and PARAGON PUBLICATIONS *Handbook for Teaching the Language Arts,* copyright 1958 by Constance McCullough, reprinted by permission of the author and Paragon Publications.

MCGRAW-HILL BOOK COMPANY *Are You Listening?* by Ralph G. Nichols and Leonard A. Stevens, copyright © 1957 by the McGraw-Hill Book Company, Inc., and Willis Kinsley Wing.

THE MACMILLAN COMPANY "The Cat," from *Menagerie,* by Mary Britton Miller, copyright 1929 by The Macmillan Company, reprinted by permission of the author and publisher.

MASSACHUSETTS INSTITUTE OF TECHNOLOGY PRESS *Psychology and Pedagogy* by E. B. Huey.

University of Minnesota "Finger Plays for Young Children," Leaflet No. 11, reprinted by permission of the Institute of Child Development and Welfare.

National Association of Elementary School Principals "Helping the Disadvantaged Build Language," *National Elementary School Principal,* November 1965. Copyright 1965, National Association of Elementary School Principals, National Education Association. All rights reserved.

National Conference of Christians and Jews, Inc. "Role Playing the Problem Story," by George and Fannie Shaftel, 1952.

National Council of Teachers of English *Language Programs for the Disadvantaged* by Richard Corbin and Muriel Crosby, 1965. Copyright © 1965 by the National Council of Teachers of English. Reprinted by permission of the publisher and Richard Corbin. *Language, Linguistics and School Programs* by Bernard J. Weiss. Copyright © 1963 by the National Council of Teachers of English. Reprinted by permission of the publisher and Bernard J. Weiss. "Instant Enrichment" by Marie E. Taylor, *Elementary English,* February 1968. Copyright © 1968 by the National Council of Teachers of English. Reprinted by permission of the publisher and Marie E. Taylor. "Reading to Meet Emotional Needs" by Paul A. Witty, *Elementary English,* February 1952. Copyright © 1952 by the National Council of Teachers of English. Reprinted by permission of the publisher and Paul A. Witty.

University of Nebraska Press Reprinted from a Curriculum for English Poetry for the Elementary Grades, 1966, by permission of the University of Nebraska Press. Copyright © 1966 by the University of Nebraska Press.

Parker Publishing Company *The Nongraded Primary School* by Lillian Glougau and Murray Fessel, 1967. Used by permission.

Prentice-Hall, Inc. Nila Banton Smith, *Reading Instruction for Today's Children,* © 1963. Reprinted by permission of Prentice-Hall, Inc., Englewood Cliffs, New Jersey.

Random House, Inc. and William Morris Agency, Inc. *Crisis in the Classroom* by Charles E. Silberman (New York: Random House, Inc., 1970). Copyright © 1970 by Charles E. Silberman. Reprinted by permission of Random House, Inc., and William Morris Agency, Inc.

Regents Publishing Company *English as a Second Language: From Theory to Practice,* by Mary Finocchiaro, 1965.

Science Research Associates, Inc. "Listening Skill Builder No. 1," reprinted by permission from the *Instructor's Handbook, SRA Reading Laboratory, IVa,* by Don M. Parker. Copyright 1959, Science Research Associates, Inc.

Scott, Foresman and Company *Language and How to Use It,* books 3 and 4, by Andrew Schiller et al. Copyright © 1969 by Scott, Foresman and Company.

Charles Scribner's Sons and William Heineman Ltd. Reprinted by permission of Charles Scribner's Sons and William Heineman Ltd., from *The Yearling,* page 279, by Marjorie Kinnan Rawlings. Copyright 1938 Marjorie Kinnan Rawlings; renewal copyright © 1966 Norton Baskin.

Sidgwick & Jackson Ltd. "Choosing Shoes," from *The Very Thing,* by ffrida Wolfe, reprinted by permission of the author's representatives and the publishers, Sidgwick & Jackson Ltd.

Tash, Merry Lee "To the Boy That Sits in Front of Me"; "Hobbies"; "Poems"; "Dear Mom"; reprinted by permission of the author and Clover C. Tash and Lloyd C. Tash.

Tucker, Susan "A Question to God," reprinted by permission of Gordon H. Tucker.

H. W. Wilson Company "Helping Children Enjoy Poetry" by May Hill Arbuthnot. Reprinted by permisison from the January 1962 issue of the *Wilson Library Bulletin.* Copyright © 1962 by the H. W. Wilson Company.

Wisconsin Department of Public Instruction *English Language Arts in Wisconsin.*

Yale University Press "Bundles," by John Farrar, from *Songs for Parents,* 1921.

dedication

This book is dedicated to the. four teachers who influenced my interest in the language arts. Elizabeth Russell taught me to be specific in my work. Paul McKee urged me to help children demand meaning from the words they use. Robert Pooley revealed to me the beauty of the English language as it is expressed in literature. Virgil Herrick caused me to question so much that seemed to be fact.

to the student

Teaching in the elementary schools involves hundreds of tasks. No one has ever made an effort to list all of them. Teachers have acquired skill in much the same way that a good parent learns to care for a family or a physician learns to treat his patients. Part of teaching proficiency comes from the memory of the way we were taught, part comes by learning from the experience of others, and part is based upon our own willingness to work at tasks that we feel must be accomplished. A methods course in the language arts is designed to prepare you to teach by having you relate your own childhood efforts to speak, read, and write to those of young learners, to inform you about what others have learned who have worked in this area, and to present ways of working with problems you will face. Some of these problems will have rather specific solutions; others are predicaments that are never completely resolved. Just as the medical profession has been baffled by the common cold, the teaching profession continues to face unsolved problems. But with better teacher training and greater awareness of child psychology, more and more children are learning to read well, write with ease, speak expressively, and think efficiently.

The problems of teaching the language skills provide the basic organization of this book. Chapter 1 describes the place of the language arts in the school curriculum, outlines the interrelationships of language and culture, and has a brief discussion of the children who will learn in our classrooms. These problems are concerned with the reason for doing things rather than with the procedures used in instruction. The following chapters emphasize the many ways teachers accomplish their goals. In these you will be able to detect my own personal philosophy. You will also find suggestions that appear to contradict this point of view. My purpose has been to present many ways to guide the learning of children. Do not hesitate to be critical of ideas and procedures presented in these chapters. Be slow to make judgments, but if some of these ideas and methods are found wanting, cast them aside and seek others.

Throughout the text specific devices, exercises, and activities are suggested. The front line of the educational battle against ignorance is in the classroom where the teacher and learner are face to face. What happens in these classroom experiences must be something read, something written, something learned. Theory is practical in that it helps a teacher determine which of many devices and techniques to use. The great unknown to anyone outside your classroom is a knowledge of the individual child with whom you work. It is your ability to know this child and combine this knowledge with the information of a methods course that will determine your success as a teacher.

P. S. A.

preface

A methods course must be about three major aspects of education. First, there are ideas and facts with respect to the objectives to be accomplished, the history of past efforts, the reasons why things are done as they are, and the people who have dedicated their efforts to the field of study. Second, there are the processes to be achieved. Some, such as handwriting or storytelling, may need further practice by those who would teach them. But the major concern with process is the analysis of those elements in reading, composition, or speech that each learner needs at his present stage of growth. The language arts are basically processes that involve techniques and attitudes basic to success in communication of ideas. Third, the course must provide the beginning teacher with information about the materials available, the means of evaluating their success in use, and practice in creating materials to accomplish the learning objectives of the classroom.

Like medicine or engineering, much that must be done will interest only those who are concerned about the problems to be solved or the project to be accomplished. Much that a physician does is dull or disagreeable unless he is concerned about the illness and welfare of a patient. The same is true of a teacher. It is the children who have a communication problem that causes teachers to seek ways of helping them or to find and create materials and activities to interest the learners enough to put forth the effort to achieve. A great deal is known about how teaching can be effective, but every teacher continues to seek more effective ways to work with learners.

We live in a language-oriented culture; we are word oriented. Mastery of the skills of language is essential to success of an individual in our society. The elementary school must assume the responsibility of assuring each child that by the time he leaves the sixth grade he will be able to learn through language in both its written and oral forms. Subject content, whether it be in literature, science, or social studies, provides the interest, the motivation, and the ideas through which the skills of communication are achieved. Throughout life an individual is able to learn the knowledge needed to make his life meaningful only in terms of his ability to use language skills. Through the skills of communication, students are able to clarify their thoughts, establish goals, plan together, and share ideas with others.

My work has caused me to visit schools in Colorado, Wisconsin, Texas, Tennessee, and California. In these schools I found teachers who were aware of the responsibilities that are the heritage of our children. From these teachers I learned much that is presented here. It was not until my work involved the training of student teachers that the need to bring this information together became apparent. This book is not intended to cover all the subject matter required for teaching the language arts. It is planned to help beginning teachers obtain successful classroom results as they start their teaching careers. With experience more aspects of the language arts will assume importance and, I hope, encourage teachers to become scholars in the true sense, dedicating some of their time and energy to the research needed in this field.

Questions have been asked at the conclusion of the presentation of each topic to encourage evaluation or application of the ideas presented. These may be used for class discussion but are primarily to encourage the student to react to the material and summarize his own ideas.

Although a vast number of books, articles, theses, studies, and reports in the language arts have been consulted in the preparation of these chapters, no attempt has been made to include references to all of them. The implication and application of such knowledge has been stressed throughout the book. A beginning teacher needs not only to know *how* to do her work in this field, but also to understand *why* certain procedures are followed. It is hoped that practice will lead to questioning, questioning to further study, and further study to improvement of instruction in the language arts.

I have learned from so many students, colleagues, and teachers that any list of those to whom I owe a debt of gratitude would be incomplete. All of them, like myself, have been repaid many times as we have watched a child read successfully, respond to a story or poem, write a sincere letter or creative story, or speak effectively in a way that reflected his own personality in a society where each respects the individuality of others.

P. S. A.

table of contents

eight Grammar (Old and New)   413

nine Evaluating and Interpreting the Language Arts Program   463

language
skills in
elementary
education

one

the language skills and the children we teach

The Wonderful Words

Never let a thought shrivel and die
For want of a way to say it,
For English is a wonderful game
And all of you can play it.
All that you do is match the words
To the brightest thoughts in your head
So that they come out clear and true
And handsomely groomed and fed—
For many of the loveliest things
Have never yet been said.
Words are the food and dress of thought,
They give it its body and swing,
And everyone's longing today to hear
Some fresh and beautful thing.
But only words can free a thought
From its prison behind your eyes.
Maybe your mind is holding now
A marvelous new surprise!

MARY O'NEILL

What Are the Skills of Language?

Let us start by thinking together about the miracle of language. A word can cause us to sink into the deepest despair or lift us to inspired behavior. Words we share with our family, community, and country become a bond that unites us.

When a way to write words was discovered, man was no longer dependent upon the memory of listeners; meanings became more uniform and understanding more certain. Written words were a link with all generations to come, and as time passed became man's link with the past. Civilizations have disappeared, leaving only ruins and relics from which we attempt to interpret earlier

1

ways of life; others, though buried under desert sands, seem almost contemporary because of written records, which tell us about their religion, education, business, and even the intimate gossip of their times.

Today more language power has been given man through such developments as television, radio, and the telephone. It is possible for one speaker to have over 100 million listeners. Distance and time are no longer barriers to the use of language. We take for granted such things as intercontinental telephone service and amateur radio operators who talk with others at sea or in other lands. Telstar has added to this power by two-way, intercontinental television transmissions between Europe and the United States.

One of the rewards of teaching is the satisfaction that results from helping a child grow in his ability to communicate ideas in speech and writing. Just as a parent proudly reports the first word the child speaks, so a teacher shares the child's development of a new vocabulary, his first written story, and his achievement when a degree of reading skill has been mastered. And just as a parent worries about the child's future, so are teachers concerned when a child is not competent in his use of language. A student who fails to achieve competence in language faces life with an unfair handicap for which the school must accept responsibility.

In many of our schools the daily program is divided among different subjects; of these reading, spelling, handwriting, and composition are in the language arts area. If separate periods are provided for literature, speech, and phonics, they are also part of the language arts program.

Although we may divide the school day into subject periods, the skills of language are used throughout the day. The receiving skills are listening and reading; the sharing skills are speech and handwriting. Each one of these skills is related to the others, both as to the mental processes involved and as to the function of each in communication. Speech has no purpose unless associated with listening; the mental processes you employ to understand and evaluate the ideas

on this printed page are almost identical to those you would use in listening to a teacher present these ideas orally.

The skills of speech, writing, reading, and listening are usually grouped together as "the tools of communication." The word *communication* has an interesting meaning. When one individual has had an interchange of thoughts or ideas with another, we say that communication has taken place. To be *in communion* means to be in a state of mutual understanding or feeling; normally, this communion is an exchange of ideas on a common basis of understanding. (Both words stem from the Latin *communis,* or "common.") If we separate the ideas shared from the writing, speaking, reading, and listening skills, the ideas become the *content* of communication. For this reason one sometimes hears the statement that the language arts have no content and must always use social studies, science, or other information in order to have ideas to share.

One result of this idea has been a tendency on the part of some to neglect instruction in the skills themselves and to concentrate on factual information; a few teachers have felt that if the child has enough to talk or write about, the skills needed will develop without planned instruction.

Others believe that the mastery of skills in the elementary school will give the child the ability and security needed to grow in knowledge. The entire lifetime of an individual who reads with ease and expresses himself clearly and comfortably is a learning experience. To attempt the mastery of many volumes of social ideas or scientific facts during the elementary school years places an artificial pressure on both teachers and students which may result in failure to provide adequate competence in language skills.

As a teacher or a future teacher you are personally concerned with communication because it is a necessity of teaching. What you are trying to do in the classroom is to communicate to children, to aid them in their efforts to communicate with you and with others. There are times when you will completely misunderstand your college teachers, just as your students will fail to understand you. Sometimes the words cause this misunderstanding. (A group of kindergarten children were quite puzzled about what the teacher meant when she asked them to "tiptoe.") More often, the same words will be used with different meanings; that is, the person speaking the word thinks of one meaning and the person hearing the word associates it with another. The fact that many of our common words, such as *run,* have many different meanings accounts for incomplete communication or a total lack of it.[1] Another factor is experience. Such words as *river, wagon, car,* and *lake* evoke different images with each of us. Only when an experience is completely shared does total communication take place. Fortunately, complete and exact communication is not always necessary for adequate understanding.

Teaching is not just telling. Communication involves more than words. The derivations of most words for teaching imply showing, showing how, showing what, or showing why. The word *teach* is derived from the Anglo-Saxon *taecean* and is akin to the German *zeigen,* "to show." In Latin *doceo* means "I show, point out, inform, tell," as does the Greek *didasko* and *deiknymi*—originally, "I show or point out," but ultimately, "I teach."

The term *art* is used to describe something that is personal, creative, and original. In contrast, the word *skill* may indicate something mechanical, exact, impersonal. When we spell a word we do not offer a creative original version of the word but merely give an exact mechanical rendition of the accepted form. Yet when we write a poem we seek to express something personal and original. Some teachers stress the skills of language instruction with emphasis upon correct usage drills, grammatical classification of words, and frequent testing. Others would place their emphasis upon the per-

sonal expression of ideas by students, feeling that in doing so they are helping them develop the art of language. A modern language program is concerned with both.

If we think of language as a code designed to carry meaning, the linguistic terms *decoding* and *encoding* are easily understood. When you listen to a speaker you decode the meaning. When you speak you encode the sounds to make meaning. Writing as speech in graphic form is an encoding process and reading as an interpretation of speech in print is a decoding process. Some prefer the term *recoding* for reading, because written symbols are turned first into sound and then are decoded. There are other ways of communicating meaning—such as gestures (body language), dance, and painting—but we are focusing attention on those directly involving language.

Listening and reading are related in that they are both means of receiving communication. Speaking and writing are related in that they are ways of expressing meaning. In use the skills are frequently related. A student writes notes as he listens or reads. A speaker interprets the listening response of those he is with. In conversation speaking and listening almost become the same process.

As a teacher you will isolate aspects of the language skills to identify specific parts and to meet the needs of individual children. When a teacher helps a child speak a specific sound with exactness, identify that sound as represented by a letter in a word, or spell the word according to a sociably accepted pattern, the larger purpose of language is not forgotten. It is through language that thought is organized, refined, and expressed. The Greek word *logos* included both the identity of speech and thought. John Dewey says,

Even if the thing is not there to represent the meaning, the word may be processed so as to evoke the meaning. Since intellectual life depends on possession of a store of meanings, the importance of language as a tool of preserving meanings cannot be overstated. . . . Without words as vehicles . . . no cumulative growth of intelligence would occur. Experience might

---

[1] The 500 most commonly used words in English have over 14,000 dictionary definitions. See William V. Haney, *Communication: Patterns and Incidents* (Homewood, Ill.: Irwin, 1960), p. 48.

form habits of physical adaptation but it would not teach anything; for we should not be able to use an old experience consciously to anticipate and regulate a new experience.[2]

For Discussion

1. Recall how the skills of language were presented in the elementary school you attended.

2. In class, try an experiment to note the difference between the sender and receiver as far as complete communication is concerned.

> The teacher says, "When I was a little girl (or boy). . . ." How old was the child you pictured in your mind?
> The teacher says, "The dog barked." What kind of dog did you picture? Age? Color?
> The child says, "My grandmother lives in the country." What picture do you see? Is the place a farm, ranch, or suburban area? How old is the grandmother you picture?

3. Use the word *strike* with as many different meanings as you can devise. Look in the dictionary to see how many are listed. How might words of this nature interfere with communication?

4. One problem of communication is the stereotyped association people have with certain words. What is your image of a teacher, scientist, Dutch boy?

5. To what extent are words only an aspect of communication? When people share ideas what are the aspects of human relationships that influence meaning?

What Are the Objectives of Instruction in the Language Program?

In education we attempt to give direction to our work by deciding what our objectives are. Teachers have stated these objectives in many ways. One statement that has been traditional and widely understood by parents is that the purpose of the elementary school is to teach the three R's: reading, 'riting, and 'rithmetic. In the minds of many these subjects are fundamental and of first importance. The fact that elementary schools were called grammar schools is further evidence of this thinking.

Contrary to some opinions, the schools of today still consider the skills of the three R's as fundamental for life success. Teachers have discovered so much about child psychology that they are able to approach the task from the learner's point of view. The more we know about a child, the better we can decide when he will need and use certain skills, when these skills will be most meaningful, and how his interests and attitudes are influenced. When these decisions have been made, a subject can be organized *psychologically*, or in the way it is learned. If we look at the skills apart from the learner and attempt to define what should come first, second, and third, we say that it is organized *logically*. You will find that in practice we use both logical and psychological organization of materials to gain the results we seek.

Behind any statement of objectives there is a philosophy. It is also true that each teacher interprets and functions with respect to any curriculum guide or textbook in terms of the values she feels are important.

To clarify the objectives of teaching the English language fifty authorities from the United States and Great Britain met at Dartmouth College in 1966. The seminar was impressed by a consultant, Sybil Marshall, who has taught children in England.[3] She protested against the traditional discipline that has called for silence in the classroom and premature emphasis on mistakes. She dwelt on the rich possibilities in the child's own exploration of language, his interest in words, his pleasure in using more of them. To illustrate, she told of a child who was stamping around the room, strumming on a toy guitar like a Beatle and singing a lyric of his own composing—"Maxi-

---

[2] John Dewey, *How We Think* (Boston: Heath, 1933), p. 234.

[3] Herbert J. Muller, *The Uses of English* (New York: Holt, 1967), p. 42.

mum capacity, maximum capacity!" The teacher's job is to supply the children plentifully with stories, poems, jingles, songs, and pictures; let them begin selecting for themselves; create an atmosphere of freedom and pleasure in which they continually use words; and take care neither to separate reading, writing, and talking nor to isolate English from the other arts. Mrs. Marshall goes so far as to say that she would ban exercises in grammar, punctuation, and spelling. In 1963 Sybil Marshall wrote,[4]

I would give them enough patterns, but not in the form of exercises. I would give them patterns in speech, in books, in poetry, and in plays. I would not subject my pupils to ten minutes a day under the ultraviolet lamp of intense grammatical exercises, but would instead seek out every patch of literary sunshine and see to it that the pupils worked and played in its warmth and light until grammatical usage and good style, the balance and cadence of sentences, and the happy choice of the most significant words soaked into them through every one of their senses. . . . It is much more important, surely, to be bursting with things to write about and not know precisely how to write them, than to know all the rules and not have anything to write.

The Denver, Colorado, Public Schools provide this framework for their English Language Program.[5]

Importance of Language

Language is so much a part of everyday human behavior that most individuals take for granted the phenomenon of communication; yet this very intricate relationship with all aspects of life reflects the vital importance of language in the development of civilization. Language not only enables man to transmit his heritage from one generation to another but also shapes and reflects his culture. Among the some 3,000 world languages which have evolved, English is unique—in its history, in its structure, in its power and beauty. By means of the free interchange of ideas through listening, speaking,

reading, and writing, English functions at its highest level as a world language in the second half of the twentieth century.

Language and Learning in a Modern World

In an age in which knowledge multiplies during every decade and in which technological advances are changing the typical worker's tasks every few years, education takes on an even greater importance than it has in the past; in a school system seeking to educate young people who can be expected to retrain themselves at least three times during their working years, learning *how to learn* takes on additional significance. The importance of the role of language in the learning process cannot be overestimated. Language plays a key role in unifying a vast and complex nation and in providing individuals with outlets for developing diverse skills and abilities.

Unity and Diversity in a Democratic Society

The dual responsibility of maintaining unity while fostering and encouraging diversity is vital to a democracy, where both the individual and his society are matters of special concern in the public education of children. Each child must achieve the common goals set forth by a democratic society, and each child must be motivated to achieve diverse and multiple goals of his own as dictated by his personal talents and interests. Unity is provided both in the common learning of all pupils (basic communication skills) and in the language needs of democratic electors (developing of the basic communication skills to a level which enables the individual to function efficiently as a participating member of a democratic society). From such a language study, pupils develop a sense of pride in their language as they gain power and experience delight in its use. Also, literature—one of the great products of the language—can be another unifying force as children experience, together, a sampling of this part of their cultural heritage; more important, the experience in literature helps children to understand themselves, their culture, and their society. Diversity is recognized through individual differences of pupils as they enter school and is fostered by good teaching which helps pupils develop individual talents; the flexibility of the English language offers a variety of means to develop creativity and to release imaginative powers.

[4] Sybil Marshall, *Experiment in Education* (New York: Cambridge University Press, 1963), p. 9.

[5] *Denver Public Schools Preliminary English Course of Study,* 1968.

Definition of English

Our language, which is constantly growing and changing, is the vehicle of thought, the key to effective learning. The study of English is the study of language in itself—a structured system of symbols—and its use in all the processes of communication. In classroom activities there is an intermingling of both receptive (listening and reading) and expressive (speaking and writing) language arts. Through the balance of emphasis on these various facets of English in daily classroom situations, the Denver Public Schools seeks to provide youngsters with skills to meet common goals of their democratic society and to challenge their diverse abilities for finding ways of living peacefully in their own world and for finding esthetic satisfaction in doing so.

Principles

The following principles reflect an attempt to translate the goals and beliefs expressed above into a form which is more practical and workable in the daily classroom environment. The principles are intended to apply to the teaching of the English language and its literature at each age level from the time the young child enters school until the young adult graduates.

1. There exists a common body of English which is taught and used in all courses at all levels of instruction.
2. Language, as social behavior, is both a structured system of symbols and a means of communication.
3. At an early age children are in possession of the essential elements of language in its spoken form. The conventions of the English language are taught on the basis of need, experience, and background of pupils as well as on previous attainment.
4. At a preschool age, native speakers have usually acquired unconsciously the basic sentence structure of the English language.
5. English has its roots in many languages.
6. A study of the history of language will reveal its dynamic character and will foster an appreciation of its literary and colloquial variation.
7. Word order is the predominant factor in the structure of the English language.
8. English takes different forms in varying situations.

9. All language skills are interrelated.
10. Use of language can develop critical thinking and self-evaluation.
11. A high correlation exists between thought and proficiency in communication.
12. Language is an instrument of personal development and social communication.
13. Language enables one to release creative potential.
14. Literature, as an art form, reveals the culture from which it springs.
15. Specific literary types have definite structure.
16. Literature has sensory as well as intellectual appeal.
17. Literature makes use of imaginative and figurative language.
18. Literature broadens experience, deepens understanding, improves judgment, and provides for esthetic response.
19. Listening to good literature read aloud enhances appreciation through sensory appeal and the union of sound and sense.
20. Facts are important only as they contribute to the understanding, as a whole, of the literary selection or any other type of communication.
21. Exposure to good speakers and writers will improve competence in communication.
22. As pupils have opportunities to recognize and experiment with structures, competence in clear, forceful, appropriate expression will be increased.
23. Composition, both oral and written, should be a challenge which enables pupils to see relationships and to draw valid conclusions.
24. Students should be encouraged to develop an inquiring mind which understands the reasoning processes and is able to interpret the evidence necessary to solve problems and make decisions.
25. Spoken language, which is basic to all communication and most widely used, occupies a prior position of importance in relation to other communication skills.
26. Pupils must be taught how to listen for directions, facts, ideas, concepts, and appreciation; for listening is more than hearing.

Structure

Thinking

Literature

Composition

Speaking

Listening

27. Listening must go beyond hearing to become a response with understanding, feeling, and critical analysis.
28. The inductive process is basic to learning.
29. Classroom emphasis should stress learning rather than teaching.
30. Classroom climate should be such to encourage constructive expression on the part of the pupil.
31. The responsibility for teaching English is shared by all teachers.

Method

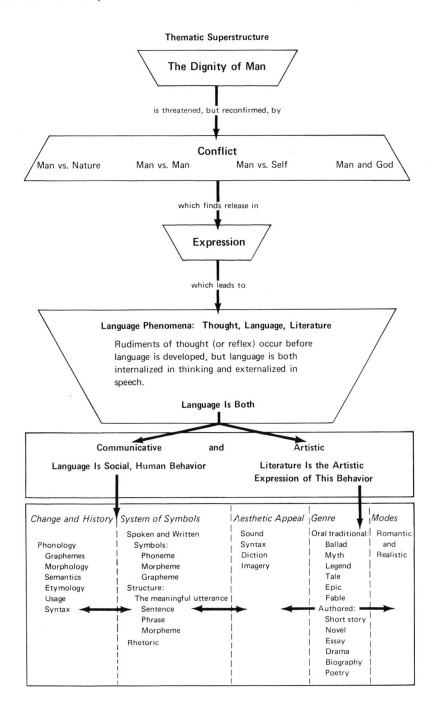

Rate your present skill or knowledge for each of the following aspects of teaching language arts as follows:	*Satisfactory*	*Improving*	*Needs Attention*

1. I understand the historical background of the language I teach.
2. I know how children master language before starting to school.
3. I know how language instruction fits into the school day.
4. I can explain how reading, writing, listening, and speaking are related.
5. I know what the National Council of Teachers of English is and have read the publications of that group.
6. I know the educational leaders in the field of language arts instruction.
7. I can give a parent a reference that will help guide the creational reading of her children.
8. I can purchase books intelligently for a classroom library.
9. I know of books that should be read to children.
10. I can hold children's attention as I tell a story.
11. I know how to share a picture book with little children.
12. I can teach a finger play to a child and explain its importance to his parents.
13. I know many things to do that will encourage children to read good literature.
14. I can involve children in dramatic play and creative dramatics.
15. I can suggest a variety of book-sharing techniques to children.
16. I know where to get information concerning a book fair.
17. I know the sources of poetry that are appropriate to the children in my class.
18. I can read poetry well.
19. I know how to direct children in simple verse choir experiences.
20. I can recognize different types of speech defects.
21. I know how to distinguish the speech defects that I can help and those that need a speech specialist.
22. I understand why it is important to listen to children.
23. I can discuss with a supervisor the importance of teaching listening in my classroom and give examples of classroom emphasis on listening.
24. I can write print script.
25. I can write neatly and legibly on the chalkboard.
26. I can write a note to a parent and not be embarrassed by my handwriting.
27. I know the reasons why I teach handwriting the way I do.
28. I know how to help a left-handed child write well.
29. I know how to teach skills of spelling.
30. I know how to individualize spelling instruction.

Rate your present skill or knowledge for each of the following aspects of teaching language arts as follows:	*Satisfactory*	*Improving*	*Needs Attention*
31. I know how to make the spelling period interesting to children.			
32. I am able to help children to write creatively.			
33. I know the relationship between oral and written composition and use it in my teaching.			
34. I understand how standards of performance are established and how to use them to foster improvement in composition.			
35. I can plan and produce an assembly program.			
36. I know what type of work in composition to expect of children in the separate grades.			
37. I understand the fundamentals of grammar.			
38. I understand the conflict between teaching grammar and functional usage in the grades.			
39. I understand the significance of readiness in all learning experience.			
40. I know how the textbooks in spelling, penmanship, language, and reading are usually organized and used.			
41. I can teach a beginner to read.			
42. I understand the strengths and weaknesses of phonics as applied to spelling and reading.			
43. I know of material designed to be used with children who are below grade level in reading.			
44. I know these magazines and read them to keep informed concerning the language arts: *Elementary English, N.E.A. Journal, The Reading Teacher, Elementary School Journal, The Instructor,* and *The Grade Teacher.*			
45. I can identify these authors of children's books: Doris Gates, Florence Means, Laura I. Wilder, Marjorie Flack, Virginia Lee Burton, Dr. Seuss, Beatrix Potter, Lois Lenski, Astrid Lindgren, Holling C. Holling, and others who have received special awards.			
46. I can plan a lesson for one period of instruction, and for three groups in a single skill for a week.			
47. I can make purposeful worksheets in handwriting and reading or know sources of such material.			
48. I can give a talk at the P.T.A. explaining the significance of the skills of language arts for children in the space age.			
49. I recognize the issues that exist in the language program and seek solutions that will work in my classroom.			
50. I am aware of the importance of research in education and seek to keep informed.			

The preceding partial inventory of teaching knowledge will help you direct your efforts as you become a teacher of the language skills. As the course proceeds you may wish to check your progress.

Beginning teachers will not find an immediate answer to the many issues found in the area of teaching children to use language. It is important for our teacher to know why authorities with equal dedication to children and to the profession of teaching do not have exact or absolute answers and why differences exist. One purpose of this book is to help beginning teachers establish their own philosophical guidelines and professional awareness of the materials and methods that will assist them to function effectively in the teaching–learning situations of the elementary school.

To be a teacher of the language program you must feel with a deep conviction that the way a child uses his language is important to him both as a student learning to communicate his needs and feelings to others and as a future adult who will require mature language skills to meet the problems of a complex society. You will need to have mastered such skills as handwriting, spelling, reading, and oral expression. Along with these basic skills you will need a sensitivity to the beauty expressed through words in poetry and prose, an understanding that words are the tools of communication with others, and an awareness that thoughts and ideas are the ends or goals for which such skills are perfected. Above all, you must possess a desire to grow in language power as you teach and work with children and as you establish yourself as an individual growing toward teaching competence.

For Discussion

1. What do you believe at this time about the following statements?

a. The schools are doing a better job teaching the fundamentals than in the past.

b. Language and spelling errors can best be corrected through drill.

c. All children in the class should have the same spelling book.

d. The fact that there are children in the fifth grade who have a reading level of third grade and below indicates that the schools have failed to teach reading properly.

2. Would you approve of instruction in social courtesy as a language arts objective?

3. How may writing about fears contribute to the emotional maturity of a child?

Hints on Pronunciation for Foreigners [6]

I take it you already know
Of tough and bough and cough and dough?
Others may stumble but not you,
On hiccough, thorough, laugh and through.
Well done! And now you wish, perhaps,
To learn of less familiar traps?

Beware of heard, a dreadful word
That looks like beard and sounds like bird,
And dead: it's said like bed, not bead—
For goodness' sake don't call it "deed"!
Watch out for meat and great and threat
(They rhyme with suite and straight and debt.)

A moth is not a moth in mother
Nor both in bother, broth in brother,
And here is not a match for there
Nor dear and fear for bear and pear,
And then there's dose and rose and lose—
Just look them up—and goose and choose,
And cork and work and card and ward,
And font and front and word and sword,
And do and go and thwart and cart—
Come, come, I've hardly made a start!
A dreadful language? Man alive,
I'd mastered it when I was five.

        T. S. W.

        (only initials of writer known)

How Do Children Learn Language?

By the time we meet the child as his teacher, a tremendous amount of learning has already taken place. Because the language the child brings to school is so important, let us start by a brief survey of what has happened during those preschool years.

By the end of the first month of life a mother can often detect pain, rage, or mere exuberance in the vocalization of the baby. Just as the baby makes random movements with his arms and legs and is in general learning some control over his body, so does

---

[6] From a letter published in the *London Sunday Times* (January 3, 1965), from J. Bland. Cited by Mackay and Thompson, "The Initial Teaching of Reading and Writing," *Programme in Linguistics and English Teaching,* Paper no. 3, University College, London, and Longmans Green and Co., Ltd., London and Harlow, 1968, p. 45.

Teachers constantly seek new ways to make their work effective. This beginning teacher is checking creative writing ideas presented by the curriculum director of his school district. (*Courtesy of California Western University.*)

he exercise his voice mechanism. At the end of four months most infants have mastered fairly well the principles basic to effective use of the vocal mechanism. They blow bubbles, chuckle, gurgle, laugh, and experiment with the use of the tongue, larynx, and breath control. This might be called the babble stage of language growth. Through it the infant learns the modification in tension of vocal chords and the positions of tongue and lips necessary to the imitation of the sounds he hears. He has command of most of the vowels and a few consonant sounds at this time. By six or seven months some children are able to make all of the consonant and many of the diphthong sounds necessary for speech. By nine months the babble softens into the rhythm of the speech the child hears around him. Actual words begin to develop at eleven or twelve months when the child's active vocabulary consists of *mama, daddy,* and one or two other words.

It is difficult to decide when babblings cease and actual words are substituted. Because it is necessary to depend on parents for records, data are not always reliable. The first words are so anxiously awaited that word formation is likely to be more imagined than real.

The first words are usually monosyllables. As soon as parents notice the first *ma, da,* or *by,* they encourage the child and soon some association of sound and situation is established. In the main the first words are interjections or nouns. Added by gestures the child is able to convey a variety of meanings with only one word. The single word *water* or *wa-wa* may mean "I want a drink," "see the bath," "it is raining," or "bottle," "glass."

First words have an emotional quality.

Communication takes many forms. Response to the expression of another need not involve words. (*Courtesy of Burbank Public Schools.*)

Vocabulary is determined by situations. Dramatic play provides opportunity to use adult words. (*Courtesy of San Diego County Schools.*)

They may express a wish or feeling, or they may express a real personal need. Interestingly enough, it is believed by some authorities that speaking the word is secondary to the general emotional status of the child at the time of using the word. As words are learned they are used to supplement body movements, emotional expressions, and other devices used to express wants. In time language becomes a substitute for certain aggressive behavior of children.

Imitation plays an important role in the child's linguistic development. Learning by imitation is shown by the fact that the child learns the language of his environment and by the fact that the congenitally deaf child cannot learn normal speech, because he is unable to hear and therefore cannot imitate sound. Of equal importance to the imitation of others is the imitation by the child of those sounds that he himself has made. Nearly everyone is familiar with the continued repetition of a sound by an infant. It is thought that a desire to hear himself talk is what contributes to this activity. When the child is in the presence of adults and accidentally or purposely makes sounds,

parents are likely to pronounce a word which approximates the sound made by the child. This is good training, because it provides an auditory strengthening and stimulates the child to remake the sound he has produced.

From a report by Brown and Bellugi on the early language of two children, we find that these young talkers concerned themselves with syntax in remarkably efficient ways.[7] Two children, a boy and a girl aged twenty-seven and eighteen months, respectively, imitated their mothers' sentences, and though they left out words, they never changed the original order of words they repeated. "Frazer will be unhappy" became "Frazer unhappy." "He's going out" became "He go out." Words and parts of words that carry meaning were retained in these and other samples from the systematically made records. "No, you can't write on Mr. Cromer's shoe" was condensed to "Write Cromer's shoe." It was never "Shoe write

---

[7] Roger Brown and Ursula Bellugi, "Three Processes in the Child's Acquisition of Syntax," *Harvard Educational Review,* Vol. 34 (Spring 1964), pp. 133–51.

Cromer." The investigators remind us that in speaking such sentences as "Frazer will be unhappy," the adult spontaneously stresses *Frazer* and *unhappy*. This is the very essence of the nature of our language. We do, indeed, stress the meaning-bearing words. Children learn the stress system as they learn to talk. Infinite numbers of repetitions make it automatic.

Dr. Walter Loban of the University of California has in progress a fascinating study of the language of the same children from their entrance into kindergarten through their graduation from high school. Results are available for the first six years.[8]

The pupils were asked in an interview to tell what they saw in a carefully selected group of pictures and what they thought about them. The responses were recorded and the language analyzed by a scheme set up by a board of linguists.

One of the major problems in any such analysis is the presence in the speech of children and young people of certain "tangles" of language. They are hesitations, false starts, and meaningless repetitions which interrupt the sentence patterns. These "tangles" were removed and studied separately from the remaining sentences. During kindergarten and the first three grades, the total group and the high subgroup showed a steady decrease in the number of mazes (35 per cent) and the number of words per maze (50 per cent). The low group, on the other hand, increased both the number of mazes and the average number of words per maze during the same four-year period. Throughout the study, the low group, writes Dr. Loban, "says less, has more difficulty saying it, and has less vocabulary with which to say it."

The high group was distinguished from the kindergarten up by the ability to express tentative thinking as revealed by such words as *perhaps, maybe,* and *I'm not exactly sure.*

The gifted sensed alternatives; the weak made flat, dogmatic statements. Although the pictures invited generalizations and figurative language, little of either was used by any of the children.

Dr. Ruth Strickland used the same analytical scheme for her study of the oral language of children from sixteen public schools in Bloomington, Indiana.[9] Her purpose was to contrast the intricacy of children's patterns of speech with the simplicity of sentence structure in reading textbooks commonly used in grades 1 through 6. The latter proved to be extremely simple in contrast to forms used by the children in their own speech. Whether they should be or not seems to be a question still in dispute.

The tremendous amount of oral expressiveness indulged in by young children is illustrated in an unusual report. Every word uttered by a girl two and one-half years old was recorded for a full day, from seven in the morning until seven-thirty at night. Here is an example of this child's expression as she sat with her grandmother.

I'm sewing a button—I found a big button, too. That's the best one. Now it'll be all right. On this side. Now I made a nightgown. Is that a knot? Helen don't have a very large buttonhole either. Cut it now. Now the button is sewed on. Now I have to get another string. Here's a pad—didy to go underneath. Here's the woolen blanket. I found it. Helen has some more sewing to do. Helen wants to set a buttonhole on it. What kind of buttonhole? What kind of buttonhole? What kind of buttonhole? That's too little. That's not very large. I'm not ready.

Speech is often a social overture (for example, asking of a question that requires no answer). Talking often accompanies action in other motor areas. The child appears bent on filling every waking moment with oral expression; indeed, it seems that talking is almost compulsive in nature.

One investigator found that in a single day his three-year-old child asked 376 ques-

---

[8] Walter D. Loban, "The Language of Elementary School Children," *A Study of the Use and Control of Language Effectiveness in Communication and the Relations Among Speaking, Reading, Writing, and Listening,* Research Report No. 1 (Champaign, Ill.: National Council of Teachers of English, 1963), pp. 8–55.

[9] Ruth Strickland, "The Language of Elementary School Children: Its Relationship to the Language of Reading Textbooks and the Quality of Reading of Selected Children," *Bulletin of the School of Education,* Indiana University, Vol. XXXVIII, No. 4 (July, 1962).

tions and that his four-year-old child asked 397.[10] This is probably somewhat high for average children, but gives an idea of why this age is referred to as the question age. As early as three years of age language serves the purpose of simple narration, with the incidents related usually being telescoped into a single simple sentence. For example, "We went downtown" may be used to cover all the exciting situations involved. Occasionally children of three can enlarge upon this, and some children of four can tell enough of an incident to hold the attention of other children. Imaginative elements often creep in, possibly as a reflection of the stories being read to children at that age. For example, a child may relate, "Once there was a big engine. It came right up to the door and asked for breakfast."

The most complicated and advanced use of language is to express reasoning: "If I don't wear my mitten, I don't get them dirty," or, "Where does my dinner go when I eat it?" As the child's experiences enlarge and as his mastery of vocabulary increases, the form of reasoning he can do becomes increasingly complex.

In content of language we find a predominance of egocentricity in the speech of young children. The six-year-old's insistent "Look at me! See me!" is familiar to every parent and teacher.

Almost all studies of children's language have noted the lateness with which pronouns are added to the child's vocabulary. It is not unusual to hear a three-year-old refer to himself as "Jimmy" instead of saying "I," "me," or "myself." Dr. Dorothea McCarthy of Fordham University conducted a study by recording responses from twenty children at each of seven age levels, from eighteen to fifty-four months.[11] She found that nouns constitute about 50 per cent of the total speech of very young children. Verbs increase from about 14 per cent of the total speech at eighteen months to about 25 per cent at fifty-four months. Adjectives increase over the same interval from about 10 to about 20 per cent. Connectives do not show up until about two years of age; after that age they steadily increase in proportion. These developmental trends explain the peculiar flavor of the very young child's speech. He typically uses many nouns and verbs, very few pronouns, and practically no connectives. His speech is thus direct, unadorned, and essentially disconnected.[12]

The rapid speech of nursery school and kindergarten children has been studied with the aid of a mechanical hand tally and stop watch. The findings indicate that children of this age level have an average verbal output of about sixteen words per minute, and an average rate of 186 words per minute while speaking. When one considers the average rate of about 100 words per minute adapted by experienced lecturers, the young child's verbalization rate is indeed high. It was further found that the child who talked the most uttered approximately seven times as many words as the child who talked the least. Boys tended to speak less than girls in a given time interval, but they spoke more rapidly when they did verbalize.[13]

Measuring the vocabulary of an individual presents many problems. Words used will be limited to the occasion or situation. Decisions must be made as to what constitutes a word. Should *chairs* be counted as a separate word from *chair,* should *moo-moo* be accepted as a word for *cow,* should one meaning of a word be counted as a separate vocabulary understanding from its other meanings?

Vocabulary studies have been made in a number of situations. Conversations have been recorded; the written material of an individual has been analyzed; children have been stimulated to write all the words they know by showing them pictures or giving them key words; lists have been used to check recognition.

One research study used a pocket dic-

[10] From *The First Two Years: A Study of Twenty-five Babies,* Vol. II, by Mary M. Shirley, Child Welfare Monograph Series, No. 7. University of Minnesota Press, Minneapolis. Copyright 1933 by the University of Minnesota, p. 327.

[11] Leonard Carmichael, *Manual of Child Psychology* (New York: Wiley, 1951), p. 476.

[12] Ibid., p. 530.

[13] Ibid., p. 553.

tionary of 18,000 words to check vocabulary. As a result it was concluded that a twelve-year-old knew 7,200 words. When another study used a dictionary of 371,000 words it was concluded that a child that age knew 55,000 words. With respect to the vocabulary of first-grade children, some studies indicate that a vocabulary of 2,500 words is normal whereas others indicate 24,000 words is normal.[14]

Repeated tests with college undergraduates indicate that their vocabulary is over 100,000 words, probably over 200,000. It would be expected that such vocabulary development would be gradual through the individual's growth. The evidence would indicate that the vocabulary of children has probably been underestimated.

An additional consideration is the fact that an individual's speaking vocabulary will differ from his listening and reading vocabularies. Children understand many words spoken to them that they never use in their own speech, and adults read words that would not be used in their spoken vocabulary.

How can such knowledge as presented here be used by a teacher? It would seem wise to extend, refine, and enhance the oral arts and skills children already possess and then to use the oral efficiency that children bring to school as the means of developing a complementary efficiency in reading and writing. Strickland takes this position.[15]

One of the errors Spanish-speaking children make is leaving out the pronoun that is needed in a sentence in which the child is asked, "Where do you live?" The child is apt to say, "Live in Chicago." Why? Because in Spanish the pronoun is inherent in the verb, and the child is carrying over into English a principle that operates in his own language. Or if you teach in Pennsylvania Dutch country, you find children utilizing a pattern which stems from Old German. A child may say, "My off is all," meaning "My vacation has ended," or he turns

a sentence around: "Pa threw the cow over the fence some hay," giving a Germanic twist to the sentence. Likewise, the little Negro child says, "Him a good dog; he go he house." We must not become mired immediately in the problems of usage because the child is following accurately almost every grammatical rule that operates in those sentences. To be sure, when he says, "Him a good dog," he has—and many children seem to have—no third-person singular in his speech, but he is using the correct verb. The first and last words you know are correct for the purpose and he has the proper word but the wrong form of it in the other two slots. We're being told over and over again *don't become overconcerned about the errors.* Notice that most of what the child is saying is correct and get at the task of tuning his ear to the parts that you want to add or change. We know that we have to do that with little children who come to kindergarten or first grade, some even from the best language backgrounds.

The culturally deprived child comes to school with deficits in learning sets and the ability to "learn to learn." Because he lacks particular experience and because he is at a relatively low level of linguistic development, he is usually not ready to begin his learning at the same level and by the same approach as is characteristic of children from less restricted cultural environments. Unless the school reshapes its curriculum and methods to begin with the child where he is, learning cannot proceed in a fruitful and meaningful way.

Present school practices do not succeed in overcoming the initial differences between culturally advantaged and culturally disadvantaged children. Instead, what start as small measurable differences in the first grade become larger each year. By the end of the sixth year of school there is a cumulative deficit in the school achievement of the culturally disadvantaged children which shows up most clearly in the tool subjects of reading and arithmetic. Deutsch defined the "cumulative deficit" in a study he conducted in 1965.[16]

[14] Nancy Larrick, "How Many Words Does a Child Know?" *The Reading Teacher* (December 1953), pp. 100–104.

[15] Ruth Strickland, *Linguistics and Language* (Denton, Tex.: Texas Woman's University Proceedings, 1965).

[16] Martin Deutsch, "The Role of Social Class in Language Development and Cognition," in Harry Passow (ed.), *Education of the Disadvantaged* (New York: Holt, 1965), p. 216.

Children who use a language other than English at home practice new English speech patterns as they participate in activities. (*Courtesy of La Mesa Public Schools.*)

In general, we have found that lower-class children, Negro and white, compared with middle-class children, are subject to what we've labeled a "cumulative deficit" phenomenon which takes place between the first and fifth grade years. Though there are significant socio-economic and race differences seen in measured variables at the first grade level, it is important to note that they become more marked as the child progresses through school. While we can accept that some of this cumulative deficit is associated with inadequate early preparation because of corresponding environment deficiencies, the adequacy of the school environment . . . also must be questioned: in a model system, one should expect linearity in cognitive growth.

It is this cumulative deficit which must be reversed early in the culturally deprived child's school career. Delayed attempts may make such a reversal impossible. Ausubel suggests that possible irreversibility in cognitive development may result from the "cumulative nature of intellectual deficit." A child who has a deficit in growth is less able to profit developmentally from new levels of intellectual stimulation. Furthermore, intellectual development becomes increasingly differentiated with age, and differentiation is based on the ability to profit from new experiences which are increasingly specialized and complex.[17]

[17] David P. Ausubel, "How Reversible Are the Cognitive and Motivational Effects of Cultural Deprivation?" in ibid., p. 309.

Continuing research in early childhood education seems to indicate that neither Head Start nor kindergarten starts early enough.

It may well be that the United States, like every other "advanced" nation, may have its spending priorities upside down. We may make much better use of our educational resources if, instead of beginning the formal education process at the age of six, we started it at two or three.

For Discussion

1. How might the parental use of "baby talk," such as "itsy bitsy bow wow," influence the speech habits of a child?

2. How might the Southern dialect of the United States have been started?

3. Why do some seek uniformity in the speech habits of children?

4. What influence has television had on the speech of children you know?

5. Listen to the questions of little children. How many seek an answer? How many are conversational openings?

6. Ask your parents to recall any words you invented and used which were understood by the family.

7. In later childhood there are many words with regard to games that are the inventions and sole property of childhood. In hide and seek we have *Allee-allee-otsen-free!* for *all in free. Dibs* means "that's mine," or *Dibs on first base* means "I get to play first base." Can you think of others?

8. How might the "cumulative deficit" of language be avoided?

How Do We Work with the Very Young Children in School?

At the age of five, each day is one of wonder and discovery. There are new things to see, new words to use, and new ideas to try. No day is long enough to see it all, and tomorrow seems so far away. As a teacher you will be amazed at children's energy and constant need for activity.

In order to work well with this age, a teacher must learn to use a very different technique from that suitable for an older group of young adults. In the Orient, a form of wrestling called judo has been developed. It is a method of using the strength and energy of an opponent so that it reacts against him. When an opponent makes a rushing attack, the master of judo estimates his force and momentum and instead of meeting it with an opposite force, attempts to direct it against the opponent himself, so that he is thrown to the floor. Although the analogy is a bit strained, it suggests how the teacher can manage the energy of young children. She should not try to stop it or even keep up with it; but she should attempt to understand it, and provide ways for directing this energy so that the child's needs are met.

A visit to a kindergarten will reveal the physical characteristics of the age. Children are active and must move their large muscles. There are room centers where movement is appropriate and which are equipped with play equipment suitable for children in this age group. Girls grow faster than boys and are frequently more mature in all respects. Because this is the age of chicken pox, measles, and mumps, there are frequent physical checkups and absences. Because vision is not yet mature, the child is protected from activities that call for frequent refocusing of the eyes. Rest periods and quiet times alternate with periods of activity because fatigue is a natural result of expending so much energy.

Intellectually these children are beginning to understand time patterns, can follow simple directions, see differences more readily than similarites, are not quite certain about the distinction between reality and fantasy, and are able to tell or retell simple stories. The teacher provides opportunities to talk about and distinguish between imaginary and real things. The group shares experiences in order to build a common background. There is freedom to ask questions. Perhaps most important of all, children have an opportunity to listen and to be aware of the things they have learned through listening.

Emotionally the five-year-old demands affection and attention. The desire to please is powerful and many ways are used to gain status. Some show evidence of fear of the unknown, and the wise teacher is careful about phobic response to punishment. At this age the threat of being sent to the principal's office can become in the imagination of a child almost equal to that of capital punishment for an adult. On the playground they become combative but are beginning to substitute language for force, using name-calling or verbal quarreling instead of hitting and kicking.

In the classroom there are outlets for emotions through dramatic play, listening to verse, and creative use of paints, clay, and paper. There is freedom to express opinions without fear of criticism and there is freedom from pressure to work beyond abilities. Help is given the child to recognize himself as an individual and to respect the individuality of others. Limits to behavior are clearly defined so that the child is aware of how things are done while sitting on the rug, while tinkering with toys or equipment, or while playing outdoors or moving in single file through the halls.

Socially, children of this age are self-centered in contact with others. They have to learn how to work in a group, find sharing of prized objects a bit difficult, and look to adults for approval.

In the classroom the children are given an opportunity to participate in group activities and to be creative in social situations by dictating stories, poems, and experiences to the teacher, who records them. Opportunities to look at the work or behavior of the group, or of other small groups, provide occasions to define limits and expectations.

The children are taught such specifics as what to reply when a visitor comes to our room and says, "Good morning, girls and boys." How may we show a visitor what we are doing? How can this block house be made better? What might we do to improve the way we played at the swing today?

Much of what is done in school at this age is important to the immediate needs of the child, but teachers must anticipate the future needs that must be satisfied as the child masters reading, writing, and other skills needed by educated persons in our society. The term used to describe this is *promotion of readiness.* Among the many factors involved in language readiness are the following:

Broad, rich experience.
Vocabulary development.
Ability to attend (stories, completion of work, participation).
Seeing likeness and difference.
Hearing likeness and difference.
Organizing thought in sequence.
Being able to classify and generalize.
Ability to follow instructions.
Ability to speak clearly.
Interest in books and experience of others.
Ability to draw conclusions.
Ability to recall details.

A wise teacher looks at the language needs of children at the kindergarten level and asks herself two questions: "What skill do they need now as they live and work together in this room?" and "What later needs will be influenced by what we do?" These children are not taught to read, spell, or write, but nearly every activity will be related to later development of these skills. As children learn to identify their own clothes hangers, as they watch the teacher put labels on objects in the room or write the day of the week on the chalkboard, each child begins to understand the meaning of reading. When a particular sound appeals to a child and he repeats it in a song or verse, he is mastering the sounds of our language which will later help him in spelling. The pictures done with great concentration at the easel are expressive experiences almost identical with writing in that they express an idea or experience visually.

From the moment the child enters the room and is greeted in a friendly manner until he leaves with a satisfactory feeling about the day, he has many language experiences. As he makes an airplane, he enjoys using the words that he has heard: *jet, pilot, hostess, fuel,* and maybe *supersonic.* As he paints the plane, color words take on meaning. A feeling of orderliness, neatness, and appropriateness accompanies his activities throughout the day In clean-up, he uses words like *over, under, behind, beside,* which have indefinite associations. Dramatic play in the home, store, and other interest centers calls for conversations which explain sentence structure, choice of words, and organization of ideas. On his walks he learns to see, listen to, and appreciate the sights and sounds of nature. When his sensory experiences are vivid, he bubbles over with ideas and loves to talk about what he saw, what he did, how things look, and how he feels.

Throughout the day the teacher finds the right moment to bring literature either to one child alone or to a group of children. As a child works with others to build a road, church, or bridge, the teacher may find an occasion to read to the group such poems as James Tippet's "Trains," "Trucks," "Tugs," and "The River Bridge." A teacher who can go to her file and find "My Dog" and read, "His nose is short and stubby, his ears hang rather low," ending with the thought "Oh, puppy, I love you so," has given the group an expression for their inner feeling. If she teaches them the action play or finger play that starts, "My dog, Duke, knows many tricks," and substitutes the name of Mary's dog, new experience is shared.

At times, the teacher is wisest who remains silent and waits for children to react. She realizes that truly educative experiences mean not only active presentation of ideas, questions, and materials, but also a quiet alertness to and observation of the child's responses to the environment and to her.

There is much "planned" listening for these children. While they close their eyes, they listen to the fire crackling, the sound of a truck passing, or an object being tapped. They listen to the teacher reading and to each other telling about the events at home. It has been said that "the child who listens is one who has been listened to." In order to serve the child's listening needs, we establish standards not only for what children will tell us but also for how they will listen. The group decides that today we will only tell about happy things, beautiful things, pets, or things that make sounds.

The very shy may tell only the teacher, the very vocal must limit himself to only one incident of his trip.

The child leaves the kindergarten with the beginnings of many skills. Among those closely related to language, one should note these:

Ability to listen:
  When a story is read aloud.
  When a speaker is telling of an experience.
  To different sounds and tones.
  To directions.
  To hear likenesses and differences.
  To rhythms.
  To gain ideas.

Ability to speak:
  In complete thoughts.
  Repeating sounds.
  Imitating good speech patterns.
  In a pleasant voice.
  Telling of his own experience.
  Showing feeling in manner of expression.

Abilities related to future reading:
  Recognizing simple sequence.
  Recognizing likenesses and differences in letter forms.
  Connecting symbols with ideas.
  Care in handling picture books.
  Interpreting the events in a picture.

Abilities related to future writing:
  Learning to use paintbrush, chalk, pencil.
  Putting teacher-made signs and labels on objects.
  Expressing oral ideas which the teacher records.
  Experimenting · with paint, chalk, crayon, and pencil in imitating writing.

For Discussion

1. How may children who have not had kindergarten be helped at the beginning of first grade?

2. What does modern research indicate with respect to teaching some children to learn to read at the end of kindergarten?

3. Are the major purposes of kindergarten important enough to justify the expense of these institutions?

4. What tests should be used to check the sight of young children?

5. Which language experiences in kindergarten might be called prereading experiences?

What Will Children in the Grades Be Like?

As children progress through the first and second grades their standards often exceed their abilities. There is much dissatisfied crumpling of paper or erasing. One writer describes this as the "eraser" age. Teachers sometimes make it a rule that all erasing will be done by the teacher in order to keep children from rubbing holes through the paper. This behavior is only one aspect of the child's awareness of criticism from peers or age mates. The world is no longer made for him alone, but for the group or gang with whom he identifies himself. What others think, the praise or punishment that others receive, and other children's opinions about things now have much greater influence on his conduct than they did previously.

There is a loss in personal freedom of expression in art and story. Where the child once wanted to paint simply what he felt or saw, he is now concerned about the effect his work will produce on others. Group judgment or practice will influence his clothes, eating habits, books read, language used, and personal conduct.

By the age of eight, definite speech patterns have developed. The eye is more adapted to the tasks of reading and writing. There is a sense of hurry and untidiness that is related to a tendency toward accidents. These accidents are also associated with curiosity and interests that outdistance caution. Exploring the unknown is a favorite activity.

Emotionally, primary children desire and seek prestige. The Cub Scout or Brownie uniform is worn with pride. Those who do not belong show jealousy, and because feelings are still near the surface, violent outbursts or sullen withdrawal can be expected at times. Boy–girl relationships are wholesome and are either at the companion level or ignored. These children look for recognition from adults through use of social courtesies and individual association, but at the same time they seek independence through peer group approval. Most want adults to keep "hands off," literally and figuratively.

The older children of this age range are sometimes referred to as being in the latency period rather than preadolescence. Because they have already mastered the basic skills they can follow their interests in all directions. Teachers of these groups are true generalists from the educational point of view. One day they may be learning how humans can breathe in outer space, the next how the United Nations is organized, and the next how the Aztec Indians told time.

In the sixth grade many of the girls have entered adolescence. They find emotions difficult to control. Trivial sights or events can cause a major crisis. Some overt emotional display may belie underlying causes. Sometimes these children cry when happy and show antagonism toward persons they admire. Ordinarily, the girls are taller and weigh more than the boys throughout the intermediate grades.

Intermediates like to plan and organize. Clubs are organized almost solely for the fun of organizing them, although such activity may express a yearning for great achievement. There is little regret when nothing of much significance happens in a club meeting. The important thing seems to be that the meeting took place. Close friends also constitute an aspect of this period and new friendships explain some of the changed classroom behavior. Elections are often little more than popularity contests. New students go through a period of popularity as individuals seek them as friends. Note passing and in a few cases actual flaunting of a boy or girl friend are other common forms of social behavior at this time.

Working with these children requires a fine balance of permissiveness and control. At times free rein must be given to permit maximum use of abilities and extension of interest. At other times the control of the adult leader must be exercised to prevent immature judgments and emotional actions. This control requires a knowledge of each individual and of the nature of group inter- action.

Beginning teachers are usually unprepared for the wide range in abilities encountered. A study in Ferndale, Michigan, showed a reading range among children aged seven of thirty-two months, whereas among those aged twelve it was 107 months.[18] The range in mental age increased from sixty-five months at age seven to 107 months at age twelve. Excluded from this study were children who had been placed in special rooms, so in some classrooms teachers would expect a greater range than this. Ferndale is a suburban city near Detroit. The range is probably similar in most American communities. This means that we must expect great variability in the results of teaching effort. There are many common interests and needs toward which teaching energies are directed, but by no effort or magic can we produce common achievement or "fifth-grade work" or "sixth-grade norms" with a total class. We have not failed as teachers nor have some children failed as students. Although teaching and learning took place, the responses were in-

---

[18] W. A. Ketcham and Rondeau G. Lafitte, "A Description and Analysis of Longitudinal Records of Development of Elementary School Children in Ferndale, Michigan," Ferndale Public Schools, 1960.

[19] Ibid.

[20] Tulare County Schools, *Tulare County Cooperative Language Arts Guide* (Visalia, Calif., 1949).

fluenced by the individual abilities of those with whom we work.

Previous studies of the growth patterns of individual children reveal that each child's pattern is uniquely his own. Some start early and continue to grow rapidly; others start late and are always behind their age mates. Yet we cannot be certain that one who starts early will be always ahead of his group. The following case study reveals why teachers hesitate to make absolute predictions.[19]

At 78 months of chronological age all of Mary's growth measurements but one were below her chronological age. Her mental age was 64 months, reading age 74 months, weight age 76 months, and height age 84 months. By 138 months of chronological age, all of her growth measurements were above her chrono- logical age. The child's IQ was 100 when she was 78 months old and 131 when she was 137 months old. By age twelve she had a reading age of fifteen although her reading did not equal her chronological age until age 8.

Such children are not unusual. Parents will sometimes say, "My boy did not like reading until he had Miss Nelson in the fifth grade." With all due credit to Miss Nelson, it is safe to assume that the child was prob- ably like the girl described above. However, it may have been the efforts of a Miss Nelson that prevented this child from accepting a self-image of being slow to learn or poor in scholarship.

Children move through this sequence of language growth in the elementary school— no two at the same rate or in the same way. The following listing of this sequence was prepared by the Tulare County Schools.[20]

Kindergarten (4½–6 years)

Listening:	Listen to peers in play groups. Develop an increasingly long atten- tion span to stories. Can remember simple directions and messages.
Speaking:	A few will still be developing speech sounds, using them correctly in some words and not in others. Use simple direct sentences. The vocabulary ranges from 2,000 to over 10,000 words.
Reading:	Interpret pictures, explore books, can identify some signs such as STOP or displayed words on television. About 1 in 600 can read children's books.
Writing:	Like to watch adults write. Experiment with crayola and paints.

Grade One (5½–7 years)

Listening:	Listen to clarify thinking or for answers to questions. Can repeat accurately what is heard. Listen for specific sounds in words and the environment.
Speaking:	Can share experiences before the group in an established way. Use compound and complex sentences. Use the grammar patterns of the home. Some speech repetition takes place as they try to remember words for ideas they wish to express.
Reading:	Read charts, preprimers and primers, and master a vocabulary of 300 to 600 words. Understand the use of many consonant sounds.
Writing:	Write names, labels for pictures, and stories to illustrate art work. The spelling applies the phonics of reading.

Grade Two (6½–8 years)

Listening:	Listen with increasing discrimination. Making suggestions and asking questions to check their understanding. Are aware of situations when it is best not to listen.
Speaking:	Have mastered all sounds of speech and use them correctly. Use some of the "shock" words of our language without complete understanding.
Reading:	Read with increasing attention to meaning, enjoy selecting their own stories, read their own writing. Usually start the year in a first reader of a commercial reading series.
Writing:	Write well with print script. Use dictionary books or notebooks as references for spelling. Seek to correct misspellings.

Third to Fourth Grade (7½–10 years)

Listening:	Are increasingly aware of the value of listening as a source of information and enjoyment. Listen to the reports of others, tapes of their own reports, and radio broadcasts with purpose and pertinent questions. Display arrogance with words or expressions they do not understand.
Speaking:	Re-enact and interpret creatively radio, movie, and story situations as they play. Speak fairly well to adults and can make themselves understood. Are praised in most school-associated social situations. Vocabulary of some children may be as high as 60,000 words.
Reading:	Read with interpretive expression. Grow in reading speed as they read silently. Most children succeed in using reading as a study skill.
Writing:	Reports are written in all subject areas. Creative stories and poems are written. Write rough copies with a willingness to recopy to improve legibility, ideas, and punctuation.

Fifth to Sixth Grade (9½–12 years)

Listening:	Listen critically for errors, propaganda, false claims. Listen to a wide variety of stories, poetry, rhyme and find pleasure in exploring new types.

Speaking: Show an increasing awareness of the social value of conversation and try to get what they want through persuasion. Become increasingly competent in the use of inflections, modulation, and other methods of voice control. Employ singing, yelling, whispering, and talking. Can conduct club meeting and present organized talks or dramatic recitations.

Reading: Show increased interest in factual material and how-to-do-it books. Many read independent of instruction. Use reading with greater purpose, such as getting information for a trip, checking references, or following a personal interest. Adapt method and speed or reading to the content and purpose.

Writing: Make between 1½ to 2 errors in each sentence at first. Find new uses for writing as they answer advertisements and do creative work. Are interested in the writing techniques of others and will note good and poor composition in the newspapers. Like to see their writing in print. Use the dictionary as a spelling aid.

Underneath all language there is a process of thinking. Language is a process of naming, giving meaning to what is seen by symbolizing the thing or event in sound and word. Work with young children and others who have come to school with limited language development reveals that their language may be the evidence of limited perception and thought. The following table reveals the language activities that involve the thought process.

Language develops in young children as they think through their experience and learn to use words to reflect the increasingly fine shades of meaning they find in it. More than fifty years ago, a pioneer in relating children's "meaning-ideas" and "word-ideas" proposed as a "universal" principle of "oral expression" that "a man is effective linguistically in those situations, and those only, in which he has often been placed, and in reaction upon which he has been constantly urged, by force of circumstances, to express himself readily and to the point." [21] If we wish to use O'Shea's law as our guide, we might then agree that our chief purpose is to provide situations or experiences for which language needs to be developed and to provide these frequently enough and with such continuity of urging or support that the child learns to express himself ever more readily and to the point.

THINKING PROCESSES AND LANGUAGE ACTIVITIES

Types of Thinking Processes	Kinds of Language Activities
1. *Relating* Linking one item of experience to another in terms of similarities and/or differences	Comparing Contrasting Differentiating
2. *Generalizing* Setting up categories or making generalizations from observed relationships among items of experience	Categorizing Generalizing Summarizing
3. *Classifying* Placing new items of experience in categories or under generalizations already set up	Classifying Defining Describing Naming Symbolizing
4. *Modifying* Enlarging categories and generalizations to accommodate new items or events of experience	Criticizing Guessing Imagining Qualifying Modifying Revising Testing

Chapters Two through Nine present many of the specific techniques used to achieve these abilities.

For Discussion

1. What events or incidents remain in your memories of the school years between

---

[21] M. V. O'Shea, *Linguistic Development and Education* (New York: Macmillan, 1907), pp. 234–35.

ages nine and twelve? Were you in a program? Can you recall a favorite book? Did you write any letters?

2. In light of what we know about child growth would it be possible to group children of similar ability at the beginning of a school year and keep them similar throughout the year?

3. Comment on this statement: "Group teaching does not mean group learning. A TV program such as *Sesame Street* may instruct millions but each individual listener responds in terms of his own background and interest. In a classroom a teacher may share a story with the total class but expects responses to differ. Individualizing instruction would not mean a separate story or explanation for each child."

What Are the Cultural Influences upon Instruction in Language?

Abilities in speaking, listening, thinking, reading, and writing are not developed apart from the group life in which each individual learner finds his securities, his values, and his language patterns.

A culture is usually considered to be the sum total of all the material achievements, customs, beliefs, and values of any group of people; it includes the people themselves and their institutions as well as their ways of communicating and interacting with each other. A culture cannot be viewed merely as an aggregate of parts but must be seen as a human society in which various aspects of the whole are interrelated in a functioning way. Art, literature, and values emerge from the group's social experiences. Thus a culture is a dynamic and changing pattern, always being created by its members and in turn always conditioning the behavior of those who create it.

The American culture pattern furnishes the wider cultural context in which all American schools function. Democratic values and methods, together with a common basic language, make it possible for the United States to be a national or political cultural unit.

Culturally determined goals in language teaching make language a social tool for such purposes as understanding oneself and other people, relating oneself to the world through literature, finding personal satisfaction through expressive and creative use of language to solve personal and group problems, developing discriminative power to detect the purposes behind the written or spoken symbols, and evaluating the reliability of the spoken and printed messages. These goals have grown out of the modern setting of cultural activities. The conditions of living in today's world make it important to listen to and evaluate a radio or TV broadcast, to read and interpret a newspaper intelligently, and to speak, write, read, and listen with concern for integrity, logic, and honesty of expression.

The establishment of newer goals in a position of primary importance demands a new cultural integration of values and events. This integration is a slow process. It is not easy for people to see that the familiar, fundamental three R's may become still more fundamental with a recognition of the purpose for which reading, writing, speaking, and other language tools are used.

The culture holds the values which determine the opportunities for learning in the schools. Such questions as who will go to school, for how long, and in what kind of building and who should teach are answered in different ways by different cultures. Laura Ingalls Wilder in *These Happy Golden Years* describes a culture which felt that a few weeks of school in midwinter was adequate.

The culture determines what the interests and experiences of schoolchildren will be. What a child reads, speaks, and writes about is influenced by the family and community in which he lives. Children are most interested in the learning activities they can experience in their learning environments.

The culture determines the meanings that children attach to words and statements. A child raised on the prairies of eastern Colorado has no experience to relate to the word *woods*. Eventually, through pictures and descriptions he has a meaning, but it will never be as complete as that of a child who has watched a forest change through the seasons, known the fun of seeking wild fruit and nuts, or participated in the gathering of maple sap. The Navajo child whose dwelling has always been a hogan does not use, hear, or read the symbol *house* with the same meaning as the child who has lived in a brick bungalow.

The culture determines when learning experiences shall be introduced and the sequence in which skills shall be developed. As knowledge from the fields of child development and social anthropology has accumulated, leaders in education are finding that the cultural patterns of age and grade expectations in a middle-class society do not always agree with what is known about children's intimate growth patterns; the culture often expects learning to occur before the child is ready for it. However, the expectations provide a strong stimulus for learning, and when the timing of the expectation is not out of adjustment with the individual's growth pattern, this cultural influence is in favor of educational achievement.

The culture tells what kind of speech is expected of both boys and girls. The little boy is respected for speaking like a male, but scolded, teased, or otherwise punished for speaking like a female. The father serves as a model of the sex culture which the boy is encouraged to learn.

A child speaks the way his family and neighborhood speak because this is the group with which he has made first identifications. To identify with a person or group means to form a strong emotional attachment. A child's first identifications are the result of his human need for love and membership in the group. When a child identifies with someone, he unconsciously imitates that person's speech patterns. He is prone to retain these early speech habits, for they give him an identification badge; they are the symbols by which he proves his belongingness to a group. The extent to which a child speaks correctly or according to the school standards indicates the patterns that are in the security-giving group life surrounding him.

It is significant to note that the social group, even more than the family, provides the pattern for speech imitations after early childhood—more specifically, the peer group to which an individual belongs during later childhood and adolescence. The school must then accept the child as he is and help him

to have pleasurable, satisfying experiences with the school group, so that he will want to change his language badge for the one used in school.

When teachers begin to understand the middle-class expectations for rapid training, they will more clearly see why early reading and writing have become symbols of status. A child who learns to read early proves his and his parents' worthiness by this important cultural achievement. Fear of losing face with their group causes some parents to pressure children into reading before they show readiness for it. Teachers, too, are sometimes sensitive to their status position and exert similar pressures on children for early reading performance.

The cultural expectation for learning to read during the first year of school experience was established at a time when children were beginning the first reader at the age of seven, eight, or even nine years. It has persisted in the culture pattern, although the age for beginning first grade has been lowered. It was once culturally acceptable to leave school without having mastered reading.

Language instruction is dependent not only upon a child's inner maturational pattern but also upon his experience background and his opportunities for learning. A teacher must respect every child's commonplace experiences. She should dignify some of the everyday incidents of life and thereby help the child feel comfortable about his own home life and group experiences. An example of how this may happen is related by a teacher of a small school. Ten-year-old Jerry, who seemed active and interested outside of the schoolroom but who had never volunteered to share any of his interests in writing, said that he "didn't want to write anything." Jerry had never been to a circus, his only experience with airplanes consisted of watching them fly overhead. He did not have a horse or a pet. The teacher's concern for Jerry's lack of interest in sharing experiences led her to a discovery. Hitherto she had asked children to write about the unusual, or the exciting, or the very, very new experiences which only certain children had. She now changed her approach and encouraged them to write about such every-day occurrences as skinning a knee, getting wet in the rain, or running a race; Jerry then made some attempts to write about these "commonplace" experiences. Later he wrote rather well about "Hurting My Thumb."

Similarly, a child who comes from a home where a foreign language is spoken or where language opportunities are limited may not be as ready for reading English. The school must both supplement and complement the cultural nurturing of language growth.

Miriam Wilt of Temple University was thinking of such children when she said,[22]

The child has vocabulary; he has experience; he has grammar; and he has *his* culture. Surely these are worth valuing and preserving. Surely these are worth using as a lever to broader, deeper, and richer goals. But more important, perhaps, than the school using what the child brings may be the effect upon the child's self-image of the school's use of what he brings. Dignity and self-respect accompany acceptance of him as he is. Proud of his heritage, he can begin to raise his sights so that his goal will always be just beyond his grasp. On the other hand, if everything he knows is wrong and everything he does is bad, he is apt to close his shell like an oyster and silently drift away to stand against the world of school rather than with and of it.

A speaker who is ashamed of his own language habits suffers a basic injury as a human being: to make anyone, especially a child, feel so ashamed is as indefensible as to make him ashamed of the color of his skin.

The National Council of the Teachers of English makes these recommendations:[23]

Many disadvantaged children and adults speak a nonstandard English dialect. Every speaker of English is a speaker of a dialect whether it is characteristic of New England, New York City, suburban Chicago, rural Georgia, Harlem, or Oakland, California. The unfortunate and unavoidable fact is that some of the English dialects are so unique as to prevent speakers from participating fully in social structure, in prosperity, in the distinct culture, or in the democracy of the United States. Our educational enterprise has as one important function the preparation of every citizen for full participation. And to the extent that a man's dialect denies him this privilege, the school must help him overcome that disability. Teachers everywhere recognize that social and economic mobility requires that a person be able to speak an "established" dialect, or standard informal English. However, no one seems to be certain what to do, when to do it, or how to go about it.

The NCTE Task Force recommends that children be permitted to operate in the dialect of their community at the lower levels of elementary school education, and that direct instruction in the use of standard informal English be begun no earlier than the intermediate elementary grades.

During the early stages of development in school, children must become acquainted with language in general, with its uses in thinking and communicating; many of these experiences must be provided through the dialect which they already speak. As children gain experience in listening to and understanding informal English, especially through contact with teachers, school programs can gradually begin to teach standard informal English.

This does not imply, of course, that children not be exposed to standard English dialect or that classroom personnel speak the local dialect. It implies that actual instruction in the use of standard English is more appropriate and effective after children have experience listening to and understanding it from television, radio, and especially, the teacher.

The lack of planned attention to oral pattern practice, to communicating ideas aloud, and to planned experiences in listening is a serious deficiency in many programs. Rigidly structured reading programs, without oral experiences using new vocabulary and sentence patterns, seem unlikely to achieve lasting growth.

The NCTE Task Force recommends that oral language receive greater stress in language instruction for the disadvantaged at all levels of education, from preschool through adult.

Only as progress is made in the use of oral language will there be substantial improvement in reading and writing. The interdependence of these language skills has been demonstrated both in research and in practice. All forms of drama, from puppetry to formal acting, and

---

[22] Herbert J. Miller, *The Uses of English* (New York: Holt, 1967), p. 61.

[23] Richard Corbin, Muriel Crosby, *Language Programs for the Disadvantaged* (Champaign, Ill.: National Council of Teachers of English, 1965), pp. 72–74.

the oral tradition of literature need to be given greater emphasis in schools.

Literature rests on a shaky foundation in programs for the specific minorities. In some areas, because literature in traditional textbooks is too difficult or too remote, it has been dropped altogether. In others, books written for younger children are pressed into service with adolescents who might know the words but who understandably reject the ideas. In still other programs, basic literacy is so urgent a goal that the entire focus is on learning to read expository and factual materials for skill development and for information. Perhaps the most uncreative solution has been to use conventional and inappropriate materials *anyhow,* because eventually they will or should be "good" for the students.

The NCTE Task Force recommends that at all levels of instruction the English curriculum for disadvantaged students include appropriate imaginative literature chosen and presented with these students in mind.

Implementing this recommendation makes necessary two sets of choices: the materials and modes of presentation. At the preschool and primary levels, reading aloud by teachers trained in oral interpretation or by recorded artists offers an important way of extending horizons, enriching cultural backgrounds, and calling attention to imaginative and figurative uses of language so untypical of many dialects in lower socioeconomic groups. As the children mature and the thematic or "substantive" content of literary materials becomes more significant, so too does the choice of materials. Although oral reading by the teacher should never stop altogether, no program can find any excuse other than inertia for not providing imaginative literature for children to read themselves. Perhaps more than anything else, the learner needs to find his own identity and to relate himself to the larger social community. Where better than through literature can students learn to rise above themselves and to extend the range of their intellectual and emotional powers?

For Discussion

1. Modern suburban neighborhoods tend to group people of similar income and aspirations. How would this influence the language instruction in the school?

2. A boy in the fourth grade of a suburban school is having trouble in reading.

The parents had planned to send the boy to live with his cousins on a farm for the summer. However, the school now plans to have a special remedial summer school. What would you advise the parents to do?

3. Children in your school use a great deal of profanity. This reflects the language heard at home. What action would you suggest to your fellow teachers?

4. The American Association of School Administrators has identified the following cultural changes that should influence school action. How would each influence instruction in the Language Arts? [24]

To make urban life rewarding and satisfying
To prepare people for the world of work
To discover and nurture creative talent
To strengthen the moral fabric of society
To deal constructively with psychological tensions
To keep democracy working
To make intelligent use of natural resources
To make the best use of leisure time
To work with other peoples of the world for human betterment

What Cultural Influences Are Reflected in the English Language?

A major factor in our culture that concerns us is the English language itself. An understanding of the development of English will help to explain the spelling of certain words, the structure of our sentences, the growth of vocabulary, and the changes in usage.

A number of the early outside influences on the language of Britain came from Rome. Julius Caesar, as early as 54 B.C., reconnoitered on British soil and established friendly contacts with various chieftains. The Roman conquest was not completed until a century later and was marked by periods of savage resistance. The completeness of the cultural impact on the Britains is not known; the many Roman ruins throughout Britain would indicate a

---

[24] *Imperatives in Education,* American Association of School Administrators; 1201 Sixteenth Street N.W.; Washington, D.C. (1966).

thoroughgoing Romanization of the country. For a period of almost 400 years the Romans were in complete control of Britain.

Later the influence of Latin was extended by the activities of the Church. By the sixth century Christianity had spread throughout all of England. Christian converts were among the Anglo-Saxons who conquered England after the Romans left; the Welsh and British inhabitants were for the most part Christians before this time.

There are over 450 words of Latin origin found in Old English; these include: *cheese* (cāseus), *mint* (monēta), *seal* (sigillum), *street* (strata), *kitchen* (coquīna), *cup, plum, inch, wine, abbot, candle, chapter, minister, noon, nun, offer, priest, inscribe* (scribere), *cap, silk* (sericus), *sack, pear, cook, box, school, master, circle, spend, paper, term, title.*

The influence of Latin has continued through the years. Sometimes the borrowed words have come through French, Spanish, or Italian, but many retain their original form or drop an ending. One recognizes the Latin derivation of words like *censor, census, genius, inferior, quiet, reject, legal, history, individual, necessary, picture, nervous, lunatic, interrupt.* The Latin prefixes *pre-, pro-, sub-, super-*, or endings *-al, -ty, -ble, -ate, -tion, -ize* are often used with words from other sources.

Of the 20,000 words in full use today about 12,000 are of Latin, Greek, or French origin.

The original speakers of the tongue from which English was born were Germanic dwellers on the eastern or European coast of the North Sea from Denmark to Holland. These Anglo-Saxons and Jutes had undoubtedly raided the British shores even before the Roman departure in A.D. 410.

When the last legions were summoned back to defend their Italian homeland, the Britons started fighting among themselves. The Jutes were called in by the British King Vostigen to assist him, after which they settled in Kent. The Saxons did not arrive until 477 or the Angles until 547. Many of these came as mercenaries lured by the promise of land, which was divided as war booty.

By the beginning of the seventh century

this Germanic language that we call Anglo-Saxon emerged from the confusion and turmoil of the British conquest to take its place among the modern tongues of Europe. Among the factors thought to have influenced this development were the wide acceptance of a single religion and the unity of the seven kingdoms to resist the Danish invasions.

The sounds of the language resembled those of modern German rather than those of modern English. The little *c* always had the hard *k* sound. The letters *j, g, v*, were not used; *f* suggested our *v* sound; *h* was more like the *ach* of German. One additional letter, þ, called *thorn*, was used for one of the *th* sounds; we still use it in such signs as *Ye Olde Shoppe.* We have lost the *u* sound and *i* has replaced *y* in many words. Nouns had four cases: nominative, genitive, dative, and accusative. Adjectives were declined to agree with the word modified. Our little word *the* could assume any one of twelve different forms to show gender, number, and case. There were only present and past tenses.

Only a small percentage of our vocabulary today is Anglo-Saxon. If one were to take 2,000 Anglo-Saxon words at random, one would find only a little more than 500 still in use; however, these would include many of our most common words, such as: *man, wife, child, horn, harp, coat, hat, glove, hall, yard, room, bread, fish, milk, house, home, hand, thumb, head, nose, ear, eye, arm, leg, eat, work*, and *play.*

The Anglo-Saxon ability to form compounds led to expressions in which the original elements are almost lost. *Good-by* or *good-bye* is a corruption of "God be with you."

Some words from the Anglo-Saxon have picturesque word origins. *Spider* means "spinner" and *beetle* "biter." *Strawberries* once were berries strung on a straw. The poll in *poll tax* is the old word for *head.*

In spite of the Latin influence in the Church, such Anglo-Saxon words as *god, gospel, lord, Holy Ghost, sin*, and *doomsday* survived. In isolated dialects some Anglo-Saxon forms have resisted change; *larned* is used for *taught, mooned* for *lunatic, hun-*

dreder for *centurion, foresayer* for *prophet,* and *gainraising* for *resurrection.*

In the year 787 piratical rovers from Scandinavia first visited England, and for more than 100 years continued to make landings primarily for the sake of pillage. In 840, thirty-five shiploads of Danes landed in Dorset; in 851, 350 ships came up the Thames and apparently for the first time wintered in England. Eventually they became so numerous that, for the sake of order, Alfred the Great made a settlement whereby half of England had its own Danish king; at one time all of England was ruled by these Danish kings. (When you say "They are ill," you are speaking old Norse, from which has descended modern Danish.) At least 1,400 localities in England have Scandinavian names.

Such words as *steak, knife, dirt, birth, fellow, guess, loan, sister, slaughter, trust, wart, window, odd, tight, skin, happy, ugly, wrong, scare,* and *though* are among our language heritage from the Danes. The *-son* of our family names replaced the *-ing* of the Saxon. (*Washington* actually means "Wasa's children's farm.")

Such doublets as *no—nay, rear—raise, fro—from, shatter—scatter, shirt—skirt, ditch—dike,* and *whole—hole* are a part of the divided language loyalties of the Islanders. The first is Saxon, the second Norse.

The future tense (which had hitherto been expressed by the present, "I go tomorrow"); the pronouns *they, their, them;* and the omission of the relative pronoun *that* in such expressions as "the man I saw" were Scandinavian introductions in our language.

The Scandinavian invasion was not limited to the British Isles. Just as the Danes were settling in England, other Norsemen were invading the coast of France. As the British secured peace by granting an area to the invaders, so those in France were granted the region centering about Rouen. These Normans accepted both the religion and the customs of the Franks. Indeed, this acceptance was so rapid that the grandson of their Viking leader Rolf (or Rollo) could not learn his ancestral language at home but was sent away to learn Norse. Thus it was that when these Normans invaded England they not only brought with them the French language but vestiges of Scandinavian as well; indeed, other languages than these were spoken by the forces under William, Duke of Normandy. There were mercenaries from Spain, Italy, and Germany.

The struggle between the hardy race which had been developed in England under the wise policies of Alfred the Great and this Norman force was a long and bitter one. The Anglo-Saxon nobility finally was reduced to the level of their own peasants. Their language was scorned and ignored as being fit only for inferiors. With their defeat, the land was divided among the conquerors.

At the dawn of the thirteenth century there were three languages in England: French was the literary and courtly tongue, Latin the language of the Church and legal documents, and Anglo-Saxon that of the market place.

Conquerors cling to their own ways as long as they plan eventually to return to their homeland. While the Normans were occupying England their forces were defeated in France, and most of them gave up all thought of returning to that land. This changed their attitude toward the Anglo-Saxons and the language they spoke. In 1349 English was reinstated in the schools, and in 1362 Parliament was reopened in English. During this time, hundreds of words came into the language. Some were words that one class might acquire from another, such as *baron, noble, dame, servant, messenger, story, rime, lay.* French law terms remain in use: *fee simple, attorney general, body politic, malice aforethought.* In our kitchens we use *sauce, boil, fry, roast, toast, pastry, soup, jelly, gravy, biscuit, venison, supper, salad, saucer, cream.* The French words *beef, veal,* and *pork* remain along with the Saxon *ox, calf,* and *swine.* Our present word *island* represents a blend of Saxon *iegland* and the French word *isle.* Among our synonyms, we have French and Saxon words in *acknowledge, confess; asemble, meet; pray, beseech; perceive, know;* and *power, might.* The words associated with the arts are French, or Late Latin through French: *amusement, dancing, leisure, painting, sculpture, beauty, color, poetry, prose, study,* grammar, title, volume, paper, pen, copy, medicine, grief, joy, marriage, flower.

Many of the terms of the modern square dance are French. When one "sashays to the corner" the word is an adaptation of chasser, which means to chase; and do si do is dos-à-dos, or back-to-back. Many military terms are French: army, navy, enemy, arms, battle, siege, sortie, soldier, guard, spy, lieutenant, rank, vanquished, conquer.

But the most important thing that happened during these years was a tremendous simplification of the language. No longer were nouns and adjectives declined. One form of each word emerged as the one most frequently used. One authority says with a note of regret that if the language had remained neglected by scholars for another 100 years it might have emerged with a great purity of expression and meaning determined on basic usefulness to a people blessed with considerable common sense.

In review, then, the English language contains words, patterns of speech, and spelling that were influenced by historical developments. Starting with the ancient Celtic, we next found the Latin influence of the Roman invaders. The basic language structure is Teutonic as introduced to the British Isles by the Angles, Saxons, and Jutes. This in time was influenced by the Danes. With the Norman invasion, we have noted both the French and continuing Scandinavian influences. Because of the Church, the Latin influence continued through the years. Although trade with other lands has influenced our vocabulary, these are the major historical sources of the English language we use today.

For Discussion

Explain this statement: "While half the words in common usage are of Latin or Greek origin, half of the words on any one page will be Anglo-Saxon in origin."

What Recent Changes Have Taken Place in the English Language?

With the development of printing, a number of important changes came into the language. The English printer William Caxton (1422?–1491) made the works of Chaucer (1343–1400) available to the general public beginning in 1477; he is famous for printing the first book in English in 1475 (*The Reccuyell of the Historyes of Troye*).

Something happens when words are reproduced in print; they achieve an importance and dignity they did not possess in manuscript form. The very act of duplication or making copies seems to grant authority to the printed word. The spelling of a word or the sentence structure that appears in such an important literary effort places the stamp of social and cultural approval upon the form; at any rate, we can trace many of our instructional problems in language to these first printed books.

One of the problems was that of spelling. The word *guest* appears as *gest, geste, ghest, gheste; peasant* as *pesant* or *pezant; publicly* as *publickly, publikely, publiquely; yield* as *yeild, yielde,* and *yilde.*

Often it was a printer's effort to make words seem more consistent or even more scholarly that determined the form used. The silent *b* in *debt* and *doubt* originated on the premise that the original Latin forms had *b.* An early form was *det* or *dette.* The *gh* in *delight* and *tight* is a result of analogy with *light* and *night.* A number of words such as *won* in which the *o* represents the sound of *u* were an effort toward spelling reform. When such words are spelled with *u* the handwriting tends to become a confusing series of upstrokes.

It has been estimated that 10,000 words were added to the language during the Renaissance, and they became widespread through the press. Shakespeare added such words or expressions as *accommodating, apostrophe, dislocate, frugal, heartsick, needle-like, long-haired, green-eyed, hot-blooded.* Words such as *capacity, celebrate, fertile, native, confidence,* and *relinquish* were called barbarisms and were understood by few readers.

No description of this time would be complete without reference to the King James Bible of 1611. It is estimated that less than 6,000 different words are used in this translation and that fully 94 per cent of these were part of the common speech of the day. The translators were apparently concerned with reaching the masses in a language that would be understood by all. Hence it was up to them to use the best-known words.

Some words are repeated with great frequency (*and* is used 46,277 times). Although there is monotony in some parts, the text is usually very clear in spite of the profound ideas expressed. While Shakespeare shows us the range of thought that can be expressed with many (15,000–17,000) words, the Bible demonstrates almost the same range with only 6,000.

Today a highly literate adult is not likely to have a recognition vocabulary of much more than 150,000 words. Of this number a few will be used over and over again. One fourth of all our spoken words consists of a repetition of the words *and, be, have, it, of, the, to, will, you, I, a, on, that,* and *is.*

Since the invention of printing, new words have been added to English in many ways. Some are borrowed from other languages; others have been created for new products; and still others seem to be accidents or the results of misunderstanding foreign speech. If a person who spoke Anglo-Saxon were to listen to us today, he would have a very difficult task understanding all that is said.

From the Italian we find these words: *design, piazza, portico, stanza, violin, volcano, alto, piano, torso, cello, vogue, serenade, trombone, broccoli, boloney, confetti* (hard candy), *cash, carnival, cartoon, studio, solo, opera.*

Spanish words include *alligator, banana, canoe, cocoa, hammock, hurricane, mosquito, potato, tobacco, rodeo, cockroach, cork, tornado, sombrero.* In the Western United States many towns, hills, rivers, are Spanish-named as a result of the early exploration and settlement in those states during the seventeenth and eighteenth centuries. The terms of ranch life and the cowboy and his vigilante equipment are usually Spanish in origin: *hacienda, mustang, corral, lasso, lariat.*

The Dutch are responsible for such words as *chapter, yacht, schooner, boor, drawl, deck, boom, cruiser, furlough, landscape, tub, scum, freight, jeer, snap, cookie, toy, switch, cole slaw,* and *yankee.*

The Arabic language gave us *candy, lemon, orange, spinach, sugar, algebra, alkali, alcohol, assassin, syrup, sofa, divan, mattress, magazine,* and *safari.*

From Hebrew, we find *camel, ebony, sapphire, seraph, cherub, cabal, rabbi.*

From India comes *loot, pundit, rajah, punch, coolie, bungalow, calico, cot, polo, thug, khaki.*

Kimono, samurai, and *kamikaze* are Japanese.

Malay gave us *caddy.*

The tribes of Africa are responsible for *gorilla, voodoo, zebra,* and probably *jazz.*

The American Indians are the creators of many of our words; among these are *moccasin, raccoon, skunk, totem, woodchuck, hominy, caucus,* and *tomahawk.* Every state contains Indian place names: *Chicago* means "a place that smells like skunks," *Peoria,* "a place of fat beasts," and *Manhattan,* "the place where all got drunk."

New words come into our language almost daily. Some are changes in the word root: *edit* from *editor, peddle* from *peddler, jell* from *jelly.* Others are abbreviations such as *pub* for *public house, cad* from *cadet, pup* from *puppy.* Some imitate other words: *motorcade* and *aquacade* from *cavalcade, litterbug* from *jitterbug, telethon* from *marathon.* We combine words to make new ones, with *smoke* and *fog* becoming *smog, motor* and *hotel* becoming *motel,* and *liquid oxygen* becoming *lox* (used for combustion of fuel in rockets).

Old words are used in new ways or as different parts of speech. A master of ceremonies is abbreviated *emcee;* this in turn becomes a verb in such usages as "Allen may emcee the show." An example of one word used to serve different parts of a sentence in the newspaper headline that reads, "Police Police Police Show."

Words change in meaning. *Harlot* once was a servant, *wanton* and *lewd* meant "untaught" or "ignorant." *Notorious* was simply "well known." A *governor* was a "pilot," *rheumatism* meant a "head cold," and a *nice person* was a "foolish person."

In the years since the war many words have been added to our language: *Cinerama, countdown, zoorama, fallout, readout,* and *sonic boom* are examples.

A recording of an astronaut's flight provides a reuse of words that have been developed in the age of space exploration. (*Courtesy of San Diego State College.*)

Modern slang is a source of new words. Often this is the private language of an age group. Expressions like "Twenty-three skiddoo" are now archaic; they are no longer part of the living language. One recent coinage, however, seems to have found a permanent place in our speech. One sees it in headlines. The President uses it and it has found a place in literature. It is the term *to goof*. It means "to make a mistake, yet know better." When one word will say that much, it probably deserves a permanent place in our language. The third edition of Webster's *New International Dictionary* does not consider this term to be slang, although similar expressions are still held to be questionable usage.

Today the opportunities for vocabulary enrichment have been both extended and accelerated by the advent of such instruments of communication as radio, motion pictures, and television. The number of radios in use has grown from about 15 million in 1950 to more than 80 million today. To this we must add the influence of almost 85 million television sets. The in-

fluence of the motion picture has been increased not only by the entertainment film in commercial theaters and drive-ins but also by those made especially for television or for instructional use in school.

The English language is truly a many-splendored thing. We are the heirs of a language of tremendous vigor and force; its extraordinary growth both as to words and geographical range is only a partial witness of the value of our heritage. It is our task as teachers not only to help children to understand the wonderful power of this language, but to guide students so that its use will enrich their lives and those with whom they live.

For Discussion

1. Make a list of new words and slang expressions as you hear them or see them in print.

2. How should we explain the use of slang to children?

3. What influence do you think paperback

books have had on the reading habits of individuals your age?

4. Find examples of good and poor English used in comic books or in television programs. Do these have any influence on the children you teach?

5. A new word was coined by the press at the time this book was being written. The first monkey had been sent into space and recovered. Within three days children across our land were talking of the *chimpanaut*. Can you identify a recent word coined in current news events?

6. How could the story of a word's origin help a child remember its spelling?

7. A few of the long words of our language may add interest to a bulletin board or discussion. Here are some: *antidisestablishmentarianism* was used in 1869 by Prime Minister Gladstone to describe the principles of those opposed to the separation of Church and State. *Honorificabilitudinitatibus* appears in the fifth act of "Love's Labour's Lost" by Shakespeare. *Floccinaucinihilipilification* means "estimation of worthless." *Pneumonoultramicroscopicsilicovolcanokoniosis* means a "disease of the lungs." *Aqueosalinocalcinocetaceoluminosocupreovitriolic* was used to describe the waters at Bristol, England.

8. Some of the language found in the Bible is no longer used. Why do we no longer use *thee, thou*, and such verb forms as *maketh?*

9. Can you explain some of these inconsistencies?

An English Test

We'll begin with box, the plural is boxes,
But the plural of ox should be oxen, not oxes.
One fowl is a goose, but two are called geese,
Yet the plural of mouse is never meese.
You may find a lone mouse, or a whole nest of
*   mice,*
But the plural of house is houses, not hice.
If the plural of man is always men,
Why shouldn't the plural of pan be called pen?
The cow in the plural may be called cows or
*   kine,*
But a bow, if repeated, is never called bine;
And the plural of vow is vows, not vine.

If I speak of a foot and you show me two feet,
And I give you a boot, would a pair be called
*   beet?*
If one is a tooth and a whole set are teeth,
Why shouldn't the plural of booth be called
*   beeth?*
If the singular's this, and the plural these,
Should the plural of kiss ever be written keese?
We speak of a brother, and also of brethren,
But though we say mother, we never say
*   mothren.*
Then the masculine pronouns are he, his, and
*   him,*
But imagine the feminine, she, shis, and shim!
So the English, I think you all will agree,
Is the funniest language you ever did see.

UNKNOWN

What Does the Elementary Teacher Need to Know About Linguistics?

The study of language in the culture of a people is an aspect of anthropology. So is the study of the way parents educate their children. Nelson Frances of Brown University describes the work of linguists.[25]

A linguist is a scientist. His subject matter is language. He is concerned with such broad questions as:

What is language?
How does it work?
What are its parts and how do they fit together?
How do languages differ and what do they have in common?

as well as with more specific questions about particular languages—their structure, history, and relationships. Around the edges of the discipline of linguistics are important peripheral studies like psycho-linguistics and socio-linguistics, whose hyphenated titles indicate their interests.

The principal occupations of the linguist relate to seeking solutions for these questions. Specifically, the "pure" linguist—

works away at theory, attempting to find the best ways to study, describe, and to some degree at least, explain the workings of language and languages;

---

[25] Bernard J. Weiss, *Language, Linguistics and School Programs* (Champaign, Ill.: National Council of Teachers of English, 1963), pp. 95–99.

goes into the field to collect material, which he gathers, records, preserves, classifies, and publishes: makes use of materials collected by others;

synthesizes concepts, ideas, relationships, etc., on the basis of such materials; teaches linguistics to future linguists and others, including English teachers.

There is also the *applied linguist*. This curious title does not mean that the linguist is himself applied to anything; it is a back-formation from *applied linguistics*. The applied linguist (who is often a pure linguist with another hat on) brings linguistic knowledge to bear on such problems as the teaching (and learning) of languages or how they can be made more efficient by

devising writing systems for hitherto unwritten languages;

helping technicians of various sorts with machine translation and other technological gadgetry (much of this kind of work is sponsored by various government agencies, including the armed forces, which are understandably interested in problems of communication);

working with psychologists, reading specialists, and others on problems of language learning and the teaching and learning of reading;

preparing dictionaries, concordances, editions, glossaries, grammars, and other similar materials for the general public or for students and teachers.

The concerns of the linguist and the teacher are often dissimilar. The linguist is primarily concerned with theories about language. The teacher is concerned with the ability of a child to speak and write effectively.

Throughout this book information from the studies of linguistics has been placed in association with the work that teachers do. The history of words, changes of word meaning, ways of writing, the new grammar, the place of dialect, the sounds in our language, the construction of dictionaries, and the teaching of a second language are discussed when appropriate to the problems of working with children.

At times teachers are puzzled by linguistic scholars who make suggestions with respect to teaching young children that are contrary to what is known about child

growth or the psychology of learning. The educators' expertness in these areas needs to balance the knowledge the linguists possess. Publishers have misused the term *linguistic* to suggest qualities in new materials that will solve teachers' problems. It is difficult to conceive of a school program that did not have some linguistic validity, because linguistic scholars are far from being in agreement. (They do not agree on the number of sounds in our language, the definition of a sentence, or the grammar of English.) This is especially true with respect to reading. Any claims of a single approach simply reveal the uninformed background of the advocator.

Teachers know that many educational problems are more related to economics, sociology, or psychology than to language. Indeed, much linguistic information explains learning difficulties without suggesting classroom procedures.

There are eight basic linguistic principles which should be observed as a teacher formulates the philosophy and practices which will apply in a classroom.[26]

First, language is a system. It is a system of complex patterns and a basic structure. There are individual units which work together with other units. Thus linguistically we look at grammar not to identify parts of speech but to learn the forms and patterns within the system. Children learn a language by learning to *use* these structured patterns rather than by analyzing them.

Second, language is vocal. Only speech provides all the essential signals of a language. The unit parts are those sounds that make a difference in meaning when used; they are called phonemes. Letters are an attempt to represent the sounds of a language. Reading is first of all a recoding of print to sound, then a decoding of the language to meaning. This is why a reading program should be based upon the child's existing language knowledge.

---

[26] Harold B. Allen, "Face East When Facing Non-English Speakers," *On Teaching English to Speakers of Other Languages,* Series I (Champaign, Ill.: National Council of Teachers of English, 1964), pp. 53–55.

The *fourth fundamental is that each language is unique.* No two languages have the same set of patterns, sounds, words, or syntax. English is neither German nor Latin. For many years our school grammar has misled students by providing Latin grammatical statements as if they were true about English. It would have been equally erroneous to have insisted that students follow the grammatical rules for German.

The *fifth fundamental is that language is made up of habits.* Our use of the system itself is on the habit level. Our ways of pronouncing a sound or ordering words in a sentence are done as automatically as walking. Teachers are not going to get anyone to speak English by telling him about the language or having the learner memorize language forms. Learning a language is governed by situations which require the use of language. The situations control the vocabulary and the syntax.

The *sixth fundamental is that language is for communication.* Language must first make sense to the user—but it must also make sense to others. If the pronunciation is misunderstood, or forms indicate a meaning other than the one intended, the language fails to communicate. This demands an audience analysis. If this is done it is apparent why standard usage is essential and at the scholarly level an exactness is necessary. Getting a job, participation in group discussions, writing to be understood require a high quality of language. While there is less concern about the best way to speak and write, there will always be a concern for grammatical adequacy to assure the exchange of meaning.

The *seventh principle is that language is related to the culture in which it exists.* Language exists in speakers who are in certain places doing certain things. Almost every trade has words and expressions understood only by the in-group. Sometimes this is called jargon, a kind of occupational slang. At other times it is highly technical language requiring similar experiences to assure communication.

The *eighth principle is that language changes.* One teacher illustrated this to a group by having the following dialogue of slang used twenty years ago recorded on a tape. The children were asked to interpret what was meant.

Slang 20 Years Ago [27]

School has been dismissed for the day.
Jim and Kathy meet outside Jim's homeroom.

JIM: Hi, Kathy! Howzit?

KATHY: Hi, Jim. Say, what gives in your class these days? Jeepers, I never saw so much junk!

JIM: Not junk, sister. Pyramids. We're building Egyptian doodads in social studies.

KATHY: How come?

JIM: It's for the glass gadget in the hall. We're going to stash the stuff in there so the other kids can glim it.

KATHY: Terrif! That's a lot more fun than eyeballing the old books all day. This brain factory's looking up.

JIM: Well, I gotta beat it now. Time to put on the feed bag. Dig ya later?

KATHY: Natch.

Current slang such as neat, square, cool, dough, bread, pad, sharp were discussed noting both established meaning and the slang interpretation.

All eight principles are important for teachers who work with children.

For Discussion

1. What is some of the educational jargon that is used by educators? Would the following terms qualify: *peer group, open classroom, homogeneous grouping, interest centers, finger play, slow learner?*

2. What are some current slang expressions used on the campus? What purpose does such language serve?

3. A modern author expresses this opinion about some of the uses of linguistics in the school. Observe a modern classroom in language and see if this statement is justified.[28]

---

[27] Anna McCormic and Norma Dove, "Teaching Slang, It's a Gas!" *Grade Teacher* (February 1969), p. 116.

[28] James Moffett, *A Student-Centered Language Arts Curriculum* (Boston: Houghton, 1968), p. 14.

Linguistics filled the bill to dispel the last wisps of progressivism and to establish the post-Sputnik age of "intellectual rigor." By a deft switch of rationale we could now go on teaching grammar, not as an aid to speaking and writing—for massive evidence forbade that—but as a "humanity" for its own sake, or as an intellectual discipline (like Latin) to develop the mind. A student who is told to learn the different kinds of "determiners" or to transform one arbitrary sentence into another arbitrary sentence might well ask, "If it's a humanity, why is it so inhumane?" It can only be a symptom of hysteria in the profession to swallow the argument that any modern grammar is a humanity or that the study of it has some special virtue for developing thinking. A study of the uniquely human ability to produce language and organize life symbolically is indeed a humanity, but that study is conducted by paying attention to everyday verbal behavior, and, in later years, by becoming acquainted with psychology, sociology, and anthropology, subjects which are hardly even touched on in the overall pre-college curriculum. Yes, language is central to human life, but grammar is a drastically small and specialized subject, limited essentially to nothing broader than syntax, that is, the relations and patterns of words in a sentence.

What Principles of Learning Guide the Teacher of Language?

Learning has been described in many ways. For our purposes it might be described as a change of behavior which persists and which is not due to maturation alone. This rules out those changes associated with the physical growing up that does influence behavior. When a child learns to substitute a carefully drawn letter in the first grade for the scribbling he did before coming to school, and uses this acquired learning as the beginning of his writing skills, he has changed his behavior in a manner that will persist.

Behavior involves more than acquired skills. It is a combination of knowledge and skill with a goal, supported by an attitude of

A study of man's effort to communicate through signs helps children become objective about their own language skills. (*Courtesy of San Diego State College.*)

confidence. As we influence the behavior of children in a learning situation we are aware of these three factors. Often our task is not to teach a skill but to establish a goal for the learner so that he will employ knowledge he already has; or it may be encouragement to instill the confidence needed by the child in directing his skills toward a goal.

To a college student it is quite possible that learning seems to mean the gathering of information and facts. A history course might be considered to provide an example of this kind of learning. Why did you take the history course? Your goal, frankly, may have been to learn more about the United States. Did it change your behavior in any way? Will it influence your actions as a citizen? Will it influence your interests as you select recreational reading? Is your attitude the same with respect to political decisions you are asked to make? Your answers may be negative to all of these questions, yet the fact remains that you chose to take the course because of some personal motivation. Usually a college instructor attempts to make his classes interesting and to motivate your participation. In the back of his mind there is the comforting thought that you are there to learn from him because he knows more than you do about that particular subject. In addition, he does not face any special problems of communication. If you do not understand his language you can review the subject matter in books or other reference materials on your own. If you fail to understand or if you compete unsuccessfully, you are notified about this in the form of a low grade.

The teacher of grade school children faces a different situation. Many a well-informed adult has failed completely as an elementary teacher because he or she could not guide the learning of immature individuals. The child is in your classroom because of cultural pressure rather than any specific decision of his own. As a matter of fact, he had no alternative but to go to school; attendance is required by law. Fortunately, he has two culturally important goals that make school an attractive place. First, the little child wants to learn to read and write and, second, he desires to be accepted and

loved. Because of this he strives to please the adults who are his associates. A child does many things through no other motivation than to please his parents or other family members and his teachers. One of the tragedies of childhood is to be in a situation where the tasks assigned cannot be accomplished in a way that wins approval.

Modern psychology has much to offer the teacher of language arts. The following five principles will emphasize some results of the work in that field which make learning more effective.

1. *The first principle is that teaching effort is most effective when the learner has a basic understanding of established goals and sees the relationship between what is taught and those goals.* A visit to an elementary classroom will reveal that the teacher knows a great deal about each child. One of her concerns is interest. As she plans she asks, "What will interest John?" Or she will remember, "Mary is very interested in insects." She also knows that children follow patterns of interests as they develop. Home, mother, baby, and fun are universal interests of the beginners. As their environment expands the interest will include neighbors, children far away, foods of different countries. Schools often plan their curriculum units around these known common interests. Such interests establish purposes for reading, writing, and research; they therefore provide goals for the child in undertaking certain tasks.

When children have rather limited interests the good elementary teacher plans situations that will arouse curiosity and questions. Sometimes a film will awaken interest in volcanoes or animals. An exhibit of pioneer objects which can be handled may lead to the study of history as the teacher desired. When this is accomplished, the teacher has motivated an interest. Sometimes a teacher is criticized for forcing interests on children rather than developing interests that already exist. The problem faced by most teachers is one of working with a large group of children rather than with just one or two. With one or two, a teacher could teach language well in association with the emerging interests of each child. With a total class a teacher faces such practical problems as meeting certain expected achievement standards and having enough material on hand to gain certain objectives, as well as the social responsibility of controlling youthful energy so that learning can receive some direction. But motivation that results only in acceptance by children of teacher-determined goals will never be as effective as goals mutually felt and accepted by both teacher and pupil. At times during the day motivation can come from each individual child; at other times it must be group determined.

The word *attainable* is significant with respect to goals. The child who is constantly asked to do more than he can accomplish with success is in a difficult position. The adult can simply walk away from the situation by resigning from a job, changing courses, or moving to another town. The child cannot meet frustrating conditions in the same way. He may misbehave or move into a dream world and ignore what is happening to him. Some will put forth extra effort to master a task for a time if they feel the pressure from home or the teacher. Eventually, for the sake of relieving tension, these children create an acceptable self-image which does not place great value on the specific skill. It is safe to say that few children are motivated for any length of time by continuous failure. Of equal importance in considering the word *attainable* is the child who achieves without effort. For some children the tasks of education present little challenge. Proficiency with the yo-yo is not an especially satisfying skill for a college student. In almost any classroom there is one child who is completely bored by the situation. Frequently we exploit these children by making little teachers out of them. This action at least recognizes their superior knowledge, although it seldom helps them toward greater educational growth. The most effective effort is put forth by children when they attempt tasks which fall into the "range of challenge"—not too easy and not too hard—where success seems quite possible but not certain.

2. *A second basic understanding about directing learning of children is that a teacher must consider individual differences.* A college classroom of future teachers studying the language arts consists of a homogeneous group. Not only have the students passed through a number of educational filters so that their ability is that of rapid learners, but they have made a common vocational choice. No elementary classroom can be made as homogeneous. Yet there are great differences within the college classroom; some students are married and have children, others have traveled widely; some belong to campus organizations, others do not. Although they may have a common interest in teaching, their other interests may vary widely.

A classroom of children will reveal differences in rate of learning, interests, social and economic backgrounds, and dozens of other factors that must be recognized. The teacher knows that the *whole* child comes to school, not just a mind to be taught. Some of the differences that the teacher considers would be the child without a breakfast, the child who is worried because he heard his parents quarreling the night before, and the child who had night terrors after seeing a late-late TV movie. The differences have a direct influence on the goals established for each child.

It should not be assumed that all instruction must be individualized because of these differences. There are common needs that the teacher considers with respect to the group. There are many similar interests based on their ages and years in school that form the basis for group instruction. The important thing to remember is that a competitive rating, which is felt to be fair in a college class, is not appropriate in many elementary classrooms. To let a child who reads very well set the expected standard for the class would be as foolish as to let the one who sings the best establish the only acceptable vocal standard for all. Yet we sometimes act as if we were saying that unless you read as well as Mary you cannot get an A in reading. A more common way of ignoring the significance of individual differences is to use an average score as the means of measurement. This is simply a mathematical manipulation that seems to have an authority far beyond any defendable reason. If we give a spelling test and add the scores made and divide by the total number of students, we can find the average score. If all those taking the test were of equal ability and aptitude, the results might indicate those who put forth the greatest effort and least effort to study the words. But if those taking the test represented the normal range in ability, the average tells us nothing. It is only as we consider the work exhibited by each child in terms of his personal idiosyncrasies that we can make any judgment worthy of a professional teacher.

It is especially important that a teacher accept individual differences as well as recognize them. Some teachers spend a career trying to make people alike in the area of reading and writing. One hears them say, "If John would only try!" the inference being that with only more effort John could be like Jane. As children advance through the school years the differences in the skills taught at school will become greater. The span of reading ability in a first grade will be small, usually ranging from six months to three years. The span of reading ability in a sixth grade will range from the second-grade level to the adult reading level. The device most frequently used to make dissimilar groups alike is to hold the top ones back by limiting material to sixth-grade books while providing special training for those "below grade level," with the assumption that through some teaching magic those who read second-grade material can be brought to the sixth-grade level.

A modern teacher is also careful as to predictions about children based upon present performance or potential level of achievement. Some "late bloomers" may eventually surpass pupils who seem far ahead of them in grade school. It is well to remember that it is only in school that success is limited to success in reading.

3. *A third basic principle of teaching children is to present the skills or understanding in situations similar to those in which they will be used.* Language is functional when it is used in conversation, reports, letter writing, listening to the radio, viewing television, telling a story, or any of the communicative acts of daily life. Effective expression, legibility in writing, correctness in usage, or thoughtfulness in listening and reading will develop only to the extent that children discover these skills to be of value in the daily, functional use of language. To isolate instruction on any aspect of language without this understanding on the part of the learner produces very limited results.

This does not mean that drill is entirely out of place in the language arts program. But to be effective the drill must be self-assigned by the learner in terms of a specific goal he desires to achieve. Drill on a specific word in spelling may involve writing the word many times, just as drill in basketball may involve shooting toward the basket over and over again.

The same is true of worksheets which involve selection of such correct usage items as *set* and *sit* or *lie* and *lay*. They are true learning devices only when the student does them with an understanding of the possible error and the desire to correct an error he has made. Some children in filling in blanks on worksheets have made the same errors year after year. The teachers have carefully recorded scores made on these assignments. Some had them corrected by the students and thought they were doing a good job of teaching. In some schools teachers will defend this procedure by saying that all judgments by their principals concerning the language arts are based on the standardized test results. The teachers feel that they are preparing the children for this measurement by such drills and in that they are correct. But it should be recognized that they are teaching for testing rather than for any functional use of the language.

An example of intelligent application of this learning principle can be found in association with letter writing. During the year the need to write a business letter will develop in connection with the work of the students. At that time instruction should be given concerning the form of such letters and careful attention should be given to their content. If the letter is actually to be mailed, children will welcome and remember the information taught.

Related to this is the care that must be

taken to assure that something once taught will be used when needed. As a new language skill is introduced it becomes a standard to be applied in all work. Throughout the year students will add to the list of standards that they expect to maintain as they write and speak. As new knowledge is employed, habits are established.

4. *A fourth basic principle of teaching is that concepts are best established by using many firsthand perceptual experiences.* How easy our task would be if it were only a matter of "telling" the child. If concepts were built by lectures, an oral reading of the law would make good citizens of all of us. Children can learn only what they have experienced. All meanings are limited by the experiences of the learner. The understanding of democracy may start from such basic behaviors as taking turns, participating in a group decision, acting as chairman of a group, or being on the Safety Patrol of a school. Eventually we hope that it will develop into an explanation of our way of life.

Fortunately the imagination of a child is so vivid that some concepts will develop as he identifies himself with characters in a story or with great men in history. Some children can do this as they read, others as they participate in role-playing dramatizations, and still others through discussion of problems and situations.

Some of the concepts are developed in association with other learning. The teacher may think she is doing a fine job teaching speech by means of a verse choir, yet the child may actually be learning to like or dislike poetry rather than to enunciate correctly. All learning situations have an emotional content. Often the feeling about a learning situation remains long after the facts taught are forgotten. One teacher reports remembering a composition he had written on Italy in the fifth grade. The contents are forgotten except that for his cover he drew a flag of Italy. He does remember vividly a mental picture of the teacher mounting his composition on the bulletin board. He also reports that since that time Italy and things Italian have always held a special attraction for him.

5. A fifth basic principle has been im-

plied in the other four but for the purpose of emphasis should be noted by itself. It is simply that *to be retained, learning must be used.* Learning for a specific situation— such as memorizing a part in a play or studying Japanese while visiting Japan— disappears in a very few years if not used. Nearly every college student reading this page once knew how to solve a problem involving square root. Now if they try to obtain the square root of any four-figure number without referring to tables, they will probably find they have completely forgotten how to do it, simply because the knowledge has not been used recently. Usually we plan instruction with respect to specific learning in what might be called a spiral organization. We start with the known, go to the new, then return to the known. We call this reteaching, reinforcing knowledge, integration of knowledge, or simply review. Seldom do we attempt to move toward the new by climbing stairs where each step represents new knowledge.

This reteaching principle places a responsibility upon the teacher. The teacher as the mature individual in the teaching–learning situation is expected to plan and select experiences that are useful to the child at his present stage of development. In the language arts curriculum of today this can be illustrated by the way phonics is taught. A few years ago the school day provided a separate period for phonics. Children were drilled in the sounds of the English language. Some were able to transfer this knowledge so that it could be used in reading and spelling. Others failed to make the transfer. In order to render this knowledge more useful, teachers were told to teach the specific phonics needed to meet a specific reading or spelling need. As soon as the child knew two words that started with the same sound he was taught to note the beginning letter and to apply its sound in a new word. Thus the immediate usefulness of phonics was apparent to the learner.

Later, when we discuss the parts of speech, we will see that this problem has reference to teaching sentence analysis. No matter how sincerely we drill children in identification of nouns, verbs, adjectives, and other parts of speech few children remember this information. For some reason we have not taught this knowledge in a way useful to the learner in the elementary grades. Application of this principle means that teachers must first find a way in which the language skills we teach children can be of immediate service to them and, second, see that it is used with frequency to prevent forgetting.

Modern psychology has taught us much more with respect to the way children learn, but the preceding five principles will help solve many of the immediate problems of a beginning teacher planning instruction for children.

For Discussion

1. State to what extent the five principles of learning discussed in this chapter are repeated in the following statements:

Principles That Influence Learning [29]

a. Learning takes place more readily if the child accepts as useful and important to him the activities in which he is expected to engage.

b. A child's learning is both richer and easier if he shares in selecting and setting the goals of learning, in planning ways to gain them, and in measuring his own progress toward them.

c. A child learns to solve his life problems, some of which he cannot now anticipate, only to the degree that he is capable of understanding and directing his own actions.

d. Learning is more efficient if it has satisfying emotional content, if feeling is supportive of thinking.

e. Firsthand experience makes a deeper impression upon a person than vicarious experience.

f. Learning is facilitated and reinforced when more than one sensory approach is used.

g. A child learns best when he is relieved of too great pressure to compete and when he feels reasonably confident that he can accomplish what is expected of him.

h. A child learns best when his failures are viewed constructively by a teacher who likes and respects him and when appropriate remedial or corrective measures are worked out with him.

i. Attitudes, feelings, values, and appreciations are learned. Every experience involves a constellation of such learnings.

j. A child learns best when his efforts are appreciated by his teacher and his classmates.

k. A child learns best when he is freed from the distractions of personal problems.

l. A child learns best when the rhythm of mental activity, physical activity, and relaxation is appropriate for him.

m. Learning opportunities are richer for children when they are not restricted to the things which the teacher already knows.

2. Carl Rogers feels that no man can teach another. At best we present situations and questions that cause the learner to teach himself. Is this what the poet Kahlil Gibran is saying in this situation from his book *The Prophet?*

Speak to Us of Teaching [30]

And he said: No man can reveal to you aught but that which already lies half asleep in the dawning of your knowledge.

The teacher who walks in the shadow of the temple, among his followers, gives not of his wisdom but rather of his faith and his lovingness.

If he is indeed wise he does not bid you enter the house of his wisdom, but rather leads you to the threshold of your own mind.

The astronomer may speak to you of his understanding of space, but he cannot give you his understanding.

The musician may sing to you of the rhythm which is in all space, but he cannot give you the ear which arrests the rhythm nor the voice that echoes it.

And he who is versed in the science of numbers can tell of the regions of weight and measure, but he cannot conduct you thither.

For the vision of one man lends not its wings to another man.

And even as each one of you stands alone in God's knowledge, so must each one of you be alone in his knowledge of God and in his understanding of the earth.

---

[29] Camilla M. Low, "Selecting and Evaluating Learning Experiences," *Guidance in the Curriculum,* Chap. 4, 1955 Yearbook (Washington, D.C.: Association for Supervision and Curriculum Development, 1955), pp. 52–65.

[30] Reprinted from *The Prophet* by Kahlil Gibran with permission of the publisher, Alfred A. Knopf, Inc. Copyright 1923 by Kahlil Gibran; renewal copyright 1951 by Administrators C.T.A. of Kahlil Gibran estate, and Mary G. Gibran.

How Do Schools Meet the Special Needs of Individual Students?

The classroom teacher does two things to meet the extreme ranges of talent and abilities encountered in some classrooms. One is to modify the requirements of the regular curriculum; the other is to enrich the content of the curriculum. Usually we modify the requirements for children who are slow in maturing or handicapped, and enrich for those who are above average or gifted. In a sense, the modification for the slow child is an enrichment for him.

With respect to the gifted, the term *enrichment* describes two types of practices. One is to give these children more advanced work. This can be done by promoting the child to a class where he works with students much older than himself, but where he finds the contest a stimulating challenge. Or the child may be kept with children his own age and yet work in books that are more difficult than those read by the other children. Thus, an eleven-year-old gifted child might be reading Shakespeare either in a fifth-grade class or with a high school group. This method is usually called vertical enrichment, because the child moves upward toward more difficult material. The other type of enrichment would be to have able children remain with their age mates but explore areas that all the other children do not share. The gifted child might study a foreign language, astronomy, or geology, or he might read avidly as he solves research problems, sharing the results with his classmates. This type of practice is called horizontal enrichment.

We do not know which method is best. The answer may be a combination of the two, or it may depend upon the child. With respect to language arts the horizontal type is more apt to meet the needs of most children. Our mission is not achieved by treating children as adults. In spite of an individual's brilliance, the adult world will seldom have a place for a fifteen- or sixteen-year-old as an equal. The years of youth are precious and brief. We seek to enrich the world of able children while they are living in it, not when they have become adults. Their needs to belong, to be accepted, and to be wanted are shared by all other young people. It would hardly be enrichment to put them in a world where neither children their own age nor adults satisfied these needs.

The term *open classroom* is now used to describe the teaching–learning situation in which the students pursue individual studies or inquire about a subject without predefined objectives. The Integrated Studies curriculum described later would be considered an open classroom situation. In *36 Children* Kohl [31] describes his work with a class in Harlem who wrote creatively of their immediate problems and after being introduced to Greek mythology invented similar explanations for aspects of life around them.

In some open classrooms, buildings have been designed so that several teachers are with a large group of children who are divided according to interests or purpose. In some there is a great deal of student tutoring working in groups of two. The room is carpeted and children may be working on the floor, in large boxes under and on tables, or sometimes outside the classroom in a comfortable secluded spot. There are many materials easily available to the learner. These may include individual sound tapes, film cassettes, games, animals, reference books, records with listening headphones, or objects being studied such as a gasoline motor. The atmosphere is one of freedom to explore as well as a sense of achievement. In some there are continuous rewards in the form of stamps or other recognition. In none is there a predetermined achievement level which would create a sense of failure. Time is usually organized by the learners in conference with the teacher. Some are far more skill oriented than traditional classrooms in that progress is based upon a sense of mastering rather than covering a book or preset curriculum.

Some teachers have always followed such a program because of their orientation to children and their educational goals. Nearly all kindergartens have been such classrooms in the past.

---

[31] Herbert Kohl, *36 Children* (New York: Signet Books, 1967).

Many schools follow a practice of "clustering" a group of above-average children in classrooms with normal students. This provides some mutual stimulation yet affords opportunities for leadership and sharing with age mates who have similar social and physical interests. Others provide "seminar classes" where small groups of gifted children work together all day. It is a growing practice to provide an enrichment program in a summer school where foreign languages, typewriting, and advance science courses are taught.

Children are usually considered intellectually gifted if they have an IQ of more than 148. In order to provide special classes many schools lower this requirement to 130. But identification of gifted students is not just a matter of high intelligence. The tests we use seem to measure abilities in mathematics, reasoning, and the use of words. Other abilities such as talent in art, music, or social leadership are not measured. Neither are such personality factors as interest, steadfastness, and emotional stability. Frequently outstanding students in science have quite normal IQ ranges.

Terman's great study of very bright children did indicate that many were equally superior in physical and social adjustment.[32] However, teachers who have worked with these children insist that things are not always well with those who have a mind with adult power despite their child's body. The very insight these children possess makes for sensitivity. The high goals they set make them extremely critical. Their abilities tend to set them apart socially, and frustrations use up some of their energy. Many are lonely as a result of isolated or adult interests. Some become bored and resentful with regimented class drill. Others suffer from overenrichment that leaves little time to live and play as normal children.

There are many activities for these children in the language program. Guided reading in the world of literature; research reports from encyclopedias; creative expression in original stories, plays, and poems; and surveys relating to a personal interest are but a few of these activities. But procedures will differ when working with this type of ability. Larger blocks of subject matter and longer periods of time are needed to permit the expression of the abilities these students possess. A vast amount of material must be made available that is beyond the needs of a regular classroom. Evaluation with these children to establish desired goals and quality of work takes considerable time and individual counseling.

There are some special problems to consider. The books these children are able to read frequently contain an emphasis upon sex or abnormal personalities that are beyond the social maturity of these children. In the areas of religion and politics comparable problems exist. These children are seriously concerned about philosophy, social questions, religion, and economics, and their interests are not to be taken lightly.

There may be a difference between highly creative individuals and those with high intelligence quotients. One study reports that creative talents do not seek conformity with teacher-approved models, nor do they seek to possess now the qualities that will lead to adult success. The investigators report, "It is as if the high-IQ children seek and like safety and security of the known while the highly creative seem to enjoy the risk and uncertainty of the unknown." These creatively gifted individuals consider high marks, IQ, pep and energy, character, and goal-directedness less important than do the high-IQ group. They do rate a wide range of interests and a sense of humor higher than the high-IQ group. Indeed, humor is marked among the creatively talented. Apparently these children do not find a comfortable place in many classrooms, yet they possess a gift more rare than intelligence.[33]

At the other extreme there are the slow learners and the handicapped. There is one

---

[32] L. M. Terman and M. H. Oden, *Genetic Studies of Genius* (Palo Alto, Calif.: Stanford, 1947).

[33] J. P. Guilford, "Convergent and Divergent Aspects of Behavior," Lecture, San Diego County, October 1960. See also his *Personality* (New York: McGraw-Hill, 1959), Chaps. 15 and 17.

POTENTIAL ACADEMIC ACHIEVEMENT OF CHILDREN WITH VARIOUS IQ LEVELS

Chrono-logical Age	Slow Learning Range				Slow Normal Range			Average
	50 IQ	60 IQ	70 IQ	75 IQ	80 IQ	85 IQ	90 IQ	100 IQ
6	Pre-K	Pre-K	K	K	K	K	K	K & 1
7	Pre-K	K	K	K	K	K	K & 1	1 & 2
8	K	K	K	K — 1	K & 1	1	1 & 2	2 & 3
9	K	K	K & 1	1	1 & 2	2	2 & 3	3 & 4
10	K	K & 1	1 & 2	2	2 & 3	3	3 & 4	4 & 5
11	K	1	2	2 & 3	3	3 & 4	4	5 & 6
12	K & 1	1 & 2	2 & 3	3 & 4	4	4 & 5	5	6 & 7
13	1	2	3 & 4	4	4 & 5	5 & 6	6	7 & 8
14	1 & 2	2 & 3	4	5	5 & 6	6	7	8 & 9

From *Design for Teaching,* Elementary Curriculum Bulletin No. 2, Dade County Public Schools, Miami, Fla., 1947.

special group that a beginning teacher needs to understand well to avoid serious errors in judgment and practice. These are the children who come from homes where English is not spoken. Common sense tells us that their primary need is a knowledge of the English language. They are not necessarily slow learners and should not be treated as such. Of course, they appear slow in a world where the printed books and all instruction are in a foreign language.

The above chart will help identify some of the expected achievements of the slow learner. It is important to note that these children are learning. The child with an IQ of 75 may be working at the kindergarten level through grade 2 but by the age of thirteen he can do beginning reading. It is important that this experience be as pleasant for him as it is for the normal child who masters the beginning reading at the age of seven or eight. The two great needs of these children are a feeling of acceptance and a sense of growth or academic achievement.

In the language program there will be a greater emphasis upon oral speech experiences based upon actually shared experiences of the group. These children need a lot of directed "doing" of the type associated with kindergarten activities. They need to handle things. Early reading will be limited to basic signs such as "Stop" and "Go." Much of the learning is situational—what we do and say

when we visit the principal's office, when we go to the cafeteria, when we watch a program.

The slow learner cannot compete with children who operate in a more rapid way. They want praise and honor as much as any individual. It should be given to them when they achieve growth or improvement. Just as the gifted need to be challenged, so do the slow. It is sometimes difficult to think of a challenge for the gifted. It is equally difficult to appreciate what may be a challenge for slow children. One student of this type in the sixth grade was using all of his ability when he wrote his name correctly.

With an understanding teacher these children become steady, stable, dependable workers in situations where the routines and tasks give them security. The three R's for these children are repetition, relaxation, and routine.

For Discussion

1. How can we explain the needs of a slow-learning child to a parent who is an average or above-average learner?

2. Why do schools sometimes hesitate to publicize the work they do with slow learners? With the gifted?

3. Does it take a gifted teacher to work with gifted children?

What Is the Integrated-Studies Program?

In British schools and a few in the United States the strongest trend is away from teaching grammar, marking papers, and using textbooks of a traditional nature and toward creative writing, dramatics, and a generally more spontaneous curriculum. Linguistics as such are not included in the language arts program in the elementary school. It is a university discipline and is considered desirable knowledge for elementary teachers but not as something to be taught or discovered by young students. The everyday verbal behavior of children represents the process for growth in language understanding and thinking. The development of thought and intellectual rigor comes in many ways as the learner symbolizes his experiences and attempts to understand the symbolization of other people.[34]

One term used to describe such programs is *integrated studies;* others are *fused, emerging,* and in some cases *individualized.* Integrated learning fills the pupils' minds not with parts of knowledge called subjects, but with a *unified area* of experience. The effects of such a program are evidenced in the students. Pupils care about what they are learning and the concern sustains them in the pleasure of hard work to satisfy felt needs. Pupils make choices (rather than accepting assignments) that concur with their developing personal interests. Pupils range widely through many firsthand experiences in the sphere of action; these are anticipated, accompanied, and followed by secondary experiences in the sphere of contemplation. Pupils use many linguistic skills in a stimulating workshop atmosphere in close relationship with other pupils and adults. The major activity is personal talk as the pupils are involved in new experiences and explain new roles. Writing serves a purpose when, after many involvements, pupils come to an understanding, or discover an underlying pattern. Pupils mature in attitude as they share experiences and interact with others

[34] P. Bartlett and E. Bates, *Impetus to Integrated Studies* (London: Ginn, 1969).

(both children and adults) in a field of common concern and discover different ways of arriving at truth. Phases in the development of man's understanding are re-enacted. Slowly from the pool of imaginative personal response in which every incoming experience is made their own there emerges a sense of the knowledge they have in common with others which, as it increases, attains the status of "a subject," too extensive for any one mind to contain. In the course of his school career the pupil may go deeply into a chosen "subject" area of experience, but the habit of integrated learning will help him draw the subject into his own personal world picture, a very different result from that where facts are approached and expected to be remembered for their own sake.

Pupils work on their own time schedule, unforced by teachers anxious for signs of progress. Progress comes in the pupil's attitude, in his mastery of himself in all his complexity and ambiguity, in his desire to grow, in his openness to experience, in his deep involvement with what really matters. This approach to education is a sincere effort to accept what is known about individual differences and the nature of a rapidly changing society in which the student will live and work.

If imaginative and well-informed teachers have been able to anticipate the learner's developing interests; provide the right response; make available helpful books, material, and equipment; and prompt pupils into rewarding directions while avoiding dead ends, integrated learning may well have taken place. But if the theme is chosen by the teacher; if the pupils are nagged into fact finding for testing or to please the teacher or to get a grade; if the teacher has preplanned every step and judges by preconceived attainment goals; if cohesion is imposed from without instead of being built up steadily in each pupil's mind from within; if the slower members of the school community are unable to see the wood for the trees; if there is no steady flow of talking, acting, reading, listening, writing, imagining, doing; if the pupils feel no pride or satisfaction in what is happening, it is quite probable that integration has not characterized the school program.

Such a program respects not only the differences between students but also those between teachers. The teacher who is best in an integrated-subjects program accepts himself, using his own gifts to enrich the classroom community, taking from others that which will enlarge his limitations, wasting no time on whether he knows enough himself, but spending it instead on finding out with his pupils. Such a teacher quickly recognizes those whose span of attention is long and those with less staying power, those capable of initiating work for themselves and those who need care and guidance, those whose efforts are ready to share with people beyond the classroom and those who should remain under his protection. This flexible approach on the part of the teacher takes into account both the interests likely to predominate in the various age groups and those an individual is likely to have.

The teacher is rarely at his desk, although for him, as for the children, relatively quiet periods are necessary for consolidation and reflection. Initiative passes between teacher and children as emphasis moves from individual to small group to class, and possibly to other classes, other schools, and interesting visitors.

Parents often wonder what goes on in school, as they piece together scraps of information from their own and other people's children. Why does the teacher not sit at his desk and see that pupils do as they are told? Are painting, dancing, acting, expeditions, and so on, really *work?* Are the children forever on the move? Does the teacher never use the blackboard to pass on his store of information in a systematic way? Has accuracy ceased to matter? These are fair questions, and the teacher is usually only too eager to answer them.

"The modern classroom is planned for maximum involvement of your children's interests," he will say. "In it the children are able to range freely, but this freedom is not to be confused with license. It gives room for individual choice among many attractive alternatives, in an atmosphere where personal need is respected and served. It gives time for satisfying results to be achieved, whether long-term or short-term. It provides an environment where suitable materials for creation and research abound, and there is no place for mere passive acceptance and rote learning."

Order imposed from without is temporary and shallow compared with the true order associated with the active investigation and quiet follow-up work that takes place in such classrooms. Children who are allowed to develop in this way are recognized by their confidence, serenity, and poise; by their intellectual curiosity, self-reliance, and perseverance in the face of difficulty; and by the range and accuracy of their imagination and powers of expression. Just as a young child explores and develops his own powers through the biological process of play, so the older pupil explores and develops *his* powers through the so-called play activities of music, drama, painting, or expeditions. Just as an infant does not learn a technique of walking or talking to make him "accurate" and efficient in these skills, so the older pupil achieves accuracy and efficiency by pleasurable practice in purposeful context.

The teacher certainly does not abdicate. What then does he do?

He encourages diversification of activity. He helps children to formulate their own questions (where once he would have "assigned" them himself).

He places the emphasis on enrichment of understanding rather than overpolished short-term products.

He judges when a pupil's "collection" of interests is ready to become a "system" and prompts realization by a timely question.

He helps to set the climate of opinion.

He secures due sympathy for the disadvantaged child.

He feeds in relevant material. (Freed from the shackles of preparing his own brief for lessons, he now has time to read and to discover.)

He values articulate, independent, adventurous young people.

"Language work" is a world away from tasks given cold, to put in the mould of a forty-minute period; it is designed to be on-going, rising quickly from a significant context, and as diverse as the range of people in the classroom. Themes, ranging forward and back through time and place, can help children to find symbols for life as they know it and to enrich and order their deeper feelings and ideas; they enable a wide variety of language powers to be brought into operation quite naturally. A workshop approach helps each pupil to find his own level and raise it as he moves through the gamut of talk, listening, drama, reading, and writing.

Although any language that children can offer must be accepted, and it is likely to be "domestic" in the first place, pupils will have been tempted into many registers and styles by the needs of richly diverse contexts:

Informal talk for problem solving, contemplating, evaluating, and role playing.

Serious discussion when using accumulated information in the service of shaping points of view.

Exposition, as when conducting people through an exhibition of work.

Tape recording in groups for playback to the class.

Play writing.

Diary writing.

Book writing.

Film script writing.

Excursions into special uses of writing, such as minutes and agenda, recipes, and so on.

Thoughts about language while evolving one's own, considering sign language, dialects, and slang.

Creative use of personal language in stories, poems, and so on.

Reading all kinds of literature.

All these activities, some directly developing personality and others helping to space and objectify clusters of interests, will form features of the "profiles" we have in mind. Language development has a chance of becoming much more coherent and swift in integrated studies, as it is readily seen as a common concern for all teachers, whatever their "subject interests."

A social by-product of integrated studies is the degree to which home and school are brought into collaboration. Now that the emphasis has been transferred from "aquiring facts" to "enlarging the child's world picture," the lore of home and street takes on a new value and shared learning is much more likely than it used to be.

Teachers do help with beginning parts and materials have been created to guide children as they start their search for knowledge.

The chart on the top of page 49 indicates what might happen simply by starting with a *street.*

A scroll map (bottom of page 49) shows the flow of interest.

The following examples of language work were the result of river study.[35]

A River Project

Hester's description of the beaver is typical of many products of research in a study of the river.

The Beaver

Beavers are found in North America, Europe and North Africa. They have five toes on each foot, with webs between the hind toes and a double claw on the second toe. There are four molars to each jaw. Their tails are scaly and rounded at the base, then broadening and flattening out to the rounded end. Their bodies are plump and covered with rich, silky fur. Beaver's lengths are normally about 2 ft. 9 ins. and their tails about 12 ins.

This animal's colour is dark brown above and slightly paler below. They are darker when wet.

Beavers live in lakes, rivers or marshes where there is running water. They build dams of branches and mud across streams so as to flood home territory and cover the lodge. Beavers swim and dive well. They do not hibernate. They eat roots, bark and water-plants, stored below ice for winter. Beavers live for approximately fifty years.

Beavers have four front teeth and they are always as sharp as knives. This is because there is a layer of orange enamel (very hard) covering them.

---

[35] Ibid.

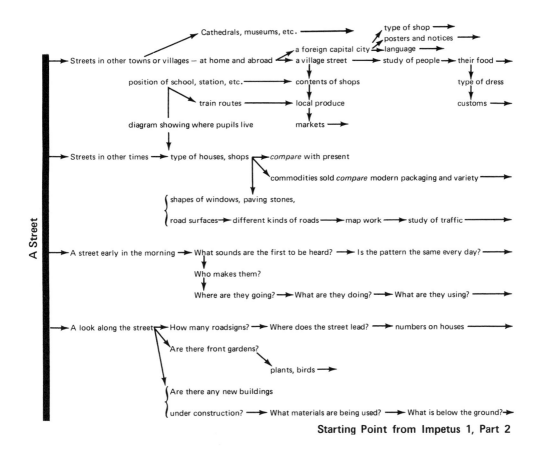

Starting Point from Impetus 1, Part 2

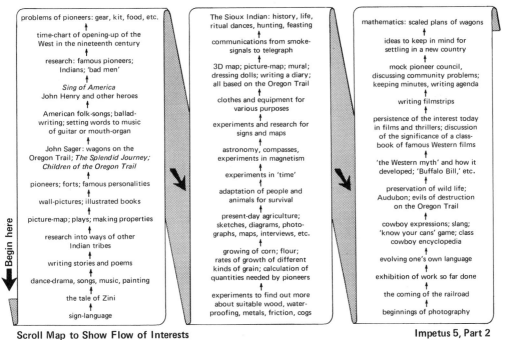

Scroll Map to Show Flow of Interests

Impetus 5, Part 2

Both illustrations are from P. Bartlett and E. Bates, *Impetus to Integrated Studies* (London: Ginn, 1969). By permission.

49

The beavers make their lodges, homes, by piling a great mass of sticks and roots in a big cone on a solid foundation at the bottom of the pond. A lodge is sometimes six or eight feet high and fourteen or more feet across its base. It is very firmly woven together.

                                          HESTER

Boys enjoyed straightforward personal recording, with maps.

We left school at about 2.45 and walked down to the river. It was a nice day and some of the other groups came. The tide was fairly high but it was going down. We saw a tug pulling two barges, and a tug pulling one barge. We saw a couple of 'pairs', a few 'eights', some 'scullers' and a 'tub four'. We saw planes and a helicopter. We also saw a bandstand and a separate tug. The water was horribly full of rubbish. There were many trees. I noticed an Elm and a Willow. We saw an emphicar on the water and I saw a police boat. Mr. N. went to fetch a girl's paper which she had dropped over the railings. There was a nice fresh breeze and all of the boys in the groups, Adrian, Richard, Kevin, Bruce and all the others went back to school but I went to the Ibis Sports Club.

'The moods' of the river seemed to make a strong impact on most children, especially in its stranger or 'sadder' aspects.

The River at High Tide

Shabby boats float
With colourful paints cracked and worn,
Slimy twigs and gnawed wood
Swirl, then motionless
To cling to the forgotten craft;
Chugging tugs
Pull heavy laden barges
While others
Ancient and condemned;
Coxon's orders
Echo the serene sky,
The rower's oar
Swishes the sunlit water;
Green ridged trees
Twist over the shadowed water,
Strong icy ripples of the tide
Reach the concrete edge.

                                          ERIC

For Discussion

1. How would an integrated-studies curriculum provide for the wide range of reading abilities found in most intermediate grade rooms?

2. What interest centers and other materials would be of value in an integrated-studies program?

3. One authority tries to get teachers started in an integrated-studies program by telling them to be lazy—"Let the children teach you." What does he mean?

4. Why might an integrated-studies program be a richer educational experience than a textbook program in a culturally deprived community? Would this be the case in a community with many educational resources?

5. In *Crisis in the Classroom* by Charles E. Silberman (Random House, 1970) there are a number of classroom examples for classroom practice in American schools. Which of these would be examples of an integrated-studies program?

Item: A fourth-, fifth-, and sixth-grade room in Lakota. A number of youngsters are writing stories, each taking off from the opening phrase "One frosty, frigid morning. . . ." On the board is a collection of a hundred or so "winter words and phrases," which the children themselves have assembled. The buzz and chatter all over the room indicate that the children are quite verbal.

Item: Another fourth-, fifth-, sixth-grade room in Lakota, filled with devices to stimulate communication of all sorts. There are sheets posted around the reading area, where children write their own suggestions for "A Good Poem to Share," "A Good Story to Read to Yourself." A "Something to Share" bulletin board is filled with the children's own snapshots, poems, stories, personal notices, and so on. Other displays of the children's writing indicate a more-than-usual degree of imagination. There is a display headed, "What is . . .?" with poems children have written on what is blue, what is gold, what is purple, and so on, trying to express how a color feels, sounds, smells, and so on. And there are stories on "What a Turkey Thinks of Thanksgiving" (a nice switch from "Why We Are Happy the Pilgrims Landed"), a collection of "Spooky Tales," essays on "My Dream School."

Item: A sixth-grade classroom in Stark-weather. Three youngsters are writing a story. To help them break away from the usual rigid classroom exercise, the teacher has one child begin by writing something that is to serve as the middle of a story; a second then writes a beginning to lead up to the middle segment, and a third completes the story.

Item: A room in Minot. A display headed "A Poem I Recommend" has a caption suggesting that those students who were interested might like to write down the poem's title, the book and page number where it can be found, and their reasons for liking the poem. Nineteen children were interested.

Item: A fourth-, fifth-, sixth-grade room in Lakota. On the wall are poems the children have written. One, by a farmer's son, begins, "I think my shadow is full of fears/Because when I go in the dark it disappears."

Item: The teacher directs a group of children in a game about circles. The children dance into large circles, small circles, tiny circles. They intersect. They form concentric circles. Then, with pencils, paper, and compasses, the children each make a "Circle Book," no two of which are alike. It is clear that they understand terms like *connecting, concentric, intersecting,* as well as subtle differences between *huge* and *large* or *small* and *tiny.*

Item: Two little girls dress up in "grown-up" clothes; together with a boy, they play house in a remarkably sophisticated manner. The two "mothers" decide on their marketing list, writing the order on a pad, and then dictating it over the phone to the grocery store clerk. The clerk takes down the order but tells them they will have to come and call for it; his delivery man has gone home. Off the girls trot, weaving on their high heels as they go. Everything is fine until it comes time to pay the bill; the clerk has arrived at one total, the shoppers another. The impasse is resolved by going to the "bead bank," a table with three sealed jars, each containing beads of a different color to represent "ones," "tens," and "hundreds," and a huge open jar containing beads of all three colors. The children arrange and rearrange the beads until they agree on the (correct) answer.

Item: A first-grade classroom. Children at several tables are working with "intellectual kits"—homemade collections of stuff organized around some common characteristic or theme. At one table a master teacher is "modeling" the Hughes approach for the classroom teacher. The process can be used for any kind of kit (teachers are encouraged to make up their own) or for any objects a teacher may use to get children talking, observing, comparing, classifying, and so on.

Each of the five children has a kit made out of a piece of bright red felt. The master teacher begins by asking the children if they can guess what's inside without looking. "It's something hard," one boy volunteers. "Mario thinks he feels something hard," the teacher repeats, asking for more replies. "It's noisy," another child suggested. "Carla shook her package and heard noises," the teacher responds. "I wonder what kind of material makes noises?" "I think it's metal," a third ventures. "Juan thinks the material is made of metal, Carla thinks the material makes noises, and Mario thinks he felt something hard," the teacher continues. "Hearing is a good way of finding out, and so is touching. How else can we find out about things?" "Looking," one child replies. "Well, then, why don't you open your kits and see what is inside." The children open the kits with gusto; each has a collection of keys of various shapes, sizes, and functions—assorted house keys and car keys, a big black wrought-iron decorative key, a small metal key that winds a toy car, the tiny key to a personal diary, and so on.

After the children have handled the keys for a few minutes, the teacher continues the lesson, asking if anyone can find two keys that look alike. Carlos offers two keys that are the same length but have differently shaped tops. "They certainly do have shafts of the same length," the teacher replies, rubbing her finger along the length of the shaft, but not translating the word directly and not correcting the child directly; instead, she works the word *shaft* into the conversation several times. For a half hour the lesson continues, as teacher and children talk about the keys, comparing and differentiating them according to size, shape, color, material, weight, and use.

Item: At another table, five children and the teacher aide are working with a kit of hinges, including among other items a door hinge, a scissors, a purse, spectacles, and a clothespin. They discuss the fact that the door hinge and the scissors are both hinges, that the scissors has a cutting edge, just like a table knife, but that the table knife has no hinge. The point of the discussion is to establish the concept of cross-classification, i.e., that objects may have membership in more than one group, sharing some but not all the characteristics of the other objects in that group.

Individual Projects or Areas of Specialization

Provision for the differences between individual students is as important at the college level as it is in the elementary school; however, it is seldom possible for a teacher at that level to know the students as well as the teacher does during the beginning years of school. As a result, individual needs must in part be met by the college students themselves. In a methods course this can be done by having each student select a problem or area which he will study with some intensity and share with the others.

At the end of each chapter there are suggested projects that you may want to select as an area of specialization, or these may suggest others to you that have occurred in your teaching. During the first weeks of the course, glance ahead at these suggestions and select one that interests you, one in which you feel you need greater understanding and competence.

One characteristic of the teaching profession is the sharing of ideas that will help others. Our educational magazines are full

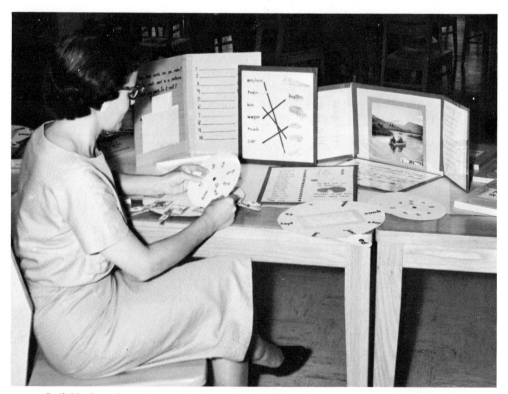

Individual needs may be met by instructional drills and games that provide a laboratory experience which emphasizes a specific bit of knowledge. The shoe-string board in the center is a familiar matching exercise similar to those in many work books. Teachers usually create such materials to use in their classrooms. (*Courtesy of California Western University.*)

of such experiences contributed by teachers. Classroom teachers welcome visiting students and will pass on material that has taken them months to develop. Few other groups are so cooperative with regard to the "secrets" of the trade. Your entire class can profit from the presentation of these individual studies; instead of one area of ideas, each student gains those of as many as there are in the class.

Some projects can best be presented by a paper which is a short summary of information learned; others require a demonstration with a puppet, story, or other device. A third type represents collections of materials, and the major value of sharing is that others may learn of sources.

Your class should decide if these should be a part of your grade. Up until now you have often worked for a high grade. Perhaps this is the time to change your objective to working for professional competence. Like the good teachers you have known you will be guided by the question, "Will this help me be a better teacher?" rather than "Will this get a good grade for me?" The chances are that the reputation you build as a professional person will be far more important than a grade.

The material in this chapter would be related to projects like the following:

1. Make a study of local place names. What was the original source and meaning?
2. Review some of the chapters in *Linguistics in the Elementary School Classroom* or *Readings in the Language Arts* by the author of this text, published by Macmillan.
3. In the book by Helen and Carlton Laird, *The Tree of Language* (Cleveland: World, 1957), there is much that will interest children with respect to the story of names and common words. Adapt some of this material for classroom use. Why do so many unpleasant word meanings start with *sn?* What words can have opposite meanings? such as hold fast and run fast.
4. Review current practices with relation to the gifted or slow-learning child as reported in course of study publications or periodicals.

Bibliography

General Books

Frazier, Alexander. *New Directions in Elementary Education.* Champaign, Ill.: National Council of Teachers of English, 1967.

Jenkins, Gladys Gardner, Helen S. Shacter, and William W. Bauer. *These Are Your Children.* Chicago: Scott, Foresman and Company, 1966.

Schlauch, Margaret. *The Gift of Language.* New York: Dover, 1955.

Todd, Vivian E., and Helen Heffernan. *The Years Before School,* 2nd ed. New York: The Macmillan Company, 1970.

Articles

Dean, Loraine. "Increase Vocabulary with the Word Elements Mono Through Deca," *Elementary English* (January 1970), pp. 49–55.

Endres, Mary, Pose Lamb, and Arnold Lazarus. "Selected Objectives in the English Language Arts (PreK–12)," *Elementary English* (April 1969), pp. 418–25.

English Curriculum Study Center. *Project English—Composing: A Process.* Athens, Ga.: University of Georgia, 1965.

Entwisle, Doris R. *Subcultural Differences in Children's Language Development.* Baltimore: Johns Hopkins University, 1967.

Keyser, Samuel Jay. "The Role of Linguistics in the Elementary School Curriculum," *Elementary English* (January 1970), pp. 39–48.

Kinder, Robert F. *The English Program K–12—The Tree and Its Roots.* Champaign, Ill.: Connecticut Council of Teachers of English, N.C.T.E., 1967.

LeGow, Marcy. "Alice in Subland," *Exceptional Children* (Summer 1970), pp. 773–75.

MacDonald, James B. *Language and Meaning.* Washington, D.C.: Association for Supervision and Curriculum, N.E.A., 1966. (*Address:* 1201 16th Street N.W.; Washington, D.C.)

Morrison, Charlotte. "A Creative Teacher Shares Notes to Trainees in a Gifted Child Training Program," *The Gifted Child Quarterly* (Summer 1970), pp. 97–105.

Ojemann, Ralph H. "Should Educational Objectives Be Stated in Behavioral Terms, Part II," *Elementary School Journal* (February 1969), pp. 229–35. Part I: February 1968, pp. 223–31. Part III: February 1970, pp. 271–78.

Strauss, Jack, and Richard Dufour. "Discovering Who I Am—A Humanities Course for Sixth Grade Students," *Elementary English* (January 1970), pp. 85–120.

Readings

College enrollment has put great pressure on existing library resources. Books of selected articles are a convenient source for students. Frequently the material in such collections is unavailable to teachers in any other form.

Anderson, Paul S. *Linguistics in the Elementary School Classroom.* New York: The Macmillan Company, 1971.

Anderson, Verna, and others. *Readings in the Language Arts.* New York: The Macmillan Company, 1968.

Burns, Paul, and Leo M. Schell. *Elementary School Language Arts: Selected Readings.* Chicago: Rand McNally & Company, 1969.

Cayer, Roger L., Jerome Green, and Elmer E. Baker, Jr. *Listening and Speaking in the English Classroom.* New York: The Macmillan Company, 1971.

Frost, Joe L. *Issues and Innovations in the Teaching of Reading.* Chicago: Scott, Foresman and Company, 1967.

Gleeson, Patrick, and Nancy Wakefield. *Language and Culture.* Columbus, Ohio: Charles E. Merrill Books, Inc., 1968.

Howes, Virgil. *Individualizing Instruction in Reading and Social Studies.* New York: The Macmillan Company, 1970.

Johnston, A. Montgomery, and Paul C. Burns. *Research in Elementary School Curriculum.* Boston: Allyn & Bacon, Inc., 1970.

Majurkiewicz, Albert J. *New Perspectives in Reading Instruction.* New York: Pitman Publishing Corp., 1964.

Petty, Walter T. *Issues and Problems in the Elementary Language Arts.* Boston: Allyn & Bacon, Inc., 1968.

Robinson, Evelyn R. *Reading About Children's Literature.* New York: David McKay Company, Inc., 1966.

Schell, Leo M., and Paul C. Burns. *Remedial Reading.* Boston: Allyn & Bacon, Inc., 1968.

Tiedt, Iris M., and Sidney W. Tiedt. *Readings on Contempory English in the Elementary School.* Englewood Cliffs, N.J.: Prentice-Hall, Inc., 1967.

Weiss, M. Jerry. *An English Teacher's Reader.* New York: The Odyssey Press, Inc., 1962.

College Textbooks

Applegate, Mauree. *Easy in English.* New York: Harper & Row, Publishers, Inc., 1960.

Ashley, Rosaland Minor. *Successful Techniques for Teaching Elementary Language Arts.* West Nyack, N.Y.: Parker Publishing Co., 1970.

Boyd, Gertrud A. *Teaching Communication Skills in Elementary School.* New York: Van Nostrand–Reinhold, 1970.

Corcoran, Gertrude B. *Language Arts in the Elementary School. A Modern Linguistic Approach.* New York: Ronald Press, 1970.

Dallmann, Martha. *Teaching the Language Arts in the Elementary School.* Dubuque, Ia.: Wm. C. Brown, 1966.

Dawson, Mildred A., M. Zollinger, and A. Elwell Gindey. *Language Learning.* New York: Harcourt Brace Jovanovich, Inc., 1963.

Drewes, Ruth H., and others. *Practical Plans for Teaching English in Elementary Schools.* Dubuque, Ia.: Wm. C. Brown, 1965.

Greene, Harry A., and Walter T. Petty. *Developing Language Skills in the Elementary School.* Boston: Allyn & Bacon, Inc., 1967.

Lamb, Pose. *Guiding Children's Language Learning.* Dubuque, Ia.: Wm. C. Brown, 1967.

Leonard, Edith M., Dorothy D. Van Deman, and Lillion Miles. *Basic Learning in the Language Arts.* Chicago: Scott, Foresman and Company, 1965.

Liebert, Burt. *Linguistics and the New English Teacher.* New York: The Macmillan Company, 1971.

Logan, Lillian M., and Virgil G. Logan. *A Dynamic Approach to Language Arts.* Toronto: McGraw-Hill Company of Canada, 1967.

May, Frank. *Teaching Language as Communication to Children.* Columbus, Ohio: Charles E. Merrill Books, Inc., 1967.

Moffett, James. *A Student-Centered Language Arts Curriculum, Gr. K–13, A Handbook for Teachers.* Boston: Houghton Mifflin Company, 1968.

Shane, Harold, and others. *Improving Language Arts Instruction in the Elementary School.* Columbus, Ohio: Charles E. Merrill Books, Inc., 1964.

Smith, E. Brooks, Kenneth S. Goodman, and Robert Meredith. *Language and Thinking in the Elementary School.* New York: Holt, Rinehart and Winston, Inc., 1970.

Smith, James A. *Creative Teaching of the Language Arts in the Elementary School.* Boston: Allyn & Bacon, Inc., 1967.

Strickland, Ruth G. *The Language Arts,* 3rd ed. Boston: D. C. Heath & Company, 1969.

Tidyman, Willard F., Charlene Weddle Smith, and Marguerite Butterfield. *Teaching the Language Arts.* New York: McGraw-Hill Book Company, 1969.

Tiedt, Iris M., and Sidney W. Tiedt. *Contemporary English in the Elementary School.* Englewood Cliffs, N.J.: Prentice-Hall, Inc., 1967.

Trauger, Wilmer K. *Language Arts in Elementary Schools.* New York: McGraw-Hill Book Company, 1963.

Wolfe, Don M. *Language Arts and Life Patterns.* New York: The Odyssey Press, Inc., 1961.

two

speech and listening

How Are Skills in Oral Communication Fostered?

The term *poorly languaged child* has been used to describe the four- and five-year-old youngsters who were assisted by the Head Start program. That program was an attempt to prepare those children whose environmental background limited their early success in school. Some of these children were from homes where a foreign language was spoken or whose oral English usage was not equal to that of other children their age. Some were from environments that were so restricted that the children's vocabulary was limited. Sometimes the term *culturally deprived* is used to describe such children. It is true that in comparison with many children the culture had not provided some boys and girls with the language traditions in the form of stories, mother goose rhymes, talk with adults, the idioms of social relations or the vocabulary meaning found in the subject content of the primary grades.

The effort to meet the needs of this group revealed the importance of adequate speech practice as the basis for developing skills in reading and writing.[1] It also emphasized the importance of language with respect to an individual's self concept and psychological identification with his society. The development of language growth has been discussed in Chapter One. Our purpose now is to note the ways the child may be assisted in

---

[1] This is not a new discovery. See Emmett A. Betts, *Foundations of Reading Instruction* (New York: American Book, 1954), pp. 6–10.

developing the skills of organizing his oral language.

The influence of the home is of fundamental importance. A child of four is probably silent nineteen minutes of his waking day.[2] Given some direction, such oral practice has great potential for learning. A study of the relationship between the early reading experiences and patterns of parent–child relationships found that children who engage in two-way conversations at mealtime with parents who encourage them to talk can be distinguished from other children denied this experience. The child in a home where the mother is frequently absent because of work or social activities may get such experience by relating with another adult, such as a grandmother or babysitter.

It is quite certain that exposure to television does not do the same thing for a child. First, the role of the child as speaker does not exist as he watches. There is limited interaction. Second, much that demands a child's attention on television is limited with respect to language. Many cartoons shown to children represent a sophisticated humor and use words which mean little to the listener. (Nearly all commercial cartoons are addressed to adults.) Third, the television vocabulary is limited to a few situations, such as the Western cowboy. It is quite possible that some television programs especially designed for children with an educational purpose as a goal might influence children's oral speech in a positive way.

Children's oral language growth responds to educational efforts in a rewarding way. One group of orphans of nursery school age made significant advances after seeing pictures that they discussed, listening to stories told by an adult, going on short excursions, and undergoing specific training involving situational vocabulary and language patterns.[3]

---

[2] Robert Brandenburg, "The Language of a Three Year Old Child," *Pedagogical Review,* Vol. XXI (March 1915), p. 89.

[3] Helen C. Dawe, "Study of the Effect of an Educational Program Upon Language Development and Related Mental Functions in Young Children," *Journal of Experimental Education,* Vol. XI, 1956, pp. 200–209.

Such simple material as nursery rhymes introduce extensive vocabulary. Forty popular ones introduce over 400 words.

Experience with young children who speak a combination of English and other languages such as some in Hawaii and the Spanish-English dialects suggests that teachers must provide a model that demonstrates desired form.

When a child asks, "Hay tees?" (What's this?), answer, "That is an elephant," rather than, "An elephant." Say, "This is a soldier's hat," not "A soldier's hat," or, "A hat." Thus the speech pattern for labeling is established. These children are helped in their understanding of generalized concepts needed for classification by the teacher using complete sentence patterns. Say, "That *color* is pink," "This *color* is red," "That *animal* is a horse," rather than, "A horse," when a picture is shown. Children will only be confused by, "This is rough; this is smooth," even when objects are handled. Use "The sandpaper is rough," "The floor is smooth."

Activities involving matching should involve more than identification. Children should say *how* things match: "Yes, the toys are the same *color*," "The wheel and the orange have the same *shape*." Be careful about the so-called big and little hands on the clock. Longer and shorter may be more accurate.

When a child gropes in his effort to communicate, such as sticking out a foot with a new shoe on it, respond, "Yes, I see your new shoe." This form of echo procedure provides the words the child needs—in this case, "See my new shoe." When a child says, "Hus got one dem flowers, dem Sann Slause —our house," the teacher says, "You have a Christmas tree at your house, too," or, "Eu-ahhee-ee me uh," the teacher can sympathize by "Yes, I saw Carl hit you."

This procedure may be extended using the child's original expression. "You have a Christmas tree at your house, too. Some of the children are making decorations for the tree. You can make some for our tree and some to take home to put on your tree."

Language vocabulary is developed by having children actively, physically involved in the demonstrations of the use of words.

Real objects rather than pictures are starting points. The children see, feel, put together, take apart, smell, listen to, eat as aids to learning language. Activities are planned to involve such motor response—the child puts his hand in *front* of him, *behind* him, *between* his legs, *over* his head, *on* his head.

A narrow focus on the right word should be avoided; as long as the meaning is clear, all should be accepted.

The ball that is beside the box may also be next to the box, at the side of the box, by the box, in front of the teacher, on the floor, on the rug, between George and the box. Remember how you felt when a teacher had a "right" answer that was so narrow that others equally correct were not accepted.

Such language activities are not a part of special drill periods but a part of every activity the child experiences. Teachers do not need to be concerned about talking too much if they know the purpose to be served by such activity.

Oral language use shows positive results even at the college level. Dillard University planned a prefreshman program to help students who wished to offset a background of limited language, little access to books, and inadequate opportunity to think about and discuss current affairs. For six weeks the students read two hours a day, talked over what they read with a teacher, and listened to a selected television broadcast and discussed it. In addition, the students studied one subject of their own choosing. Such a program uses the techniques which research and common sense suggest are important for the development of language power and thinking.[4]

Reports of three major research efforts suggest methods that any teacher might use.

A group of Spanish-speaking first-graders in San Antonio, Texas, was studied in terms of their problem of learning to read English.[5] In addition to the language problem, observation revealed a lack of experi-

ence related to the material in the reading texts; a short attention span; general unfamiliarity with such tasks as using a pencil and scissors; minimal auditory and visual discrimination (many seemed unaware of or indifferent to differences); lack of information (even when using Spanish) about such topics as their names, how many were in their family, and so on; fear or apathy toward the school environment and the world around them; and inability to classify objects and follow a sequence of directions even when given in Spanish.

To bridge the many needs of these children the audiolingual techniques were applied to specific science learnings relating to things in the environment such as weather, animals, and materials. The approach was inductive and used objects. The task was to accustom the pupils to the basic language structure. "Is this a _____?" "Yes, it is. It is a _____." From this pattern in which the children had individual objects to use, the teacher eventually moved to words with generalized meanings (for example, *shape*). But more was needed than just language patterns in English. These children needed a sense of pride in what they did know, so Spanish was studied in some groups with the purpose of showing that the children had learned to use Spanish and therefore could learn English. Self-esteem and self-confidence were obvious needs for the children.

A series of lessons was planned with that objective. The place to start seemed to be the child's name. For these children the name needed to be more than a label pasted on an object, as would be implied in the pattern, "What is your name?" "My name is _____." Instead the name should be treated as a part of the child, which is implied in the pattern, "Who are you?" "I am _____." In the lesson the child answered the teacher's question, "Who are you?" only after looking into a full-length mirror. In responding he checked by pointing to himself. A variation was to have others respond to questions about the child before the mirror; they would be asked, for example, "Who is he?" The word *teacher* and the teacher's name were introduced similarly.

---

[4] Frank Jennings, "For Such a Tide Is Moving," *Saturday Review,* May 16, 1964.

[5] Anne O. Stemmler, "An Experimental Approach to the Teaching of Oral Language and Reading," *Harvard Education Review,* Vol. XXXVI (Winter 1966), pp. 45–49.

The use of "talking dolls" permitted some objectivity. A reading booklet based upon the oral language was developed with the title "All About Me." It contained such items as, "What color is your hair?" "My hair is _____."

A group of twenty-four sixth-grade students who were severely retarded in reading skills was drawn from three classrooms to form a special group that met for a forty-five-minute period each day.[6] Sixteen had IQ's below 90; half of the group had been in several schools; ten had attended kindergarten; three had speech defects. Careless enunciation and poor English usage were generally characteristic of the group. In class these children seldom participated in discussions.

Books ranging in difficulty from first through fourth grade were made available. Each student selected a book. Help was given with respect to difficult words. At the end of thirty minutes the children met in small groups to tell about the story they had read. At first the recounting of the story was completed in two to four minutes, but by the end of the twelve weeks, ten and twenty minutes were required. In time the students visited other classes to tell a favorite story.

By the end of the first three weeks many students had ceased asking for help on individual words and were attempting to pronounce them through their knowledge of phonics. Grammar errors decreased as the demand for telling a story forced the children to read for ideas and language phrasing. There was classroom restlessness during the first weeks and at times when new books were brought to the classroom. During the last weeks there was no restlessness and groups grew quite independent of the teacher. The reading gains on tests were impressive but the great difference was the confidence with respect to discussion and willingness to make oral reports that the children exhibited in their regular classroom.

The third study involves 400 teachers in Pennsylvania who are attempting to create an on-going curriculum of oral communication in regular classrooms.[7] As a result of this effort a number of suggestions to other teachers can be made.

First, *grading of performance must be eliminated.* Most teachers make the mistake of using the same kind of instruction for communication skills that they would use in subjects which call for a mastery of cognitive material. Communication is intrinsic in personality. A student who fails history fails a subject, whereas a student who fails in communication fails as a person. One does not learn to communicate by learning about communication, although such learning is important. Communication skills must be developed in real situations in which a goal is realized because of communication.

Second, *care must be taken with criticism.* Criticism has often come from the teacher or the "wolf-pack" class when the teacher, in an effort to check listening, asks, "What suggestions would you make to the speaker?" The capable student is not helped and those who need help are threatened. Criticism should be a private consultation not often possible in school. A more effective method is to provide a chance for the student to analyze his goals and determine how well he has achieved them. A teacher might point out some aspects of success. It does not help to learn of one's ineffectiveness if there is no way to improve. It is helpful to look at a specific skill, such as voice tone or wording of an opening or a question, because the learner may focus on that element without putting his personality on the line. The teacher becomes a consultant rather than a critic.

Third, *there must be an opportunity for the student to talk with the teacher privately.* The teacher must establish a channel for feedback. Student diaries, private evaluations, setting up "talking tables" are a few such devices. The teacher must see his role as that of motivator, persuader, and facili-

---

[6] Richard P. Sawyer, "Better Speech for Better Reading," *Elementary School Journal,* Vol. LXV (April 1965), pp. 359–65.

[7] Gerald M. Phillips, "Oral Communications Program" (University Park, Pa.: Pennsylvania State University, 1968).

tator. The student must trust him and the teacher must understand the goal of the student.

Fourth, *the student must determine his own goals and choose the methods by which he works to achieve them.* The teacher assists the student by helping him break big goals down to manageable units and put minor goals in proper perspective. These goals may be in any area of the curriculum. Competition with others or asking all to act at the same pace have been discredited. The function of the teacher is to participate with the child in the communicative transaction, not to control or coerce participation on the teacher's terms. The teacher manipulates the environment to create opportunities and activities, but he does not manipulate the students. The situation as seen by the student determines the progress that will be made. The interaction between the teacher and student influences any technique used.

Activities such as the following provide opportunity to develop oral communication skills.

Sharing an experience orally gains form when purposes are well defined. (*Courtesy of the Burbank Public Schools.*)

News Time

Have individual students become experts on a person of their choice, such as the President, an astronaut, a sports figure, a music group, the governor, the mayor. When appropriate the class is given a briefing about the activities of the person.

Have individuals or small groups follow a single problem or activity and keep a bulletin board or notebook about which they report periodically. Suitable topics might include air pollution, effects of DDT on animal life, political changes in other countries, Africa (or a single country), college unrest, the new school building, the new bridge, the strike.

When a student reports a news item he might first locate the place on a map, put two words (or more) on the board that might be new to the class, ask a question at the end, give a question to the teacher to be put in a listening test at the end of the week. Such procedures help the child prepare his report with the listeners in mind.

All news reporting for a time may be centered on a large topic until the students become expert; such topics include the election, the war, our national policy, use of leisure time, animals in the news, humor in the news, human interest stories, and characters in comic strips. Slower groups should use news of the class and home. This can be dictated and written as *Our Day* or *Our Week* for future reference. This should be done at the end of the period.

Editorials have a place in News Time. In turn, each one who wishes might talk on "How I think TV could be improved," "Why I think ten-year-old students should be in bed by 10 o'clock," "Our school lunch program needs to be changed," "Safety hazards in our school," "Our school needs _____," "My parents understand me," "Ugly spots in our neighborhood that can be changed," "There should be a special period for _____," "Let's write to the mayor (governor) about _____."

Interviewing and Surveying

Planned interviews provide exceptional opportunities for oral communication prac-

tice. The child will need help setting up the questions, which should be written.

Children are often asked, "What did you do at school today?" The teacher might introduce interviewing with such a question (which would also prepare the children to do a good public relations job at home). Preference surveys are a common commercial practice. A committee might make a preference survey of the class with respect to favorite toothpaste, soap, cold drink, music, or television program.

This activity may be extended to planning interviews with the principal (ask him what he does), the superintendent of schools (have him come to the classroom), the school secretary, the janitor, the oldest person in a child's family or neighborhood, or a neighbor with a hobby (tropical fish, cooking, collecting). Interviewing others in the class in order to write a short biography increases the interest in reading biographies and in the author's techniques.

Surveys provide an equally interesting extension of the interview. Each child might interview one adult on a problem and pool the results. Such questions as the following might be used: "What do you think is the greatest problem our city must solve?" "If you were my age, what business would you prepare for?" "What gives you the most enjoyment?" Some surveys can be made without interviews, such as, "How many cars stop between 8 and 8:30 A.M. for the traffic patrol?" "What is the most popular make of car in the school parking lot?"

To give meaning to the occasion the interview and survey may be used during such special weeks as Education Week, Book Week, Safety Week, or such days as Poetry Day, Veterans' Day, Arbor Day. On Arbor Day a nursery might be visited to learn what trees grow well in the area or a survey of different varieties of trees in one block might be made.

Demonstrations and Directions

Children who have traveled can demonstrate a skill they learned (instead of "What I did on my vacation"). This might involve the use of chopsticks to eat, Japanese paper folding, hobby or craft projects, magic tricks, slides, post cards or photographic talks, care of plants or pets, experiences earning money (newsboys and baby-sitters have adventures and problems).

Teach the class a game to play on a rainy day or at a picnic, or imagine you were telling an Eskimo about baseball, football, tennis, horseshoes, and so on.

Play "How do I get there?" One child asks how to get to a place in the community, school, or state. Volunteers who answer may be given one to five points for their accuracy, simplicity, and brevity.

Talks on "How does it work?" stimulate a great deal of research either in books or through field trips. A vocational slant can be given by interviewing neighbors and parents on "What do they do at the _____ (bakery, movie theater, clinic, service station, supermarket, and so on).

Selling, Describing, Persuading

Your Scout Troop is selling cookies (or peanuts, tickets, and so on). What should you say as you go to potential customers?

Take any object in the room, including clothing worn, and make a commercial for it such as one you might hear on the radio.

Describe "The car (Bicycle) I want," "The dress I need," "The best meal I remember," "My grandparents," "My old school."

You need a quarter (a larger allowance, a new pair of shoes, and so on). What would you say to your parents?

Creative–Imaginative Situations

Many suggestions for creative writing are effective in increasing the oral vocabularies of some children impressively.

Show any three objects and ask how they might be related. Examples of such objects might be a pen, paper, and book: a book, lamp, and toy; a picture of a house, a dog, and an airplane. Let the children think of the most unrelated objects possible and show how they might be associated through imagination. A salt shaker, old tire, and worn hat might be a challenge. A student

teacher brought a sack to school with three strange items in it. She explained, "I found these in the old house I bought. What do you suppose the people were like who lived there?"

To make children aware of the ordinary it might be good for some classes to start the day a least once each week with a creativity exercise. Such an exercise might proceed from the following questions:

1. What would happen if you woke up and the ground was covered with red snow?
2. What would happen if we could talk with insects?
3. What would happen if you had an experience like Rip Van Winkle and today was a day twenty years from now?

Role-playing experiences are exceptional opportunities for language growth. The child must project his personality into that of another. This may require changes in dialect, age, sex, class, or color.

A friend borrowed a book from you. When he returns it you see that someone has spilled ink on it. What do you say? Why?

Newspaper accounts can be made into role situations by asking, "If you had been _____ what would you have done?"

Telephoning

In many communities the telephone company will arrange a conference interview for a class. It may be with a local author, an official, or another classroom—sometimes in a distant state. The entire class can listen while individuals participate. All aspects of telephone courtesy and use can become a part of the preparations of such a call.

Some schools select a student to help in the principal's office at noon hour. A specific task is to answer the telephone and take messages.

As a science activity, two fourth-grade boys in Poway, California, installed a telephone between their classrooms. As an independent reading activity students read aloud

Oral composition should be practiced in all curriculum areas. (*Courtesy of the Burbank Public Schools.*)

to each other on the telephone during a scheduled period.

Tutoring

Speaking–listening activities are prominent in many tutoring situations. One child may check another with respect to beginning sounds in a series of words which may be on separate cards or in sentence blocks. Sets of cards with similar pictures on them may be given two people, a screen put between them. One describes the picture on his card in such a way that the other identifies the picture from the description. Each card identified is surrendered. Reading along with another to assist with words or simply reading a story aloud may be a rein-

forcement for a student who has recently mastered a skill or a step in reading development.

Attention to the following aspects of speaking, accompanied by training and practice, can assure teachers of the continuous growth of students in their command of spoken English: [8]

- **Vocabulary.** Words are the basic units of spoken language. Experiences of home, school, and community provide the opportunity for an ever-expanding vocabulary. But command of words, except in limited numbers, does not arise by itself. Children

---

[8] From English Language Arts in Wisconsin, Robert Pooley, Project Director, Madison Department of Public Instruction, 1968, p. 160.

need to be led continually to recognize new words, to relate them to context, and to practice their use in purposeful communication. Ideally each child should have an opportunity to speak briefly and to use new words every day. Conscious encouragement by teachers can do much to expand vocabulary.

- **Voice.** Many children need sympathetic guidance in developing a good speaking voice. Pitch should be brought within a reasonable range and volume adjusted to the class group. Frequent practice in choral reading and speaking can allow the teacher to note and correct voice deficiencies of individual pupils without the embarrassment of a solo performance. Since boys' voices change with adolescence, they need readjustment of pitch and volume in junior high school and early senior high school years. Great tact is required in helping such students.

- **Bearing.** Standing easily and gracefully before others is difficult for children and is a particular problem for young adolescents. Much of their reluctance to speak before a group arises from this factor. From the primary grades on, every possible opportunity should be seized to make appearance before others a natural classroom situation. Children should take it for granted that they will perform before their fellows as pantomimists, oral readers, actors in impromptu plays, makers of oral reports, and expressers of ideas. Where such experience is habitual, much uneasiness will disappear. By private conference the teacher can help an awkward child assume a better posture, use his hands more freely, and acquire relaxation before a group.

- **Planning.** Children's speaking progresses from the utterance of a few scattered ideas to the presentation of a well-planned, organized discourse. This progression seldom happens by accident. Therefore, training in organization is an important factor in the growth of speaking. It begins with the child's arranging a few items he wishes to express in an order which he deems best for his purpose. The second stage is the formation of a brief outline on paper to allow the speaker to present his ideas in an order which he has planned in advance. The culmination is the highly organized outline of a prepared speech in which a central idea is supported by properly subor-dinated contributing ideas. The latter stage is for mature students only; in general, a simple card outline will suffice.

- **Sentence patterns.** Oral sentences are much more loosely constructed than written sentences. Nevertheless, there is a definite growth in spoken sentence patterns which marks the experienced speaker over the beginner. Young children often get into "mazes," which are confused patterns they cannot complete. An illustration: "This boy, he didn't understand this man, well, so he, I mean the man, took and. . . ." This kind of pattern confusion can be reduced by helping students make shorter statement units and avoid vague references like "this boy," "this man," etc. Thinking sentences before speaking them also tends to improve spoken sentence structure. Learning to begin sentences with clear, unmistakable subjects is another aid. There is no need to make speech sound like written English. Speech can be free and informal, but expressed in those simple patterns of the English sentence which avoid confusion of structure and reference.

- **Audience response.** Very often, schoolroom speaking practice becomes a dialogue between pupil and teacher. The wise teacher will direct the pupil's speech to his fellow students and will expect critical but friendly listening. When possible the teacher should retire to the audience, training pupils to conduct the speaking exercises as well as participating in them. The teacher will help each pupil become aware of his audience, learn to speak to it, and become sensitive to its reactions. As the speaker learns to direct his remarks to a live audience, he will increasingly recognize how he is "getting across." His own desire for success is the best motivation.

One of the important aspects of speech is the observation of certain courtesies between speaker and listener. Many of these can be taught indirectly by the teacher in his own speaking to students as individuals or as a class. Preserving the dignity of the individual, no matter how young, refraining from unnecessary interruption of a speaker, using courteous terms when addressing students (even when one is provoked!) and encouraging the expression of independent views are important courtesies of speaking. It is of little use to teach as lessons what one violates in practice.

One principal reported the following experiences with emphasis upon oral language for a culturally limited or different group.[9]

Vocabulary building goes on constantly as teachers chart key words for children, promote dictionary skills, utilize the resources of the special teachers, tell stories and have children re-tell them, use jokes, riddles, conversation, discussion, telephoning, reading and poetry.

Two effective media for promoting vocabulary growth and fluency of expression have been 1) the intercom for students to give the daily news and special announcements and 2) the Storytellers Club where children learn to how to tell stories.

When using the intercom, children learned to listen to one another as they took turns giving the daily news reports. They also learned how to write to get attention and the importance of saying things in a variety of ways in order to keep attention. They grew in confidence and prestige when they identified themselves as the announcers.

The children selected the announcers and showed astuteness in their selections. They did not only select the good readers; they selected the children who needed recognition. When selections were made this way, the need to excel was important. Some children memorized their scripts by studying them with the family at night. Others asked parents to come to school to listen to them as they made the announcements.

The Storytellers Club met weekly with its membership drawn from grades three through six. It started quite simply. For the children its major goal was to tell stories to children in kindergarten and first grade. For the teachers, the goals were to

1. Encourage reluctant readers by having them read simple material with no stigma attached.
2. Get more inflection in children's voices.
3. Promote vocabulary.
4. Develop thinking.

In an environment where relationships are good, deprived children seem to say by their actions, "I don't understand everything my teacher says, but I like her and I am trying to talk like her and to do the right things." Doing the right thing is important to children from the least favored neighborhoods. They usually like their teachers very much and want to please them. Teachers have strong influences on attitudes and behavior as well as on the acquisition of skills and the development of concepts.

Knowledge of the structural parts of the English language (parts of speech, kinds of sentences, etc.) is not essential in the elementary school, and there certainly is little evidence to indicate that such knowledge improves the grammar or usage of children whose language background is poor.

Successful changes in language patterns are being made by teachers who:

- Set good examples in their own oral expressions, since children tend to imitate adults.
- Realize that the cultural setting of the home has a definite influence on the language skills of children. Changes will be made more slowly when children have regular contact with teachers, parents, and playmates who express themselves understandably in more than one idiom. These children find it more difficult to recognize "good English" and "bad English."
- Provide many opportunities for oral expression in order to develop aural consciousness of forms and construction. Children need much practice in using preferred forms in regular class activities as well as in controlled practice.
- Emphasize what the child says rather than how he says it. We are dealing with thinking when we deal with language. More acceptable expressions can be emphasized at another time when a child is not developing a thought.
- Help vocabulary and fluency to develop by providing many firsthand as well as vicarious experiences. Words and expressions that children repeat do not always have correct meaning for them.
- Encourage children to convey feelings and ideas through their own original efforts, especially through the media of letter writing, diaries, and short stories. This will bring increasing satisfaction as the gap is narrowed between their speaking and writing vocabularies and between their oral structure and skill in manipulating words and structures in writing.

In the exciting, interesting, accepting climate of the classrooms of sensitive and creative teachers, children who come from disadvantaged backgrounds search for meanings and find op-

---

[9] Theda M. Wilson, "Helping the Disadvantaged Build Language," *National Elementary School Principal* (November 1965), pp. 456–59.

portunities to imagine, to exchange ideas, to think, to discover, and to create. As they listen, speak, read, and write, they develop their own individualities and form the basic foundations for their futures.

They have inherited the right to express themselves. They are becoming free to do that with clarity and with confidence.

For Discussion

1. A city child may have a cultural background quite different from those presented in reading textbooks. The same would be true of a rural child with a Mexican or Indian heritage. Why have we been reluctant to prepare early reading material for these children? If it were to be done, what content would you put in such books?

2. Current textbooks for language instruction contain a great deal about the linguistic history and structure of English. Is this content more appropriate to social science than a language text? How much help does the teacher find in current textbooks with respect to oral composition?

What Should Be Taught About Listening?

The prophet Jeremiah (5:21) laments that his people "have ears but hear not." In a less strenuous vein a teacher once complained to me, "The children all have that tuned-out look." A marriage counselor reports that the most frequent complaint by either spouse is, "You're not listening to a thing I say!" Nonlistening may be a natural defense against the bombardment of partially useless information and sound that assaults the ear in our mechanized society. Or nonlistening may be the result of limited auditory perception and understanding on the part of an audience. For some people, listening to music may be only a pleasant physical experience comparable at best to basking idly in the sunshine; for others the music may have a deep intellectual and spiritual significance, involving perception of inner harmonies and complex rhythmical patterns.

No one questions the importance of listening as a means of learning for boys and girls. Paul Rankin's pioneering study showed that high school students in Detroit spent 30 per cent of the time they devote to language each day in speaking, 16 per cent in reading, 9 per cent in writing, and 45 per cent in listening.[10] Miriam Wilt more recently found that elementary school children spent about two and one half hours of the five-hour school day in listening.[11] This was nearly twice as much time as their teachers estimate the children spent in listening. Some feel that in the usual classroom the chances are about 60 to 1 against any given pupil speaking, compared to the possibility of others speaking and a pupil listening.

Undoubtedly, there is as wide an individual difference in the area of listening as in other skills. We speak of some people as being auditory-minded in contrast to others who are visual-minded. Speech and music teachers have long been aware of the differences among children in hearing specific sounds.

It has been suggested that some of these differences are culturally determined. Some sociologists explained the fact that boys in the elementary school are apt to have more reading problems than girls by the observation that in many families the mother talks more frequently with the little girl than with the little boy. The result of such "preferential" talking according to the theory is that girls are more advanced in language than boys of the same age, especially in the primary grades. In Japan, just the opposite has been noticed. Little girls were long considered academically "inferior" until it was realized that the boy child was getting much more attention at home and at school. In some classrooms over 80 per cent of the questions were being directed to the boys

[10] Paul T. Rankin, "The Importance of Listening Ability," *English Journal,* Vol. 17 (October 1928), pp. 623–30.

[11] Miriam E. Wilt, "A Study of Teacher Awareness of Listening as a Factor in Elementary Education," *Journal of Education,* Vol. 43 (April 1950), pp. 626–36.

Directions given through prepared tapes provide directed listening exercises. (*Courtesy of the La Mesa Public Schools.*)

until the inequity was brought to the attention of the teachers.

Another cultural influence upon listening is provided by radio and television. Kindergarten teachers are reporting that children come to school with a much wider knowledge than the curriculum assumes. In India, where there is a high degree of illiteracy, one might assume that the population would be relatively uninformed about world events. This, however, is not the case. The availability of free radios in many community teahouses has resulted in a surprisingly well-informed adult population.

Don Brown suggests that the terms *learning* and *listening* are both limited in meaning, and that the gerund *auding,* based on the neologic verb *to aud,* more accurately

describes the skill that concerns teachers. "Auding is to the ears what reading is to the eyes." If reading is the gross process of looking at, recognizing, and interpreting written symbols, auding may be defined as the gross process of listening to, recognizing, and interpreting spoken symbols.[12]

David Russell uses the following formula to contrast reading and auding further.[13]

---

[12] Don Brown, "Auding as the Primary Language Ability" (unpublished dissertation, Stanford University, 1954).

[13] D. H. Russell and E. F. Russell, "Listening Aids Through the Grades" (New York: Bureau of Publications, Teachers College, Columbia University, 1959).

Seeing is to Hearing
as
Observing is to Listening
as
Reading is to Auding

To aud, then, would mean to listen with comprehension and appreciation.

Children *hear* the whistle of a train, the chirp of a bird, or the noise of traffic. They *listen* either passively or actively to a popular song or news broadcast. But when they listen attentively to a teacher to follow directions, or to get facts from a classmate's report, or to understand two sides of a debate, they may be said to be *auding,* for they are listening to verbal symbols with comprehension and interpretation. Throughout this discussion, however, the term *listening* will be used in referring to the response that Brown describes as auding.

Different levels of listening are really different degrees of involvement. Some activities to be as satisfying call for much less involvement than others that demand a high degree of dedication. The following situations are examples of listening levels in terms of different purposes.

1. Hearing sounds of words but not reacting to the ideas expressed: a mother knows that Joey is speaking.
2. Intermittent listening—turning the speaker on and off: hearing one idea in a sermon but none of the rest of it.
3. Half listening—following the discussion only well enough to find an opportunity to express your own idea: listening to a conversation to find a place to tell how you handled a child.
4. Listening passively with little observable response: the child knows the teacher is telling them once again how to walk in the hall.
5. Narrow listening in which the main significance or emphasis is lost as the listener selects details which are familiar or agreeable to him: a good Republican listening to a candidate from another party.
6. Listening and forming associations with related items from one's own experiences: a first-grade child hears the beginning sound of *Sally, says,* and *said,* and relates it to the letter *s.*
7. Listening to a report to get main ideas and supporting details or follow directions: listening to the rules and descriptions of a new spelling game.
8. Listening critically: a listener notices the emotional appeal of words in a radio advertisement.
9. Appreciative and creative listening with genuine mental and emotional response: a child listens to the teacher read *Miracle on Maple Hill* and shares the excitement of sugar making.

These levels overlap, but they do describe listening with respect to situations that teachers know. In the classroom it is possible to guide a child's listening so that his auding may be selective, purposeful, accurate, critical, and creative, just as we guide growth in the skills of reading.

A. Social Listening [14]
  1. Listening courteously and attentively to conversation in social situations with a purpose. K–6
  2. Understanding the roles of the speaker and listener in the communication process. K–6
B. Secondary Listening
  1. Listening to music that accompanies rhythms or folk dances. K–6
  2. Enjoying music while participating in certain types of school activities such as painting, working with clay, sketching, and handwriting practice. K–6
C. Aesthetic Listening
  1. Listening to music, poetry, choral reading, or drama heard on radio or on recordings. K–6
  2. Enjoying stories, poems, riddles, jingles, and plays as read or told by the teacher or pupils. K–6
D. Critical Listening
  1. Noting correct speech habits, word usage, and sentence elements of others. K–6
  2. Listening to determine the reason "why." 1–6

----

[14] Board of Education, *Reading and Language in the Elementary School* (Gary, Ind.: Gary Public Schools, 1962).

3. Listening to understand meanings from context clues. 1–6
4. Listening to distinguish between fact and fancy, relevance and irrelevance. 1–6
5. Listening to draw inferences. 1–6
6. Listening to make judgments. 1–6
7. Listening to find new or additional information on a topic. 2–6
8. Listening to find the answers to specific questions which require selectivity and concentration. 4–6
9. Listening to interpret idioms and unusual language. 5–6
10. Listening objectively and appraising to determine authenticity or the presence of bias and inaccuracies. 5–6

E. Concentrative Listening (a study-type listening)
1. Listening to follow directions. K–6
2. Perceiving relationships such as class, place, quantity, time, sequence, and cause and effect. 4–6
3. Listening for a definite purpose to elicit specific items of information. 4–6
4. Attaining understanding through intent listening. 4–6
5. Listening for sequence of ideas. 4–6
6. Perceiving a speaker's or a group's main objective and organization of ideas. 4–6
7. Taking notes of important facts. 4–6

F. Creative Listening
1. Associating meanings with all kinds of listening experiences. K–6
2. Constructing visual images while listening. K–6
3. Adapting imagery from imaginative thinking to create new results in writing, painting, and dramatizing. 1–6
4. Listening to arrive at solutions for problems as well as checking and verifying the results of the problems solved. 4–6

Listening in some respects is more difficult than reading. In the process of reading, a strange word may be the signal to stop, look at other words in the sentence or pictures on the page, or refer to the glossary. In listening this is not possible. One must make a hasty guess as the speaker continues, rethink what the speaker has said while keeping up with the current ideas being spoken. Most college students know

the experience expressed by a freshman when he commented, "I was with him until he mentioned the macrocephalic measurement, then he lost me." Children too have their "frustration level" in listening. The "tuned-out look" familiar to teachers is a signal with respect to either the interest or difficulty of spoken content.

The fact that we listen from six to ten times faster than a person can talk means that dedicated concentration must be practiced in some listening situations to avoid distractions. The printed page demands attention and can be read at a rate of speed equal to that of our mental reactions. In listening this happens only if the listener disciplines himself to attend to what the speaker is saying. Interruptions to an oral explanation by a classroom visitor, outside noises, or any disruptive incident mean the explanation must be repeated. Once listening is accepted as important the learner must accept the responsibility to put forth an active listening effort to learn. This activity should equal the effort to gain information from reading.

One element that makes listening more difficult than reading is that a person usually listens for the main idea rather than specific parts. In reading, one has a record of the specifics and usually remembers where they may be located. In listening, the speaker has designed the material to highlight a major idea which he wants the audience to remember. To do this he uses facts, stories, and emotional appeals. These are recalled only if the listener relates them to the total effect of the talk. Church sermons and college lectures are good examples; a person may tell a friend that he heard a good sermon or lecture, but when asked what was said may be able to recall only that it was "about brotherhood."

Related to this is the problem of listening to a discussion or conversation. Such speech is frequently disorganized as the speakers explore various ideas or aspects of a topic. Strange to say, people seem to remember as much or more from such situations as from a well-organized lecture. Apparently the careful organization and fixed pattern lulls some listeners into a comfortable enjoyment which is less involving than the disorganized rambling that permits or requires involvement with random changes of topic or subject matter.

Many bad habits develop in the listening area. Both children and adults have a way of avoiding difficult or unpleasant listening. Every parent knows the "Surely, he is not talking about me!" attitude of a child who is being corrected. Emotions interfere with listening to ideas. "Who is he to be saying that?" "They will never convince me that those ugly things are art," and, "How would she know, she's never been a mother!" are emotional statements that reveal limited reception.

It is interesting to note the wide variation of response to a distraction in a classroom. A lawn mower operating outside the window or music being played in the next room will command the complete attention of some and be ignored by others. Some individuals have a habit of seeking distraction even though they may be interested in the speaker or topic.

The expression of ego is as obvious in listening as it is in the constant use of *I* in speech. This is especially obvious in little children. A teacher or speaker will be telling about a trip to Europe or showing a cowboy lariat. A hand will pop up and a child will volunteer, "Tomorrow is my birthday," or, "We have some baby chickens at our house." For some this is an innocent way to "say something, too." Usually it is an indication of lack of interest in others. Adults will be listening or participating in a conversation about a topic, then suddenly will say, "I think I'll have my hair done tomorrow," or, "When do we eat?" Or there may be a subtle attempt to impress, as in, "When I was in Mexico," or, "The President said to my cousin."

Teachers are frequently poor listeners. For some, teaching limits their interests to such an extent that they dismiss many subjects prematurely as "uninteresting." At one University Club the matron said she felt sorry for many of the people who lived there. "They are such specialists they cannot listen to each other." Some teachers develop the habit of not listening for ideas but are always judging the manner of expression or organization of speech. They are actually evaluating or grading the manners of those they hear.

Good listening habits involve not only thinking with the speaker but anticipating the direction of his thoughts, objectively evaluating the verbal evidence offered in terms of the speaker's purpose (rather than arguing with it item by item as it is presented), and reviewing mentally some of the facts presented. Taking notes of ideas or phrases helps many people. There are others who find note taking a distraction. Some report that they find the ideas in their notes rather than in their heads. Brief summaries are probably better than detailed stenographic reports.

There is no more attentive listener than the child who asks a question that truly concerns him. These are probably the most "teachable moments" in any classroom. Choosing the question to ask a visitor or the principal or when planning material before a unit sets the stage for careful listening. Before oral reading, attention is assured if children are listening in order to answer a question. A good story writer builds this interest or suspense into his plots. The reason the reader gets involved in a story is usually because he wants to know how a problem will be solved.

In the classroom the language arts teacher wants to be sure that the listening experience will be worth the children's time and effort. The sharing period can be improved by having each child think first of his audience and how he wants them to respond. At one time this period was considered valuable simply as a spontaneous period of free expression. At the beginning that may be its purpose. But such items as, "I have a new petticoat," or, "our cat had kittens," belong in the free conversational exchange of children rather than the crowded school curriculum. The following suggestions provide the same practice in language but add a concern for the listeners.

1. Share the signs of the change of a season noted while going to and from school.

2. Share things that happened at home or play that were pleasant or humorous.
3. Share the most important thing that happened on a trip.
4. Share one toy by telling about it or demonstrating its use.
5. Share something good or kind that a person has done.
6. Share the local or national news. Some classrooms have a television committee, a radio committee, and a picture committee. These children report events they have learned from these sources. In the intermediate grades some teachers provide the clippings from which children select their reports. Others give a little quiz at the end of the week on the news reported. Sometimes better preparation will result if the listeners may ask one question about a report. Two standards should apply—the news must be told rather than being read orally, and it must not concern crime.
7. Share something an individual has made.
8. Share a riddle or joke (after first checking with the teacher).
9. Share a fact or interesting bit of knowledge about a bird, rock, stamp, coin, insect, star, airplane, sea shell, object from a foreign land, book, or "believe-it-or-not" item.
10. Share a new word and its meaning or history. This might be a word in a foreign language if there are children from homes where a foreign language is spoken.

Material shared is better if children have to plan ahead a bit. Children might sign on the chalkboard today for sharing tomorrow, or each row may have a day which is their sharing day. The teacher is responsible for the quality of material shared in literature. If children are to listen to material read, it should be material that offers true enrichment. Poetry appropriate to the child's interests that is read well will reveal the beauty of words. Stories that add stature to the child's value concepts should be told and read.

The responsibility of the listener should be discussed. There is the point of courtesy to a speaker that all children understand. It is only the Golden Rule applied to speech—"you listen to me and I will listen to you." Listening for meaning is just as important as reading for meaning. A listener may *disagree* but should not *misinterpret*. Causes of misinterpretation might be discussed with benefit to both speaker and listener.

The attitude of the teacher toward listening will influence children. Teaching is as much listening as telling. We listen to discover interest and needs. Those trained in nondirective guidance know how important it is for the therapist to listen. The psychologist listens a great deal as the patient talks. A good salesman listens to discover what customers want. The wise teacher listens to encourage the expression of children. At times a teacher listens because a child, or parent, needs an audience for a personal concern. The following suggestions will help in such situations.[15]

1. Take time to listen. When someone is troubled or needs to talk, give him the time if at all possible. It will help clarify communication between you.
2. Be attentive. Let tirades flow uninterrupted. Try to indicate that you want to understand.
3. Employ three kinds of verbal reactions only—"H-m-mm," "Oh," or "I see." Remain silent, nodding to show understanding. (College professors frequently work with a pipe at this time, cleaning it, etc.) If the talker is unreasonable, restate what he said, putting it in the form of a question.
4. Never probe for additional facts. There is a difference between willingness to listen and curiosity. Your purpose in therapeutic listening is seldom to obtain information.
5. Avoid evaluating what has been said.

---

[15] R. G. Nichols and Leonard A. Stevens, *Are You Listening?* (New York: McGraw-Hill, 1957).

Material prepared with the listener in mind adds to the educational result in all curriculum areas. (*Courtesy of the Burbank Public Schools.*)

Avoid moral judgments and the temptation to advise. The talker is getting his problem clear through talking and then must define alternative solutions.

6. Never lose faith in the ability of the talker to solve his own problems. The talker is really talking things over with himself as he talks with you.

Start instruction in listening by establishing standards. The discussion might be centered about situations where listening is important: You are a waiter taking an order; you are to go to the principal's office with a message and return with his; you are to interview a famous person; you are to report on a news broadcast. These imaginative exercises could lead to an inventory of listening habits. A checklist like the following may be used:

1. Do I get ready to listen?
2. Do I give the speaker my attention?
3. Do I think with the speaker?
4. Can I select the main idea?
5. Can I recall things in order?
6. Can I follow directions?
7. Can I retell what I hear?

Children learn from discussions of this nature that a good listener is polite, gets the facts, listens thoughtfully, listens for a reason, and makes intelligent use of what he hears.

The use of listening posts and the tape recorder has provided substantial aid in teaching listening. The following lesson is from a current textbook for the fourth grade.[16] Determine what skills are taught by such a lesson.

These classroom activities emphasize the skills of listening:

1. Develop a routine of giving directions only once in a lesson. Select one subject, introduce the challenge of a "One-Time Club" or "First-Time Club" with respect to assignments or directions. If a child misses the first time, he is not a club member but may get the information from a member. For some groups the teacher

[16] Andrew Schiller and others, *Language and How to Use It,* Book 4 (Glenview, Ill.: Scott, Foresman, 1969), p. 90.

This group is listening to a recorded story while one child shows the book being presented. Teacher-made tapes should give directions as to page and guide the examination of pictures as well as the words of the story. (*Courtesy of the Burbank Public Schools.*)

might say, "I will give the assignment only once, then I will ask some of those in the 'First-Time Club' to repeat what I have said."

2. Use oral tests frequently that require more than one-word answers. Dramatize the test if the group responds to that type of motivation by imitating the pattern of a television quiz program.

3. Ask children to review the work of the previous day in a subject for a child who was absent.

4. Practice oral summarization of the information presented in a film.

5. Read a descriptive paragraph, have children paint or draw the picture presented, then read the story again as a check.

6. Play a listening game by giving increasingly difficult instructions to one child and then another. To the first child you might say, "Peter, take the apple from the desk and place it on the chair." To the next child, "Fred,

take the apple from the chair, show it to Mary and return it to the desk." The game increases in difficulty until someone fails to follow directions correctly.

7. Ask the pupils, in pairs, to interview each other on hobbies or special interests. After the interviews talk about the possibilities of learning by this method. Discuss the advantages and disadvantages of interviewing as compared to reading.

8. A game called "Efficient Secretary" is designed to challenge children to write entire sentences from dictation. The sentences are read only once. At first the sentences are short but they are increased in length as the child's ability increases. This exercise has a natural correlation with spelling.

9. Second-chance listening is valuable in the social studies. The teacher reads an informative article, which is followed by questions. After this the article is read again and children

check their answers or answer the questions a second time.

10. The game "Lost Child" is good for both oral description and listening. One player is the policeman. Another player describes someone in the room who is his "lost child." If a class member can guess who it is before the policeman does, the two exchange places.

David H. Russell and his wife have collected a group of listening activities called *Listening Aids Through the Grades,* published by the Bureau of Publications, Teachers College, Columbia University, New York, N.Y.

For Discussion

1. A visual-minded individual is one who remembers things that he sees. An auditory-minded person would be one who remembers what he hears. Which of your memories are most vivid—things you hear or see?

2. Do you know of any way of measuring individual differences in this respect? How might it be done by a classroom teacher?

EMPHASIS
This lesson gives children further practice in visualizing while they listen. It is a step up over previous exercises in that both the objects described and the identifying terms will be new to children.

EXPLANATION
List these words on the chalkboard: *jump scooter, whirligig, muff, foot stove, tailor's goose, quern, piggy churn, hex signs.* Tell children that the words are names of the objects pictured on page 90. Invite pupils to read the two paragraphs on the page to learn a little more about these objects.

Since the appearance of many objects described in this lesson will be strange to pupils and the names will be equally strange, you may want to (1) let children listen with their books open, and/or (2) let pupils jot down brief clues while listening (such as "piggy churn —looks like a pig").

Give boys and girls explicit instructions that they are to make only two notes concerning each object: (1) the name of the object, and (2) one characteristic that will help them to remember how it looks or how it works. Children should not be allowed to take unlimited notes, or the purpose of note-taking is defeated.

For your convenience, the articles are identified below.

1. jump scooter   5. tailor's goose
2. hex signs   6. muff
3. whirligig   7. quern
4. foot stove   8. piggy churn

After children have made their responses and checked them with each other's opinions, replay the record as a final check. Exercises 1 and 2 on pages 97-98 of this *Guidebook* are extensions of this lesson.

Let's Listen

All the objects on this page played some part in the life of early America. Most of them have passed from daily use. You may guess the purpose of some from looking at the pictures, but how many can you name?

Listen now to a description of how these things were used and what they were called.

What Is the Relationship Between Listening and Reading?

Both reading and listening require the learner to have a readiness for accomplishment. This includes his mental maturity, vocabulary, ability to follow sequence of ideas, and his interest in language.

In general, the purposes of reading and auding are both functional and appreciative. In functional reading and auding, children are concerned with finding facts, getting a general idea, following directions, or putting the material to work in some way. In appreciative reading and auding, children are ready to enjoy a selection for its own sake— a story for its humor, or a poem for its expression. Or they may combine function and appreciation in reading or listening with a view to creating a dramatization.

In both reading and auding, the word is not usually the unit of comprehension but it affects comprehension of the phrase, the sentence, and the paragraph. Children must hear certain key words clearly (e.g., *world* vs. *whirled*) if they are to understand an oral passage, and they must see them clearly (*bond* vs. *board*) if they are to read them exactly. But along with exact perception in both activities must go understanding of word meaning. The grasp and interpretation of both oral and written paragraphs depend upon understanding the meaning of individual words in their context and in varied relationships.

In both reading and auding, the unit of comprehension is either the phrase, the sentence, or the paragraph—rather than the single word. Comprehension is aided if the speaker or writer avoids common errors of pronunciation, spelling, and usage. Both reading and auding make use of "signals" in the form of written or oral punctuation.

In addition to an exact, literal understanding of a sentence or passage, both reading and auding may involve critical or creative interpretation of the material. In both situations the receiver may critically question the reliability of the source, the relevance of the argument, or the emotive power of the language employed. In both cases the receiver may utilize his previous experiences to combine the materials into some fresh, original, and personal interpretation.

Reading and auding may take place in either individual or social situations. Critical, analytical activities often flourish best in the individual situation; creative and appreciative reactions under the stimulus of the group situation. Analysis of the propaganda devices in a political speech is easier reading the printed version of the speech in a quiet room than listening to the speaker deliver it in a crowded hall. Conversely, appreciation of the choral reading of a poem may be heightened by an enthusiastic group response.

In order to improve reading, each listening skill should be followed by its reading counterpart. As students advance, the material used for these activities should necessarily become more difficult in order to meet their growing needs. The listening–reading skills need to be approached through direct and indirect instruction, with more emphasis on the direct than has been the practice in recent years.[17]

Some modern readers provide listening exercises in the teacher's manual:[18]

"Sue's big brother, Jerry, has made a model airplane. He is going to fly it in the contest Saturday. The contest is going to be at White Park. Prizes will be given there for the best made airplane, the airplane that flies the longest, and the airplane that makes the best take-off and landing. One of the prizes is a motor for a model airplane. Jerry hopes he can win that.

"Here are the questions: What I read said, 'Sue's brother, Jerry, has made a model airplane. He is going to fly it in the contest Saturday.' Who is meant by the word *he* in those lines, John? . . . Yes, the word *he* means Jerry. What is meant by the word *it* in those lines, Carl? . . . Yes, the model airplane.

"Then what I read said, 'The contest is going to be at White Park. Prizes will be given there for the best made airplane, the airplane

---

[17] Donna M. Mills, "Listening in Grades Four Through Eight," *Reading and the Language Arts* (Chicago: University of Chicago, 1963), pp. 59–61.

[18] Paul McKee, *Reading for Meaning; Come Along,* Teacher's Manual (Boston: Houghton, 1957).

Listening Goal	Reading Activity
1. To discriminate and locate phonetic and structural elements of the spoken word.	Use selections with rhyming words.
2. To discover and to identify sounds, words, or ideas new to the listener.	Close eyes and identify sounds—man-made as well as natural. The tape recorder can be used.
3. To listen for details in order to interpret the main idea and to respond accurately.	After listening show the main idea, with details radiating from it.
4. To listen to a selection for the purpose of answering a previously stated question.	
5. To listen for the main idea when stated in the topic or key sentence.	Have the key sentence occur in various positions.
6. To discriminate between spoken fact and opinion.	Listen to selections. Students write *Fact* or *Opinion*. Discussion and reading to verify should follow.
7. To distinguish between relevant and irrelevant details.	List relevant details in one column and irrelevant ones in another.
8. To listen to select the type of writing: narrative, descriptive, or expositive.	Use various sentences and paragraphs. Students select type.
9. To listen to music to determine mood.	After listening, select and discuss words which could be used to reflect the same mood.
10. To listen to poetry or prose to determine mood.	After listening, select and discuss words and phrases that were used to set mood.
11. To listen in order to visualize a scene.	After listening, draw the scene. Follow this by reading to verify the visual concept. Discuss.
12. To determine oral story sequence.	a. Ask for the sequence of events for a paragraph heard. b. Listen to a story and act out the story sequentially (possibly with puppets).
13. To list the stated facts used to obtain an inference.	Stated facts } Inference
14. To listen in order to understand space and time relationships.	
15. To associate descriptive ideas heard with more concrete objects and life situations.	Listen to descriptions of familiar people and determine the identities.
16. To draw conclusions or form opinions based on facts heard.	Use discussions on a topic followed by conclusions drawn. Group decides the validity of conclusions.
17. To recognize bias.	Use the tape recorder and reproductions of speeches and commercials. What indicates the bias? Are *all* facts given?

that flies the longest, and the airplane that makes the best take-off and landing.' What did I mean by the word *there* in those lines, Jim? . . . Yes, I meant White Park.

"The last two sentences said, 'One of the prizes is a motor for a model airplane. Jerry hopes he can win that.' What does the word *that* mean in those lines, Ann? . . . Yes, it means the motor for a model airplane."

Deciding Which of Several Meanings a Word Has in Statements

"When Harry said, 'It's a long way to our house from here,' the word *way* meant distance. When Paul asked, 'Which way do we go from here?' the word *way* meant direction. When I say, 'I like the way in which you are fixing your hair,' the word *way* means manner.

"Listen while I read three sentences to you. Decide what the word *way* means in each sentence.

"Here is the first sentence. 'John swims in the same way that Bob swims.' What did I mean by the word *way* in that sentence, Ben? . . . Yes, I meant manner.

"Here is the second sentence. 'Which way is the zoo from here?' What did the word *way* mean in that sentence, Ruth? . . . That's right. It meant direction.

"Here is the third sentence. 'It's not a very long way from our house to Betty's house.' What did the word *way* mean in that sentence, Carl? . . . Yes, it meant distance.

"You can see that one word can have many different meanings. To decide what a word means each time it is used, you have to think of the meaning of the words that are used with it."

For Discussion

1. Why is it often ineffective to correct the behavior of children by giving the class a lecture?

2. What listening experience had the greatest learning effect on you?

How May Correct Usage Habits Be Established?

Correct usage is concerned with proper form. The agreement of verb and subject in number and tense, the form of the pronoun in various positions in the sentence, and the word order in sentences are some of the situations that present learning problems of proper form. The child who says, "I done my work" is using the wrong verb form. Another who says, "Him and me are friends" is using the wrong form of the pronoun. Children use these forms because they hear them at home, on television, and in the playground.

First of all, the teacher will encourage the child to enjoy his natural language. He will be accepted, no matter what he says or how he says it. His language is a verbal expression of his thoughts and feelings. If we reject it, we reject him. Furthermore, we reject by implication the family who has taught him to speak and with whom he has strong emo-

tional ties which he needs as he develops as a human being.

A child's speech patterns are discovered by encouraging him to talk. During these early school years the content of his "talk" will often be centered about himself, his home, and his family. At first the teacher will accept the child's own word groupings, if they are in communication units, whether or not he considers them to be complete. But he may also listen for and take note of patterns of substandard usage which can be brought to the children's attention later.

Important as it is to accept the child, immature patterns of usage and all (or along with his immature patterns of usage), we cannot leave him here. As he develops to take his place in his ever-widening world, a corresponding development in his language patterns will be necessary. We can provide for this continuous sequential growth through carefully organized instruction.

At this point individual deviations will be handled with respect for the child. He is aided in expressing himself by modeling his speech after a classroom dialect. The teacher may say something like, "I understand what you mean, but in our classroom we say it this way," and then give him the substitute form. The time and manner in which these substitute forms are given depend upon the feeling of belonging that the child has in his classroom, a state to which the teacher will always be sensitive.

The teacher's attitude, too, plays a major role in achieving a standard classroom dialect. If the teacher is consistent in what is expected from the class and communicates this expectation firmly yet kindly, the pupils will respond with their best. The teacher will want to carry over this consistent attitude into the other subjects as she continues incidental correcting throughout the day.

Forms which might help to establish the classroom dialect would include the following:

1. A transition from all "baby-talk" and "cute" expressions.
2. The acceptable uses in speech and writing of *I, me, him, her, she, they,* and *them.* (Accepted: "It's me.")

3. The appropriate uses of *is, are, was, were* with respect to number and tense.
4. Standard past tenses of common irregular verbs, such as *saw, gave, took, brought, stuck.*
5. Elimination of the double negative: "We don't have no apples."
6. Elimination of analogical forms: *ain't, hisn, hern, ourn, hisself, theirselves,* and so on.
7. Appropriate use of possessive pronouns: *my, mine, his, hers, theirs, ours.*
8. Mastery of the distinction between *its* (possessive pronoun) and *it's* (it is, the contraction). (This applies only to written English.)
9. Elimination of *this here* and *that there.*
10. Approved use of personal pronouns in compound constructions: as subject (*Mary and I*), as object (*Mary and me*), as object of preposition (*to Mary and me*).
11. Attention to number agreement with the phrases *there is, there are, there was, there were.*
12. Elimination of *he don't, she don't, it don't.*
13. Elimination of *learn* for *teach, leave* for *let.*
14. Avoidance of pleonastic subjects: *my brother he; my mother she; that fellow he.*
15. Sensing the distinction between *good* as adjective and *well* as adverb (for example, "He spoke well").

The English language is constantly changing. The meaning difference between *shall* and *will* that is still taught in language books has for all practical purposes disappeared in usage. The use of the pronoun *whom* has reached the stage where those who do use it frequently do so incorrectly, and the word is seldom used in conversation.

There are very few research studies available on the proper grade placement of usage practice. Those that do exist are usually surveys of city courses of study and textbooks. This means that teacher judgment, as much as any other factor, has influenced the grade placement. Textbook writers must consider the practical problem of the total amount of material to be put in a book. As a result, the teacher may find an item such as *take–took* listed in an index with three page references. Further examination will reveal that frequently these refer to one sentence in a test of ten items in which the child has to make a choice between two forms. Frequently children guess the correct form in such an exercise, even though they misuse the verb in their own speech and writing. *If a child is making an error the teacher must plan more corrective instruction than that found in many textbooks.*

A peculiar problem of usage errors is the fact that a child who has correct speech in the primary grades may start making errors in later grades. Perhaps this is because he hears incorrect usage on television and in the playground, or reads it in comic books. Exercises in the textbook may help to counteract this factor by reinforcing existing correct habits.

One other factor concerning textbook drill material should be noted. The sentence may require the child to select between *was* and *were.* If the problem is only one of selecting between the singular and plural it will not serve the child who says, "You was," or, "If I was." The drill or test should concern the error the learner makes.

To change a usage habit three things are necessary: the error should be identified, oral practice should be stressed until the established form sounds correct, and written practice should be given to maintain the desired habit and to test the learner. Oral exercises provide opportunities in listening to the correct form. The drill is for the listener as well as the speaker. "Game" situations like the following provide such practice.

A child cannot learn to *improve* his language unless he first feels free to *use* language. Errors in the use of language, therefore, should be called to his attention only after he feels accepted by the group and sufficiently self-confident so that correction will not silence him. The spirit in which corrections are made is perhaps the most important single factor in the child's language development.

These steps have proved effective in practice:

1. Listen to the children talk and note the type of errors common to the group and to individuals.
2. Select the most glaring ones for correction.
3. Choose a few errors at a time for concentrated effort.
4. Call attention to the correct use of words as well as to errors in usage.
5. Correct the child at the time the error is made, but after he has finished what he had to say.
6. Follow a period of oral expression with a short drill period in which the child hears the correct form repeated several times.
7. Play games in which the correct form is used over and over again.

Note how Mary is complimented on correct word usage in grade 1. The children were saying "I got" repeatedly. Mary said, "I have."

TEACHER: I am so glad to hear Mary say "I have." It sounds pleasing to my ears.

This approval made the others eager to use "I have."

The children correct a common error in grade 2:

TEACHER: This morning I heard someone say, "The bird he was building a nest." Let's all think of something you have seen a bird do and see if we can leave out the *he*.
CHILD 1: The bird was feeding his babies.
CHILD 2: The bird was hopping on the ground.
TEACHER: This morning I heard someone say, "This here book is mine." It would sound better to say, "This book is mine." Let's all take something out of our desks that belongs to us and tell about it.
CHILD 1: This pencil is mine.
CHILD 2: This chalk is yours.

The children begin to drop *ain't* when assisted to make proper substitutions.

TEACHER: Lately I've been hearing some of you say, "I ain't got a pencil. I ain't

going with you." Does anyone know a better way of saying it?
CHILD 1: I haven't a pencil.
CHILD 2: I'm not going with you.
TEACHER: That's better.

Using toy telephones for conversation between two children is a helpful device to alert teachers to discover inappropriate usage such as "Me and my brother," or "I seen." [19] Here, too, we detect baby talk which has been permitted in the home. Many of our five- and six-year-olds come to us unable to sound several of the consonants. A few examples are *fadder* for *father, Zimmy* for *Jimmy, yittle* for *little, won* for *run.*

By listening and speaking to each other in the form of these "pretended" phone calls, children grow in the knowledge of a standard classroom dialect. The tape recorder is also a valuable instructional aid at this point as the child is able to hear his own voice and listen to it critically.

The best drills to teach English as a foreign language are known as pattern practice drills. The drills are something like the following: Suppose the teacher wants to make automatic the use of *there are* and *there is.* The problem, of course, is that the student wants to say, "There is two spoons on the table." We can set up a series of key frames thus:

There's one spoon on the table.
There're two spoons on the table.
There's a spoon on the table.
There're some spoons on the table.
There're several spoons on the table.

The teacher will say each one of these sentences and then ask the class to repeat each orally. Next she can ask for individual repetition. Then she can extend the exercise by giving a series of cues—words which will substitute in the patterns: *toast, dishes, bread, glasses, forks, two vases, several napkins, some food,* and so on. This can be varied further as follows:

---

[19] Throughout this chapter, examples have been drawn from *English Language Arts* in Wisconsin; Robert C. Pooley, Project Director, Madison, Wisconsin; Department of Public Instruction; William C. Kahl, State Superintendent of Schools, 1968.

CUE: How many spoons are there on the table?

RESPONSE: There're two spoons on the table.

CUE: Is there a spoon on the table?

RESPONSE: Yes, there's a spoon on the table.

CUE: There's. . . .

RESPONSE: There's a spoon on the table. There's a dish on the table.

CUE: There're. . . .

RESPONSE: There're forks on the table.

Or take another example: Our problem here is that the student says "them things." We can set up a series of frames as follows:

I don't like that thing.
I don't like those things.
That book's on the table.
Those books er on the table.

The students will repeat these and similar frames after the teacher, and then the teacher can proceed thus:

CUE: That man is my friend. (*Men.*)

RESPONSE: Those men are my friends.

CUE: That thing is on the table. (*Things.*)

RESPONSE: Those things are on the table.

Later a student may provide cues.

"Chain Practice" can be played to substitute *he doesn't* for *he don't*. In this game each child asks a question, and the child in the next desk responds and then forms the question for the next, who then responds and forms a question for the next child, and so on. The teacher may ask the first question:

TEACHER (*to David*): What doesn't David like to do?

DAVID (*to teacher*): David doesn't like to mow the lawn.

DAVID (*to Marilyn*): What doesn't Marilyn like to do?

MARILYN (*to David*): Marilyn doesn't like to wash the dishes.

MARILYN (*to Laura*): What doesn't Laura like to do?

Chain practice is more fun if it moves along quickly.

An imaginative pupil or the teacher may make a puppet for this activity by coloring a face on a lunch size bag with the mouth at the bottom of the sack so that the puppet can appear to be talking. Children may take turns talking for the puppet. The teacher will ask the puppet (the pupil) questions which he will answer using standard classroom dialect. Here the pupils will practice negative answers.

TEACHER (*to puppet*): Albert, do you have any candy?

ALBERT (*to teacher*): No, I haven't any candy.

TEACHER (*to Albert*): Albert, do you have any marbles in your pocket?

ALBERT (*to teacher*): No, I haven't any marbles in my pocket.

The responses to the teacher's questions are intended to replace "I haven't got no . . ." or "I ain't got no . . ." with the more desirable "No, I haven't any . . ." Albert might develop as a special character who makes the errors the class is committing.

The next language game is designed to substitute deviant words with acceptable ones (such as *isn't* for *ain't*). The teacher will list some words on the chalkboard. For example,

troposphere	ionosphere
scientific	satellite
barometer	prediction
humidity	forecast
atmosphere	thermometer

These are scientific words which might be selected for a sixth-grade class that had become familiar with them in science. One student is chosen to begin. He thinks of one of the words on the list. Then he begins by saying, "What word am I thinking of?"

CLASSMATE: Is it *humidity?*

STUDENT: No, it isn't *humidity.*

ANOTHER CLASSMATE: Is it *prediction?*

STUDENT: No, it isn't *prediction.*

This game may be scaled down to almost any level by the use of more simple words.

A sixth-grade class prepared the following material:

Script for an Exercise Using *Did* and *Done* Correctly

Good morning. This is station WDSC bringing you another in the series called "Aids to English Usage." Have you ever heard a person say, "I done wrong"? Now, does this sound like a good use of English to you? How about saying it this way? "I have done wrong." The use of *did* and *done* causes a lot of children trouble, so this morning we are going to try and help you use these two words correctly. Listen to the following sentences. Can you explain why we use *done* instead of *did?* Does the word *done* seem to stand alone?

1. I have done the job well.
2. We have done the work quickly.
3. They have done the lesson well.

In these sentences did you notice that *done* has a helper word, *have?* When used, as it was in these sentences, *done* requires a helper word. The word *did* may stand alone. Listen and you will see that *did* stands alone.

1. I did the work for the teacher.
2. We did our homework in the kitchen.
3. Our class did well in arithmetic this week.

Did you notice that the word *did* was able to stand alone? It did not need a helper word. Now, listen to this story and try to fill in the missing word. The speaker will pause when he comes to a place where you could use either *did* or *done.* Write the correct word on your paper. Number your answers from 1 through 5 so we may correct them afterwards. Let's begin the story.

John said to Bob, "Look, I (*pause*) my work paper already." Bob laughed and said, "You are slow, John. I have (*pause*) my paper already. Mike has (*pause*) his paper, too." Mike looked up from his desk and smiled. "I (*pause*) mine when the teacher was going over the problem." It looks like all three boys have (*pause*) their lesson well.

Now I shall repeat the story so that you can proofread your answers before we grade the exercise. (*Repeat story.*)
The correct words are: (1) *did,* (2) *done,* (3) *done,* (4) *did,* (5) *done.* Did you get them all correct? Tune in tomorrow for a special lesson on two more demons, *saw* and *seen.* See you then.

Children at the intermediate level can learn a manner of speaking for the classroom and still retain a homely dialect which they learn from their parents. They can also begin to appreciate other dialects. For example, stories spoken in dialect once spoken in the South have been preserved. In some

classes the familiar Uncle Remus stories might be used. At the onset children may be reminded that most Negroes no longer speak this way. If the teacher feels comfortable with the dialect, she may read the stories to the children; if she is uneasy about the pronunciation, she may use records.

The lesson may be structured this way: Tell the children that these stories are different from other stories they have heard and that they will have to listen carefully to the way that the storyteller uses words. Explain who the speaker is. The first listening is just for the fun of the story. *The Wonderful Tar Baby* or the language patterns in the regional books by Lois Lenski would be a good beginning.

After the reading or the record is finished, children will want to talk about it and tell about different ways of talking which they have heard or regional dialects to which they have been exposed. The record might be played a second time for the children to listen for interesting ways of expression which they hear. A second lesson could be set up by asking the children to look in the library for stories using dialects. Give them some help by suggesting that they might find conversations between Southern people or between Western people. Suggest that people from different areas have a dialect the children will find different from their own. Set a time for the children to read the dialects that they have discovered for themselves.

A whole week could be devoted to dialects if the children become enthusiastic about them. The music teacher could help out by giving some time during music to songs with lyrics in dialect. For instance, songs by Stephen Foster or some Western cowboy ballads offer excellent experiences in dialect. Stories using dialect could be written by some children.

For Discussion

1. How can correct usage be stressed without establishing the discourteous habit of correcting each other? Should children ever correct adults?

2. Are there programs on television, such as "What's My Line?" that could be adapted for classroom use?

What Voice Qualities Should a Classroom Teacher Possess?

Speech instruction in the elementary classroom starts with the voice of the teacher. The tone used, the manner of speaking, and the vocabulary employed all influence the quality of instruction. A voice that is too low to be heard or that has a high, irritating quality produces classroom tension and behavior problems. A monotonous voice robs literature of the emotional content that makes it interesting. Voice is a major aspect of personality. When we think of someone as gracious or poised, our judgment is partly based on that person's voice and vocal expression.

The teacher's words carry meaning not only because she conceives and expresses her thoughts accurately, but also because her voice is properly attuned and controlled to convey this meaning. The tonal quality of her voice may make the difference between interested and inattentive children. A thin voice gives an impression of weakness, causing the listener to shift his attention. Clarity of enunciation and resonance quality or timbre determine whether or not a teacher's directions and suggestions will be followed. The teacher's voice is of greatest value when it is calm yet firm, well modulated yet sufficiently loud to be heard in a busy classroom, and suitably inflected to convey the varied feelings and emotions encountered in oral reading.

There are two ways to discover how you sound to others. One is to make a tape recording and then to listen critically to yourself. The other is to cup your hands behind your ears and read aloud either a paragraph of a story or a verse of poetry. If the results are not pleasing, there are a number of things you can do about it.

Start by learning to control your breathing and posture. Standing "tall," head up, shoulders back, and breathing deeply will do much to improve the sound of your voice. Listening attentively to people whose voices you find attractive while consciously imitating some of the patterns of speech will also help. Speaking with relaxed throat and lips well apart helps to produce full, rounded tones, as does proper sitting and standing. Barring a physical deformity in the throat or mouth, anyone can learn to speak distinctly and agreeably.

Voice modulation means a "toning down," or tempering, of the voice to avoid nasal twang, harshness, stridency, shrillness, or shouting. A man with a high-pitched voice sounds feminine; conversely, a woman with a hoarse or low-pitched voice sounds masculine. Speech exercises can help remove these defects by providing a pattern of speech to imitate that will modify the disturbing qualities. At first one may feel a bit self-conscious saying, "How now, brown cow?" over and over again, but this exercise is just as therapeutic as those used in a gym class to correct posture.

Relaxation is fundamental in all speech training. Not only the muscles used for speech but all other parts of the body as well should be free from tension in order to produce relaxed, clear voice tones and harmonious coordination of the many elements comprising the speech mechanism. Relaxation may be gained by perusing a quiet story or a short poem or by gazing upon a restful scene or painting.

Flexibility and control of the lips are important in the projection of correct "labial" sounds. Proper placement of the tongue is essential to the production of well-rounded vowels and to the formation of distinct, clear consonants and other "velar" and "glottal" sounds. This type of exercise is best done at home. The object is to "throw" the sounds toward the back of the room and to imagine that they are bouncing off the wall. The sounds should be thrown with an explosive breath effort.

ba,
ba, be;
ba, be, bi;
ba, be, bi, bo;
ba, be, bi, bo, boo.

The same exercise may be used with *p, m, v,* and *f* as well. The poem below provides practice in lip movement.

Antonio

Antonio, Antonio
Was tired of living alonio.
He thought he would woo
Miss Lissamy Lu,
Miss Lissamy Lucy Malonio.

Antonio, Antonio
Rode off on his polo-ponio.
He found the fair maid
In a bowery shade,
Sitting and knitting alonio.

"Oh, nonio, Antonio!
You're far too bleak and bonio!
And all that I wish,
You singular fish,
Is that you would quickly begonio."

Antonio, Antonio,
He uttered a dismal moanio;
Then ran off and hid
(Or I'm told that he did)
In the Antarctical Zonio.

LAURA E. RICHARDS

Flexible tongue practice can be obtained by the same type of exercise used for the lips:

ta,
ta, te;
ta, te, ti;
ta, te, ti, to;
ta, te, ti, to, too.

These letters may also be used: *l, n, d, k, g.*

Insufficient breath and lack of volume are often the speech characteristics of timid, insecure individuals. With a group or alone, the timid can be reassured through the device of projecting himself into a character. Have these children pretend to be newsboys crying, "Extra! Extra! Read all about it." Or peddlers selling fruit, "Big, ripe bananas. Buy your bananas here!" Or cheerleaders, "Team! Team! Team! Fight! Fight! Fight!" Of equal value and far easier is singing many familiar songs which help the individual project his voice and interpret feelings.

The roof of the mouth or hard palate is a cavity that amplifies sound vibrations in addition to giving them a strong and more pleasing quality. Voice resonance can be cultivated by the way the oral cavity is used. Dull voices are frequently associated with dull faces. A smile and a happy state of mind will help increase resonance. Humming is also good for this purpose.

Intonation and emphasis give variety to the voice. It may come down emphatically at the end of an important idea, or go up in suspense and wonderment. Parts of words, entire words, or complete phrases may be lowered or raised.

Practice in Raising or Lowering the Voice [20]

Read the following sentences up and down as they are written:

```
                      hear me?
        do        you        Stop
1. Don't   that! Do              I say.
   Put             not
    it    here,          there.
2.      up          down
                    I'll
     you          here          there.
3. If    don't come       come
              do?      help you? Thank
   How   you    May
4.    do           I            you.
   That's              What is
                            rodent?
5.      an  unusual  animal.    it? A
```

Make the voice go up or down as the lines indicate:

1. Police horses are trained by encouragement, not by punishment.
2. He was a bully, not a hero—a cheat, not a conqueror.
3. You would vote for that stupid, that hateful, that impossible beast?
4. Here were strangers to face, tasks to conquer, opportunities to grasp.
5. The game was almost a landslide for our boys.

[20] Agnes Frye, "Syllabus for Speech," mimeographed (Sacramento, Calif.: California State Department of Instruction, 1956).

Emphasize the underlined word and note the change in meaning of the sentence:

1. I am going to the show.
2. I am going to the show.
3. I am going to the show.
4. I am going to the show.

Read the different interpretations of this sentence:

1. Naturally he'd like some cake. (of course he would)
2. Naturally he'd like some cake. (whether anyone else does or not)
3. Naturally he'd like some cake. (but he can't have any)
4. Naturally he'd like some cake. (he wouldn't need much)
5. Naturally he'd like some cake. (he wouldn't like bread)

Carrie Rasmussen suggests that teachers use the following questions to decide how qualified they are in the speech area of the language arts: [21]

Do my visible actions add meaning to my words?
Does my facial expression reinforce my words?
Is my whole body alive?
Do I appear free physically?

Do I talk loud enough to be heard easily?
Do I pronounce my words carefully?
Is my voice pleasant?
Is my tone quality (pitch) good?
Does my voice have variety?
Do I speak clearly?

Do I know what I am talking about; is my information accurate?
Is my vocabulary good?
Do I understand my audience—one, four or forty in number?
Do I make clear what I am saying? Is my choice of words good?

Do I try to understand others?
Do I talk too much?
Do I know how to listen?
Do I know how to make things interesting?

Do I have a sense of humor?
Do I get the other person's point of view?

Do I have ideas?
Do I know how to create things?
Do I know how important creating is in the life of man?
What do I know about Creative Dramatics?
Am I teaching poetry in my class and are they enjoying it?
What do I know about discussion, storytelling, giving a talk?
Can I direct a play?
Can I integrate one subject with several others and make it fun?

You can tell from this that Rasmussen considers speech far more inclusive than voice. Her definition is an interesting one: [22]

Speech is the blending of those elements: thought—mental processes; language—the molding of thought and feelings into words; voice—carrying thought and words through vocal sound to someone else; action—bodily bearing and response and listening. Speech is designed to transmit belief, emotion, or attitude on the part of the speaker, and our chief reason for speaking is to arouse corresponding ideas, meanings, and actions in others. It is sometimes called a code, but whatever we call it, we use it almost constantly; it is one of our most necessary tools.

For Discussion

1. Should a teacher who moves from Georgia to California attempt to change her speech pattern to conform to her new classroom?

2. Should college students with speech faults, such as lisping or high-pitched voices, be admitted to a teacher-training program?

3. Observe a classroom. Note the different tones of voice the teacher uses as she explains material to the total class, talks with an individual child, or gains attention of a group.

4. Do you have a speech habit that you would not wish children to imitate?

5. Can you tell from a person's voice if he is tired or emotionally disturbed?

---

[21] Carrie Rasmussen, *Speech Methods in the Elementary School.* Copyright 1949 The Ronald Press Company.

[22] Ibid., p. 8.

What Speech Activities Are Presented in the Primary Grades?

Some children come to school who have not yet mastered all the sounds of our language. Studies indicate that we can expect this development of speech sounds: [23]

Age	Consonants
3½	p, b, m, h, w (lip sounds)
4½	d, n (tip-of-the-tongue sounds)
5–5½	f, j, w, h, s, z
6–6½	v, th, sh, zh, l
7–7½	ch, r, th (voiceless)
8	such blends as pl, br, st, sk, str

The sounds most frequently defective are: *s, z, sh, zh* (as in pleasure), *ch, j, th, l, r, wh,* and the *-ing* ending which is shortened to *-en.*

With young children the following letters have more than names—they are given a personality to focus attention on the sound

they represent. In order to do this, key words or sounds are used as the children practice the sounds. Naming objects in pictures and talking for dolls or animals aid sound identification.

Some sounds are twins. They look the same when we make them but some sounds whisper in words and some talk out loud: *p–b; t–d; k–g; f–v; th–th; s–z; sh–zh; ch–j.* The second is the "talker" because it adds the vibration of vocal chords.

Ear training is important if the children are to improve speech habits. Until they hear the difference between the way they are pronouncing a word or producing a voice sound and the way it should be pronounced or produced, they will not change their pattern of speech. Ear training to develop auditory discrimination for the sounds of speech is the first step in speech correction and improvement.

Do not try to correct an *s* or *r* before easier sounds have been mastered. Instead, give much ear training on these sounds. Of course, there is no sense working on blends if the *l* and *r* have not been perfected.

A picture test can be made by the teacher to check the child's ability to say the initial

---

[23] Irene Poole, "The Genetic Development of the Articulation of Consonant Sounds" (doctoral dissertation, University of Michigan, 1934), p. 60.

Lip sounds	p	the *pop* sound (not *puh*)
	b	the *bubble* sound (not *buh*)
	m	the *humming* sound
	w	the *soft wind* sound
	y	the *smile* sound
Lip-breath sounds	h	the *little puff* sound
	wh	the *big puff* sound
Tip-of-the-tongue sounds	t	the *ticking watch* sound
	d	the *tapping* sound
	n	the *spinning* sound
Back-of-the-tongue sounds	k	the *little cough* sound
	g	the *gurgle* sound
	ng	the *ring* sound (*ding-a-ling, ting-a-ling*)
Lip–teeth sounds	f	the *cross kitty* sound
	v	the *airplane* sound
Tongue–teeth sounds	th	(as in *this*) the *flat tire* sound
	th	(as in *the*) the *motor* sound
Teeth sounds	s	the *steam* sound
	z	the *buzz* sound
	sh	the *baby's asleep* sound
	zh	the *vacuum cleaner* sound
	ch	the *train* sound
	j	the *jump* sound
Tongue and voice sounds	l	the *bell* sound
	r	the *rooster* sound

Sack puppets and a cardboard-box stage stimulate a purposeful use of language for this class. (*Courtesy of the San Diego City Schools.*)

consonants. Frequently, an alphabet book or picture dictionary will provide the pictures needed. These are suggestions that might be used: *h*, hat; *m*, man; *wh*, whistle; *w*, wagon; *p*, pig; *b*, ball; *n*, nail; *y*, yellow; *t*, table; *d*, day; *k*, kite; *g*, gun; *ng*, ring; *f*, fish; *v*, valentine; *l*, lamp; *th*, thumb; *th*, feather; *sh*, shoe; *zh*, tape measure; *s*, sun; *z*, zebra; *r*, rabbit; *ch*, chair; *j*, jar.

A still more comprehensive test uses separate pictures for each sound in all three positions—initial, medial, and final. As the teacher points to the picture, the child names it, with the teacher recording all errors. Teachers may make this test themselves with pictures cut from magazines, or they may purchase any of the commercial tests that are available. Many authorities

feel that at the kindergarten level testing for errors in the initial position only is sufficient.

An individual test that is interesting for the child is a story using the rebus method of picture insertion. The tester reads the words and the child "fills in" by giving the words for the pictures. One in the Los Angeles City Speech Course of Study goes like this: "Jimmy sat up in (picture of bed). He looked through the (window) at the bright (sun). It was time to get up. He put on his (coat) and (pants) his (stockings) and (shoes). He put his magic (ring) on his (finger) and went downstairs." The story continues until all sounds have been tested.

Auditory discrimination is an essential skill in both reading and spelling. These lessons indicate how the sounds may be isolated in words.[24]

Words Beginning with S—Paper Bag Game

Teacher, "Today we are going to play a guessing game. In each of these paper bags is a toy or an article. The name of each thing starts with *s* as in sun. One person will be it. He will peek into one of these bags and give you one clue about what he sees. He might say, 'I see something we wear.' Then we will take turns guessing what he saw." (These items can be in the paper bags.)

scissors   sock   sailboat   stick   soap   star salt (small package as served on airplanes)

"The game must be played using complete sentences. When you guess, you say, 'Is it _____?' putting in the name of what you want to guess. The person who is it must answer you using the name of what you have guessed. If after everyone has had one turn and no one has guessed correctly, a second clue will be given."

(Stress the need for all questions and answers to be complete sentences using the forms: Is it a _____? No, it is not a _____! Depending upon the ability of your group, you may wish to add the following step in the lesson.)

"Let's write the names of all the things we have guessed and any other words we have used that begin with *s* sounds. Tell me what to write on the chalkboard."

Note: The lesson that follows should be used soon after this one.

Initial, Medial, and Final S Words— Paper Bag Game

Teacher, "The game today uses words that have *s* sounds in the beginning, the middle, and the end. Your main clue is that there is an *s* sound somewhere in the word you are to guess. The things in the paper bags all have an *s* sound somewhere in their name."

(See preceding lesson for detailed instructions for playing this game.) The items in the paper bags can be

basket   bus   sunglasses   nest   stone   purse mouse

[24] Mary Smith, *Listening Habits and Speech Sound Discrimination,* Alameda County Schools Department, Haywood, California, 1963.

(Stress the need for all questions and answers to be complete sentences using the forms: Is it a _____? No, it is not _____. Write the words they have guessed and have the class tell whether the *s* is in the beginning, middle, or end of the word.)

Auditory Discrimination Between S and Z

Teacher, "The letter *s* makes more than one sound. Sometimes it says *s* and sometimes it says *z*. When it says *s*, we blow air through our closed teeth. When it says *z*, we do it the same way except our voice box vibrates or wiggles. Put your hand on your throat near your "Adam's apple" or voice box (larynx). Say s-s-s-s. You do not feel movement there. Now say z-z-z-z. Feel your voice box wiggle? *Scissors* is a word that has lots of s's. See if you can tell which ones say *s* and which ones say *z*. Hold your throat as you say *sizorz.* Yes, it begins with *s* and has a *z* sound in the middle and on the end."

(Put these words on the chalkboard in *mixed* order and have the children tell you whether they belong in the *s* column or *z* column.)

S column	Z column
sister	rose
salt	houses (note that both s's have
seven	the *z* sound in the plural of
house	house)
this	his
guess	flowers
school	please
sleep	does
just	ears
said	nose
across	these
	present

"Now, let's read each column aloud holding our throats to check to see if we have them right."

Note: This lesson is particularly helpful for children with Spanish and certain other foreign backgrounds. It should be repeated until the children thoroughly understand and can distinguish between these two sounds. You can develop many word lists for this type of lesson from reading, spelling, and other subject matter vocabulary.

Speech activities are involved in all phases of the curriculum. Singing, dramatic play, storytelling, finger plays, sharing time, and puppet plays and poetry reading stimulate and provide practice for speech improvement.

The following games are speech-centered and may be used with positive results in the primary grades.

Treasure Chest

Place several small objects in an attractive box. The names of these objects contain specific sounds. For the development of the sound of *k* the chest might contain a car, comb, kite, cane. Children take objects from the chest and say their names correctly.

I See Something You May See

A child makes three statements to describe something he sees. Children guess what it is by saying, "Do you see _____?"

Lip-Reading Game

Teacher: "I am going to say names of children in the class but I am not going to use my voice. Watch for your name. Stand when your name is said on my lips."

CH Guessing Game

Guess the answer. Example: Two sides of the face (cheeks). Where you go on Sunday (church).

I Have Something in My Sack

In a large box put many small paper bags in each of which is a small toy.

The names of the toys may contain specific sounds for improvement. A child chooses a sack from the box, peeks in, and discovers his toy. He then describes the toy without naming it. The child who guesses correctly then chooses a sack from the box and the game continues.

Telephone Games

One child orders from a list of toys and telephones order to Toy Store. He then goes to the storekeeper and asks if his package is ready. Storekeeper answers, "What is your name?" "My name is _____." "Yes, your package is ready," etc.

Fishing Game

Select pictures representing words which contain sounds you have been working on. Put paper clips on each picture, then put pictures in a pail or box. Attach a magnet to a string hanging from a pole. After lifting the picture out of the pail, the child tries to say the name of the picture. If he does, he keeps the picture; if he does not, he must put picture back (after having practiced it a little) and try again.

Sound Ladder or Word Ladder

Draw an outline ladder on paper or on the blackboard. Place syllables you are practicing or words on each rung of the ladder. Child begins at bottom and climbs ladder by pronouncing each of the words or syllables correctly. The game is to see if he can climb to the top and back down again without "falling off." If he misses he must start at the bottom again.

Animal Talk

The sounds: *quack-quack, moo-moo, baa-baa, oink-oink,* and *peep-peep* are good for lip movement. Pictures of animals may be shown and the children imitate that animal. A story may be told about a farmer and when an animal is mentioned the children make the proper sounds.

Noisy Cards

Make picture cards that suggest sound effects. The pictures are face-down in a stack. A child takes the top card. Questions and answers should be in sentences.

Child: "My picture says _____. What do I have?"

Answer: "Do you have _____?"

Child: "Yes, (or no) I have a _____."

A Listening Story

Negative practice is important in checking the child's knowledge of sounds. Ask children to raise their hands when they hear a sound error as you read. Have them identify the error, and then give the correct sound.

Sound Boxes

Collect and place in boxes small objects starting with easily confused sounds; example *s-z, th-s, th-f, w-r.* Review the contents of the boxes periodically, letting children use names of objects in sentences.

I See Something

Use sound boxes mentioned above. Teacher says, "I see something in this box that starts with _____." Child chooses object and says, "Is it a _____?"

Mailman

Pictures of objects containing sound being worked on are placed in envelopes.

A very effective device is to sketch a large profile on a cardboard, indicating the lips, teeth, palate, and bottom of the mouth. Omit the tongue. Cut out the cardboard to show the mouth cavity. Make a red mitten for your right hand. As you teach a sound, use your gloved hand in the open mouth cavity to simulate the tongue. Move it against or between the teeth, bunch it up in the back, curl it up to the palate for /r/, or indicate movement from one sound to another.

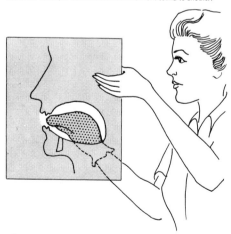

From Mary Finocchiaro, *English as a Second Language: From Theory to Practice* (New York: Regents, 1965), p. 54. By permission.

Child: "Mr. Mailman, please look and see if you have a letter for me."
Mailman: (Gives child envelope) "Yes, I have a letter for you."
Child: (Opens envelope) "My letter has a _____ in it."

Balloons

(especially good when working on "L")

Make colored paper balloons about six inches in diameter with a string fastened to each one.

FIRST CHILD: I am the balloon man. Balloons! Balloons for sale!
Who will buy my balloons?
SECOND CHILD: I will buy a balloon.
FIRST CHILD: What color would you like?
SECOND CHILD: I would like a _____ balloon.

(Continue game until all balloons have been chosen.) After all balloons have been chosen, ask for them to be returned by colors, using only the lips to form the words without a voice. Do not exaggerate lip movements when forming the words.

For Discussion

1. Should a child be expected to read a word containing a sound that is not present in his speech?
2. Should a child be expected to read a word containing a sound that he cannot or does not hear?
3. What games would you suggest that a child play at home who has not mastered the major speech sounds?
4. Why are you no longer aware of the difference between such sounds as *th* in *this* and *throw?*
5. How might singing games help in the development of a child's speech?

How May the Classroom Teacher Help Children with Speech Defects?

"Speech is defective when it deviates so far from the speech of other people in the group that it calls attention to itself, interferes with communication, or causes the possessor to be maladjusted to his environment." [25]

About one of every ten children in the public schools has a speech defect as defined above. About half of these defects are relatively simple problems, such as substituting *wun* for *run* or saying *pay* for *play*. The remaining are more serious. These include hearing impairment, physical defects such as cleft palate, stuttering, and delayed speech resulting from psychological causes. The first group can be cared for by a classroom teacher, the second needs the help of a specialist. However, many of those receiving special training will be in regular classrooms and in all other respects their education is the responsibility of the regular teacher.

In all cases early recognition and treatment of the defect will help the child. Even if some of these defects cannot be corrected, the child, like other handicapped individuals, can be shown how to adjust to his limitations. The teacher can aid in this recognition, but in so doing she must also recognize and be able to distinguish between those defects that can be corrected and those that cannot. It is as unprofessional to attempt to remove some of these speech defects without special training as it would be to treat serious illnesses without medical training.

Parents and regular teachers can assist the child in correcting simple articulation errors. Articulation errors of sound substitution, addition, and omission may be identified in a number of ways. Conversation, questions, counting, and naming the days of the week or objects in a room will reveal the existence of the error. Further identification of the habit can be made by test sentences or pictures of objects which contain the sound in different parts of words. Sometimes the child can say the sound in some words that he fails to articulate in others.

The first step toward correction is to have the child recognize his error and decide to change it. The teacher might say,

John, sometimes you use a sound in a word that other people do not use. Listen while I read a story and pronounce some words the way you do. I'll put my hand behind my ear when I say those words. Then I'll read the story again and say the words as others do. If you hear the difference put your hand behind your ear. You say "shine crackers," others say "fine crackers." Here are two pictures of a fine cracker. One has a X across the picture. Listen to me. If I say "fine cracker" hold up the picture without the X. If I say "shine cracker" hold up the one with the X.[26]

Once errors have been identified by the one making them the emphasis is upon listening. "It is not sufficient to isolate and identify the correct sound during the preliminary period of ear training. The student must be stimulated with the sound so thoroughly that it may almost be said to ring in his ears." [27] Names, faces, symbols, stories are used to identify the incorrect sounds. Discrimination consists of comparing and contrasting the correct and incorrect sounds both in isolation and in incorporation within regular speech. Without the ability to differentiate correct sound from incorrect sound, the student becomes discouraged and treatment becomes blind drill. The following therapy involves ear training to the extent that the learner hears himself. Hearing his own error is the foundation for corrective habit formation.

Some speech problems are beyond the treatment of the classroom teacher. The teacher will have children with such problems in class and needs to understand some of the problems these children have.

Cleft palate designates the pathological condition in which the roof of the mouth has failed to grow together before the child was born. Surgery can correct this, but sometimes the condition is neglected until after the child has developed speech, when correction requires relearning breath control. Ordinarily a classroom teacher is not trained to meet this problem but she may

[25] Charles Van Riper and Katherine G. Butler, *Speech in the Elementary Classroom* (New York: Harper, 1955).

[26] Charles Van Riper, *Speech Correction* (Englewood Cliffs, N.J.: Prentice-Hall, 1964), pp. 243–44. (Contains many additional suggestions.)

[27] Ibid., p. 251.

have such a child in her class. The sounds made by these children are distorted, because they have no sounding board except the throat and nose chambers. A film is available, titled "The Wisconsin Cleft Palate Story," which might be used to help a child's parents understand this problem or to enlist the aid of others. During the long period of re-education that follows a cleft-palate operation these children need patient understanding by teachers, parents, and their peer groups.

Malocclusion denotes a failure of the teeth to mesh—usually at the front of the mouth. During the intermediate grades this is a frequent condition of new teeth in the as yet undeveloped jaw. A large number of these situations adjust themselves with growth. It is a frequent (and expensive) practice to correct malocclusion during the junior high school years. Mrs. Eleanor Roosevelt, one of the most beloved women in American public life, who for years had protruding front teeth which affected her speech, had the condition corrected late in life.

Probably the most misunderstood of all speech defects is *stuttering*. In this situation the speech is only a symptom of a deeper psychological cause. Correction is not a matter of speech alone. The most important thing for all teachers to remember about stuttering is that it is caused by pressure and tension at some critical moment in a child's life. The tragedy is that stuttering is sometimes caused by the school itself. Strange to say, in our culture it is more frequent among boys than among girls. Equally strange is the fact that stuttering does not exist at all in some cultures. At times when the child is facing considerable speech development, as at the age of three or in the first grade, ideas sometimes come faster than the sounds or words can be recalled and produced. Nearly every child "clutters" or says "ah-ah-ah" while seeking the word. Concern by parents or teachers during this period seems to cause some to stutter. These children are so robust that we may forget their inner sensitivity. A remark of concern, such as "I am afraid John is going to stutter," overheard at this time may actually cause

stuttering. Even an attempt by the parent to correct the speech by saying "Stop and start again" may cause damage.

Because stuttering is misunderstood, parents of older children frequently think they are clinging to a childish habit and can stop stuttering if they want to. Stutterers can usually sing, speak, or read in a group; take part in a memorized play that involves them physically (such as sweeping with a broom); and talk while dancing without stuttering. Increased language facility that is the result of much writing and a growth in psychic confidence and security usually helps a person who stutters.

The most important thing a classroom teacher can do for a stutterer is to help him accept this defect without embarrassment. The child who can accept this speech pattern as one accepts being left-handed is a long way toward satisfactory educational and social adjustment. These suggestions may be shared with the child's parents:

1. Do not provide words, finish a sentence, or act impatient when listening to a stuttering child.
2. Do see that the child is not subject to physical or emotional strain. "Stuttering is the weak and weary nervous system protecting itself from complete exhaustion."
3. Do praise the child's efforts and make him feel both worthy and loved.
4. Do not put the stuttering child in an exciting and highly competitive position. Overly ambitious parents or those who expect high behavior standards sometimes create ulcers for themselves at the same time they make a stutterer of their child. Far too many stutterers are the sons of highly ambitious professional men.
5. Do not correct or reprimand the child for stuttering or call attention to it. He is already building up fears in meeting speech situations and is extremely conscious of his trouble. Anticipate some speech situations—such as telephoning, meeting strangers, answering questions—and provide confidence-building practice.

The group is planning an original puppet play which they will create and then present. (*Courtesy of the Burbank Public Schools.*)

6. Help him accept himself as a stutterer. "Sure I stutter sometimes but I'm trying to get over it" is a healthy attitude. All of us on occasion do what the stutterer does more frequently.

For Discussion

1. There are other speech defects than those described here. Can you describe some of them?

2. Would you advise a parent to send a child with a speech defect to some of the special speech camps held during the summer months? What would you want to know before doing anything?

3. Would there be any advantage in clustering all children with speech defects in a few rooms?

4. A child with a speech defect in your classroom has been accepted by the other children as a humorous clown. The speech-defective child likes this role and plays it well. What actions would you take?

5. One teacher reports, "My A/V Club is a very small group, usually six boys. I have had students with speech deviations, and find that these boys feel free to participate in oral discussions and demonstrations, and have overcome a great deal of their timidity about speaking as they become interested in operating the equipment." How would you justify such a grouping based upon speech needs?

How Does a Teacher Work with Children Who Do Not Speak English?

Some schools place children who do not speak English in special orientation classes regardless of grade until language is mastered. For little children a year of "prefirst" following kindergarten is considered essential. When the problem concerns only a single child, a buddy system in which the buddy is changed at times usually works well. This is an excellent learning experience for the English-speaking child in that he is forced to note the structure of his language.

While the great stress will be upon listening and reproduction of oral language, there will be some reading. Anyone who has traveled in a foreign country knows that it is easier to read some of the basic signs than it is to speak the language.

The very first day of school the foreign-speaking child has one word in common in both languages—his name. His experience with language should begin with this one word. First the teacher must make sure that the child recognizes his name orally. Some parents use a different name or an abbreviation but give the school the full formal name. This results in difficulty for the child. Frequently the teacher pronounces the name differently from the way the parents do.

The teacher presents the name cards by attaching one set to the child's table or chair or coat hook, and teaches the child to find his own place. Then she gathers them in small groups and presents the cards, holding one up, saying the name, and handing it to the child. The following games provide needed practice. Although designed for Spanish-speaking children, these activities are appropriate for any child learning the English language.[28]

1. *Mailman* (tests the "mailman"). A child who is chosen to be mailman tries to pass out the name cards of his group, giving each one his own card. If a recipient gets the wrong card and does not realize it, the teacher may call for an inspector to check on the mail delivery. The game is good because it involves no competition.

2. *Going to the Store* (tests each participant). The teacher places all the name cards of the group in the pocket chart. She then calls a child to "go to the store" and get his name. This is especially valuable when there are names which begin alike, as it calls for careful discrimination. It can be varied by telling the child to get another child's name.

3. *Storekeeper* (tests the storekeeper). The teacher places all the names in the pocket chart. One child is the storekeeper. The others go up one by one, say their names, and the storekeeper tries to give out the correct card. If he misses, the one to whom he gave the wrong card is the new storekeeper. This game provides opportunity to teach new English phrases orally, such as "Good morning," "What do you want?" "I want," and "Thank you."

4. *Find the Stranger* (tests discrimination of each participant). The teacher uses a double set of name cards. She arranges each line in the pocket chart so that it contains two identical names and one different name. The children in turn study one line and point out the stranger.

5. *Find the Twins* (tests discrimination of each participant). Using a double set of name cards, the teacher arranges the pocket chart so that each line contains three different names, one of which is repeated. The children in turn study one line and point out the twins.

It is usual for most first grades to have many labels around the room, such as *window, door, books,* and so on. If the class will contain many non-English-speaking children it is better not to put up these labels at the beginning of the term, for the child may associate the label with the language they know. The words should be used in every possible classroom situation before being presented in written form. The first word chosen might be *chair.* When the teacher can say the word *chair* and get a satisfactory response from the child, such as touching the chair or pointing at it, she is

[28] Margaret E. Gott, "Teaching Reading to Spanish Speaking Children" (unpublished thesis, San Diego State College, 1955).

ready to present the word. She presents a card to the child with the word *chair* on it and attaches a duplicate card to the chair. The child then takes the card to the chair to prove that it is identical, saying the words as he does this. This is called *matching* and will be used in many other lessons.

In presenting the nouns, it is best to present the singular form first and avoid the plural as much as possible. In Spanish, the final *s* is usually preceded by a vowel, and it is difficult for the child to pronounce the plurals which have a consonant preceding the *s*. There is also another difficulty because the final *s* sometimes has a *z* sound. When the plural form is used in the course of schoolroom activities, the teacher should try to establish the correct pronunciation as soon as possible.

The following list of words is divided according to the number of pronunciation difficulties. They should be presented slowly and practiced in enjoyable situations. They provide the Spanish-speaking child with the satisfaction of reading achievement while he is learning speech.

A. *Few Pronunciation Difficulties:*

ball	game	chair	toy	crayola
clay	house	nail	clock	playhouse

B. *One Pronunciation Difficulty:*

table—*bl*	paper—final *r*
door—final *r*	saw—*aw*
window—short *i*	box—short *o*
book—short *oo*	car—final *r*
paint—final *nt*	airplane—no vowel
pencil—short *i*	between *rp*
rug—short *u*	top—short *o*
	crayon—*on*

C. *Two Pronunciation Difficulties:*

hammer—short *a,* final *r*
sharpener—*sh,* final *r*

D. *Three or More Pronunciation Difficulties:*

blackboard—short *a,* final *d,* no vowel
between syllables
puzzles—short *u, z,* final *s*
playthings—*th,* short *i, ng,* final *s*
scissors—short *i, zr,* final *s*

picture—short *i, tu,* final *r,* no vowel between *ct*
drawing—*aw,* short *i, ng,* no consonant sound between syllables

Games

1. *Matching* (tests discrimination of each participant). This should be played with no competition and in the slow group should involve much bodily movement. Each child is handed a card and tries to match it with the label on the object before the teacher rings her bell. When he finds the correct object he stands quietly until his turn to read his word to the group.

2. *Where Are You Going?* (tests recognition of words by each participant). In this game the teacher holds up a card and asks a child, "Where are you going?" He tries to remember the word on the card and points to the place where he is going to try to match it up. Then he is given the card and goes to prove the correctness of his recognition, matching the word with the proper label and reading it aloud. If he is in error, he is allowed to go about the room and hunt for the correct label. This game teaches silent reading with comprehension.

3. *Picture Match.* The teacher prepares a set of small pictures mounted on cards about 3×4 inches and places the pictures in the pocket chart. The children try to place the word cards under the correct pictures. A card incorrectly placed is checked against the labeled object in the room. The children may place one card in each turn, or one child may try to place them all. If this game is used at the stage where the child has been taught only two words, and then each new word added to the set, there will be no confusion.

After the words *door* and *window* have been taught, the teacher may play an oral language game of "Open the Door. Open the Window." This may be done first in the group with a cardboard house and later in the room. The words *open* and *shut* need not be presented in printed form, for they seldom occur below primer or first-reader level. The child hears the word *the* in the complete sentence first. Later the teacher uses it just with the noun. She shows the cardboard house and says, "The door." The child points to the door. After the child has shown that he is familiar with the article in oral language, the time has come to present it in written form.

For the first presentation the teacher says the words *the door* while showing the phrase on a card, and a child responds by indicating the door. The label on the classroom door has only the noun. Some bright child sees this at once and calls the teacher's attention to it. Her card is different! The teacher then holds up the card with the noun only, saying "door," then holds up the other saying "the door." Ask children to add *the* to other words.

Pictures drawn by the children supply a good medium for the first sentences. The child brings his picture to his small group to show. If he knows no English he can quickly learn to hold it up and say, "See." The children will quickly learn to express appreciation for the picture by saying, "Oh! Oh!" These words are easy for the child to say. The teacher can employ them many times daily. She should use only a simple paraphrase of the meaning of *pleasure* and *approval* at first; later on she can add *excitement, dismay,* and *disapproval.*

A number of pictures are now placed in the chalkrail or hung along the chalkboard. Then the children learn to indicate their own by saying, "my boat" or "my airplane." The teacher can very easily facilitate this by having all the children or all the group draw the same thing. The word *my* is also easily taught, as soon as the children know the word *chair,* by having each child indicate his chair with his name on it and say, "My chair."

On the wall or on a bulletin board the teacher arranges an ever-changing display of children's pictures. As the child shows his drawing he says, "See my boat." The teacher selects, with the children voting, a picture of the day, and puts it up, writing on the tagboard label what the child said, "See my boat." The child goes to the bulletin board, points to the picture and says, "See my boat." The teacher then indicates the label, and moving her whole arm under the line of

words in a horizontal position from left to right, repeats the phrase. Some pictures are left up for several days and the children play matching games with the duplicate labels. Two or three pictures may be mounted on large sheets of tagboard or paper and hung on the chart rack with the labels printed below. These are the first experience charts used by the children.

The New York City Schools have summarized their experience as a result of working with many emigrants from Puerto Rico in the following: [29]

The elementary school child will learn English better if he is placed in a class where the majority of the children are English-speaking. This arrangement builds into the language learner's day a natural and forceful motivation for speaking English as well as many native models of English speech to which he may listen and respond.

The language learner's classmates should be English-speaking children of average and above average academic ability in order to give him a verbally stimulating environment and classmates whose attitudes toward learning are positive.

The language learner will adjust better if he is placed as closely as possible and desirable with his age peers, regardless of his previous schooling.

English will be learned best if taught by a native speaker of the language.

The classroom teacher needs special assistance in acquiring the skills of teaching English as a second language as well as additional instructional aids.

Teachers who have an understanding and appreciation of the cultural heritage of their language learners are more apt to relate better to their pupils and thus establish a better climate for the teacher-learning process. Children who are learning English as a second language should not be referred to as "culturally deprived" regardless of the economic status of their parents. The term "culturally diverse" appears to be more accurate.

The terms *oral* and *aural* are difficult to contrast as we speak English. For that rea-

---

[29] Reprinted from *Hispania,* Vol. XLIX, No. 2 (May 1966), pp. 293–96. Excerpts from a presentation given at the San Diego Conference on the Teaching of English to Speakers of other Languages, March 12, 1965.

son *audiolingual* is used to describe the oral approach to teaching language. In a sense this is no more than a planned drill-centered repetition of the way a child would learn English as a native. There is one important difference. The learner knows another language pattern and thought organization. Young children accept such differences and seldom make comparisons except in vocabulary. An older student does continue to think in his first language and translate thought and words into the second. Space permits only a summary of suggestions for those who use the audiolingual approach. It should be noted that highly motivated adults sent to the English Language Institute at the University of Michigan were able to speak a workable oral English in about three months. During the War many in the Armed Forces learned oral Japanese as a result of intensive work for about six months. No effort is made to teach the reading of a language until the oral patterns and vocabulary are mastered. The following are tips for teaching English through the audiolingual approach:

1. Limit the English to experiences the learners know.
2. Repeat the sample language patterns rather than isolating individual words. (Piaget says all people learn language from the whole to the part.)
3. Repeat the pattern several times before asking a learner to say it. Move around the group so that all can see your lips and face while speaking.
4. Always use the normal speed and natural conversational intonation. Exaggerations will be imitated.
5. Add variety to the responses by having the groups speak—one table or row, then the boys, then the girls, and so on.
6. If you speak the learner's language, use it sparingly and only when gesture, pantomime, pictures, objects, or other materials have failed.
7. Do not rush the learner. Speed should not be a factor in gaining early responses.
8. If you isolate a word or sound in order to correct an individual, repeat

the entire language pattern naturally and have the pupils do this as well.
9. Move from individual, to group, to individual, and so on. All should be involved, instead of waiting for a turn.
10. After three or four efforts to correct an individual, go on to others. Later return to the first pupil after he has heard the others.
11. Individual differences, short attention spans, and monotony of drill call for variety. Sing a phrase, act a phrase, let students move about. Do not advance rapidly. You are establishing habits that take years of practice.
12. Postpone reading and writing in all forms until language patterns are established. In time some reading and writing may maintain skills. Don't be tempted to seek a quite busy classroom that may mean the learners will never gain the oral practice needed.
13. Use routine (some order of practice) and avoid oral directives. Gestures can be used for *you speak, you listen, you stand, you sit* if such words would distract from the practice.

A practical problem of working with children whose language is limited is reported by a principal.[30]

Fighting and name-calling are problems in areas where children and adults are not articulate enough to be able to discuss differences of opinion and to reconcile them. A principal helped some children to make words work for them by keeping a small tape recorder on her desk. When children were sent to her office because of fighting, they followed a simple formula:

1. Tell exactly what you did even if you feel it was wrong.
2. Tell what you might have done differently.
3. Decide what you are going to do about it.

As the children talked, she recorded each version, and if they came to no agreement on what could be done about the dispute, she played the tape for them to hear each account. The play-

---

[30] Theda M. Wilson, "Helping the Disadvantaged Build Language," *National Elementary School Principal* (November 1965), p. 44.

back always had a profound effect. When children had to listen and were not grouping words, they found it easier to solve their problems.

She noticed that these phrases were generally used as children told what happened:

"talking about my mother"
"got all big and bad"
"got up in my face"
"get off my back"
"flipped me"
"rooted me"

The principal helped the children to see that these phrases did not specify what had happened, and the children were encouraged to be more specific. They learned to tell events in sequence. The principal learned that what are common meanings to certain groups are uncommon in general use. In communicating with people, one must understand the implications of what is said as well as what is meant.

For Discussion

1. Why have many adults studied a foreign language for the purpose of reading it rather than speaking it?

2. Would it be wise to have foreign-speaking children learn to read their language prior to reading English? What is their learning goal?

3. The term *bicultural* is used with respect to new programs in Texas. In what respect does such a concept include more than language? What reasons can you see for seeking a one-culture population?

How May Oral Reading Skills Be Improved?

A good oral reader is eager to share with his listeners something that seems important. It may be new information, an experience, a vivid description, an interesting character, a bit of humor, or a poetic phrase. Without a motive of this kind, oral reading is impersonal and lifeless. The reader should know his audience's interests and needs and interpret the material accordingly. To read aloud well, the reader must have mastered the skills of perception so that he recognizes words quickly and accurately. Equally important is ability to group words together in thought units and to read smoothly. To help his listeners grasp the author's meaning, the reader uses various devices. He highlights new ideas through the use of emphasis; makes clear the transition from one idea to another; indicates by proper phrasing the units of thought within a sentence; relates the ideas of a series by keeping his voice up until the end is reached; and indicates climax by force and vigor of expression.

Most teachers will grasp at this point and ask, "Does such reading take place in the elementary school?" They are thinking of the slow, halting oral reading of the reading circle. Day by day teachers have urged children to read as if they were talking, to read to find the answer to a question, or to read the part of a story they liked best. But seldom has such reading produced anything like that described above. It was usually thought good if the child knew all the words. Nor was anyone in the listening group charmed by what was read. After all, they had read the same material.

Unfortunately, most oral reading in a classroom has been for the single purpose of evaluation. In addition, there has been an emphasis on speed as an indication of growth. Children have sat before machines to increase eye movement, have taken timed tests, have been taught how to skim, and have been given vast amounts of materials to read for information. Little wonder, then, that few read well orally.

The skills of oral reading are most naturally developed in the reading of plays. The reading of plays adds many values to reading: it enlists the delight in dramatization which appears in the everyday make-believe of all children; it enriches imagery in the reading of fiction; it provides disciplines not found in other types of reading; it enhances comprehension, vocabulary development, phrase reading, expression, and general speech skills.

Children of all reading levels may be cast in a play. Undiscovered personality qualities are often brought out in play reading. When a child is "someone else" while reading a play, new and delightful aspects of his per-

Carefully prepared oral reading is an excellent small-group activity. (*Courtesy of the San Diego City Schools.*)

sonality are revealed. Plays are good for reducing shyness in timid children and for finding sympathetic qualities in aggressive ones. Plays allow discussion of personal qualities, manners, habits, and ethical choices without self-consciousness on the part of pupils or moralizing by the teacher. The children can talk objectively about the actions of the characters, knowing that the roles they have played are only "make-believe."

Play reading requires disciplines not encountered in other reading. Alertness to timing of speeches, coming in on cue, keeping one's place on the page, reading words and phrases correctly, expressing oneself well—these and other factors are recognized by the child as important in the success of the play.

The motivating power of the true audience situation is always found in play reading. Comprehension is assured; the child cannot interpret his lines unless he understands them. Phrase reading is improved by play reading. The child who is inclined to read a word at a time or to ignore commas and

periods in oral reading will strive for complete phrases and attend to punctuation when he interprets his role. Improvement of expression through emphasis, pauses, and interpretation of mood and feeling is the main outcome of play reading.

Modern elementary readers contain plays designed to achieve these goals. But children need more experience with this form of literature than that provided in a reading series. Those in the format of radio plays provide excellent practice in oral skills. The radio format is modern and appeals to the children. It also has great appeal for the teacher, since costumes and scenery are not needed.

College students enjoy reading this one, although it is planned for the intermediate grades.[31]

Read the following play to yourself in order to get the meaning and *feeling* of it.

There is nothing difficult about the words or the lines.

---

[31] Donald D. Durrell and B. Alice Crossley, *Thirty Plays for Classroom Reading* (Boston: Plays, Inc., 1957).

As soon as you have read the play decide who will take the different parts.

Now practice reading aloud together. Your big job is to see that each person comes in on time.

Betsy, Clem, and the Wise Woman all get impatient with Noodle at some time or other. *Be sure you show this impatience in your voice.*

Noodle is not very bright. His speech is slow and hesitant. *Try to sound stupid as you read his lines.*

After you have read the play over two or three times, decide together how well you are doing these things:

1. Does Noodle sound stupid?
2. Does Betsy sound quick, alert and confident?
3. Are your voices clear and loud enough to be heard?
4. Are you pronouncing every word carefully?
5. Is each person ready to come in "on cue" with his lines?
6. Are you paying attention to the punctuation?

If you cannot truly say yes to these things, get busy and practice again.

Don't read the whole play. Work on the parts that are not coming right.

When you are sure you are ready to read the play for others, let your teacher know. You can then decide with her when it is best to read to the class.

A Kettle of Brains

adapted from an old folk tale by
Gweneira M. Williams

Characters

(*2 boys, 1 girl, 1 woman, and the narrator*)
NARRATOR
NOODLE, *a stupid boy who wants a kettleful of brains.*
CLEM, *Noodle's friend who is trying to help him to get some brains.*
THE WISE WOMAN, *who is old and a little impatient with Noodle. She is really poking fun at him.*
BETSY, *a smart girl who decides Noodle needs her care.*

NARRATOR: Noodle, a stupid boy, is being brought to the hut of the Wise Woman.

His friend, Clem, is showing him the way. Noodle is hanging back.

NOODLE (*fearfully*): But I'm afraid.

CLEM: You want brains, don't you?

NOODLE: I need a whole kettleful, I do.

CLEM: Well, then, go to the Wise Woman's hut there and knock at the door. Maybe she knows a way to get you some brains.

NOODLE: Aw, Clem, I'm scared.

CLEM: Noodle, don't be more of a fool than you can help, will you? Go on!

NOODLE: Hello, in there!

WISE WOMAN: What do you want, fool?

NOODLE (*hesitantly*): Well . . . well . . . well . . .

CLEM: Noodle, you're a fool.

NOODLE (*hopefully*): It's a fine day, isn't it?

WISE WOMAN: Maybe.

NOODLE: Maybe it'll rain, though.

WISE WOMAN: Maybe.

NOODLE (*gulping*): Or on the other hand, maybe it won't.

WISE WOMAN: Maybe.

NOODLE: Well, I can't think of anything else to say about the weather. But, but . . .

WISE WOMAN: Maybe.

NOODLE (*in a rush*): The crops are getting on fine, aren't they?

WISE WOMAN: Maybe.

NOODLE: The cows are getting fat.

WISE WOMAN: Maybe.

NOODLE: Wise Woman, I thought maybe you could help me.

WISE WOMAN: Maybe.

NOODLE (*desperately*): I need brains. Do you have any to sell?

WISE WOMAN: Maybe.

NOODLE: What d'you mean, maybe?

WISE WOMAN: Maybe I have and maybe I haven't. It depends on what kind of brains you want. Do you want a king's brains?

NOODLE (*astonished*): Ooh, no!

WISE WOMAN: Or a teacher's brains?

NOODLE (*startled*): Lawkamercy, no!

WISE WOMAN: Or a wizard's brains?

NOODLE: Heavens to Betsy, no!

WISE WOMAN: Well, what kind do you want?

NOODLE: Just ordinary brains. You see, I don't have any at all!

WISE WOMAN: Maybe I can help you.

NOODLE: Maybe? How?

WISE WOMAN: You'll have to help yourself first.

NOODLE (*eagerly*): Oh, if I can, I will.

WISE WOMAN: You'll have to bring me the thing you love best.

NOODLE: How can I do that?

WISE WOMAN: That's not for me to say. But when you bring it here, you must answer a riddle for me, so I'll be sure you can use the brains.

NOODLE: Oh, gosh to goodness!

NARRATOR: Noodle hurried home and now we see him dragging a big bag toward the Wise Woman's hut.

NOODLE (*eagerly*): Here it is, Wise Woman.

WISE WOMAN: Here's what?

NOODLE: The thing I love best.

WISE WOMAN: What is it?

NOODLE: My pig!

WISE WOMAN: Well, now that you're here, can you answer this riddle?

NOODLE: I'll try.

WISE WOMAN: Tell me, what runs without feet?

NOODLE (*stupidly*): Maybe . . . caterpillars?

WISE WOMAN (*angrily*): Idiot! You're not ready for brains! Come back again when you've decided what you love next best!

NOODLE (*thoughtfully*): What runs without feet? . . . Gosh I loved my pig best. What do I love best after him? . . . I know! My hen, my little hen! Wait a minute, hey, wait! Just wait a minute! I'll be back in a jiffy! Wait!

WISE WOMAN: Burn, fire, burn,
      Burn to a turn,
      One thing's sure as sky and fire,
      Fools never learn!

NOODLE: Here it is! Wait, here it is! Gosh, my goodness, heavens to Betsy, wait! Don't sell that kettle of brains! Here it is!

WISE WOMAN: Here's what?

NOODLE: Here's the thing I love best next to my pig!

WISE WOMAN: What is it?

NOODLE: My hen!

WISE WOMAN: Are you ready to answer me another riddle?

NOODLE (*bravely*): I'll try!

WISE WOMAN: Well, tell me this. What is yellow, and shining, and isn't gold?

NOODLE (*hopefully*): Cheese, maybe?

WISE WOMAN: Fool! . . . What do you love best next to your hen?

NOODLE (*crying*): What'll I do? What'll I do? I've lost the two things I love best! And I still haven't any brains! Whatever will I do now? They were the only two things I loved in the whole world! . . . Who are you?

NARRATOR: As Noodle looks around helplessly a girl comes in. When she sees him, this is what she says.

BETSY: Well, for heaven's sake!

NOODLE (*still crying*): Who are you?

BETSY: My name's Betsy. What's the matter with you?

NOODLE: Oh, I wanted some brains.

BETSY: Why?

NOODLE: I don't have any.

BETSY: Well, where did you think you could get some?

NOODLE (*sobbing*): The Wise Woman in there said she'd give me some if I brought her the things I loved best in the world.

BETSY: Well, did she?

NOODLE: No-o-o!

BETSY: You poor fool, why not?

NOODLE: I c-c-c-couldn't answer the r-r-riddles sh-sh-she asked m-me!

BETSY (*kindly*): There, there, don't cry. Don't you have anyone to take care of you, silly?

NOODLE: No.

BETSY: No one?

NOODLE: No one.

BETSY: Well, I wouldn't mind taking care of you myself!

NOODLE: Lawkamercy!

BETSY: Well?

NOODLE: You mean . . . (Hesitating) *marry* me?

BETSY: Well, yes.

NOODLE: Can you cook?

BETSY: Yes.

NOODLE: Can you sew?

BETSY: Yes.

NOODLE: Can you scrub?

BETSY: Yes, I can. Will you have me? I'd be a good wife.

NOODLE: Well, I guess you'd do as well as anyone else.

BETSY: That's fine.

NOODLE: But, but . . .

BETSY: But what?

NOODLE: What shall I do about the Wise Woman?

BETSY: Let *me* talk to her!

NOODLE: Oh, no, no!

BETSY: Why not?

NOODLE: I'm afraid!

BETSY: I'm not! Don't you need brains?

NOODLE: Well, yes.

BETSY: Come on, then, come on!

WISE WOMAN: What do you want, young woman?

BETSY: Brains for my husband here!

WISE WOMAN: Your husband, eh?

BETSY: We're going to be married.

WISE WOMAN: Does he love you the best of anything in the world?

BETSY: Go on, tell her!

NOODLE: I reckon I do.

BETSY: I'm not! Don't you need brains?

WISE WOMAN: Not so fast, not so fast. He'll have to answer the riddles first.

NOODLE (*sadly*): Oh, the riddles.

BETSY (*unafraid*): What are they?

WISE WOMAN: What runs without feet?

NARRATOR: Betsy nudges him and whispers something. Noodle speaks.

NOODLE: Well, my goodness, water!

WISE WOMAN: H'm.

BETSY: Give him the next riddle.

WISE WOMAN: What's yellow and shining and isn't gold?

NARRATOR: Betsy whispers something to Noodle. He answers again.

NOODLE: Well, heavens to Betsy, the sun!

WISE WOMAN: H'm. Here's the third riddle. What has first no legs, then two legs, then four legs?

NARRATOR: Noodle looks at Betsy. Betsy makes swimming motions with her hands. Then she whispers something.

NOODLE (*happily*): A tadpole!

WISE WOMAN (*crossly*): That's right. Now go away!

NOODLE: But where is the kettleful of brains?

WISE WOMAN: You already have them.

NOODLE: Where? I can't see them.

WISE WOMAN: In your wife's head, silly. The only cure for a fool is a good wife. And you have one . . . or will have one. I can't help you any more. Be off with you! Good day!

NOODLE: Maybe she's right. . . . You'll marry me, lass? I won't have any brains if you don't.

BETSY: Of course I will! I have brains enough for two, anyway! Come on!

THE END

There are other ways of practicing oral reading. One very good practice in many schools is that of having children in the intermediate grades prepare a library book which they read to a small group in the kindergarten or first grade. One fourth grade motivates this by keeping a record of "Books I Have Read to Others."

Some selections in great literature especially lend themselves to oral reading. The whitewashing of the fence in *The Adventures of Tom Sawyer* is written as if it were a play. Some of the scenes in *Freddie the Pig* by Walter R. Brooks consist almost exclusively of conversation that makes delightful oral reading.

For the lower grades parts of *Pooh* by A. A. Milne may be presented as a Readers' Theater. *Charlotte's Web* can be an excellent assembly or P.T.A. program, with a narrator and four readers sometimes reading dialogue and at other times reading exposition.

Have three members of the class read the following from *Tom Sawyer* to demonstrate the fun of oral reading.

NARRATOR: When school broke up at noon, Tom flew to Becky Thatcher and whispered in her ear:

TOM: Put on your bonnet and let on you're going home; and when you get to the corner give the rest of 'em the slip and turn down through the lane and come back. I'll go the other way and come it over 'em the same way.

NARRATOR: So the one went off with one group of scholars, and the other with another. In a little while the two met at the bottom of the lane, and when they reached the school they had it all to themselves. Then they sat together, with a slate before them, and Tom gave Becky the pencil and held her hand in his, guiding it, and so created another surprising house. When the interest in art began to wane, the two fell to talking. Tom was swimming in bliss. He said:

TOM: Do you love rats?

BECKY: No! I hate them!

TOM: Well, I do, too—*live* ones. But I mean dead ones, to swing round your head with a string.

BECKY: No, I don't care for rats much, anyway. What *I* like is chewing gum.

TOM: Oh, I should say so. I wish I had some now.

BECKY: Do you? I've got some. I'll let you chew it awhile, but you must give it back to me.

NARRATOR: That was agreeable, so they chewed it turn about, and dangled their legs against the bench in excess of contentment.

TOM: Was you ever at a circus?

BECKY: Yes, and my pa's going to take me again sometime, if I'm good.

TOM: I been to the circus three or four times—lots of times. Church ain't shucks to a circus. There's things going on at a circus all the time. I'm going to be a clown in a circus when I grow up.

BECKY: Oh, are you! That will be nice. They're so lovely, all spotted up.

TOM: Yes, that's so. And they get slathers of money—most a dollar a day, Ben Rogers says. Say, Becky, was you ever engaged?

BECKY: What's that?

TOM: Why, engaged to be married.

BECKY: No.

TOM: Would you like to?

BECKY: I reckon so. I don't know. What is it like?

TOM: Like? Why, it ain't like anything. You only just tell a boy you won't ever have anybody but him, ever ever *ever*, and then you kiss and that's all. Anybody can do it.

BECKY: Kiss? What do you kiss for?

TOM: Why, that, you know, is to—well, they always do that.

BECKY: Everybody?

TOM: Why, yes, everybody that's in love with each other. Do you remember what I wrote on the slate?

BECKY: Ye—yes.

TOM: What was it?

BECKY: I shan't tell you.

TOM: Shall I tell *you?*

BECKY: Ye—yes—but some other time.

TOM: No, now.

BECKY: No, not now—tomorrow.

TOM: Oh, no, *now*. Please, Becky—I'll whisper it, I'll whisper it ever so easy.

NARRATOR: Becky hesitating, Tom took silence for consent, and passed his arm about her waist and whispered the tale ever so softly, with his mouth close to her ear. And then he added:

TOM: Now you whisper it to me—just the same.

NARRATOR: She resisted for a while, and then said:

BECKY: You turn your face away so you can't see, and then I will. But you mustn't ever tell anybody—*will* you, Tom? Now you won't, *will* you?

TOM: No, indeed, indeed I won't. Now, Becky.

NARRATOR: He turned his face away. She bent timidly around till her breath stirred his curls and whispered,

BECKY: I—love—you!

NARRATOR: Then she sprang away and ran around and around the desks and benches, with Tom after her, and took refuge in a corner at last, with her little white apron to her face. Tom clasped her about her neck and pleaded:

TOM: Now, Becky, it's all done—all over but the kiss. Don't you be afraid of that— it ain't anything at all. Please, Becky.

NARRATOR: By and by she gave up, and let her hands drop; her face, all glowing with the struggle, came up and submitted. Tom kissed the red lips and said:

TOM: Now it's all done, Becky. And always after this, you know, you ain't ever to love anybody but me, and you ain't ever to marry anybody but me, never never and forever. Will you?

BECKY: No, I'll never love anybody but you, Tom, and I'll never marry anybody but you—and you ain't to ever marry anybody but me, either.

TOM: Certainly. Of course. That's *part* of it. And always coming to school or when we're going home, you're to walk with me, when there ain't anybody looking—and you choose me and I choose you at parties, because that's the way you do when you're engaged.

BECKY: It's so nice. I never heard of it before.

TOM: Oh, it's ever so gay! Why, me and Amy Lawrence—

NARRATOR: The big eyes told Tom his blunder and he stopped, confused.

BECKY: Oh, Tom! Then I ain't the first you've ever been engaged to!

NARRATOR: The child began to cry.

TOM: Oh, don't cry, Becky, I don't care for her any more.

BECKY: Yes, you do, Tom—you know you do.

For Discussion

1. It is reported that high school and college students dislike reading aloud in class. Can you explain why?

2. Because reading ahead of the voice with the eyes is necessary in oral reading, do you think oral reading can be done by children having reading difficulty?

3. Give reasons for agreeing or disagreeing with this statement: "Oral reading at sight of new material is the most difficult of all reading tasks."

Books of Plays Designed for Oral Reading

Durrell, Donald D., and B. Alice Crossley. *Thirty Plays for Classroom Reading.* Boston: Plays, Inc., 1957.

Kissen, Fran. *Bag of Fire, The Straw Ox, The Four Winds.* Boston: Houghton, 1941–1952.

Schneideman, Rose. *Radio Plays for Young People to Act.* New York: Dutton, 1960.

Stevenson, Augusta. *Dramatic Readers.* Boston: Houghton, 1930–1954.

Ward, Winifred. *Stories to Dramatize.* Anchorage, Ky.: Children's Theater Press, 1952.

What Is the Place of Dramatics in the Classroom?

Creative dramatics starts with the simple, natural play of the preschool or kinder-garten. Here the children play house in the roles of father, mother, child, and the lady next door. In these roles the children try out the vocabulary they hear spoken in the situations of the adult world around them. There is no better way to teach children the social amenities of greeting and farewell. Teacher suggestion as to what should be said is usually welcomed and frequently sought. Some of the more imaginative children will provide patterns that others will imitate.

Children will observe the storekeeper, bus driver, and waiter with new interest after playing any of these roles in the classroom. Although the teacher is seldom imitated in the classroom, playing school is a favorite home activity. Parents frequently know many of the teacher's mannerisms and practices as a result of this. However, most children seem to invest the role of teacher with a crossness and severity that is more a part of childhood's folklore than actuality. The influence of television will reveal itself in the children's acting. Where once children saw a movie once a week, they now see one daily. It is only natural that free play will reflect some of the behavior they observe. To avoid some of the noise and violence it is well to establish through discussion and practice the "acting" techniques that are appropriate to the classroom.

As the children get older the influence of television can be converted to an asset. No generation of children has had wider experience with dramatic form. Many children by the age of twelve have seen more of the great dramatic personalities and literature than past generations have known in a lifetime. The attention-getting exposition, the involvement of the main character with a problem, the gradual working out of that problem, and the final resolution become almost second nature after so much familiarity with this form. Many of the favorite children's programs, such as those of some TV comedians, usually follow a theme as simple and obvious as that of old folk stories so that the concept of unity, which once seemed such a difficult idea, can be easily understood. Unfortunately, some of these comedy shows have a degree of sophistication of theme and action that is inappropriate for the classroom.

A few items to use as props help children give realism to a role. An apron establishes a grandmother, just as a cane identifies a grandfather. A hat makes a boy a man and nothing gives a girl more maturity than a long skirt.

Creative dramatics in the school has no concern that children become "actors," nor that story plays be produced for a guest audience. In some situations the presence of an audience may make the children self-conscious of their roles as actors, rather than assist the process of creating the play. The stage may be the front of the classroom but the whole room may be involved, in order to indicate a change of scene. Aisles

are used as roads, scenery is drawn on the chalkboard, and tables become bridges, mountain tops, or castle towers.

In the primary grades the attitude is one of creative play. "Let's play that story," the teacher will suggest. "Who wants to be the mother bear?" Some children are quite content to be a tree in the forest, others will need suggestions as to what to say, but the values of released imagination, language practice, and dramatic interest are always there.

In the intermediate grades children imagine that they are the Pilgrims or pioneers. Such dramatics frequently become organized to the extent that the main ideas are outlined, children experiment with different scenes, select the ones that seem most

A feather in our hair and drums to beat helps us to feel like Indians. (*Courtesy of the La Mesa Public Schools.*)

effective, and actually write a script that is later presented as a formal production.

Sometimes a formal dramatic play is created by children. Bernice Carlson suggests the steps in writing a script.[32]

One way to think of history is to think of typical scenes during certain periods of time. Social study books have chapters on "Visiting a Farmer Along the Ancient Nile River," "A Peep into an Athenian Home," "A Day in a Roman School." History books often picture life in early Colonial homes, log-cabin life, life on the trail West.

This kind of information can provide background material for a historical play, but it is not a play unless something happens to people in the scene. The event may be typical, but it must be important to the characters involved. There must be a problem, and it must be solved.

Supposing we choose a historical scene familiar to us all—pioneers moving West. What can we picture on the stage? It can be a scene with families gathered around the campfire for the evening meal. Some folks are singing, women are preparing food, children are chasing each other and laughing. Someone announces that it's time to eat.

What happens? A family discovers that their little Janie is missing. Everyone panics.

"I thought she was with you."

"When did you see her last?"

Her father starts to rush out into the night to get her. Men grab him and hold him back. What kind of search party shall they send out? How close are the Indians?

The leader's voice booms out above the hubbub. "Order! Order! I'm in command here. We won't do a thing! Not a thing, until we ask Almighty God to help us think straight in this crisis."

At the end of the prayer, while heads are still bowed, little Janie and an Indian boy enter. She runs to her mother, waving a rag doll. Some men grab the Indian, accusing him of capturing the child, being a spy, leading other Indians to their camp.

Of course, the child explains that he is her friend, Red Feather. The Indian tells that he found the child emptying the drawers of a discarded dresser. He had allowed her to keep

the doll she found and had ridden with her on his pony to the camp.

"See my dolly," says the child.

"Oh, yes," says her mother. "I see your dolly. I see you. But most clearly I see that Red Feather is our friend."

If you use this plot for a play, you can tailor it to the needs of your group, having as many pioneers as you have would-be actors. Picture each character as an individual and write the dialogue as you would when dramatizing a story.

The play which follows pictures a different situation in this Western scene. A young couple moving West in a covered wagon realize that they must discard some furniture in order to lighten their load enough for their weary oxen to pull the wagon. Heavy tables and chests must be thrown out. But must they discard little things, too? What about the little French clock they are carrying in a small crate? Would it help very much to discard that?

The husband thinks it would. The wife knows that she has chosen a rugged life as a pioneer, yet she hates to give up every pretty thing. Who could help them decide what to do? How about their guide? Who might he be? Let's choose Jim Bridger, and study his character.

Jim was a trapper, guide, and champion tall-tale teller. Adding a tall tale to the play might enliven it, if we can find one that fits into the plot. We read tall tales and run across one that Jim told about the eight-hour echo that woke him up every morning. We don't know how he happened to tell the story. Maybe he used it first to prove a point when talking to a young couple like the ones in our play.

Telling a tale to prove a point would be in keeping with Jim's character. When he was alone in the wilderness, he did a lot of thinking. When he came back to civilization and mixed with people, he was slow to speak. He chose his words carefully, trying not to hurt anyone's feelings. His manners, in general, were not polished; but he always made a point of being extra polite to ladies, never forgetting to tip his hat when he said "Howdy," and remembering to say "Ma'am" most of the time.

If a couple were to ask him to settle a family argument, he probably wouldn't want to take sides. He'd say something that would relieve tension and prove his point in a roundabout way. We can use the story of the eight-hour echo, if it fits into the dialogue.

Now we have the setting, the characters, the problem, and a possible solution. We can begin to write the dialogue.

[32] Bernice Carlson, *The Right Play for You* (Nashville, Tenn.: Abingdon, 1960).

Jim Bridger and His Eight-Hour Echo

Characters

Molly Howe, pioneer; *Henry Howe,* pioneer; *Jim Bridger,* guide

SCENE: *The plains during the time of the great movement to the West. Like many other people,* MR. *and* MRS. HOWE *now know that they cannot take all of the things with them that they had hoped to take. They have already discarded some of their furniture in an effort to lighten their load.* MRS. HOWE *is holding a little wooden box which she doesn't want to give up.*

HENRY: Molly, I've told you. The wagon is broken.

MOLLY: Yes, Henry, I know.

HENRY: We have only one wagon left.

MOLLY: Yes, Henry.

HENRY: One wagon holds less than two wagons. We have to get rid of everything that we don't actually need.

MOLLY: I know, Henry. I discarded the chest that Papa made for us.

HENRY: Yes.

MOLLY: And Grandmother's rocker. Mama wanted to keep that for herself. Then she said, "You need something comfortable in your new home. Take the rocker."

HENRY: There never was room for that rocker!

MOLLY: I know it now. But there is room for this little box.

HENRY: It's more than room, Molly. It's weight. The horses can pull so much and no more.

MOLLY: The box doesn't weigh much, Henry. Just feel. (*She hands box to* HENRY, *who weighs it with his hands and gently places it on the ground.*)

MOLLY (*showing how loose her skirt is*). I've lost ten pounds, I'll bet, since we started. Likely, I'll lose ten more. Then the horses can pull me and the box. (HENRY *shakes his head.*) Then I'll walk, Henry. I've got to save this little box! (*He shakes his head.*) It's the French clock that Aunt Hettie brought from Paris. It's the only pretty thing I've got

left. Please, can't I have something pretty in my new home?

HENRY: Molly, nothing will be pretty if we don't get to California.

MOLLY: If you don't need a pretty clock, how are you going to tell time? Your watch was stolen in St. Louis.

HENRY: I know that it was stolen. (*Looks off stage.*) Here comes Jim Bridger. Let's ask him if we need a pretty little old French clock in California. Hi, Jim. Come here.

JIM (*entering and taking off hat, bowing slightly*). Howdy, folks! Hear your second wagon broke down.

HENRY: We're unloading all we can. Tell us, Jim, do we need a pretty little old French clock in California?

JIM: Can't say about California. I don't need one where I winter up in the mountains.

HENRY (*to* MOLLY). See? I told you.

MOLLY: You don't need a clock at all, Jim? How do you tell time?

JIM: I got an echo.

MOLLY and HENRY: An echo?

JIM: Yep, an eight-hour echo.

HENRY: Jim, what do you mean?

JIM: When I yell something, in exactly eight hours the echo yells it back to me.

HENRY: Jim!

MOLLY: How does that serve as a clock?

JIM: When I go to bed, I yell, "Get up, Jim!" In exactly eight hours, the echo says, "Get up, Jim!"

MOLLY: Really, Jim?

JIM (*with fingers crossed*). Really.

HENRY: You don't need a clock at all?

JIM: Not at all. I just think of things eight hours early and yell to my echo. When it's time, my echo yells back to me.

MOLLY (*seriously*). Jim, what do you do on a very rainy day when there's no sun and you're camping in a place where there's no eight-hour echo?

JIM (*rubbing head and thinking*). Well, then I sorta wish I had a clock.

HENRY: A little old French clock?

JIM: Any kind of timepiece to tell me if the hours are long or just seem long. (*Takes a few steps away. Then turns.*) You know, one winter when we were holing up in a big log camp, a pork eater had a clock with chimes. It was mighty cheerful, hearing those chimes ring out each hour in the wilderness.

MOLLY: See, Henry.

JIM (*quickly*). But I don't need a clock at all when I'm camping with my eight-hour echo.

MOLLY (*sweetly*). Henry, supposing we don't build our house near that eight-hour echo?

HENRY: Then it might be handy to have a clock.

MOLLY (*brightly*). You mean? (HENRY *nods and picks up clock.*)

HENRY (*handing clock to* MOLLY). See if you can find a safe place to pack it. It might be nice to hear those chimes ringing in the wilderness even if we do settle near an eight-hour echo.

MOLLY: Thank you, Henry! Thank you, Jim. (*Exits quickly.*)

HENRY (*half disgusted, half amused*). An eight-hour echo! (JIM *winks and shows crossed fingers.*) No wonder people say, "You can't argue with Jim Bridger!"

JIM: Or a woman.

Writing the Play for a Different Cast

You can write this play for the specific players who want to act in it. If you want more characters, introduce a child or two. Let them listen to the argument for a minute, then run and get Jim Bridger. As they enter, they might say, "Pa! Ma! Here's Jim Bridger. Ask him what we need in California." You can also add "walk-ons," men and women who stop to say "Howdy" to the Howes and remark about the broken-down wagons, etc.

If you want an all-male cast, use Jim Bridger, Henry, and a teen-age nephew who is on his way to California to live with his sister. He has promised to bring the clock, and he wants to keep his promise.

If you want to have two women, eliminate Henry. Introduce a mother and her daughter, who argue about the clock. The mother, now a widow, wants to lighten the load and cut out every ounce she can. The daughter wants to take the clock to California.

Staging the Play

A bare stage can represent the plains. If possible, have some discarded furniture on the stage. You do not need a clock, as it is in a wooden box.

To costume the play, copy the dress of pioneers whom you have seen on TV. Mountain men wore big-brimmed hats, turned up on one side. (Sew the edge of the brim of a cowboy hat in one small place to the crown of the hat.) They also wore long-sleeved shirts, and tight pants. Henry wears a work shirt and pants. Molly wears a long-sleeved blouse and a long skirt, a little too big for her at the waist.

It may help some students to start with simple pantomime, such as pretending to walk through deep snow or falling leaves; pretending to eat ice cream, a pickle, or cotton candy; pretending to toss a baseball, a chunk of ice, a hot potato, or a pillow. Stand facing another student and act as his reflection in a mirror, moving slowly at first and then faster.

From such pantomimes move to sketches involving one-way dialogue. For example, you get a telephone call inviting you to a party, telling you that your parents were in an accident, informing you that you won a contest, announcing that your team lost.

Situations involving two or more may be suggested by the teacher. For example,

1. Your friend has asked you to go to the movie; your mother has said you must stay home. She is nearby.
2. A shy schoolmate has just returned from being ill and absent from school and you want him to feel at home at school again.
3. You are taking a test and a schoolmate asks for your help.
4. A classmate has just had a religious holiday. You want to know about it.
5. Your mother wants you to go to camp but you want to stay home.
6. You have borrowed a camera and broken it. Return it to the owner.
7. Your class is going to elect a president. You want a friend to run, but he is reluctant.

One of the uses of dramatic play is to help children with personality problems. A boy with effeminate traits may develop more "manliness" by playing the role of a cowboy or Santa Claus. A girl lacking grace and poise may gain a measure of these when cast as a beautiful princess. A shy child may vent repressed feelings when she plays a wicked witch.

Ordinarily the group decides who will take the various roles in a play. After discussing what a character should be like, it is wise to have different individuals "try out" for the part. The king should walk with lordly mien, speak deliberately and quite loud because of his vast authority, and perhaps flourish a wooden sword. After such a character is established in the minds of the children, let them take turns feeling like a king or whatever character is being developed. At the beginning most teachers cast parts by type. This means using the child whose personality most nearly fits the part. But after children have had some experience with dramatics there will be opportunity to use the story to help a child with a social or personality problem. All the parts, however, should not be assigned on a "problem" basis or children will lose interest. One case of "play therapy" at a time is enough for most teachers to handle.

Sociodrama is closely related to group dramatics as an aid to personality adjustment. Its main purpose is to assist children in being aware of the feelings and problems of others. "How does it feel to be the only child in a room not asked to a party? Let's act it out in a story." The situation may be centered in any problem: the child who acts as a bully and mistreats little children, the child who does not speak English, the lonely lady who complains about the noise children make.

Children sometimes write stories that lend themselves to role playing. This example was guided and supervised by Barbara Celse of the Orange County, California, Schools.[33]

Work at Home

My name is Jim and I want to tell you a story of my life.

My house has six living in it. They are my mother, father, brother, sister and brother-in-law. The reason my brother-in-law is living with us is because they are fixing their house.

---

[33] George and Fannie R. Shaftel, *Role Playing, The Problem Story* (New York: National Conference of Christians and Jews, 1952), pp. 69–70.

I want to write this story because I don't think it's fair. Every night after six people have dinner at the house, they go to the other part of the house. My mother says, "Do the dishes, son." I am the only living thing in the kitchen. I have to do the dishes and they go watch TV.

The class role-played this story. Jim, who wrote this problem, did not participate in the first enactment. However, he helped arrange the seating at the dinner table.

A. Family Around the Table

(*The adults did most of the talking. They tried to find someone else to do the dishes.*)

MOTHER: Well, I think Jean (*older brother, aged 19*) should stop gadding around every night with his girl friend. He should help, too. Now Jean, you just stay home tonight and do the dishes. It won't hurt you.

JEAN: I got a date. Why doesn't Pat (*married sister*) help?

(*They suggested everyone in the family at one time or another. They also proposed: That everyone take turns.*
That a dishwasher be bought—but this was immediately vetoed because of cost.)

At this point, the class questioned Jim to get more information about the family. It was discovered that:

- Sister just had a baby.
- Jean (the older brother) works all day and sometimes helps build a house at night. He's engaged.
- Father and brother-in-law work on the house they are building at night.
- Jim gets paid for doing the dishes.

B. Family Around the Table

(*In this second enactment Jim plays his own role.*)

FATHER: Well, I think the women should wash the dishes.

JIM: (*to brother*) Why don't you help out?

JEAN: I'm too busy.

JIM: But I want to see my TV program. I think he should help.

JEAN: You need the money more than I do.

BROTHER-IN-LAW: I don't think Jim should

have to do it all. Let's do them before we go to the house.

FATHER: Well, you know, you aren't going to be living with us much longer. Your house is almost finished. It will be different then.

Then the class again began to question the family members.

To Jean:

Question: Why don't you bring your girl friend over and both of you help?

Answer: We'll be all dressed up!

Question: Well, she can wear an apron. I do.

Answer: Gosh, I work all day. I have to have some time for fun. Besides, I help on the house some nights, too.

To Mother:

Question: Why don't you help?

Answer: I work all day, too. Jim gets paid for this job.

To Jim:

Question: How long does it take you to do the dishes?

Answer: Last night it took me about two hours!

Question: You don't know how to do them! I—

The discussion then became a sharing of experiences in dish-washing, and rules for efficiency in doing the job.

The final consensus of the class's thinking was:

• Jim should have help sometimes.
• He needs to be more efficient.
• He could arrange his time better.
• Everybody has some job to do.
• And, furthermore, Jim gets *paid* to wash those dishes!

Puppets are used as a vehicle for dramatic work in all grades. Some shy children find it easier to project their language through a puppet actor. Certain dramatic effects can be achieved with puppets that make the productions much more satisfying. Animal actors, folklore characters, magic changes and exotic areas (such as the bottom of the sea) are much easier to manage with puppets than with human actors. Somehow the simple plays written by children seem more spirited when given with puppets.

Puppets should be kept simple. Figures on a stick, sacks on the fist, and even the toy hand puppets that can be purchased are better than elaborate string marionettes. Marionette making is an art rather than a language project. The time taken to make and manipulate these figures does not stimulate enough language activity to warrant the effort.

Formal dramatics, involving the memorization of a well-written play, have many values for children able to participate in them. The discipline of memorization, the work on characterization, the team spirit developed in presenting the material, and the gratifying applause of a truly appreciative audience are valuable experiences. The beginning teacher is often tempted to start with a play that is too difficult. The professional children's theaters with well-equipped stages and trained staffs can produce elaborate plays with such apparent ease that a teacher is tempted to try the same in the classroom. Don't do it unless you are willing to spend hours rehearsing after school, devote week ends painting scenery and making costumes, and act as a military policeman during rehearsal and the performance. Perhaps in a summer school or with an especially talented group you can realize your ambitions. In the meantime, be content with less professional material. By all means avoid plays that require large casts or run more than an hour.

Plays such as *Why the Chimes Ring, Strawberry Red, King of Nomania, Knights of the Silver Shield, Elmer, Cabbages* are favorites for the junior high school age group. The little plays published in the magazines *Grade Teacher, Instructor,* and *Plays* are widely used in the lower grades and are relatively simple to prepare. Most children will learn their parts in six or eight readings. By the time of the production most of the children will know all the lines. Get mothers involved in making costumes, and on the day of the show have at least one adult supervise children backstage who are not performing. If make-up is used, keep it simple. A little rouge on the cheeks, a dab of lipstick, and a stroke or two with the grease pencil will transform most child actors sufficiently. No matter how well it is put on, a beard never looks right on a child. Crepe hair applied with spirit gum, available at all theatrical supply stores, is about as satisfactory a method of "aging" as any.

Most scenery problems can be solved by using sets of folding screens on which the outline of a forest, window, or fireplace has been drawn in colored chalk or water colors. Children's imaginations are so vivid that anything more than this is lost effort. Various sound effects are available on records or they can be put on a tape and amplified at the proper time.

Children are usually excited after a performance. If possible, plan to have a post-performance period with refreshments and general relaxation while costumes are put away and other details attended to. Children are seldom ready for a scheduled class after a play, and the wise teacher will recognize this fact in making plans. Avoid showing concern over forgotten lines or things that did not go just right, but instead find much to praise.

Radio and television scripts offer excellent possibilities at the elementary level for group composition and speech. The definite pattern in which action and dialogue must be cast gives pupils a needed support as they plan what scenes the cameras should focus on, or what sounds the microphone can pick up. In a television script the scenes for the cameras ("video") are placed on the left-hand side of the page; the words spoken, music, and sound effects ("audio") are placed on the right, opposite the scenes they will accompany.

The First Thanksgiving, below, was first produced in the school auditorium by a fifth grade and then on local television.[34] The script is actually a continuity sheet.

Children should be told to speak in a clear and natural voice, without "rushing" their lines yet moving along as though they were talking normally to other students. They should not try to imitate or exaggerate. This does not mean, however, they should not strive to get some feeling into their voices.

On most educational television shows, all colors are seen as shades from black to white. Blacks, grays, and light grays give good contrasts. Pure white is not good since it produces a halation effect and configuration is lost. However, this does not exclude murals and drawings done in color, but if you are preparing "props" for the show, use blacks, grays, and light grays in order to obtain contrasts that are desirable. Values are easier to control with these colors than with yellows, reds, blues, and greens.

Lettering on posters should be large and simple, not less than 2 inches in height. Remember that lower case is more legible than

[34] Minneapolis Public School Board of Education, *Communications,* 1953.

Video	*Audio*
1. Announcer.	1. Opening announcement.
2. Pupils stage left.	2. Short reports on Pilgrims settling in Massachusetts.
3. Play given stage right and center; scenes as follows:	3. (Dialogue from play.)
4. The Lullaby: Mistress Hopkins at home, taking care of her baby when Squanto arrives.	4. Squanto tells Mistress Hopkins that Governor Bradford and Chief Massasoit have agreed upon a feast of Thanksgiving.
5. Squanto exits. Mother and baby at home.	5. Mother sings Old Lullaby.
6. Other Pilgrim mothers and children come to visit Mistress Hopkins.	6. Women discuss the coming feast.
7. Priscilla enters. Priscilla and children begin preparations for the feast.	7. Priscilla directs the children in preparation for the feast.
8. Priscilla sends two boys on an errand.	8. Priscilla sends boys out to get corn.

(The script continues through ten more scenes and ends as follows.)

Video

21. Governor Bradford advances and holds out hand to Massasoit.

22. Massasoit shakes Governor's hand, nodding head solemnly. Then waves his hand toward distance, as if game had been laid down there.

23. Governor Bradford exists followed by Standish, Massasoit, braves, Squanto and pilgrims.

24. Pilgrims and Indians worship, Elder Brewster leading meeting. Tithing man has a stick with rabbit's foot on one end and hard ball on the other. Pilgrims seated on benches. Taller Pilgrim men stand in rear. During service the tithing man quietly touches a small girl who has fallen sleep with her head on her neighbor's shoulder.

25. All stand and sing.

Audio

21. *Gov. Bradford:* Welcome, Massasoit! Welcome to the great Sachem! Welcome to all your braves. The palefaces (gestures toward Pilgrims) welcome the Red Men. We are happy to be here.

22. *Massasoit:* Massasoit brings heap buck, turkey, rabbit for white man's feast.

23. *Gov. Bradford:* We thank you. And now follow me (*beckons*). I will show you to your tents till the feasting begins.

24. Elder Brewster offers prayer.
"Lord, we come before Thee, now,
At thy feet we humbly bow,
Oh do not our suit disdain,
Shall we seek Thee, Lord, in vain?
May the Lord abide with us till our next meeting."

25. Song ("O God, Beneath Thy Guiding Hand")

26. SIGN OFF

capitals. Do not use "fancy" lettering. Try to use black letters when possible.

Prints or photographs can be used to show specific objects, scenery, or people. They should be mounted on 11- × 14-in. board, preferably horizontally.

Normally there are at least two TV cameras on each show; one takes all "placement" or long shots and the other the close-ups. This is important to know, for if you want to show something you have made you must hold it a little above waist height, tilted slightly forward to prevent glare— very steady for about 10 to 15 seconds in the direction of the close-up camera.

For Discussion

1. Do you feel that every child in a classroom should have a part in a program presented for an audience?

2. You work in a school where assembly programs and PTA programs are assigned to teachers a year in advance. As a result the teachers put on elaborate productions and compete with each other. This year you have drawn the Christmas assembly. What would you do?

3. You have a class with many emotionally disturbed children. These children come from broken homes, attend clinics, and so on. Should you attempt creative dramatics?

4. In order to encourage participation and expression, teachers sometimes permit or encourage children to participate in activities of questionable taste. Should a second-grade girl dance a Hula and sing *Lovely Hula Hands?* The love songs that constitute the popular music of the day have their place, but should one be sung by primary children simply because their childish innocence adds cuteness? Sometimes boys appear on TV singing in the manner of popular singers whose facial and bodily expressions accentuate the sexual suggestions of the lyrics. Are there aspects of taste and propriety that students might discuss with respect to such programs?

How Is Courtesy Taught in the Language Arts Program?

The first lesson in the first book published in the Korean language after the close of World War II had to do with the way a child should greet his parents and grandparents. Although Orientals may have a greater regard for the social amenities of family life than Americans who still think of themselves as hardy pioneers, there is nevertheless a growing concern for courtesy in our country. Some states have laws requiring that manners and morals be taught in the schools. Other courses of study list courtesy as one of the values to be sought as an objective. Because certain aspects of courtesy depend on a proper use of language, most textbooks in the language arts include lessons on this topic.

A part of the awkwardness of children in a social situation arises from not knowing the proper thing to say. Greetings, introductions, apologies, interruptions, and expressions of appreciation involve established patterns of language. At first these may be taught as examples to be imitated. "Say bye-bye," a mother urges the infant. Or the parent will, by asking the child, "What do we say when someone gives us something?" eventually elicit a "thank you."

A student teacher working with a group of small children knows that it is a disturbance when an adult enters the classroom. Naturally, children are curious about the stranger. The teacher can maintain control, keep the class moving ahead, and teach some courtesy by stopping a minute and saying, "Girls and boys. This is Mr. Jones from the college. He is here to watch me teach. What do we say when we have a visitor in the room?" The children chorus, "Good morning, Mr. Jones," then return to their work. In upper grades a monitor will go to the visitor, show him where to sit, and hand him a copy of the book in use. Then at a convenient time the teacher greets the visitor. Many states require that a record of all visitors be maintained. Even if this is not required it provides an interesting way to greet a visitor. Prepare a "Visitor's Register." Have a child make an attractive cover for it. After the visitor has registered, it is sometimes good to have the courtesy monitor introduce him to the class.

Courtesy instruction will seem a bit silly to children unless it is presented in terms of situations. These situations should reveal the need for some type of social convention.

At the time when the school is having an open house or a parents' evening, present the problem of just how we should introduce a parent to the teacher, a parent to a classmate, or one child's parents to other parents.

In a social studies class there will be times when opposing opinions must be expressed. How do we express disagreement without offending people or starting an argument? And if we should offend a person, how can we express our apologies? It will interest children to learn how these problems have been solved in other lands. Many of our concepts of courtesy reflect our democratic belief that everyone has certain rights and freedoms. We do not avoid direct contests in athletics even though we know someone will lose, whereas the Oriental feels that "loss of face" is tantamount to personal ruin. His only choice is to avoid direct contests and find indirect ways of expressing his ideas.

There is no better place to discuss table manners than in a health class. Start with problems like this: "Do you like to sit at a table where someone is messy with food? Talks with his mouth full? Shouts and plays at the table?" Lessons about the use of knife and fork, setting the table, refusing food you don't like, discussing certain topics at the table, and even ordering food at the restaurant all involve language skills in this area.

In the third grade, children are growing in social awareness and are anxious to know ways of behaving. Etiquette that requires girls to precede boys through doorways, to walk "on the inside," and to make the initial greeting does not seem quite so trivial at this age as it may later. A party at Halloween or Valentine's Day can be rich in lessons in courtesy. Some classes make little guidebooks on good manners.

Basic to all courtesy are two concepts, respect and kindness. Respect is shown to our parents and to older people, to our country and its flag, to those who serve us, and to our friends and neighbors. Much of courtesy consists in the application of the Golden Rule in an awkward situation. Kindness covers a broad area of human virtue and includes good will, compassion, generosity, and love for one's fellow man. Rudeness is the opposite of kindness in that it makes another person suffer. Even following the rules of etiquette can be unkind if it causes others to be embarrassed. The story of Queen Victoria blowing on her soup to cover up a guest's bad manners can be told as a true act of courtesy. Merely following the accepted forms can make us appear as if we considered ourselves superior to all others.

Both respect and kindness are expressed when we speak of consideration of others. This must go much deeper than the language aspect, but knowing the language is a way of establishing the behavior desired as well as the inner sensitivity that is true courtesy. There is no more courtesy in a curt or thoughtless "thank you" than in the thoughtless salute of a new recruit in the army. But a salute that reflects respect, alertness, and a dedication to service is the heart of military courtesy.

Again the importance of example must not be forgotten. The teacher's everyday manners will provide many object lessons in this area. It might be well for the children to know more about the teacher's prerogatives and responsibilities. Although it is usually not courteous for a child to criticize his schoolmates, it is quite another

thing for a teacher to overlook their shortcomings. Consistency is the key to success.

Some teachers, too, need to "mind their manners." The hasty lunch hour, eating alone, or being too much apart from social activities can develop poor table manners. A friend who works for the F.B.I. says he can always identify teachers by the way they eat. Teachers may also reflect ungraciousness in accepting favors. Hundreds of requested letters of recommendation have been received by teachers without a word of thanks to those who wrote them. Teachers sometimes accept dinner invitations as though these were a part of their salary. There is no reason why a teacher should not do something in return. If anyone else in our society is invited out to dinner, appreciation is expressed by a reciprocal invitation, a little gift of flowers or candy, or at least a pleasant thank-you note. Even a bachelor can invite people to dinner at a restaurant.

Boorish behavior is always offensive because it betrays callous disregard for the feelings of others. Men in education who depend on profanity, salty anecdotes, and expansive exuberance at conventions to prove they are "regular fellows" may succeed in proving quite the opposite. The

---

Concepts to Discuss

People use good manners and courtesy because they make living and working together more enjoyable.

What things can we do to make our classroom more enjoyable?
1. Hang up clothes on hangers.
2. Clean up spilled paint and water.
3. Leave the easel clean and ready for the next person.
4. Keep desks clean and neat.
5. Respect the rights of others. Try to help other people.
6. Equipment in the room belongs to all of us. We each have the privilege of using it, and the responsibility of taking care of it.

Learning Activities

The children can be asked to speculate on what the room would be like if no one used manners and courtesy.

Why Have Good Manners, filmstrip (Eyegate House), gives many ideas on why people use good manners.

Children will mention most of these specifics and probably add many more.

The song "It's Good to Share" (*New Music Horizons, Book III,* p. 70) fits in nicely.

Young America Films' *We Plan Together* is an excellent filmstrip to use prior to committee work.

The group will profit from planning and executing a "model" work and clean-up period. Afterwards, the values of all working to achieve a common purpose can be pointed out.

Flag Courtesy

Why do we show respect for our country's flag?

1. To show that we are thankful for our country.

How do we show respect for the flag?

1. When giving the pledge, stand and face the flag, place right hand over heart.
2. When the flag is brought into a room, stand and remain standing until the flag is in place in its holder.
3. When the flag is raised or lowered on the flagpole, stand still, face the flag, and place hand over heart.
4. When the national anthem is played, face the flag and salute. If the flag is not displayed, face the music, but do not salute. (This holds true only for "live" music, and is generally not done if the music is recorded.)
5. Cubs and Brownies, when inside a room, salute instead of placing hand over heart, only if they are in full uniform.

The film *The Flag Speaks* will make an especially valuable contribution. It discusses our national pride for the flag, and demonstrates correct flag courtesy.

Members of the class who are Cub Scouts or Brownies can be called upon to share what they know about flag courtesy.

The filmstrip *Flag Etiquette* (Young America Films) will provide an excellent summary of what has been learned.

A committee can be formed to learn and demonstrate these rules for the class. This might also be shared at an assembly.

This is a good time to learn or relearn "The Star-Spangled Banner," and "America, the Beautiful."

---

woman teacher who overdresses, overspends, or overeats may in fact be disclosing a sense of insecurity. Unless they take steps to correct these personality disorders, such teachers cannot be very successful in teaching courtesy. Even the young child can see the type of persons they really are.

The plan on these pages was used successfully in teaching good manners in a third

grade. Start by helping children to know that the real basis of good manners is sincerity; that merely being familiar with the "rules" won't tell us what to do in every situation. Sometimes we simply don't know the precise rule to apply, but as long as we are sincere our behavior will be appropriate.

As the children's outlook begins to widen, the transfer to situations outside the room

---

Concepts to Discuss

What are some things a good citizen tries to do on the playground?

1. Learn the rules of the game, and play according to the rules.
2. Observe safety rules for the swings, slide, and other equipment.
3. Avoid picking fights.
4. Try to include new children in games. Do not tease.
5. Take care of school equipment.
6. The equipment belongs to everyone at our school, therefore all must share it.   •

Learning Activities

The filmstrip *Good Manners at Play* (Eyegate House) is a helpful aid to introduce playground manners.

Have a problem-solving discussion centered around difficulties that can be prevented by learning and knowing rules.

A small committee can undertake the writing down of game rules. These could be put on a hektograph master and reproduced.

Another group might prepare a bulletin-board display on playground manners.

Dramatic play to demonstrate several ways of handling a "touchy" situation.

Role playing might be used in regard to the "new child" on the playground.

Use filmstrip *New Classmate* (Popular Science Films).

can be made. The playground is a real testing ground for social amenities. Here the conflict between serving one's own desires as opposed to being considerate to others is especially marked. Even though children know the correct thing to do, they cannot always bring themselves to do it. The very child who contributes the best ideas in the classroom is often the one who fails most to "practice what he preaches." It is obvious that boys and girls will need understanding guidance in utilizing what they learn during this phase.

Having given consideration to the social amenities that come into use in the classroom and on the playground, the children can now be guided into a study of manners and courtesy on a broader scope that includes the whole school, and the school's personnel.

Concepts to Discuss	*Learning Activities*
Why do we need to use courtesy and manners, in other places, at school?	Some of the ideas that were developed in answer to this same question for the room and playground can be reviewed and enlarged upon.
1. Use of good manners will make our school a more enjoyable place.	
Besides the teacher, who are some of the people at school who need our help in order to do their jobs?	This will be a good opportunity to invite resource people to the classroom.
1. The principal.	The principal may be asked to explain the "whys and wherefores" of the various school rules. She might also help develop a cooperative attitude toward these.
2. The school secretary.	She can tell of her job, and its complexities. The need for manners in the school office should be emphasized, as her job is often complicated by children who forget to use good manners.
3. The custodian.	The school custodian will appreciate the opportunity of talking to the group. He can help them in many ways by stressing the need for conservation of paper and soap in lavatories, explaining the need for respecting property, etc. He may also wish to express his appreciation to those who help him keep the school clean.
4. Patrol boys and school safeties.	Because the patrol boys and safeties make such a valuable contribution to the school, they should be given a chance to speak to the group.
What can we do to help these people help us? 1. Be courteous and remember that what they say is to help us. 2. Follow the rules because rules are like manners in that they help everyone get along better.	Children are naturally grateful for things done for them. They may want to discuss ways of expressing their gratitude to the people who have come to the room and helped them learn. This can lead to a consideration of *ways* of saying "thank you."
	The language period can be used to study the mechanics of letter writing. Emphasis should be placed upon individuality.
When someone has done something nice for you, what can you do to show you appreciate it? (Children need to be introduced to other ways besides verbal thanks.)	Children should see this as a pleasurable activity rather than a disagreeable task.

Concepts to Discuss

1. Write "thank-you" notes.
2. Make things to show our appreciation.
3. Do something.

Are there other times and places at school when we need to use good manners and courtesy?

1. The cafeteria:

   Wait in line patiently.

   Use good table manners.

(Table manners are fully discussed under "Manners at Home.")

2. Auditorium.

   Find seat and sit down quietly.

   Give attention to the program.

   Applaud politely.

3. Corridors.

   Walk on the right side.

   Say "excuse me" when necessary.

   Keep voices low.

   Look where you are going, or go where you are looking.

4. The school bus.

(The school bus deserves special consideration, since difficulties often arise in such situations where children are without close supervision. Children need to know that certain behavior is very dangerous on the bus. Riding the bus is a privilege which, if not respected, may be lost.)

Why do we *especially need* to use courtesy and manners on the school bus?

1. Safety factors.
2. Buses are usually crowded. Consideration for others helps make it a pleasant trip.

How can we show respect for public and private property?

1. By treating it as if it were ours.
2. Public property is just like school equipment. We all have a share in maintaining it.
3. You may be trespassing if you are on someone's private property without the owner's permission. (Teacher may explain that the property owner is entitled to certain legal protection from trespassers.)

If you find something which you think someone has lost, what is the right thing to do?

1. Do everything you can to find the owner.
2. The more valuable a thing is, the more reason a person has to try to find the owner.

Learning Activities

Committees can be organized so that each child is given the chance to say "thank you" in his own way. Some groups may write "thank-you" notes, while others express their gratitude by making things such as clay paperweights, calendars or pictures.

The filmstrip *Good Manners at School* (Eyegate House) discusses many situations at school calling for the use of good manners.

This will provide an opportunity for small-group work. Each group may choose a specific situation such as the auditorium, etc. They can find out what manners and courtesies are in order at these places. A report can be prepared and a presentation given to the class such as: a puppet play, illustrated talk, and so on.

See instructional material section for appropriate verse.

A good lead-in discussion might be centered around what the bus driver does for us.

An excursion will provide the best learning opportunity for this concept.

Teacher share the "Golden Rule," or similar object story.

Role playing in a given meaningful situation such as this: Several children are picking flowers as they wait for the bus. What would you do if you were the person who planted these flowers and how would you feel about this?

A spontaneous puppet play can be used in connection with lost-and-found concepts. This can demonstrate how the loser feels and how the finder reacts.

For Discussion

1. Do you think that a "courtesy week" would be effective in a school? What would you suggest as activities?

2. What understandings should children have concerning telephone courtesy?

3. Who had the greatest influence on your own habits of courtesy? Your mother? Father? Scout leader? Teacher?

4. In the primary grades it is sometimes effective to have a "boy of the day" and "girl of the day." Sometimes these children wear a special badge or crown. This is an honor which is given as a reward for desirable behavior. Would such a device work with intermediate-grade children?

Suggestions for Projects

1. Evaluate parliamentary procedure as a speech activity and illustrate its use.

2. Show how certain radio and television program ideas or techniques might be adapted to classroom use.

3. Evaluate educational television and illustrate how a class might prepare a program for broadcast.

4. Plan a way to use puppets to gain better speech habits.

5. Discuss and illustrate how the sharing time may be made an effective language learning experience.

6. Evaluate some of the listening tests. Examine the Brown-Carlsen Listening Test, World Book Company (9–12) California Auding Test, Council on Auding Research, 146 Columbia Avenue, Redwood City, California (9–12), Listening Test, Educational Testing Service, Princeton, New Jersey, four levels.

7. Make a courtesy handbook to use in an intermediate classroom.

8. Make a collection of speech drills and verse to use with children who have articulation problems.

9. Some school systems have "listening posts" in some rooms. These consist of sets of earphones which the child uses while a recording is played. Investigate the literature relating to these or evaluate one in use.

Bibliography

Books

Eisenson, Jon, and Mardel Ogilivie. *Speech Correction in the Schools,* 3rd ed. New York: The Macmillan Company, 1971.

Phillips, Gerald M., Robert E. Dunhem, Robert Brubaher, and David Butt. *The Development of Oral Communication in the Classroom.* Indianapolis: The Bobbs-Merrill Co., Inc., 1970.

Possien, Wilma M. *They All Need to Talk.* New York: Appleton-Century-Crofts, 1969.

Pronovost, Wilbert, and Louise Kingman. *The Teaching of Reading and Listening in the Elementary School.* New York: David McKay Company, Inc., 1959.

Van Riper, Charles. *Speech Correction,* 4th ed. Englewood Cliffs, N.J.: Prentice-Hall, Inc., 1964.

Wyatt, Gertrud L. *Language Learning and Communication Disorders in Children.* New York: The Free Press, 1969.

Articles and Pamphlets

Biloon, Jean, Althea Rieff, and James Yantsos. *Experimental Language Arts Instructional Guide in Listening and Speaking,* Ramapo Central School District No. 2, Spring Valley, N.Y.

Brantley, Mabel, and Mary McCullough. "Story Telling Styles of Young Children," *Illinois Journal of Education* (December 1968), pp. 32–36.

Burks, Ann T., and Polly D. Guilford. *Wakulla County Oral Language Project* (May 1969), pp. 606–11.

Carlson, Ruth K. "Raising Self-concepts of Disadvantaged Children Through Puppetry," *Elementary English* (March 1970), pp. 349–55.

Gallagher, Betty. "Teachers' Attitudes and the Acceptability of Children with Speech Defects," *Elementary School Journal* (February 1969), pp. 277–81.

Landry, Donald L. "The Neglect of Listening," *Elementary English* (May 1969), pp. 599–605.

MacKintosh, Helen K. *Children and Oral*

Language, Joint Statement of A.C.E.I., A.S.C.D., I.RA, N.C.T.E., 1964.

Material Development Center. *Teaching English as a Second Language* T.E.S.L. Project Materials, Teachers College, Columbia University, 1965.

Moreney, Anne S., Joseph M. Wepman, and Sarah K. Hass. "Developmental Speech Inaccuracy and Speech Therapy in the Early School Years," *Elementary School Journal* (January 1970), pp. 219–24.

Orange County Superintendent of Schools. *Speech Activities in the Classroom, Grade K–8.* 1104 W. 8th Street, Santa Ana, Calif. (1965).

Smith, Mary L. *Listening Habits and Speech Sound Discrimination.* Alameda County Schools; Haywood, Calif. (1963).

Sturak, L. A. *Bibliography of Listening Post Materials for Primary Grades.* San Diego City Schools; San Diego, Calif. (1969).

Wright, Betty Atwell. *Urban Education Series.* New York: The John Day Company, Inc., 1965.

three

discovering children's literature

What Is the Purpose of Teaching Literature in the Elementary School?

John Stuart Mill once said, "The imagination is that which enables us, by a voluntary effort, to conceive the absent as if it were present, the imaginary as if it were real, and to clothe it in the feelings which, if it were indeed real, it would bring us along with it. This is the power by which one human being enters into the mind and circumstances of another." This ability to interpret life is a skill that can be cultivated and extended. All children do not have the same power of imagination. As some grow older it seems to diminish rather than grow. The literal-minded intermediate child needs help to strengthen his skills of imagination, his ability to empathize with others, his ability to see himself "from the outside."

Teachers hope that their efforts in literature instruction will lead children to find in books an understanding of the richness of life, with all its experiences and its feelings, that will enlarge their own lives. Reading about others who solve problems similar to those found by the reader can help him to feel confident about his own ability to face life. Each person needs to feel that he belongs, has a contribution to make, and will be respected by others. Stories do this in many ways. It is comforting to know, for example, that others feel the same way about a situation as you do or that others are sometimes motivated by envy, as the reader himself may be. When the story indicates an honored way of behaving, the reader feels confident because he too would have acted

Book jackets help create an interesting bulletin board. (*Courtesy of the Burbank Public Schools.*)

that way. Contrasting one way of living with another helps a reader to appreciate qualities in both.

There is a literary culture that is the right of all children and that is an aspect of reading skill. For understanding, the child must know the meaning of such sayings as, "Don't be a dog in the manger," or, "He is a regular Tom Sawyer." One textbook cannot give all that is needed, but the heritage of folk literature should be a discovery of young readers. Many selections in contemporary reading programs are designed to lead to wider personal reading. The classic plots and themes found in such tales as "Cinderella," "Puss-in-Boots," and "Snow White" are a part of the literary background needed to understand the many stories based upon overcoming evil with wit or innocence, gaining success in spite of great odds, and changing the ugly into the beautiful.

Certainly the child learning to read needs to know that reading can be a pleasure whether reading is in the form of listening to material well read or participating in silent or oral group reading. Children should also know the pleasure of personal writing, which can be stimulated by literature.

In the early years of a reader's life the emphasis should be upon verse, fable, and folklore. For some children the only literary abilities to be developed will be to identify reading material by such classification. Eventually children will note the different ways stories start and end, that some characters seem real and others remain as flat as the paper in the book, and that some writers, by the use of words, make the reader feel happy or sad. All of this in time becomes an awareness of writing style. When a child discovers that a single writer writes a kind of story that he is able to identify, the reader has made a basic literary discovery.

Teachers who wish to extend emphasis on literature should limit their efforts to the following types of analysis.

1. *Character.* What are the clues to characters suggested in the writing? From what is said or the action taken, what inference can be made about the individual? Why does the character act the way he does? What are his values? Did anyone change in the story? Why?
2. *Setting.* Can you see where the story is happening? How do those in the story

act because of the setting? Is there a basic struggle between the people in the story and the nature of the place where they live?

3. *Mood–feeling–tone.* What words are used to tell you how the writer feels? What is the tone of voice of the story-teller? Is it serious? Humorous? Is this a true experience?

4. *Story pattern.* What story would you tell if you had only the first paragraph to guide you? Can you tell what happened by reading only the last paragraph? Is there a theme or lesson that the writer is illustrating? Who is telling the story? What difference does it make?

The teacher's goal is to enhance what is read, such as discovering the subtle bits of humor and character that might be lost as the reader becomes involved in the plot.

The child's appetite for more reading can be stimulated by

1. Guiding the child to reading which will broaden and deepen his experiences.
2. Fitting the library book to the child, not the child to the book.
3. Bringing masterpieces of children's literature from the past and those of the present into proper perspective.
4. Challenging, but not pushing, the child.
5. Waiting with wisdom and patience for the child's own pattern of reading growth to unfold.

Teachers have encouraged wide reading by using the following procedures:

1. *Storytelling and oral reading* of carefully made selections from various types of literature that children might otherwise miss. Certain books or passages from books for increased appreciation of skillful use of language, vivid characterization, or dramatic incident are savored best when they are shared.
2. *Book talks,* including introductions to authors, illustrators, background material, stories behind stories, and sampling of passages to broaden reading interests and add zest to reading.
3. *Round-table, thought-provoking discussions* to help children discover for themselves the deeper meanings and values that transcend the plot in good books. This does not mean overanalysis, which would destroy the pleasure of a good story for children, but it does mean a voluntary sharing of the fresh, individualized interpretation of the universal truths of a good story as a child sees them in relationship to his own experience.

4. *Literature* presented in such a way as to vitalize and enrich all areas of study and school experience so that children will come to recognize reading for pleasure and self-enlightenment as a natural part of living. Teachers should not feel that every literary experience must be followed by a related activity. However, frequently the interest of the children and the nature of the literature enjoyed guide individuals or groups quite naturally into creative writing, art experiences, creative drama, quizzes about authors or stories, or other interpretive activity.

There is a place for personal reading in the curriculum. This is an opportunity for the child to follow his interests and read for his own enjoyment. Many teachers feel that motivating such reading through records, visits to the library, book talks, and other such activities constitutes an adequate program. Others feel that children need guidance to find the books that have lasting merit. Few children will read more than 400 books of children's fiction in their lifetime. It is important that some of these be true literary experiences.

The enjoyment of a few books *in depth* may be the guidance needed. The following plans illustrate efforts to do this: [1]

A class of second graders had just returned from a trip to the zoo and in small informal groups were discussing the animals they had seen. As the teacher walked from group to group, he assumed the role of an interested listener. As he listened, he observed the expressions of the children. Noticing a very

---

[1] English Language Arts in Wisconsin, Robert Pooley, Project Director, Madison, Wisconsin, Department of Public Instruction, 1968.

puzzled look on Jamie's face, he asked him if something was puzzling him.

"How do they catch the big bears?" Jamie wanted to know.

The teacher answered that perhaps the other boys and girls were wondering, too, and he asked the boy to save his question for the literature period on the following day, at which time he would read a story which would answer the question.

The next day the teacher was prepared to answer Jamie's question as well as to share with the class *The Biggest Bear*. Having called on Jamie to repeat the question for the class, the teacher explained that he thought Jamie's question would be answered as they listened to and enjoyed the story *The Biggest Bear,* by Lynd Ward.

As the teacher read the story and shared the illustrations with the interested group around him, the children gasped as they learned that Mr. Pennell had killed three bears and therefore had three bearskins nailed to his barn, but Johnny's family had none. Like Johnny, the children became more and more attached to the bear cub in the story. The antics of Johnny's bear as he grew bigger and bigger brought intermittent squeals of delight and gasps of horror, especially details of the chaos in mother's kitchen and the damage in father's shed. They sympathized with Johnny as his father explained that the bear must go back to the woods.

"The bear really liked Johnny, didn't he?" a child exclaimed.

"Yes he did! But now Johnny had to do something that was very difficult for him to do," explained the teacher.

The sad-eyed audience gave visual testimony that they experienced vicariously what Johnny was feeling as he and his father took the bear into the forest, and all three fell into a bear trap. How delighted the students were to eventually find that some kind men would take care of Johnny's bear if Johnny would let them have him for the zoo.

At this point the teacher asked Jamie if he knew one way of capturing bears for the zoo. The teacher was pleased when Jamie replied, "They set traps; but I hope all people are as kind as these zoo people were."

The teacher could tell that the children were anxious to talk about the book and he therefore asked the question, "Was there any part of the story you liked best?" He called on extrovert Tommy, who was wildly waving his hand.

"I liked the part where Johnny took the bear in all directions. May I make a map of Johnny's trip with the bear?" he asked, "and can I call on someone else to answer next?"

When the teacher nodded his head, Tommy called on Larry, who only now was emerging from his shell. Larry timidly smiled and said that he liked the part when Grandpa Orchard said, "It's better to have a bear in the orchard than an Orchard in the bear." The group laughed with Larry because they liked him and were happy that he was no longer afraid to share his ideas with them.

The teacher then presented these questions and watched the children's reactions in order not to destroy the pleasure they had derived from the story: "When Johnny first found the bear cub, why didn't he kill him? After all, he did want a bearskin for their barn." "Was it all right for Johnny to have the bear for a pet?" "Why did Johnny try to do what his daddy wanted him to do even though it was hard for him?" "How did Johnny feel?"

At the close of the lesson a young girl asked if she could take the book home to share with her little brother, and when others echoed this request, the teacher knew that *The Biggest Bear* would be one of their favorite stories.

The next day another child brought his record of *The Biggest Bear* to share with the group, and once more the class relived the story.

In one intermediate class, . . . the story *The Good Master* by Kate Seredy [was used]. The teacher asked someone to find Hungary on the map, to locate Budapest and the Hungarian Plains. The time that this story takes place was discussed. (Prior to World War I.) To bring out the plot the teacher asked such questions as these: When Kate arrived at her uncle's ranch, what tomboy actions surprised the family? What caused her to become more gentle in her ways?

The teacher also asked questions about the characters in the story: What was tomboy Kate like? Who was her best friend? Why was he called The Good Master?

The teacher usually helped the children become aware of the plot of the story or the book by direct questioning. The plot of *Wheel on the School* was brought out by this question: How do Lina and the people of the Dutch fishing village get the storks back? In *My Side of the Mountain* by Jean George, the children by discussion saw that Sam had dozens of problems to solve in living off the land for a year. In reading *Hans Brinker* by Mary Mapes Dodge, the teacher helped the children identify the

A library corner in the classroom supplements the school library. (*Courtesy of the San Diego County Schools.*)

main plot by asking: Why does everyone try so very persistently to restore Raff Brinker's memory?

Characterization was handled in this way. In reading *And Now Miguel* by Joseph Krumgold, the children followed Miguel's experiences as he grows up to be a man in his father's family. Through questions such as these the plot unfolded in *Mary Poppins* by L. Travers: Mary Poppins was a magical character, vain and stern. Would you like Mary to sit beside you? Why? To direct their thinking about the plot of *Johnny Tremain* by Esther Forbes, the teacher asked the children how the story would be different if Johnny lived today. In discussing *Henry Huggins* by Beverly Cleary, the teacher asked, "Have you experienced some of the frustrations Henry had? How did Henry meet his problems?" In an activity to develop plot for

The Secret Garden by Frances Burnett, the teacher suggested that the children portray Mary's bad temper by role playing, and he asked them why they thought she acted as she did. The episode of Christmas at the Cratchits in *The Christmas Carol* by Charles Dickens lends itself to this activity: By reading expressively, can you portray the feeling of Bob Cratchit, Tiny Tim, and others in the family?

To help the children become sensitive to the mood, the teacher guided their thinking with such questions as: At the beginning of the story, what particular feelings did the family have about Kate's actions? What was the feeling at the end of the story? The teacher recognized that the preceding discussion led up to an understanding of the theme of the story. He continued: What causes Kate to become gentler in her ways?

The teacher then presented ways to develop perception of the setting of a story or a poem. For *Blue Willow,* the children made a mural to show the setting. Attention to illustrations and the author's name suggested the setting for *Crow Boy* by Taro Yashima. Pictures and slides were used to show the environment for the story *Wheel on the School* by Meindert DeJong. A recording and filmstrip provided setting and mood for the story *The Sorcerer's Apprentice* by H. H. Ewers, translated by Ludwig Lewisohn. In the study of *The Silver Llama* by Alida S. Malkus, pictures of Peru were helpful. A sense of time and place setting was developed for *The Tree of Freedom* by Rebecca Caudill by making a table map of clay showing the mountain and the passes in Kentucky at the beginning of the westward movement. These Wisconsin children were familiar with the setting of *Caddie Woodlawn* by Carol Brink and they enjoyed finding descriptions of familiar scenes. In *King of the Wind* by Marguerite Henry, the teacher explained that Mrs. Henry lives in Virginia and asked the children why they thought the author could write so vividly about horses. In *Paddle to the Sea* by Holling C. Holling, the children quickly discerned how the illustrations show the beauty of the Great Lakes, the St. Lawrence, and the Atlantic.

The teacher developed sensitivity to mood in these stories by asking appropriate questions: How is a mood of suspense created in *Matchlock Gun* by Walter Edmonds? In *Call It Courage* by Armstrong Sperry, the children felt the excitement of being marooned on a desert island and sighed with relief at the outcome of the story. They admired the courage of Mafatu. They were asked these questions: What makes this story exciting? What other feelings do you have as you read the story? In *The Story of Doctor Dolittle* by Hugh Lofting, although the animals are continually in trouble and fear, the story is very humorous. The children were asked: Why is this story so funny? Do you like this kind of humor?

An awareness of theme was developed by discussion of the main idea in a story. In *Beatinest Boy* by Jesse Stuart, the teacher asked, "What is the relationship of the boy and his grandmother?" In reading *Apple and the Arrow* the children were asked how the Swiss people won their struggle for freedom against the Austrian tyrant, Gessler. Before reading *Door in the Wall* by Marguerite De Angeli, the children saw a filmstrip which showed the fortification of a castle so that they would be better able to visualize the difficulties of the small invalid boy who was able to save a castle.

In recent years one of the great changes in publishing emphasis has taken place in the area of children's literature. Today nearly every major publishing house has a children's editor who selects or develops manuscripts for books suited to the interests and abilities of modern children. There are some publishers who specialize in books for young readers. In 1970 over 3,000 titles were published for children and youth in the United States.

In all of this material there is much that is of only temporary importance, as is true for the many volumes published for adults. But it is quite possible that many books of real worth go undiscovered because busy teachers and parents do not have the time to keep informed in this rapidly expanding field.

An early task for one preparing to teach is to explore this segment of the children's world. At first, read at all grade levels in order to note the type of material available and the quality of writing and illustrations. Later concentrate on the grade levels that most concern you.

A source of information is the *Children's Catalog* published by The H. W. Wilson Company, New York. This is primarily a reference work for use in libraries. In it are listed the books considered of highest merit published recently as well as those of enduring value of the past. If you are establishing a library for the first time, you will find in it a special list recommended for initial purchase as a nucleus for future growth. The *Children's Catalog* is too expensive for individual purchase by a teacher but should be available in a school district that spends funds for library books.

In order to recognize merit and to direct the attention of the public toward children's literature, a number of awards are made each year. The John Newbery Medal is awarded for a book that is considered the most distinguished contribution to American literature for children.

The Caldecott Medal honors the best-illustrated book for children.

There are other awards which call attention to books of merit. These include The Laura Ingalls Wilder Award and The Regina Medal. In Canada there are two Book-of-the-Year-for-Children medals. The Hans Christian Andersen Award is an international children's book award. In England the Carnegie Medal and Kate Greenway Medal correspond to the Newbery and Caldecott awards in the United States. There are awards given in France, Germany, Norway, Sweden, and Switzerland for outstanding children's books published each year in these countries.

The book reviews that appear in *The Horn Book, Saturday Review, Childhood Education, Elementary English, The New York Times,* and *The Christian Science Monitor* provide another source of aid in selecting books for children.

The Children's Book Council, located at 175 Fifth Avenue, New York, promotes the nationwide Book Week. Posters, book jackets, wall charts, and other materials are available for school use at very low cost.

With all this emphasis upon the new it must not be forgotten that we share a great cultural heritage from the past. There are constant references in our language which assume that we know the meaning of such expressions as *my man Friday, the golden touch, the patience of Job, and whitewashing the fence.*

Anthologies of children's literature contain collections of old and new verse, fairy tales and folktales, short selections from modern writers, notes on authors and illustrators of children's books, and excellent suggestions for their classroom use. In time most elementary teachers will want to purchase one of these anthologies to keep on their desks as a constant source of classroom material. A book of this nature is as basic to good instruction as chalkboard and chalk, but some districts hesitate to spend funds for individual teacher references. In that case the teacher has no choice but to purchase the book as a basic tool of the profession and use the expense as a tax deduction.

The *Anthology of Children's Literature* by Edna Johnson, Evelyn R. Sickels, and Frances Clark Sayers, published by Hough-ton Mifflin Company, and *Story and Verse for Children* by Miriam Blanton Huber, published by Macmillan, are outstanding single-volume collections. Mrs. May Hill Arbuthnot has several books: *Time for True Tales, Time for Fairy Tales, Time for Poetry,* and *Children and Books,* all published by Scott, Foresman and Company.

A number of special bibliographies have been issued to help teachers locate material appropriate to the need of a child. Some of them are periodically brought up to date. The following are helpful: *Reading Ladders for Human Relations* by Muriel Crosby, 1969 (Washington, D.C.: American Council on Education); *Behavior Patterns in Children's Books* by Clara J. Kircher (Washington, D.C.: Catholic University Press); *About 100 Books, a Gateway to Better Group Understanding* by Ann G. Wolfe (New York: The American Jewish Committee Institute of Human Relations); and Ethel Newell, "At the North End of Pooh: A Study of Bibliotherapy," *Elementary English* (January 1957). Leland Jacobs of Columbia University has provided a series of four programs for adults about children's books which is available in *How to Choose Children's Books,* Board of Missions of the Methodist Church Service Center; 7820 Reading Road; Cincinnati, Ohio 45237. Mrs. Elvajean Hall, Coordinator of School Libraries of the Newton, Massachusetts, Public Schools, maintains a current list of books dealing with human problems which is free upon request to Campbell and Hall; Box 350; Boston 17, Massachusetts.

In the area of children's literature we are endowed with great riches. Our problem is to spend it with wisdom.

For Discussion

1. What sources of information concerning new books for children are available in your teaching community? What responsibility must a teacher assume for this information to be used?

2. Would you consider such old favorites as *Mrs. Wiggs of the Cabbage Patch* or *Black Beauty* appropriate for modern children?

3. How do you explain the popularity of series books with young readers?

4. Comic books are a favorite form of leisure reading for some children. Are they of literary merit? How should such material be handled in school?

5. Have you had an experience that would justify the following statement?

As children, most of us were turned off and away from literature by teachers' instructions to read selections of prose or poetry to find their "true" meaning—dissecting, analyzing, and finally giving succinct summaries of what the authors were attempting to communicate to us. We came to view literature not as an encounter with life as it is or might be, but as a formal, dull learning experience in which the teacher engaged in literary criticism with an uninvolved audience.[2]

6. Can you recall reading any book that influenced your beliefs or attitudes?

7. How concerned should parents and teachers be when they discover children reading books that are vulgar or suggestive? What countermeasures would you suggest?

8. Why should certain subjects, such as death, union labor, working mothers, and deceitful bankers and businessmen, be taboo in children's literature?

9. Does the following statement contradict the ideas presented in this section?

Children read books, not reviews. They don't give a hoot about the critics; They don't read to find their identity; They don't read to free themselves of guilt, to quench the thirst for rebellion, or to get rid of alienation; They have no use for psychology; They detest sociology; They don't try to understand Kafka or *Finnegan's Wake;* They still believe in God, the family, angels, devils, witches, goblins, logic, clarity, punctuation, and other such obsolete stuff; They love interesting stories, not commentary, guides, or footnotes; When a book is boring, they yawn openly, without any shame or fear of authority; They don't expect their beloved writer to redeem humanity. Young as they are, they know that it is not in his power. Only the adults have such childish illusions.[3]

---

[2] May Hill Arbuthnot, talk given at Rancho Sante Fe, California, 1966.

[3] Isaac Bashevis Singer, as reported in *Saturday Review,* March 21, 1970, p. 18.

How Can Teachers Involve Parents in the Literature Program?

Our objectives in the teaching of literature will never be realized if our efforts are limited to what can be accomplished in the school day. Appreciation of literature as a personal enrichment takes time. The rhythm of the school day, with its schedules and demands, is not right for some literature. It is when the reader is alone, unscheduled and undisturbed, that a story can truly live. But children will complain that they do not have time to read at home. There is so much time needed for music lessons, homework, chores —and television. Once the "rhythm of the night" was the inspiration of storytelling. Parents shared the stories of their youth and children discovered the world of imaginative writers. Today the rhythm of the night has come to mean the sound of ricocheting bullets on television, the wearisome exhortations of announcers, and the tasteless prolixity of commercials. Somehow we must work with parents to find time for children to read. Our first task is to show parents the values of literature in contrast to the thirty-minute exercises in violence of TV drama. Annis Duff's book *Bequest of Wings* tells of the joys shared by a family as modern books were used in the home. If a teacher cannot get parents to read this book, it might be wise to discuss it with them at a parent–teacher meeting or conference.

Most parents will respond to the teacher's appeal for their help in providing good books for their children. Explain to them why we need so many children's books and how difficult it is to secure the right ones. Suggest that at Christmas or on a birthday they buy a book for their child which might be shared with the class. A group of parents and teachers might suggest a list of books to be purchased or the criteria to be followed when buying books for children.

Ownership of a book means a great deal to a child. A recent study asked the members of a sixth-grade class to list their three favorite books. The final list failed to correspond to any bibliography of children's books but one element was noted. If a child owned a book it was listed as a favorite.

Another way of making parents aware of the material available for children is a planned summer reading program. As summer approaches, a fifth-grade class might ask the sixth grade to suggest books that they would enjoy. The fifth-graders should also note the books their class has enjoyed but which some members have not had time to read. From these two sources each child might select six or eight books that he plans to read during the summer. A simple folder or notebook can be made and used for an early report at the beginning of the next school year.

When parents sponsor a book fair they discover the modern world of children's literature. Material for such an enterprise can be secured from the magazine *Scholastic Teacher* (50 West 44th Street, New York).

Parents are sometimes concerned about the expense of children's books. It does seem like an extravagance to pay $3 for a picture book that only takes twenty minutes to read. Nancy Larrick, in *A Parent's Guide to Children's Reading*, makes an important point by comparing the costs of good books with toys, and then pointing out that long after the toys are broken or discarded the books are still available for rereading. This is one criterion to use in buying a book. Will it be worthy of rereading? If not, don't buy it. There are other sources for books of only temporary interest.

There are good, inexpensive books available. *Scholastic Magazines* publishes a series of paperback books for children. These are reprints of the finest modern books available. The E. M. Hale Company of Eau Claire, Wisconsin, also publishes reprints of outstanding children's books. Some of the "grocery-store" or "supermarket" books are also good. A committee of the P.T.A. might evaluate some of these and suggest a few for purchase.

" 'Tis a strange sort of poverty to be finding in a rich country." These are the words spoken by an immigrant lad in Ruth Sawyer's *The Enchanted Schoolhouse*. Though his words refer to the inadequate and dilapidated school facilities to be found in a wealthy and thriving city in America, they can well apply to America today—a land wealthy with a multitude of fine books that children and parents have not discovered.

For Discussion

1. What influence would this poem have on the parents of the children you teach?

My Mother Read to Me

Long ago on winter evenings,
I recall, my mother read;
There beside our old base-burner
Just before my prayers were said.

Here she gave me friends aplenty,
Friends to fill my life for years;
Meg and Jo and Sister Amy
For little Beth I shed my tears.

Scrooge and Tim and Mrs. Wiggs
Robin Hood and Heidi too,
Young Jim Hawkins and his treasure
Saved from Silver's pirate crew.

Can it be that one small lady
Could, just by her magic voice,
Change a room so, in a twinkling
To the scenes from books so choice?

Poor we were, as some might count us,
No fine house, our clothes threadbare,
But my mother read me riches
From the books she chose with care.

Now in times of fear and struggle
When woe and want about me crowd,
I can use reserves of courage
From the books she read aloud.

E. H. FRIERWOOD

2. Is involvement through concern for the reading of all children a better approach than one of concern for a specific child?

How Is Poetry Presented in the Modern Curriculum?

Our culture is rich in poetic tradition. In many communities there is a Longfellow School or one named for Lowell, Whitman, Field, or Stevenson. The respect for poetry was reflected in the curriculum of the recent past which frequently specified selections that were to be studied and memorized in each grade. Some schools had as many as 100 "pieces" to be mastered in the seventh and eighth grades.

The purpose of this requirement was to ensure that each child would know this aspect of our cultural heritage. Although it was recognized that some of this material was beyond the understanding of the students, and that memorization added a burdensome routine, teachers sincerely felt that eventually this material would enrich the lives of individuals. Many adults today get great satisfaction in reciting "Abou Ben Adhem" or "Snowbound." Some will say, "This poem did not mean much to me when I was in school but each year I seem to enjoy it more." On the other hand, some who were taught this way learned to detest poetry and still think of it as a disciplinary activity.

Poetry in the curriculum of the past was frequently associated with programs. One learned a piece to recite on Friday afternoon or at a parents' meeting. Grandparents especially were delighted with this accomplishment and usually rewarded the speaker with an appropriate gift. Contests were held in which all the participants recited "The Highwayman." Audiences would spend an afternoon listening to ten or more elocutionists repeat the same selection.

Good poetry is sometimes found in popular magazines and daily papers. Although many of these are of transient value, some very good material undoubtedly goes unrecognized in the great mass of published verse. Some of the more talented poets of our day may turn to songwriting or prose because of the greater financial returns involved. Just as such poems as "Trees" and "America, the Beautiful" have been made into fine songs, the lyrics of many popular songs have merit as verse.

In this environment poetry in a modern classroom serves many purposes and needs. It is used to enrich all curriculum areas. Modern anthologies contain a great deal of verse appropriate to the age and reading level of the child for whom the book is intended, although this places a severe limitation on the choice of material. May Hill Arbuthnot has a useful collection in *Time for Poetry* which the teacher reads to children rather than having them read it aloud themselves.

Most teachers today start with the children with whom they work rather than with a collection of poetry which they feel must be mastered. They recognize the truth of Carl Sandburg's statement,

Poetry for any given individual depends on the individual and what his personality requires as poetry. Beauty depends on personal taste. What is beauty for one person is not for another. What is poetry for one person may be balderdash or hogwash for another.[4]

The teacher seeks to present material that will meet the immediate appreciation level of students as well as build sensitivity for growth in appreciation. Many teachers keep a file of poetry and draw from it when appropriate throughout the school day. As the seasons change, verses are used to express the children's feelings, or to call attention to the flight of birds or the budding of our pussywillow. Holidays are made special days through poems that may be used as the theme of a bulletin board display. In social studies, the life of the Indian becomes personalized as the group recites a Navaho prayer or chant. On the playground the ideals of fair play and good sportsmanship are remembered because a verse suggests meaningful behavior. Throughout each day and year the child grows in perception and understanding through the planned use of poetry. He learns to listen to words for both meaning and sound. He finds that some words create an atmosphere that is sad or frightening, whereas others have a warm and lazy effect.

To accomplish this the teacher starts with herself. Teachers who experience the most difficulty at the beginning are those who have a love for great poetry yet are unwilling to discover the appreciation level of the children with whom they work. Walt Whitman's "When Lilacs Last in the Dooryard Bloom'd" will not be accepted by a class that delights

---

[4] Carl Sandburg, *Early Moon* (New York: Harcourt, Brace, 1930), p. 20.

in "Little Orphan Annie" by Riley. The most important consideration in selection of material is to avoid any value judgment as to what children *should* like. Stated positively, the most important consideration is to discover what they do like.

Start by reciting poems to the children that you know by heart. Avoid any discussion of word meanings. Children do not need to understand every word in order to enjoy a poem. After you have recited it, a child may ask what a certain word means. If he does, by all means tell him in a sentence or two. Then repeat the poem a second time. Select for your memorizing a few of the very best children's poems.

Reading poetry to the children requires preparation. The teacher should read the verse aloud to herself, note the punctuation, the mood of the poem, and any unusual expression or words. Before reading aloud, a few remarks help the listener orient himself. Introduce "Little Orphan Annie" in this manner: "Here is a poem your parents liked, and I think you will like it, too. There are a few words like *hearth* and *rafter* that you may not know; they mean. . . ." Then the teacher might ask a few questions after the first reading. Appropriate ones would be, "Why do you suppose the author repeats the words *If you don't watch out?* Notice how they are written in the poem to show how they might be read." After showing the children the printed poem, another question would be, "How do you feel when you hear the words *the lamp wick sputters and the wind goes whooo?* What was the writer trying to do?" If the children wish, the teacher might read the poem a second time, then place it on the reading table for those who wish to read it themselves.

Some children will bring poems they have found and offer to read them to the class. Others will respond to the invitation to bring poems for the teacher to read. Reading poetry aloud is difficult and many children do not do it well. As a result it is a deadly listening experience. We want to develop good listening habits, but there are better ways of doing it than by forcing attention to poorly read poetry.

The poems found in children's readers are much more fun to read if they have first been heard with pleasure. These selections are the basis for instruction concerning the oral reading of poetry, but that instruction should follow an appreciative listening. Good oral reading is largely imitative and the example followed should be a worthy one. It is the poet who has to speak through the oral reader. It is not the reader speaking poetry. May Hill Arbuthnot gives this advice about one of the problems teachers face.[5]

If you discover a group of children or young people who groan, "Oh, not poetry!", it means one of several things. They have been fed poems too old, too difficult or too "precious" for them. Or they have been set to analyzing poetry—finding all the figures of speech, marking the meter, putting the poem into their own words, picking out the most beautiful line or some such nonsense. The cure for these victims is, take it easy. Begin with nonsense verse or the simplest and most objective verses about everyday experiences and activities. After all, you don't start children's musical experiences with symphonies and sonatas. Even John Ciardi, a serious adult poet and poetry critic, starts his own children with nonsense or humorous verse. But please note his verses are never banal doggerel, but skillfully written by a master craftsman.

Another starting point for reluctant poetry-tasters is the narrative or story poem, long or short. The rapid, on-going meter of verse heightens the sense of action and makes the ballad irresistible to children. From "The Night Before Christmas" for the youngest, to the gory old Scotch-English ballads for the oldest, the story poem will hold them enthralled.

In conclusion, never forget that, like music, poetry is an aural art. It should be spoken and heard to be fully understood and enjoyed, so read poetry aloud whenever you have a chance. Even at your loan desks, have a book of poems on hand, show it to your youthful customer and say casually, "Listen to this and see if you like it," and read a short one. Even our young teenage sophisticates, when they hear poems vigorously and unaffectedly read, say wonderingly, "Read it again." While the children bounce enthusiastically and cry, "Sing it again!" That is your reward.

---

[5] May Hill Arbuthnot, "Helping Children Enjoy Poetry," *Wilson Library Bulletin,* 36 (January, 1962), p. 377.

Sometimes a poem is presented by having it read well by the teacher or pupil, then read in unison by the class. At other times a carefully prepared lesson plan helps children identify with the purposes of the poet and the beauty of language used.

The following sample lesson plan is intended to be just that, samples or suggestions, and nothing more. It is not a guide to be rigidly adhered to but an outline to be expanded upon or altered to meet the demands of the individual teaching situation.[6]

Grade 4: Sample Lesson Plan for Teaching Margaret Widdemer's *"The Secret Cavern"*

Objectives

1. To introduce the poetry of introspection.

2. To point out how the speaker's character is revealed through the imaginative experience of the poem.

3. To lead the child to introspect, i.e., to reason about himself, his desires, his imaginative experiences, his actions.

4. To indicate to the child the close affinity that usually exists between his natural desires (his likes and dislikes), his imagined experiences and his actions.

5. To point out to the child that in many cases when his actions run counter to his desires and plans it is a result of his having thought (reasoned, intellectualized) about those planned courses of action, a result of his visualizing the actions and their consequences. He decided beforehand that the desired action would be wrong or unwise.

Presentation

1. Introduction: Life would be quite dreary if we didn't have any pals or playmates, wouldn't it? I am sure I would be unhappy and lonely if I didn't have any friends. I like to be around people, but there are also times when I like to be alone. Sometimes when I am alone I like to read; sometimes I like to think; and sometimes I like to let my imagination wander. Perhaps some of you can tell me what you like to do when you are alone?

2. After the children respond, continue: I would like to read a poem to you about an adventurous boy who liked to let his imagina-

tion wander. See if you can tell why I think he is an adventurous boy.

The Secret Cavern *

Underneath the boardwalk, way, way back,
There's a splendid cavern, big and black—
If you want to get there, you must crawl
Underneath the posts and steps and all.
When I've finished paddling, there I go—
None of all the other children know!

There I keep my treasures in a box—
Shells and colored glass and queer-shaped rocks,
In a secret hiding-place I've made,
Hollowed out with clamshells and a spade,
Marked with yellow pebbles in a row—
None of all the other children know!

It's a place that makes a splendid lair,
Room for chests and weapons and one chair.
In the farthest corner, by the stones,
I shall have a flag with skulls and bones
And a lamp that casts a lurid glow—
None of all the other children know!

Some time, by and by, when I am grown,
I shall go and live there all alone;
I shall dig and paddle till it's dark,
Then go out and man my pirate bark:
I shall fill my cave with captive foe—
None of all the other children know!

MARGARET WIDDEMER

3. Discussion: Now can any of you tell me why I think he is an adventurous boy? (Responses will probably be related to the dark cavern. If children are unfamiliar with the word "cavern," explain its similarity to "cave." The children may suggest the "treasures," "chests," "weapons," "flag with skulls and bones" and the "pirate bark.")

4. Why do you suppose there is just one chair? (The boy wanted this as his very own secret place.)

5. Do you think he truly wants to live there all alone when he is grown? What tells us in the poem that he really does like to be around other people? (He is going to fill the cave with "captive foe.")

6. I am going to read the poem again, and this time I want you to notice what kinds of pictures the poem helps you to see. (Read the poem again. Children often close their eyes

---

[6] *A Curriculum for English Poetry for the Elementary Grades* (Lincoln: University of Nebraska Press, 1966), pp. 21–28.

---

* From *Little Girl and Boy Land* by Margaret Widdemer, copyright, 1924, by Harcourt, Brace & World, Inc.; renewed, 1952, by Margaret Widdemer. Reprinted by permission of the publishers.

while creating images. The atmosphere must be such that the children are relaxed and feel free to close their eyes or put their heads on their desks, if they wish.)

7. Now let's talk about the mental pictures the poem helped us to see. (The children will probably describe the cave, the colorful treasures, and so forth. Try to elicit responses about the feelings they experienced while listening. Girls, especially, may think the dark cave seems "spooky." The sensation of "dampness" may also be mentioned by the children. The sound of the paddle of the boat as it swishes in the water is a possible response. At this point the children may be eager to paint or draw the scenes which you and they have pictured.

8. Creative writing: Just think of all the pictures and feelings we have been talking about. By choosing certain words the poet was able to help us see these pictures. Let's see if we can think of a picture we might like to paint using words. We've had so many good ideas about the poem, about secret places and being alone that I think we would all enjoy painting some pictures with words. You might like to describe a place you know—a cave, a treehouse, a quiet place or perhaps your own room. We will need two sheets of paper. We will call one our "Idea Paper." We will jot down on this paper ideas that come to our minds. Then we may want to think about our ideas for a while and decide how we'd like to put them together. Some of you may want to write a paragraph that will make a picture for us, or help us to "hear" certain sounds. Some of you may want to write a poem using your ideas. Perhaps some of you already have a short story in mind. I see that everyone has his "brush" (holding up pencil) and his "canvas" ready (hold up paper), so let's start "painting." (The teacher who takes this time to write creatively along with the children will see many satisfying results. The experience seems to become more enjoyable and worthwhile to the children when the teacher is writing also. After their poems or paragraphs are finished, the children may want to exchange papers for proofreading or to form into small groups to read them aloud. Compositions could be recopied for a bulletin board or a composition booklet. The central objective is to make certain the experience has been enjoyable for the children and that they feel their compositions are noteworthy.)

Although the feeling for poetry is often caught rather than taught by the informed and enthusiastic teacher, the schools should provide for ever-increasing depths of appreciation. It is not enough to expose children just to the poems they can feel and readily understand. We must expose them also to "a sense of a margin beyond, as in a wood full of unknown glades, and birds and flowers unfamiliar," as Andrew Long said in his introduction to the *Blue Poetry Book*.

Teachers need to expose children to ever-increasing depths of appreciation. Listed below are some specific ideas and suggestions of poems to use to help children understand the concepts.[7]

1. Enjoyment of rhythm, melody, and story.
   a. *Rhythm*
      "Barbers' Clippers," by Dorothy Baruch—child listens for rhythm in this unrhymed poem.
   b. *Melody*
      "Sea Shells," by Amy Lowell—hear the sea in the alliteration of *S*.
   c. *Story*
      "The Little Elfman," by John Kendrick Bangs—hold a conversation between a child and a puppet elf.
2. Appreciation of seeing one's own experiences mirrored in poetry.
      "Choosing Shoes," by Efrida Wolfe—children tell how they felt when they went shopping for shoes and compare experiences.
3. Projection into a world other than that in which one lives.
      "Radiator Lions," by Dorothy Aldis—a child who lives in a home may be helped to understand George's predicament, living in an apartment, housing unit, etc.
4. Understanding of symbolism and hidden meanings.
      "Boats Sail on the Rivers," by Christina Rossetti—see clouds as ships and rainbow as a bridge.
5. Sensitivity to patterns of writing and literary style.
      "Merry-Go-Round," by Dorothy Baruch. If this poem is put on a chart, young children can note that the shape of the lines as well as the words convey the movement of the merry-go-round.

---

[7] Oakland, California, Public Schools, *Find Time for Poetry*. Primary Curriculum Supplement (July, 1960).

For Discussion

1. Why do teachers sometimes start with poems they feel children should like rather than starting with what children do like?

2. What contemporary poetry do you respond to? Share some of the words of popular songs or of the popular poems of Rod McKuen in class. If children are to find satisfaction in poetry the teacher must find and present poetry that gains a response equal to that she feels toward poetry that speaks to and for her.

3. Why is it unfair to ask children to name a favorite poem?

4. Why do teachers feel more secure presenting a poem that is by a recognized poet than one containing ideas and rhyme that children enjoy?

5. Should sentimental verse or rhymed doggerel be considered subliterature to be ignored by the school?

6. Do you agree with J. A. Cutforth, a famous teacher in England, when he says,[8]

It is impossible to teach poetry. One could, I suppose, attempt to do so by giving a series of instructions on the rules of prosody, but that is not what we are trying to do. All we can legitimately hope to do is to make a child interested in poetry. If we use poems as a vehicle for exercises in comprehension or grammar, we are not only defeating our own ends—for poetry will at once degenerate into a mere school exercise—but we are defeating the poet's aim, which is much more important. In the last analysis, he wrote to please.

How May a Verse Choir Encourage the Classroom Use of Poetry?

The oral reading of poetry has long been a tradition in the British Isles. The verse choir in some areas is as highly organized as an orchestra. High and low voices are balanced to gain special effects and the number in a choir is limited to certain voice quali-

ties. A performance by such a group is as effective as that of a singing choir. We do not seek the same standards with verse choirs in the elementary school. Our primary object is to delight those who are taking part rather than to perfect a performance for the entertainment of others. In accomplishing this the result will be a satisfying self-expression that leads to a high degree of appreciation of the material used.

In achieving this primary objective there are a number of parallel benefits. The shy child feels that he is a contributing member of the group. He is able to participate in a public appearance without any agonizing emotional pressures. The greatest benefits are in the area of speech. The values of precise enunciation and careful pronunciation are obvious to the most slovenly speakers. The slow or fast speaker is made aware of the effect of such speech on the listener. Not only is the quality of voice tone brought to the level of awareness but those whose voices are unpleasant receive needed attention.

From the beginning the approach should be one of enjoyment. With any group start with familiar material so that there is no problem of memorization. A favorite with all ages is "Hickory Dickory Dock." After writing it on the chalkboard the teacher might point out that the poem has the rhythm of a clock ticking. Then add the words, tick-tock three times at the beginning and end.

Tick-tock, tick-tock, tick-tock
Hickory Dickory Dock
The mouse ran up the clock
The clock struck, One!
The mouse ran down
Hickory Dickory Dock.
Tick-tock, tick-tock, tick-tock

The teacher might say, "Now watch my arm. I will move it as if it were a clock pendulum or metronome. When I go this way, say *tick*, and this way say *tock*. Let's practice it once to see how much we can sound like a clock." After one round of

[8] J. A. Cutforth, *English in the Primary School* (Oxford, England: Basil Blackwell, 1956), p. 28.

We dressed like this when the verse choir performed for the P.T.A. (*Courtesy of the San Diego County Schools.*)

practice, go ahead: "That was fine! Now we will have one row be a clock and tick all the way through the verse while the rest of us say it. Notice that we must pause after the *dock* to allow time for a *tock* sound. We might say the last *tick-tock* very softly as if the clock were stopping."

Later a way might be discussed to emphasize the word *one*. Sometimes emphasis is secured by having only one person say the word, sometimes by clapping hands or ringing a bell, and sometimes simply by having everyone say it louder.

Another verse with a dramatic effect is one with a "wind" idea in it. Have the entire group hum to sound like a wind blowing, then while some continue to hum, the verse is said with the humming quietly fading away at the end. Most children will know "Who Has Seen the Wind?"

Who has seen the wind?
Neither I nor you;
But when the leaves hang trembling
The wind is passing through.

Who has seen the wind?
Neither you nor I;
But when the leaves bow down their heads
The wind is passing by.

CHRISTINA ROSSETTI

Before saying a verse together it is wise to note the punctuation. If a group pauses at the end of each line an unpleasant singsong effect destroys the meaning of the poetry. Sometimes this can be avoided by a slight pause after words that should be emphasized, such as *seen* in the first line or *leaves* in the third.

Usually the signal, "Ready, begin" is used for primary children. A hand signal can serve the same purpose. A closed fist opening might be the sign to start.

The simplest type of choral reading is that using a refrain.

Red Squirrel

Unison:	*Flip-flop!*
Solo:	*Without a stop*
(very	*A red squirrel runs*
rapidly)	*To the oak-tree top.*
Unison:	*Whisk, frisk!*
Solo:	*He is so shy,*
(slowly)	*He hides himself in*
	The leaves near by.
Unison:	*Hip, hop!*
Solo:	*With acorns brown*
(fast)	*In his furry cheeks*
	He hurries down.
Unison:	*Snip, snap!*
Solo:	*The nuts he cracks*
(slowly)	*With his long, white teeth*
	As sharp as tacks.
Unison:	*Pip, pop!*
Solo:	*He sits quite still*
(slow, then	*Eating his goodies*
very rapidly)	*Then runs down the hill.*

GRACE ROWE

The Christmas Pudding

(Read faster and faster with each line.)

Solo:	*Into the basin put the plums,*
Refrain:	*Stirabout, stirabout, stirabout.*
Solo:	*Next the good white flour comes,*
Refrain:	*Stirabout, stirabout, stirabout.*
Solo:	*Sugar and peel and eggs and spice,*
Refrain:	*Stirabout, stirabout, stirabout.*
Solo:	*Mix them and fix them and cook them twice,*
Refrain:	*Stirabout, stirabout, stirabout.*

LILLIAN TAYLOR

Funny the Way Different Cars Start

Solo 1: *Funny the way different cars start.*
Row 1: *Some with a chunk and a jerk,*
Row 2: *Some with a cough and a puff of smoke Out of the back,*
Row 3: *Some with only a little click— With hardly any noise.*

Solo 2: *Funny the way different cars run.*
Row 4: *Some rattle and bang,*
Row 5: *Some whirrr,*
Row 6: *Some knock and knock.*
Girls: *Some purr*
Boys: *And hummmmm*
All: *Smoothly on with hardly any noise.*

DOROTHY BARUCH

The Giant Shoes

Solo 1: *There once was a Giant who needed new shoes,*
Refrain: *Left! Right! Tie them up tight!*
Solo 2: *Said he, "I'll go to the shoestore and choose."*
Refrain: *Left! Right! Tie them up tight!*
Solo 3: *"High ones, and low ones, and black one and brown."*
Refrain: *Left! Right! Tie them up tight!*
Solo 4: *"Give me the biggest you have in the town."*
Refrain: *Left! Right! Tie them up tight!*
Solo 5: *The shoeman said, "These are the biggest I've got."*
Refrain: *Left! Right! Tie them up tight!*
Solo 6: *"Take them and try them and keep them or not."*
Refrain: *Left! Right! Tie them up tight!*
Solo 7: *"They fit," said the Giant, "and squeak, I'll buy them."*
Refrain: *Left! Right! Tie them up tight!*
Solo 8: *He wore them all year 'cause he couldn't untie them,*
Refrain: *Untie them! Untie them!*
Solo or Group: *He wore them all year 'cause he couldn't untie them.*

EDWINA FALLIS

The Meal

Solo:	*Timothy Tompkins had turnips and tea.*
Row 1:	*The turnips were tiny He ate at least three.*
Row 2:	*And then, for dessert, He had onions and ice.*
Row 3:	*He liked that so much That he ordered it twice.*
All:	*He had two cups of ketchup, A prune and a pickle.*
Solo:	*"Delicious," said Timothy. "Well worth a nickel."*
Row 1:	*He folded his napkin And hastened to add,*
All:	*"It's one of the loveliest breakfasts I've had."*

KARLA KUSKIN

Another simple form is the two-part arrangement. One half of the children say one part and the other half the other part. Question-and-answer poetry is often used for the two-part arrangement.

Whistle, Whistle

Boys: *Whistle, whistle, old wife,*
         And you'll get a hen.
Girls: *I wouldn't whistle if you gave me ten.*
Boys: *Whistle, whistle, old wife,*
         And you'll get a flower.
Girls: *I wouldn't whistle if you gave me a*
         bower.
Boys: *Whistle, whistle, old wife,*
         And you'll get a gown.
Girls: *I wouldn't whistle for the best in town.*
Boys: *Whistle, whistle, old wife,*
         And you'll get a man.
Girls: *Whhhh! I'll whistle if I can.*

TRADITIONAL

A third arrangement is the line-a-child pattern. Each child has a chance to speak one or more lines by himself. In some poems certain lines can be spoken by individual children and other lines can be spoken in unison.

The Song of the Pop-Corn

Unison: *Pop-pop-pop!*
1st Child: *Says the pop-corn in the pan;*
Unison: *Pop-pop-pop!*
2nd Child: *You may catch me if you can!*
Unison: *Pop-pop-pop!*
3rd Child: *Says each kernel hard and yellow;*
Unison: *Pop-pop-pop!*
4th Child: *I'm a dancing little fellow.*
Unison: *Pop-pop-pop!*
5th Child: *How I scamper through the heat!*
Unison: *Pop-pop-pop!*
6th Child: *You will find me good to eat.*
Unison: *Pop-pop-pop!*
7th Child: *I can whirl and skip and hop.*
Unison: *Pop-pop-pop-pop!*
             pop!
                  Pop!
                     POP!!

LOUISE ABNEY

The most difficult of all choral reading is that involving the total group. Much practice is required in speaking together;

in drilling upon articulation, enunciation, inflection, and pronunciation; and in blending the voices into workable balance while maintaining satisfactory timing. Sometimes it is wise to divide a class into high and low voices. Some of the Bible materials, such as Psalm 121 or the Christmas Story of Luke 2:1–16, lend themselves to this type of presentation.

Bundles

(Good for stressing enunciation)

A bundle is a funny thing
It always sets me wondering;
For whether it is thin or wide,
You never know just what's inside.
Especially on Christmas week,
Temptation is so great to peek;
Now wouldn't it be much more fun
If shoppers carried things undone?

JOHN FARRAR

Listen to the Wind

Listen
To the wind
Listen to the wind
Listen to the wind
Wind, wind, wind, wind
He's roaring up the hill
And whirring around the house
He's whistling round the corners
And rattling all the doors
A blustering, boisterous
Monstrous sort of wind
Listen to the wind
Wind, wind, wind, wind
Listen to the wind
To the wind
Sighing.

MARY M. GREEN

Aeroplane

1st Group: *There's a humming in the sky.*
             There's a shining in the sky.
2nd Group: *Silver wings are flashing by*
             Silver wings are shining by.
All: *Aeroplane*
             Aeroplane
             Flying high.
1st Group: *Silver wings are shining*
             As it goes gliding by.

2nd Group:	First it zooms
	And it booms
	Then it buzzes in the sky
	Then its song is just a drumming.
All:	A soft little humming
	Strumming
	Strumming.
1st Group:	The wings are very little things
	The silver shine is gone.
2nd Group:	Just a little black speck
	Away down the sky.
All:	With a soft little humming
	And a far away humming
	Aeroplane
(softly)	Aeroplane
	Good by.

MARY M. GREEN

The American Flag

Solo:	There's a flag that floats above us,
	Wrought in red and white and blue—
	A spangled flag of stars and stripes
	Protecting me and you.
Unison:	Sacrifices helped to make it
	As men fought the long months through—
Boys:	Nights of marching
Girls:	Days of fighting
Unison:	For the red and white and blue.
Girls:	There is beauty in that emblem
Boys:	There is courage in it, too;
Girls:	There is loyalty
Boys:	There is valor
Unison:	In the red and white and blue.
Solo:	In that flag which floats unconquered
	Over land and sea
	There's equality and freedom
Unison:	There is true democracy.
Solo:	There is glory in that emblem
	Wrought in red and white and blue—
Unison:	It's the stars and stripes forever
	Guarding me and guarding you.

LOUISE ABNEY

Little Echo

All:	Little Echo is an elf		
	Who plays at hide and seek.		
	You never, never find him.		
	But you can hear him speak:		
Low:	Hello	High:	Hello
Low:	Hello	High:	Hello
Low:	I'm here	High:	I'm here
Low:	Come near	High:	Come near
All:	I'm here.		

LOS ANGELES CITY SCHOOLS

W-O-O-O-O-O-W-W !

Slow with hint of eeriness	Away in the forest, all dark-some and deep,
	The wolves went a-hunting while men were asleep;
Medium— more like conversation	And the cunning Old Wolves were so patient and wise,
	As they taught the young cubs how to see with their eyes,
	How to smell with their noses and hear with their ears,
	And what a wolf hunts for and what a wolf fears.
Low, warningly	Of danger they warned: "Cubs, you mustn't go there— (pause)
	It's the home of the Grizzily-izzily Bear."

W-O-O-O-O-O-W-W !

Medium— like conver-sation but a little more quick	The cubs in the pack very soon understood
	If they followed the wolf law the hunting was good,
	And the Old Wolves who'd hunted long winters ago,
	Knew better then they did the right way to go.
	But one silly cub thought he always was right,
	And he settled to do his own hunting one night.
	He laughed at the warning— said he didn't care (pause)
Slow and soft	For the Grizzily-izzily-izzily Bear!

W-O-O-O-O-O-W-W !

High— brightly	So, when his elders were not on the track,
	"I'm off now!" he barked to the cubs of the pack.
	"I'll have some adventures— don't mind what you say!"
	A wave of his paw—and he bounded away.
Low—slow, breathlessly	He bounded away till he came very soon,
	Where the edge of the forest lay white in the moon,
Slowly—softly, deliberately	To what he'd been warned of —that terrible lair (pause)
	The haunt of the Grizzily-izzily Bear!
Mournfully	W-O-O-O-O-O-W-W !

Slowly and sorrowfully

He same . . . and what happened? Alas! To the Pack
The poor silly wolf-cub has never come back,
And once, in a neat little heap on the ground,
The end of a tail and a whisker were found,
Some fur, and a nose-tip—a bristle or two,
And the kindly Old Wolves shook their heads for they knew.

Voices reach crescendo in these final lines

It was all of his nice little feast he could spare, (pause)
That Grizzily-izzily-izzily Bear!

W-O-O-O-O-O-W-W !

NANCY M. HAYES

Locomotive

Unison:	Mobs of people
	Lots of noise
	Rattling baggage.
	Porter boys.
	Grinding brakes.
	Shifting gears
	Merry laughter,
	Parting tears!
Solo:	All ab-o-o-ard! All ab-o-o-ard!
Dark:	Slowly
	Slowly
	Turning,
	Massive engine moving on.
Medium:	Smoking
	Smoking
	Higher
	Higher
	Smokestacks hurl the smoke anon.
Light:	Fuel
	Fuel
	Fire
	Fire
	Faster
	Faster
	Speed
	Speed!
Unison:	Got to reach my destination.
	Got no time for hesitation.
	Have to please the population.
	I am working for the nation.
	Hurry, hurry to my station.
Medium:	Past the valleys, past the hilltops.
	Past the river, past the pond.
	Past the farmhouse or the city
	Quickly covering the ground.

High:	I'm racing the sun
	I'm racing the moon
	I'm racing the stars
	I'm faster than time
Low:	The mountains clear away for me.
	They build a bridge across the sea.
	The iron weight above my wheel
Medium:	Trembles even rails of steel
Dark:	Through tunnels, black, a sooty black
	Wth dusty smoke and grime.
Light:	Faster, faster, night's decending
All:	I must reach my place on time!

RODNEY BENNETT

Solo parts should be used to encourage all children rather than to display a few stars. Frequently solo parts should be spoken by small groups of three or four whose voices are similar.

After children are interested in choir work they will accept some special speech exercises, such as rolling their heads for relaxation, or such tone exercises, as saying *ba, be, bi, bo, bu* toward the front of their mouths. If the teacher starts with these, most children think they are ridiculously funny and no worthy results are achieved.

A verse choir should perform because it motivates both effort and interest but the teacher must avoid the temptation to use material beyond the appreciation level of the children or material unworthy of memorization. At Christmastime little children in their night clothes with candles make an appealing group. A sixth-grade graduation class might prepare a patriotic verse, "I Am an American," from *Book of Americans* by Stephen Vincent Benet. Inviting visitors from another room to hear a choir perform is as motivating as more elaborate presentations.

For Discussion

1. What were some of the poems you memorized in the elementary school? Why did you memorize them?

2. Are the words of any current popular song of poetic quality?

3. Why are so many poems and songs written by men rather than women?

4. What would you do with a poem a child brought to school that you considered unworthy of the class?

5. Do you feel that a more analytical approach to poetry should be made in the intermediate grades than that suggested in this chapter?

6. What type of tests should be given children with respect to poetry taught?

What Verse May Be Used with Young Children?

The action verse or finger play is found in all cultures. The Chinese have them, our American Indians have them, and new ones are invented daily. Friedrich Wilhelm August Froebel, the father of the kindergarten, collected many of his time and called them mother's-play. You may recall the delight you felt as your mother .moved your toes and said, "This little piggie went to market, this little piggie stayed home," etc. We suspect that one of the most interesting experiences of childhood is that of self-discovery, and these verses reflect the charm of that experience. The following are among the best known:

Pat-a-Cake

Pat-a-cake, pat-a-cake, baker's man
Make me a cake as fast as you can.
Roll it, prick it, and mark it with T,
And put it in the oven for Tommy and me.

Thumb Man

Thumb man says he'll dance,
Thumb man says he'll sing,
Dance and sing my merry little thing,
Thumb man says he'll dance and sing.
[Also Pointer, Tall man, Ring man, Little man.]
Where is thumb man? [Hold hands behind back.]
Where is thumb man?
Here I am. [Fist forward with thumb standing.]
Here I am. [Other fist forward, thumb standing.]
How do you do this morning? [Wriggle one thumb in direction of other.]
Very well, I think you. [Wriggle other thumb.]
Run away, run away. [Hands behind back again.]
[Can be sung to the tune of "Are You Sleeping?"]

In using action plays, it is better to use too few than too many. The fun seems to be in repetition of the familiar favorites.

The teacher first demonstrates the entire verse, then asks one or two children to come to the front and do it with her. After that, each line is done by the group and repeated until a few have mastered it. Needless to say, parents delight in watching a verse choir use these materials.

After these become old favorites, children will want to make up their own. To do this, start with a movement such as holding up an arm with the fist closed.

"This is an airplane searchlight,"
[Arm held up, wrist bent.]
"It turns to the left," [Open the fist.]
"It turns to the right," [Open the fist.]
"And the airplane came home" [Movement of both hands of airplane landing.]
"On a dark, dark night."

Other movements might be holding hands together to indicate something closed, fingers raised as candles on a cake, fingers "walking" to indicate movement either on the table or for an insect on the bend of the arm or opposite palm, fists pounding to indicate marching, building, or loud movements. Soon total body action is needed and eventually one reaches simple pantomime.

When using nursery rhymes, children's names may be substituted for the rhyme characters. Let each child select the person he wants to be, to avoid this being used in a way that might hurt the child. Let children join in on a repeated refrain. This may also be done in such a story as "Little pig, little pig, let me in!" "No, no, no, not by the hair of my chinny-chin-chin." Space permits only a few here. One class found over 200 known to children in the schools where they were student teachers.

Little Jack Horner

Little Jack Horner sat in a corner
[Sit straight in chair; left hand held in lap in the pie.]
Eating his Christmas pie.
[Pretend to eat pie with right hand.]
He put in his thumb and pulled out a plum
[Stick thumb of right hand into pie; pull out the plum.]
And said, "What a good boy am I!"
[Hold hands high in air.]

Flag Salute

(This salute to the flag may be used the first semester in school; then gradually introduce our national salute.)

The work of my hands
    [Cup both hands in front of you.]
The thoughts of my head
    [Both hands on top of head.]
The love of my heart
    [Hands folded over chest.]
I give to my flag.
    [Extend hands and arms toward flag.]

Two Dickey Birds

Two little dickey birds sitting on a wall;
    [Fists clenched, thumbs erect.]
One name Peter, the other named Paul.
    [Nod one thumb, then the other.]
Fly away, Peter; fly away, Paul.
    [One hand, then other moved to behind back.]
Come back, Peter; come back, Paul.
    [One hand, then the other reappears.]

Five Little Squirrels

Five little squirrels
Sitting in a tree,
The first one said,
"What do I see?"
The second one said,
"I smell a gun."
The third one said,
"Quick, let's run!"
The fourth one said,
"Let's hide in the shade."
The fifth one said,
"Oh, I'm not afraid."
But—bang! went the gun
Away they did run!

Little Turtle

There was a little turtle.
    [Upper right index finger.]
He lived in a box.
    [Place in cupped left hand.]
He swam in a puddle
    [Move finger in circle.]
He climbed on the rocks.
    [Move up on left fingers.]
He snapped at a mosquito.
    [Snap right hand in air.]
He snapped at a flea.

He snapped at a minnow.
He snapped at me.
    [Snap toward self.]
He caught the mosquito.
    [Close right fist in air.]
He caught the flea.
He caught the minnow.
But he didn't catch me.
    [Point toward self, shake head.]

Two Telegraph Poles

Two tall telegraph poles
    [Pointer fingers erect.]
Across them a wire is strung.
    [Second fingers outstretched to touch between pointer fingers.]
Two little birds hopped on.
    [Thumbs to position against "wire."]
And swung, and swung, and swung.
    [Sway arms back and forth from body.]

Caterpillar

Roly-poly caterpillar
Into a corner crept,
Spun around himself a blanket,
Then for a long time slept.
Roly-poly caterpillar
Wakening by and by—
Found himself with beautiful wings,
Changed to a butterfly

Itsy, Bitsy Spider

Itsy, bitsy spider went up the water spout.
    [Hands make a climbing motion; or thumbs on index fingers of opposite hands, one after the other.]
Down came the rain and washed the spider out.
    [Drop hands.]
Out came the sun and dried up all the rain.
    [Arms circled overhead.]
Itsy, bitsy spider went up the spout again.
    [Make "spider" motion again.]

Grandmother

Here are grandmother's glasses,
    [Circle thumb and finger, each hand, over eyes.]
Here is grandmother's hat.
    [Fingertips together on head.]
This is the way she folds her hands
And puts them in her lap.

Ready for Bed

This little boy is ready for bed.
   [Hold up forefinger.]
Down on the pillow he lays his head.
   [Place finger in palm of opposite hand.]
Covers himself all up tight,
   [Fold fingers over forefinger.]
Falls fast asleep for the night.
   [Cock head toward shoulder, close eyes.]
Morning comes, he opens his eyes,
   [Quickly lift head, open eyes.]
Throws back the covers with great surprise,
   [Open palm to uncover forefinger.]
Up he jumps and gets all dressed,
   [Quickly raise forefinger off palm.]
To hurry to school to play with the rest.
   [Move finger off to the side.]

Five Little Soldiers

Five little soldiers standing in a row
Three stood straight and two stood so,
Along came the captain, and what do you think
They all stood up straight just as quick as a wink.

Five Little Pumpkins

Five little pumpkins sitting on a gate.
The first one said, "My it's getting late!"
The second one said, "There are witches in the air."
The third one said, "But we don't care."
The fourth one said, "Let's run, let's run!"
The fifth one said, "Isn't Halloween fun?"
"Woo-oo-oo" went the wind, out went the light.
Those five little pumpkins ran fast out of sight.

Supervisors and principals sometimes use finger play as a means of establishing acceptance on the part of little children. A principal who can teach a new one in the kindergarten will always be welcome. Froebel saw in this common interest a mystic relationship. Perhaps he was right. But it is obvious that these simple verses help children to speak better, notice sounds in words, learn about rhyming endings, and gain social recognition in a way that is pleasant to both the child and the teacher.

Action stories may be developed after the pattern of the old nursery rhyme in which one child says, "I went upstairs," and the other child replies, "Just like me." A leader tells a part of a story and the remainder of the group do the action saying at the same time, "Just like this."

LEADER: Goldilocks went for a walk in the forest.
GROUP: Just like this.
LEADER: She stopped to look at a bird.
GROUP: Just like this.
LEADER: The bird said, "Cheer up! Cheer up!"
GROUP: Just like this, "Cheer up! Cheer up!"

After reading the story *Copy-Kittens* by Helen and Alf Evans, the children may want to act it as it is reread. Other stories of this nature may be "played" as the beginning of creative dramatics.

For Discussion

1. How may a culturally different child be encouraged to practice new speech patterns through finger play?

2. What contemporary activities might be made into body play? Do the following suggest pantomime: airplane beacon, cars parking, flowers blooming, airplane landing?

3. How are finger plays related to the chants of childhood used when jumping rope or playing games? See Ione Opie and Peter Opie, *The Lore and Language of School Children* (London: Oxford University Press, 1959), or E. Brooks Smith and others, *Language and Thinking in the Elementary School* (New York: Holt, Rinehart and Winston, 1970), pp. 40–42.

What Values Are There in a Teacher's Poetry File?

A poetry file assures the teacher of having interesting material available. Most teachers prefer to put in the file a few old favorites which they know will be used. Without a file it sometimes takes hours to locate such well-known verses as E. L. Thayer's "Casey at the Bat" or Joaquin Miller's "Columbus." I remember visiting a school where everyone was searching for the latter poem. The principal greeted me by asking, "Do you remember that poem about Columbus that has the words 'sail on—sail on' in it?" At the time none of us could think of the author.

After teaching the same grade for some time, some teachers prefer to put favorite verse in a notebook classified by the months. The beginning teacher usually finds a card file most convenient. Then as the teacher borrows and clips, she selects those that are most useful. Nothing is so discouraging as to remember that you saw a clever verse which could be used in your class and not be able to locate it a second time. Clip and file until you have a collection that meets your needs.

There are many ways to organize such a collection. One heading might be *Holiday Poems*. Later these might be divided under the title *Halloween, Christmas, Valentine's Day*. Although there are many poems related to this topic, it is sometimes difficult to find one appropriate to your group.

Another broad category for a poetry file would be that of *Curriculum Enrichment*. In time this too could be divided into the various subjects.

In the first grade one teacher used the following poem while her class was studying the post office:

A Letter Is a Gypsy Elf

A letter is a gypsy elf
It goes where I would go myself;
East or West or North it goes;
Or South, past pretty bungalows,
Over mountain, over hill,
Any place it must and will,
It finds good friends that live so far
You cannot travel where they are.

ANNETTE WYNNE

In science these might be used.

Clouds

Over the hill the clouds race by
Playing tag in a blue, blue sky;
Some are fat and some are thin,
And one cloud has a double chin.

One is a girl with a turned up nose
And one wears slippers with pointed toes;
There's a puppy dog too, with a bumpity tail,
And a farmer boy with his milking pail.

Sometimes they jumble all in a mass
And get tangled up with others that pass,
And over the hill they go racing by
Playing tag in a blue, blue sky.

HELEN WING, *The Christian Science Monitor*

Cloud Names

Cumulus clouds
Drift over the sky,
Fluffy as soapsuds
Bellowing by.

Along the horizon
In layers of light
The stratus clouds glow
In the sunset bright.

Cirrus clouds hang
So loosely together
Their cottony film
Means a change of weather.

Nimbus clouds threaten
With blackness of storm
Shut the door, light the fire
Be cozy and warm.

LOS ANGELES CITY SCHOOLS

One of the major reasons for having children write poetry is to act as a release for strong feelings. Poems that express these feelings for children probably act the same way. There are some children who will find these poems delightful "because they say exactly how I feel." As a category for a poetry file they might be listed under *Expression of Strong Feelings*.

One Day When We Went Walking

One day when we went walking,
* I found a dragon's tooth,*
A dreadful dragon's tooth,
* "A locust thorn," said Ruth.*

One day when we went walking,
* I found a brownie's shoe,*
A brownie's button shoe,
* "A dry pea pod," said Sue.*

One day when we went walking,
  I found a mermaid's fan,
A merry mermaid's fan,
  "A scallop shell," said Dan.

One day when we went walking,
  I found a fairy's dress,
A fairy's flannel dress,
  "A mullein leaf," said Bess.

Next time I go walking—
  Unless I meet an elf,
A funny, friendly elf—
  I'm going by myself!

VALINE HOBBS

Choosing Shoes

New shoes, new shoes,
  Red and pink and blue shoes.
Tell me, what would you choose,
  If they'd let us buy?

Buckle shoes, bow shoes,
  Pretty, pointy-toe shoes,
Strappy, cappy low shoes,
  Let's have some to try.

Bright shoes, white shoes,
  Dandy-dance-by-night shoes,
Perhaps-a-little-tight shoes,
  Like some? So would I.

                    But
Flat shoes, fat shoes,
  Stump-along-like-that shoes,
Wipe-them-on-the-mat shoes,
  That's the sort they'll buy.

FFRIDA WOLFE

Presents

I wanted a rifle for Christmas,
I wanted a bat and a ball,
I wanted some skates and a bicycle,
But I didn't want mittens at all.

I wanted a whistle
And I wanted a kite,
I wanted a pocketknife
That shut up tight.
I wanted some boots
And I wanted a kit,
But I didn't want mittens one little bit!

I told them I didn't like mittens,
I told them as plain as plain.
I told them I didn't WANT *mittens,*
And they've given me mittens again!

MARCHETTE CHUTE

Probably the most charming of all poetry for children is that which takes the commonplace and then because of some rare insight of an adult into the child's world we have a chance to rediscover the simple ways of life again. It is childlike rather than childish. In your poetry file you will want a section on *Enrichment of Daily Life.* Those who work with primary children will especially want material by Dorothy Aldis. Another author for this age is Aileen Fisher, who wrote this favorite:

Coffeepot Face

I saw
my face
in the coffeepot.
Imagine
a coffeepot *face!*

My eyes
were small
but my nose was NOT
and my mouth
was—every place!

AILEEN FISHER

Probably the best-known verse of this type is this by Annette Wynne:

Indian Children

Where we walk to school each day
Indian children used to play
All about our native land,
Where the shops and houses stand.

And the trees were very tall,
And there were no streets at all,
Not a church and not a steeple,
Only the woods and Indian people.

Only wigwams on the ground,
And at night bears prowling round—
What a different place today
Where we live and work and play.

ANNETTE WYNNE

An example of poetry without rhyme that creates a mood is this poem by Beatrice Schenck De Regniers:

Little Sounds

Underneath the big sounds
underneath the big silences
listen for the little secret sounds.
Listen.
ts ts
That is the little sound of the sugar,
The little loaf of sugar
deep inside the cup of hot black coffee.
ts ts
That is what the sugar says.

Listen for the little secret sounds.
Sh! be very quiet and listen.
tck tck tck tck tck tck tck tck
That is the little sound of your father's watch.
tck tck tck tck tck tck tck tck
It makes such a tiny hurrying scurrying sound.

Listen for the little sounds always.
When a pussycat licks her fur
can you hear a little sound?
When someone is licking an ice-cream cone
can you hear?

Did you ever hear
a rabbit biting a lettuce leaf?
a cow switching her tail?
a tiny baby breathing?

Listen
to the little sound of
a letter dropping into a letter box,
a pin falling to the floor,
a leaf falling from a tree,
dry leaves crunching under your feet.

Listen to the little secret sound
of a pencil writing on paper,
of a scissors snipping your fingernails,
of a flower stem breaking when you pick a
  flower.

Listen for the little sounds always—
Listen.

BEATRICE SCHENCK DE REGNIERS

Primary teachers will want a special section for poems that can be told with the flannel graph. "Waiting at the Window" by A. A. Milne requires only three figures: two raindrops and a bright yellow sun. When the teacher first shares the poem, she guides the drops down. On the next telling, a child may do so. Eventually some children will learn the poem because it is so much fun to tell with these flannel figures.

Another that lends itself to a flannelboard presentation is "Mice," by Rose Fyleman.

Mice

I think mice are rather nice
Their tails are long,
Their faces small,
They haven't any chins at all,
Their eyes are pink
Their teeth are white
They run about the house at night
They nibble things they shouldn't touch
And no one seems to like them much,
But we think mice are nice.

ROSE FYLEMAN

Those verses which suggest a way to act will always be popular with teachers. Some of these suggest standards of conduct, others are gentle reminders, and a few use a bit of ridicule to guide behavior.

Little Charlie Chipmunk

Little Charlie Chipmunk was a talker
Mercy me!
He chattered after breakfast
And he chattered after tea
He chattered to his sister
He chattered to his mother
He chattered to his father
And he chattered to his brother
He chattered till his family
Was almost driven wild
Oh, Little Charlie Chipmunk
Was a very tiresome child.

HELEN COWLES LE CRON

Three Cheers for Peter

When Peter eats a lollypop
He doesn't walk or run or hop
He sits upon the bottom stair
Or in the kitchen on a chair
He doesn't try to chew or bite
Or swallow chunks; he just sits tight
And sucks. And he is careful not
To let it make a sticky spot
On furniture. Three cheers for Peter
He's a good safe candy eater.

ALICE HARTICH

You will find many verses that are worthy of a poetry file simply because they are fun and add humor to life. This would include limerick, nonsense verse, and those with clever use of words. The whimsical couplets of Ogden Nash are recorded with musical background. Children especially enjoy his "The Panther" (which ends with "Don't anther") and his "The Octopus."

A bit of wise-cracking doggerel like this has its place in your file:

Modern Light

Twinkle, twinkle little star
I know exactly what you are
You're a satellite in the sky
And why my taxes are so high.

Another group of verse in your file would be that which helps the child relate himself to all nature. In the fall there will be a time when children will sense the rhythm of nature when you read to them Rachel Field's "Something Told the Wild Geese." Once I observed a group of students on a hike who had earlier discovered a deer track on the road and were now listening with true appreciation to "The Tracks" by Elizabeth Coatsworth. The following poem employs delicate and sensitive imagery.

Soft Is the Hush of Falling Snow

I like the springtime of the year
When all the baby things appear;
When little shoots of grass come through
And everything is fresh and new.

But, oh, I like the summer, too.
When clouds are soft and skies are blue
Vacation days are full of fun
I like being lazy in the sun.

But when the fall has once begun
I'm glad that summer then is done
I love the frosty biting air
The harvest yield seen everywhere.

But winter is beyond compare
For though the world seems black and bare
It's rest time for the things that grow
And soft is the hush of falling snow.

EMILY CAREY ALLEMAN

This one would be appropriate for Arbor Day:

Trees

Trees are the kindest things I know;
They do no harm, they simply grow.
And spread a shade for sleepy cows,
And gather birds among their boughs.
They give us fruit in leaves above
And wood to make our houses of.
And leaves to burn on Halloween;
And in the spring new buds of green.
They are the first when day's begun
To touch the beams of morning sun.
They are the last to hold the light
When evening changes into night.
And when the moon floats in the sky
They hum a drowsy lullaby
Of sleepy children long ago.
Trees are the kindest things I know.

HARRY BEHN

Poetry has often been the form in which writers have presented an ideal or expressed religious thought. You will want a section of such inspirational material.

A Prayer for Little Things

Please, God, take care of little things,
The fledglings that have not their wings,
Till they are big enough to fly
And stretch their wings across the sky.

And please take care of little seeds,
So small among the forest weeds,
Till they have grown as tall as trees
With leafy boughs, take care of these.

And please take care of drops of rain
Like beads upon a broken chain,
Till in some river in the sun
The many silver drops are one.

Take care of small new lambs that bleat,
Small foals that totter on their feet,
And all small creatures ever known
Till they are strong to stand alone.

And please take care of children who
Kneel down at night to pray to you
Oh, please keep safe the little prayer
That like the big ones asks Your care.

ELEANOR FARJEON

Even arithmetic has been a subject for writers:

Counting

Today I'll remember forever and ever
Because I can count to ten.
It isn't an accident any more either,
I've done it over and over again.

I used to leave out five and three
And sometimes eight and four;
And once in a while I'd mix up nine
As seven or two, but not any more.

I count my fingers on one hand first,
And this little pig is one,
And when old thumb goes off to market
That's fine, and one of my hands is done.

So when I open my other hand
And start in counting again
From pick up sticks to big fat hen,
Five, six, seven, eight, nine and ten.

HARRY BEHN

The effect of reading a poem like "I Wish" by Nancy Byrd Turner or "A Mortifying Mistake" by Maria Pratt after a dull arithmetic period will justify all your efforts to create a poetry file.

A Mortifying Mistake

I studied my tables over and over, and
  backward and forward, too;
But I couldn't remember six times nine, and
  I didn't know what to do,
Till sister told me to play with my doll, and
  not to bother my head.

"If you call her 'Fifty-four' for a while, you'll
  learn it by heart," she said.

So I took my favorite, Mary Ann (though I
  thought 'twas a dreadful shame
To give such a perfectly lovely child such a
  perfectly horrid name),
And I called her my dear little "Fifty-four"
  a hundred times, till I knew
The answer of six times nine as well as the
  answer of two times two.

Next day Elizabeth Wigglesworth, who always
  acts so proud,
Said "Six times nine is fifty-two," and I nearly
  laughed aloud!

But I wished I hadn't when teacher said,
  "Now Dorothy, tell if you can."
For I thought of my doll—and sakes alive!—
  I answered, "Mary Ann!"

MARIA PRATT

Poetry which will help us understand other cultures is needed. Poems of this type follow.

From Korea:

Song of Five Friends

How many friends have I? Count them:
Water and stone, pine and bamboo—
The rising moon on the east mountain,
Welcome, it too is my friend.
What need is there, I say,
To have more friends than five?

They say clouds are fine; I mean the color.
But, alas, they often darken.
They say winds are clear; I mean the sound.
But, alas, they often cease to blow.
It is only the water, then,
That is perpetual and good.

Why do flowers fade so soon
Once they are in their glory?
Why do grasses yellow so soon
Once they have grown tall?
Perhaps it is the stone, then,
That is constant and good.

Flowers bloom when it is warm;
Leaves fall when days are cool.
But O pine, how is it
That you scorn frost, ignore snow?
I know now your towering self,
Straight even among the Nine Springs.

You are not a tree, no,
Nor a plant, not even that.
Who let you shoot so straight;
What makes you empty within?
You are green in all seasons,
Welcome, bamboo, my friend.

Small but floating high,
You shed light on all creation.
And what can match your brightness
In the coal dark of the night?
You look at me but with no words:
That's why, O moon, you are my friend.

author unknown

From Senegal:

Forefathers

Listen more often to things rather than beings.
Hear the fire's voice,
Hear the voice of water,
In the wind hear the sobbing of the trees,
It is our forefathers breathing.

The dead are not gone forever.
They are in the paling shadows
And in the darkening shadows.
The dead are not beneath the ground,
They are in the rustling tree,
In the murmuring woods,
In the still water,
In the flowing water,
In the lonely place, in the crowd;
The dead are not dead.

Listen more often to things rather than beings.
Hear the fire's voice.
Hear the voice of water.
In the wind hear the sobbing of the trees.
It is the breathing of our forefathers
Who are not gone, not beneath the ground,
Not dead.

                              author unknown

Children need to recognize the poetic appeal in material without rhyme.

Good Night

Many ways to spell good night.

Fireworks at a pier on the Fourth of July
*   spell it with red wheels and yellow spokes.*
They fizz in the air, touch the water and quit.
Rockets make a trajectory and gold-and-blue
*   and then go out.*

Railroad trains at night spell with a
*   smokestack mushrooming a white pillar.*

Steamboats turn a curve in the Mississippi
*   crying in a baritone that crosses lowland*
*   cottonfields to a razorback hill.*
It is easy to spell good night.
*   Many ways to spell good night.*

                              CARL SANDBURG

Theme in Yellow

I spot the hills
With yellow balls in autumn.

I light the prairie cornfields
Orange and tawny gold clusters
And I am called pumpkins.
On the last of October
When dusk is fallen
Children join hands
And circle round me
Singing ghost songs
And love to the harvest moon;
I am a jack-o'-lantern
With terrible teeth
And the children know
I am fooling.

                              CARL SANDBURG

Sharing poems related to the same topic will help children see the different point of view that each of us brings to a situation.

In these poems each writer is talking about houses. Do they agree in any way? Then share with them "Sometimes a Little House Will Please" by Elizabeth Coatsworth, "Our House" by Rachel Field, "Our House" by Dorothy Brown Thompson, and "Song for a Little House" by Christopher Morley.

Teachers will find that the building of such a file increases their own appreciation of poetic expression. However, what has been said concerning individual differences of pupils applies to teachers as well. If you do not truly feel some pleasure and delight in sharing poetry with children, possibly it will be well for you to spend time on those aspects of the curriculum about which you are enthusiastic. In a few cases you may learn with the children or from the children. Start where you are, even if the only poetry that stirs you in any way is the "Star Spangled Banner" or "Home on the Range." That is a beginning.

For Discussion

Evaluate two poems for preschool children, two for boys in the third grade, and two for a sixth-grade class. This bibliography will locate the sources for you. (Note that asterisked items are for primary grades only.)

Aldis, Dorothy. *Hello Day.* New York: G. P. Putnam's Sons, 1959.

————. *All Together.* New York: G. P. Putnam's Sons, 1952.

*————. *Is Anybody Hungry?* New York: G. P. Putnam's Sons, 1964.

Austin, Mary. *The Sound of Poetry.* Boston: Allyn & Bacon, Inc., 1963.

Behn, Harry. *The Little Hill.* New York: Harcourt Brace Jovanovich, Inc., 1949.

————. *Windy Morning.* New York: Harcourt Brace Jovanovich, Inc., 1956.

————. *The Wizard in the Well.* New York: Harcourt Brace Jovanovich, Inc., 1956.

————. *Cricket Songs: Japanese Haiku.* New York: Harcourt Brace Jovanovich, Inc., 1964.

Cole, William, ed. *Humorous Poetry for Children.* Cleveland: The World Publishing Co., 1955.

————, ed. *Beastly Boys and Ghastly Girls.* Cleveland: The World Publishing Co., 1964.

————, ed. *The Birds and the Beasts Were There: Animal Poems.* Cleveland: The World Publishing Co., 1963.

————. *Oh, What Nonsense!* New York: The Viking Press, Inc., 1966.

————. *Poems for Seasons and Celebrations.* Cleveland: The World Publishing Co., 1961.

* De Regniers, Beatrice Schenk. *Something Special.* New York: Harcourt Brace Jovanovich, Inc., 1958.

Fisher, A. *Cricket in a Thicket.* New York: Charles Scribner's Sons, 1963.

————. *Going Barefoot.* New York: Thomas Y. Crowell Co., 1960.

————. *Like Nothing at All.* New York: Thomas Y. Crowell Co., 1962.

* Frank, Josette. *Poems to Read to the Very Young.* New York: Random House, 1961.

Kuskin, Karla. *Alexander Soames: His Poems.* New York: Harper & Row, Publishers, 1962.

————. *In the Middle of the Trees.* New York: Harper & Row, Publishers, 1958.

————. *Square as a House.* New York: Harper & Row, Publishers, 1960.

————. *The Animals and the Ark.* New York: Harper & Row, Publishers, 1958.

————. *The Rose on My Cake.* New York: Harper & Row, Publishers, 1964.

Lewis, Richard. *In a Spring Garden.* New York: The Dial Press, Inc., 1965.

————. *The Moment of Wonder: A Collection of Chinese and Japanese Poetry.* New York: The Dial Press, Inc., 1964.

Livingston, Myra Cohn. *I'm Hiding.* New York: Harcourt Brace Jovanovich, Inc., 1961.

————. *See What I Found.* New York: Harcourt Brace Jovanovich, Inc., 1962.

* ————. *Wide Awake.* New York: Harcourt Brace Jovanovich, Inc., 1959.

McCord, David. *Far and Few.* Boston: Little, Brown and Co., 1925.

————. *Take Sky.* Boston: Little, Brown and Co., 1961.

Merriam, Eve. *Catch a Little Rhyme.* New York: Atheneum Publishers, 1966.

————. *It Doesn't Always Have to Rhyme.* New York: Atheneum Publishers, 1964.

————. *There Is No Rhyme for Silver.* New York: Atheneum Publishers, 1962.

Milne, A. A. *Now We Are Six.* New York: E. P. Dutton & Co., Inc., 1927.

————. *When We Were Very Young.* New York: E. P. Dutton & Co., Inc., 1924.

Nash, Ogden. *A Boy Is a Boy.* New York: Franklin Watts, Inc., 1960.

————. *Custard the Dragon.* Boston: Little, Brown and Company, 1959.

————. *Parents Keep Out.* Boston: Little, Brown and Company, 1951.

————, ed. *The Moon Is Shining Bright as Day.* Philadelphia: J. B. Lippincott, 1953.

————. *The Pocket Book of Ogden Nash.* New York: Pocket Books, Inc., 1955.

O'Neill, Mary. *Hailstones and Halibut Bones.* Garden City, N.Y.: Doubleday & Company, Inc., 1964.

————. *People I'd Like to Keep.* Garden City, N.Y.: Doubleday & Company, Inc., 1965.

————. *What Is That Sound?* New York: Atheneum Publishers, 1966.

————. *Words, Words, Words.* Garden City, N.Y.: Doubleday & Company, Inc., 1966.

Should a Teacher Read to Children?

There are many books that children enjoy and need to know before they have achieved the ability to read them independently. "Ear literacy" is far ahead of reading literacy throughout the elementary school. But there is more to justify reading aloud to children than just the child's inability to read. Shared experiences act as bridges between those involved. The quiet moments with a parent while Huckleberry Finn drifts down the Mississippi, or with an entire class as the teacher leads them through *Alice in Wonderland* or Dorothy's wonderful land of Oz, establish kindred spirits and high morale.

In many schools throughout the nation teachers read selected books to children. In the intermediate grades the first fifteen minutes after lunch is usually set aside for this purpose. While the pupils relax after strenuous play, the teachers read from old and new classics. Favorites include Lewis Carroll's *Alice in Wonderland,* Joel Chandler Harris' *Uncle Remus Stories,* Virginia Sorensen's *Miracles on Maple Hill,* L. Frank Baum's *The Wonderful Wizard of Oz,* E. B. White's *Charlotte's Web,* Betty MacDonald's *Mrs. Piggle Wiggle's Magic,* Kenneth Graham's *The Wind in the Willows,* Walter Edmond's *The Matchlock Gun,* Glen Round's *Blind Colt,* Lucretia Hole's *The Peterkin Papers,* Armstrong Sperry's *Call It Courage,* Hildegarde Swift's *Railroad to Freedom,* Alfred Olivant's *Bob, Son of Battle,* Rudyard Kipling's *The Jungle Book,* Howard Pyle's *Otto of the Silver Hand,* Glen Round's *Ol Paul the Mighty Logger,* A. Sommerfelt's *Road to Agra,* Margot Benary-Isbert's *The Ark,* Mark Twain's *The Adventures of Tom Sawyer,* and the many books about space travel.

One factor in reading difficulty is dialect. Some stories written for children are almost impossible for them to read aloud because they have no way to relate the dialect of the book to their experience. Only a teacher can present the *Uncle Remus Stories* properly (and then only with practice).

There are only a few hints that the teacher needs to remember to be a good oral reader.

First, enjoy the story yourself. If it is a book that you do not mind rereading as each new group of children comes to your room, you can be certain not only that the book is worthy of your efforts but that your appreciation will be sensed by the children. Second, interpret the mood and differentiate between the principal characters in dialogues; be a bit dramatic when the plot is exciting, but don't explain the action while reading. Let some of the new words be interesting enough for the children to discover their meaning from the context; if there is a moral, let the listener discover that too. Third, because of time limitations, scan a new book and note the good stopping places. Sometimes it spoils a story just as it does a movie to come in late or to have the film break in the middle of a scene. Finally, always keep in mind that your purpose is to guide the children toward an appreciation of good literature and excellent writing. This period is not a time to spend with material of only passing interest or mass-production quality. Let the children read the detective series or *The Scouts on Patrol,* but don't use these precious periods for such material.

Reading a picture book to little children requires special preparation. The books for kindergarten and primary children must be selected with care. Although little children will respond to almost any material presented by a teacher whom they love and respect, it should always be kept in mind that the materials read establish the standards the children will form for later reading. A book such as *Petunia* by Roger Duvoisin presents animals with childlike characters with which the child easily identifies. Humanized machines such as *Mike Mulligan and His Steam Shovel* or *The Little Engine That Could* tie together the worlds of fantasy and realism. The humanized animals of the old, old favorite *Peter Rabbit* continue to charm children because of their intimacy with all living things. Rhyme adds charm but is not necessary. To be avoided at this level are stories with dialect; fairy tales of giants, dragons, and cruel stepmothers; and stories that are overemotional or overexciting in tone.

The story should be short or in episodes that cover easily divided parts. Establish standards as to behavior during story reading. Routines should be known to all so that stories are expected at certain times or at a certain signal. Children should not be expected to stop an especially interesting activity without a "getting ready" or "finishing up" time. At the beginning, some teachers prefer to start the story hour with only a part of the group.

To regain a wandering child's attention, call him softly by name, or smile directly at him to bring his attention back to your voice. In some groups, the more mature may need to work together. This may be the beginning group for the story hour while others rest or color. The teacher usually does as much telling as reading, using the pictures in the book to guide the questions and interest of the listeners.

Although it may be handled well by some teachers, the retelling of the stories read by a child seldom holds the attention of other children. A story book brought from home should be identified as "Billy's book." After the teacher has examined the material, she may feel that the stories are appropriate for the group. Otherwise, a chance to see and talk about the pictures usually satisfies everyone.

To help some develop better habits, two children may be chosen to sit on each side of the teacher. These children in turn help show the pictures in the book. A special honor on a birthday or when there is a new baby at home might be to select an old favorite for the teacher to read that day. It is well to remember that some children have never listened to a story read to them before coming to school.

One of the major purposes of presenting a book to a child of this age is to enable him to select the book to peruse with pleasure by himself. Watch children as they thumb through a new set of library books. They will pick one up, glance through a few pages, then discard it for another. In many classrooms it is wisest to put books on the library table only after they have been read to the children. With this experience, the child can make a meaningful selection. Here

are nine suggestions for reading a picture book.

1. Gather the children closely around you either on low chairs or on the floor.
2. Sit in a low chair yourself.
3. Perform unhurriedly.
4. Handle the book so that children can see the pages at close range.
5. Know the story well enough so that you do not need to keep your eyes on the page at all times.
6. Point out all kinds of minute details in pictures so that pupils will look for them each time they handle the book later on.
7. Encourage laughter and spontaneous remarks.
8. Make illustrations as personal as possible by relating them to the pupils' own experiences.
9. Impart your own enjoyment of the book.

Many teachers feel that there should be no interruptions the first time a story is presented. With a picture book the reader and listener are involved in a rhythm of learning the words and seeing the pictures. The reader does not intrude anything, such as explanations of word meanings or personal reactions. Only her voice bridges the words and pictures of the story and the child. For some children and some books this is the only way a story should be read. In many cases the first reading of a story should proceed in this way so that the total book experience will be felt by the child. For some listeners attention could be diverted to an incident or picture that might interfere with the purpose of the author. For other books and other children careful attention to detail and involvement through personal association with story incidents enriches the experience. Experience will determine the most effective procedure for a new teacher.

Here is the way one teacher presented *Wag Tail Bess* by Marjorie Flack.

Boys and girls, the name of our story today is *Wag Tail Bess.* [*Run fingers under the title from left to right.*] Can anyone tell me what

Picture books are enjoyed when presented at eye level. Some should be seen first, then heard; some listened to, then examined; and others presented with a rhythm of listen and look. (*Courtesy of the Burbank Public Schools.*)

kind of a dog this is on the cover? [*Accept all suggestions.*] Maybe the story will tell us. [*Open the book.*] This is an envelope that shows that this book belongs to the library. This little card in the envelope says our class has the book and this slip of paper tells us when the book must go back to the library. This is done to remind us that other children would like to read the book when we have finished it. That is why children should not tear out such things. Sometimes inside the cover of a book there are very interesting pictures that tell us what the book is about. What do you see on these end papers? Yes, there is the dog again. There is an old friend of ours. Do you remember Angus? Do you think those are ducks or geese? Maybe the story will tell us. There is one other little animal on this page. Yes, there is a little kitten. You can just see his tail. [*Turn the page.*] This is the title page. There again is the title, "Wag Tail Bess." And this is the name of the person who wrote the story, Marjorie Flack. At the bottom it tells the name of the company that published the book. [*Turn the page and read.*]

Once there was an Airedale puppy. (*Aside:* Yes, you were right, John, the dog is an Airedale.) Once there was an Airedale puppy and she was named Wag Tail Bess because her mother's name was Bess and her father's name was Wags. But Wag Tail Bess never wagged her tail or stuck up her ears or smiled as an Airedale should, so she was called plain Bess.

Bess was so shy she was afraid of almost everything although she was big enough to know better. [*Look at the pictures of Bess.*] See how afraid she looks. [*Continue reading.*] When Bess was outdoors she was afraid to come indoors, and when she was indoors she was afraid to go outdoors. When Bess was taken walking she was afraid to walk forward, so she would try to walk backward, and when she couldn't go backward—she would lie down. [*Show the pictures.*] See how Bess would pull back. Notice the other dogs looking at Bess. What do you suppose they were thinking? [*Continue reading.*] Bess was even afraid to eat her dinner. She would sniff at it on this side and sniff at it on that side, until at last she would get so hungry she would gulp down her dinner without chewing it at all. [*When you reach the words* get so hungry, *read them slowly and show them to the children.*] Then Bess would be afraid because her tummy ached. [*Look at Bess.*] This is the way she would eat. This is the way she felt when her tummy ached. [*Continue reading.*] At nighttime Bess was afraid of a strange, black creature. Sometimes it was small and sometimes it was large, but always it would stay with Bess wherever she went; crawling on the floor and climbing up the stairs and down the stairs, and sometimes on the wall. What do you think it was? [*Show the picture.*] Yes, it was her shadow. How do you feel about Bess? Don't you feel a little sorry for her?

One day when Bess was outdoors because she was afraid to go indoors, she heard these sounds come from the yard next door: "Meowww! Quack, Quack! Wooof-Wooof!" [*Show the picture and repeat the sounds as you point at the words. Turn the page while the children are still watching the page. Read while they look.*] Then up in the tree jumped a cat! [*Again while they are looking at the book turn the page and while they look, read.*] Through the hedge came scuttling a duck, then came [*again read while they watch the action of the story in the pictures*] another duck! And then came [*turn the page*] Angus! (See the ducks and the cat and Angus. What will happen now? Well let's read and see.)

The foregoing excerpt is enough to show how one teacher would conduct a typical story hour session. Such a procedure takes time but it is effort well invested. A teacher who takes such pains to ensure her pupils a pleasant acquaintance with a picture book is providing those pupils with many later periods of recurring pleasure. They will relive in imagination all the activities she described, enjoy again the color and detail of the pictures, and rediscover familiar details in the scenes she has pointed out. The book will become a familiar friend which they will enjoy again and again.

The list of books that follows, prepared by Marie Taylor, has been classroom tested. However, success in one situation does not guarantee a response in another.[9]

---

[9] Marie E. Taylor, "Instant Enrichment," *Elementary English* (February 1968), pp. 229–33.

Kindergarten

Angelo the Naughty One, by Helen Garrett. Viking, 1944. Children love this story about a boy who hates to take baths.

Angus and the Ducks, by Marjorie Flack. Viking, 1944. A favorite picture book about a sassy, little Scotty. Other books in the series are *Angus Lost* and *Angus and the Cat.*

Bedtime for Frances, by Russell Hoban. Harper, 1960. A badger child tries to delay bedtime just as other children do.

The Biggest Bear, by Lynd Ward. Houghton, 1952. A Caldecott Medal Book about a boy's pet bear cub that becomes overwhelming when he grows up. *Nic of the Woods,* by the same author, is equally successful as a dog story.

Blueberries for Sal, by Robert McCloskey. Viking, 1948. Anticipation is strong in this story about Sal and her mother, and little bear and his mother, getting all mixed up while gathering blueberries.

Contrary Woodrow, by Sue Felt. Doubleday, 1958. About kindergarten and Valentine's Day.

The Country Bunny and the Little Gold Shoes, by DuBose Heyward. Houghton. 1939. A favorite Easter story.

Curious George, by H. A. Rey. Houghton, 1941. Only one of many monkey stories: *Curious George Flies a Kite; Curious George Learns the Alphabet; Curious George Goes to the Hospital;* and others.

Daddies, by Lonnie C. Carton. "Tender, amusing rhymes about daddies and their children."

Edith and Mr. Bear, by Darr Wright. Doubleday, 1964. All the Darr Wright books are highly recommended by one of our staff.

George and the Cherry Tree, by Aliki. Dial, 1964. One of the few simple picture books available for seasonal demand.

The Happy Lion, by Louise Fatio. McGraw, 1934. All the people who visited the zoo were the lion's friends until he got out of the cage. More titles in this series.

Make Way for Ducklings, by Robert McCloskey. Viking, 1941. A family of mallard ducks makes their home in the middle of Boston. Outstanding Caldecott Award book.

May I Bring a Friend? by Beatrice S. De Regniers. Atheneum, 1964. Children are carried away as each successive caller at the queen's tea party is more ridiculous. Rare illustrations and delightful rhymes.

No Roses for Harry, by Gene Zion. Harper, 1958. Indomitable Harry knows no self-respecting dog would wear a sweater with roses, even one knitted by Grandma.

Paddy's Christmas, by Helen Monsell. Knopf, 1942. A bear story with the subtle meaning of Christmas.

Read-to-Me Storybook, by the Child Study Association of America. Crowell, 1947. Excellent collection of contemporary stories for young children.

The Red Balloon, by Albert Lamorisse. Doubleday, 1957. An imaginative picture book that leads to discussion.

Rosebud, by Ed Emberly. Little, 1966. Delightful turtle story.

Swimmy, by Leo Lionni. Pantheon, 1963. Like *Rosebud,* a book for sharp eyes. *Inch by Inch,* by the same author-illustrator, uses the concept of size.

Told under the Blue Umbrella, by the Association for Childhood Education International. Macmillan, 1933. Excellent collection of recommended stories for children.

First Grade

Andy and the Lion, by James Daugherty. Viking, 1938. Andy, who likes to read about lions, meets one on his way to school. The thorn-pulling episode is a modern version of *Androcles and the Lion.*

Babar and Father Christmas, by Jean deBrunhoff. Random, 1949. A fine introduction to the other Babar books. Children squeal when Babar falls through the roof.

The Five Chinese Brothers, by Claire Bishop. Coward, 1938. A modern classic. Exaggeration and repetition delight youngsters.

The Gift of Hawaii, by Laura Bannon. Whitman, 1961. A little Hawaiian boy has "a great big love for his Mamma."

Hailstones and Halibut Bones, by Mary O'Neill. Doubleday, 1961. Intriguing book of verse that invites creativity with color.

Jeanne-Marie Counts Her Sheep, by Françoise. Scribner's, 1951. A simple story, picture, counting book.

Katy No-Pocket, by Emmy Payne. Houghton, 1944. An amusing story of how a mother kangaroo solves the problem of having no pocket.

Nine Days to Christmas, by Marie Hall Ets. Viking, 1959. A Caldecott book about a Mexican Christmas, introducing the pinata.

A Pocketfull of Cricket, by Rebecca Caudill. Holt, 1964. A quiet story about a boy's affection for his pet cricket and the first day of school.

Red Is Never a Mouse, by Eth Clifford. Bobbs, 1960. A book of color.

Ski Pup, by Don Freeman. Viking, 1963. Hugo, a Saint Bernard rescue dog, accidentally becomes a ski dog.

The Snowy Day, by Ezra Jack Keats. Viking, 1962. An experience in visual perception. A little boy tries out the snow.

The Story about Ping, by Marjorie Flack. Viking, 1933. A little duck in China does not wish to get a spank if he is the last one on board.

Time of Wonder, by Robert McCloskey. Viking, 1957. One can feel the fog and the other sensations of beach life at the ocean.

Where the Wild Things Are, by Maurice Sendak. Harper, 1964. A very imaginative monster book about a little boy who gets even after being sent to his room.

Whistle for Willie, by Ezra Jack Keats. Viking, 1964. Willie's day is full of the small discoveries of all children.

Second Grade

And to Think That I Saw It on Mulberry Street, by Dr. Seuss. Vanguard, 1937. Nonsense rhyme about a street where the ordinary becomes the extraordinary.

"B" Is for Betsy, by Carolyn Haywood. Harcourt, 1939. The day by day incidents in the Haywood books make them completely realistic and entertaining. At the end of the year good readers will enjoy reading them.

The Bears on Hemlock Mountain, by Alice Dalgleish. Scribner's, 1952. Everyone told Jonathan there were no bears on the mountain. Suspense mounts as Jonathan crosses the mountain.

Brighty of the Grand Canyon, by Marguerite Henry. Rand, 1953. Highly recommended, this story of a lone burro found by an old prospector has magnificent drawings of the Grand Canyon.

Charlotte's Web, by E. B. White. Harper, 1952. The gentle friendship of a pig, a spider, and a little girl who could talk to animals.

Clown Dog, by Lavinia Davis. Doubleday, 1961. A boy defends his dog in a new neighborhood until his pet becomes a hero by discovering an orphaned fawn.

Crow Boy, by Taro Yashima. Viking, 1955. A shy Japanese boy is recognized by his classmates through his teacher's understanding.

Down, Down the Mountain, by Ellis Credle. Nelson, 1961. Two Blue Ridge Mountain children want creaky-squeaky shoes more than anything else in the world.

Easter in November, by Lilo Hess. Crowell, 1964. A surprise Easter story about an unusual breed of chickens that hatches colored eggs.

Lentil, by Robert McCloskey. Viking, 1940. Lentil's harmonica saves the day. Illustrations large enough to be seen by the class.

Little Runner of the Longhouse, by Betty Baker. Harper, 1962. A much needed easy treatment of Iroquois life.

Marshmallow, by Clare T. Newberry. Harper, 1942. A pet cat cannot understand when a little white bunny comes to live at his home. Exceptional illustrations, fine story.

Mike's House, by Julia Sauer. Viking, 1954. Most second graders have been introduced to *Mike Mulligan and His Steam Shovel,* by Virginia Burton, and will chuckle at this story of a boy who makes no compromise with any other book.

Millions of Cats, by Wanda Gág. Coward, 1928. How does a little old woman choose one from millions of cats?

Reindeer Trail, by Berta and Elmer Hader. Macmillan, 1959. "How the fleet-footed reindeer brought to Alaska by the friendly Lapps, save the Eskimos from starving."

The Story of Helen Keller, by Lorena Hickel. Grosset, 1958. This version of a great lady's life is simple enough to be enjoyed by second and third grades.

Tom Tit Tot, illus. by Evaline Ness. Scribner's, 1965. The comic illustrations fit the "gatless" girl in this refreshing variation of Rumpelstiltskin.

Two Is Company, Three's a Crowd, by Berta and Elmer Hader. Macmillan, 1965. Fine to use when the geese are migrating. The story of how Big John and his wife feed a few and soon have more than they can handle.

Third Grade

The Borrowers, by Mary Norton. Harcourt, 1953. If you can't find your stamps or thimbles, the Borrowers are probably using them for pictures or footstools. One third grade constructed a home for the little people.

The Courage of Sarah Noble, by Alice Dalgleish. Scribner's, 1954. The true story of a brave little girl who, in 1707, went with her father into Indian territory.

Dancing Cloud, the Navajo Boy, by Mary Buff. Viking, 1957. Excellent story of Navajo life with striking full-spread illustrations.

The Enormous Egg, by Oliver Butterworth. Little, 1956. Young Nate Twitchell finds an oversized egg in his chicken nest that hatches into a baby dinosaur and complications.

Henry Huggins, by Beverly Cleary. Morrow, 1950. All the Henry books enthusiastically recommended.

Homer Price, by Robert McCloskey. Viking, 1943. Each chapter is its own story. *The Doughnuts* and *Super Duper* are samples of the humor.

The Indian and the Buffalo, by Robert Hofsinde. Morrow, 1961. This author has given us much authentic Indian material.

The Limerick Trick, by Scott Corbett. Little, 1960. Kerby needs to write a limerick to win a contest. A chemical mixture solves one problem but leads to another when Kerby finds he can't stop rhyming.

The Light at Tern Rock, by Julia Sauer. Viking, 1951. Excellent Christmas reading. A boy learns patience the hard way when he is forced to spend Christmas tending the lighthouse beacon.

Little House in the Big Woods, by Laura Ingalls Wilder. Harper, 1953. The entire Wilder series, depicting the author's childhood in the mid-west, is highly rated and always enjoyed.

Little Navajo Bluebird, by A. N. Clark. Viking, 1943. A fine picture of present day Navajo life.

Mary Poppins, by P. L. Travers. Harcourt, 1962. Remarkable things happen when Miss Poppins blows in as the new Nanny.

The Matchlock Gun, by Walter Edmonds. Dodd, 1941. Historical fiction set in the Mohawk Valley during the French and Indian War. A boy is left to protect the family when the father answers the call for help from a settlement under attack.

The Nightingale, by Hans C. Andersen; illus. by Harold Berson. Lippincott, 1963. A fine retelling of a favorite story.

The Nutcracker, translated by Warren Chappell. Knopf, 1958. An excellent selection for Christmas. May be used with the music.

The Otter's Story, by Emil Liers. Viking, 1953. Like *The Beaver's Story,* recommended as an absorbing, unsentimental animal story.

Paddle-to-the-Sea, by Holling C. Holling. Houghton, 1941. An Indian boy carves a toy canoe and launches it in the waters of northern Canada. The story traces its journey through the Great Lakes, over the Falls, into the Atlantic. Striking illustrations showing landscape and industry native to the area.

Tatsinda, by Elizabeth Enright. Harcourt, 1963.

A fantasy with weird creatures, strange names, and a little girl pursued because she is different.

A Weed Is a Flower: the Life of George Washington Carver, by Aliki. Prentice, 1965. Fine introduction to biography.

Fourth Grade

Away Goes Sally, by Elizabeth Coatsworth. Macmillan, 1934. Sally moves from New England to Maine wilderness in the original house trailer—a log cabin on runners.

The Bee Man of Orn, by Frank Stockton. Holt, 1964. A man wishes to live his life over. The surprise ending delights the children.

The Children of Green Knowe, by L. M. Boston. Harcourt, 1955. A beautifully written fantasy. Children will differ about what is real and what is imagined.

Chitty-Chitty-Bang-Bang, by Ian Fleming. Random, 1964. A magic car becomes a boat or airplane when the family escapes from gangsters. Highly recommended.

Ice King, by Ernestine Byrd. Scribner's, 1965. Sensitive story of a friendship between an Eskimo boy and a bear orphaned by hunters.

The Magic Bed-Knob, by Mary Norton; in *Bed-Knob and Broomstick.* Harcourt, 1957. Sheer fantasy about English children and their magician friend who gets the book off to a fine start when she falls off her broomstick and sprains her ankle.

Mama Hattie's Girl, by Lois Lenski. Lippincott, 1953. This regional book gives meaning to the place of the Negro in the North and South and is also excellent for the relationship between child and grandmother.

Misty of Chincoteague, by Marguerite Henry. Rand, 1947. A captivating horse story that begins with Pony Penning Day, still held on Chincoteague Island.

The Moffats, by Eleanor Estes. Harcourt, 1941. A family story full of humorous incidents. The Halloween chapter is hilarious.

Navajo Sister, by Evelyn Lampman. Doubleday, 1956. Excellent tale about the adjustment necessary when Navajo children leave the reservation for boarding school.

Pippi Longstocking, by Astrid Lindgren. Viking, 1950. A Swedish story about an uninhibited little girl who lives by herself and does only what she pleases in very unusual ways.

The Shy Stegosaurus of Cricket Creek, by Evelyn Lampman. Doubleday, 1955. George is the dinosaur who escaped extinction.

Strawberry Girl, by Lois Lenski. Lippincott, 1945. A realistic story about a family of Florida Crackers; strong regional background.

Stuart Little, by E. B. White. Harper, 1945. Ths mouse-man has been a "smash" in one fourth grade. "Good for the first day of school."

Wind in the Willows, by Kenneth Grahame. Scribner's, 1961. A classic that few children will enjoy unless it is first shared aloud.

The Witch of Blackbird Pond, by Elizabeth Speare. Houghton, 1958. Excellent background of Puritan America and the witchcraft movement. A Newbery Medal winner.

Young Mark Twain and the Mississippi, by Kane Harnett. Random House, 1966. One of the excellent Landmark Series.

Fifth Grade

And Now Miguel, by Joseph Krumgold. Crowell, 1953. Authentic picture of sheep raising in New Mexico and a boy who longs to become a man.

The Animal Family, by Randall Jarrell. Pantheon, 1965. A mystic story of a woodsman, a mermaid, and the animals. Like *The Children of Green Knowe,* children will puzzle over the story.

Call It Courage, by Armstrong Sperry. Macmillan, 1940. A South Sea Island boy, shamed by the tribe, redeems himself by his bravery. Adventure at its best.

The Complete Peterkin Papers, by Lucretia Hale. Houghton, 1960. The uninhibited Peterkin family find solutions peculiar only to them. Ridiculous humor.

Farmer Boy, by Laura Ingalls Wilder. Harper, 1933. "Good to show how people lived before modern conveniences." Early New York State.

The Gold-Laced Coat, by Helen Fuller Orton. Lippincott, 1934. Fine to read before a field trip to an early American fort. This setting is Ft. Niagara.

The Island of the Blue Dolphins, by Scott O'Dell. Houghton, 1960. Based on the actual life of the sole inhabitant of the island, this Newbery winner has had great appeal for intermediate grades.

Li Lun, Lad of Courage, by Carolyn Treffinger. Abingdon, 1947. A courageous boy proves himself by achieving the impossible on a mountain.

Miss Pickerell Goes to Mars, by Ellen MacGregor. McGraw, 1951. Miss Pickerell shuddered at the thought of a Ferris wheel or stepladder. Her jaunt on a spaceship is a complete surprise. One of many in a series.

Pancakes-Paris, by Claire Bishop. Viking, 1947. A realistic story about a typical friendship between a French boy and American soldiers during World War II. A little French vocabulary.

Road to Agra, by Alic Sommerfelt. Criterion, 1967. Boy and sister make a long journey to gain help from World Health Association.

Shadow of a Bull, by Maia Wojciechowska. Atheneum, 1964. The future is decided for the nine-year-old son of a famous bull-fighter when he is born. A fine treatment of a child's reaction to public pressure in a setting rare to children's literature. A Newbery Award winner.

The Talking Tree, by Alice Desmond. Macmillan, 1949. A fine book for the study of Alaska; about totem poles and a young Tlingit Indian who must reconcile past with present.

Twenty and Ten, by Claire Bishop. Viking, 1952. Twenty school children in France befriend ten Jewish children fleeing from the Gestapo during World War II.

Sixth Grade

Adam of the Road, by Elizabeth Gray. Viking, 1942. An interesting picture of life in 13th century England.

Aunt America, by Marie Halun Block. Atheneum, 1963. Life behind the Iron Curtain. Children need to understand the concepts of freedom.

The Bronze Bow, by Elizabeth Speare. Houghton, 1961. An unusual setting portraying the hatred of the Jews for their Roman conquerors during the time of Christ. Used before Easter each year by one fifth-grade teacher. A Newbery Medal book.

The Christmas Carol, by Charles Dickens. Many editions. The descriptive flavor of Dickens' words are not heard in the television versions.

The Door in the Wall, by Marguerite deAngeli. Doubleday, 1949. A crippled boy, despairing in a society of medieval knighthood, triumphs over his handicap. Excellent background for monastic and feudal study. A Newbery winner.

Follow My Leader, by James Garfield. Viking. A boy adjusts to blindness at the age of eleven.

The Incredible Journey, by Shelia Burnford.

Little, 1961. Fascinating adventure of a motley group of animals traveling together.

It's Like This, Cat, by Emily Neville. Harper, 1963. Sophisticated sixth graders will enjoy this story of New York City and a boy who never quite understands his parents, and vice versa. A Newbery book.

The Loner, by Ester Wier. McKay, 1963. Excellent character study of a boy who travels with migrants until he meets "Boss" and desperately wants to please her. Fine picture of sheep raising.

Martin Rides the Moor, by Vian Smith. Doubleday, 1965. A wild pony is the salvation of a boy deafened by an accident.

My Name Is Pablo, by Alice Sommerfelt. Criterion, 1966. Youth problems in Mexico City.

Onion John, by Joseph Krumgold. Crowell, 1959. A close friendship develops between the boy and the town junk man. Excellent human relations: humorous but realistic.

Second Hand Family, by Richard Parker. Bobbs, 1965. An up-to-date treatment of teen age interests. Concerns a group who play rock and roll. Enjoyed by pre-teens.

The White Panther, by Theodore Waldeck. Viking, 1941. A fast-moving story about a panther stalked by man and beast because he was born white.

A Wrinkle in Time, by Madeleine L'Engle. Farrar, 1962. Science fiction at its best.

For Discussion

1. Can you recall the names of any of the books your teachers read aloud to your class in school?

2. Do parents still read aloud to children at home?

3. What other sources are available for read-aloud stories?

4. How would you handle the criticism that reading aloud to a class is just entertaining the children when you should be teaching them?

5. Review the section on storytelling for children with special needs as presented in Lena L. Gitter, *The Montessori Way* (Seattle, Wash.: Special Child Publications, 1970, pp. 164–206). (The address of Special Child Publications is 71 Columbia St., Seattle.)

How May Book Reports Be Effectively Used in the Classroom?

Surveys of the school subject preferences of children usually reveal that language class is rated the favorite by one in ten, but is the least liked by about three in ten. Within the specifics of the language course the item most frequently listed as the least preferred is book reporting. It is probably safe to assume that book reporting has not been a very popular activity with many children.

There are a number of reasons why this may be so. At one time children were required to read a prescribed number of books from a specific list each month or each report-card period. The books were frequently not appropriate to the readers and the motivation was one of coercion. It may not have been so distasteful to read the books, but to be required to review them in prescribed uniform style was an artificial writing assignment. Frequently whole classes would cheat as they shared reviews or copied from book summaries found in libraries.

Dr. Charles Boehm, State Superintendent of Public Schools in Pennsylvania, expressed a concern of many teachers when he wrote: [10]

Why don't more students seek . . . out [good books]? Because we discourage them. We make reading a penalty. We insist that our pupils write book reviews, naming the principal characters and important events in a format unchanging for a hundred years. So our youngsters read the short, the concise, the easily remembered books. And teachers should be the last to criticize them. The challenging, the thought-provoking books are to be shunned because teachers want only dates and names.

A related reason for the unpopularity of this activity is what has been described as the "F.B.I. approach" to literature. The teacher's purpose might be stated: "Has the child really read the book? Has he just leafed through or looked at the pictures? He must answer certain questions so I'll be sure that he read it."

---

[10] C. Boehm, "What You Don't Know About Your Schools," *Saturday Evening Post* (May 14, 1960), p. 37.

Another approach is that of account keeping. This listing of books often incorporates a competitive spirit. The slow reader is naturally going to feel embarrassed if others read ten books while he reads only two.

In a third grade one teacher reports stimulating a high interest in books which the children were to select independently. A rule accepted by the group was that once a book selection was made, that book was to be completed. One child selected an excellent but long and difficult book. She was still reading this while other children were on a second or third book. Because a public record was kept, this had an effect. The next book she selected was short and had many pictures. Because the element of competition is difficult to eliminate, this factor can be corrected by allowing a number of points for each book, so that the more difficult ones will be allotted more points and thus will not be avoided.

There are many worthy purposes for book reports. First, reports are a way of learning from the reading of others. When a child has had a reading adventure or learned some interesting information, others like to share it with him. Second, reading can be motivated by a report. One child's stamp of approval on a book will encourage others to want to read it. "Even the boys will like Laura," exclaimed one child after reading *Little House on the Prairie*. Third, reports meet a social need. Sharing the fun of *Freddie, the Detective* is as important in the conversation of fourth-graders as discussing the current best seller is among adults. Fourth, specifics need to be noticed for complete appreciation. Such specifics can include an author's use of words, descriptive passages, or illustrations. Fifth, reports give recognition to children. For many children reading a book is an achievement. Each one is a trophy that attests to greater mastery of a complex skill that has been put to use. Sixth, reports tell the teacher about the child's interests and needs. Misinterpretation or confusion revealed in a report indicate special needs that guide the teacher in planning work with the child. Although literature is largely for enjoyment and appreciation, the reading process can be observed and help can be given in its improvement so that further experiences in literature will prove more satisfying and rewarding.

In all grades, both oral and written reports are used. Oral reports require careful direction and planning to be worthy of the attention of the class. Time required to prepare peep shows, cartoon strips, dioramas, dressed characters, flannelboard figures, and other such accessories for book reports is often questioned. Some children have both the time and interest needed to make such comment and such visual devices add to the effectiveness of a presentation. A balanced approach in terms of the over-all needs of a child must play a part in any consideration by the teacher.

Primary children may give book reports as a part of the sharing period. Or an opening exercise one morning a week might emphasize books they find interesting. At such times teachers make suggestions like the following: Show only the cover of a book and tell why the reader liked it. Show one picture and incite curiosity as to what is happening in the story. Show a sea shell, leaf, model airplane, space ship, or rock, that some books explain. Show a flannelboard figure or a picture for a part of a story read by a child. Form a book club and follow a simple outline in making reports. Such an outline might include:

1. What kind of a story is it? Is it true?
2. What is it about?
3. Is it about this country or some other? When did it happen?
4. What are the pictures like?
5. Is the book easy to read?
6. Who wrote the story? Do we know any other stories by that person?

These items are only suggestive. Certainly every book does not fit into the use of each question. Any item by item checking can become monotonous. We merely want to help children become conscious of the many qualities that books have and the substance that develops real appreciation of literature.

The following forms have been used by teachers:

READ FOR FUN

Name _____ Date _____

Book title _____

Main character _____

People who like
_____animal stories
_____stories about children
_____stories about _____

_____adventure stories
_____funny stories
_____exciting stories

will like this book.

Did you enjoy this book? _____

It was
_____easy to read.
_____hard to read.
_____just right.

(Used in Grade 2)

(Grades 3 and 4)

BOOK REPORT

Name of book _____

Author _____

Illustrator (if any) _____

Name some of the characters: _____

_____

Tell which character you liked best _____

_____

_____

The part of the book I liked best was _____

_____

_____

_____

_____

Do *one* of these things:
  1. Tell your class part of the story.
  2. Make a picture.
  3. Make something suggested by book.

My name is _____ Room No. _____

Intermediate children have a wider range of possibilities with respect to book reports, both because of greater maturity in oral language and in writing facility and because of greater breadth of reading interests. The purposes of reporting are to interest others in expanded reading, to share information, to communicate the pleasure of ideas from reading, and to emphasize the achievement of having read a book that was significant for one reason or another to the reader. Often children themselves have useful suggestions for accomplishing these purposes. The person who read the book pretends to be one of the characters. The audience is to guess the name of the book from what he says or does. A series of clues may be given and the listeners and observers may write down the name of the book opposite the number of the clue. These guessing games give all children a chance to participate. Or a group of children may present a panel. They may discuss a book they have all read, or the subject "Dog or Horse Stories I Have Liked."

A good way to emphasize authorship is to have a "Lois Lenski Day" or a "Newbery Award Day (or Week)." Students may be curious to find the qualities that made certain books worthy of awards. Such qualities as characterization, picturesque words, descriptive passages, ingenious plot, appropriate illustrations, imaginative humor, and range of experiences take on meaning and importance as children learn to recognize them. The group might create an award for a favorite book.

An oral synopsis of a story is good practice in arranging events in sequence and in learning how a story progresses to a climax. It also helps children who are interested in writing stories of their own.

Broadcasting a book review over the public-address system or radio is a challenge for careful preparation and ingenuity in planning sound effects, background music, or dramatic reading. Clear enunciation and good voice modulation will also be important.

Telling a story, telling about a new book, or reading a small excerpt to another class may be good for the child who wants to share the experience, and it may stimulate the audience to learn more about the book or others by the same author.

During an informal "book club" session the students meet in small groups and talk about books they have read. The object is to whet the book appetites of the group.

An oral comparison of two books related in theme is a good exercise in critical evaluation. The problems of the Negro girls in *Shuttered Windows* by Florence Means and *Mary Jane* by Dorothy Sterling might be compared; so, too, the humor in the *Paul Bunyan Stories* might be compared with that in *Pippi Longstocking.*

Such projects as constructing a miniature stage, making preparations for a television show, planning and decorating a bulletin board, dressing dolls as book characters, impersonating book characters, and planning quiz programs about books may all on occasion stimulate interest in both oral and written reports. Displaying such related objects as a cowbell for Heidi, wooden shoes for Hans Brinker, a Japanese doll, travel pictures, or pioneer relics are good devices for variation in vitalizing both reading and reporting. In social studies the study of a country can be personalized through a story character, thus providing broader understanding of both the literature and the geography of the country.

Written reports may take many forms. Letters of appreciation may be written to authors or librarians. A letter to a friend or relative recommending a book should actually be mailed. Advertisements may be written for the school paper, a bulletin board, or a book jacket. Short reviews may be written for "We Recommend" bulletin boards or for "Before You Read" or "My Opinion" scrapbooks. Sometimes the local paper will publish well-written book reviews. Some classes keep a file of brief summaries which is consulted when a child wants a certain type of book. These are usually limited to a few sentences. Some children like to keep a "Personal Reading Notebook" in the form of a diary, like the one on the following page.

Teachers have developed many techniques to encourage children to read widely. A bulletin board on which each child has a small book in which to record the titles and authors of each book read is quite popular. Sometimes this is done on a bookshelf and each child has a cardboard-bound book cover in which to do his recording so that the bulletin boards are not occupied for such a long period of time. One class used the space idea by putting the name of each new book read on a small paper satellite. The caption was, "We Are Really Orbiting."

Children sometimes are inclined to limit their reading to a single interest. To encourage a more balanced reading program, teachers sometimes use a reading wheel which is divided into areas of biography, foreign lands, animals, science, adventure, or folklore. As each child reads a book his name is placed in the proper area on the wheel. The object is to have one's name in each area. Scott, Foresman and Company, Chicago, provides a free wall chart designed to encourage a well-rounded program in reading. The *News-Journal* of North Manchester, Indiana, has several forms of "My Reading Design" which also serve this purpose.

Another plan to widen the reading interest involves the use of a map. The object is to "Take a World Cruise" or "See America First." Books appropriate to each region are suggested. Sweden might be represented by "The Sauce Pan Journey," France by "The Big Loop." After a book is read about one country or area the child moves on to the next until the tour is completed.

Bulletin boards or charts frequently motivate the reading of a book. The teacher might make a list under the title, "These Are Miss Smith's Favorites." A group of children might list others under such titles, "Books Every Boy Should Know," "We Recommend for First Purchase," "Interesting Travel Books," "Girl's Favorites," "Books to Grow On," "Books About This Area."

In most situations the reading is more important than the reporting. The teacher needs to know the quality of the child's reading to be sure he is getting the most from each reading adventure. This can be done in class situations through observances of a child reading independently, in teacher–pupil conferences, and in some of the discussions and

PERSONAL READING NOTEBOOK

Here are some ways in which information about the things in my book have helped people:

_____

_____

_____

Below are some unsolved problems or questions (about things in my book) which scientists are still working on:

_____

_____

_____

I recommend this book because _____

_____

Name _____ Date _____

MY BOOK REPORT

Title _____

Author _____ Number of pages _____

Illustrator _____

The biographer (one who writes about a real person) tells the following childhood incident in the life of his subject:

_____

_____

_____

The subject of the biography is:

_____

The following people were important in helping this real person to grow into a famous adult:

_____

_____

A problem which this person had to overcome was:

_____

This person overcame his problem in this way:

_____

_____

This person had the following characteristics which I admire:

_____

_____

I think the most exciting adventure which this person had was:

_____

_____

_____

reporting that he does. There is no need for a report on every book. Some children need more of these reporting experiences than other children. In the final analysis the best reports may be a child's heartfelt spontaneous statement, "Miss Jenkins, do you know another like that?"

For Discussion

1. If your state has a Reading Circle try to learn these things about it. How are books selected? What motives are given the children for reading these books?

2. Do you feel the criticism of book reports is justified in terms of your own experience?

3. How can we prevent embarrassment for a child who must read books much below the reading level of others in the class?

4. Do you think book reports might be individualized? One child might limit his report to those new words he learned; another might limit his to finding an interesting sentence.

How Do Teachers Become Effective Storytellers?

There are no basic rules to ensure the proper telling of a story. Some of the greatest story craftsmen cannot agree as to best methods to use. Storytelling is as individual an art as acting or playing a musical instrument. Each person must develop his own techniques, style, and selection of stories to suit his taste and abilities.

There are a few basic considerations, however, upon which most storytellers agree. First, the story must be appropriate to the audience. The very young child likes simple folk tales, but he does not respond to stories that are completely make-believe, with goblins, elves, and fairies. He does not understand the completely abstract. There must be some elements in the story that relate to his personal experiences. In the story of "The Three Bears" we have chairs, beds, bowls of soup, and activities which are familiar. Having them associated with bears adds mystery and

adventure but the events are familiar, everyday experiences. The child accepts the unreal because it is close enough to the real world he knows.

Little children love rhymes and jingles and many old story favorites have a marked rhythmic quality. In stories this rhythm is the result of repetition of words and phrases in a set pattern. Such phrases as "Not by the hair of your chinny-chin-chin," or "Then I'll huff and I'll puff and I'll blow your house in," always bring delighted responses.

Children like to play with words. That is the way words become more meaningful and a lasting part of their vocabulary. Children cannot keep from repeating "a lovely, light, luscious, delectable cake" as the teacher reads "The Duchess Bakes a Cake." In telling some stories the teller prepares the listeners by saying, "This story contains some wonderful new words. One of them is _____ which means _____; another is _____ which means _____. Listen for them." One or two words presented before a story would be enough. The story will do considerable teaching by providing context for the words.

Make-believe is most important to children in the years from six to ten, because it helps them understand the world about them and increases their imaginative powers. In the stories that they read and hear the youngsters are the heroes, at least for the time being. They know they are pretending, but as the story unfolds, each boy is Jack the Giant Killer and each girl is Cinderella.

Second, the storyteller knows that some stories are good to tell and that other stories are better to read such as *Winnie the Pooh* or *The Jungle Book*. A story for telling must be simple and direct. The plot must be strong and develop rapidly. In storytelling there is no place for long analyses of characters or situations. The mental pictures must be supplied by a few words or a phrase. Each incident must be vivid and clear-cut in the listener's mind. The climax must be emotionally satisfying. This can be a surprise, the solution of a problem, or something achieved.

The charm of simplicity can best be learned through experience. We know that children respond to cumulative repetition, such as one finds in "The Gingerbread Boy." They want the characters to talk. Descriptions are simple because children supply so much with their own imaginations. Good must triumph, but it is all right for the bad people to be very bad as long as in the end they are punished. Some prefer stories of animals to those with people in them. For many, the gentle stories about raindrops, flowers, and insects are a new discovery in contrast to the rapid pace of television and movie cartoons. A story that lasts six or eight minutes is quite long enough and many favorites take less time than that.

"The Three Little Pigs" is an example of a good story for telling little children. Each step is an event. No time is spent in explanation or unnecessary description. The story tells what the characters did and said and the events are linked in the closest kind of sequence. There are no breaks and no complexities of plot. Each event presents a clear, distinct picture to the imagination.

Ordinarily it is wisest not to change traditional stories. If you question any element in a story it is usually best to select another story. There is a trend in the direction of removing much of the horror aspects of the old folk material. The three bears are now friendly bears. They are provoked by Goldilocks because she enters their home without permission. The wolf now chases Red Riding Hood's grandmother into a closet instead of devouring her. In the original version of the "Three Billy Goats Gruff" the troll had his eyes gouged out and was crushed to death. In the modern version he is merely butted into the river and swims away unscathed, never to return. The first two of the Three Little Pigs are no longer eaten by the wolf but make an exciting escape to the house of the wise pig.

Any idea that may cause the young child to lie awake at night is best omitted from the program. It is well to discuss make-believe with children. Let them be assured that there are really no dragons and that wolves are unlikely visitors in the suburbs. Even such innocent stories as "Little Black Sambo" have caused nightmares of being chased by a tiger. Much depends, of course, on how seriously the story is read.

Another common theme in many of the old tales is the cruelty of stepparents and other kin related by remarriage. Stereotypes which stigmatize kin, old age, or social groups have no place in the story hour.

A discussion before reading some of these stories can take care of such questionable elements. The story of a good stepmother like Abraham Lincoln's provides a balance to "Cinderella." There are many good and kind old ladies to offset the cruel old hag in Hansel and Gretel. Teachers should remember that the horror that an adult senses in a story such as "Snow White" is quite different from a child's point of view. Torture and even death have only incidental significance for many children. Death is frequently an acceptable solution to a problem. Children play Cowboys and Indians, "good guys" and "bad guys," with violent shouts, agonizing mock deaths, and melodramatic hardships one moment and listen with rapt attention to a poem of delicate beauty the next.

Sometimes children themselves will suggest changes in these stories. This frequently happens as they dramatize a story. Another interesting variation on the traditional material is to put the characters in a new situation. Make up a story of visiting the Three Bears for Christmas or let Cinderella go to school.

Third, a storyteller knows that preparation is needed to make a story vivid to listeners. After a careful reading, put the story aside and think about it until you can picture the story to yourself, clearly in all details. Check any doubts by reading the story again. It is better for a beginning storyteller to know a few stories well than to attempt so many that none can be told with complete confidence. The "tell it again" quality of stories is a great safeguard for beginners. Any storyteller is almost sure to tell a story better each additional time he tells it. A beginner might plan an introduction, plan the sequence of the events, plan an ending, and then practice telling it aloud by himself.

And fourth, a storyteller knows that the audience must be comfortable and free from interruptions during the story, and that the story must end before the audience becomes weary or bored. Wait a few moments before starting a story so that there is a hush of expectancy in the room. If some children are inattentive or noisy, pause until quiet is restored. If many grow restless it is quite obvious that you have the wrong story. Don't blame the children, just say, "I guess this isn't the right story, so let's stand up and stretch." Then go on with some other group activity such as marching, singing, or finger play. Start another story only when there is expectancy and readiness for wholehearted listening.

Certain devices can be used to hold the attention of listeners. When Hans Christian Andersen entertained the children of Denmark with his stories, he used to cut out silhouettes in order to make his characters more vivid. In ancient China the storyteller would cast shadows to illustrate the characters in his tales of magic and ancient ways. The modern movie cartoon favorites use a combination of silhouette figures and movement to hold attention. In the modern classroom the flannelboard provides the story-teller with the means of achieving similar types of movement, magic, and characterization.

As the child listens to the storyteller, his visual attention is focused on characters and movement as figures are moved about on the flannelboard. These figures are cutouts representing the main characters. On the back of each item used, the storyteller pastes a bit of flannel or sandpaper so that it will adhere to the flannelboard.

Flannelboard stories should be looked upon as a means of stimulating the imagination and improving the quality of oral language of children. Many teachers find that permitting children to make their own flannelboard stories and telling them helps children to expand their language power, self-confidence, and creative talents. Another propect is the emotional release that can be observed in some children as they plan, cut out, and manipulate figures to illustrate some story they especially like or that they create.

A flannelboard aids both the storyteller and the listeners. (*Courtesy of the Burbank Public Schools.*)

Although the term *flannelboard* is used here, the device may be made with felt or coat lining. Those made for children's games are sometimes sprayed with "flocking." A store that specializes in window-display materials will have this for sale. If flannel is used, get the heaviest available. Coat lining is usually obtainable from a dry goods store. If you have a large bulletin board which you wish to cover, use felt or coat lining. This will cost about $10 or $12. Each figure needs to have a large piece of flannel or felt glued to the reverse side. Then as it is placed on the board the teller should run his fingers over the figure, causing it to adhere to the board. Some use rough sandpaper or flocking on the figure. For some figures bits of flannel about an inch square in three or four places serve to hold better than one large piece.

Children seem to respond better to cutouts made of bright and heavy construction paper than to drawn figures. Apparently cutouts allow more scope for the imagination. However, illustrations cut from books and made into figures for the flannelboard also appeal to them. In a sense this type simply transfers the book illustrations to the flannelboard. Faces and clothes can be drawn with ink or wax crayon, or made of bits of construction paper pasted to the figure.

Some stories need scenic backgrounds—a big woods, a lake, a castle. Rather than make these of paper it is easier to draw them with crayon on a large piece of flannel. Then the figures will stick to the scenery as the story is told. Regular outing flannel that costs about 49¢ a yard is good for this purpose.

Most flannelboards are made of plywood or heavy composition cardboard about two feet wide and three feet long. The felt or flannel should be about 3 feet by 4 feet in order to allow adequate overlap on the back of the plywood. Staples from a regular paper stapler will hold it well. Do not glue the flannel to the board, as the glue reduces the static charge that causes the figures to adhere. The size should be large enough to hold the figures, but not so large that it is uncomfortable to carry or awkward to store away. Some teachers like to have handles on the board, others hinge them so they will fold. It costs about as much to make a board

as to buy one. The only advantage to a home-made one is that you have exactly what you want.

The following story is a flannelboard favorite: [11]

Queer Company

A little old woman lived all alone in a little old house in the woods. One Halloween she sat in the corner, and as she sat, she spun.

Still she sat and
Still she spun and
Still she wished for company.

Then she saw her door open a little way, and in came

A pair of big, big feet
And sat down by the fireside.
"That is very strange," thought the little old woman, but—

Still she sat and
Still she spun and
Still she wished for company.

Then in came

A pair of small, small legs,
And sat down on the big, big feet
"Now that is very strange," thought the old woman, but—

Still she sat and
Still she spun and
Still she wished for company.

Then in came

A wee, wee waist,
And sat down on the small, small legs.
"Now that is very strange," thought the old woman, but—

Still she sat and
Still she spun and
Still she wished for company.

Then in came

A pair of broad, broad shoulders,
And sat down on the wee, wee waist.
But—

Still she sat and
Still she spun and
Still she wished for company.

---

[11] Paul Anderson, *Flannelboard Stories for the Primary Grades* (Minneapolis: Denison, 1962), and Paul Anderson, *A Second Book of Stories to Tell* (Minneapolis: Denison, 1969).

Then in through the door came

A pair of long, long arms,
And sat down on the broad, broad shoulders.
"Now that is very strange," thought the little
old woman, but—

Still she sat and
Still she spun and
Still she wished for company.

Then in came

A pair of fat, fat hands,
And sat down on the long, long arms.
But—

Still she sat and
Still she spun and
Still she wished for company.

Then in came

A round, round head
And sat down on top of all
That sat by the fireside.

The little old woman stopped her spinning and
asked

"Where did you get such big feet?"
"By much tramping, by much tramping," said
Somebody.

"Where did you get such small, small legs?"
"By much running, by much running," said
Somebody.

"Where did you get such a wee, wee waist?"
"Nobody knows, nobody knows," said Some-
body.

"Where did you get such broad, broad should-
ers?"
"From carrying brooms," said Somebody.

"Where did you get such long, long arms?"
"Swinging the scythe, swinging the scythe," said
Somebody.

"Where did you get such fat, fat hands?"
"By working, by working," said Somebody.

"How did you get such a huge, huge head?"
"Of a pumpkin I made it," said Somebody.

Then said the little old woman,
"What did you come for?"

"YOU!" said Somebody.

The following techniques should be used as a story is told with the flannelboard:

1. Place the flannelboard where it will remain securely in a place that can be seen by all students. The chalkboard is good if the group is in a small circle seated before it. An easel is better if the board must be seen by an entire room. If children are seated on a rug they must be farther away from the teacher than when she uses a picture book. Those in front will be under a strain looking up if too near the board.

2. Arrange the figures to be used in the sequence needed for telling the story. It is best to keep them in a folder away from the sight of the listeners. Otherwise, some of the surprise and suspense is lost as they are introduced. A manila folder used in file cabinets makes a good container. Staple a pocket on one side of the folder to hold the figures and staple the story to the other side.

3. There is a tendency to look away from the listeners to the figures as they are placed on the flannelboard. Of course, this is necessary. Try to use this movement to direct the listeners' eyes but turn back to the audience as you tell the story. Otherwise, you will find yourself talking to the flannelboard, thus creating a hearing problem for your audience.

4. Plan your follow-up before you tell the story. Are you going to evaluate the story? Are you going to have them retell parts of the story? Are you going to have the children create a favorite story? When a story ends in the classroom it is a bit different from the ending of a play in the theater or a television program. The audience is still with you. Instead of going home or turning on another station you must plan the transition to the next school task.

In the Orient there are still storytellers who earn a living walking along the street. They signal their approach by tapping two pieces of wood together. Each child offers a small coin and is given a piece of hard candy. While he eats the candy, the storyteller entertains with some of the famous folk stories of the land or the latest adventures of Mickey Mouse. As the story unfolds, the storyteller illustrates it by a series of color prints from books, or hand-drawn pictures. These *Kami-she-bai,* or picture stories, might well be used in our own country.[12]

Stick figures and simple puppets used as characters in a story or as the teller of the story will hold the attention of those children who need something to see as well as to hear. An important object in a story such as a lamp, old coffee mill, glass slipper, shaft of wheat, apple, miniature rocker, spinning wheel, or toy sword may be used. Some stories depend for an explanation on the core of an apple, the way a seed or feather is formed, or the shape of a flower or leaf, since the fable was a means of explaining a fact of nature. And one should not neglect the chalkboard or simple stick figures to illustrate a scene or character.

In addition to a pleasant voice, clear speech, adequate vocabulary, and a relaxed appearance, today's storyteller needs the resources of inner grace which comes from sincerity and a respect both for the audience and for the art of storytelling. When you have a clear visual picture of each character and scene, know the plot thoroughly, can establish a mood for listening and are able to end the story so that your audience is satisfied, you are a good storyteller.

For Discussion

1. Do you think that every child should have a contribution to make in the social situations of his life by being able to tell a joke, relate a humorous family experience, do a trick, or tell a story at the campfire? In what ways does such an ability influence personality?

2. How can we find time in the school day to provide opportunities to tell stories and listen to them?

3. Should the oral interpretations of literature be limited to fiction and poetry?

---

[12] Sets of Kami-she-bai pictures may be obtained from the Tuttle Publishing Co., Rutland, Vt.

Suggestions for Projects

1. Review ten books which might be read by children in a single grade to improve their understanding of a foreign land or an ethical value (a different book for each country or value).

2. Review ten books which might be read by children in a single grade to improve their historical or geographical concepts of our country.

3. Make a collection of twenty-five poems that will interest boys in grades 5–6. Indicate in general how such poetry would be introduced and used.

4. Make a collection of ten poems appropriate to the purposes of a verse choir at a grade level.

5. Select three stories or ballads that might be dramatized by children.

6. Make a bibliography of dramatic material to use in the intermediate grades.

7. Indicate the skills needed and how they may be developed with regard to the dramatic presentation of a play.

8. Collect a group of ballads or stories that might be read aloud while a group presented the action in pantomime.

Bibliography

Books

Arbuthnot, May. *Children and Books,* 3rd ed. Chicago: Scott, Foresman and Company, 1964.

Chambers, Dewey W. *Storytelling and Creative Drama.* Dubuque, Ia.: Wm. C. Brown Co., 1970.

Duff, Annis. *Bequest of Wings.* New York: The Viking Press, Inc., 1959.

Duff, Annis. *Longer Flight.* New York: The Viking Press, Inc., 1959.

Fenner, Phyllis. *The Proof of the Pudding.* New York: The John Day Company, Inc., 1957.

Guilfoile, Elizabeth, and others. *Adventuring with Books: A Booklist for Elementary Schools.* Champaign, Ill.: National Council of Teachers of English, 1966.

Haviland, Virginia. *Children's Literature: A Guide to Reference Sources.* Washington, D.C.: Library of Congress, 1966.

Huck, Charlotte, and Doris Young. *Children's Literature in the Elementary School.* New York: Holt, Rinehart & Winston, Inc., 1967.

Kingman, Lee. *Newbery and Caldecott Medal Books.* Boston: Horn Books, Inc., 1965.

Larrick, Nancy. *A Teacher's Guide to Children's Books.* Columbus, Ohio: Charles E. Merrill, 1960.

Sawyer, Ruth. *The Way of the Story Teller.* New York: The Viking Press, Inc., 1962.

Sikes, Geraldine. *Children's Literature for Dramatization.* New York: Harper & Row, Publishers, 1964.

Smith, James Steel. *A Critical Approach to Children's Literature.* New York: McGraw-Hill Book Company, 1967.

Whitehead, Robert. *Children's Literature: Strategies of Teaching.* Englewood Cliffs, N.J.: Prentice-Hall, Inc., 1968.

Articles and Pamphlets

Cohen, Dorothy H. "Word Meaning and the Literary Experience in Early Childhood," *Elementary English* (November 1969), pp. 914–25.

Gilpatric, Naomi. "Power of Picture Books to Change Child's Self-Image," *Elementary English* (May 1969), pp. 570–74.

Helson, Ravena. "Fantasy and Self Discovery," *Horn Book* (April 1970), pp. 121–34.

Hundler, June. "Books for Loving," *Elementary English* (May 1970), pp. 687–92.

Highland Park Independent School District. *English Language Arts* (1967). Address: 7015 Westchester Drive; Dallas, Texas.

four

handwriting

Among all the Inventions of Mankind none is more Admirable, necessary, useful or convenient than Writing, by which a Man is enabled to delineate his very Conceptions, communicate his Mind without Speaking, and correspond with his Friend at ten thousand Miles distance, and all by the Contrivance of twenty four Letters. Viz.t Aabc.&c

---

What Are the Objectives of Handwriting Instruction?

Teachers influence the writing of children by example, by planned lessons, and by establishment and maintenance of standards. To do this teachers need to be able to use acceptable print script and cursive writing, diagnose the individual needs of children, and plan experiences to meet those needs. Teachers do this by understanding the nature of the task to be done, the materials and tools used, and current procedure and philosophy; acquiring the personal skills needed; and understanding the range of individual differences among learners.

Teachers then must become masters of the craft as well as teachers of handwriting. The chapter thus will focus on the handwriting of the college student preparing to teach as well as providing the history and research that explain contemporary classroom practices.

The purpose behind the statement that handwriting should be viewed as a means of expression and not as an end in itself is to focus the attention of teachers and learners on the message rather than on the penmanship. This is a proper emphasis. There is no reason to master penmanship unless one wishes to communicate by writing. Unfortunately, some have interpreted the statement as a justification for neglecting instruction in the mechanics of writing. The inconsistency of this thinking is revealed when we look at typewriting. Here, too, the skill is a means of expression. But for a period when the skill is being mastered it becomes a legitimate end to study the habit-forming routines that constitute the skill.

The psychology of habit formation in teaching handwriting is similar to that used

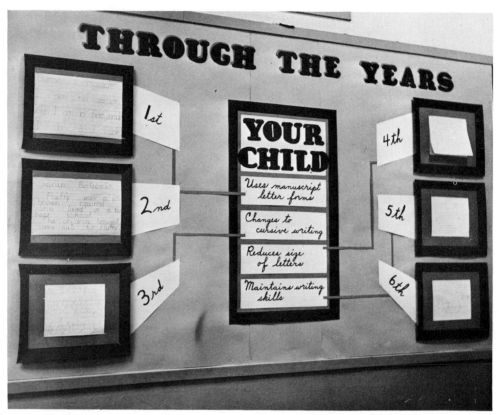

Both students and parents profit from an explanation of the achievement expected in handwriting. (*Courtesy of the San Diego City Schools.*)

in a sport like golf or tennis or in a skill like piano playing. The learner must first decide to seek mastery of the skill area. After that each specific movement receives critical attention and drill. In tennis the coach will first illustrate a stroke, then repeat it in slow motion, and finally have the class perform each movement that he has demonstrated. He may even take the learner's arm and guide it through the movements if a correction is needed. The stroke will be practiced separately and in connection with other movements previously taught. In the same way the piano teacher will have the child play simple melodies and then do specific scale exercises to gain the finger control desired. This psychology is different from that involved in the usual concern of teachers with meaning and understanding.

Watching an athletic coach at work would be of great help to a handwriting teacher.

One would observe that the coach is enthusiastic about the game and concerned about the actions of each player. He praises good plays but also points out errors. Both are analyzed to make the players aware of their actions, using demonstrations by the coach and selected players. Rewards or trophies are given to the winners. Above all, it should be noted that athletic skills are perfected through a great deal of individual practice, as well as by actually playing the game.

Although handwriting in the air is justly questioned as it is sometimes done, it is a valuable way to establish accurate perception of the movements to be made. The young writer must have a mental image of the letter or word he is to achieve and the movements needed to create it. Slow-motion imitation of the teacher's movements or oral directions is like slow-motion drill in an athletic game. A teacher cannot face the class and demonstrate writing without reversing the child's view of what is being done. As a teacher writes a letter on the chalkboard she has the class follow her movements, usually on paper but sometimes in the air, as if writing on an imaginary chalkboard. Class observers check variations that indicate confusion or faulty movements. Children learn a great deal from such careful observation of each other. At times, tracing over letters can correct faulty perception or habits.

Because we are concerned with muscular development and physical maturity in handwriting, there are some factors in the growth patterns of children that should be considered in our teaching. The primary child frequently lacks the muscular coordination needed for writing. The powers that are developed are in the big muscles and nerve centers rather than in the small muscles of the fingers. We accept the dominant handedness of little children, which is usually observable at the age of three but may not be fully developed until the age of eight. Because farsightedness is the normal vision of young children we avoid long periods requiring close work with small details. Patterns of progress will differ widely during the primary grades, but girls will usually be more mature than boys.

Instructional implications based upon these factors would include the following practices: The little child is encouraged to work with clay, finger paint, or other materials that require finger coordination. Large muscles are used by using chalkboard letters about 3 inches high. The paper used has spaces of ½ inch between lines. The width used corresponds to the sidewise span of the forearm of the child. Soft chalk and thick, soft lead pencils are used. Speed is never emphasized. Careful attention is given to the physical comfort of each child. Copy work, which forces constant refocusing of the eye, is avoided. This especially applies to work on the board which the child copies on paper. No effort is made to keep the entire class together for instruction. Each child sets his own progress pattern. The aptitudes or skills of boys and girls should

not be compared. Early writing efforts are usually characterized by great deliberateness.

In the intermediate grades the children gain greater control over both large-muscle activities and eye–hand coordination involving the small muscles. These are the years that influence lifetime habits with regard to musical instruments, skill with tools, and handwriting. The longer attention span results in a willingness to accept drill and repetition if the children understand the final goal. As the boys approach adolescence the rapid growth of the hands may cause a deterioration in their handwriting. At this stage handwriting can be improved by exercises involving ovals, push-pulls, and writing exercises to music. Older children sometimes express their egos through highly individualized writing, such as ringing the *i*'s instead of dotting them, making triangles of loops below the lines, or crossing the *t*'s in unconventional ways. Insistence on standard practices in school papers is not unreasonable.

As children mature, their handwriting becomes smaller. In grade 4 it becomes standardized according to the system used, with concern for exact proportioning of letters being a part of the instructional program. Ballpoint pens or fine-point fountain pens are introduced. Much of the drill is self-assigned as the result of comparing work with a standardized writing scale, which reveals various types of handwriting defects. Speed is gradually encouraged. To secure peer-group approval, writers' clubs are organized; good writing is displayed and rewarded. Children with severe handwriting problems are usually encouraged to use print script rather than to continue with cursive writing.

As with all skills there will be great personal variation, but in general, most schools attempt to meet these goals at the following grade levels:

By the end of kindergarten, most children may be expected to possess the following knowledge concerning handwriting:

1. Writing is a form of communication. It is language shared through signs.

Signs, names, and other written symbols have meaning.

2. In some cases, a child will be able to write his first name.
3. There will be some familiarity with the forms of print-script writing as the teacher uses it in recording children's stories, labeling pictures, or writing names.

By the end of grade 1, most children may be expected to

1. Write in print-script form all letters, both capitals and lower case.
2. Write their name and address.
3. Write simple original stories.
4. Understand and practice proper spacing between letters of a word and between words of a sentence.

By the end of grade 2, a child should

1. Be able to do good print-script writing in daily lessons.
2. Know about margins, heading of paper, and spacing.
3. Write a friendly letter.
4. Know the correct use of the terms: capital letters, period, question mark, comma as used between city and state and in dates.
5. Write print script with apparent ease.

By the end of grade 3, a child should be able to

1. Use both print script and cursive writing to meet his daily needs.
2. Write his own name, his school, city, and state in cursive style.
3. Analyze and improve his own written work.
4. Write with reasonable speed.

During grade 4, the child should be able to

1. Write correctly friendly letters (one or two good paragraphs).
2. Write notes to friends and classmates.
3. Write original stories, poems, plays, and programs.
4. Show evidence of retaining manuscript writing as a supplementary tool.
5. Meet the grade standards as indicated on a handwriting scale.

6. Recognize and correct his errors in letter formation.

By the end of grade 5, the child should be able to

1. Write a business letter.
2. Take notes in class.
3. Plan and present written reports.
4. Use pen and ink neatly.
5. Attempt writing on stationery without lines.
6. Meet grade standards with regard to legibility and speed (fifty to sixty letters per minute).

By the end of grade 6, the child should be able to

1. Proofread and rewrite many first writing efforts.
2. Take pride in submitting neat, orderly papers in all class work.
3. Meet grade standards of legibility and speed.

About ninety minutes a week are spent on direct practice of writing in the primary grades. In the upper grades practice periods of sixty minutes a week, divided into three twenty-minute periods, are common. Some schools have thirty minutes each day for handwriting. This period is used for writing school reports as well as practicing on handwriting techniques. Other schools combine handwriting and spelling in an alternating schedule.

In grades 7 and 8, the language teacher should devote some time to writing instruction each week. Teachers of all subjects should check and grade papers for neatness and legibility in handwriting. Ideas and the willingness to express them are more important than mechanics, but a carelessly written paper should be handed back to a student to be done over and a grade should be withheld until the second paper is handed to the teacher. The second effort should be accepted if it is an improvement.

Much that we teach with respect to handwriting is the result of tradition. In the past "copperplate" (examples engraved on copper plate for printing by the early writing masters) writing was extensively used.

Business schools taught the Spencerian Script, which was a beautiful, ornate writing, closely related to that devised by the Dutch teachers. Systems based on "arm movement" became popular in the schools. These consisted of a carefully organized series of exercises designed to train the individual to write rhythmically. The writing arm rested on the forearm muscle, and finger movement was avoided. One of the reasons for the wide acceptance of this method is that much of the fatigue associated with long periods of writing was avoided. The exercises consisted of a series of continuous ovals and "push-pulls," or were designed to give practice in writing individual letters and their parts. Students were encouraged to complete sets of exercises of high enough quality to receive certificates of merit and pins awarded by the publishers.

Some have criticized exercises of this type as being so unrelated to actual writing as to be isolated skills; one may learn how to make ovals but not necessarily how to write. A discouraged teacher is apt to accept such criticism and justify neglect of writing practice. On the other hand, there is a great deal of evidence that writing drills did produce excellent and even beautiful handwriting or calligraphy. Many students were actually self-taught by the manuals because their teachers were not masters of the system. While all students did not become calligraphers, it should be noted that neither did all become excellent readers, mathematicians, musicians, or artists.

Nearly all systems used today involve a modification of those in the past. At the end of this chapter you will find listed the materials available for penmanship instruction.

The reform movement in penmanship instruction that was started in England by William Morris (1834–1896) is still growing. This is an effort to return to the forms used at the time of the Renaissance. In the schools of England one finds systems based on this influence. That of Marion Richardson is an extension of the use of "print-script" writing in the primary grades. It is called Italic writing. This is a form of print which was first used by Aldo Manuzio in Italy during the Renaissance; Virgil was the

first author printed in this type (1501). The current revival is based upon the desire to find a script that is both beautiful and legible, but that still expresses individuality. No claim is made concerning speed. Italic writing uses a flat pen held at a 45-degree angle which gives a thick descending line and thin ascending line. The oval, rather than the circle, is its basic movement. Many of the letters appear connected and may be if the writer wishes.

Experiments with the typewriter in the elementary school date back to at least 1927. All such studies have indicated that children enjoy the experience and achieve some skill in the use of the machines. Kindergarten teachers report that as a prewriting experience it is an effective way to teach letter names and aspects of visual discrimination. Gifted children in the upper grades profit from summer schools that have courses in typing. The typewriter appears to provide a bridge between their advanced ideas and the lack of physical maturity for a large amount of handwriting.

It would be impractical to assume that typewriting skill would replace the need for learning to write either print script or cursive writing. The ability to write a neat, legible hand with reasonable speed and with-

Sing a song of sixpence,
Pocket full of rye;
Four & twenty blackbirds
Baked in a pie.
When the pie was opened
The birds began to sing
Wasn't it a dainty dish
To set before a King.?

An exercise in modern italic script, as used in many European Schools.

out strain is essential in the modern curriculum.

Modern trends in handwriting instruction reflect current understanding of factors in child growth and recent study. None can be said to be universally acceptable or based on such absolute information that future change would be impossible. In comparison with the past, these changes may be observed:

1. Cursive writing is losing its place as a recognized part of the early primary program. The simpler forms of manuscript or print-script writing are preferred. Print script is being accepted as desirable writing in all grades.
2. Children no longer trace letter forms except under critical circumstances.
3. Children who show a strong preference for writing with the left hand are no longer required to learn to write with the right hand.
4. The use of the rhythmical aids is discouraged. The size and shape of the various letters are so different that an absolute conformity to set rhythm is unnatural.
5. Accessory drills that presumably contribute rhythm and freedom in muscular movement are minimized. Ovals and related exercises are used much less than in the past.
6. There is less emphasis on speed in writing.
7. Fountain pens and ballpoint pens are used in classroom practices.
8. Such incentives as penmanship certificates and pens are not widely used, although still available.

For Discussion

1. How can children be led to appreciate the importance of learning to write skillfully?
2. What information do you find in children's encyclopedias that might be used for classroom research on the alphabet?
3. Find an example of Spencerian writing, or, if possible, one who can write this script. Defend the modern point of view that such art is not needed in writing.
4. What is the basis for objections to the use of colored ink or ballpoint pens in adult writing?
5. How would a school use a special penmanship teacher?
6. Would it be desirable to require all teachers to pass a blackboard writing test before granting them authority to teach?
7. Make a collection of handwriting samples written by children in other countries. Contrast the quality of handwriting demonstrated.
8. In the Orient the writing instruments such as the brush and ink are regarded as works of art. Should we try to develop an attitude that writing is an art form?

How Is Print Script (or Manuscript Writing) Taught?

Print-script writing (also called manuscript writing) started in England. In 1919 Miss S. A. Golds of St. George the Martyr School, London, published a copybook called *A Guide to the Teaching of Manuscript Writing.*

In 1922 a course taught by Marjorie Wise of England at Columbia University introduced print script to the American schools. Since that time the use of this simple form of lettering has been accepted in nearly all the schools of the United States.

The term *cursive* means "running" or "connected"; the terms *print script* and *manuscript* refer to writing in which each letter is separately formed, as in printer's type.

The major differences are contrasted on the next page.

The use of print script in the primary grades has been accepted because of the following reasons: Primary children learn only one alphabet for reading and writing. With its three basic strokes—i.e., circles, arcs, and straight lines—print script is easier for the young child to learn. Print script is more legible than cursive and with practice may be written rapidly. Children who master print script do a great deal more writing of a creative nature than children who must master the cursive form. The major disad-

Manuscript	*Cursive*
Letters are made separately.	Letters are joined.
Pencil is lifted at the end of each letter or stroke.	Pencil is lifted at the end of each word.
Letters are made with circles, parts of circles, and straight lines.	Letters are made with overstrokes, understrokes, connected strokes, and ovals.
Letters are spaced to form words. Space between letters is controlled by the shape of the letter. The *i* and the *j* are dotted and the *t* crossed immediately after the vertical stroke is made.	Spacing between letters is controlled by the slant and manner of making connective strokes. The letters *i* and *j* are dotted and the *t* crossed after the completion of the word.
Letters closely resemble print and are, therefore, legible and easy to read.	Letters are unlike those on the printed page.
Small letters and capitals are different except for *c, o, s, p, v, w, x,* and *z*.	Small letters and capitals are different.

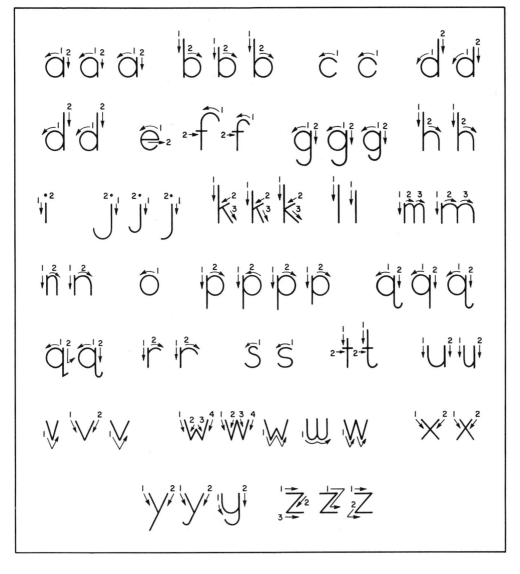

vantage of using print script would be the fact that a transfer to cursive writing must be taught later.

Recent surveys indicate that some schools do not require children to change from this script to cursive writing in the upper grades unless they desire to do so. The majority make the change in the third grade. In others the change is made in the second grade. Those favoring no change give these reasons: Print script is a legible, easily produced form of writing that with practice can be written as rapidly as cursive writing.

Those who change do so primarily because children indicate a desire to write like grown-up people do and because of the greater speed possible with the cursive form.

There are three kinds of experiences which lead to writing readiness. The first group can be described as manipulative experiences. These are designed to strengthen muscles needed for writing and to gain control over tools used in writing. Children develop the small muscles of the hands through playing with toys, dialing the telephone, setting the table, changing a doll's clothes, putting puzzles together, cutting with scissors, finger painting, and clay modeling. They draw or scribble with chalk at the chalkboard or with crayons on large sheets of paper. It is well to remember that scribbling is writing and that it is the child's first means of identifying himself with the writing process until he is ready to be taught the letter forms. In the eighteenth and early nineteenth centuries Johann Pestalozzi (1746–1827) had children draw geometric forms on slates as he told stories. These were actually exercises in writing readiness.

The second group of experiences is designed to increase the child's ability in the use of language. It is futile for children to learn to write before they can express their ideas orally. Beginners must have many experiences that stimulate the desire for self-expression. As they listen to stories and poems, look at pictures, dictate stories and letters, or make up songs they should be encouraged to comment freely. As children see their ideas written by the teacher in a letter or invitation, writing becomes a magic tool for extending speech. With this recognition comes not only an understanding of the usefulness of writing but a strong personal desire to perform the writing task.

The third group consists of those experiences designed to give practice to the basic movements of writing itself. These are usually started at the chalkboard, where only large muscles are involved. The purpose is to understand certain letter forms and how they are created. Circles are first drawn by the children. They are given directions as to the starting place. Following this, the children are asked to look at the number 2 on the clock. When a circle is made it is best to start where the 2 would be if you were making a clock. Children draw clocks, doughnuts, balls, soap bubbles, and Halloween faces, or they "set" a table with a circle for the plate and lines for the knife, fork, and spoon. Some like to attempt such advanced circles as a string of beads, a bunch of grapes, a Christmas tree with ornaments, an umbrella, or a cat.

Combination of circles and straight lines can be made by drawing a square wagon with wheels, making a turkey with tail feathers, or making stick figures with round heads.

As children transfer this activity to paper, some supervision is necessary to establish certain habits. All lines are made from top to bottom and left to right. All circles are started at the two o'clock position or where one would start to make the letter *c* and move toward the left.

As soon as possible—even at the readiness period—writing should say something. Children should be encouraged to label their picture of a cat with the word; the letters *c a t* might be copied from a teacher-made example. The child should know the names of these letters before writing them and should realize that he has made a word when he finishes. Thus, knowing the letter names and the ability to read what is written are a part of writing readiness.

One teacher introduced writing to a small group at the chalkboard in this manner: She first placed her chair close to the board and sat as she wrote, in order to make it more convenient for the children to watch as they stood about her. She was writing at their eye level. The teacher said. "Today we are going to write. We must first learn to hold the chalk so that it will make a soft, white line. If it squeaks, it is trying to tell you that you are not holding it right."

The teacher then demonstrated how to hold the chalk, first in the right hand and then in the left. "Good writers do it this way. I put my pointer (index) fingertip at the end of the chalk, the middle fingertip next to it, and my thumb underneath. Now let's see if you can do this." After each child had held the chalk, the teacher continued: "I am going to write the name of one of the children in our reader. Watch and see where I start each letter." The teacher wrote each letter slowly, calling attention to the letters that start at the top line and the letters that start in between the lines. "Now I will do it again," the teacher told them. "You will tell me everything I must do." The children, with teacher prompting, directed the action through a second writing of the word. The original word remained on the board as a guide and reminder. "Let's see how well we have written," the teacher remarked. "Bobby, draw your fingers along the bottom of the letters to see if they sit tight on the line. Are they all right? Mary, draw your finger along the tops of the low letters to see if they are even. And now, Jack, check the tall letters to see if they start at the top line."

After these checks to sharpen visual discrimination had been made the teacher continued. "I want each of you to find a place at the chalkboard. I have written the lines on the board. Find the line that is even with your eyes. That is the one you will write on. Find your place and then write the same word that I did." The teacher gave individual help as needed. With some groups it would be better to have one child demonstrate what is to be done before the others try. After each child had appraised his work the teacher had them write the word a second time.

Other similar lessons teaching spacing between words, as well as other words and letters, should be done at the board before writing on paper is started at the desk.

If a section of the board can be reserved, writing practice during free time will be a popular activity. The teacher can put an assignment at the top of the space such as "Write the names of three boys," or "Write three words that start with B."

When making the transition from chalkboard to paper—and until the child is able to write correctly from memory—he must have a copy from which to write. The copy should be made on the same kind of paper that the child uses. The letters should be well formed. The amount of work will be controlled by the amount of time free for supervision, as well as by the fatigue factor. Most children tire after writing for about ten minutes.

Various systems of print script form the letters in different ways. Usually a school system selects one program and attempts to have a common form throughout all grades. Spacing is a problem in all systems. The instruction to leave the space of the letter *o* between words, and of one hump of the *n* between letters means little to beginners. Teachers frequently say "one finger between letters and two fingers between words." The

problem is that letters made of straight lines should be closer together than those with curves, in order to give the illusion of uniform spacing throughout.

All writing that is made available to the child for observation or for copy should be properly spaced and aligned. Occasional comments by the teacher may be used to strengthen the child's impression of well-spaced letters and perfectly straight lines. But in the early stage of writing instruction, the child needs to concentrate chiefly on getting a clear visual image of the letters he writes and on learning the correct order of making the strokes. After the child has learned to form the letters properly, there will be plenty of time for him to master the art of letter arrangement.

The paper should be placed directly in front of the child, parallel with the lines of desk or table, rather than at a slant. The paper is moved as the child writes. Soft lead pencils or crayons are used. Ordinarily, a child can write easily while seated in a properly fitted chair and desk. Some small children write better if they can stand while writing. This is especially true if they are writing on large or oversize easel paper.

Early handwriting instruction should use whole words that have real meaning for the children—words they are interested in and that are easy to write. It will probably be necessary to contrive ways to bring in words like *queen, quiet, quail, fox, fix, box, excuse, zebra, zoo, buzz,* and *dozen,* in order to teach the letters *q, x,* and *z,* which are not frequently used. The entire alphabet must be taught.

One recent study indicates that the lower-case letters present the following order of difficulty for beginners: [1] *l, o, i, f, x, s, t, v, r, g, a, b, h, j, p, n, m, z, q, k, y, d, c, e, w, u.* These were not reproduced from memory, but copied. From memory *p, q, b,* and *d* would give more trouble. Many programs present the letters in similar groups. One text teaches *o, a, d, q, g, b, p, c,* and *e* as

---

[1] E. B. Coleman, "Collecting a Data Base for a Reading Technology," *Journal of Educational Psychology,* Monograph, Vol. 61, No. 4, Part 2 (August 1970).

Group One. The letters that use straight lines are Group Two: *l, t, i, f, j, n, m, r, h, u.* The remaining letters are taught later: *v, w, y, r, z, k,* and *s.* The letter *s* is taught as a continuous series of curves. The capital letters are usually taught in association with children's names. Those identical in shape with their small letter counterparts would be the simplest. These are *O, C, S, V, X,* and *Z* in most programs. Making an ABC book gives practice with capital letters and reinforces the phonics program.

The following are frequent errors: rounding straight lines and angles, making letters upside down and backward, forming lines so that they do not meet at the proper places, and making incomplete letters. There errors can be prevented by careful initial teaching, although all children make some errors when involved in the thought of what they are writing. With respect to closure errors it is easier for children to join the circle and straight line strokes if the *c* rather than the complete oval is used for parts of the letters *a, d, b, g,* and *q.*

One factor that governs the formation of some print-script letters is that of ease of transfer to cursive writing. The reason for starting the letter *e* with the straight line, then the circle, is simply because that is the way the cursive letter is formed. It may well be that it is wiser to consider the letters in one alphabet unrelated to the other. Certainly this seems to be true of the capital letters, except for the fact that both proceed from left to right.

As the teacher writes she should call attention to details, naming the letters and commenting on the size, shape, and direction of strokes. She should watch the child write the word, comment favorably on letters well formed, and give additional instruction when it is needed. If a particular letter proves difficult, the child should give it additional practice. When introducing letters in a word for the first time, or isolating a difficult letter for study, the teacher may give more time to demonstration and discussion; thus: "The *t* is a tall letter. We start at the top, go down, and try to make it very straight. We cross it near the top from left to right. The *t* is not quite so tall as an

l, but it is taller than *i,* or *m,* or *n*" (depending on which letter the children already know).

At this point it is well for the teacher to bear in mind that when a child begins to write, he cannot remember everything he has been told. Only two things are essential: he must form the letters in fair approximation to the copy, and he must make every stroke in the right direction as he forms his letters. If he cannot do both, he probaby is not ready to write and would profit more from nonwriting activities at this time.

The practice of tracing, except in special problem cases, has been questioned. If the child cannot make the strokes without the tedious, time-consuming muscular drill involved in tracing, he is hardly ready for handwriting instruction. And if the child, in tracing, puts all his attention on the segment of line that he is attempting to follow at the moment, he loses sight of the letter or word as a whole, and so at the end of the lesson may be able to write no better than at the beginning.

There are programs such as the one in Hawaii and that published by Lyons and Carnahan that do a great deal of tracing. Additional study needs to be done to determine the effectiveness of such practice.

In learning to write, as in other kinds of growth, children pass through the same general stages of development. But the rate of progress and the time at which each level of achievement is reached will vary according to the individual differences of the children themselves. The rate of learning among the children in any one class may range from slow to normal or fast. It is not uncommon for a child to start slowly and then pick up speed as he matures, or for another to start rapidly and then "slow down'" later. Nevertheless, at any given time there will be enough children with similar needs to make some group instruction possible. In writing, as in reading, groups must be small enough to permit close personal supervision of each child's work by the teacher. This is true whether the writing is done on the board or on paper.

A good lesson in handwriting contains five elements: (1) visualization, (2) analysis, (3) practice, (4) comparison or evaluation, and (5) correction.

Note the following in teaching the child to write his name.

1. *Visualization.* The teacher has prepared a card (3 × 5) with the name of each child. "I wonder how many can read each other's names. As I go through the cards, the person whose name it is will call on another child to read it. After all have been read, I will give you your name cards."

2. *Analysis.* "How many have an *e* in their name? Jane, show us how to make an *e*. This is one letter that does not start at the top. Does anyone have a *g* in his name? Gregory, show us how to make a *g*. That is another letter that does not start at the top. Look at each letter in your name. Are there any you think we should practice?"

3. *Practice.* "Now go to the board and put an *x* at the eye-level line where you will start. Write your name once. When you have finished, go over your name card and see if each letter is correct."

4. *Evaluation.* "How many have all the letters on the line? How many have all the letters right? How many have the space between letters right?"

5. *Correction.* "Now let us write our names once more and make them better. You are to keep the name card at your desk and use it whenever you wish to write your name."

In the first grade many lessons in handwriting will require the teacher to prepare a worksheet. Normally these worksheets should meet the following standards:

1. The learner's attention will be focused on a few handwriting difficulties.
2. The worksheet will contain enough guidance so that possible errors will not be practiced.
3. While the drill is on a single element, the practice should result in the feeling that something has been written.
4. There should be enough practice to give a sense of purpose to the lesson, but not so much that there is physical strain.

The first thing on the worksheet should be the letters or word demonstrated by the teacher. There may be arrows or other markers to show where the writer starts each letter and to show the direction of the strokes. The first stroke might be in red, the second in yellow, and the third in blue.

The second part of the worksheet may consist of practice on one or two letters. An example should be given and spaces should be made indicating how many "copies" of each letter are required.

Finally, these letters should be put together to form a word or sentence. Sometimes only part of a word is given, with blanks left for the missing letters. Other worksheets may indicate by a picture what word is to be written. As soon as the child is ready the writing should become personal. The worksheet may start a letter by having printed on it: "Dear Santa, please bring me. . . ."

The next step is to have the children do a great deal of personal writing, using model alphabet charts to guide the writing. "Homemade" greeting cards provide writing practice. These cards may then be sent to a child who is ill or used for birthdays, Christmas greetings, Mother's Day remembrance, or Valentine's Day. Labeling also provides excellent writing practice. Children can make flash cards for reading drill. But best of all are the stories written to illustrate a picture or to entertain the group. We will discuss such stories later under creative writing.

There are standardized scales to evaluate print-script writing. However, few children can use them. A chart that asks the child to check the following elements will serve for most evaluation needed at this grade:

Did you make each letter the way it is on the chart?
Are your letters on the line?
Are your down strokes straight?
Are your round letters like a circle?
Did you leave enough space between words?

There are a number of devices that teachers use during this period to add interest to the writing practice. Here are some of them:

Ask the children to listen carefully to a word description to see if they can identify

PEANUTS ® By Charles M. Schulz

(Courtesy of United Features Syndicate. By permission.)

a letter which is on the alphabet chart. The teacher says, "I am thinking of a small letter that is made with a circle and then a tall stick." The child who identifies *d* goes and writes it on the board. The teacher then describes another letter.

The teacher asks, "Who can find the letter that comes before *m*? What is its name?" The child who identifies the letter may write it on the board. A variation is to ask, "What letter comes after *m*?"

Each child in turn goes to the front of the room and gives his name and initials. "My name is Robert Smith. My initials are R. S." Then he writes them on the board. Or a child may write a classmate's initials on the board and have the class identify the person.

A magic slate can be made with transparent acetate sheets from a novelty store. Insert a sheet of paper with the letters, words, or numbers you wish the child to practice. The children trace over these with a crayon—or better, write under the examples. These can be used many times because the crayon marks can be wiped off.

One teacher starts her group by saying, "We are going to make pumpkins today. Watch how I make one." The teacher uses the guide words "One around." After the children have made a row of pumpkins, the teacher says, "Let's put our pumpkins beside a fence post. Now look again," the teacher says, "because you have made the letter *a*."

Another teacher talks about the letters that are done only on one floor such as *a, c, e, m*. Other letters are upstairs letters like *b, d, h,* and *l*. Basement letters are *g, j, p, y*.

Sometimes children do a better job of alignment if they are told, "Let's see if we can keep our letters sitting straight on a shelf."

After the children have spent several lessons on lines, circles, their names and single words, one teacher starts with a sentence such as, "I am a boy." After the unlined paper is distributed the children are asked to fold the paper in half lengthwise, then fold the bottom half to the center fold. This provides folded lines to follow. The children write the sentence on the bottom fold and then draw a picture in the top half to illustrate their sentence.

For Discussion

1. Why is it important that early writing practice result in a word?

2. Primary pencils do not have erasers. Children are told to put a line through an error and write it again. Do you think erasers should be available? Give reasons for your answer.

3. Why should cursive writing instruction be postponed for all children in the first grade?

4. Plan a worksheet that will provide for the steps in a writing lesson suggested in this chapter or evaluate a worksheet in a commercial workbook designed to teach handwriting skills.

How Do Teachers Guide the Child's Learning as He Transfers from Print Script to Cursive Writing?

Although there are some school systems that make no effort to teach any form of writing but print script, the majority do introduce cursive writing in either the late second grade or third grade. This change is more the result of response to cultural tradition than to educational merit. We have enough evidence to indicate that with practice, print-script writing can be written as rapidly as cursive writing. It remains a legible and easy form of writing. It also assumes enough personality so that signatures in print script are now legal. There are usually two reasons given for the change. One is that children are attempting to imitate the cursive writing they see and need direction to do it correctly. The second is that parents disapprove of older children's use of print script. There are no studies known to this writer that indicate if either of these arguments is valid.

There are some schools such as those in Hawaii that start with cursive in the kindergarten. The children use typewriters when they wish to reproduce material similar to that in their readers. The reason given is that the final goal should determine the initial instruction. In such schools there is no reason for lessons concerned with the transition from print to cursive.

There is a strong traditional force within the teaching group. Upper-grade teachers use cursive writing. They seem unwilling to change. Thus the child must change to conform to the teacher's writing pattern. Another factor in this situation is that it represents a teaching specific which seems to indicate educational growth. Teachers often like to introduce something new; the home reaction is generally that "children in Miss Smith's class are certainly making progress."

Certainly it makes sense for the child to use print script as often as possible after having mastered this skill. Children will more readily express their ideas in the written form throughout the second and third grade if they use print script. Rather than start the transfer late in the second grade, which means that children will be subject to unsupervised practice during the summer months, it seems wisest to start the transition in the third grade. Even then total transfer should not be rushed in the third grade. Children should continue to write spelling words and answers to test questions in the form of writing that is easiest for the individual. Even after cursive has been mastered there will be occasions throughout all grade levels to use print-script skills in such exercises as filling out forms, writing invitations, and designing greeting cards or posters.

The major aspect of readiness for training in cursive writing is the ability to read words written in this script. Members of the family will frequently teach a child to "write" rather than "print" his name. Teachers will start using cursive to present assignments and words in the spelling lessons. Children play games with their sight vocabulary in both printed and cursive forms. Other factors—such as desire to write, adequate physical development, and the ability to use print script—should be considered. Slower children who are just beginning to understand how to read should not face the additional problem of learning a new way to write.

A few children will make the transfer in imitation of the writing of parents or older children. The change is made with very little guidance, and penmanship instruction is only a matter of perfecting the new forms. These children do not need to follow any of the instructional patterns suggested here.

The transfer to cursive should conform to the principle of moving from the simple to the complex. Experience indicates that the small or lower-case letters should be introduced first, in the following order: *l, e, i, t, u, n, m, h, k, w, o, b, v, x, y, j, f, s, p, r, c, a, d, g, q, z.*

Capital letters, with the exception of *I*, should be taught in association with the children's names. Rather than drill on all of them in grade 3, it is best to practice them in usage with an example and teacher guidance.

The best equipment to use is an ordinary lead pencil at least 6 inches long, with soft lead (No. 2). The paper should be ruled. Because some children have a tendency to write too small, wide-ruled paper is usually used. Space lines such as two faint lines dividing the space into thirds between the regular lines of the paper aid most children. Usually the lines are closer together than that used for beginning manuscript writing. This sequence is followed in many schools:

Grade 1	At first unruled paper (without lines), 12- × 18-inch, folded.
	Later, 1-inch ruled paper.
	Later, ruled ½-inch light and heavy, long way.
Grade 2	9- × 12-inch, ruled ½-inch alternating light and heavy lines.
	Ruled 1-inch light, long way.
Grade 3	At first ½-inch alternating light and heavy lines.
	Later, ⅝-inch one space for tall letters.
Grade 4	Reduce to ½-inch as children are ready.
Grades 5, 6	Ruled ½-inch, reducing to ⅜-inch.
	⅜-inch spacing.

It is good classroom management to have a jar of sharpened pencils ready (having been prepared by a monitor) so that a pencil with a broken point can be exchanged for a new one without class interruption.

Slanted cursive writing is best introduced as a completely new form of writing. Before distributing paper to the class, the teacher might make remarks like this:

Many of you have noticed that your mothers and fathers do not use print-script writing. Some of you have written your name or a few words in this writing. You will see how this writing differs from the writing we have been doing. I will write the name of our town on the board in this new writing. You will see that the letters are slanted and joined. We have been writing with our papers directly in front of us. It will be easier to write this new way if you slant your paper. For those who are right-handed, the paper should slant to the left, with the bottom corner pointing toward your heart. If you are left-handed, the paper should slant to the right.

The exact position for each person will differ according to arm length. These variations may be suggested to the individual as the teacher observes his writing.

The first step is to make guidelines to use in letter formation. The teacher might say,

Watch while I make some lines on the board. Notice how each line slants the same as the other lines. I want them to slant only a little. I am going to leave a space between each pair of lines. Now you may make three pairs of slanted lines.

The first letter we make will be the letter *l*. I will start on the bottom line, cross the bottom of the slanted line, make a curved line to the top and then come down the guideline and finish with a small curve. Now, you try it. Make an *l* with each guideline.

Now, make three more pairs of guidelines and this time we will make two letter *l*'s that join. We might say, "Up, around, straight down; up, around, straight down."

Observe to see that the letters are neither too wide nor too thin. In the second lesson, demonstrate the letter *e,* using only half of a slanted line as a guide. Use the same three steps. Follow this with the letter *i.*

The third lesson introduces the letter *t.* Start by making guidelines on two-thirds of the writing space. The cross on the *t* is one-half the distance between the top and bottom writing lines.

The children should now start to use these letters in words.

The teacher might say,

"I am thinking of some words that use the letters we have practiced. If I put the guidelines for the words on the board, I wonder how many of you will be able to write the word. Copy the guidelines on your paper before you write the word.

Yes, the words are *ill* and *tell.* Can you think of another word that we can write with these letters? Yes, we could write *tile.* What guidelines will we need? See how many other words you can think of, using *i, e, l,* and *t.* We'll compare lists after I have helped some children with their writing.

Some children will think of only two or three. Possible words include *little, let, lie, lit, tie, title, tell, it, ill, tilt, eel,* and *tee.*

The fourth lesson introduces the letter *u.* Start by making two short guidelines in groups of three. Use guide phrases such as "up, down, around; up, down, around."

The letter *n* is made with groups of two small guidelines. This letter begins with a hump that starts a space before the first

Direct assistance should be given in guiding handwriting practice. (*Courtesy of the San Diego City Schools.*)

guideline. Guide words such as, "hump, down, hump, down, up" may be used.

The letter *m* is made with groups of three guidelines. The first stroke is the hump, a space before the first guideline.

Now a number of words may be written. "Instead of starting with guidelines, write the word, then put in the slanted guidelines to see if you have the proper slant. I wonder how many words you can make using *i, l, t, e, m, n,* and *u.*" Practice on these letters should continue several days.

The fifth lesson introduces the letter *h.*

This is a combination of *l* and *n.* As a guide one needs a long line and a short line.

Write words: *hit, hen, hill, him, the, then them.*

The letter *s* presents a special problem. Some prefer a square as a guide rather than a slanted line. The upstroke goes to the corner of the square and the downstroke follows straight down before making the curve.

The sixth lesson introduces the term *bridge.* The new letter is *w.* Start by making groups of three lines as for *m.* The teacher might say, "We will make the letter *w* by starting as if we were making the letter *u*. At the end, we go up once more, then make a bridge. This bridge sags a little. The letter *o* does not need a guideline but the bridge should be stressed. For the letter *b* we need only a long line as a guide. We first make the letter *l* then close the ending by coming around as one would make an *o* and end with a bridge."

Words to write: *will, bill, we, be, wet, bet, tub, new, bum.* Practice several days on words with the *bridge*. Note that when *e* and *i* are after a letter with a bridge, they start in a different way. The letter *r* is a bridge with a point. Difficult combinations at this point are *os, or, ox, ve, br.*

The next letter to study is *k*. This letter is like *h*. It starts as if one were writing *l*, then instead of a letter like *n*, one goes around and makes a little circle, then comes down to finish the letter.

If one covers a part of the letters *k* and *h*, one should see *l*.

The letters *a, g, d,* and *q,* contain the oval, which is the most difficult aspect of transfer from manuscript to cursive. One reason for insisting that when learning manuscript the child starts his circles at the 2 o'clock position is to aid in this transfer.

Start by having the child make a series of "eggs that tip or leaves on a stem." If short slanted lines are used, start at the top of these guidelines, make the oval by returning to the starting point, then follow the guideline down to make the connecting stroke.

Another method that might be described as "connected print script" would be handled in the following manner: Have the child print a word like *good*. Then have the child trace the word he has printed, without raising his pencil. This, of course, means that he will connect the letters. As the child retraces give him directions, such as: "Around, down, make the tail on the *g;* now, without raising your pencil, go up and over to the top of the letter *o*, around the *o*, and without raising your pencil, slide over to the other *o* and around the *o;* without raising your pencil, slide over to the round part of the letter *d;* go around and up on the stick stroke, down again, and add a tail stroke." Next let the child try to write the word *good* without retracing the print script.

Only letters which connect almost automatically should be taught by this connective method. The following primary words have letters which are easy for children to connect:

1. act	21. goat	41. hut	61. pail
2. add	22. gold	42. it	62. pat
3. all	23. good	43. lad	63. path
4. at	24. got	44. laid	64. pig
5. auto	25. ha	45. lap	65. pool
6. call	26. had	46. late	66. pop
7. cloth	27. hail	47. laugh	67. pot
8. cloud	28. hall	48. lip	68. pull
9. cold	29. hat	49. little	69. put
10. cup	30. hill	50. load	70. tag
11. cut	31. hid	51. log	71. tail
12. dad	32. hit	52. lot	72. tall
13. did	33. hog	53. oat	73. tap
14. dig	34. hold	54. o'clock	74. till
15. do	35. hole	55. oh	75. to
16. dog	36. hood	56. old	76. too
17. dot	37. hop	57. out	77. tool
18. dug	38. hot	58. pa	78. tooth
19. glad	39. hug	59. pad	79. up
20. go	40. hunt	60. paid	

in	in	in
it	it	it
call	call	call
put	put	put

The letters *b, e, f, r, k, s, z* must be taught as specific difficulties. The cursive that results from the method is vertical. Slant is obtained by turning the paper. Some teachers prefer to introduce this method by using dotted lines to show the cursive form on top of the print script. Children trace over these dotted lines as they master the new form.

The teacher starts with words containing letters that are alike in cursive and print script. These would contain the small letters *i, t, o, n, m, e, h, l, u, d, c* and the capital letters *B, C, K, L, O, P, R, U*. A word is written in print script on the board as an example for the children to observe. The word *it* would be printed at a slant. The teacher then adds a "reach stroke," going to the first letter and from the first to the second. An ending stroke for the word is added. Then the teacher says, "Now I am going to do it without patching (guiding dots). Reach for the *i*. Now make the *i* lean right back against the reach line. Reach high for the *t*. Lean the *t* right back against the reach line. Reach up as high as the *i* to end the word. Now cross the *t* in the middle and dot the *i*. Let's do it again but this time you tell me what to do. First we will put in patch lines then we will do it without patching." After this each child practices at the board.

This type of lesson is repeated with *in, me, he, let, nut, do, cut, ice, mud, hut, den, cent, nice, home, mile, come, then, did*. Each lesson contains these steps: the word is written first in slanted print script, reach strokes are patched in, the word is written without patching, and children steer the teacher's chalk through the word before writing it under supervision. Practice cards are provided which illustrate these steps for all the other letters. In the independent writing of the children during this period both cursive and print script appear. Both are expected—and permitted.

In the past, music was used a great deal as students practiced penmanship exercises. Experience with music as an aid to manuscript writing indicates some serious limitations. The music puts a premium on speed that is unnecessary and frustrating. The major practice should be with words, and because each letter has a different rhythm, no music is of the proper beat for words. Little children respond to music with total body movement that interferes with writing.

When parents ask about teaching their children to write at home the teacher may explain thus:

If a child writes before he is ready, he frequently develops a feeling of tension, grips his pencil too tightly, and builds up a dislike for writing. Then too, a young child's muscles are not developed enough for successful writing. Therefore he should use large pencils and crayons. These are provided in school. Writing at school is supervised to avoid poor habits, such as gripping the pencil too tightly, incorrect letter formations, and poor position.

If, however, the child is eager to write and seems ready, parents might give the child a large, soft pencil or crayon and unlined paper, and teach manuscript letters using

capitals only at the beginning of proper names. (Send a copy of the specimen alphabet to the child's home.)

For Discussion

1. Why do you consider the second, third, or fourth grade the best place to make the transfer to cursive writing?

2. Which method of transfer do you prefer? Why?

3. Make a worksheet to be used during this period of writing instruction.

4. Try writing to music. Do you feel that it would aid instruction?

5. Write a letter to parents explaining the handwriting program in your school.

How May Good Cursive Writing Be Achieved and Maintained?

There are a number of well-planned, modern handwriting programs available for use in schools. Some school systems, like those of Hawaii, Minneapolis, Detroit, and Philadelphia, have prepared programs for their own use. The first step toward achieving good cursive writing is to select or devise a system of handwriting and then follow it with determination and consistency.

The New York City schools group for related teaching those letters with similar structure. In the related groupings that follow, some of the letter forms are analyzed for teaching. The letters *SSD* refer to straight slanting downstroke in all letters except *c* and *o*.

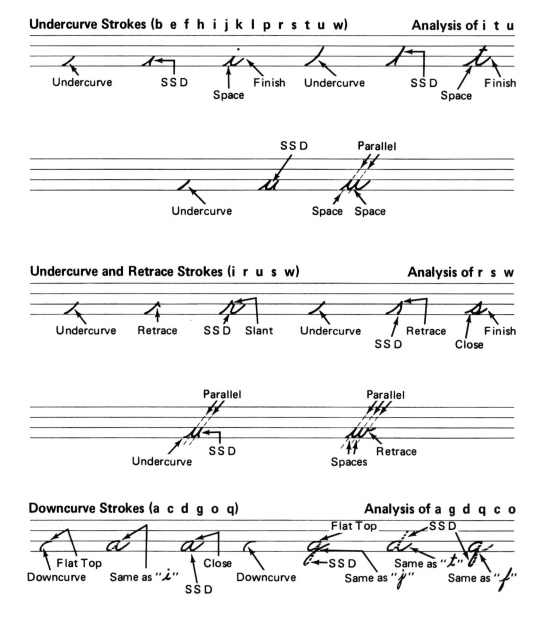

Undercurve Strokes (b e f h i j k l p r s t u w)   **Analysis of i t u**

Undercurve   SSD   Finish   Space   Undercurve   SSD   Finish   Space

SSD   Parallel

Undercurve   Space   Space

Undercurve and Retrace Strokes (i r u s w)   **Analysis of r s w**

Undercurve   Retrace   SSD   Slant   Undercurve   Retrace   Finish   SSD   Close

Parallel   Parallel

Undercurve   SSD   Retrace   Spaces

Downcurve Strokes (a c d g o q)   **Analysis of a g d q c o**

Flat Top   SSD

Flat Top   Close   SSD

Downcurve   Same as "*i*"   SSD   Downcurve   Same as "*j*"   Same as "*t*"   Same as "*f*"

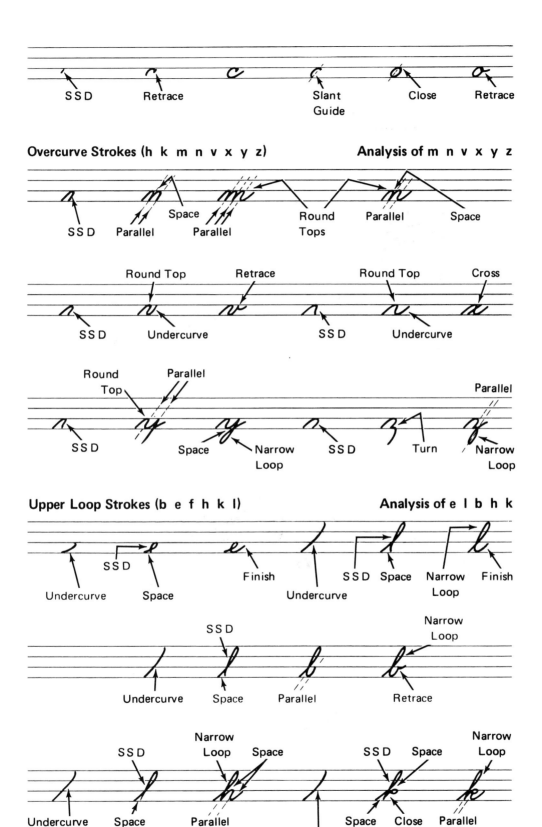

SSD Retrace Slant Guide Close Retrace

Overcurve Strokes (h k m n v x y z)

Analysis of m n v x y z

SSD Parallel Space Parallel Round Tops Parallel Space

Round Top Retrace Round Top Cross
SSD Undercurve SSD Undercurve

Round Top Parallel Parallel
SSD Space Narrow Loop SSD Turn Narrow Loop

Upper Loop Strokes (b e f h k l)

Analysis of e l b h k

Undercurve SSD Space Finish Undercurve SSD Space Narrow Loop Finish

SSD Narrow Loop
Undercurve Space Parallel Retrace

SSD Narrow Loop Space SSD Space Narrow Loop
Undercurve Space Parallel Undercurve Space Close Parallel

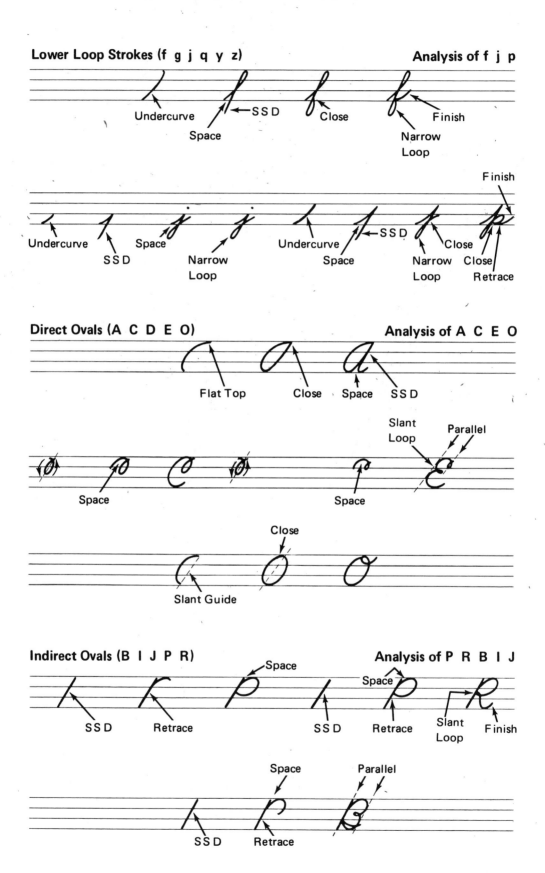

Lower Loop Strokes (f g j q y z) Analysis of f j p

Undercurve Space SSD Close Finish Narrow Loop

Finish

Undercurve SSD Space Narrow Loop Undercurve Space SSD Narrow Loop Close Close Retrace

Direct Ovals (A C D E O) Analysis of A C E O

Flat Top Close Space SSD

Slant Loop Parallel

Space Space

Close

Slant Guide

Indirect Ovals (B I J P R) Analysis of P R B I J

Space Space

SSD Retrace SSD Retrace Slant Loop Finish

Space Parallel

SSD Retrace

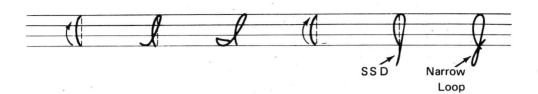

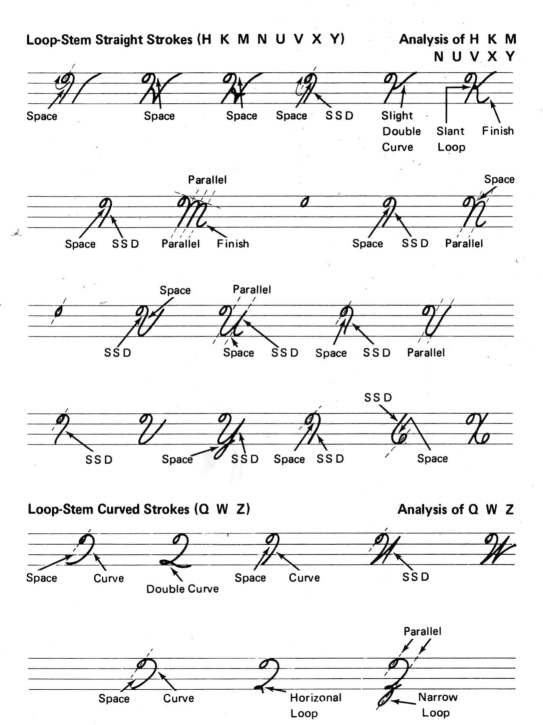

Loop-Stem Straight Strokes (H K M N U V X Y)

Analysis of H K M N U V X Y

Loop-Stem Curved Strokes (Q W Z)

Analysis of Q W Z

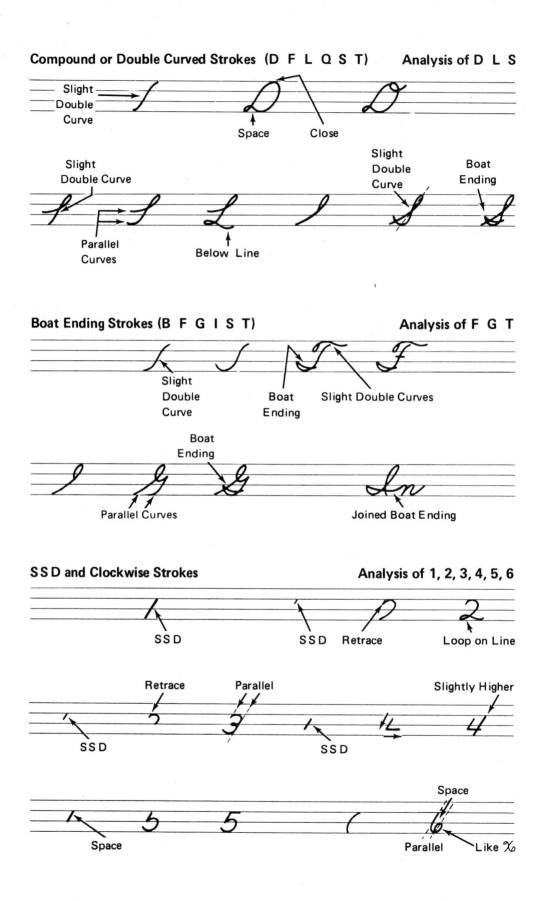

Compound or Double Curved Strokes (D F L Q S T)　　　Analysis of D L S

Slight Double Curve

Space　　Close

Slight Double Curve

Parallel Curves

Below Line

Slight Double Curve

Boat Ending

Boat Ending Strokes (B F G I S T)　　　Analysis of F G T

Slight Double Curve

Boat Ending

Slight Double Curves

Boat Ending

Parallel Curves

Joined Boat Ending

S S D and Clockwise Strokes　　　Analysis of 1, 2, 3, 4, 5, 6

SSD

SSD　Retrace

Loop on Line

Retrace　　Parallel

Slightly Higher

SSD

SSD

Space

Space　　　　Parallel　　Like 𝒳

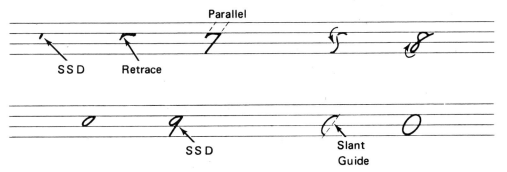

Determination is needed because so often the short time allowed for handwriting practice gets crowded out of the school day. In most intermediate grades only about sixty-minutes a week divided into three twenty-minute sessions on Monday, Wednesday, and Friday are available for handwriting drill. This is enough time if the practices stressed are consistently followed in all the writing of the child. These short sessions are usually planned to provide practice on a single element in writing. It may concern the formation of a letter, spacing, alignment, slant, connecting strokes, or ending stroke. After the teacher has demonstrated the element and the group has discussed the writing problem presented, the students usually follow an exercise in a copybook. After this is completed a comparison is made between the students' work and the example for the purpose of evaluation. The motivation is usually based on the student's desire to gain recognition through excellence or to improve a weakness.

Frequently only those who have special handwriting problems participate in the classwork, whereas those who have no special needs use the time for independent writing. One disadvantage of many programs is that they use as examples a higher quality of writing than is normally achieved. Indeed, the same examples serve for the sixth grade that are used in the third. The Minneapolis schools have solved the latter problem by selecting examples for each grade from children in that grade. These have been reproduced in a handwriting scale for each grade. Sample One is of the very best and is labeled "You have reached your goal. Your writing is very good." Below the example attention

is called to the word shapes, spacing, and letter formation, with the teacher's suggestion on how to score a writing sample that is similar to it. Sample Two says, "You are on the right track. Your writing is satisfactory." Sample Three says, "You are on the right track. You need to improve." Attention is called to some of the errors in the samples as well as the good qualities. Number Four says, "You are on the wrong track. You need help." Again the errors are noted. Each child has an individual Handwriting Record which is based on the above scale and other charts. Each grade level has a series of lessons—sometimes described as writing tricks—designed to improve items checked in the record.

The following example of the cursive writing lesson plan for grades 5–6 is taken from the New York Public Schools.

Over-All Class Aim

To maintain proper spacing between letters.

Specific Aim

To refine the formation of the small letters with rounded tops.

Motivation

The teacher shows the class a piece of written work in which many words are illegible (postcard or envelope returned because of illegible address; spelling, composition or social studies papers). On the lined chalkboard, she copies some of the incorrectly written words and writes the correct form next to each. She discusses with the children the causes of the difficulty encountered in reading the words and guides them to the conclusion that the main cause is essentially the pointed tops in certain letters. They also note that other elements, including poor spacing, make words difficult to read.

The teacher writes the letters *m, h, v,* on the chalkboard and adds, at the children's suggestion, other small letters which should have rounded tops, as *n, y, x.* The teacher and children decide which of these letters to re-analyze and practice in order to help them improve the writing of all small letters with rounded tops.

Procedures

Teacher:

Writes the letter *y* on the lined chalkboard and discusses it as she writes. . . .

Reviews with the children posture and position of paper and pencil.

Children:

Copy the letter, compare it with the teacher's model, note any deviation, rewrite it correctly if necessary, and then write it three or four times more.

Dictate to the teacher, for writing on the chalkboard, words in which the letter occurs at different places, e.g., *you,* by, *eye.*

Copy these words and check specifically for the correct formation of the letter *y* and the spacing between letters.

Teacher:

Moves about the room to assist a few children individually.

Children:

Dictate to the teacher, for writing on the chalkboard, a sentence which includes the practice letter and possibly other letters in the related group; e.g., T*he* bo*y*s *h*elp eac*h* ot*h*er i*n m*an*y* ways.

Copy the sentence from the chalkboard once or twice depending upon their individual speed.

Evaluation

The teacher helps the children to compare their letter *y* in the sentence with their practice writing of the letter. They also note the rounded tops of the related letters in the group. In addition, they compare a piece of writing from their folders with their practice paper to note the improvement in the writing of these letters.

Assignment

The children plan to pay particular attention to the writing of the letters with rounded tops in copying their reports for the class newspaper.

There are handwriting scales available with nearly all commercial programs. Children find these difficult to use in analyzing their own writing. There is no reason why any class or school cannot collect enough writing samples to develop its own standards or expectancies for each grade. The standardized scales can be used by teachers as they make judgments concerning the samples selected. Probably the most scientifically constructed scale is that devised by Leonard P. Ayres and published by the Educational Testing Service of Princeton, N.J. A major consideration is general quality of writing rather than specific style. This is difficult to determine if the writing being judged is vertical or backhand. Most individuals making such appraisals are also influenced by the formation of certain letters, such as capital *R* or small *r.* Noble and Noble and the Palmer Company have scales that diagnose specific writing problems of children practicing the methods published by these firms. The Zaner-Bloser Company makes available a small dictionary of letter forms which each child uses. This dictionary presents the letters of their system with a space for the child to make his own examples. These can be used as a record of a child's progress. As the child compares his present writing with his past work he can note progress or weakness. This comparison serves much the same purpose as a standardized scale.

Writing samples should be collected from each child at least four times during the year and kept in a collection of other examples of his work. Some teachers ask the child to write, "This is a sample of my writing on October 1." This inscription is folded back so that it is not visible when the child later writes, "This is a sample of my writing on January 1." Direct comparison can be made to see if skills are being maintained or improvement made. Both examples of writing are folded back when the child writes a third or fourth time on the same paper. Such a sample is especially helpful when talking with a parent about a child's work.

The following form, prepared by the Sheaffer Pen Company, is an example of an individual diagnostic device. It is designed to help children establish goals for their work in handwriting as well as establish meaningful standards.[2]

PUPIL SELF-ANALYSIS SHEET

A. Here is how I write when I am in a hurry:
   (Write: "This is a sample of my writing")

_____

_____

B. Here is how I write when I do my best writing:
   (Write: "This is a sample of my best writing")

_____

_____

_____

C. I would mark my fast writing: (circle one grade) Excellent   Good   Fair   Poor
   I would mark my best writing: Excellent   Good   Fair   Poor

D. Here is my analysis of my handwriting:

	EXCELLENT	GOOD	FAIR	POOR
1. SLANT .... Do all my letters lean the same way?	____	____	____	____
2. SPACING .... Are the spaces between letters and words even?	____	____	____	____
3. SIZE .... Are all small letters evenly small and tall letters evenly tall?	____	____	____	____
4. ALIGNMENT .... Do all my letters touch the line?	____	____	____	____
5. LOOPS .... Are l, f, h, g, y, k, b well formed?	____	____	____	____
6. STEMS .... Are all my downstrokes really straight?	____	____	____	____
7. CLOSINGS .... Are a, d, g, o, p, s closed?	____	____	____	____
8. ROUNDNESS .... Are m, n, h, u, v, w, y rounded?	____	____	____	____
9. RETRACES .... Are t, i, d, p, m, n retraced?	____	____	____	____
10. ENDINGS .... Do my words have good ending strokes without fancy swinging strokes?	____	____	____	____

[2] *My Handwriting Quotient* (Madison: W. A. Sheaffer Pen Company, 1960).

In the handwriting period there will be times when the entire group will be working on the same problem—perhaps that of word endings or alignment. Because all have a like purpose, group diagnosis is effective. Project samples of the writing on a screen by means of an opaque projector. Because the purpose is to seek means of improvement rather than being graded, most children will welcome the attention and suggestions concerning the next step they should take to improve. At first, attention should be directed toward one or two specific points. After using this type of diagnosis for some time, any aspect of the child's writing may be the basis for suggestion. A plastic transparent overlay will help some children examine specific letters. These are available with most handwriting systems. Another device is to cut a small hole in a piece of paper and examine the child's writing one letter at a time.

Those who write well should receive recognition. There should be a place to exhibit "our best work." Some teachers have rubber stamps made so that they can place *excellent* or from one to four stars on a paper. We know that intermediate children respond to such praise and that all learners work better if they know the work will be evaluated.

Regardless of the system used, the following five elements enter into the handwriting program; a chart of these made for the classroom can act as a constant reminder:

1. *Formation.* Each letter should be made and joined correctly according to whatever penmanship system is followed. Examples of letters that cause trouble can be shown on this chart.
2. *Size.* This is to remind them of the need for uniformity in size regardless of the type of letter.
3. *Slant.* The problem here is usually one of consistency.
4. *Alignment.* Letters that go above or below the line get mixed with other writing and thus are very difficult to read.
5. *Spacing.* Even spacing is necessary for

rhythmic reading. This chart, based on the program of the New York City schools, emphasizes these ideas.

The final judgment concerning handwriting should be based upon the child's daily written work. Occasionally, before and after children complete a written assignment, make a class inventory of writing needs. Have the students look at their papers while you record by number (not name) the results on the chalkboard. Use the following inventory of writing habits:

Alignment
    How many had
        correct top alignment?
        uneven top alignment?
        correct bottom alignment?
        uneven bottom alignment?
        writing under the line?
        writing over the line?
Letter Spacing
    How many had
        correct letter spacing?
        uneven letter spacing?
        letter spacing too close together?
        letter spacing too far apart?
Word Spacing
    How many had
        correct word spacing?
        uneven word spacing?
        word spacing too close together?
        word spacing too far apart?

The secret of continuous improvement is to establish a feeling of achievement. This can be done by setting specific attainable goals. When a goal is achieved, celebrate it fittingly. (While one can hardly recommend leading a snake dance through the halls whenever the whole class learns to make a good capital *A*, it is no less of an achievement than winning a basketball game.) Examples of such objectives that the entire group can eventually achieve are

• Write the small letters of the alphabet correctly four times, joining the letters to each other. The teacher (or a committee) can be the judge until an acceptable exercise is received from each member of the class.

Guiding Rules for Cursive Writing of the Small Alphabet [3]

1. In the lower-case alphabet, every letter, except *c* and *o,* must have a *straight* down stroke, slanting from right to left.

    The downstrokes are not straight.

    The downstrokes are straight.

2. The *space* between two letters should be wide enough to hold an *n* without the up-stroke:

    "n spaces" between letters

    Spaces are too narrow.

    Spaces are too wide.

3. All downstrokes must be parallel.

    Downstrokes are parallel.

    Downstrokes are not parallel.

4. All letters must rest ON the line.

    Letters rest ON the line.

    Letters do not rest on the line.

5. Letters must be of uniform and proportionate size.

6. The *total* slant of the writing should be parallel to the diagonal of the paper, whether by right-handed or left-handed writers.

- Write sentences using words with difficult letter joinings, such as *bring, arrows, written, following, uncommon, bewitched, disturbance, suited,* and *delighted.*
- Write sentences using these words: *there, their, they're; here's, hears; were, we're, wear; your, you're.*
- Copy a short poem.
- Write a good thank-you letter.
- Write the alphabet in capital letters.

- Write the addresses of three friends as they would appear on an envelope.
- Write five quotations.
- Make a directory of the class showing names, addresses, and telephone numbers.
- Keep the minutes as a secretary of a meeting.

[3] Max Rosenhaus, "You Can Teach Handwriting with Only Six Rules," *The Instructor* (March 1957), p. 60.

The following sentences contain *all* the lower-case letters of the alphabet. When written a few weeks apart the student may evaluate his progress.

1. The violinist and the zither player were equally fine so the judge marked both excellent.
2. At the zoo, the children saw an ibex, a jaguar, a kangaroo, a flamingo, and a very queer bird called a pelican.
3. The writer moves the hand quickly but smoothly across the page, watching the sizes of the letters and joining them expertly.

Many schools purchase an alphabet strip which they place over a chalkboard to act as a constant point of reference for children as they write. This technique can be effective if it is made significant to the children. Some teachers have pictures drawn to go with each letter. In the lower grades the drawing may be an apple for *a,* but the upper grades may require something more challenging to illustrate such words as *avocado* or *astronaut.* Unfortunately, the space over the chalkboard is an awkward point of reference. For some children the details of the letters are lost because of vision problems. Some programs provide individual desk cards which are used by the children when they need to recall how a letter is made. In practice these are more effective than the alphabet strip.

There are two types of children who must be provided with such individual references. One is the left-handed child who needs examples that apply to his pattern of writing. The other is the transfer student who has mastered a system other than the one being taught in the new school. To require that such children change to the system taught in the new situation is an example of educational inefficiency.

The following lesson, prepared by Naiman, was designed as part of a rapid review program with intermediate-grade children.[4]

---

[4] Nathan Naiman, *A Blitz Handwriting Program* (San Diego, Calif.: Oak Park School, 1960).

Finishing Strokes

Ending the last letter of each word with a good finishing stroke makes our handwriting look much better. Most of these strokes swing up with a slight upward curve to the height of the letter *a.* The curve of the final stroke is downward on the letters *g, j, y* and *z.*

Part 1

Look at yesterday's sample of your best handwriting. Look for the final stroke or "tails" on every word that you wrote on this sample. Put the number of tails that you left off here: _____ Count every tail that is poorly shaped or that reaches above or below the height of the letter *a.*

Part 2

Now put your name on the right of the top line of your paper. Put the date just below your name. On the third line just to the left of the center, put the title, "Handwriting." Skip the next line. Using good finishing strokes, write the following sentence three times:

Paul said, "The big brown fox quickly and slyly jumped over the lazy dog.

Skip a line and then write the following words, ending them with good tails:

month because windy high kite string west held fell oak broke away will where an hold east air

Part 3

Again, look at yesterday's sample of your handwriting. Copy those words needing tails and put good tails or finishing strokes on them. Look closely at the ending of each word to see that you are improving your final strokes.

Using Good Slant in Handwriting—Lower Loop Letters

Proper slant in handwriting is very important in the making of lower loop letters. Be sure the slanted part of these letters is straight. The lower loop letters are: *g, j, p, y* and *z.*

Part 1

Take the written work. Put the guide sheet under it. See if the lower loop letters have the correct angle of slant. How would you grade your slant? Is it excellent, good, fair or poor? _____

Now look at the finishing strokes. Put a check by those that do not reach as high as the letter *a*.

Part 2

Today we will practice good slant on the lower loop letters. Put your name on the upper right on the top line of your paper. Put the date just below your name. On the third line just to the left of the center, put the title "Handwriting." Skip the next line.

_____

_____

Carefully write a line of each of these lower loop letters:

g, j, p, q, z

Here are some words that have lower loop letters. Write each two times:

gag   pipe   gang   jig   pig

Write this sentence two times: "The big pig danced a jig."

Part 3

Now look at all of the writing you have done today. See if all of your lower loop letters reach half way below the line. See if they have straight backs. Circle those which are poorly formed. Practice writing those words that you circled. How would you grade today's work? Is it excellent, good, fair, poor? _____

Spacing in Handwriting

After one word has been finished, a space is left before the next word is written. This space is just about as wide as the small letter *a*. This space should never be larger or smaller than this.

Part 1

Look back at the sentences you wrote in earlier lessons. See if the spacing between words is about as wide as the letter *a*. Are you leaving too much space or not enough? How would you grade your spacing on these sentences? Is it excellent, good, fair, or poor? _____

Part 2

Put the heading on your paper.

Now here are some sentences for you to write. Be careful to leave a uniform space between your words. Write each sentence twice:

The quick brown fox jumps over the lazy dog.
Whatever is worth doing at all is worth doing well.
Well begun is half done.

Here is a sample of good spacing:

_____

_____

Part 3

Skip a line and write the following:

"Here is another sample of my best handwriting. I am careful with finishing strokes, slant, letter size, and the spacing between letters."

Compare this writing with the writing in the first lesson. Is it better, just as good as, or poorer than this first lesson? _____

The following are other suggestions with respect to handwriting instruction in the intermediate grades which come from experienced teachers.

1. Make the paper on which the final writing will appear have special significance. Make mimeograph copies of a flag, holiday picture, or school letterhead on good-quality "mimeo" bond paper. Explain that the number of copies is limited and that the paper should not be used for the exercise until each person feels that he is prepared. Sometimes attractive stationery will serve the same purpose.

2. Hold a writing clinic with one or two of the best writers acting as "doctors" for specific letters.

3. Exchange handwriting samples with other schools, both in the United States and in other countries.

4. Suggest to parents the value of a good writing instrument as a birthday or Christmas gift.

5. Make art designs formed of alphabet letters.

6. Have an "Each One Teach One"

week, during which each child teaches one letter and its formation to another child or small group. Let the children devise worksheets or lessons for this. One fifth grade produced a textbook titled, "How to Write Well."

The most important handwriting problem is that of illegibility. Illegible handwriting is due to seven errors: (1) faulty endings, (2) incorrectly made undercurves, (3) mixed slant, (4) failure to give letters in the *a* group proper slant, (5) incorrect formation of the initial stroke of such letters as the capitals *W, H, K*, (6) incorrect endings in final *h, m, n*, and (7) failure to make the downstroke of *t* and *d*.

End strokes as spacers between words improve the legibility of writing more than any other single device. One writer claims that attention to this factor can improve legibility by 25 per cent.

Ability to make the undercurve of the letter *l* alone improves the shape of many related letters and brings about the orderly appearance of written paragraphs.

The letters that extend below the line should show the same slant as those above the line. The principle of parallel slants brings about harmony in handwriting.

Many letters exhibit an initial stroke shaped like a cane. The stroke consists of two parts, a loop and a downstroke. These should be made so as to conform to the slant of the other letters. There are eleven letters to which this principle applies.

When *h, m*, or *n* appears at the end of a word, there is a tendency to slur the last two strokes. Emphasis upon precision in making the last downstroke in writing these letters and in the final upstroke removes a common fault. The letters *t* and *d* constitute a special application of the *l* principle. Once the relationship of these letters to the *l* principle is recognized, errors in letter formation are eliminated.

The letters *e, a, r*, and *t* cause the most confusion. Such combinations as *be, bi, br, by, bo, oe, oi, os, oc, oa, ve, va, vo, vu, we, wi, wa, ws*, and *wr* also cause trouble. The demons of handwriting are *a* that looks like *o, u*, or *ci; l* that becomes *li; d* that appears

as *cl; e* like *i* or the reverse; *m* and *n* like *w* and *u; t* like *l* or *i*; and *r* like *e* or *n*.

To make children aware of certain legibility difficulties have them do the following:

1. Write the words *add, gold*, and *dare* and analyze the letters *a, d*, and *g*. What happens if the letters are not closed at the top?
2. Write the words *no, nail, make*, and *name* and analyze the letters *m* and *n*. What happens if the top is not rounded?
3. Write the words *it, tin, nine*, and *trip* and analyze the letters *t* and *i*. What happens if the letters have open loops?
4. Write the words *late, let*, and *lend* and analyze the letters *l* and *e*. What happens when the loops are not open?
5. Write the words *up, under*, and *run* and analyze the letter *u*. What happens when the tops of *u* are not pointed?

Some writing habits must be changed to increase legibility. Children who write *gt, ot*, or *ju* with short connecting strokes should be told to "swing between each letter" or "spread your letters out like an accordion." At first the distance should be exaggerated, then modified to proper spacing. If a child continues to write all letters close together, let him practice his spelling words on a regular sheet of ruled tablet paper but with the lines vertical rather than horizontal. There should be one letter between each line.

A tight grip on the writing instrument may produce tense, slow writing. The writer can be helped by having him wad a sheet of paper into a ball. This is held by the lower fingers against the palm of the hand. Such a practice seems to direct the pressure from the pen.

Speed is the great enemy of legibility. We can think as fast as 250 words a minute and write about twenty-five. Yet eventually some rhythmic speed must be attained.

Drills to increase speed may be of these types:

- Write one letter. *nnnnnnn*
- Write difficult letter combinations which tend to decrease speed of writing—*e, i, r* following *b, w, v.*
- Write easy word or words— *the to it run sun*
- Write words with thought associations *sunsunsunsun* clap hands, green grass, blue sky
- Write one- or two-minute time tests.

Suggested sentences containing twenty letters are

Working for speed is fun.
She will meet you at home.
Write all papers neatly.

Suggested rate per minute

- Grade 4, with pencil: forty-five letters or better.
- Grade 5, with pen: fifty-five letters or better.
- Grade 6, with pen: sixty-five letters or better.

If a child persists in poor writing, it may reflect an emotional problem. In such cases it is wise to forget about handwriting instructions until the basic problems of the child are cared for.

When the writing problem is due to a bad habit in holding the pen, the interesting and inexpensive plastic writing frame available from Zaner-Blower may prove helpful. This device positions the writing instrument and aids the necessary retraining.

The basic cause of illegible handwriting is carelessness. The solution is to make handwriting so important that the learner will care enough to do it well.

For Discussion

1. How can a bulletin board be used to motivate good writing?
2. What should be the attitude of a teacher whose handwriting is not a good example for the children?
3. How can a "Good Writers' Club" or a "Pen Pal Club" motivate good handwriting?
4. Give arguments for and against awarding handwriting certificates.

What Provisions Should Be Made for the Left-Handed Child?

It is seldom very satisfying to be a member of a small minority or to be considered "different" from other people. The left-handed person faces both these problems. In our population the left-handed number from 4 to 11 per cent of the population. The range of these figures may be explained by the extent of tolerance of left-handedness in the segment of the population surveyed. Where no effort has been made to convert the left-handed individual to right-handed writing we have higher percentages than in those places subject to more pressure to change. (In a society where table manners, writing tools, and student desks conform to the assumption that everyone is right-handed, the left-handed individual certainly is at a disadvantage.)

To expect or require a left-handed person to become right-handed makes no more sense than expecting a right-handed person to develop left-handedness. There are many outstanding left-handed persons, ranging from Leonardo da Vinci to former President Harry S Truman. The term *sinistral* used to describe a left-handed person comes from Latin and simply means left-handed. (Unfortunately, the term *sinister* is closely related and has an unpleasant connotation.) Sinistrals in school should have the same individual respect that we advocate for all children.

Once we acknowledge the right of a child to write with his left hand, we then have the task of finding ways to help him do this well. The usual way that left-handedness is revealed is through the individual's activities. Observation of a child while he is using a pair of scissors, bouncing and catching a ball, putting marbles into a jar one at a time, eating with a spoon, or using a hammer and saw will reveal the dominant hand. If a child uses both hands with equal ease we say that he is ambidextrous. Because of the general convenience that it will provide, these children are taught to write with the right hand.

It is not easy to determine true dominance for some children. They may have a left-eye dominance and still be right-handed. Some children should be referred to trained clinicians to determine true dominance.

A number of simple tests have been suggested to help determine mixed dominance, left-eye preference with right-hand preference, or right-eye preference with left-hand preference. Cases of mixed dominance are evidenced in the problem some children have in keeping their paper in the "arm track." They seem to be maneuvering their paper constantly to try to keep it in place.

The preferred eye can be determined by having the pupil sight a coin on the floor through a cardboard cylinder held at arm's length. The coin is sighted with both eyes open. First one eye and then the other is covered as he looks at the coin. When the dominant eye is covered, the coin can no longer be seen through the cylinder.

A more elaborate device to determine motor-visual preference and to stimulate the development of controlled vision in the eye on the same side of the body as that of the dominant hand is the Leavill Hand-Eye Coordinator produced by the Keystone View Company, Meadville, Pa.

At one time it was felt that forcing children to change from left- to right-handedness would cause stuttering and other psychological tensions. Some experiments seem to indicate that it is not so much the change as the way the change is directed. Although there is no clear-cut evidence that cerebral nerve damage does take place when a child's natural handedness is tampered with, there is equally little evidence that it does not. As teachers we must ask ourselves this question: Is right-handed writing so important that we are willing to risk creating speech trouble, neuroses, or other evidence of emotional disturbance? The answer is usually no.

Some of the difficulties faced by the left-handed person learning to write a system devised by right-handed individuals can be experienced by a right-handed person who attempts a few left-handed exercises. Draw a series of squares, first with the right hand and then with the left. Note that the "pull strokes" with the right hand are "pushing strokes" with the left. These strokes involve different muscles according to the hand used. Then observe a right-handed individual writing. He starts at a mid-body position and writes in a natural left-to-right movement, away from the body. An attempt to imitate this will reveal why a left-handed child copying a right-handed teacher will write moving away from his mid-body position toward his natural direction, or right to left. The result is mirror writing, which is completely legible to the writer but can be read by the rest of us only when held up to a mirror. Correction is made by explaining to the child that he must conform to the left-to-right pattern so that others can read what he writes. Have him copy individual words and letters, always starting at the left side of the paper. This will take considerable time because he is being asked to learn to write words that seem backward to him. Eventually, as these children master reading, the problem disappears. Sometimes it is wise to postpone writing instruction temporarily until reading is well established.

Another result of imitating right-handed writing is that the child develops an awkward writing position. In order to hold a pencil or pen in exactly the way a right-handed person does, a left-handed child may twist his hand around to a backward or upside-down position. Some actually write upside down.

It is very difficult to help these children once such awkward writing positions are well established. The first requirement is that both the child and his parents want to correct it. Without this desire the results of any teaching effort will be limited. For the child it is almost a punishment. Some will write quite well in the "backward" position, but for many it will mean uncomfortable writing for a lifetime.

Start by adjusting the position of the paper and arm. Place two tape markers on the desk or writing table. Have the child rest his left arm between these two tapes. This will prevent the arm from swinging out. Another tape can be used to indicate the proper position for the paper. Provide a long pencil or ballpoint pen as the writing instrument. Have the child hold this about an inch and a half from the point. The first exercises should be tracing over letters and words written by a left-handed individual. A considerable amount of writing should be done at the chalkboard; it is practically impossible to use the upside-down position there. The teacher might even guide the hand movements to assure the correct response. These children should have a card of letters written by a left-handed person for personal reference at their desks. If the child who has reached the fifth grade is using an awkward position, it is sometimes best to let him continue. Urge instead that he learn to use the typewriter as soon as possible. Some school systems have special summer classes in typing for such left-handed children. Here the left-handed have an advantage over right-handed people; the standard typewriter keyboard was designed by a left-handed person.

There is little experimental evidence to guide a teacher in developing a writing program for the left-handed child. Teachers with experience suggest the following procedures.

Group the left-handed together. This makes it easier to supervise instruction and prevents a tendency to imitate right-handed individuals.

Begin instruction at the chalkboard where close supervision can be given. An error caught early can prevent the formation of a bad habit. Stress left-to-right movement and the starting place when writing each letter. Circles should be made from left to right in manuscript, even though this may seem awkward at first.

When the left-handed child starts writing on paper, it may be wise to have him place an arrow as a "traffic signal" at the beginning of his writing to assure the teacher that he is starting at the correct place and proceeding in the correct left-to-right direction. A left-handed child may be a good helper to another left hander.

The child learning to write manuscript with his left hand places the paper directly in front of him, just as the right-handed individual does. It will be necessary for him to move the paper frequently as he writes; this is the task of the right hand. Accordingly the writer should be seated at the left-hand side of a table—or alone at an individual desk rather than sharing a table with a right-handed child. Once these first steps have been mastered, the left-handed child might continue writing print script throughout the grades. In the second grade his print script may develop a natural slant if he slants his paper as he will later for cursive writing so that his left hand follows a natural arc while moving from left to right. Otherwise some feel that he should be started on cursive immediately. Why should he be required to learn two different systems developed for right-handed people?

The natural arc of the left hand as it rests on the desk should determine the position of the paper for cursive writing. The upper right corner of the paper will be in line with the centerline of the body. Children can be told that the bottom corner should point "toward their heart." In shifting the paper the right hand presses down on it, holding it firmly until one line is finished, and then moves it up for the next line. The left hand slides lightly along the line of writing while the paper is kept stationary.

The pen or pencil is held with the thumb, index, and middle fingers. It should slant toward the writer's left shoulder. The pen should be held a little higher than would be the case for a right-handed writer, so that the child can see what he writes and avoid running the left hand over the written material. Some teachers place a small rubber band around the pen to indicate where to grip the instrument.

A good ballpoint pen is a better writing instrument for the left-handed person than a pen with a steel nib. The ballpoint does not dig into the paper with the upstrokes, and the ink dries immediately. Avoid cheap ballpoints that are too short, or those that must be held in a tight grip because the sides are too smooth. A strip of adhesive tape on the barrel helps to keep a pen from slipping.

Copy for the left-handed writing exercises should be directly in front of the writer, not on the chalkboard. At first some children need to have their hands guided through the proper movements. If a single letter is reversed in any writing, take time to work on that letter alone.

Let the child determine his own letter slant after you have established the proper position of the paper for him. Most left-handed children seem to prefer a vertical form of writing. A few find a backhand more natural. Because our objective is legibility and ease of writing, slant should not be predetermined for the left-handed.

Special attention may need to be given to the letters *O, T, F,* and *H* to prevent the use of sinistral strokes. Because upward strokes are difficult for some left-handed writers, they may be eliminated on the letters *a, c, d, g, o, q* when they begin a word.

A complete set of writing exercises is available for left-handed children learning cursive writing. These exercises were written by Dr. Warren Gardner and are available from the Interstate Press, 19 North Jackson Street; Danville, Ill.

A special meeting with parents of left-handed children is of value. Stress at this meeting the normalness of being left-handed, stress the problems relating to changing handedness, and give a demonstration of proper left-handed writing.

Research by E. A. Enstron justifies the conclusion that

pupil success in writing with the left hand is basically a problem of teacher understanding. When we know how to help *beginning* left-handed writers, they will, in all normal situations, learn to write successfully with speed and ease, and their writing will have the usual forward slant. There is no need for a left-handed pupil to be stigmatized as an "odd-ball" by writing in a different, absolutely unnecessary, difficult-to-read style.

Many left-handed individuals resent as much discussion as provided here with respect to their writing. "What is the problem?" they ask. And we can truthfully answer, "For many left-handed individuals, there is no problem."

For Discussion

1. What advantages and disadvantages does a left-handed teacher have?

2. Would it be wise to have all left-handed children in the intermediate grades meet together for handwriting instruction?

3. Spain, Italy, all Iron Curtain countries except Czechoslovakia, and most of the Oriental world permit only right-handed writing. What religious references are the basis for such a rigid demand?

Suggestions for Projects

1. Assemble enough samples from one classroom or school to construct a handwriting scale. This might be a scale for judging the manuscript writing of children in the third grade, the writing of left-handed individuals of the same age, or of boys in the sixth grade.

2. Investigate the materials used in England to teach "italic" writing. That published by Ginn and Company (London) is widely used. Dillons University Book Store, 1 Mallet St., London, is another source of such materials.

3. Investigate the use of the typewriter by elementary school students. When is typing taught? How is the skill used by a child in the regular classroom? What special teaching programs are available?

4. Plan a display that will explain the handwriting program of your school to the public.

5. Make a comparison of the various handwriting programs now on the market. What are the essential differences with regard to philosophy, equipment, letter-formation drills, and special features?

6. Make a case study of an individual with a handwriting problem.

Bibliography

Books

Handwriting Made Easy—Teacher's Manual and Refresher Course. New York: Noble & Noble Publishers, Inc., 1957.

Articles

Anderson, Dan W. "What Makes Writing Legible," *Elementary School Journal* (April 1969), pp. 365–69.

Enstrom, E. A. "Those Questions on Handwriting," *Elementary School Journal* (March 1969), pp. 327–33.

Erickson, L. Ward, and R. B. Woolschlager. "Typewriting in Elementary School?" *N.E.A. Journal* (October 1962), pp. 54–56.

Furner, Beatrice A. "The Perceptual-Motor Nature of Learning in Handwriting," *Elementary English* (November 1969), pp. 886–94.

Hart, Leo. "Typing Belongs in the Elementary Curriculum," *Business Education World,* Vol. 40 (January 1960), pp. 9–11.

Horton, Lowell W. "Illegibilities in the Cursive Handwriting of Sixth Graders," *Elementary School Journal* (May 1970), pp. 446–49.

Leavitt, Jerome E., and Frances Sigborn Hein. "My Mother Writes Terrible," *Elementary School Journal* (November 1969), pp. 74–78.

Lewis, Edward R., and Hilda P. Lewis. "An Analysis of Errors in the Formation of Manuscript Letters by First Grade Children," *American Educational Research Journal* (January 1965), pp. 25–35.

five

reading

What Reading Skills Are Taught in the Language Arts Program?

In recent years millions of dollars have been spent in research attempting to determine the best methods and materials for the teaching of reading. Important differences between programs with different emphasis were found, but none of these differences was as significant as the fact that different teachers using the same materials or methods produced a greater range of results than that found between any of the programs studied. Some teachers, because of unique abilities to understand the needs of a learner and relate the materials available to those needs, were successful in developing reading abilities regardless of method.

This does not mean that reading methods and materials are unimportant. It does mean that a competent teacher, using materials in which she has confidence, is essential to a successful program in reading instruction. If the teacher knows *why* she is using a certain book with a child or *why* she is helping a child master a specific reading skill, she is operating at a professional level that assures results. The beginning teacher starts by being a technical assistant, learning the nature of the reading process, the vast range of materials available, and the ability to direct the growth of children learning a skill that will open the world of knowledge to them.

Linguistically speaking, reading is a recoding and decoding process, in contrast with speaking and writing which involve encoding. One aspect of decoding is to relate

the printed word to oral language meaning, which includes changing the print to sound and meaning. An alphabetical language such as English presents sound clues in its written language. These sounds may be represented by total words, word groups, letter combinations such as *ing,* or single letters. A child learning to speak a language usually associates sounds with meanings. This means he hears sounds as words or sentence parts. A child's first association between writing and reading is usually based on meaning. The child of three or four can select his favorite record or book through visual clues; he knows the names of stores, streets, and some commercials on TV as words, not the individual letter sounds in words. Many teachers introduce the individual sounds only after the child can read certain words. The known words then are studied to note how they start or end. This is sometimes called the look–say word method of teaching reading. In contrast with this would be a program that started with the alphabet and progressed through spelling to words.

For some reason, starting with a small group of familiar sight words and then going to individual sounds of the alphabet is considered by some an unphonetic approach to reading. Yet it is the most widely used approach to beginning phonics found in reading textbooks.

Some languages are written in a manner that does not contain a sound clue. Most of these started with a form of picture that has been simplified. The characters of Chinese illustrate one form of such writing. You can read the meanings, at the right, even though you have no idea of the way the Chinese pronounce the words.

There are ideographs in our language as well. The $ sign contains no clues to its sound but you know its meaning. All our numbers are ideographic. The symbols 9, 10, 11 contain no sound clues but represent only meanings.

There are children in our schools whose perception and memories are such that the basic vocabulary is learned as whole words. Usually such children do well in reading until the third grade, when the expanded subject matter exposes them to a wide vo-

cabulary. At that time their lack of word-attack skills becomes of critical importance.

One hears that reading is only interpreting "talk" written down. At the beginning steps of reading this is a useful way of explaining printed symbols to children. But words, like ideographs, are more than printed sound symbols. It is equally true that reading is a matter of interpreting thought in print.

Few books read by adults are printed "talk." Certainly I have never talked in the manner I am writing this textbook. When the teacher works with comprehension and understanding as reading skills, he has a controlled situation that permits him to prepare the oral language and the experience background of the reader which is essential to interpret the thought presented by the writer. It does not matter if these are called reading–thinking skills, as listed in many courses of study since 1900, or creative or critical reading skills as in more recent publications.

A part of our problem in the language arts is that the term *reading* can be used with many meanings. Some of these have to do with purpose, such as *oral* reading, when a writer's ideas are projected through speech; reading that describes an *area* in the curriculum; reading that means *action* and may refer to anything from a child's telling what he sees in a picture to a judge's interpretation of a point of law. A child may read a word by changing it to sound which he recognizes in his language, or he may change it to

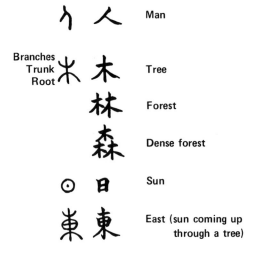

Man

Branches
Trunk
Root

Tree

Forest

Dense forest

Sun

East (sun coming up
through a tree)

sounds and discover that it is still meaningless. Another may understand a word's meaning without being able to pronounce it. In terms of response the word means different things. Sometimes the response is careful and profound thought, at other times it is an imaginative fantasy. There may be great emotional feeling in the response on only casual notice of the material.

Eventually all these aspects of reading are mastered by most students. But to the beginner the problem is one of looking at words in their printed or written form and discovering the meaning intended by the one who wrote them. Reading is the method by which we communicate to ourselves—and sometimes to others—the meaning contained in printed symbols.

In some literature the authors seem to assume that "reading" is the ability to look at printed symbols and change those symbols through phonics to oral reading. One author boasted of his ability to do this with Czech printed material, although he had no idea what the sounds meant. It is possible for reading to be so taught that attention is called to the words themselves rather than to the meaning they should convey.

Reading may be thought of as looking *through* words to the fields of thought *behind* them. The degree of relationship between the meaning of the writer and the interpretation of the reader determines the accuracy of the reading. The meaning is not on the printed page, but in the mind of the reader. Thus meaning will differ, because each reader possesses different experiences in terms of which he interprets the words.

To the beginner each word represents a puzzle to be solved. A word like *mother* or *baby* presents little or no difficulty because the meaning is definite, the words are familiar, and the feelings associated with the words are usually pleasant. A word like *fruit,* however, which can mean *apples, bananas, oranges, grapes, lemons,* or *peaches,* is a different problem. A word like *here,* which may mean *at school, by the teacher, where to stand, on the desk,* or almost any place, is a puzzle indeed. Then there are words like *at,* which even the teacher cannot define without talking a long time. Some printed words

are interesting visually, such as *look,* which has a pair of eyeglasses in the middle, and *oh,* the first letter of which is the shape of the mouth when you say it. Each new word that is recognized and remembered is a satisfying experience when one is six and learning to read.

From the teacher's point of view the process is one of repetition, encouragement, reteaching, searching for material, making special material, being pleased by the success of some, and being concerned about the failure of others. Teachers do not expect beginners to identify words that are strange in meaning or new to their oral language. Effort is directed toward the establishment of word-recognition skills that will help a child change the printed words to their proper sounds and meanings, which are already part of his oral vocabulary. The focus of teaching effort is on the individual child. Reading is not taught to a child but rather a child is taught to read.

A beginner probably remembers each word through the same kind of association process that an adult uses in recalling the identity of people. Such factors as age, hair color, size, profession, place of meeting, and topic of conversation serve as memory aids. If we are seeking to recall a person's name we use these factors as clues. In much the same ways a child learns to look for certain clues that will help him to recognize the message of the printed word. Five types of reading clues are taught as a part of a child's word-attack skills.

Context clues are found in the picture, in the meaning of known words in the sentence, or in the oral discussion of the class. It is always wise to discuss the pictures in a story first or the children will move their eyes away from the new word to look at the picture for help. If the oral discussion has set the story in Africa, the child may use that clue to understand a new word when he comes to it.

Among the different kinds of context clues one finds: [1]

---

[1] Homer J. Carter and Dorothy J. McGinnis, *Teaching Individuals to Read* (Boston: Heath, 1962), pp. 84–85.

Definition

The unknown word is defined in the descriptive context. For example: A house on a boat is called a *houseboat.*

Synonym

This type of contextual clue consists of a known synonym for the unfamiliar word. For example: Mother was angry and father was *irate* too.

Familiar Expression

This type of clue requires a background and knowledge of common expressions and acquaintance with familiar language patterns. For example: She was as proud as a *peacock.*

Experience

Children and adults may depend upon their experience and mental content to supply the meaning of the new word. For example: The color of grass is *green.*

Comparison or Contrast

The unknown word may be compared or contrasted with something known. For example: John is extravagant, but his brother isn't. John's brother is so miserly he could almost be called *penurious.*

Summary

The new or unknown word may summarize the ideas that precede it. For example: Down the street they came. First there were the girls twirling batons, then the marching band, and then the men in uniform. It was a *parade.*

Reflection of Situation or Mood

The general tone of the sentence or paragraph provides a clue to the new or unknown word. For example: The clouds were black and ominous. Occasionally streaks of lightning slashed the sky while low rumblings of thunder could be heard in the distance. Silhouetted against this threatening background was the dark and foreboding house where I hoped to secure refuge against the storm. Without warning, a strong feeling of *apprehension* gripped me.

Phonetic clues will be discussed in the *section on phonics.* None of the reading programs widely used today neglects the importance of this knowledge. Phonetic clues should probably be called linguistic clues because both individual sounds and the language flow of words, sentences, and story are involved. The details of teaching these clues will be discussed on pages 233–246.

Word-form clues are sometimes called configuration clues. These are the forms of the word that give it some identity. *Christmas* and *grandmother* are relatively easy words because of their meaning and length. *Elephant,* with its silhouette or shadow of tall and long letters, may be recognized because of its form. For some words these configuration clues render little assistance. Words like *such, said,* and *word* have similar silhouettes or, as some teachers say, have like shadows. Recent studies suggest that beginners use these clues far less than experienced readers. It may well be that with a few exceptions word-form clues should be taught above the second grade.[2]

Structural clues are those noticed in common endings such as *-ing, -ed* or *-tion.* Compound words contain structural clues when children recognize the two combined words. The ability to use prefix and suffix meanings or to recognize the root word represents an advanced use of these clues. See page 213.

Sight words are those that must be memorized through repetition. Words with indefinite meanings, such as *of,* those with difficult phonetic combinations, such as *one,* and some proper names are examples of sight words. Children with keen visual memories will usually learn almost all primary words by sight. Certain words need many repetitions before they are mastered. Words like *here, there, who, what,* and *where* are especially difficult. Others will be remembered after only a few repetitions.

Dictionary skills are sometimes referred to as a reading clue. Certainly for older students the dictionary is a way of determining the meaning of a word.

---

[2] Johanna P. Williams, Ellen L. Blumberg, and David Williams, "Clues Used in Visual Word Recognition," *Journal of Educational Psychology* (August 1970), pp. 310–15.

Structural analysis and phonic analysis are different in content and application. Phonics is concerned with the sound elements in words; structural analysis, with the units that make up the structure of a word or that change the meaning of a word. Structural analysis can be put into effect more rapidly than phonic analysis; it does not take as long to perceive whole structural units in a word as it does to sound out letters or letter combinations. Structural analysis is most useful from third grade on where children frequently need to pronounce new words of two or more syllables. Pupils should be encouraged to use structural analysis first in attacking an unrecognized word, and if that does not work, then to use phonics. The two should be combined frequently.[3]

CLASSIFICATION OF WORD STRUCTURE ELEMENTS TOGETHER WITH EXAMPLES AND WORD RECOGNITION PROCESSES

Words in a Compound Word	Stem or Root Word	Inflectional Forms	Prefixes	Suffixes	Possessive Forms	Contractions	Syllables
Example: snowman	Example: joy	Examples: Words changed by adding s—cats es—boxes ed—walked ing—walking er—sweeter trainer est—sweetest	Examples: re—return dis—disappointed	Examples: ment—amusement less—helpless	Examples: John's hat the girl's doll	Examples: didn't aren't haven't	Examples: dan ger wis dom
Children learn to identify the two separate words in a compound word as snow, man, when having difficulty in reading a compound word.	Children learn to look for the stem word in words changed by adding affixes as joyful, enjoyed, enjoyment as needed when meeting unrecognized words.	Children learn to recognize and pronounce these endings when encountered in reading words.	Children learn to recognize prefixes and their meanings when encountered in reading words.	Children learn to recognize suffixes and their meanings when encountered in reading words.	Children learn to identify possessive forms by noting apostrophe s in reading words.	Children learn that the one word stands for two words, and that the apostrophe shows where a letter was left out.	Children learn the concept of a syllable, and learn several ways of dividing words into syllables, when reading words.

[3] Nila Banton Smith, *Reading Instruction for Today's Children* (Englewood Cliffs, N.J.: Prentice-Hall, 1963), p. 216.

In practice, clues are combined. Word form and phonics are combined in locating the base word and the ending in a plural like *birds*. Even sight words often contain a structural or phonetic clue that an individual child will use to remember the word.

In addition to these word-attack skills, skills relating to thinking about what is read are of equal concern. The word-attack skills enable the reader to examine a printed word and determine its language sound and meaning. The *skills of response* help the child organize and interpret what the writer has said. These refer to understanding the main idea expressed, noticing details that add meaning, determining whether the idea is true, and noting the personal responses of appreciation. Another group of skills is usually called the *study skills*. These include the ability to locate information, read maps and charts, and select pertinent information.

Meaning is closely related to purpose or incentive in reading. A problem or question leads to meaningful reading experiences.

- Read to find out what discovery the character made, what the character did, what happened to a particular character, or to answer the questions the group had about Indian life or space flight. (Reading for details or facts.)
- Read to find out why it was a good title, what the problem is in the story, what the character learned, and to summarize what the character did to achieve his purpose. (Reading for main ideas.)
- Read to find out what happened in each of the parts of the story, what happened first, second, and third—each step taken to solve a problem, scenes and events for dramatization. (Reading for sequence or organization.)
- Read to find out why the characters feel the way they do, what the author is trying to show us, why the characters changed, what qualities the characters had that helped them succeed or caused them to fail. (Reading for inference.)
- Read to find what was unusual about a character, what was funny in the story, or whether the story was true. (Reading to classify.)
- Read to find out how the character changed, how his life is different from the life we know, how two stories are alike, how the character is like the reader. (Reading to compare or contrast.)
- Read to find out whether the character was successful or lived by certain standards, whether you would like to do what the character did or work the way he did in the story. (Reading to evaluate.)

A modern reading program seeks a content so interesting and so related to what is known about children that it serves as the instrument for the mastery of the reading process. Recent material recognizes the importance of relating content to the familiar family life of the reader. Urban children are interested in folk and traditional literature, but they also need stories with which they can identify in terms of their daily experience.

At one time I worked with some children in Colorado with a Spanish-language heritage and culture. I recognized that the Midwestern upper-middle-class children of the textbook were inappropriate for the group. As an alternative I chose stories that dealt with humanized animals. One hot afternoon, in the midst of a slow-paced and dull class, a delightful little boy put his book down, looked up at the ceiling, and sighed in complete honesty, "I'm so tired of reading about chipmunks!" He needed something about the problems of his life. It would have been better to have used newspapers or material the children had dictated than the books I had selected.

The reading process involves a number of specific skills, such as the use of word-analysis techniques. At times the mastery of process is the focus of instruction, but it is not the end purpose of a reading program— which is to help the child attain a level of reading that will enable him to acquire, organize, and share ideas as an intelligent member of society.

For Discussion

1. What sight words might a child learn from watching television? Should such words be used in beginning reading instruction?

2. In what sense would the term *reading* be synonymous with *thinking?* Are there thinking skills that should be taught? In what way is thinking influenced by reading? Is the detection of propaganda a reading or thinking skill? Is the response to poetry a reading or thinking activity? Is it a learned response?

What Are the Basic Reading, Language-Oriented, and Individual Approaches to Reading Instruction?

The term *basic reading* is usually applied to a planned program of instruction presented in a series of books written by an author or group of authors and presented by a single publisher. Because the publisher has the missionary task of spreading the author's ideas about reading instruction, there is a tendency to stress one or two ideas in order to gain distinction. In order to teach reading, competing series in basic reading contain much that is similar. However, each series will have methods as well as content that differ from others. One will stress a carefully selected vocabulary or phonetic controls. Another will emphasize the teacher aids in the manual or workbooks that will make the task "easier." Still another will emphasize content of stories, which may correlate with social studies or be selections from children's literature.

Basic reading series usually have one or two reading-readiness books, three or four preprimers, a primer, a first reader, and two books for each grade up to grade 6. Each book has its own workbook. Some series use the workbook to present the new words before they are encountered in the textbook. Others use the workbook for additional practice, testing, and independent reading. A few series introduce some words in the readiness books. Between forty-five and sixty words are used in the preprimers. All of these are used in the primer. A primer usually adds 90 to 100 words and the first reader 140 to 160 to complete a total of about 300 words in the first grade. Second readers will add from 350 to 600 words and the third readers from 600 to 900. The total number of words used in the primary readers of different authors varies from about 1,100 to 1,800. A number of additional words are derived from these basic words lists. The actual number of different words the child will see in print in the first three grades will range from 2,500 to 4,000.

There are two reasons for the careful control of vocabulary in a modern series. First, a small sight vocabulary can become the foundation for development of phonetic and structural analysis skills. Second, it makes it possible for the child to read something that satisfies him without too much difficulty. Piano lessons are planned in much the same way. Simple melodies provide a feeling of accomplishment and the reading of notes can be limited to simple techniques.

Each reading series contains a different vocabulary, but a large percentage of words in all series will be from the first 1,000 of the Thorndike Word List. This is a study of 20,000 frequently used words in children's books and is referred to by all publishers.

Words that are taught in one series and used in another are called overlap words. If *come* has been taught in one preprimer, the child will be able to read it in another. Notice the overlap words in five first preprimers listed at the top of p. 216.

The following facts should be noted. No two series use exactly the same vocabulary. Words such as *come, look, and,* and *here* do overlap. Although no single book contains more than twenty-one words, the number of different words in these first preprimers is sixty-five.

Because of these facts teachers find it best to go through the preprimers of one series first; then the preprimers of other series may be used for free reading while a child is studying in the primer.

The question of vocabulary control involves all materials available for classroom use. Simple library books with controlled vocabulary are being produced in great numbers. If this vocabulary does not have considerable overlap with the basic readers, the children may find it difficult. However, word count alone does not determine the interest a child has in certain material. A child may find a book of great interest to him not as difficult as a vocabulary study would indicate.

Overlap of Vocabulary in Five Preprimers

A	B	C	D	E
Tom	go	Tip	Ted	Bill
ride	Dick	no	run	come
Betty	help	here	jump	see
fast	look	come	Sally	and
Susan	Jane	Jack	Boots	Linda
Bunny	Sally	is	Mother	Ricky
see	Puff	not	to	here
Flip	here	with	come	Rags
and	Spot	me	look	run
Mother	run	Janet	at	fast
come	oh	find	and	to
airplane	at	home	Father	midnight
the	me	go	play	me
can	Tim	the	splash	look
Pony	get	ball		work
Father	down	will		at
apple	jump	you		home
get	come	I		can
toys		and		
		play		

Schools sometimes adopt one basic series and then use books from other series as supplementary readers. This usually means that equipment such as flash cards and workbooks for the basic series is available. A common practice is to use three basic series in some grades to take care of differences in ability. The major advantage gained is in the area of content. Children in each group have their own stories. Then, too, some series may be better adapted to a slow group than to a fast group. However, attempting to follow three different manuals and plan three different types of lessons is a burdensome way for a beginning teacher to start.

From the child's point of view a reader is interesting or "good" according to its content. But the teacher looks upon the stories as the vehicle whereby certain skills are developed. The writers of a basic series first determine the method of teaching, which they build into the teacher's manual. Stories and vocabulary are selected that will best support the method employed. The manual is the key to the teacher's success. A student beginning to teach starts with the manual of the series used, adjusts the suggestions in terms of what is known about the children, and adds material when needed. Although the manual is not a teaching plan, it does make suggestions for use as such. Basic reading instruction is a carefully organized activity designed to develop specific reading skills as well as an intensive consideration of the writer's ideas. Reading instruction is not a race to get to the end of a book or to cover a great mass of material in a short time.

Efforts have been made to organize the reading skills into levels of development. A textbook series often considers the reading-readiness and preprimer books as being level 1. The primer would be level 2. Because modern series have divided the second and third grades into two levels, there are seven levels of skill development in the first three grades. Charts showing the plan of skill development may be secured from the textbook publishers. In practice, the reading skills do not develop in such an orderly fashion. The language we use has a less apparent order of difficulty than, for example, arithmetic. The following chart indicates five levels of development in reading. Although the first two are considered primary, some children will go beyond these levels in the second grade.

The Developmental Stages in Learning to Read [4]

At the first stages of reading instruction a number of innovative practices are being tried. Books designed for basic reading are used but in addition to the methods given in the basic reader or as a replacement for these methods, the Initial Teaching Alphabet, special linguistic or phonic materials, or the Language Experience approach are being used.

The Initial Teaching Alphabet was developed by Dr. James Pitman, whose father developed the Pitman shorthand system years ago. It extends the twenty-six letters of our alphabet to an alphabet of forty-four letters, making it possible to present early reading material with a high degree of sound–letter correspondence. Transition to the regular alphabet is made in the second or third year. The I.T.A. helps assure the initial success of a child learning to read.

Because the environment cannot be controlled so that children using such a system are not also aware of regular orthography, it has been difficult to test the results of this method scientifically. Although it simplifies the sound system of the language, the material does add to the writing problem of first grade by requiring the children to learn a system that will be used for only a short time. In addition, all writing in the environment of the child, such as the names of stores and toys, the books their parents read aloud, and so on, is in regular spelling. The incentive to learn the regular alphabet cannot be suppressed. Nearly all children read in a gross way frequently encountered signs, such as *stop, go, Safeway, Sears, corn flakes, Milky Way.* Phonetic irregularities are not a major factor in reading confusion. It may be that idiographs such as the Chinese use are actually easier for beginners to read than a system based upon sound.

Some linguists have created beginning reading materials that use words with phonic regularity, such as, "The cat sat on the mat,"

V — **THE STAGE OF REFINEMENT IN READING ABILITIES, ATTITUDES, AND TASTES**

This stage may continue from the upper elementary grades well into adult life. In it the individual develops a differentiated attack on reading problems in line with his varied purposes for reading. He extends his reading interests and develops tastes for more worthwhile materials in current publications and recognized literature.

IV — **THE STAGE OF EXTENDED READING EXPERIENCE AND RAPIDLY INCREASING EFFICIENCY**

Children at this stage are no longer restricted to simple content because of limited vocabulary and are able to read material of such quality that interest motivates effort and increases power and independence. Children are capable of using a variety of texts in solving problems if they are trained in the techniques of setting up the problem, searching for authoritative answers, and of pooling, evaluating, and summarizing their findings.

III — **THE STAGE OF RAPID PROGRESS IN BASIC READING SKILLS, HABITS, AND ATTITUDES**

During this stage a child increases his sight vocabulary and develops ability to recognize new words by context, by association, by known parts, or by more detailed analysis. He begins to read with understanding a greater variety of materials. He forms the habit of reading independently for information and for pleasure. He develops the desire to share pleasant reading experiences with others and sees some of the possibilities of using reading in problem-solving activities.

II — **THE INITIAL READING STAGE**

This is the stage in which the children are taught to read material based on their current group experiences. The simple content involved may be that of science or events of daily living. Charts or booklets made by the teacher are used. It is important at this stage that children come to realize that their reading yields information useful to them in their activities and to feel that reading is fun. Habits of reading from left to right and from line to line are begun. Some practice in locating sentences is provided. Children are encouraged to note the distinctive configuration of words of special interest or of unique form and to compare words with like beginnings. At this stage, a basic reading vocabulary is established upon which to build as progress is made.

I — **THE PREREADING STAGE**

This is the stage during which the children engage in a program of experiences designed to develop mental, physical, emotional, and social readiness for reading.

---

also with the purpose of assuring success for the child as phonic generalizations are being established. But the restrictions of such a system result in stories far from the natural language of a first-grade child. There is not much satisfaction in reading, "Ann had a bag," "Nat had a nag." The first-grade child cannot write such material for he lacks the linguistic knowledge to do so. In some programs this material is presented in the programmed style of teaching-machine materials. Highly motivated students sometimes respond to the novelty of such presentations. There are many contributions that a knowledge of linguistics can make to the teaching of reading, but material of this nature is no more linguistic than are reading programs that emphasize meaning or the natural language of the child.

---

[4] *The Elementary School Program in California XXVI,* No. 2 (Sacramento: State Department of Education, April 1957), p. 19.

THE AUGMENTED ROMAN ALPHABET

æ	b	c	d	cc
face	bed	cat	dog	key

f	g	h	ie	j	k
feet	leg	hat	fly	jug	key

l	m	n	œ	p
letter	man	nest	over	pen

r	s	t	ue	v	w
red	spoon	tree	use	voice	window

y	z	ʒ	wh	ch
yes	zebra	daisy	when	chair

th	th	ʃh	ʒ	ŋ
three	the	shop	television	drink

ɑ	au	a	e	i	o
father	ball	cap	egg	milk	box

u	ω	ω	ou	oi
up	book	spoon	out	oil

THE NEW SINGLE-SOUND ALPHABET

A	Λ	Λ	B	C
at	ate	all	bow	cell say

C	D	E	Ǝ	Ǝ
chair	dip	hen	he	her

F	G	H	⊬	⊥
fast	goat	hat	bit	bite

J	K	L	M	N
jaw	kiss	low	music	no

Ʌ	Ω	Ω	Φ	Θ
king	lot	old	look	out

G	P	R	S	T
boy	pipe	run	sure	table

Θ	⊥	U	U	W
thirst	there	up	due	you

V	W	Σ	Y	Z
vest	wig	azure	yes	zebra

© 1961 FCCA

ʃhe littl red hen

Wuns upon a tiem littl red hen livd in a barn wiʃh her fiev chicks. a pig, a cat and a duck mæd ʃhær hœm in ʃhe sæm barn. cech dæ littl red hen led her chicks out tω lωk for fωd but ʃhe pig, ʃhe cat and ʃhe duck wωd not lωk for fωd.

⊥U L⊬TL RED HEN

Wunc upΛn u TΔm L⊬TL RED hen L⊬vd ⊬n u born w⊬Θ hƎR FΔv Ɔ⊬kc. U p⊬G u kat and u duk mΔd ⊥ER hΩm ⊬N ⊥u cΛm born. Ɔ dΛ L⊬TL RED hen led hƎR Ɔ⊬kc ΘT TΩ LΩk FΛR FΩD. but ⊥u p⊬G, ⊥u kat, and ⊥u duk wΦd not LΩk FΛR FΩD.

Logic supports the many efforts to reform the way we spell, but it becomes less practical every year as the amount of printed material increases using the established patterns. The impact of the child's environment invalidates efforts to control experimentation with new alphabets.

Early identification as an author is a powerful motivation to write. (Courtesy of the San Diego County Schools.)

One of the oldest methods of introducing reading instruction is through writing. The so-called spelling approach to reading was one application of this approach. In Belgium after World War I and in Korea after World War II there was a great lack of reading materials to use with children. In both countries children started by writing about their own experiences and thus created reading material for others.

In the *Elementary School Teacher* for October, 1900, there is an account of the work of the Francis Parker School in Chicago.[5]

The children learn to read as they learned to talk, "from a desire to find out or tell something." From the child's point of view, learning to read is incidental to other things in which he is interested. After performing some experiment, or perhaps after working in the garden or

---

[5] E. B. Huey, *The Psychology and Pedagogy of Reading* (Cambridge, Mass.: M.I.T. Press, 1968), pp. 298–99.

observing things in nature, the children gather to tell what has been done, and the teacher writes their statements on the board. The child reads, this, knowing its meaning already, and takes the printed account, perhaps, to read to his parents at home. Below is a selection from one of these children's stories of a trip to a farm, the story being illustrated by photographs taken during the trip:

Reading Lesson on the Farm at Thornton

October 2, 1897, we went to visit a farm.
It was a beautiful day.
There was a deep blue sky above us, with not a cloud in it, and cool, fresh air around us.
We had bright sunshine all day long.
"The nicest day of all the year!" said Fritz.
The farm we visited is 15 miles from our school.
It is on Halsted Street.
We might have gone all the way in wagons, but that was too slow for us.
It only took us 42 minutes to go on the train.
Then we were only one mile and a half from the farm.
Big hay-wagons were waiting for us at the station.
Oh, what fun we had going to the farm!
We passed a big limestone quarry.
We wanted to see it, but we could not stop for that.
We passed some beautiful oak woods.
We wanted to gather leaves, but we could not stop for that.
We passed a great yard full of horses and colts.

In recent years the Language Experience approach, published by Dr. R. Van Allen and available through Encyclopedia Britannica Press, has revived interest in this method.

Eventually the children read the books prepared for basic reading programs. One purpose for reading is to enjoy the experiences, both real and imaginary, of others, and it is unrealistic to expect children to produce material that equals the tales and verse of our cultural heritage. In some classrooms the children are permitted to write without reference to correct form, which can result in the development of poor writing habits. The growth of reading skills and

interest may be limited by problems created by writing requirements, for reading and writing skills are not parallel learnings for all children.

The reason teachers have turned to a program of individualized reading instruction is because of the range in abilities found in the normal classroom. It is not uncommon for the thirty-five children in a fifth-grade room to have a range that extends from below that of average third-grade readers to above that of average ninth-grade students. In such situations the teacher divides the class into groups for instruction. The books or assignments for each group will be determined by the reading achievement of the individuals in that segment of the class. In a small rural school that has one teacher for all the grades, similar grouping practices are followed. It is customary for an able second-grade child to read with those in the third or fourth grade. The term *personalized reading* is sometimes used to describe such practices.[6]

A special method of individualizing instruction within a classroom has been identified by the terms *self-selection* and *language approach*. The self-selection program allows each child to seek whatever reading material stimulates him and work at his own rate with what he has chosen. The major elements of a self-selection reading program include the following:

1. Children themselves select their own reading materials.
2. Children read at their own rate.
3. Teachers work almost entirely with individuals.
4. The best elements of recreational reading and one-to-one skill teaching are combined.
5. Groups are organized not by ability but by purpose or goals.

Individualized reading is not a single method of instruction but rather a plan of

[6] See Willard C. Olson's, "Seeking, Self-Selection, and Pacing in the Use of Books by Children," *The Packet* (Boston: D. C. Heath Co., 1952), for an interesting projection of the expected range of abilities to be found in a classroom.

organization. Nor does individualized reading eliminate the use of groups. Instead, it changes the way groups are organized, how long they exist, and what their purposes are.

The child does not decide whether or not he will participate in developing skills, what materials will be supplied, what skills he will work on, or any other matter that pertains to professional competence. This is the teacher's role. An individualized reading program is planned, designed, and organized into an instructional program. Individualized reading is not recreational reading. Recreational reading does not usually involve reading instruction. In individualized reading, definite provision is made for the teacher to teach, for the children to read aloud to the teacher at reasonable intervals, and for reading instruction to take place daily.

Materials are a basic consideration of individualized reading. If children are to have any degree of self-selection, then materials in large quantities must be available. It typically means that a hundred or more titles might be found at any one time in the classroom. Material for individualized reading includes, of course, all book varieties: basal texts, supplementary readers, library books, texts in the various subject fields, trade books, pamphlets, brochures, teacher-made and pupil-made materials, magazines, and newspapers.

Management procedures and arrangements in individualized reading are flexible. The teacher does have well-defined purposes; goals are firmly fixed in mind, and an organization and structure are provided which release children to learn. But materials, time allotments, and procedures are used and developed in terms of the individual learner's growth in reading and self-development.

Usually teachers plan scheduled periods to meet the following objectives:

1. For selection of reading materials.
2. For individual reading conferences between teacher and pupil.
3. For independent activities for children not reading independently.
4. For class or small-group discussion and sharing.
5. For children in pairs or small groups to engage in creative work growing out of common reading.
6. For small groups or the whole class either with the teacher or independently to develop needed skills and to work on common difficulties in reading.
7. For children to read independently.

Time allotments vary. No two teachers work exactly the same way, nor are all of these activities provided each day. Some teachers set aside special days for certain activities; other teachers have them for short times throughout the day.

The typical daily program follows a routine of this nature: The teacher gives some direction to the class as a whole before starting other activities. During this time the children have an opportunity to raise questions about their work, to clarify committee work assignments, to decide reading plans, and to get a clear understanding of the day's plans.

Depending on the day's purpose, planned activities, and needs and interests revealed, the teacher would work in one or more of the following ways:

1. Hold individual reading conferences while others work on independent activities.
2. Work with a small group on a particular skill while others read independently.
3. Hold individual reading conferences while some children read independently and others work in pairs or small groups on creative activities.
4. Circulate to provide help as children read independently, carry on other independent activities, or work in groups.

Balance in the program is maintained by looking at the daily activities for a period of time. Some teachers keep a diary to record past activities and plan future programs. In this way they soon discover that a fixed daily routine is not necessary to achieve desired results with each pupil contact.

Grouping is flexible in time span and composition. Some groups work only a day together, others longer. Depending on their needs, some children may participate in several groups at a time or perhaps none at all. After reviewing her notes the teacher recognizes a common need and plans a group activity; or after four or five reading conferences, volunteers are designated to form a group. Test results may indicate good possibilities for group work. Groups are formed in different ways but always for a specific task at a particular time. When the purpose is accomplished, the group is disbanded. Grouping frequently occurs in individualized reading, but it is organized to focus on the individual learner.

Direct attention is paid to skills in individualized reading. The skills are no different from those found valuable in any basic reading program. The emphasis is on determining which skills are to be developed in individual children, and how much practice each should have.

Procedures used for skill development vary from day to day, but teachers generally find these basic steps helpful:

1. Provide individual guidance during the reading conference.
2. Perform group work with children who share a common need.
3. Encourage pupils to assist each other—working in small groups.
4. Divide the class into practice groups alternating teacher guidance and self-responsibility.
5. Make plans for the entire class.

Any program which encourages children to read in many areas for a variety of purposes at different speeds demands some kinds of records. In individualized reading many types of records are useful:

- Running diaries of reading activities.
- Individual plans for reading, sharing, or activity.
- Records of reading difficulties—new words, meanings of words, development and completion of comprehension worksheets, and so on.
- Kinds and amount of reading.

The teacher keeps individual cards or a page in a notebook for each pupil, recording dates when books were started and finished, difficulties encountered, strengths noted, attitudes, and personal observations.

Although some teachers prefer an individualized reading program, it is a growing practice to combine group and individualized programs. Some of the students may follow a basic reader as it was planned by those who created the series; others may follow an individualized program guided by the teacher.

For Discussion

1. Would any material that the teacher had not read be used in an individualized program?
2. Would it be possible for certain skills to be neglected in an individualized program?
3. Individualized reading is noncompetitive. Does this mean that the poor reader might be a poor reader in an individualized program and not recognize the fact? What would be gained in such a learning situation?
4. Would it be possible for a teacher to direct her major effort toward the needs of the lower third of a class and neglect the upper third in an individualized program?
5. What factors make a book easy or difficult for a child?
6. If there were no reading textbooks, what material might be used to teach a child to read?
7. Why is the comic book format avoided in reading instructional material?
8. How many different words would be taught if the three preprimers of three different reading programs were used?
9. Why would a third-grade teacher want to use a first reader that had not previously been used? Should there be certain books of simple reading difficulty reserved for use in the upper grades?
10. If a new series of readers were to be purchased in a system, why would it be efficient to use this material in grades above that for which they had been written as well as at the level for which they were intended?
11. Is supplementary reading instruction the same as recreational reading?

How Has the Readiness Concept Influenced Instructional Practice in Reading?

In the development of each child there is a time when his language facility, experience, or social development would indicate that the child is ready for an aspect of reading instruction. The following checklist indicates the aspects of readiness that a teacher would consider in the first grade. Some of these factors are developmental and cannot be influenced directly by instruction, whereas others, of course, may be influenced by the work of the kindergarten.

Checklist for Reading Readiness [7]

	Yes	*No*
Physical Readiness		
1. Eyes:		
a. Do the child's eyes seem comfortable? (Does he squint, rub eyes, hold material too close or too far away from eyes?)	————	————
b. Are the results of clinical test or an oculist's examination favorable?	————	————
2. Ears:		
a. Does he respond to questions or directions, and is he apparently able to hear what is said in class?	————	————
b. Does he respond to low-voice test of twenty feet, a whisper test of fifteen inches?	————	————
c. Is his audiometer test normal?	————	————
3. Speech:		
a. Does he speak clearly and well?	————	————
b. Does he respond to correction readily?	————	————
4. Hand-eye coordination:		
a. Does he make his hands work together well in cutting, using tools, or bouncing a ball?	————	————
5. General health:		
a. Does he give an impression of good health?	————	————
b. Does he seem well nourished?	————	————
c. Does the school physical examination reveal good health?	————	————
Social Readiness		
1. Cooperation:		
a. Does he work well with a group, taking his share of the responsibility?	————	————
b. Does he cooperate with the other children in playing games?	————	————
2. Sharing:		
a. Does he share materials without monopolizing their use?	————	————
b. Does he share his home toys with others?	————	————

[7] David Russel, et al., *Manual for Teaching the Reading Readiness Program,* rev. ed. (Boston: Ginn, 1961), pp. 55–57.

	Yes	*No*

c. Does he wait his turn in play or games?

d. Does he await his turn when classwork is being checked by the teacher?

3. Self-reliance:
   a. Does he work things through for himself?

   b. Does he work without asking teacher about the next step?

   c. Does he take care of his clothing and materials?

   d. Does he find anything to do when he finishes an assigned task?

4. Good listening:
   a. Is he attentive?

   b. Does he listen rather than interrupt?

   c Does he listen to all of a story with evident enjoyment so that he can re-tell all or part of it?

   d. Can he follow simple directions?

5. General:
   a. Does he take good care of materials assigned to him?

   b. Does he follow adult leadership without objection or show of resentment?

   c. Does he alter his own methods to profit by an example set by another child?

Emotional Readiness

1. Adjustment to task:
   a. Does the child see a task (such as drawing, preparing for an activity, or cleaning up) through to completion?

   b. Does he accept changes in school routine calmly?

   c. Does he appear to be happy and well adjusted in school work, as evidenced by good attendance, relaxed attitude, pride in work, eagerness for a new task?

2. Poise:
   a. Does he accept a certain amount of opposition without crying or sulking?

   b. Can he meet strangers without unusual shyness?

Psychological Readiness

1. Mind set for reading:
   a. Does the child appear interested in books and reading?

   b. Does he ask the meanings of words or signs?

   c. Is he interested in the shapes of unusual words?

	Yes	*No*
2. Mental maturity:		
a. Does the child's mental test show him sufficiently mature to begin reading?	_____	_____
b. Can he give reasons for his opinions about work of others or his work?	_____	_____
c. Can he draw something to demonstrate an idea as well as children of his own age?	_____	_____
d. Is his memory span sufficient to allow memorization of a short poem or song?	_____	_____
e. Can he tell a story without confusing the order of events?	_____	_____
f. Can he listen or work an average length of time without restlessness?	_____	_____
g. Can he dramatize a story imaginatively?	_____	_____
3. Mental habits:		
a. Has the child established the habit of looking at a succession of items from left to right?	_____	_____
b. Does he interpret pictures?	_____	_____
c. Does he grasp the fact that symbols may be associated with pictures or subjects?	_____	_____
d. Can he anticipate what may happen in a story or poem?	_____	_____
e. Can he remember the central thought as well as important details?	_____	_____
4. Language:		
a. Does he speak clearly?	_____	_____
b. Does he speak correctly after being helped with a difficulty by the teacher?	_____	_____
c. Does he speak in sentences?	_____	_____
d. Does he know the meanings of words that occur in pre-primers and primers?	_____	_____
e. Does he know certain related words such as *up* and *down, top* and *bottom, big* and *little?*	_____	_____

The child's language ability develops and extends in environments which encourage individual expression. The slow-to-start would benefit from experiences in listening, observing, looking, talking, interpreting; experiences in feeling, seeing, smelling, hearing, identifying; experiences in musical and rhythmic expression; experiences in dramatic play and game activities; talking over, sharing, telling stories, singing songs, chanting rhymes, and many other experiences to develop free and easy oral expression.

What kinds of activities tend to put an emphasis on mental development? [8]

Observation. Many opportunities for individual and group participation should be provided to check on the accuracy and

_____

[8] Salome Brown, "The First Grade Child Not Quite Ready for Reading Instruction," *Reading in Action in the Sixties,* Western Washington State College Bulletin, Bellingham, Wash., January 1965.

understandings children gain through observing, watching, noting, interpreting, perceiving, listening, touching, smelling, tasting. Activities such as:

1. Ask the children to tell what they saw on the way to school.
2. Play a musical record. Have the children tell what they heard.
3. Provide many different kinds of materials—such as lace, burlap, velvet, and brocade—and have the children describe the material and tell how they feel.
4. Have them listen and identify different sounds they hear in the classroom.
5. Ask the children to identify the smells they might notice on a trip to the grocery store.

Observations may be visual, auditory, kinesthetic, or in combination.

Interpretation. Children need to be given opportunities to interpret their environments. Interpretation is a process of putting meaning into and taking meaning from an experience. Children interpret their experiences in the light of their past experiences. We all recall the experiences of the six blind men and an elephant. A picture, a story, a trip, or a book may provide the medium for interpretation.

1. Have the children look at a picture of clouds. Is it summer or winter? A fair sunny day or a rainy day? What makes you think so?
2. Have the children observe a new book. What kind of story do you think this will be? Will it be a happy story? Will it be a funny story?

Classification. Classifying calls for examining, grouping, bringing about order. Classifying involves the process of analysis and synthesis. Children have to think on their own to come to a conclusion or decision on classification. Collections of pictures may be used again and again for different kinds of grouping. The classification may be weather. The children then place the pictures into

groups according to pictures of summer and pictures of winter.

Comparison. Perceptive observation is sharpened through comparison. Children need to be aware of likenesses and differences. Children may compare many things, such as a bird and an airplane, two pictures, two stories which have been read by the teacher, two songs the children sing, a tree and a bush, two pets, two holidays.

Imagination. The drawing of mental pictures calls for inventiveness and originality. Children need to create, to invent, to pretend. Imagining can free a child to leave a prosaic environment and go into a world of make-believe and creativeness. The imaginative teacher can develop many activities such as the following: What would you do if you could fly? If you were an elephant? If you were a teacher? If you were a president? What would you do if you had a dollar? If you had a lot of money? Where would you spend the winter if you were a bear? If you were a grasshopper?

Other activities would include collecting, organizing, making associations, dramatizing, predicting, investigating, hypothesizing, making assumptions.

The chart on the following pages will help teachers follow up the diagnostic results of the inventory questions.[9]

At all levels of reading there is a readiness factor that concerns meaning. Are you as a teacher ready to read the following selection and understand its meaning?

While the doctrine of the Trinity remains a mystery over which subtleties may be endlessly poured out as intellectual libations, in its total tangible effect it is an admonition that pure monotheism is not enough, whereas tri-theism is too much; the true idea of God lies between them; it must at least contain a procession out of the infinite reserve into the life of the universe of men, and without abandoning its absolute selfhood.[10]

[9] Battle Creek Public Schools, Battle Creek, Michigan.
[10] Hocking Hibbert Lectures, "Living Religion and a World Faith" (London: G. Allen, 1940), p. 273.

READING READINESS HANDICAPS AND THEIR CORRECTION

Handicap	Evidence of Handicap	Helpful Procedures
Low in general intelligence	MA is below 6–0 on a test. IQ is below 90 on a test. Seems lacking in curiosity. Ideas seem vague and confused. Comprehension is poor. Range of information is poor. Unable to give explanations. Language development is retarded.	Mental age will increase steadily as child gets older. If child has been handicapped by poor environment, sometimes shows increase in IQ with good schooling. If MA below 5–0 or IQ below 80, may take a year or more to become ready for reading instruction. General readiness work with little emphasis on reading until child has reached MA of at least 6–0 is recommended.
Poor memory	Forgets instructions. Unable to recall events of story. Memory span below 4 digits or words. Poor memory for visual details. Memory is tested in various ways in Gates, California, Betts, Monroe, Stevens, Van Wegenen tests.	Give motive for wanting to remember; send on errands with oral messages. Tell a simple story; ask child to retell story after other children have done same. Play memory games: One child says something, 2nd tries to repeat it; if correct, he takes lead. Several objects on table. Child who is "it". turns back, tries to tell which one was removed. Have children inspect picture. Remove picture, ask for list of things in picture.
Inability to follow directions	Needs repetition of directions. Becomes confused if given more than one direction at a time. Look for evidence of low intelligence, language handicap, or poor hearing. Difficulty in following directions on any readiness or intelligence test.	Give directions slowly and clearly. Gain child's attention before starting. Play "following directions" games. At first, give one direction at a time, then two, then three. Allow children to take turns in giving directions for games and other classroom activities. Check for possible hearing difficulty.
Poor attention	Does not listen when directions are given. Tires of activity quickly. Is very distractible. Seems dreamy, absorbed in own thoughts.	Check for possible hearing difficulty. This is normal in young children. Watch for signs of restlessness and change to another activity. For individual activities, give a seat away from other children. Give opportunity to tell his stories and ideas. In general, provide interesting activities.

Handicap	*Evidence of Handicap*	*Helpful Procedures*
Poor visual perception	Insensitive to similarities and difference in pictures, words, letters. Draws and copies drawings poorly.	Practice in clay modeling, drawing, cutting around outlines. Assembling picture puzzles. Finding missing parts in pictures. Describing pictures in detail.
	All readiness tests contain subtests to measure visual perception.	Exercises for noting visual similarities and differences, such as those in reading readiness workbooks. If very poor, delay reading. Check for possible visual deficiency.
Poor auditory perception	Seems to have poor hearing but does well on hearing test. Speech is indistinct or defective. Does not recognize rhymes.	Provide a good model of speech. Encourage accurate pronunciation. See suggestions under "Defective speech."
	Is insensitive to similarities and differences in word beginnings or word endings. Cannot recognize (or blend) a word if it is sounded out.	Much use of rhymes, jingles, poems, and songs. Call child's attention to difference between two words which he confuses. Play "word family" games. One child says a word; next child has to say a word which begins (or ends) same way. Say a list of words. Have child listen for one that does not sound like others.
	Tests of auditory perception are included in Gates and Monroe tests.	Many teachers do much of their training in auditory or phonic readiness after children have begun to read.
Poor general health	One or more of these: overweight; underweight; pale, looks anemic; listless, tires easily; frequent colds; mouth breather; poor posture; other signs of poor health.	Recommend a thorough medical examination. Take special precautions to avoid strain and fatigue for frail or sickly children. Give rest period.
	Report from physical examination or nurse.	Discuss with mother the child's eating and sleeping habits. Check up to see that defects are corrected.
Physical immaturity	Child is very short for age.	In some cases where evidence of endocrine deficiency is present, medical treatment speeds up growth. Child should not be teased or made to feel conspicuous.
	Child looks much younger than his age.	If child is generally immature, retention in kindergarten may be advisable.

Handicap	Evidence of Handicap	Helpful Procedures
Poor vision	Does poorly on vision tests. Teacher observes that: eyes tear or become bloodshot; child squints or closes one eye to see better; gets close to board or chart to see; complains of headaches.	Refer for eye examination. If glasses are needed, see that they are obtained and used. Place in a favorable seat. If difficulty is severe, sight-saving activities and materials may be necessary.
Poor hearing	Does poorly on whisper or watch test. Teacher notes that child: has a chronic ear infection; seems inattentive; misunderstands directions; asks to have statements repeated; comprehends better in conversation than at usual classroom distances.	Refer to an ear specialist or hospital clinic. Give child a favorable seat. Speak slowly and distinctly to child. Emphasize visual approach in reading. Poor hearing is no reason for delay in starting reading, unless other handicaps are present.
Poor muscular coordination	Clumsy: poor at walking, running, skipping, hopping, dancing, climbing stairs, throwing, catching. Often drops and spills things. Poor hand–eye control in using scissors, crayon, pencil.	Be patient; clumsiness and slowness are not intentional. In severe forms, lack of coordination may be sign of neurological difficulty. Refer for medical examination. Rhythmical games to music: dancing, skipping, etc. Rhythm band. Show careful ways of holding objects. Simple types of handwork: cutting, pasting, coloring, clay or plasticine, weaving, construction. Use of manipulative toys: pegboards, form-boards, etc.
Poor cultural background	Parents are uneducated, ignorant. Foreign language is spoken at home. Home is lacking in common cultural assets: telephone, radio, magazines, books, etc.	If possible, encourage taking adult education courses. Provide a good model. Give rich oral language abilities (see following). Explain to parents desirability of child's hearing and speaking English at home. Provide rich, varied experiences (see following).
Meager background of experience	Child's experience is confined to own neighborhood. Unacquainted with traditional rhymes and stories. Range of information very limited.	Plan a sequence of visits; school itself; stores, fire station and other points of interest in neighborhood, more distant parts of community, the zoo, a farm, etc. Develop new concepts and vocabulary during trip and in subsequent discussion.

Handicap	*Evidence of Handicap*	*Helpful Procedures*
		Make use of pictures and lantern slides. Provide rich experiences in classroom. Encourage children to bring pets and possessions to school, sharing experiences. Have appropriate, simple units of activity. Read stories and poems to children. Children retell and dramatize stories.
Limited vocabulary	Limited comprehension. Has difficulty finding words to express his ideas; uses circumlocutions. Nearly all readiness and intelligence tests contain vocabulary tests.	Vocabulary develops normally out of rich, varied experiences (see pages 13–20). Acting games. Teacher says a sentence, children (taking turns) act it out. Different games can be played in which children act out nouns (animals, etc.), verbs (walk, run, hop), adverbs (quickly, quietly), prepositions (under, behind, in). Pictures are used for introducing new concepts. Children list all words they know of one type (tops, pets, flowers, etc.). Those not generally known are described and illustrated.
Poor use of language	Speaks in one or two words, or in fragmentary sentences. Uses immature speech forms ("I runned," etc.). Uses awkward or confused word order. Uses undesirable speech forms which are characteristic of his cultural background.	Put child's idea into a complete sentence, have him repeat it. All statements should be in complete sentences. Correct gently grammatical errors, awkward constructions, slang, etc., by stating child's idea in more appropriate language; praise him when he repeats teacher's statements. Provide opportunities for natural growth in language ability through free conversation, group discussions, telephone conversations, radio broadcasts, composing group stories, telling experiences, dramatization of stories.
Defective speech	Speaks too fast, runs words together. Lisping Baby talk; defective pronunciation of consonant sounds. Marked hesitation, stammer, or stutter.	Speak slowly and distinctly to children. Encourage child to take his time. Promote relaxation. Is normal in children who have lost baby teeth. If marked, requires special training in production of speech sounds. Mild cases usually clear up without special attention. This is a problem for a speech correctionist or psychologist. Classroom teacher should encourage relaxation, rhythmical activity, freedom from strain.

Handicap	Evidence of Handicap	Helpful Procedures
Emotional stability	May be shown in: shyness, timidity, excessive self-consciousness.	Do not rush timid child into group activities; give him time to become used to school.
	Quick temper, tantrums, stubbornness, negativism, extreme restlessness.	Remove over-excited, rebellious, stubborn or angry child from group temporarily, provide a quiet individual activity.
Emotional instability	Extreme sensitivity; crybaby.	Teacher should show warmth, liking for the child, appreciation.
	Specific nervous habits.	Underlying cause of nervousness needs to be removed.
	Poor concentration.	Severe cases of emotional instability should be referred to a psychologist or mental hygiene clinic.
Lack of self-reliance	Child makes excessive requests for help.	Encourage child to try to do things. Provide help and support when needed.
	Child gives up quickly when he meets difficulties.	Build self-confidence through experience of success in a graded series of activities, starting with very easy ones.
Poor group relations	Child is bossy; picks fights and quarrels.	Remove from group temporarily. Look for cause in the home situation.
	Submissive, shy, afraid to speak up.	Ask child easy questions. Praise generously. If too shy to talk in front of group, allow to recite to teacher privately.
Bad family situation	Interview with mother or older children in family. Look for evidence of: poor discipline—too harsh, too lax, or inconsistent. Quarreling and dissension. Child is unloved. Child is overprotected.	When family situation is very bad, parents should be encouraged to seek help of social service agency or mental hygiene clinic. Some mothers are receptive to tactfully given suggestions concerning discipline and child management.
Lack of interest in reading	Child seems restless, uninterested, when teacher reads or tells stories.	Language may be too difficult or ideas too strange for child's comprehension. Vary type and difficulty of stories. Provide library table with interesting picture and storybooks. Read stories from books in class library. Have a bulletin board. Post simple notices, etc. Build simple reading stories from children's own experiences. Praise generously the first signs of interest or attempts to read.
	Child shows no interest in books or in learning to read.	

Readiness is determined by interest in the topic, familiarity with the vocabulary, and the intellectual ability to respond to the ideas.

Concepts such as the following from fourth- and fifth-grade books will cause reading difficulty unless the teacher anticipates the language background of the students and helps provide meaning for these terms:

- Most of the *infectious* and *contagious* diseases are caused by *bacteria*.
- Birds help to keep the *balance of nature*.
- The *red corpuscles are racing through the capillaries*.
- Business and industry were *paralyzed*.
- Science has *unlocked the greatest force in nature*.

Such figures of speech and strange terms often cause trouble, but the child may also not be aware of the meanings of simpler terms. If the child understands the term *stag* to mean a boy without a date, imagine the meaning that might be read into Scott's line, "The stag at eve had drunk his fill."

Often it is the thought, rather than the words, that requires a readiness to understand. Even a beginning reader can recite Hamlet's "To be or not to be," but to understand these words requires a psychological orientation far beyond the child's mental capacity.

For concepts to be clarified after reading there must be teacher planning prior to reading. However, such clarification is also a part of long-range readiness training in that the children form a habit of demanding meanings that make sense as they read. Other long-range readiness practice may be illustrated by the way primary grades provide readiness for the work study skills of the intermediate years. Getting the main idea essential for the study of social studies and math, as well as outlining in language, can be started in the primary grades by listening to decide what is the best title for a selection. Drawing conclusions can be presented in terms of listening to decide what will happen; the important skill of understanding association between ideas can be presented in terms of noticing the meaning of such words as *it, there, they,* which are referents to persons or things in preceding sentences.

As the children mature, the responsibility with respect to readiness for meaningful reading is shared with them by the teacher. In all areas of the curriculum the teacher accepts responsibility for these tasks:

- Help students construct the concepts which are needed to understand what is read.
- Express the assignment in questions that are stated and organized cooperatively by the teacher and the pupils. Such cooperative activity defines the assignment, sets purposes which motivate the reading, and provides opportunities for the pupil to evaluate and organize ideas read.
- Provide for individual differences in reading by supplying some books that can be read by poorest readers and other books which satisfy the best readers.
- Set purposes for the discussion and additional activities which give the pupil opportunities to evaluate, organize, and plan for the retention of ideas gained through reading.
- Give attention to each pupil's deficiencies in the reading–thinking jobs. The point of breakdown in locating information, arranging ideas, and so on, must be diagnosed for each student.

In classroom practice the readiness concept has led to some specific ways to handle individual differences. These include (1) dividing the class into groups of children with similar needs, (2) creating reading material that will interest older children yet will not be too difficult in terms of word-attack skills, (3) planning so that children will learn from each other, (4) providing special rooms for those who need additional instruction, (5) individualizing all reading instruction in a single classroom, (6) organizing the curriculum as a nongraded primary school, (7) planning summer school programs that are both remedial and enriching.

Because the normal distribution of reading ability will present an achievement range

TYPICAL GROUP ORGANIZATION

	Group III (6–10 pupils)	Group II (10–14 pupils)	Group I (10–14 pupils)
Characteristics	These pupils tend to cluster below grade level in achievement. They often have major reading difficulties. If they are below average in intelligence, they may be working at capacity. They lack interest in reading and seldom participate willingly in independent reading activities.	These pupils tend to be average achievers in reading. They progress steadily. They usually enjoy reading, but may not participate actively in personal interest reading. They have a good span of attention.	These pupils tend to exceed grade level expectancies. They are alert, curious, usually rapid readers, and complete assignments quickly. They can work on long assignments and engage in problem solving; they enjoy reading, possess language facility, and have broad interests in reading.
Needs	These pupils require more oral reading, much work with easy material to gain fluency, review of word-attack skills, and assignments that are short, specific, and varied. Frequent encouragement and much motivation is needed. A diagnosis of cause of difficulty should be made if possible.	The needs of these pupils are similar to those in Group I, but with fewer extended assignments and somewhat less difficult work. They may need considerable encouragement in independent reading activities. They need careful and consistent skill development.	These pupils need more silent reading, less oral reading, challenging assignments, much supplementary and enrichment work, high level vocabulary activities, and thought-provoking comprehensive questions.

Pupils are changed from one group to another as their needs change.

of three to five years, three groups are a common pattern of classroom reading instruction.

For Discussion

1. Readiness is used in the sense of judging the maturity of a learner and in the sense of preparing the learner. Give an example of each practice.

2. In what situations do you feel it justified to delay instruction for a child who is ready to read until more in the class are at the same stage of development?

3. In Sweden, Denmark, and Norway children do not start to school until the age of seven. What could be the reasons for such practice?

4. Some children come to school who have taught themselves to read. What explanation can be given for such achievement?

5. Under what circumstances might it be better for a child to spend a summer on a farm than to attend a summer school?

What Is the Place of Phonics in the Language Arts Program?

Phonetics and *phonics* are terms which are often confused in meaning. Phonetics is the science of speech sounds in actual use. Phonics is the application of phonetics in the teaching of reading and spelling. The phonetic symbol in speech for the s sound would be the same in all these words: bus, kiss, scene, vase, face, psalm, listen, schism, six, answer, city. Yet in the use of phonics a child must remember that the sound is made by different letter combinations. The sound element is called a phoneme. In the words listed above the sound /s/ is a phoneme.

One point must be understood from the beginning of any discussion of phonics. Communication involves an exchange of meaning. It is quite possible for a child to learn to sound out the letters of a word like *d-a-w-k-i-n,* but unless the sounder then associates the word with its meaning (stupid), he is not reading. Similarly, the child may spell a word without knowing its meaning.

Three groups are working independent of each other in this room. The teacher has made specific provisions on the chart to guide the work of one group while she is working at the reading circle. The third group studies independently. (*Courtesy of the Burbank Public Schools.*)

In such a case all that he has done is to write a design with letters of the alphabet. Although phonic skills can be used in such meaningless ways, it does not follow that they are valueless skills. Indeed, the ability to use the sounds of our language as it is written, combined with a demand for meaning, is basic to both reading and spelling.

Heilman reminds us of this when he says: [11]

_____

[11] Arthur W. Heilman, *Teaching Reading* (Columbus, Ohio: Charles E. Merrill Books, 1962), p. 261.

In the sentence, "The man was attacked by a marbohem," everyone reading this page can sound out mar-bo-hem, but no one knows what attacked the man since saying mar-bo-hem does not convey meaning to the reader. Words can be substituted for marbohem and some readers would still have trouble with the meaning even though they successfully analyze the speech sounds in the words. For example:

1. The man was attacked by a peccary.
2. "   "   "   "   "   " freebooter.
3. "   "   "   "   "   " iconoclast.
4. "   "   "   "   "   " fusilier.
5. "   "   "   "   "   " hypochondriac.

Analysis is only a tool for use in the reading process and should not be confused with the process. It is a valuable technique in reading, but is not in itself a method of teaching reading.

Phonics instruction starts in the area of speech. With immature children, any speech fault, such as the confusion of sounds in some words (as *wed* for *red*, although the child says the *r* sound in *road* correctly), requires corrective instruction. With older children, careless habits of pronunciation such as *gimme* for *give me*, *negstor* for *next door*, or *put nearly* for *pretty nearly*, must be corrected before phonics knowledge can function in spelling. In addition to these corrective measures, the child must be helped to identify individual letter sounds in different positions of a word. It is not necessary for a child to be able to pronounce all the sounds of the language before he can start learning the symbols of the sounds he does make correctly.

The teacher must understand how this knowledge will be used before attempting to teach sound and letter association to children. In reading, children use phonics to do these major reading tasks:

1. To identify the initial sound of a word.
2. To divide a word into syllables in pronunciation.
3. To check a guess when a strange word is identified from context.
4. To identify prefixes and common endings.
5. To identify the word root.

The phonics problem in reading is that of changing printed letters to sound and then giving meaning to that combination of sounds which makes a word. Without a meaning clue this process is difficult; if the word is completely unknown to the child it is almost impossible. Simple words like *adage* and *adobe*, *table* and *tablet*, or *tamable* and *tamale* require distinctions of pronunciation that are not easily discoverable by phonetic analyses.

On the market today there are programs which teach sounds independently and then apply them to words. Some start with vowels, others with consonants, and still others with consonant–vowel combinations, such as *fe*, *fi*, *fo*, *fu*. When this material is well taught, children memorize many of the sounds and alphabet letter associations of our language.

In application of the sounds, this material usually ignores the many nonphonetic words which are common in our language, such as *was*, *been*, *have*, *come*, and *you*, and does use those that can be built phonetically, such as *gun*, *sun*, *fin*, *mold*, *ill*, *dill*, and *kill*, which are not very useful in the reading material of the primary grades.

A more serious problem is that the skills learned do not apply to the analysis of longer words. The ability to sound *pat* simply does not apply to *patriot*, *pathetic*, and *patience*.

In the classroom one observes wrong teaching practices concerning phonics. Some teachers confuse visual similarity with sound similarity. Words like *grow*, *snow*, *low*, and *grown* are included with exercises on the *ow* sounds in *owl*, *cow*, and *clown*.

Finding little words in big words gives a sound clue less than half the time, yet teachers persist in telling children to look for the little word. There is no sound like *an* in *thanks*, *fat* in *father*, *is* in *island*, *of* in *often*, or *all* in *shall*. Finding the little word may give a false sound value as *bat* in *bathe*, *am* in *blame*, *doze* in *dozen*, and *row* in *trowel*, or prevent proper syllable identification as *am* in *among*, *even* in *eleven*, and *beg* in *began*. Finding the base or root word is quite another matter. Finding *father* in *fatherly* or *forget* in *unforgettable* is quite different from attempting to find *fat* in *father* or *table* in *unforgettable*. Take any page of material and note the little words in the big ones. In the previous sentence a child might find *an* (any), *age* (page), *at*, *ate*, *mat* (material), *an* (and), *no*, *not* (note), *he* (the), *it*, *lit* (little), *or* (words), *on* (ones). In none of these is the meaning of the small word a clue to the meaning of the large word. If a child considers *no* as a meaning, the meaning of the little words read into the larger word could create confusion or establish a habit of not seeking meaning.

An observation of a class in first and second grades will reveal that the teachers do a great deal of prompting with phonetic clues. Suppose the child is trying to read the word *mumps*. After getting the initial sound the teacher will say, "It rhymes with *jumps*." With that help the child says the word. It should be noted that alone he would never have been able to provide the clue, "It rhymes with *jumps*." If he could do that, he could have read the word. We do not know if such figuring out with teacher clues helps the child remember the word. Some evidence indicates that the beginning sound and meaning are all some children need. If they cannot identify the word, it should be told to them and be taught as a sight word along with some nonphonetic words, such as *laugh, each,* and most proper names or place names.

Basic reading series differ considerably in their use of phonic material. Some use any device that will work with specific new words as they are introduced. One new word will

be remembered by the shape, another by the fact that it starts with the *m* sound, still another because it rhymes with a known word. Other programs attempt to teach patterns of attack that the child should use with each new word.

At present the following sequence of learning is commonly followed:

Kindergarten or Preparatory Period

1. Listening to and understanding oral language.
2. Recognizing names that begin alike.
3. Recognizing the beginning sound of a word.
4. Recognizing letters and word differences.
5. Matching letter and word forms.

Phonetic generalizations require practice and reteaching before they become independent skills. (*Courtesy of the Burbank City Schools.*)

6. Expressing speech sounds and using language.

11. Three-letter blends: *str*.
12. Contractions.

Grade 1

1. Hearing and recognizing in words the following single consonants in the initial position *b, c* (hard sound only), *d, f, g* (hard sound only), *h, j, l, m, n, p, r, s, t,* and *w*. Omit *k, v, x, y,* and *z*.

2. Hearing and recognizing in words the speech consonants *ch, sh, th,* and *wh;* the consonant blends such as *sk, sm, sn, sp, st, sw, tw, br, bl, gl, pl, fr, tr* in initial positions.

   Any one of the initial sound items may be introduced as soon as the pupil knows two or more words which begin with that item.

Grade 2

1. Introduce *v* and *y* in addition to reviewing the initial consonants presented in first grade, and later present *q* and *k*.
2. Continue learning of blends *gr, fr, cr, dr, bl, cl, gl, sw, tw, scr,* and *thr*.
3. Emphasize the short vowel sounds.
4. Introduce the long vowels (the terms *vowel, long,* and *short* are used).
5. Teach the speech consonants in final position.
6. Introduce the vowel blends *ow, ou, oi, oy, ew, au, aw, oo*.
7. Teach the double vowels *ai, ea, oa, ee, ie, ay, oe*.

Grade 3

1. Maintenance of single consonants and consonant blends.
2. Silent letters in *kn, gh, wr*.
3. Variant consonant sounds *c, g, s, z, ed,* and *t*.
4. Continuation of work on double vowels.
5. Influence of final *e*.
6. Vowels followed by *r*.
7. Prefixes *a-, be-,* and *un-*.
8. Suffixes *-y, -ly, -er, -est, -less, -ful, -en*.
9. Division of words into syllables.
10. Alphabetization.

Grades 4, 5, and 6

1. Maintenance of all previously taught skills and addition of appropriate difficulties.
2. Prefixes *dis, ex-, in-, out-, re-, trans-, un-*.
3. Suffixes *-eenth, -ese, -ical, -ion, -ous, -ship, -sun, -ty*.
4. Placement of accent on words divided into syllables.
5. Use of key words for pronunciation in dictionary.
6. Use of diacritical marks.

A recent survey of studies on generalizations in phonics drew these conclusions: [12]

Certain generalizations appeared to be commonly taught but to have very limited usefulness according to the included studies. The following fell in this category:

The vowel in an open syllable has a long sound.

The letter "a" has the sound (ô) when followed by "e."

When there are two vowels, one of which is a "final e," the vowel is long and the "e" is silent.

In many two and three syllable words, the "final e" lengthens the vowel in the last syllable.

When a word ends in "vowel-consonant-e," the vowel is long and the "e" is silent.

When two vowels are together, the first is long and the second is silent.

If the first vowel sound in a word is followed by a single consonant, that consonant usually begins the second syllable.

When two sounds are separated by one consonant, divide before the consonant, but consider "ph," "ch," "sh," and "th" to be single consonants.

It is recommended that teachers be particularly cautious when instructing children in situations in which these generalizations might apply in two or more specific ways

---

[12] Lou E. Barmeister, "Usefulness of Phonic Generalizations," *The Reading Teacher* (January 1968), pp. 350–56.

until oral recognition is achieved. For example, the following generalizations might be helpful:

Single vowels are usually short, but a single vowel may have a long sound in an open syllable (approximately 30 percent of the time), especially in a one syllable word.

If a word ends in "vowel-consonant-e" the vowel may be long or short. Try the long sound first.

The following generalizations are those from the studies which seemed most useful, except for the "final e" generalization and the phonic syllabication number 2 generalization. The latter two generalizations were formulated by the current author as a result of the findings of the utility level studies.

Consonant Sounds

1. "C" followed by "e," "i," or "y" sounds soft; otherwise "c" is hard (omit "ch"). (certain, city, cycle, attic, cat, clip; success)
2. "G" followed by "e," "i," or "y" sounds soft; otherwise "g" is hard (omit "gh"). (gell, agile, gypsy; gone, flag, grope; suggest)
3. "Ch" is usually pronounced as it is in "kitchen," not like "sh" as in "machine."
4. When a word ends in "ck," it has the same last sound as in "look."
5. When "ght" is seen in a word, "gh" is silent. (thought, night, right)
6. When two of the same consonants are side-by-side, only one is heard. (dollar, paddle)

Vowel Sounds—Single Vowels

1. If the only vowel letter is at the end of a word, the letter usually stands for a long sound (one syllable words only). (be, he, she, go)
2. When "consonant + y" are the final letters in a one syllable word, the "y" has a "long i" sound; in a polysyllabic word the "y" has a "short i" (long e) sound. (my, by, cry; baby, dignity)
3. A single vowel in a closed syllable has a short sound, except that it may be modified in words in which the vowel is followed by an "r." (club, dress, it, car, pumpkin, virgin)
4. The "r" gives the preceding vowel a sound

that is neither long nor short. (car, care, far, fair, fare) [single or double vowels]

Vowel Sounds—Final "Vowel-Consonant-e"

When a word ends in "vowel-consonant-e" the "e" is silent, and the vowel may be long or short. (cape, mile, contribute, accumulate, exile, line; have, prove, encourage, ultimate, armistice, come, intensive, futile, passage)

Vowel Sounds—Adjacent Vowels

1. Digraphs: When the following double vowel combinations are seen together, the first is usually long and the second is silent: ai, ay, ea, ee, oa, ow (ea may also have a "short e" sound, and ow may have an "ou" sound) [main, pay; eat, bread; see, oat, sparrow, how]
2. Diphthongs (or blends): The following double vowel combinations usually blend: au, aw, ou, oi, oy, oo ("oo" has two common sounds). [auto, awful, house, coin, boy, book, rooster]
3. "io" and "ia": "io" and "ia" after "c," "t," or "s" help to make a consonant sound: vi*cio*us, par*tia*l, musi*cia*n, vi*sio*n, atten*tio*n (even o*cea*n).

Syllabication—Determination of a Syllable

Every single vowel or vowel combination means a syllable (except a "final e" in a "vowel-consonant-e" ending).

Syllabication—Structural Syllabication

These generalizations take precedence over phonic syllabication generalizations.

1. Divide between a prefix and a root.
2. Divide between two roots.
3. Usually divide between a root and a suffix.

Syllabication—Phonic Syllabication

1. When two vowel sounds are separated by two consonants, divide between the consonants but consider "ch," "sh," "ph," and "th" to be single consonants. (assist, convey, bunny, Houston, rustic)
2. When two vowel sounds are separated by one consonant, divide either before or after the consonant. Try dividing before the consonant first. (Consider "ch," "sh," "ph," and "th" to be single consonants).

[alone, select, ashamed, Japan, sober; comet, honest, ever, idiot, modest, agile, general]

3. When a word ends in a "consonant-l-e" divide before the consonant. (battle, treble, tangible, kindle)

Accent

1. In most two syllable words, the first syllable is accented.
   a. And, when there are two like consonant letters within a word the syllable before the double consonant is usually accented. (beginner, letter)
   b. But, two vowel letters together in the last syllable of a word may be a clue to an accented final syllable. (complain, conceal)
2. In inflected or derived forms of words, the primary accent usually falls on or within the root words (boxes, untie) [Therefore, if "a," "in," "re," "ex," "de," or "be" is the first syllable in a word, it is usually unaccented.]

For Discussion

1. What arguments are given to justify a separate class in phonics in a first-grade room?

2. Why might the phonetic principles of a language be more apparent to one who can read than to one learning to read? Have you mastered the reading of a foreign language? If so, how did phonics help?

3. Why are phonics generalizations useless to a beginner?

4. Can you explain the following inconsistencies?

Our Queer Language

When the English tongue we speak
  Why is break *not rhymed with* freak?
Will you tell me why it's true
  We say sew *but likewise* few;
And the maker of a verse
  Cannot cap his horse *with* worse?
Beard *sounds not the same as* heard;
  Cord *is different from* word.
Cow *is* cow, *but low is* low,
  Shoe *is never rhymed with* foe;
Think of comb *and* tomb *and* bomb;
  And think of goose *and not of* choose;
Think of comb *and* tomb *and* bomb;
  Doll *and* roll, home *and* some;

And since pay *is rhymed with* say,
  Why not paid *with* said, *I pray?*
We have blood *and* food *and* good;
  Mould *is not pronounced like* could
Wherefore done *but* gone *and* lone?
  Is there any reason known?
And in short it seems to me
  Sounds and letters disagree.

LORD CROMER

How Are the Consonant Sounds Taught?

To use a consonant sound in reading the child must do two things. First he must identify the sound of the letter, then he must use that sound in combination with the other letters to make a word.

In order to identify the sound of *b,* this type of exercise or combination of them may be used. There are others used in workbooks and suggested in teachers' manuals.

1. The teacher says, "Listen to find in what way these words are alike: *ball, bell, bent, bill, book.* Yes, they all have the same sound at the beginning."
2. "Now look at these words while I say them: *ball, box, beg.* In what two ways are they alike? Yes, they sound alike at the beginning and start with the same letter. The letter is *b.*"
3. "I am thinking of a girl in class whose name begins with *b.* Who is she?"
4. Here are some pictures of toys. Which one's start with the letter *b?* (*ball, bed, bat, bus*)"
5. "Listen while I say a sentence. Name the words that start with *b.* 'The big ball is baby's. Bobby will buy a book.' "
6. Put a marker on each picture that starts with *b.*

button	box	cane
cat	basket	book
banana	duck	bonnet

7. "I am thinking of something that is good to eat that starts with *b.* Can you name it?"
8. "Say 'Little Boy Blue' and 'Baa Baa

Games provide additional drill with word recognition skills. (*Courtesy of the Burbank Public Schools.*)

Black Sheep.' When you hear a *b* hold up a finger."

9. Mark *b* on four letter cards. Do the same for some of the other letters. Put them all together. Show the letter *b*, have the children find others like it. Or place all letters that are like it in a row.

10. The teacher says, "I am thinking of a *b* word that rhymes with *fall, cone, maybe, cat.*"

Once the sound is identified in words and associated with the letter, then the task is to substitute the sound into a word in a way that helps identify the word. This type of substitution exercise is widely used. The teacher reviews the sound. "You know these words on the board: *ball* and *big*. I have put a line under the new word in the sentence: The apples are in the box. With what letter does it start? Yes, it is a *b*. What sound does it have? What is the sentence talking about? What words do you know that will make sense that start with a *b?*"

Sometimes the substitution must be made in other parts of the word. "What letter does the new word start with in this sentence? Daddy has a new *job*. Yes, it is a *j*. What word do you know that would make sense? No, it is not *jet*. Look at the last letter in the new word. What sounds does it have? Does *jet* have the sound of *b* at the end? Can you think of a word that would make sense that starts the way *jet* does but has a *b* sound at the end?"

Or the sentence may be *Mary has a red ribbon*. "No, the word is not raincoat. What letters are in the middle of the word? What words do you know that start with an *r?* Use that sound and the other words to read the new word."

Special practice in substitution should be done with exercises like this: "You know these words: *ball, big*. You also know these words: *get, look*. What new word do we make when we take away the *g* in *get* and put a *b* in its place? What new word do we make when we take away the *l* in *look* and put a *b* in its place?"

In order to construct this type of exercise follow these steps:

Start with words that contain the letter on which the children are to practice. In the above example start with *book* and *bet*. Then change them to words such as *look, took, cook* and *get, jet, let*. Select the one that is best known by the children. These words can be used in substitution exercises for the letters indicated:

c	not, ball, now, look
f	ball, box, can
l	dog, tip, not
n	cap, hot
p	will, not, get, can, big
w	bent, hill, lake
s	get, funny, no, Jack
t	Jack, ball, down, can, look
r	can, make, fun

j	will, big, may
k	will, sick, deep
wh	tip, kite
st	sand, make, may, jump, sick, keep
str	may, feet, like
sh	take, not, look, my, mine, make
bl	bed, show, came
pr	hide, mint
cr	sleep, show, back, thank, down, just
cl	down, hear, Dick
i	(short) but, better, fast, had, let, lamb, lock, pull
	(long) none, done, rope
e	(short) but, ball, band, follow, bunch, full, hold, not, sat, shall
ea	bad, but, fast, hit, not, sat
ee	but, choose, did, said, stop
a	(short) ten, pet, trick, dish, fun
a	(long) time, while
o	red, put, cut, let
o	mist, ride, wire
oo	feet, head
u	big, bad, cap, dog, hit, not, pop
oa	get, cut, bet
th	first, jump, tick
tr	may, got, cap, just, made, by
tw	dig, fine, girl

Another form of substitution exercise asks the child to choose between two words in a sentence.

Write the word *live* on the board. "Who can read this word? Tell me what happens to the word *live* when the first letter is changed." Write *give* under *live*. Have the new word pronounced. Then ask the children to select the proper word in these sentences:

John and Paul $\frac{give}{live}$ on High Street.

John will $\frac{give}{live}$ Paul a cake.

"Can you tell these new words that are made from words you know?" Write the words *dog, get, night,* and *cake* on the board. Substitute *l* for the first letter in each of these words. Follow this by having the children select the proper word in a sentence using these words.

Consonant blends present some difficulties. The major error to avoid is that of adding an extra vowel sound at the end of the blend. *Clear* would become *cul-ear, blue* becomes *bul-oo, scream* becomes *sker-eam,* and *stream* becomes *struh-eam* or *stur-eam.*

In presenting the consonant blends through many listening experiences, William S. Gray believes that there is an advantage in presenting all the possible blends involving an identical consonant letter in a group, as *bl, cl, fl, gl, pl,* and *sl.* In this way children will become aware that the consonant *l* is often used as a blender. This is true as well of the letters *r* and *s.*[13]

In some words a trigraph, or three consonants blended together, can be sounded before the vowel sound, as in *scratch, stream, splash, sprint, scream.* At the end of words there are many possible combinations of two or more consonants which form blends in words such as *bulb, self, held, hard, large, earth, spark.*

To develop skill in attacking new words through the visual and auditory recognition of consonant blends, proceed as follows:

1. Write *bring* and *bread* on the chalkboard. Have the words pronounced and the letters *br* underlined in each word. Say: "Listen as I say *bring, bread* again. Do the letters *br* have one sound or two?" Call attention to the sound of *b* in *ball* and *r* in *ride.* "Let me hear both sounds when you say *bread, bring.*" Have several children in turn repeat the words.

"Listen as I read some sentences to hear other words that begin with the same two sounds as *bring.*" Read the following sentences, pausing after each for a child to repeat the *br* words.

Throw the *broken branch* in the *brook.* The *bridge* over the *brook* is not *broad.*

Write the following sentences on the chalkboard and have them read silently and orally. Help the group to identify *brook* by comparison with *bring* and *book.*

Bring this *book* to the *brook.*

────────────
[13] W. Gray, *On Your Own in Reading* (Chicago: Scott, Foresman, 1961).

Go *down* to the store and get some *brown bread.*

2. Use the method given in the preceding activity to develop recognition of the consonant blend *tr.* Use the known words *train, tree, truck* and the following sentences on the chalkboard:

Will you *try* to make my *train* go? *Dick* can do a *trick* with his *truck.*

3. Provide each child with a pair of cards 1 × 4 inches on which has been written *br* or *tr.* Ask the children to listen as you pronounce the following word groups and to hold up the card that has the two letters with which all the words begin.

tr: traffic, trick, traveler, trip, tractor
br: break, brothers, breakfast, brook

Drill on consonants and blending can be done with a "word wheel." Two circles are cut from heavy paper or oak tag. One is larger than the other. The upper circle has a consonant or consonant blend aligned with a slot which exposes the remainder of the word on the other disk. As the top disk is revolved, the words are formed for the pupil to call.

Picture dictionaries or student-made charts are helpful. The children may gather pictures, bring them to school, and paste them on the page in the dictionary where the appropriate beginning consonant sound is printed, or on the chart labeled with that consonant. This should be a group activity because children usually tire of making individual sound dictionaries.

An initial consonant game based on "word families" provides a check on a child's understanding. The student has a card on which an entire word is written or printed. Used with this card are a number of single-consonant cards which may be placed one at a time over the initial consonant to make another word. For example, if one uses the word card with the word *man* on it, the consonants *p, r, t, f, b, c,* and *v* may be written on the smaller cards. By superimposing each small card on the first letter of *man,* the child may form the words *pan, ran, fan, ban, can,* and *van.* When not in use, the small cards may be clipped to the larger one.

Exercises in which the child writes an initial consonant to complete a word, and then says the word, give him the opportunity for *seeing, saying, hearing,* and *doing* activities. These are effective in all phonics work and are particularly good in corrective work. Such an exercise appears here:

Directions: Write the initial consonants indicated in each of these words. Then say the words.

m	c	b
_____ad	_____at	_____all
_____other	_____ome	_____ig
_____ud	_____old	_____oy
_____ay	_____up	_____ack
_____eat	_____ar	_____ox
_____op	_____all	_____ell
_____ill	_____ap	_____ut
_____it	_____an	_____ook

In studying individual consonant sounds, there are many word-card devices that can be used. A card is made so that the initial consonant shows only when the card is folded. When the card is unfolded, a key picture replaces the initial consonant. For example, with the word *cat,* when the card is not folded, the child sees the key picture of a cat and the element *at;* when it is folded, the *c* appears, making the word *cat.*

One of the card devices resembles the first one mentioned for use with initial single consonants. It differs only in that there is a consonant blend which may be superimposed on the initial letter of a *known* word to make a *new* word. For example, the known word may be *black.* On separate cards, the consonant teams *tr, st,* and *cr* are printed. By manipulating these cards, the child can make *track, stack,* and *crack.*

Children may easily make their own individual consonant key cards by using heavy folded paper. One side of the card contains the consonant. When the card is opened, the picture and key word appear. These cards serve as excellent helps when children are still learning the initial consonant sounds and need frequent help with them. On the back of the folded card a simple sentence is written to help the child to see the word in context.

A knowledge of the consonant sounds is one of the most helpful ways phonics can be used in reading. Teachers frequently ask the children

to ignore the vowels but to use only the consonants in sounding a word. A sentence in which all vowel letters have been omitted can be read by most children. For example: Th__ m__ther w__s s__ h__pp__ t__ f__nd h__r ch__ld wh__ h__d b____n l__st th__t sh__ cr____d.

For Discussion

1. Why are some children able to pronounce words and still not read with understanding?

2. It has been suggested that the letter *c* be dropped from the language except in the combination *ch.* Why should such a suggestion be made?

3. Is it necessary to teach all the consonant blends or is blending a skill to be mastered with a few examples and applied to all?

How Do Children Learn to Use the Vowel Sounds?

The first step in use of vowels is the ability to recognize *a, e, i, o,* and *u* as being letters that represent vowel sounds. As recognition is being mastered the children should also understand that when these letters make the same sound as their names we call them long vowels and put a straight line over them. The letters *a* and *I* are little words that children know. The *e* in *be* and *o* in *no* are long because we hear the letter names in them. The long *u* as in *use* (verb) and *Utah* is quite rare in the basic reading vocabulary.

One authority suggests the following pattern of instruction with respect to the short *a.*[14]

Step 1 (see). Print *bad, can,* and *hat* on the board. "Here are three words we have learned to read. Look at the middle letter in each word. Do all these words have the same letter in the middle? What is that letter? Is it a vowel?"

Step 2 (hear). "Now I am going to say six words. Listen for the sound you hear in the middle of each word. Say *map, bad, rag, can, last,* and *hat.*" (Slightly elongate but do not isolate the sound of the vowel *a.* Do not print

---

[14] Paul McKee, *Come Along,* Teacher's Manual (Boston: Houghton, 1967).

these words or try to teach pupils to read them.) "Did all those words have the same sound in the middle?"

Step 3 (associate). Point to the words on the board. "Let's all look at these three words and say them together. In what two ways are all three words alike?" (They all have the same letter and the same sound in the middle.) "That sound is the same as the sound we hear at the beginning of *and, am,* and *at.* It is one of the sounds that the vowel *a* very often has in a word. It is called the short *a* sound."

Step 4 (apply). "We have now learned the short sound that the vowel *a* often has in words. Let's see if we can use that vowel and its short sound to decide what some new words are." (Print *but* on the board.) "What is this word? Now watch while I take out the vowel *u* and put the vowel *a* in its place." (Erase the *u* and print *a* in its place to make *bat.*) "Who can tell us what this new word is?" (Follow the same procedure to change *cut* to *cat, him* to *ham, put* to *pat,* and *top* to *tap.*)

The short *e* is one of the most difficult phonetic elements a child is asked to master. Here is one way of presenting it:

(Print *men, bed, get, let, red,* and *neck* on the board.) "Let's look at these words and say them together." (Point to *men.*) "What is the vowel in this word?" (*e.*) "Do you hear the long *e* sound or the short *e* sound in *men?*" (The short *e* sound. Continue in the same way with the remaining five words.) "What did you notice about the *e* in each of these six words? (Each *e* has the short sound.) "When *e* is the only vowel in a word and it is followed by one or more letters, the *e* usually has the short sound." . . . "Let's use what we have learned about the short *e* sound to help us read some words that we may not know." (Print the following short sentences on the board.)

Ben had a pet dog named Shep.
Shep sat up to beg for his bones.
Ben put a bell in Shep's pen.
Shep could make Ben hear the bell when
    he wanted to be fed.

Then say: "In the sentences on the board, some words are underlined. Read the sentences to yourself. Use what you know about the short sound of *e* to help you decide what the underlined words are. Be sure the word you decide on makes sense in the sentence. Will you read the first sentence aloud?" (Have two or more pupils read each sentence aloud. Then have one or two pupils read all four sentences aloud.)

Ea presents a special problem because it may be either long or short. Print the words *ready, head,* and *breakfast* on the board. "Let's look at these words and say them together. What two vowels are used together in these words?" (*ea.*) "Do you hear the long *e* sound or the short *e* sound in these words?" (The short *e* sound. Print *clean, cream,* and *read* on the board. Point to *clean*). "What is this word?" (*clean.*) "Do you hear the short *e* sound or the long *e* sound in *clean?*" (The long *e* sound. Treat *cream* and *read* in the same way as *clean* was treated.) "The vowels *ea* usually stand for the long *e* sound. When you see the vowels *ea* in a word you don't know, try the long *e* sound first for those vowels. If that doesn't give a word you know, try the short *e* sound.

"Let's see whether we can use what we know about the sounds of the vowels *ea* to help us read some words that we may not know." (Print the following sentences on the board.)

Ann went to one store for some *beans,*
    some *bread,* and some *meat.*
She went to another store for some *white*
    thread.

Read the sentences on the board to yourself. Use what you have learned about the sounds that the vowels *ea* can stand for to help you decide what the italicized words are. "Will you read the first sentence aloud?" (Have two or three pupils read each sentence aloud.)

With upper-grade students the first step is to discover the nature and extent of the child's knowledge of vowels. Write four or more familiar words on the board and ask the students to identify a vowel sound that may appear in only one or two of them. For example, write on the board the words *cake, man, ran,* and *made.* Ask the child to say the words to himself. Then ask in which words he hears the short form of the sound *a.* Some of the vowel elements and some suggested words that may be used in the exercise are the following:

Short		*Long*	
Sound of		*Sound of*	
a	cake, man, ran, made	*a*	late, band, mail, catch
e	bed, deep, feet, bread	*e*	fresh, green, neat, left
i	give, light, mind, twin	*i*	city, did, find, hide
o	lot, hop, joke, hope	*o*	both, toast, cloth, chop
u	jump, music, mumps, use	*u*	puppy, puff, use, mule

There are some rules that will help a few children. Rather than ask them to remember these rules, it is wiser to place them for reference somewhere in the room. Of course, this should be done only after they have been made meaningful.

Rule 1.   If you do not know what sound to give to a vowel, try first the short sound. If you do not get a word that makes sense, try the long sound of the vowel.

This rule is most useful with the short words of our language and does have considerable consistency in books that follow a controlled vocabulary. There will be some vowels that will be neither long nor short. When the child discovers one, the teacher might explain this. There is no reason why the child needs to learn all the variations of the vowels before he has the help of a dictionary.

Rule 2.   When a word has only two vowels and one of them is *e* at the end of the word, the first vowel is usually long.

This is the old "silent *e*" rule. It is least helpful when most needed. Such exceptions as *gone, have, love,* and *come* are introduced early in primary reading. One teacher called this *e* "company that had come for a visit." Then she would say, "Once there was a little girl named Elizabeth but at school people called her Betty. But whenever her name was on a program or the minister came to visit, her friends called her Elizabeth. That is the way with some vowels. When they are alone they have one name but when they have company they have another." I suspect this satisfies the teacher more than the children, but it might help some who need a reason.

Rule 3.   When a word has only one vowel and it is the last letter in the word, the vowel is usually long.

Such a rule would only help with the little words such as *me, be, go, no, so,* but there are also *to, ha, ma,* and so on.

When a child does not recognize one of the vowel sounds, the same steps that were used in teaching the consonants may be followed. The *first step* is to help the child hear the sound. Print on the board the words: *an, and, am, at.* Say, "We know these four words. Let's say them together. Now listen while I say them again. What did you notice about the way these words begin? What other words do you know that begin with the same sound?" (With some vowels it is wise to use the medial position such as *bad, can, bat.* In this case the children are asked to note that the words sound alike in the middle. Other words they might recall are *had, ran, sat, fat, cat.*)

The *second step* is to see the letter and associate it with the sound heard.

The *third step* is to substitute the letter and sound to make new words. Use the words *fed, miss.* Substitute the *a* as heard in *an, am* to make *fad, mass.*

The following words may be used for this step:

long *a*	bone, hole, glide, woke
short *a*	bread, quick, fed, hitch
ai	boat, bread, get
aw	drown, flew, down
short *e*	beat, pack, flash, him
ee	boat, did, stood, had
long *i*	bend, spoke, race, grape
short *i*	bud, butter, fast, wet
long *o*	clever, grape, mile, sale
short *o*	bag, rid, map, left
long *u*	late, done, care, fame
short *u*	back, hill, dance, desk

Many combinations of two vowels are used to represent vowel sounds. Teachers often use a rule, "When two vowels go a-walking, the first one does the talking." This is to help the child use a long *e* sound in words like *meat* and *bead*. Overdependence on this generalization can lead to mispronunciation of many words. A better warning might be, "When two vowels go a-walking, there's danger a-stalking."

The danger is that the two vowels are blended together in a diphthong or that two vowels may form a digraph in which one vowel sound is made. The last vowel rather than the first may be the sound made. Vowel combinations which form diphthongs are *oi* as in *boil*, *oy* as in *boy*, *ou* as in *mouse*, *ow* as in *crowd*. Two vowels together which make a digraph may have the sound of the first or the second vowel. *Ai* as in *mail* and *aisle*, *ea* as in *beam* and *steak*, *ie* as in *pie* or *believe*, *ui* as in *suit* or *guide*. The digraph may not present the long sound of either vowel as in *head, foot, fruit, canoe, would,* and *could*.

A basic generalization that children need to make about vowels in both reading and spelling is that they have a variety of pronunciations but that outside of certain exceptions there are patterns of pronunciation and spelling that will help them.

The following activities (1 through 9) are practical for drill with vowel sounds.[15]

1. When introducing the long and short sound of vowels, write the word *dim* on the blackboard, and ask the children to tell you the word. Then add an *e* and ask the children to tell you the word. Do this with several words until the children notice that a final *e*, although silent, makes the long *i* sound. Divide the class into two groups. One group looks in books for words with short sounds. The other group finds words where the final *e* makes the other vowel long.

2. For a long-and-short-vowel game, collect pictures of objects with long and short vowel sounds, such as *bell, shoe, cat, cone,* and *glass*. Paste these on 3- × 5-in. cards and place in a box. Paste a picture of a short-sound vowel word in the lid and one of a long-sound vowel word in the bottom. The children sort the cards and put them in the

¹⁵ Selma E. Herr, "Phonics Clinic," *The Instructor* (May 1957), pp. 35–39. (Available as a reprint.)

right places. Later use words instead of pictures. Provide a key for self-checking.

3. Play a detective game to find the silent letters. Prepare a list of words from reading or spelling lessons. The children circle the letters that are silent: *before, coat, high, blue, leaves.*

4. List several words on the blackboard. The children rewrite them, substituting another vowel for the one given: *went, want; wish, wash; dish, dash;* and so forth.

5. Give the group a duplicated list of words. They add another vowel to make a new word: *mad, made, maid; led, lead; din, dine.*

6. Everyone numbers his paper. The teacher says, "I am going to say some words that have either a long or a short sound of *a* in them. When I say the word, write *S* on your paper beside the number of the word if the *a* has a short sound. Write an *L* if the word has a long *a* sound in it." Be sure that the words are short and, of course, familiar.

7. Eight words (*bow, brow, cow, how, now, plow, sow,* and *allow*) are the only words primary children need with the *ow* sound. They meet these words in which *ow* has the sound of long *o—blow, crow, flow, glow, grow, know, low, mow, row, show, slow, snow, throw, tow, sow,* and *below*. Once their meaning is clearly understood, have several activities to provide further study. Put them on flash cards and show. Have the children stand up if they have an *ow* sound, sit down if they have an *o* sound. (Notice that *bow* and *sow* are in both groups.)

8. Make separate flash cards for practice on phonic irregularities. Have a bulletin board with pictures and words that have unexpected sounds. Let children pair off and show the cards to each other. For variation show them in the opaque projector. Avoid words with many irregularities.

Duplicate a list of common words involving the hard and soft *c*. Read over the list with the group, then have the children write the words in two separate columns. Do the same thing with *g*.

9. Present *ar, er, ir,* and *ur* separately, rather than treating the vowels alone. Use

groups of words such as *sir, were,* and *blur* to show that *ir, ur,* and *er* have the same sound. Point out that with *ar,* the *r* usually says its own name.

For Discussion

1. Identify a common vowel sound in these words: *fur, fir, mother, cellar, myrrh, word, journal, search, cupboard, colonel, acre, avoirdupois, were.* What is it called?

2. Should phonics instruction start with the vowels? Examine a series that does, such as that published by Economy Press of Oklahoma City.

How Are Reading Skills Taught at the Primary Level?

The first step in word recognition is to help the child realize that the printed letters represent language. In preprimers the story is told through the pictures. The children discuss what is happening, and at first the teacher reads what the book characters are saying. As the story progresses and one of the characters is calling to his mother (or dog or baby) the teacher asks, "What would you say if you were the boy in the story?" Eventually a child will say, "Come here, Mother." "That is exactly what the story says," explains the teacher. "Now you read the words that tell us what the boy says."

The clue used here is the context or meaning clue. Through repetition of the words the child eventually remembers what the word says whenever he sees it. Some words cannot be developed from the meaning alone. Such words as *said, at, was, am, is,* and *blue* must be learned through planned repetition.

The beginner seldom depends on sound clues alone to recognize a word but uses the sound represented by a letter in combination with meaning or word form. As soon as the child knows by sight two or more words that start the same way, he has a clue to the sound of all words beginning with that letter. Some letter–sound associations seem to be used by most children. The consonants *m, s, b, t, n,* and *j* appear to be quite easy as sound clues.

The first reading level corresponds to the time children are reading in the preprimers of a basic series. Programs that use other introductory procedures, such as writing, would postpone some of these activities until later.

Primary sight vocabulary is based on words that the children use frequently and with meaning in their oral language. Familiar objects in the room are labeled. Words to be presented emerge from the discussion and are written on the board or on the chart. "This is what Dick said," the teacher comments as she writes, "Come Jane. Come here." "Who will read these words for us?" Then the word will be used in other situations until it is repeated many times and the children recognize it without prompting. Small cards with words printed on them are used. The children place the words on the proper article in a picture. Or the words are distributed and in turn each child puts his label on the proper article in the room. A box of variety-store items may provide the models. Names of the articles are pasted on a large cardboard designed to lie flat on the table. The children in turn place their article on the correct word. Color names are learned by matching two cards—one with only the name, the other with the name and color. The children in turn place their article on the correct word.

Word form clues are indicated in a number of ways. Have the children notice the form of a word, its general length, shape, size, and configuration, without reference to individual letters. This is always done with a left-to-right motion of the hand under the word. After a short sentence, phrase, or word is read to the children, the word or words are displayed. The children are then asked to choose one of several pictures that illustrates what the word says. After a word is shown to the children, it is taken away. Children then close their eyes and try to "see" the word. Check by showing two words and have the children select the one they saw first. During this period words of unlike appearance are used, such as *name,*

Both auditory and reading vocabulary grow out of planned experiences. The child is matching a word card with the label on the objects (shells) as a part of a game exercise. (*Courtesy of the San Diego County Schools.*)

bed, funny. Attempting to distinguish between words that look alike, *this* and *that* or *funny* and *bunny,* will only cause confusion at this time.

Structural analysis starts with the *-s, -ing,* and *-ed* endings on words. Emphasis is placed on the part of the word that helps a child to remember which is the base or root word. Too great an emphasis on these endings will cause children to start looking at the wrong end of the word. The left-to-right habit of observing words can be stressed by presenting some words for drill in this fashion:

$$help + s = helps$$
$$or \quad help + ed = helped$$

or by direct contrast:

help	help
helps	helped

Phonetic analysis at this time is directed toward auditory discrimination. Speech jingles that repeat sounds should be used. If two or more words start with the same sound, the fact should be noted. Names that start the way words do provide a personal association with a sound. The emphasis is still on hearing parts of words, hearing the beginning of a word, or hearing the ending of a word. Names of letters are still being learned by some children during this period.

In preprimers the story is told with the pictures, while the reading is usually what the characters in the book say. Some stories are more easily reviewed if the pages are mounted in sequence like a cartoon strip. Have the children tell the story, then have them read what the story people are saying. Many series have the first preprimer in the form of a big book. This can be used for group instruction without the physical handling of the reading material during the initial introduction periods. When the child does get his own book it is a tremendous psychological experience for him to be able to read the first story independently.

The preprimer level will be completed by many children during the first half of the year. Some children will remain at this level throughout the first grade; a few need to start at the preprimer level in the second grade.

Most children arrive at primer level after reading the preprimers of the basic series. Children are ready to read a primer story when their interest has been aroused, their previous experiences have been keyed in with the story, and their speaking vocabularies have become adequate to deal with the concepts. Guided discussion and sharing of experiences pertinent to the story to be read give the children experience in talking and listening and develop readiness. A motivating question before silent reading helps children to read for meaning. Good reading and study habits are developed during the silent reading of the story. The children learn to identify their own problems of word recognition and comprehension and ask for help when needed. In the beginning, a lesson may consist of only one page of a story. As reading skills are developed, the children can manage larger units.

Discussion following silent reading helps the children to clear up comprehension problems. They can enjoy the humor of the story together and discuss relationships of characters. The teacher is able to check comprehension further by asking questions.

Rereading may be done after the silent reading of each page or after the reading of the entire story. The motivation of rereading should be to find the answer to a question, to find out how the characters felt, to enjoy the story, or to find the most interesting parts.

With respect to phonics, the children and teacher start to build a chart of "key" words to use in working out new words. This chart is built slowly, adding words as they are met in reading.[16]

The following single-consonant chart is a typical example. Words used on the chart should be words in the reading series being used. One series would use *work* instead of *wagon;* another, *look* instead of *little.*

Bb	baby	Nn	not
Cc	come	Pp	pet
Dd	dog	Qq	quack
Ff	father	Rr	run
Gg	go	Ss	something
Hh	house	Tt	toy
Jj	jump	Vv	valentine
Kk	kite	Ww	wagon
Ll	little	Xx	
Mm	mother	Yy	yellow
		Zz	zoo

(The word after *x* is omitted because the children will encounter *x* mostly at the end of words, as in *box.*)

From the very beginning, children should be taught how to skip over a word and then think it out from context, because they must necessarily do a great deal of this in later independent reading. After the student becomes familiar with the sounds of initial consonants he should be taught to check his guessed word with the beginning sound of its printed form. The following procedure is suggested as one means of helping him acquire this skill.

In the sentence "Tom saw a bird fly to the ground," we assume that *fly* is the only word which the child does not know.

TEACHER: Look at the word. What is another word that starts with the same sound?

CHILD: *Fun.*

---

[16] Devices presented here are from many sources, the major one being the 1960 Language Arts Course of Study of Grand Rapids, Mich. Other suggestions came from teachers in classes taught by the author.

TEACHER: What does a bird do that starts like *fun?*

CHILD: *Fly.*

TEACHER: Now read the sentence again to see if the word fits.

The purposes and exercises below are appropriate at the primer level.

At the first-reader level the children show more independence in reading. They are able to read and grasp the meaning of longer and more involved stories, to use context clues, to predict outcomes and draw conclusions in stories, to feel success and joy because they have a substantial reading vocabulary. Many children are at this level at the beginning of their second year in school, others will have mastered this material by the end of the first year.

In auditory and visual discrimination the children begin to recognize initial consonant blends such as: *bl*—black, *fr*—friend, *sp*—spell, and *dr, gr, pl, st, tr.* Words are added to a chart of consonant blends as they are

Purpose	*Exercise*

To develop greater comprehension emphasize reading for meaning.	From a pack of cards with words on them, choose the ones that fit in each of the following sentences:
	
	See the _____ red car.
	  (little)
	Find _____ big cars for me.
	  (two)
	Find a big _____ ball.
	  (red)
	
	Draw a picture illustrating a riddle. Copy the riddle and paste it below the picture.

To develop auditory and visual discrimination, encourage meaningful associations of sight words through the use of picture clues.	Make cards with a picture on one side and the word on the other side. Say the word and then turn the card over to see if it is correct.
To develop the use of structural analysis as a means to better word recognition by providing opportunities to recognize the variant *s.*	Provide pictures of two boats with the words *boat* and *boats.* Have the children look at the pictures and put a circle around the correct word. Repeat with many different pictures.

The same words beginning with a capital and small letter are like two completely different words to first graders. You can put two lists on the board:

come	not
do	Do
Not	will
Will	Come
Go	go

Touch two children and say a word. The children go to board, frame the word, and say it. Have a child touch and say the word in the first column and another child find it again and say it in the second. Direct a child to draw lines between the two words that say the same thing. Ask a child to erase the words he can say. Later these same words may be used in sentences on the board. This should give further meaning to words and provide an added reading situation.

met in reading. Some will not be met until second-reader level. The consonant blend and digraph chart would appear like this:

bl	black	*sh*	she
br	brown	*sk*	skate
ch	children	*sm*	small
cl	clown	*sn*	snow
cr	cry	*sp*	spell
dr	dress	*st*	stop
fl	flag	*sw*	swing
fr	friend	*th*	this
gl	glad	*tr*	train
gr	green	*tw*	twin
pr	pretty	*wh*	white
sc	scat		

Children at the first-reader level begin to learn the following final consonant sounds:

d	red	*g*	pig	*k*	book		
l	wheel	*m*	him	*n*	hen		
p	up	*s*	us	*t*	bat		

Picture dictionaries made by the children will reinforce most of the consonant sounds as well as establish a dictionary concept. Such an activity might be an early home-work assignment. Use a notebook or single sheets that may later be assembled. At the top of each quarter space the child may paste a picture of some familiar object. Each object picture must start with a different sound. He then cuts words starting with those sounds from old magazines and pastes them in the correct column.

With respect to word structure children begin to recognize the *-ed, -d, -ing* and *-s* endings. After the children have studied a

story with the teacher, sentences such as the following may be written on the board:

> The man stopped at the house.
> The big black bear walked in.
> The baby climbed on his back.
> The children marched around the room.
> The door opened.

The teacher then gives the following directions:

> Draw a line under the word that tells what the man did when he came to the house.
> Draw a line under the word that tells how the bear came in.
> Draw a line under the word that tells how the baby got on the bear's back.
> Draw a line under the word that tells what the children did.
> Draw a line under the word that tells what the door did.

The teacher will then call attention to the endings of all the words underlined on the board. The teacher says, "Very often we come to a word that looks like a new word to us when it is really an old word with *-ed* on the end of it. I'll write a word on the blackboard and then I'll ask one of you to write *-ed* on the end of the word and tell what it is after you have changed it." (*Writes such words as* help, look, call, walk, *and so on.*) Individuals write *-ed* on the end and pronounce the word.

The following exercises may be used at the first-reader level:

Purpose

To check the children's understanding.

Exercise

Write the best word on each line:

1. A rabbit _____ in a hole under a tree.
   live lived
2. The rabbit said, "I _____ I had red
   wish wished
   wings."
3. He _____ in the Wishing Pond.
   look looked
4. The rabbit _____ around three times.
   turn turned
5. He _____ home to show his wings to
   start started
   his mother.

Purpose

To develop the ability to comprehend more involved stories, provide opportunities for answering questions about a story. Children may be urged to make inferences with exercises like this.

Comprehension of words may be checked in a game of this nature.

Classification exercises will also check comprehension.

Exercise

Draw a circle around the correct word.

Dick liked Spot.	Yes	No
Sally was happy.	Yes	No

Play "Going Places":
A pack of cards, placed upside down at the front of the room. Two or three players are chosen. A starting line and finish line are designated. Each in turn takes a card from the top of the pack. One may read, "Take two steps." "Take one big step." Another, "Go back one step." "Jump." "Stay where you are." A "Run" card allows the child to go to the good line at once and win.

Put these words under the correct heading:

Things to Wear		*Things to Ride*
coat	train	cap
boat	horse	mitten
airplane	dress	hat

The Reading Lesson

During reading instruction the teacher must be concerned with the attention span of individuals in the group, the need for physical movement, the handling of material, and the activities of the remaining members of the class, in addition to the immediate aspects of the lesson. Handling of these details is indicated in the following lesson. A group of students in a class of Dr. Constance McCullough created this material. The story being read is "Little Red Riding Hood." [17]

The teacher and pupil activities are indicated first; then an explanation of the points remembered by the teacher is given as the class proceeds throughout the lesson.

The first aspect of the lesson is to build a common background for the group and to build the forms and meaning of the vocabulary used in the story.

1. The children are in a circle in the front of the room. The teacher starts by asking, "How many of you have ever been to the woods?" "What is it like in the woods?" "Are there

woods near here?" "How is it different from the town or city?"

Set the mood for reading. Develop unfamiliar concepts. Find out what is known; have children inform each other; determine what, if anything, you must explain to them. Contrast is an effective teacher.

2. "Our story today is about a girl who lives near the woods. Read this silently as I write it and be ready to read it aloud." Write: The little girl lives near the woods. As you start to write the *w* for *woods,* say "woods," for this is the one word the children do not know. (If the word were polysyllabic, like *hunter,* you would say "hunt" as you wrote the *h* and say "er" as you wrote the *er.*)

Silent reading before oral encourages efficient reading unimpeded by lip movements. Stand to one side as you write, so that *all* can see. Seat children so that this is possible. Say new words as you write them, so that children may have *simultaneous* impressions of the word from ear and eye. Write the word in a phrase or sentence so that it appears in a normal setting, making normal demands upon the reading eye and providing clues for later identification.

3. "Let's all read it together." Run hand under the sentence as the children read, to stress left-to-right observation.

[17] Constance McCullough, *Handbook for Teaching the Language Arts* (San Francisco: Paragon Publications, 1958).

All children thus experience seeing, hearing, saying—of the new word in a setting that emphasizes its meaning as well as its form. Unison activity tends to keep all children involved, watching and thinking.

4. "The little girl's name was Little Red Riding Hood." Write, and say as you write, Little Red Riding Hood. "Let's all say it." "Who can find the new word in this name and frame it and say it for us?" Child comes up, puts hand on either side of "Hood" and says "Hood." "Is he right?" "Let's read that word together." Pass hand under word as they read.

Children watch you write the words and are forced to observe them from left-to-right. Their first impression, at least, cannot be reversed or confused about which word says what. Have children take special notice of the new word. Framing of the words focusses the attention of the group and shows clearly which word the child thinks he is "reading." "Is he right?" makes whole group think and react rather than being silent and passive spectators. "Who can find" rather than "John, show us" puts all children on their toes.

5. "Red Riding Hood met someone in this story. You can solve the word for yourselves. Watch carefully as I write and be ready to read the phrase." Write: met a hunter. The children know *hunt* and *-er* from word analysis training. Pause to give children time to read. "Who will read it for us; Bill?" Bill comes up, frames phrase and reads. "Is he right?" "How do you know? Jane?" Jane explains that the word contains *hunt* and *-er*. She comes up, frames separate parts and says them as she does this. "Let's read the phrase together." Have children discuss what a hunter does, what he might be hunting, etc. Show picture if necessary to clarify idea.

Have children solve for themselves the words that follow principles of word analysis they have learned. All children should engage in word analysis which they have been taught. Those who don't understand can learn from another child's explanation. All experience multisensory approach to the word in a meaningful setting. Develop concept of *hunter*.

6. Suppose that all words that are new in the story have been introduced as above. On the chalkboard now are the sentences and phrases: The little girl lives near the woods, Little Red Riding Hood, met a hunter, carried a basket, a big wolf. The teacher says, "Let's read together now the phrases and sentences on the chalkboard." Some children will need much repetition

of the words, others very little. For extremely slow readers (learners), the teacher may not even introduce the story itself that day, but invent a story of her own on the chalkboard and pocket chart, which gives additional practice with new words and phrases.

7. *Comprehension check:* "Who can find, frame, and read the line that tells where someone lives? Jerry?" "Who can find the phrase that tells whom she saw in the woods? Janet?" "Who can find the name of our little girl? Buster?" "Who can find the phrase that tells about a man? Dick?" "Who can find what Little Red Riding Hood took with her? Jo?"

Recognition of the word should stress its meaning as well as its form. Here, you are not just testing one child; you are giving others a chance to see and hear the words again. Make sure that all are watching, not tying shoestrings.

8. *Word recognition check:* "Stand when you think you can find, frame, and read to us one of our new words. Pat?" Do this for all the words. "We read our words from left to right. Underline the new word from left to right as you say it." (Pat doesn't know what to do.) "Janet, will you help him?"

Change of position relieves physical fatigue and keeps children with you. Young children need these changes more frequently than older. Chair-scraping, wiggling, and inattention are your signals. Stress left-to-right direction. Give children experiences in helping each other. Encourage them to feel that being shown the way is help rather than negative criticism or a cause for embarrassment.

9. *Flash-card exercise:* Have flash cards containing words they know and the new words, so that you can build phrases and sentences with them. Sit to the right of the pocket chart so that you will not cover the cards as you set them in from left to right. "I am going to make a story; but, instead of telling it to you, I am going to have you read it to me. Watch carefully and be ready to read my first sentence."

Maintain the left-to-right observation of print by the order in which you insert the cards. Give children a purpose for watching before you start. Children who know what is expected of them are more apt to do it.

10. Put into the pocket chart the cards: I went into the woods one day. Have a child read the sentence. Have all stand who agree that this is right. Add other sentences similarly. Finally,

have whole story read, then new words identified.

Do not summarize here the story they will read in the book; make a different story. Physical relief through movement is provided again if needed.

11. "Now, I am going to show you some words. If you recognize the word I show, stand." Show *hunter.* Children stand. "Jim, will you read it for us?" "Let's all say it together: *hunter.* Be seated. Are you ready for the next word?" Etc.

Test of word recognition without context fosters careful study of the word. Speed is not nearly so important as care, here. Call on one child; otherwise, children who don't know the word will stand for the honor of looking smart and get away with it.

12. *Chalkboard exercise:* This can be similar to the pocket chart exercise or a variation such as: Trees grow in the woods; A hunter shoots animals. "I shall write a sentence on the chalkboard. If you can read it, stand." Have a child read it. "Is this a true statement? Do trees grow in the woods? Can you prove it?" Have the child show the picture you used for the concept of woods earlier, showing the trees in the woods.

These sentences make children think of the meanings of the new words. Have an established signal such as standing, raising hand, to reduce chaos. When true-false statements are given, always require proof. Otherwise, you are teaching guessing, not reading or thinking.

13. *Chart or newsprint exercise:* Prepare a story on a chart, using the new words. Have the children read it to you and reread parts in response to your comprehension clues. Or have children make up their own cooperative story using the new words. Draw stick figures on the chalkboard and have child read the sentence your picture refers to. Have child pantomime a meaning and have another child read the word or sentence so illustrated.

Words are best learned in meaningful settings of known words. Repeated exposures to the new words in varied settings finally cause learning. Creative expression is an effective way of cementing impressions. The drawings provide interest of guessing and variety for the same old purpose; getting the child to read the sentence. Pantomime also lends variety and gets the wiggliest temporarily off the squeaky chair.

The second aspect of the lesson concerns the directed reading of the story.

14. "Who would be a good person to pass books today? Petunia?" "Let's open our books to the table of contents. How many have found the page with the table of contents on it? George, you could find it faster with the book right-side up. There; that's right," "Look down the page, now, for the name of our new story, *Little Red Riding Hood.* Let's read the name of our story and the page it is on aloud, together: *Little Red Riding Hood,* page forty-five."

Keep the books safely tethered until you need them. Make passing the books an honor—incidentally, another reason for good behavior and attention. Some children get D in reading because they get A in horseplay. Much better than drawing attention to George would be a quiet signal to him or turning his book. Give him credit when he does it right.

15. "Who will write our page number on the chalkboard? Angus?" "In which half of our book will we find page forty-five? Esther?" "When you have found the page, study the picture at the top of it and be ready to tell me what you see."

Do this if writing numbers is still difficult for the children. Help children judge how far back into the book to look for a page. Reading the table of contents is learned by using every opportunity to read it. Even primers have a table of contents.

16. "What is happening in the picture?" (Little Red Riding Hood is talking to a lady—must be her mother. Little Red Riding Hood must be ready to go to the woods—she has her basket her mother is just filling with cookies and she has her little red riding hood on.) "Who is talking in the picture?" (her mother) "Read the first page and be ready to tell what her mother said." "Look up when you are ready." Aside to Everett: "Are you sure you read it carefully and know the answer?" "What did Mother say? Alec?" (Take this here baskit to gramma's and doan say nuttin to strangers and come straight ta home.)

This general question brings out main idea and some details, whereas "Who is in the picture" gives you just one detail. In guiding the reading of young readers, give them something to look for in a paragraph, a page, or in two pages. Older readers (such as high third or fourth grade average readers) may have a purpose set for reading an entire story alone. In all cases, however, a purpose is set. Children need to learn to read for a variety of purposes. Therefore, try to vary the objective of the reading throughout the lesson,

17. "Why do you think she wanted Grandmother to have the cookies?" "Why did she warn Little Red Riding Hood about strangers and coming straight home?" "Who will read what she said and make it sound the way she must have said it?" "Let's look at Joe and listen while he reads, to hear how she sounded." "What do you think Little Red Riding Hood will say? Let's read the next page to find out." Proceed through the story, asking questions and discussing points, until the end.

Make children aware of the human relationships and feelings, reasons behind behavior. Oral reading should have a listening audience. Oral reading is optional here, depending upon how much is needed for practice. Oral reading here serves the purpose of increasing children's awareness of mother's feeling and concern. Have children predict events. Here, again, a purpose is set for silent reading. The third aspect of the instruction is to provide purposeful rereading of the material.

18. "We talked yesterday about how Little Red Riding Hood's mother felt about her going into the woods alone. How do you think Little Red Riding Hood herself felt? Find the place that makes you think that, and read it aloud to us."

A single reading of a basal reader story does justice neither to the story nor to the learning of the new words. Basal reading experience should give the child more insight into the story meaning than he would have derived alone or in one reading. "Intensive reading" is the term.

19. "Let's listen carefully while Harry reads and decide whether that part does show that Little Red Riding Hood was happy and excited as Harry said. . . ." (Harry reads.) "Do you think Harry is right? Does any other place in the story make you think that she was glad? Billy?" Etc. "Why do you think she was happy and excited? Any other reasons?" "Did Little Red Riding Hood remember everything her mother said? How many of you think she did? No one? Find the place that makes you think she didn't. . . . What should Little Red Riding Hood have done instead of stopping to talk?" (Children can act this out if you wish, to get the feeling for situation.) "What kind of person

do you think Little Red Riding Hoood was?" Various answers here will lead to reading various parts for proof. Put the adjectives used by the children on the chalkboard. "What words describe your idea of the wolf?" Put these in parallel column.

Oral reading should have an audience that listens for meanings. Children should not always watch the page as a child reads aloud, for this practice puts the children's attention on the accuracy of the reading rather than on the ideas expressed. Have the audience either look at the speaker, "breast" their books, or hold their fingers in the partly closed book. In any case, impress the children with the fact that this is a *listening* time.

Purposeful rereading time is a time for asking questions which require a variety of types of comprehension, skimming to find answers, and oral reading activities.

20. As children discuss wolf's characteristics, have them notice these points of plot in relation to him: "Why did the wolf use a special voice, as Esther said, when he talked to Little Red Riding Hood? Why did he tell her to pick a bouquet? Why didn't he eat her then instead of going for her grandmother? Pretend you are the wolf talking to himself about what he did and what he is going to do. Who would like to do that? Did the wolf succeed in fooling Little Red Riding Hood when he sat in bed dressed like Grandmother? No? Find the place that makes you think she began to doubt."

Make children aware of cause and effect, motives and results, effect of certain choices upon plot. Have children grasp the point of view of each important character. Give children the experience of skimming for evidence.

21. "Do you think this story could really have happened? Why or why not? What in the story seems real? What seems untrue to life? What do we call a story like this?" "If your grandmother were in trouble in her home, would a hunter come to rescue her? Who would? Who protects us? Who could give her the best help?" Have the children observe that the kind of helper would depend on grandmother's trouble: illness, burglary, fire, etc.

Have the children judge the real as opposed to the fanciful. Have them learn the terms applied to fanciful tales of this kind. Feature the relationship of the story to the child's own living.

22. "We can take better care of our grand-mothers than Little Red Riding Hood could in the woods." "Do you think this story is a story of today or of long ago? Do you get any clues in the pictures or the story that make you think this? What are they?" "Why do you think this story was called Little Red Riding Hood? Can you think of a better name for it? What if this story appeared in a newspaper. . . . What would the headline be?" (Hunter De-Grandmothers Wolf.)

Protect the children from nightmares! Study the illustrations for a purpose. Have children express the main ideas in a variety of ways.

The fourth aspect of the lesson provides practice and application of skills taught.

23. "The author of this story had a good way of telling how things looked and acted and felt and tasted. How did he say Little Red Riding Hood skipped down the path? (like ·a bouncing ball) How did he say the wolf's eyes looked when he saw the cookies?" (like two ripe plums) Write these expressions on the chalkboard, under one another. "What do you notice about these two lines?" (They both begin with "like." They both liken something to something else to make it clear.)

Skill-building of various types (word recognition, word analysis, comprehension, interpretation, study skills) is done in five- or ten-minute exercise periods. Preferably they are done at the end of a period (group meeting), so that you may assign individual follow-up work at the children's desks to prove individual grasp of the work done. Usually reader manuals suggest from two to five such exercises. You should use all of them at some time during the days involved in the story, unless you are sure that the children can do them well enough without practice. Each exercise is a link in a chain of learnings. To leave one out is to risk worse performance later on, or forgetfulness of the technique. Reading skills rust out from disuse.

24. "As I pass out these sheets of paper to you, read the directions at the top to see what authors can do with words. Will you read the directions to us, Henry?" "What does that mean we should do? Yes, we are to read each sentence, find it in our story, and complete it. Read the first one to us, Bill." (Little Red Riding Hood skipped down the path like a

_____ _____.) "What should we write in the blanks? . . . Yes. Now you are to do the others in the same way. At the bottom of the page you are to write your own endings to sentences. You are to tell how you think Little Red Riding Hood looked as she skipped down the path. What could you say she looked like when she skipped?" "These expressions are called similes." Write *similes* on the chalkboard. Have the children repeat the word with you. Face them so that they can see your lips.

Help children read directions. Have one child read aloud, or all in unison. Don't assume they know what is meant. Ask them to tell what is meant. Go through the sample with them. This is creative work. Each lesson desirably has some imitative activity and some creative; something that takes a short time, something that takes time, thought. Use the technical term the children will have to become accustomed to in later work. Strange words are better grasped when the lips of the speaker can be seen.

25. "Now, who will tell us what he is going to do on this page? Douglas?"

Have a child tell what the job is, in summary, so that no question remains.

26. "Does everyone understand? If you finish early, what can you do?" Have a list of activities somewhere on a chart or on the chalkboard which are legitimate uses of reading time if a child finishes early.

Waiting for the class causes restlessness if a child finishes early. Use reading time for reading activities, not bead stringing, sawing, unrelated to reading.

27. Later, either that day or at the next meeting with the group, go over the papers with the children, either individually or as a group. "Who will read the first sentence? Do you all agree with his answer? No? What do you have, Jerry? How can we find out who is right? Let's look in our books and find the place. Now, read it aloud, please, to us, Jerry."

Rereading of the papers provides another reading experience. Proofreading to find one's own rights and wrongs is more effective for learning than teacher-marked papers. Teach the children to refer to authority rather than languish on a "tis-taint" basis.

28. The following exercise was designed to make children aware of author's style, to give

them a new language tool of their own, and to reexperience the words of the story. As you read this story of life in the woods many years ago, was there anything you wondered about that the story did not tell? List the questions the children ask. Decide where they might find the answers. This may lead to a visit to the library, the reading of books you have collected on woodland animals, etc., the seeing of a film, the listening to a story you read—then having the children tell what they found out. Perhaps, then, having collected this information, they will wish to express it in pictures or in a scrapbook as well as in discussion. Other creative activities might be such as these: to have the children pretend they had been Little Red Riding Hood and write or tell the story as it would have happened to them; to write the story cooperatively as a news story; to write a story about another wolf, etc.; to make illustrations for the story the child makes up.

Enrichment activities are of two kinds: informal and creative. Informational activities are those which add to the child's knowledge. Creative are those in which he expresses his own ideas regarding the story. Both are important and desirably we should have both in a lesson plan for a story. Children should have the incentive of being read to as well as the work of reading for themselves. Creative work can be a natural outcome of research activities. Telling a story involves the use of concepts being learned; sometimes reveals misconceptions which must be straightened out. Writing a similar story means writing the new words the children are still trying to master—an effective left-to-right experience with the new symbols. Drawings or other artistic expression related to reading not only give children a pleasant association with reading but crystallize impressions for the child and reveal any misconceptions to the teacher.

For Discussion

1. Observe a first-grade teacher at work. Note the similarities between what she does and what was described above.

2. Would it confuse a beginning teacher to attempt to explain all aspects of a lesson that she has taught?

3. To what extent could these activities be imitative of those of an experienced teacher without one's knowing the reason why they are done and still be a part of a good teaching performance?

4. Do you agree that vocabulary is best developed in situations that require its use, or would you plan lessons involving lists of new words for lessons similar to spelling lessons for vocabulary development?

5. Would you defend the use of special-skill textbooks in addition to the readers being used?

6. Do you think that primary children should make greater progress in reading than we now expect? How might this be done? What factors other than reading skill should be considered in instruction?

7. Defend or criticize this statement: "The teacher should spend as much time finding the right reading material for a child as instructing him in reading."

8. Would it be possible for two different children to use different clues to recognize a word? If possible, illustrate different ways of recognizing a word.

9. Children may recognize a word that is familiar in their language but they must identify a word that is strange in meaning as well as form. What skills are more associated with identification than recognition? At what grade levels are identification skills used?

10. Although some children will have mastered much of the reading process by the end of six months, we know that it is quite normal for others of equal mental ability to reach the fourth grade before this happens. How can we explain this to parents? How can we give these children praise and recognition in a nonreading activity? What are the children learning that is as important as learning to read?

11. Studies of highly gifted children (150 IQ and above) reveal that a common pattern for them to follow in reading development is to be average or below until the late third grade. How can this be explained?

12. What special problems does a child face in learning to read when he comes from a home where English is not spoken? What are his major educational needs? Should such children be grouped with slow-learning children from English-speaking homes?

How Are Charts Used in Reading Instruction? [18]

Many children enter first grade with great enthusiasm for learning to read. Some fully expect to read the first day. We know that the best quality of learning takes place when there is thirst for it. If a class "has its mind set" on wanting to read, there is a simple way to begin that not only satisfies the eager child but also paves the way for the more formal type of reading. The first group experience to be recorded and read may be as simple as a brief record of play. It might look like this:

We played dodge ball.
It was fun.

The teacher may need to create the brief statements of the very first recorded experiences. Very soon, however, children catch on to the idea and there is ready response to: "What might we say about what we did?"

Interest span of first graders at the beginning of the year is very brief so care must be taken to get a few brief statements on the blackboard rather rapidly. Then with the teacher using the pointer to help scan the line from left to right, the group repeats what has been written. Then the pointer moves to the beginning of the next line and moves smoothly to the end of the sentence as it is read with the teacher. There is no stopping at words. It is saying what has been said, with attention to two lines of symbols that are as unfamiliar to the children as the scratchings on the Dead Sea Scrolls would be to most adults. After it has been read once or twice the teacher might say, "That is reading and you can do it." Her enthusiasm and pleasure reassures the children that reading is fun and they anticipate their next experience. That would be enough for one time and the group would proceed to other types of activities. During the day the teacher might copy the sentences on a sheet of newsprint and bring it out just before the children go home. Again they would read it together

with the teacher and go home with the feeling that they had learned to read, just what they had expected to do, and parents are convinced from the first day's report that the children are off to a good start.

Each day new experiences are recorded. The teacher gives guidance in getting variety into the sentences, in keeping them simple, and in supplying appropriate words or phrases as needed. Sometimes charts are reread from day to day as long as interest is maintained. They are discarded as they lose significance.

This classroom example will illustrate a part of the teacher planning that takes place as an experience chart is developed.

The children have completed the construction of a barn. The teacher considered possibilities for stories which would include words from the reading list such as:

Look, look.	See, see.
Look at our barn.	See our barn.
It is big.	It is green.
Hay, horses, and	It is white.
feed are in it.	Animals live in the barn.

These two stories, thought out by the teacher, should be compared with the story finally composed by the group. The teacher guided the children to make up their story and accepted their contributions, even though she had several ideas as to how it might develop. The preplanning helped her to control vocabulary and length, even though the resulting story dictated by the children was different.

With this preparation the teacher guides the children's discussion:

TEACHER: What are some of the things we could write about our barn?
CHILD 1: Bobby, John, and Mary helped to make it.
CHILD 2: It is big.
CHILD 3: It is painted.
CHILD 4: I helped.
CHILD 5: I saw one. It was red.
TEACHER: What color is ours?
CHILD: White and green.
TEACHER: What is in a barn?
CHILD 1: Horses.

---

[18] Much of this material is from curriculum publications of the Madison, Wis., and Long Beach, Calif., Public Schools.

Dictated stories grow out of a common experience. Seeing one's own language in print takes much of the mystery out of early reading attitudes. (*Courtesy of the Burbank Public Schools.*)

CHILD 2: Food for the animals.

CHILD 3: Cows to be milked.

TEACHER: You've told many interesting things about our barn. Do you think we could tell in a story the things which are most important?

CHILD 4: You mean a story like we did about the trucks?

TEACHER: Yes.

CHILD 3: Yes, a story like the truck story.

As the teacher asks questions in logical order and the children respond, their sentences are written on the chalkboard by the teacher.

TEACHER: You've made a fine barn. What could you say to make others look at the barn?

CHILD 2: See our barn. (*Teacher records.*)

TEACHER: That would make us look, wouldn't it?

TEACHER: What color is it?

CHILD 1: White and green.

TEACHER: What can you tell about the colors in a sentence?

CHILD 3: It is white and green. (*Teacher records.*)

TEACHER: What is kept in the barn?

CHILD 4: The farmer goes in there.

TEACHER: That's right. Is that where he lives?

CHILD 4: No, but the horse does.

TEACHER: Yes, and what else would we find in the barn?

CHILD 2: Hay.

CHILD 3: Feed.

TEACHER: Who can give us a sentence with the things you mentioned in it?

CHILD 1: The farmer stays in the barn sometimes; the horse, the feed, and hay are in the barn.

TEACHER: You've included everything that

was said. Would it be all right if I left the farmer out since he doesn't live there, and say, "Hay, feed, and horses are in the barn"? (*Teacher records.*)

CHILD 1: Yes.

TEACHER: We've said many good things about the barn. Let's read the story together, and as we are reading, maybe you can think of a title for the story. (*Class reads together.*)

CHILDREN: (*In unison.*) See our barn. It is white and green. Hay, feed, and horses are in the barn.

TEACHER: Does someone have any idea for our title?

Titles are not necessary for all stories. When they are used the teacher will guide children to select a title quickly.

CHILD 1: See Our Barn.

CHILD 2: The Green and White Barn.

CHILD 3: Our Barn.

TEACHER: Shall we use that one?

CHILDREN: (*In unison.*) Yes. (*Teacher records "Our Barn" above the story.*)

Follow-up activities may include such things as drawing a picture to illustrate the story; work on such basic words as *look, at, our, it, big, see;* writing one sentence or word, and, of course, rereading the story the next day.

In making charts, keep the printed matter well centered so there is a balance of space around the story. The print must be large enough so that it can be easily read by all the children. It is a good idea to draw very light lines if newsprint is used, or to scratch lines with a pin if oaktag is used. Tall letters should be about 3 inches high and small letters about an inch and a half. An inch should be allowed between lines. Use a medium-sized felt pen to do the lettering and be sure to make correct letter forms with proper spacing between letters and between words.

In addition to group-experience charts other types of charts are needed.

Picture Charts. For variety a large colorful picture may be introduced and short sentences written about the picture. Sometimes the class will dictate short sentences telling about the picture; later, when a sizable sight vocabulary has been established, the teacher may bring in a surprise illustrated story using words the children know.

Weather Charts. The first type of recording might be: This is a sunny day; or, Today is cloudy. Children might advance to: Today is December 4. It is cloudy and cold. We saw snowflakes this morning. It may snow tonight.

Sometimes symbols for clouds, wind, sun, rain, and so on, are inserted in slots on a chart. If turnover pages are kept, at the end of the month children may count the number of cloudy days, and so on. The days of the week may be added to such a chart as time goes on. The months of the year as well as temperature readings may be added as children are ready for such experiences. Third-grade children might have a rather complete weather record including the direction of the wind and barometric readings.

News Item Charts. As children share news with the class a teacher might record such items as:

Linda has a baby brother.
Paul's father went to Chicago.
Barbara has new shoes.
Jim has a birthday today.

As the year advances the news might extend to what is happening in the community and in faraway places.

Planning Charts. These may start with something as simple as:

We will listen to a story.
Next we will play a game.
Then we will sing.
Our work period comes next.

As time goes on such charts could include specific directions the group will follow such as:

Tomorrow we will make butter.
We will need:

— — —
    etc.

A listing of names of those responsible for

bringing certain things or doing each of the tasks involved may be included.

Directions for a new game, social studies procedures, choice of work experiences, household duties, and rules for fair and safe play may go into various charts which the children play a part in planning.

Record Charts.   Record charts would indicate progress or growth. There might be a height and weight chart. One might indicate the changes that take place as children observe bulbs or plants grow and bloom. Another might keep the scores of games that are played from time to time. Still another might record the names of stories the teacher reads so it can be referred to for later choices of favorites. Later in the year records can be kept of books the children read, of achievements in other learning activities, and of items they might wish to include in a "First-Grade Yearbook."

Reference Charts.   A color chart to which children may refer when they are learning colors; a number chart; a picture dictionary type chart for word recognition; a phonics chart; a bird or flower chart are all examples of the reference chart.

In summary, the use of charts with young children serves the following purposes:

1. Classroom-created charts give the reading process real meaning and significance, because the children's own experiences are the basis for them.
2. The mechanics of reading are practiced. These include:

   a. Left-to-right eye movement.
   b. The sweep from the end of one line to the beginning of the next.
   c. The significance of words and sentences.
   d. Observation of the use of simple punctuation.

3. Children are helped to see that reading serves many purposes.
4. Much language development takes place (producing clear, simple sentences; expansion of vocabulary;

thought organization; putting events in proper sequence).

5. Charts can serve as a beginning in the development of perceptual clues:

   a. As certain words are used repeatedly, they can be identified and used on flash cards to become fixed as sight vocabulary.
   b. Whole sentences can be printed on oaktag strips so children can match them on the chart to note likenesses and differences.
   c. Children note that many words start alike. As these words are said they hear the likenesses in beginning sounds and you have an introduction to phonics.
   d. As the beginning of a sentence is read, children anticipate what follows and this becomes groundwork for use of the context clue in later reading.
   e. Children understand that the picture at the top of the chart is a clue to what the printed matter relates.

There are limitations in the use of charts. Charts seldom accomplish within themselves all that we hope to do in the area of reading. The range of words used on charts is very broad. No attempt is made to teach all the words used. Only those that are used commonly are pulled out and used on cards to become sight words and a part of each child's reading vocabulary. Of course, some children will learn many words simply by seeing them used on the various charts— which is to be encouraged. Charts do not provide for all the development of perceptual clues. Charts merely serve to introduce, to reinforce, or to make use of such clues that are developed in the reading program.

For Discussion

1. Some authorities feel that one weakness in a chart story is that no new meaning is revealed to the child as he reads such material. "It is as if the child has written a letter to himself." Do you agree or disagree with this point of view?

2. Some teachers construct the chart story with the children, then cut up the story to create flash cards. What would be their purpose in such a procedure?

3. Some teachers have created chart stories which they use year after year. This saves the time taken to create a story and provides simple reading material for practice. What weakness would you see in such a program? What strength?

4. Could adequate charts be made by putting words in a pocket chart so that sentences were formed? What would the children miss in a chart so constructed?

What Plans Must Be Made for Independent Work in the Primary Grades?

With any type of individualized instruction the teacher has the responsibility of planning work that will keep the rest of the class busy while the teacher works with a small group. The basic reading series provides in the workbook purposeful individual activities. When the basic workbook is not available, it is a growing practice to employ outstanding teachers during the summer months to produce this type of material for a district. If the material created meets a local need with special content, the time is well spent. If, however, the material is merely a copy or adaptation of existing published work, the effort may be questionable professional conduct. There are companies that provide master copies of worksheets printed with a special ink so that they can be reproduced. Although these may not be directly related to the material being taught, a busy teacher will often find them better than those she might hurriedly produce. Some manuals for basic readers now recognize this problem and suggest work that is designed for reproduction.

When worksheets are used, demonstrate to the children how to mark each activity when the work is first presented. The vocabulary of the directions sometimes must be taught. Later only brief directional sentences need to be addressed to the pupils until they are able to read and carry out the directions independently. There are often general directions or questions at the beginning of a page. They are there for the purpose of motivating pupil reading of the text. They require thought, and oral responses are expected; the pupils write on the lines provided or on lined paper. Enrichment suggestions may require children to use books and materials other than their reading textbooks. A teacher's daily reading plans should include the reminder to provide all needed materials.

In order to establish standards with children on how to obtain the materials necessary to complete enrichment activities, discuss the location of books, desirable traffic patterns as children move about the room, the way items are returned to the proper places. Some work-type activities may be too varied for the slow groups. If so, use only the portions that are suitable. Use the remainder at another time when the teacher is able to be with the groups.

Independent activities should be checked by the teacher to give children a feeling of security in accomplishment and to know the day-by-day effectiveness of pupil work. The teacher will then know what to review and when to provide additional independent work. A quick check may be sufficient on some days, but a detailed evaluation should be made at least twice a week. Papers sent home should be carefully checked; errors should be marked.

A sample and an analysis of a good reading worksheet appears on the next page.

To provide additional oral reading the independent reading circle has been established by some teachers. In late first grade the children who are in the top group are permitted to form an independent group that reads to each other without the teacher being present. The material provided is easy reading for the children involved. For children working in a basic first reader the group may read from a preprimer of a series not used in their previous work. The leader has a set of cards with the names of those in the group. These are rotated to determine who will read next. Should a child need help with a word, the leader calls on members of the group to help.

Analysis of a Good Reading Worksheet

BOOK: *Finding New Neighbors*   "Baby Bears," 110–117

NAME_____

Read pages 110–117 carefully so that you can discuss these questions:
1. How did the bears feel about Iva?
2. Why were the bears happy at the end of the story?
3. Do you think this story could really have happened? Why or why not?

Adequate space should be provided when writing is required.

Guide questions should establish purpose for reading. Answers should be *oral*, not written.

Number the following sentences in the order they came in the story:
_____ The bears were given a home in the cottage.
_____ A man found two baby bears in the forest.
_____ The bears enjoyed doing their tricks for the children.
_____ The bears played tricks on people in the entire neighborhood.
_____ The man carried the bears in a hat.
_____ A hunter took the bears to the city.
_____ The hunter sold the bears to the circus.

Activities should require thought. Writing should be kept to a minimum.

R usually gives a vowel a special sound if it comes after the vowel in the word, as *ir* in *stir*.
Say each word softly and circle each vowel-with-*r* sound that you hear.

her	for	herd	burn	river
girl	acorn	circle	turtle	squirt
barn	story	far	purple	cart

Word study skills should be practiced after they are taught at the circle.

Usually you can tell how many syllables are in a word by softly clapping the rhythm as you say the word. Write on the line before each of the following words the number of syllables it has. (Avoid excessive picture drawing.)

_____ only	_____ important	_____ shell	_____ promise
_____ village	_____ apron	_____ slowly	_____ which
_____ market	_____ molasses	_____ bananas	_____ curtains
_____ mind	_____ sneeze	_____ doctor	_____ swish

Fast workers should be encouraged to make additional contributions to the class by finding and sharing interesting and pertinent information.
For the "Early Birds": Can you find some interesting facts about bears? Look in your science books or in the dictionary.

Because being a member of such a group is a special privilege, these children must assume responsibility for their own behavior. At the designated time the children form a circle in a secluded corner of the room. Monitors distribute the books which are stored in that area. Each child has a marker which is left at the page where the reading will start. In turn, the students read aloud. At times the teacher may visit the group or ask them to tell the class about the story they are reading. The period lasts for fifteen to twenty minutes. In second grade, all groups may participate, limited only by available material, and in the third the low group. The other third-grade groups profit more by individual reading of library books.

Individual games which provide drill are needed to supplement worksheets. Each game must be taught at the circle, then placed on a shelf to be chosen by the child when he is given that opportunity. Any worksheet that involves drawing lines to match a picture and a word, a singular and plural form, a contraction and the two words that form it, words that start alike, or words that rhyme may be put on a shoestring board. This is a heavy piece of cardboard with two parallel lines of words written on it. A shoestring is attached to the words in the first column and a brad or a hole put near the words in the second column. Instead of drawing a line the child connects the shoestring between the appropriate words. After the board is checked the strings are disconnected and the drill may be used by another child. Sometimes rubber bands can be used as well as shoestrings.

Another way of matching words is to use clothespins. The snap-type clothespin is used. On a card one list of words is presented. The words to be matched are written on the clothespins. The child snaps the pins opposite the appropriate words. Each cardboard should have a cloth bag attached, which contain the pins to be used in that drill. Clothespins can be used in many exercises which would require the child to fill in a blank. Prefixes or suffixes might be on the clothespins while the base word is on the card. Beginning consonants may be on the clothespins and the remaining part of the word on the card. Sentences may be on the card, with a word omitted. The proper word would be selected by the child as he reads it on the clothespins and snapped next to the sentence that it completes.

Boxed drills have a game appeal. The most convenient boxes for these games are hosiery boxes. Stores will usually save them for a teacher if she requests them. The directions for the game are pasted in the top of the box. Sometimes the correction key can be included so that these will be self-correcting. The box may contain a picture with words on small cards to be placed on the

object named. There may be a series of questions which the child answers yes or no by putting all the yes's on one side and the no's on the other. The sentences on the strips of cards may be reassembled to tell a story. Vowels may be put in their proper places in words. Old workbooks and readers may be cut up and put in these boxes in the form of dozens of interesting game drills.

A manila folder with a pocket or envelope to contain the cards with the words, vowels, or sentences used in the exercise is another convenient form. The following type of exercise is used:

Make a cardboard folder with space for short vowels on one side, for long vowels on the other. On small pieces of cardboard, words with both long and short vowels are written.

To Play: The pupil places the words on the right page. When not in use, the word cards may be placed in the pockets at the bottom. Folders for each vowel may be made by choosing words from pupil's needed vocabulary.

Sentences using words often substituted for one another are used.

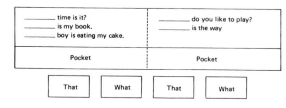

To Play: Place word cards in proper places on blank lines. One pupil checks another. Pupil works game by putting prefix and suffix cards in proper blank and pronouncing words.

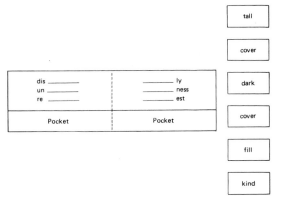

Make folder and cards. Choose card that makes a word for each blank. Say the new words.

Some teachers make their own magic slates out of a sheet of heavy cardboard (9 × 12 inches) and a sheet of clear acetate the same size. The acetate is taped to the board at both sides but left open at top and bottom. A skill-building exercise slipped between the board and the acetate sheet can be marked with a china-marking pencil. The pencil marks rub off easily with a cloth, leaving the slate ready for another child to use. Both the acetate and china-marking pencils can be purchased at art supply stores.

Acetate envelopes made of two transparent sheets fused together are obtainable at most stationery stores. These envelopes will accommodate two exercise pages placed in the envelope back to back, with perhaps a thin sheet of cardboard between them for stiffening.

Worksheets which present a word over and over again in context provide better drill practice than flash cards. It is possible for a child to recognize a word in isolation and not be able to read it in a sentence. The meaning in flash card drill is sometimes ignored. Thus it becomes important that teachers find ways of presenting work material that serves this purpose yet is easily evaluated and administered.

For Discussion

1. How may parents be involved in the creation of some of the materials described?

2. There is much discussion of teaching machines at this time. In what sense is an independent work device a teaching machine?

3. Evaluate some of the following devices as independent reading equipment:

Garrard Press; 119 West Parke Avenue; Champaign, Ill.

    Basic Sight Vocabulary Cards. Grades 1–3

    Consonant Lotto. Grades 1–4

    Group Sounding Game. Grades 1–8

    Picture Word Cards. Grades K–1

    Group Word Teaching Game.

    Syllable Game. Grades 2–4

    Vowel Lotto. Grades 1–4

    Sight Phrase Cards. Grades 1–4

Kenworthy Educational Service, Buffalo, N.Y.

    Doghouse Game. Grades 2–4

Steck Company; Box 16; Austin 61, Texas

    Reading Essentials Reading Aids. Grades 1–3

How Is Reading Taught as Children Advance in Primary Reading Skills?

Children at second-grade level are beginning to develop independence in word recognition, realization of the many happy experiences that they get from books, and understanding that reading can help them to solve problems and to satisfy their curiosity. Growth in reading skill continues through exercises of the following nature to achieve the purpose stated. The exercises are illustrative. Similar ones constructed for drill purposes would be longer and at a difficult level to challenge the student.

Identification of specific words and phrases as parts of a total sentence relates new vocabulary to known speech patterns. (*Courtesy of the Burbank Public Schools.*)

Purpose	*Exercise*
To develop comprehension and provide opportunities for children to make judgments.	Read and choose the correct reason:
	Jane liked to read books about birds. One morning she saw a book about birds in Mr. Brown's store. Jane wanted the book. She went home for money because _____.
	She had to pay for the book. She wanted to buy candy.
Provide opportunities for children to find the main idea of a story.	Choose a sentence that tells what a story is about.
	What would be a good name for this story? What did we learn by reading the story?

Purpose	*Exercise*
Provide opportunities for children to remember logical sequence.	Review the action in a story using such words as *first, then, next, after that,* and *finally* in brief sentences. Then skim the story to note words or phrases that cue the reader to the time when certain events occurred and how long a period of time the events covered.

Number events in correct sequence:

_____ Bill went to school.
_____ Bill got out of bed.
_____ Bill ate his breakfast.

Provide opportunities for children to make inferences.	Underline the best answer to the question:

Mr. Hill put a dish of food outside his back door. He called his dog, but the dog did not come. So Mr. Hill left the food near the door and went into the house.

Soon a big brown dog came by. When the Hills' dog came home, he did not find any dinner.

Why didn't the Hills' dog find his dinner?

Mr. Hill did not feed him.
A cat ate the dinner.
A big brown dog ate it.

Provide opportunities for children to perceive relationships of time and place, manner, sequence, cause and effect.	After reading a story, underline the correct phrase.

When did Tom hide?

during the night
before breakfast
at noon

Where was father working?

in the yard
near the tree
near the river

Provide opportunities for children to experience sensory images.	Choose the words to use when talking about the weather:

branch	voice	penny
cloudy	cold	stormy
mother	sunny	rainy

Purpose	*Exercise*
To develop vocabulary through the understanding of fundamental concepts; provide opportunities for children to understand related values.	Fill in the blanks in the following sentences: Apple pies are _____ than apples. Mother's pies are _____ than apples. Jane liked apple pies the _____ of all. good better best
Provide opportunities for children to use chronological sequence.	Fill in the blanks: Wednesday is the _____ day of the week. (fourth) Jane is the _____ child in the row. (third)
Provide opportunities for children to understand complementary concepts.	Supply the proper word: Pies are made by a baker; clothes are made by a _____. A cat runs on its legs, but a car runs on _____.
Provide opportunities for children to strengthen the ability to perceive analogous relationships.	Cross out the word which does not belong: house door road roof eight dress ten four lunch dinner nail breakfast
Provide opportunities for children to develop the ability to anticipate meaning.	Write on the line a word that makes the sentence true: The color of the grass is _____. The name of the dog is _____. Write on the line a word that makes the sentence true: Jerry wanted a _____. Tom _____ home. Mother gave _____ a new doll. Mary went boat
Provide opportunities for children to develop an understanding that a word may represent more than one meaning.	Notice that some words have more than one meaning: a bank of snow money in the bank post a letter a fence post an Indian trading post

Purpose

Provide opportunities for children to identify sounds and the meanings of homonyms.

Exercise

Insert the correct homonym cards in the blank spaces on a large chart:

A _____ has horns.
Betty is a _____ little girl.
Do you like a _____ sandwich?
I will _____ you at the corner.
I _____ my dinner at twelve o'clock.
Jane has _____ pennies.
This book is _____ my brother.
Two and two are _____.

deer	dear	meat	meet
ate	eight	for	four

Draw a line from the word in the first column that sounds the same as the word in the second column.

bear	mail
male	blew
sail	bare
blue	sale

The first two weeks of the second school year should be spent in reviewing the subject matter of the first grade. At the end of this period the teacher will have discovered children which are not yet able to make use of these skills in attacking unknown words. Such children may be grouped together and given instruction suited to their needs.

The remainder of the class can begin their work with the short and long sounds of the vowels. The ability to make intelligent use of the long and short sounds of vowels in attacking unknown words has been acquired with difficulty by the average and below-average child. Therefore, these sounds should be developed with particular care.

The order of development of the word elements and phonograms depends on the difficulties the children encounter in their reading and on words used for study in drill or practice periods. For example, one group working in a practice period with such words as *harder, start, sharp,* and *arms* would profit from a study of the phonogram *ar,* whereas another group who finds words such as *mouth, shout,* and *loud* difficult should study the phonogram *ou.*

1. To develop the short sound of *a:*

a. The short sound of *a* must be introduced.

TEACHER: What sound do you hear first in these words? (*Points to such familiar words as* at, am, apple, *and while the children pronounce them.*) See if you can hear that sound in these words. (*Points to such words as* cat, ran, sat, fat, back *as different children pronounce them.*) What sound do you hear first in these words? (*Points to* at, am, *and so on.*) Which letter in these words has the same sound? (*Points to* cat, ran, sat, *and so on.*) Think of another word in which you hear that same sound. (*Write words on the blackboard as they are given.*)

b. At another period such a list as the following may be written on the board:

bag	tap	bad
pan	sad	lap

TEACHER: Yesterday we found out the sound of this letter. (*Write* a *on the blackboard.*) What was it? Find that letter in these words. (*Individual children point* out the letter *a* *in the different words*.) That letter has the same sound in these words that it had in *apple* and *at*. See if you can think of all the sounds in the first word and tell us the word.

Have various children respond as the different words are indicated. If a child calls the word *bag, bad,* have him give the sound of the final letter *g* and then say the word as a whole. The child should never be allowed to pronounce the word as *ba-aa-gu* or *baa-gu,* but should *think* the separate sounds and pronounce the word as *bag.*

c. The following exercise will help children differentiate between the long and the short sounds of *a* in words with which they are familiar. In arranging work of this type, the teacher must include *only known words.*

Write on the blackboard a list of words such as the following:

can	play
had	sang
baby	fat
last	place
stand	bank
name	stay
ran	apples
ate	that

Individual children should take turns pronouncing these words and drawing a ring around those words where the *a* sounds like the *a* in *at.* Such an exercise may later be hectographed and used for independent seat work. The short sounds of the remaining vowels may be developed similarly.

2. To develop the long sound of *a* review the words in which *a* has a short sound.

TEACHER: Sometimes the letter *a* has another sound. Listen for the sound of *a* in these words. (*The teacher will point to and pronounce such familiar words as* ate, make, came.) What was the sound which you heard in every word? What is this word? (*Write* at *on the board.*) Now what is it? (*Change* at *to* ate.) What did I do to change the sound of *a?* (*Do the same with* mad *and* made.) What is the difference between these words? (*Write* cap *and* cape *on the board.*) What is this

word? (*Point to* cap.) What is this one? (*Point to* cape.) What have we found out?

A child should be able to state the generalization in words such as these: When there is an *e* on the end of a word with *a* in it, the *a* says its own name.

3. To develop the long sound of *e,* review the short sound of *e* in such known words as *pet, left, held, went, nest, get, hen, tell,* and so on.

TEACHER: Here are some other words with *e* in them. (*Points to the following list of familiar words on the chalkboard:* wee, three, weeks, sleep, feet.) Find a word that means very small. (*Child points to* wee *and pronounces it.*) Find a word that is the name of a number, and so forth. The other day when we studied words like *pet* and *hen* we found one sound that *e* has. Sometimes it has a different sound. Listen for the sound of *e* in these words. (*The teacher pronounces* wee, three, *and so forth, very distinctly.*) What sound do you hear? When *e* changed the sound of *a* where did we find the *a?* Instead of coming at the end of the word, where does the second *e* sometimes come in these words? That is another thing we must remember when we are working out new words for ourselves. (*Follow this by changing* met *to* meet, step *to* steep, fed *to* feed, *and so on.*)

4. To develop the phonogram *ay,* write such words as the following, which the children have already encountered in reading, on the board.

play   stay   gray   away

TEACHER: Find the word that tells the color of the squirrel. Find the word that tells what the squirrel liked to do. Find the word that tells what Sally wanted the squirrel to do. Find the letters that are the same in all four words. (*Individually children may frame* ay *in each of the four words.*) See if you can find out for yourselves what these words are. (*The following words are written on the blackboard and the children are helpel to work them out independently as already described above.)*

gate	sale	fade
lame	tame	fake

An exercise such as the following will be of value in helping the children discriminate independently between long and short vowels, and at the same time, grow in the skill to use contextual help effectively. The following exercise would not be used until the long and short sounds of the letters *a*, *e*, and *i* have been developed.

Read each sentence. Look for the word which belongs on each line. Write the word on the line.

One morning Tom _____ up.
             wake woke
He _____ out of bed.
   got goat
"I _____ I am not late," he said.
  hop hope

TEACHER: Listen while Billy pronounces the words and see if you can hear the sound of those letters. What is it? Here is another word with that same sound in it.

(*Write* say *on the board.*) What is it? I'm going to change *say* into a new word. Watch and see if you can read the new word. (*Erase* s *and write* m.)

Continue to change the initial consonants, using d, h, l, p, r, w.

To provide opportunities for discriminating between words containing the phonogram *ay,* after the phonogram has been developed, a seat work exercise of the following type may be given:

Write the word that makes the sentence true.

1. One _____ Tom went to
       pay way day hay
   the farm.
2. He rode all the _____ in a
         day say may way
   car.
3. He saw the cows eat _____.
         lay hay pay ray
4. One cow _____ down in the
       lay hay pay ray
   barn.

5. Tom said, "_____ I try to milk
        way say may ray
   a cow?"

Application of word-attack skills is achieved through the following activities:

Purpose	*Exercise*
Develop the ability to perceive visual and auditory differences; provide opportunities for children to hear the sounds of letters.	Listen to the teacher pronounce a series of words, most of which rhyme. Clap hands when a nonrhyming word is heard.

Complete orally very short rhymes begun by the teacher.

   The funny clown
   Jumped (*down*)
   How much does a farmer pay
   For a wagon load of (*hay*)

Listen to and imitate the sounds of animals, birds or machines.

   tick-tock of the clock
   ch-ch-choo of the train
   peep-peep of a chicken

Purpose	*Exercise*
Provide opportunities for children to recognize the letters and combinations of letters.	Use rhyming words to fit content. lunch-punch Soon it will be time for _____. He made a hole with a _____. matter-fatter Do you think it will _____. If you are a little _____.
Provide opportunities for children to blend sounds in order to pronounce unknown words.	Complete the rhyming word at the left. Then write the correct word in each sentence. (*clown*) Billy had a little br_____ puppy. The king wore a gold cr_____. The bright sun made Sally fr_____.
Provide opportunities for children to recognize vowel sounds and identify them.	Underline the vowels in each word: thing — find red — let solo — long sang — sun ball — day he — she hop — wing mind — hat
Develop the ability to analyze the structure of words and give the children opportunities to become aware of endings such as *-er, -est, -s, -ed, -ing,* and *-es.*	Add *-s, -ed,* and *-ing* to the end of the word *shout* to make new words to fit in the blanks. Fisherman Bill heard some _____. It was Jack. He _____ again and again. "Who can be _____?" asked Fisherman Bill.
Give the children opportunities to learn the structure of compound words.	Combine the words in the first column with those in the second column to make compound words. after — way door — ball air — noon gold — fish class — room base — plane Make a list of the compound words in a paragraph in a reader.

Purpose

Give the children opportunities to learn to identify contractions.

Exercise

Match contractions with the words from which each was contracted.

she'll	it is
it's	she will
won't	cannot
can't	will not

Purpose

Give the children opportunities to learn possessive forms.

Exercise

Write the name of the person who owns these things:

Jane

Jane's dog _____
The girl's doll _____
My mother's dress _____
Tom's cat _____
Father's car _____

Purpose

Develop the ability to alphabetize; provide opportunities for children to alphabetize words by the first letter.

Exercise

Write the correct word in each blank.

A pilot flies in it.   a_____
We read it.   b_____
It is a baby bear.   c_____
It can bark.   d_____

Children may be challenged to go on as far as they can with other clues.

The Third-Reader Level

When children come to the third-reader level, they have already met many words of more than one syllable, some of which they have learned as sight words. They have had experiences in listening to spoken words to identify the number of parts in each. At the third-reader level the term *syllable* is introduced. The children are beginning to develop skill in noting the number of syllables and whether the vowel is long or short.

At the third-reader level they have a directed-reading class daily—a time when they work with the teacher in reading groups or individually for basic reading instruction. During the silent reading, they receive help when needed in attacking new words.

By the end of the third-reader level, the children have gained much skill in attacking words independently. They should use and apply these skills in all school work. Periodic checks must be made to be sure previous learnings are not forgotten.

Purpose

Develop the ability to interpret the written page; give children the opportunity to follow written directions.

Exercise

Follow simple directions written on slips of paper or on the chalkboard.

Walk to the window.

Perform several written directions in the order given:

Write *go* on the chalkboard.
Tap Teddy on the head.
Walk around a table.
Open the door.
Sit down.

Purpose	*Exercise*
Give children the opportunity to arrange words into sentences.	Unscramble a jumbled sentence written on the board. Choose teams. Unscramble several jumbled words. The team unscrambling them first wins.
	Play "Grab Bag": Choose an envelope containing words that will make a sentence. Arrange the words in order.
Give children the opportunity to interpret ideas by planning riddles.	Compose riddles:

I start with *w*.
I live in a frame.
I am in schools, homes, and stores.
What am I?

(A window.)

| Give children the opportunity to skim to find something quickly. | After reading orally in class, take turns pantomiming a part of the story for others to find in the book. The first one finding it may read it aloud. |

Find the one element that is not right in each paragraph:

Sam's mother was getting dinner. She cooked beans, potatoes, meat, and rubber, and she made a cake.

Tom and Betty were playing in the snow. They both wore warm clothes. Betty had on her winter coat, mittens, woolen scarf, pajamas, and a cap.

Tom had on a warm sweater, his sister's dress, his mittens, cap, and boots.

| Give children the opportunity to interpret a story and follow the sequence of events. | Interpret through dramatization a story studied and read during a directed reading class. |

Choose a chairman to lead the discussion and to direct the play. Discuss what should be done to make the story into a play.
List important events in proper sequence. Discuss what the characters would do and say. Draw pictures of each main event in a story. Arrange them in sequence. Write a sentence about each.

| Give children the opportunity to form sensory images. | Answer questions such as the following: |

What would *smell* this way?
spicy_____   sweet_____
strong_____   unpleasant_____

Purpose	*Exercise*

What would *feel* this way?

furry_____   soft_____
smooth_____   prickly_____

What would *taste* this way?

sweet_____   bitter_____
sour_____   salty_____

To develop the ability to clarify and learn new meanings and provide opportunities to enrich vocabulary.

List all the words possible which describe a familiar object.

Draw a circle around the word that means the same as the underlined word:

My brother <u>hurt</u> his hand.
repaired   injured
I listened to his <u>tale</u>.
story   music

To develop functional understanding of word relationships and provide opportunities for children to organize and classify types of things.

Draw a line under the family name of a group of words:

lamb   beef   <u>meat</u>   pork

Draw a line through the word that does not belong in each group:

book   <u>girl</u>   page   word

Arrange a list of words in categories:

Animals	*Food*	*Clothing*
bear	coat	antelope
milk	shoes	trousers

Provide opportunities for children to perceive relationships of time, place, manner, and sequence.

Arrange the following words and phrases in the proper column:

Where?	*When?*	*How?*
in the car	under the tree	
later	into the school	
one day	in his room	
with a bang	every night	
everywhere	at the window	
that morning	as fast as he could	
fast		
this noon		

Provide opportunities for children to strengthen meaning associations.

Respond with the opposite of a given word:

forget (remember)   laugh (cry)
tired (rested)   cross (happy)
top (bottom)   hot (cold)

Purpose	*Exercise*

Provide opportunities for children to discriminate in multiple meanings.

Choose the correct word for each sentence:

wraps   patch   change

See the pretty strawberries in the

_____.

Did your mother _____ your dress?
Put your _____ in the cloakroom.
My sister _____ her Christmas presents. _____ your shoes.
The clerk gave me the right _____.

Develop an awareness of phonetic elements and provide opportunities for children to discriminate between hard and soft sounds of g.

In each sentence fill in the blank with the word which has the soft sound of *g:*

The _____ was eating the
     goose   pigeon
seeds.
The _____ came from Sue's
     message   gift
aunt.

Fill in the blank with the word which has the hard sound of *g:*

We could see the beautiful _____.
              bridge gate
The _____ animals crowded close
   strange   greedy
together.

Provide opportunities for children to discriminate between hard and soft sounds of c.

List these words in the proper column:

Soft c		*Hard c*
take	cellar	dancing
circus	cups	package
count	cabbage	ice
lettuce	city	cap

Provide opportunities for children to organize and develop phonics rules.

The Phonics Express: Write a phonics rule on each car. Add new cars as new rules are learned.

Develop an awareness of the meaning and sound of prefixes and suffixes, and skill in identifying root words and structural changes; give the children the opportunity to learn how new words are formed by adding suffixes or prefixes to known root words.

Form known root words with alphabet blocks or scrabble tiles. Add a prefix or suffix to the root word and discuss the change in the meaning of the word:

	kind			fair	
un	kind		un	fair	
	kind	ly		fair	ly
	kind	ness		fair	ness

Purpose

Exercise

The children in a word study period have worked with a group of words such as the following which have been written on the board by the teacher:

raccoon	enough
waddles	hardly
several	perhaps
hollow	special

TEACHER: I am going to write some things for you to do on the board. (*After the teacher writes each of the following directions she calls upon a child to respond. The other children check the response.*)

Put a cross before *waddles*.
Draw a line between *several* and *perhaps*.
Draw a line below *enough*.
Draw a ring beside *special*.

In each sentence there is a group of words which told you exactly *where* to put your mark. Look at the first sentence. Draw a line under the words which told you where to put the cross. (*Continue in this way with the remaining sentences.*)

Read the first word that is underlined in each of those sentences. What do you notice particularly about those words?

Opportunities should frequently be provided which will necessitate careful attention in detail in following written directions. These procedures offer suggestions for work of this kind and at the same time call attention to the prefix *be-*,

Very often we find *be* at the beginning of words just as it is here. Think of some words you know which begin that way. (*Write on the board such words as* because, begin, become, behind, *and so on, given by the children.*)

This may be followed at a later period by an exercise in which the children must discriminate between words with the prefix *be-* and so give careful attention to meaning. Such an exercise as this must, of course, be based on the actual experience of the group.

Write the right word on each line:

1. Tom sits _____ Joe.
   because   behind   belong
2. Mary sits _____ Sally and Jane.
   between   began   become

Purpose	*Exercise*

3. The table is ___._____ the
    between   begin   below
   clock.
4. The Indian dolls _____ to
    become   belong   beside
   Dick.
5. Tom is at home_____
    between   beneath   because
   he has a cold.

The ending *-ful* as it changes the form of known words may be presented in this manner.

Choose phrases from the child's reading, such as *very kind and faithful, a very useful work animal, a wonderful sight.*

TEACHER: In the first phrase find a word which tells you that the elephant was trustworthy. What is it, Ellen?

In the second phrase find a word which tells you what kind of a work animal the elephant was. What is it, Jim?

In the third phrase find a word which tells you that it is a marvelous sight to see elephants at work. What is it, Dick?

What interesting thing do you notice about those three words? Underline the part that is the same in all three.

Read the word that you have left if you leave that ending off each word, Clara.

Very often in our reading we will find words that end in *-ful*. Let's make a list here on the blackboard of words which you know that end in *-ful*. (*Such words as* thankful, thoughtful, careful, *as they are given by the children.*) What meaning is added by the ending *-ful* to the root words?

Identify root words and structural changes which may be necessary for adding suffixes.

An exercise like this one may be used:

Place many cards on a table and root words that have been changed when suffixes were added.

circling	smoky
happily	racing
noisy	writing

Ask the children to identify the root word in each and tell what happened when the suffix was added. If the right response is given, the child takes the card. The child who has identified the most words wins.

Purpose	*Exercise*
Develop skill in recognizing syllables and learning to apply rules, provide practice in applying known rules of syllabication as an aid in the pronunciation of words.	Make fish-shaped cards (2½ × 4½ inches). On each write a one-, two-, or three-syllable word. Attach a paper clip to the tail. Place mixed-up cards, word down, on a table. With a magnet pick up a fish. Look at the word, say it applying known rules, and tap out the syllables, with a louder tap for the accented ones.

Place words on large cards. Use colored string as dividers between the syllables of the words.

fur/ni/ture	au/to/mo/bile
ta/ble	ap/ple

Develop skill in alphabetizing, provide experiences for children to associate first-letter word position in the alphabet.

Place the words listed below in the proper column:

abcdefg	*hijklmnop*	*qrstuvwxyz*
happy	when	
little	Judy	
ladder	cried	
apple	Tim	
girl	inch	
sorry	tall	

Provide experiences for children to alphabetize by the first and second letters.

Write a set of cards by having each child write his first name on one. Spread the cards on a table and pick them up in alphabetical order. At first alphabetize by only the first letter, later the second.

Choose a card on which three words beginning with the same letter have been written. While holding it so that others can see it, read the words in alphabetical order. If it is done correctly, keep the card until the end of the period.

slipped	chasing
strong	company
splash	carpenter

Number in ABC order the three words on each line below:

_____people	_____outdoors
_____window	_____almost
_____look	_____close

Exercises such as those that have been described are used as a step in a reading lesson. The teacher's plan will be based on the materials read by the children. This plan outline is suggested for *groups reading at or above third-grade level*. How might the plan be modified for an individualized program?

Third-Grade Lesson Plan

Date_____   Group_____

Book_____   Pages_____

MOTIVATE FOR CIRCLE ACTIVITIES.

_____

CHECK COMPREHENSION. (Use guide questions as a basis for discussion.)

_____

_____

_____

PURPOSEFUL ORAL READING. (To support a point, to share an exciting portion, and so forth.)

_____

_____

_____

DEVELOP OR REVIEW SOME WORD-ATTACK OR COMPREHENSION SKILLS

_____

_____

_____

MOTIVATION OF NEW MATERIAL. (*Arouse interest.* Tie the story to children's own experiences and extend by using children's experiences to relate or contrast. Develop the meaning of any concepts that may be outside the reader's experience.)

_____

Select words from the new vocabulary that should be presented to the group. (Words are prewritten on board or chart. Introduce the words in sentence or phrase form.)

_____   _____   _____   _____

_____   _____   _____   _____

Ask questions to guide silent reading. (Have these listed on the chalkboard, a chart, or a worksheet. These questions usually determine the purpose for which children read. See "Guiding Group Activities" for examples.)

_____

_____

_____

Explain independent reading activity. (See "Guiding Group Activities.")

_____

_____

Indicate activities for early finishers.

_____

Reading for a specific purpose is an aspect of group instruction. A second or third reading, thus motivated, adds to individual reading efficiency. (*Courtesy of the Burbank Public Schools.*)

Supplementary Reading

Because supplementary reading books reinforce rather than introduce the basic reading skills, pacing in the supplementary books should be accelerated. Approximately four to six weeks will be required to complete a reader, depending on the length of the book and the ability of the pupils.

It is a good plan to progress systematically through the book. In planning supplementary reading, the teacher gives less attention to detailed presentation of the new vocabulary and skills. Reading assignments should be considerably longer than in the basic program. It may be necessary to use several supplementary books before the group is ready to move up to the basic reader at the next level of difficulty. Caution should be exercised in moving a child into the basic reader before he is ready.

The period of supplementary reading affords an excellent time for a child with changing needs to move to a group where his needs can be better met. For example, if the child consistently misses three or four words on a page, his needs will probably be met by moving him to a level where he can succeed. If the material presents little or no challenge to a child, he should probably be moved to a more difficult level. It is usually advisable to make a gradual move by letting him work for a time in both the old and the new groups.

The elements of a lesson taught from a supplementary reader involve added emphasis on comprehension and interpretation of what has been studied. A maximum of silent reading and a minimum of writing exercises should be included in periods of independent study. If study-type exercises are provided in the reader, they should be carefully selected to serve the purpose of the lesson. How would you modify this third-grade lesson?

I. *Text:* Charles E. Merrill, *Treat Shop*

A. *Purposes:* To build comprehension skills, to build oral reading skills, to review skills of structural analysis, to increase vocabulary, and to appreciate the author's ability to create feeling.

B. *Assignment* (*at previous circle period*).

1. Pages 56–71 were to be read silently. Pupils were instructed to be prepared to answer these questions orally:

   a. What problem did the Tollivers have? How did they solve the problem?
   b. Why did Joey appreciate his job more at the end of the story than at the beginning?

2. Children were given the following written assignment: Reread the selections to find the page numbers and the paragraph numbers that tell:

   a. Why the Tollivers decided to get rid of the cats.
   b. How the Tollivers' house seemed with no cats around.
   c. Why the cats caused no more trouble at mealtime in the Tolliver house.
   d. Why Joey was discontented in the city.
   e. How Joey felt when he first reached the farm.
   f. Why Joey changed his mind about life on the farm.

C. *Procedure* (*at the reading circle*).

1. Check on work prepared independently.

   a. Build interest: "In what ways were the two stories you read yesterday alike? Have you ever felt like Joey?"
   b. Discuss guide questions.

2. Do purposeful oral reading.

   a. Set a standard: "Today, let's try to make our reading sound just like we're talking."
   b. Check assignment that was prepared independently by having pupils read to prove a point.
   c. Evaluate in terms of standards.

3. Build word-study skills.

   a. Review the meaning of *un* as a prefix.
   b. Write the following words on the chalkboard:

      unnecessary   unsuccessful
      uncomfortable   unpack

   c. Identify the root word and the prefix in each of the four words.

4. Motivate the new story.

   a. Read the introductory poem on page 73 aloud. Ask, "Did you ever see a fairy? Why is it fun to read about elves and giants today?" Discuss pictures briefly in the first two stories.
   b. Show a book of *Grimms' Fairy Tales.*
   c. Suggest that pupils who enjoy the stories in the reader will probably enjoy other fairy tales.
   d. Introduce key words of vocabulary (prewritten on the board).

      better weather powerful *crow*
      beautiful *bray*   *goblins*
                         screamed
      fine *mouser*   The *Bremen*
                         Town
                         Musicians

   e. Present guide questions (list

on chalkboard, chart, or worksheet).

(1) Why do you think the shoemaker and his wife were good people?

(2) Tell why the title "Bremen Town Musicians" does not fit the story.

5. Make assignment.

a. Read pages 74–85. Be able to discuss the guide questions.

b. Reread the stories. As you do, list the page number and the paragraph number for each story that has:

A sad part.
An exciting part.
A funny part.

For Discussion

1. Under what circumstances would you retain a child at grade level because of a reading deficiency?

2. What values do you see in a prefirst-grade year between kindergarten and first grade?

3. If a class were grouped on the basis of equal reading skill development at the primary level, how long would they stay that way?

What Activities May the Teacher Use in the Circle to Promote Interest and Practice?

There are usually five steps in a primary basic reading lesson. The first is a preparatory or readiness phase in which the concepts needed to read the material are developed and new words are introduced. A part of this period is to arouse the interest of the student.

The second phase involves a guided reading of the material. This is usually silent and then oral, followed by a discussion. The manuals provide well-planned questions which establish purposes for the reading and check on comprehension.

After the total story is completed there is a discussion which involves additional comprehensive check and interpretation of the story.

The fourth step is drill on word-recognition skills.

The fifth is an application of what has been learned, an enrichment or a creative application of the information or skills mastered.

Although the manuals are rich in suggestions, teachers need resource materials to review the vocabulary of the previous day, to provide interesting drill on new words, and to meet special needs of children.

The following suggestions were made by a group of experienced teachers in a summer school class. Select only a few that seem to appeal to the group you teach. Although children like a little variety, too much may be overstimulation.

1. List on the chalkboard words that may be causing difficulties. Give meaning clues and challenge the children to find the correct word, as, "Can you find a word that means something we do with our eyes?" (look or see). "Can you find a word that joins other words?" (and). "Can you find a word that means a color?" (brown, etc.). When children get the idea of clues relating to the meaning of words, each child who guesses the correct word may give the clue for a next word for the others to guess. This may be done with phrases, too. In this way the children are not merely calling out words but are associating them with meanings, which is fundamental in reading.

2. One child is asked to leave the room momentarily. The others agree on a word from a list on the chalkboard. The first child returns and is given a pointer. He points to one of the words and says, "Is it 'wagon'?" The children respond with, "No, it is not 'wagon'" or "Yes, it is wagon," as the case may be. In this way all children's attention is focused on the words and all maintain interest in the repetition that takes place.

3. Divide the class into two, three, or four groups with a balance of fast and slow learn-

ers in each group. Present a pack of troublesome words to each group and challenge them to help one another until all members of the group can be checked individually on the entire pack. Those who know all the words are eager to help the slow learners during free time or whenever there is time before school starts or during bad-weather recesses. Group records may be kept and the competition continued as more words and phrases are presented in other packs.

4. Troublesome words during a reading-class period are recorded on the chalkboard. Allowing five to eight minutes at the end of the class time, check each child before he proceeds to his seat. Those who are most likely to know the words are checked first and the slow learners remain for more help. Words of which some children are not sure may be put on flash cards and given to the children to work on at home or during free moments with other children.

5. The children sit on the floor in front of their chairs. Each child in turn is asked to recognize a flash-card word or phrase. If he identifies it correctly he sits up on his chair and the teacher proceeds around the circle of children on the floor. This gives slow learners more chances for help. If a child does not know the word or phrase, a child who is seated on a chair is challenged. This keeps all children attentive, as those seated in chairs do not know when they may be called upon; if they cannot give immediate response they are again seated on the floor.

6. Place four or five difficult words along the chalk tray. Have the children repeat the words with you several times. Then have all children close their eyes while you remove one word. Mix up the remaining words. Then the children are to open their eyes and determine which word is missing.

7. Give each child a flash card with a word that he has found especially difficult. Have him take a good look at it. Then call out three words and the children having those words are to place them on the chalk tray. All the children then say the words, after which the teacher mixes them up and the original children go up and get their own words and identify them.

8. Each child is given several flash cards.

The teacher calls out an initial sound and children having words starting with that sound place them on the chalk tray. Errors are detected and children who do not respond correctly are helped.

9. Each child stands behind his chair. A flash card is placed on each chair. A child who needs help with the words is chosen to identify them. He picks up each card he can identify correctly. These are handed to the teacher. The children standing behind the chairs on which words appear that the child does not know may go with the child to a corner of the room and help him learn them. The game is repeated with the remaining words and another slow learner is helped.

10. A word is printed on the chalkboard beside the name of the child who has been having difficulty with that word. It is his "word for the day." Frequently during the day at odd moments the teacher challenges him to identify it.

11. The semicircle of chairs on which the children are seated is referred to as the streetcar. One child is chosen as the conductor. He stands behind the first chair. A word is flashed and if the conductor can identify it before the child on the chair he moves on behind the next chair and another word is flashed. If he is first to identify each word all around the class he goes to his seat for other activity. If a child on the chair is first to identify a word that child becomes the conductor and exchanges places.

12. Children are given one or two flash cards. The teacher calls for words that rhyme with a given word, or words that are action words, or words that are foods, or number words, or people's names, and so on.

13. At the end of the reading class period the difficult words from the lesson are printed on the chalkboard. A child is given an eraser and asked to identify one of the words. If he says it correctly he may erase it and go to his seat. Another child is asked to identify another word, and so on until all words have been erased.

14. A list of ten difficult words is printed on the chalkboard. Each child starts at the

bottom of the list and sees how far up he can go identifying the words. When he misses a word, his initials are placed beside that word and the next child starts at the bottom. If a child can identify them all, his initials are placed at the top of the list. The second time the children who missed a word are asked to identify the word they missed and then proceed up the list until they reach the top.

For Discussion

1. Would any of the foregoing devices be useful in a tutorial situation in which the children worked in teams of two to drill each other?

2. Would any of the foregoing devices be useful in the home where a parent wanted to help a child in reading?

What Reading Problems May a Beginning Teacher Anticipate?

A number of problems may surprise and dismay the beginning teacher. Space does not permit a discussion of all the special and remedial techniques used. These situations, which are accepted as normal by the experienced teacher, include the following:

- Children frequently lose the place while they are reading.
- Children continue to move their lips during silent reading.
- Children reverse words such as *on* and *no* or *stop* and *spot*.
- Children finish the worksheets too soon or not at all.
- The books seem too difficult for a child.
- Children will not read loudly enough to be heard.
- Children say the words but do not understand what is being read.
- Children doing seatwork keep interrupting the teacher when she is working with a group.
- A child fails to recognize a word in a story even though he always knows it when it is used on a flash card.

- The mother wishes to teach the child out of the basic reader.

Children continue to lose their place for three reasons. (1) The width of the line of type (or *measure*) may be too great in proportion to the point size so that the eye cannot follow the line without "wandering" to the beginning of the next line. Newspaper columns are designed to permit rapid reverse eye movements for adults. Adults frequently lose the place when the reading lines of small type extend longer than five or six inches. In all cases, however, the size of the type is a factor, as well as the *measure,* or length. Reading textbooks are usually designed with these factors in mind but the library books that children read aloud are sometimes difficult typographically. The otherwise excellent books of Holling C. Holling, such as *Paddle to the Sea* and *Magoo,* illustrate this problem. A related physical factor is the placement of illustrations on the page so that they tend to draw the eyes away from the beginning and ending of the line. (2) The second situation that causes children to lose the place is related to interruptions in reading. The interruption may be a difficult word. The reader may look at the picture on the page or in the previous paragraph in order to find help and then be unable to scan rapidly to the place where he is reading. A question from the teacher or a correction that causes the reader to look away from his material to the chalkboard or a chart is a common occurrence. (3) The third situation is boredom of the child in the teaching situation, sometimes resulting from waiting his turn to read in a large group of slow readers or from lack of interest in the story. Books seem to grow heavier when held for a long period of time, and merely following the page while others read aloud is not a highly motivating situation.

Teachers sometimes have students use strips of heavy paper as place markers. These are held under the line the child is reading to guide his eyes. This can be done comfortably only when the child is at a table or desk. In a circle children must rest their books on their laps, steady them with one hand, guide the marker with the other, and bend their bodies into unnatural shapes in order to read. Place markers are a great help when kept clean and used in situations where the children are physically comfortable. Sometimes it is better for the teacher to go to the child's desk or table rather than have him come to the circle.

Oral reading of information material is usually difficult. Beyond the primary level a child should not be asked to read orally unless the material has first been read silently. The skilled oral reader actually scans ahead of the material he is voicing. This is a specific skill developed in the middle grades.

Lip movement or vocalization is natural for a beginner in the reading of any language. Adults studying a foreign language can be observed moving their lips as they silently pronounce the words they read. Many adults do not move their lips, but according to physiologists vocal cords are unconsciously activated by the speech center in the brain and take on all the necessary configurations as in actual audible speech. College students complain of "tired throats" after a night of study without realizing that this silent reading may actually be the cause. Silent voicing of all words results in slow, plodding reading.

At first, all silent reading means "saying the words to yourself." In the third grade and beyond, children are encouraged to scan material for the ideas presented rather than the sounds written on the page. Although many are taught to do this before third grade, it is at this level that the child usually has mastered the basic reading skills and faces the need for such a skill in extensive reading situations.

To remind children that their lips are moving, teachers sometimes have them hold a pencil on the upper lip as they read. This will make them conscious of any lip movement. An extended reading of simple material for the enjoyment of the ideas usually develops adequate speed of reading that causes the vocalization to be reduced or to disappear.

The problem of deciding which books are easy or difficult is a puzzle indeed. The use of various readability formulas is discussed in connection with children's literature. The concept of frustration levels of reading refers to the number of new words a child must be told as he reads. If there are more than three in any sequence of nineteen words, the books are considered difficult. Intermediate children face one new word in every ten because of the rapidly expanding vocabulary of the textbooks used. Such factors as print size and leading (from the lead metal used to make spaces between lines) cause printed material to look either easy or difficult. The attitude of the reader is important. When children say that a book is "too easy" their judgment may be influenced wholly by this factor of typographic appearance. The subject matter is also a factor in a child's judgment of a book. A book about "Cowboy Sam" may be accepted by a fourth-grade reader while an animal fable in a more difficult vocabulary will be rejected.

Each child has a level at which he can succeed and grow. To find this instructional level the teacher should:

1. Estimate the child's reading level from his previous records and tests.
2. Choose a book one level lower than the estimated level.
3. Choose a page approximately one third from the front of the book.
4. Have the child read orally without preparation 100 running words. (Use a shorter passage if testing at a low reading level.)
5. Record as errors the following:
   a. Substitutions.
   b. Mispronunciations.
   c. Words pronounced by the teacher.
   d. Repetition of more than one word.
   e. Insertions.
   f. Omissions.
6. Test at the next lower level if the child misses more than one out of twenty running words.
7. Test at a higher level if he reads fluently.

The child's instructional level has been found when he averages no more than five errors out of 100 running words. This method does not check comprehension, but it is an easy device for grouping. When groups are formed, the teacher can check comprehension. If a child consistently fails to comprehend 75 per cent of the material read, he should be moved to a less difficult book.

Modern reading programs provide plateau reading experiences or absorption periods during which no new vocabulary difficulties are added. These periods are designed to fix skills previously taught or to provide opportunity to increase reading speed. Frequently neither the teacher nor the child, strange to say, recognize these periods as easier than others.

In some cities kits of materials relating to a unit topic are prepared for a class. In theory, these books are selected to care for the wide reading range of the normal classroom. While the extremes of very simple and difficult are relatively obvious, the intermediate range is difficult for both teachers and children to distinguish. Intermediate readers are especially confusing. Some fourth-grade books seem more difficult to certain children than others designed for the sixth grade.

The child who reads *was* for *saw* is obviously starting at the wrong end of a word. A clear understanding at the start of reading instruction of where to start to look at a word will prevent this. Noticing which words are alike at the beginning is a readiness exercise that is widely used. Too much emphasis on rhyming will cause children to look at the wrong end of a word for a reading clue. The tendency to reverse a word, which is revealed when a word like *no* is read as *on,* may apply to other words, even though the child pronounces the misread word correctly. A great emphasis upon phonetic formulas like *will, dill, sill* may cause the child to look at the *-ill* first, then the beginning. When he does this to all words it is natural that confusion as to the word meaning and pronunciation results.

Worksheets provide extra drill, simple tests, and independent activity. Certain types are unpopular with teachers. The most undesirable are those that require the child to cut and paste. This type of activity can seldom be done without supervision. Prob-

ably the most difficult are those that have a story cut into parts which the child is asked to rearrange in logical order. (This is a good activity but should be done as a boxed individual game.) Nearly all worksheets provide an opportunity for children to add a colored sketch when they complete the work. This may be a device to keep children busy while the teacher works with others.

Routines that provide the child with a place to put his work when finished and something to do while others complete the work are established by wise teachers. One teacher has three folders, one for each group. As soon as a child completes his work it is placed in this folder. The work is corrected that evening and returned to the children in the reading circle the next day. Those who finish their papers are permitted to read a library book, go to an interest center in the room (usually with established rules on how many may be in one place), or select an individual game. When workbooks are used, the drill sheets for the day are removed. The child cannot be expected to care for all the material that he does not use or need in these books. Normally they are an awkward size for desks and difficult for little hands to handle. Individual cardboard folders in which worksheets are inserted are especially helpful when some of the work is done in the circle where there is no adequate support to mark worksheets.

It is well to anticipate the reasons children come to the teacher for help. Perhaps there is a child who makes a practice of not listening to directions, or one who does not easily comprehend them when they are given. This child might be asked to repeat the directions after you have given them so everyone will be sure they know what to do (and you will know that he understands). Then a check must be made to see that everyone has a pencil or other needed materials. Seating the children far enough apart will eliminate complaints of copying or annoyances. Then it can be explained to the children that, because they know how annoying it is when someone interrupts their group procedures, it will be a good policy to rule out interruptions except for extreme emergencies. When interruptions do take place, the teacher needs to be firm in her judgment as to whether the interruption is a real emergency. Especially at the beginning of first grade the interruptions are often merely to get attention, and such interruptions should be discouraged at the outset. Be sure that after a group has finished reading you recognize good independent workmanship. Children need attention and praise but help them to understand that there are occasions when the needs of the group are more important than the needs of individuals.

The soft-voiced child has many desirable qualities, but he may be a source of distraction to other children if he cannot be heard beyond the first row. Low-voiced tones may be based on shyness or fear of making an error. Some beginners have been so frightened by wild rumors of school disciplinary methods that they practically refuse to talk.

Teachers put these shy children in small groups, sometimes bolstering their confidence by giving them a reading partner or letting them sit next to the teacher. Dramatic play, use of flannelboard characters, verse choir, and singing help this type of child.

More of a problem for a beginning teacher is the loud child with a short attention span. Each one of this type is different. Some are the center of attention at home and expect to be accorded the same status at school; some get no attention at home and therefore demand it at school. The "grasshopper" interests and activities of such children can disturb an entire classroom and create extreme tension for the teacher. No child should be permitted to interfere with the learning of others or take the satisfactions out of teaching. Some of these children belong in private schools. Establish a few patterns of behavior and insist that they be followed consistently. Some of these patterns will be negative. The more effective will be those that suggest alternate activities for the undesirable ones. It is not a teaching weakness to permit these children to act as leaders in the few classroom practices which they like. If activity is an essential, such errands that must be made to the principal's office may be assigned to this type of child. Chores like wrapping or unwrapping books from the central office or serving as playground monitors use up some of the boundless energy of these children. Peer judgment has some influence, but do not place the responsibility for disciplinary decisions on the other children.

Some children in the second or third grade develop the ability to verbalize the words of the reader without any clear understanding of what is being said. Sometimes these are children with a foreign-language background. They apparently have mastered all the word-attack skills except that of understanding word meaning. These children are sometimes good spellers as well. Each word is an interesting design in type rather than a thought symbol. Rather than more reading and writing these students need a great deal of speaking and listening with meaning. Word calling happens at all levels of education. As the attitude of demanding meaning is developed—not just meaning in the abstract, but the specific meaning of the speaker or writer—this type of verbalizing disappears. Too great an emphasis on scope or speed of reading may develop an attitude of "covering ground" rather than assimilating thoughts or comprehending ideas. Exercises that require rephrasing or finding words of similar or opposite meaning focus attention on what the words mean rather than how they are pronounced.

I once asked a child how he knew the word was *the* on the flash card and he said, "I always remember that the card with *the* on it has a bent corner." Such a remark may indicate that flash-card drills often become too detached from word meanings. As each word is presented it is well to give the children a chance to use it in their own sentences. Attention is then drawn to the first letter of the word and to any peculiarities in the word form, such as preponderance of tall letters, length of the word, and so on. If several copies of the flash card are available, it is best to mix them with other words and call upon children to find all the cards that have the word *the*. Then give each child a book and ask him to find the word, put his finger under it, and raise his other hand. After you have checked to see whether they are correct, the children of one group can be looking for another *the* while you are busy with a second group. Another form of drill is achieved by placing cards along the chalk tray and giving such clues as "find the card that has a girl's name on it," "find the word that joins other words together," "find a color word," or "find an action word," so that children think about word meanings as they recognize them.

More and more schools are adopting the policy of not sending home the book used for basic reading instruction until the child has completed this book at school. A child attempting to follow the suggestions of two authorities, his teacher and his mother, can become confused. Some mothers are excellent teachers but there are many who in their zeal "push" children too much and take the joy from the reading experience. Coercion or prolonged sessions of reading when the child wishes to do something else tend to destroy the best teaching efforts at school. Belittling remarks or sarcasm from older children exaggerate a beginner's errors and lower the self-esteem of a sensitive child. The child who needs the most help with reading at school seldom benefits from home instruction. The careful diagnosis of individual problems is a professional task not to be attempted by a well-meaning parent. Supplementary readers and library books which provide practice on reading skills taught at school are designed to be read at home. Because these will contain some words that do not follow phonetic principles, parents might be informed that they can be of most help to their child by listening to the stories he reads, praising his efforts as he struggles with new words, and prompting him occasionally so as to avoid long pauses. Shared reading experiences, in which parent and child alternately read parts of bedtime stories from newspapers or books, are among the most precious memories of childhood.

For Discussion

1. The content of much primary reading consists of stories about children with a pony, Daddy's new car, or grandmother's big farmhouse. Children of lower socioeconomic groups seldom read about situations similar to their own. In what way may this influence reading instruction?

2. Do you think that television has influenced children's interest in reading? How might the teacher influence home television habits?

3. At times it may be necessary to use a textbook that the child has already used in a previous grade or in another school. How can you justify this to the learner?

How Is Reading Instruction Directed in the Intermediate Grades?

Teachers seek to achieve the following purposes in the reading program of the intermediate grades:

1. Continue development of word-recognition skills started in the primary grade. There will be many at this level who are operating at second- and third-grade levels of reading. Some of normal ability follow a delayed pattern of achievement in reading. For a number of reasons, about one boy in ten does not read comfortably until late in his tenth or eleventh year of age. A part of this is lack of purpose. Apparently the reading materials of previous years did not appear worth the effort to read them. But now that he needs to read directions to make model airplanes or is exploring vocational interests, reading assumes a new importance.

2. Develop discrimination with respect to reading material. This involves elements of critical judgment, appreciation of literary quality in writing, and the ability to select materal needed to solve a problem from material less important.

3. Teach the reading skills needed in association with the school program. Intermediate children need to practice increasing reading speed, skimming, using the index or other aids to locate material, and interpreting new concepts, terms, and representation of ideas such as graphs. The dictionary is studied in detail.

4. Help the child integrate all the language art skills so that they reinforce each other. The close association of these skills may be noted in these parallel columns of skills:

Listening—Reading Skills	*Speaking—Writing Skills*
Getting the main idea	Finding the topic sentence
	Paragraphing
	Note taking
Reading for details	Outlining
	Giving directions
	Organizing ideas in sequence
	Summarizing
Determining author's meaning of a word	Vocabulary development
	Use of dictionary
	Dramatic interpretation
Using context skills	Understanding sentence structure and paragraphing
Word-analysis skills	Spelling
Oral reading	Pronunciation
	Enunciation
	Dramatic interpretation
Interpreting poetry	Choral reading, creative writing
Visualization	Descriptions
Understanding modifiers and referents	Use of pronouns, adverbs, adjectives, clauses, and phrases
Drawing conclusions	Logical organization of material
Social sensitivity to ideas presented	Expressing emotional feelings

In the classroom the teacher uses sets of basic readers, library books, weekly and monthly magazines, and daily newspapers to teach reading. At the beginning of the year it is wise to use a reader at least one grade below the level of the children as a review reader. This gives the teacher a chance to get to know the students without discouraging those below grade level. It is normal that from one fourth to one third of an average fifth-grade classroom will be able to read only third- or fourth-grade material. Social studies books and some science books will be difficult for many to read until concepts are established through experience that provides meaning and language experience.

Intermediate teachers soon learn that many of the study skills, such as drawing conclusions, reading for detail, getting the main idea, and locating information, are developed in materials other than the reading textbook.

Intermediate readers are a source for some of these skills, but the major contribution is made in the area of literature.

Because a great range of ability exists in any intermediate class, lesson planning is usually done in terms of groups with similar needs. These steps in a reading lesson are suggested in most basic programs.

1. Motivate the silent reading of the new story. Pictures, questions, and the experience of the child or teacher are used to arouse interest. At this time teachers anticipate and present some of the language and vocabulary needed to read the story.
2. A few of the key concepts and words are introduced. Seldom is it necessary to present all new words, because the children need to practice the word-attack skills they know. Some of these

Older children frequently study books designed for younger children in order to establish skills. In such a case the book must be one not previously studied. (*Courtesy of the San Diego City Schools.*)

skills may be used in the presentation of the new words as review or re-teaching.

3. Any related work in the form of workbooks, chalkboard work, or follow-up assignment is presented and explained.

4. The activities at the circle or with the group are developed. These may start by the teacher's checking previously assigned work. This work may remain with the student for further practice or be collected for checking. The story that has been read silently is then discussed. This discussion will involve questions concerning the main idea, evaluating characters and conduct, drawing conclusions, enjoying humor or literary style. Oral reading is often a part of this period as children clarify points, read dialogue for expression, choose parts, or check understanding.

Interest and purpose in the next lesson are established. Some of the new words may be analyzed or checked for meaning. Nearly every lesson provides some opportunity to strengthen phonetic and research skills.

Before leaving the group, the teacher asks some child to repeat the assignment as a means of reinforcing the memories of others. Circle procedures need variations to avoid monotony. One device that seems to appeal to intermediate children is to create problem-solving situations rather than having the teacher always provide answers and directions.

Certain activities of the class must follow established routines. These involve handling papers, distribution of books, and movement within the room. After a group has left the circle, the teacher will require a few minutes of time to check the work of those who remained at their desks.

In order to encourage and guide recreational reading, at least one period a week should be devoted to this type of activity. This may involve the entire class or only a single interest group, depending on the type of books being read or the level of reading. Those reading at an easier level often hesitate to talk freely about books that other children have already read.

Other special needs may be provided for in weekly one-hour periods. Those who are working in a skill text which is below grade level or in special editions of the *Reader's Digest* may meet several times during a week for special instruction.

To determine the needs of students a teacher may secure information about students from available guidance records. To obtain standardized test scores quickly in vocabulary, comprehension, and speed, investigate the Nelson Silent (grades 3–9) and Nelson-Denny Reading (grades 10–college), tests, published by Houghton Mifflin Co. in Boston, Massachusetts. These require only thirty minutes of time (ten for vocabulary and twenty for comprehension), provide both percentile ranks and grade levels, and demand a minimum of teacher work in scoring because of a carbon answer sheet.

For additional analysis of other aspects of reading, the following are suggested.[19]

1. For a complete phonics summary use: McKee Phonics Inventory; Houghton Mifflin Co.; Boston, Mass. Botel Informal Inventory found in Morton Botel's *How to Teach Reading* published by Follett in Chicago.
2. For an estimated comprehension level use:
   Gray Oral Reading Test published by The Bobbs-Merrill Co.; Indianapolis, Indiana.
3. For a test of phonogram understanding use *Remedial Reading Drills* published by George Wahr Publishing Co.; Ann Arbor.

4. To establish an individual reading level use *Wide Range Achievement Test* published by Chas. L. Story Co.; Wilmington, Delaware.
5. For an easy determination of intelligence use *The Quick Test* published by Psychological Test Specialists, Missoula, Montana.
6. For suggestions to follow diagnosis use the *Stanford Diagnostic Reading Test* published by Harcourt Brace Jovanovich.
7. For suggestions to prepare for standardized tests use *Reading Skills Workbooks* published by Evansville Public Schools; Evansville, Indiana.

Test results should be explained to each student to help plan the next step needed. A child eventually will recognize his needs in this area as he does in other activities and accept his work as something he seeks rather than that imposed by the authority of the teacher.

It will help many students to discuss a story or unit in advance to set goals in terms of what they know about the subject, to anticipate what might happen, and to establish oral vocabulary appropriate to the topic.

Lessons on vocabulary are often needed. A successful technique would be to have each student survey the material to be read to locate new words and then to build his own individualized vocabulary. To do this Word Profiles (3 × 5 cards) may be set up in this manner:

word	definition derivation original sentence
front of card	back of card

Cards enable the student to manipulate words better than if they are listed on a notebook sheet. Cards can be filed after mastery of a word has been achieved; new ones can be added easily. Students can hand their packs to classmates for partner testing.

This approach to vocabulary will result in a better list than one taken from the book by the teacher.

Intermediate grade children like the idea of "cracking paragraphs," which implies

---

[19] These suggestions are through the courtesy of Dr. J. E. Sparks, Chairman, Reading and Study Skills Department; Beverly Hills Unified School District; Beverly Hills, California.

Topic Noun	General Statement	Specific Statements
The word around which the entire paragraph revolves.	The main idea; the topic sentence.	The details; the facts that support the general statement.

reading paragraphs for complete understanding.

The student needs to find the topic noun, the word or phrase around which the paragraph revolves. Then the reader finds the sentence that makes the most general statement possible about the topic noun. This is the topic sentence or main idea.

In about 90 per cent of nonfiction or textbook paragraphs, students may expect to find this main idea in the first sentence. In the remaining paragraphs, this main idea may be in any sentence (often last) or it may be implied.

After much experience with finding main ideas in paragraphs, students could search for the details or the specifics, primarily found by asking *who, what, when, where, why,* or *how* about the general statement.

Until students can "crack paragraphs" with competence in independent, silent reading, they may do it in small groups using charts or using this teacher-made material.

A teacher provides a large number of highly structured paragraphs from books at levels from grade 4 through high school to be used for practice by those needing it on 5×8 cards. The students complete the information in the chart above.

Those students who are experiencing a secure knowledge of content of reading matter should learn to probe that content in depth through critical reading–thinking skills.

Questions may involve three levels of thinking:

Level 1. Literal, concrete thinking.
Level 2. Abstract, interpretive thinking.
Level 3. Elaborative, creative thinking.

For example:

That February up in the woods was one to be remembered. The wind moaned and shrieked around the corners of the cabin, but the boys were warm and cozy inside. In some of the blizzards it wasn't easy to do the chores, but the boys were toughened to it. The cattle crowded together for warmth under their shelter and came through in good shape.*

1. Literal. How did the wind sound? How did the boys feel? Why did the cattle crowd together?
2. Abstract. Why would it be difficult to do chores in some blizzards?
3. Elaborative. Why was it important that the cattle come through in good shape? Why do people choose this type of work?

Diagnostic teaching depends upon continuous evaluation by both the teacher and learner. The usual methods used are informal tests, oral questioning, and student reports. In addition the student should be learning to evaluate his own achievement. When an error of understanding is made he must analyze why he misunderstood. Did he skip an important word? Did he use the wrong meaning for a word? All errors are simply learning opportunities when handled in this way. At no time should the learner be concerned about being better than another reader. He may know this as he would in any other activity, but such comparison is not the basis for diagnostic teaching.

Conclusions from evaluation by a learner may be similar to the following: "This book is too difficult—I need to know more about finding root words—I need to know how to locate words in the dictionary—I need to learn how to locate places on a map—The illustrations will provide meaning clues—This writer does not organize carefully—I want to find out more about a topic."

Self-determined "next steps" by teacher and learner provide the motivation for continuous growth in reading skills.

A positive approach would be a record such as, "Today I learned _____."

---

* Verne T. Davis. *Times of the Wolves* (New York: Morrow, 1962).

Another way to do this is to keep records at times of only the things that were done right until the recognition of needs loses any negative feeling in much the same manner an athlete uses when he says, "I need to practice _____," or a businessman says, "I need to improve _____."

In order to free the teacher's time to meet individual and group needs, purposeful work must be found for those at their desks. Some able children like to prepare challenging materials for others to read. These may be a series of questions concerning an article from a magazine or newspaper. If mounted in a manila folder, the article on one side and questions on the other, they may be used many times or sent to another room. The circulars children receive when they write to firms or communities are also interesting reading experiences when prepared in this fashion. There are well-planned workbooks for all the intermediate grades. Although few classes would use one of these for all students, small sets of this material will save hours of teacher time as she helps children who have been absent, who need special help, or who are above average and need challenging material.

The following activities have been found to be of value as seatwork practices:

- Reread the first paragraph of the story. Answer the following questions:
1. Who are the characters introduced?
2. Where does the beginning of the story take place?
3. When does the beginning of the story take place?
4. What problem is being introduced?
- Make a list of the leading characters in the story and skim story to find descriptive phrases of each.

Appearance	Characteristics
Action	Expressions
Feelings	Attitudes

- Write a description in your own words, one for each character.
- Choose your favorite character. Pretend you meet this person. Write a conversation you might like to have with this person.

- Choose two characters in the story. Write a conversation between them.
- Choose a character from this story and one from another story your class has recently read and write a conversation between them.
- Choose one location mentioned in the story. Make a list of all descriptive words and phrases used in the text about this location.
- Write in your own words a description of this place.
- Read the ending of your story. Make a picture as you see the scene.
- Choose a title for the picture. Write a short paragraph to go with the picture.
- Read the first three paragraphs of the story and make an outline of them:
1. What is the first paragraph about?
   a. People
   b. Places
   c. Action
2. What is the second paragraph about?
   a.
   b.
   c.
3. What is the third paragraph about?
   a.
   b.
   c.
- Skim the story and make lists of words ending with *-ing, -ed, -s, -es*. Decide if any words are examples of the following rules, and if so, list the examples under the rule number.

Rule 1. If a word of one syllable ends with a single consonant by a single vowel, the final consonant is usually doubled before a suffix beginning with a vowel is added.

Examples: run, running; fun, funny; hop, hopping

Rule 2. When a word of more than one syllable ends with a single consonant preceded by a single vowel, the consonant is usually doubled before adding a suffix beginning with a vowel when the accent is on the last syllable.

Examples: omit, omitted

Rule 3. If a word ends with a single consonant immediately preceded by more than one vowel, the final consonant is not usually doubled when a suffix is added.

Examples: weed, weeded; dream, dreaming

Rule 4. If a word ends with two or more consonants or a double consonant, the consonants are usually retained when adding the suffix.

Examples: jump, jumped; dress, dresses

Rule 5. If a word ends with silent *e,* the *e* is usually dropped before a suffix beginning with a vowel is added.

Examples: hope, hoped

Rule 6. In words ending with *y* immediately preceded by a consonant, the *y* is usually changed to an *i* before a suffix is added.

Examples: cry, cries

Rule 7. Words ending with *y* retain the *y* when a suffix beginning with *i* is added.

Examples: hurry, hurrying

Rule 8. If a word ends in *y* immediately preceded by a vowel, the *y* is usually retained when a suffix is added.

Examples: play, played

- Choose words from the story that will go with the following:

1. Words telling how high.
2. Words telling how low.
3. Words telling how fast.
4. Words telling how slow.
5. Words telling when.
6. Words telling where.

- Look through the story and study all illustrations. Skim the story and choose one or two sentences as titles which you feel are appropriate.
- Read the story again. Choose a scene as a subject for a peep box. Make a peep box for this scene.

- Reread the story. List the scenes presented. Make characters for each scene to use on flannelboard. Practice the story using the pictures to illustrate.
- Work with a committee to choose one scene from the story which can be told in pantomime. Plan for one pupil to read from text while others pantomime what happens.
- Choose one character from today's story and one from another story you have read. Plan a meeting of these two characters. Decide what you would have them doing at this meeting. Paint a picture of this scene. Choose an appropriate title. Write conversation.
- Choose an experience one of the characters had in the story. Write about an experience you have had similar to this.
- Choose a situation as described in the story. Write a myth or a "whopper" about this situation.
- Write a personal, newsy letter to one of the characters in the story telling about your activities and inquiring about something the character has been doing.
- Write a personal letter as from one character to another. Write an answer to the letter as from the other character.
- Make up a limerick about a person, place, or thing mentioned in the story.
- Make a sequence chart of things that happened. You may want to make illustrations to go with the chart.
- Choose a scene in the story. Make stick puppets to go with this scene and plan to put on a show for the class.
- Choose a character. Pretend something he owns that has been mentioned in the story has been lost. Write an advertisement for the "lost and found" column of the daily paper.
- Write riddles using characters, places, or objects from your story.
- Pretend you are the news editor of the daily paper published in the city where the characters of the story live. Write articles which may appear in this paper mentioning the doings of these characters. Plan some headlines, and so on.

- Choose one of the characters who is in trouble. Write a short play for the class to act out, using the other characters as needed.
- Look for words in the story and list them under the following headings:

dr   tr   fr   fl   bl   cl   sl   st   sw
st   sw   sn   sm   cr   gr   pr   br   qu
pl   sp   spr str thr ch   sh   wh   th

- Look for words ending with *ck, ng.*
- Look for words ending with: *al, aw, ai, ay, oa, oi, oy; ow* as in *slow; ow* as in *cow; ar, er, ir, ur.*
- Find words starting with soft *g,* hard *g,* soft *c,* hard *c.*
- Find words illustrating the following:

1. Silent *e* at the end of the one-syllable word.
2. Silent vowel in a word in which two vowels come together.
3. Silent letter in double consonants.
4. When *c* or *g* is followed by *e, i,* or *y,* it usually has the soft sound.
5. When there is only one vowel in a one-syllable word it is usually short unless it is at the end.

- Find words that have root words within them.
- Find compound words.
- Find hyphenated words.
- Find words to which you can add *-y, -ly, -er, -est, -ful, -en, -able.* Make the new words by adding these endings.
- Find words that start with *re-, un-, be-.* Find other words to which these prefixes may be added. How are they related in meaning?
- Find contractions in the story such as *I'm, what's, we're, that's, haven't, there's, aren't.*
- Find words that end in *e* to which *-ing, -ed, -est,* or *-y* may be added to form new words. Make new words by adding these endings. Note that the *e* must be dropped in adding these.
- Look for figures of speech in the story. Explain the meaning.
- Choose single words that describe each character. In a column to the side of these lists, write words that are opposite in meaning. For example: happy, sad; laugh, cry.
- List all the words on a certain page that express action; things a character did.
- Tell briefly why you think each character did the things he did in the story.
- Use the table of contents in the reader to find another story similar to this one and tell why you chose that particular one.
- Read in some source book in the room more information about something mentioned in the story.
- List all the words of whose meanings you are not sure. Find them in the dictionary or glossary if the book has one. Choose the meaning you think best applies to the use made of the word in the story.
- Write statements from the story for others in the class to decide whether true or false. Be sure you know the correct answer.
- Write sentences for others in the class to complete.
- Find passages in the story that make you feel sad, happy, drowsy, excited.
- Find parts of the story you feel are humorous.
- Write a fable, legend, or fairy tale about some incident or character in the story.
- Look back through the book. List the stories you have read under the following headings: fanciful tale, biography, true story, realistic.
- Find words that begin with *dis-, en-, in-, un,- re-.* Words that end with *-ion, -ist, -ment, -ant, -er, -ance, -ish, -able, -ful, -less.* Note the influence of these elements on meaning.
- Select an advertisement or news story and note the words that have emotional appeal in them.
- Take a circular of a city or park and make a series of questions that a visitor might find answered in this circular. Clip a week's TV schedule from the Sunday paper. Make a series of questions that might be answered by reading this schedule. Read an advertise-

ment of something you would like to buy—a bicycle, toy, car. What questions are *not* answered in the material?

For Discussion

1. When should children be permitted to read library books in the classroom?

2. Should a child in the sixth grade who reads as well as an adult be expected to participate in the reading class?

3. Why do you feel a teacher is justified, at the beginning of the year, in having the better readers do a great deal of oral reading in the social studies and science classes?

4. Why are some more likely to enjoy reading circulars they have received in the mail, or a Scout Manual, or an item in *Popular Science Magazine,* than a story in the reader?

5. Examine some of the study skills such as reading for details, drawing conclusions, and getting the main idea in association with the content subjects. Find examples of reading details in a mathematics problem, in a science experiment, and in a geography book. Would it be possible for a child to use the skill in one area and not in another? What factors are operating to make these situations similar or different?

6. In the *Reading Teacher* (October 1965), a Detroit teacher tells of using the words of songs by the Beatles for reading instruction with retarded readers. The ten songs had a total of 173 words, used 1,072 times. Of the 173 words, 139 appear in Dolch's Word List. There is much repetition, *I* appears fifty-four times, *you* sixty-four times, *love* fifty-three times. Would such a program help such a child establish word-attack skills? What popular songs of today might be used in such an approach?

Bibliography

Books

Betts, E. A. *Foundations of Reading Instruction.* New York: American Book Company, 1956.

Brown, Roger. *Words and Things.* New York: The Free Press, 1959.

Bush, Clifford L., and Mildred H. Huebner. *Stratagems for Reading in the Elementary School.* New York: The Macmillan Company, 1970.

Durkin, Dolores. *Teaching Them to Read.* Boston: Allyn Bacon, Inc., 1971.

Gray, W. S. *On Their Own in Reading.* Chicago: Scott, Foresman and Company, 1960.

Heilman, Arthur W. *Teaching Reading.* Columbus, Ohio: Charles E. Merrill Books, Inc., 1962.

Huey, Edmund Burke. *The Psychology and Pedagogy of Reading.* Cambridge, Mass.: M.I.T. Press, 1968 (1908).

LeFevre, Carl. *Linguistics and the Teaching of Reading.* New York: McGraw-Hill Book Company, 1964.

McKee, Paul. *The Teaching of Reading in the Elementary School.* Boston: Houghton Mifflin Company, 1960.

Robinsen, A. Alan. *Reading and the Language Arts.* Chicago: University of Chicago Press, 1963.

Schonell, Fred. *Psychology and Teaching of Reading,* 4th ed. London: Oliver and Boyd, 1961.

Sleisenger, Leonore. *Guidebook for the Volunteer Reading Teacher.* New York: Teacher's College Press, Columbia University, 1965.

Smith, Nila B. *Reading Instruction for Today's Children.* Englewood Cliffs, N.J.: Prentice-Hall, Inc., 1965.

Stauffer, Russell G. *Directing Reading Maturity as a Cognitive Process.* New York: Harper & Row, Publishers, 1969.

Articles and Pamphlets

Bruinks, Robert H., William G. Luckes, and Robert L. Gropper. "Psycholinguistic Abilities of Good and Poor Reading Disadvantaged First-Graders," *Elementary School Journal* (April 1970), pp. 378–85.

Burke, Carolyn L., and Kenneth S. Goodman. "When a Child Reads—A Psycholinguistic Analysis," *Elementary English* (January 1970), pp. 121–29.

Emans, Robert. "Phonics: A Look Ahead," *Elementary English* (May 1969), pp. 575–82.

Feeley, Joan T. "Teaching Non-English-Speaking First-Graders to Read," *Elementary English* (February 1970), pp. 198–208.

Goodman, Yetta M. "Using Children's Reading Miscues for New Teaching Strategies," *The Reading Teacher* (February 1970), pp. 455–59.

Harris, Albert J. "Key Factors in a Successful Reading Program," *Reading Teacher* (January 1969), pp. 69–76.

Jenkinson, Marion D. "Reading—An Eternal Dynamic," *Elementary School Journal* (October 1970), pp. 1–10.

Oliver, Marvin E. "Key Concepts for Beginning Reading," *Elementary English* (March 1970), pp. 401–402.

Rutherford, William. "Learning to Read: A Critique," *Elementary School Journal* (November 1968), pp. 72–83.

Sartain, Harry W. "Do Reading Workbooks Increase Achievement?" *Elementary School Journal* (December 1961), pp. 157–162.

Smith, Nila B. "The Many Faces of Reading Comprehension," *Reading Teacher* (December 1969), pp. 249–60.

Willis, Benjamin C. "Communication Skills, Games, Techniques and Devices—Grades K-1-2-3," Board of Education, City of Chicago, 1964.

six

written composition

How May Imaginative or Creative Writing Be Motivated in the Primary Grades?

The young child has three major avenues of expression for his ideas: he can tell them orally, act it out, or paint a picture. This is where the teacher starts. The child may tell about a personal experience, tell what he thinks is happening in a picture, tell a story about an object, such as a sea shell. Sometimes the experience is completely oral. The teacher makes suggestions about words, important ideas, or the way the story was told. At other times the child makes the picture first, then tells what is happening in the picture. This provides a focus for him in determining which of his ideas are important and which are subordinate.

"What would be a good name for Jane's story?" the teacher asks. After several suggestions have been made the teacher turns to Jane. "Which one do you like best?" After Jane has decided, the teacher writes the name for all to see. With this beginning, children will soon be dictating stories which the teacher writes and the child reads. As the teacher writes she points out where she begins and how each sentence ends. "I'll put the first word here, then go to the right. This is the end of the sentence so I will put a period here." A "book" of these stories is placed on the reading table so that children can read again the stories they have written.

Creative writing can be a class-wide experience or the efforts of a small group or an individual working alone with the teacher. Such experience usually follows a discussion

Ideas and freedom to express them have priority over mechanical correctness in this classroom. In time the child will seek correct form and willingly work to achieve the skills needed because he wants to write and knows that such discipline is needed to reach his goal. (*Courtesy of the San Diego County Schools.*)

period where children "think together" and express themselves freely. In the small-group method, the members work faster and the interest factors and feeling of success are high. The teacher is immediately able to supply needed words or correct spelling, to stimulate thinking, and to build curiosity. In turn, other groups will work with the teacher. Writing experiences of the entire class now involve a common topic such as "Thanksgiving." During the discussion period, words that might be used are placed on the chalkboard. Specific aspects suitable for writing might be listed, such as "My Favorite Thanksgiving," "A Turkey's Ideas About Thanksgiving," "Why I Am Thankful." Thus the individual compositions will vary although using a similar vocabulary.

Children learn many things when they write. They become familiar with selecting, eliminating, and arranging words and with proofreading, or correcting errors. The first efforts usually contain misspelled words, incomplete sentences, and meager punctuation and capitalization. The first stories are not corrected, but as the child reads his story to the teacher, his voice indicates beginnings and endings. He then adds, with the teacher's help, his own periods, question marks, and capitals. After children have written many stories and write with ease, the teacher and child correct the first rough draft. The child takes the initiative in finding his errors, or in completing the spelling of a word where only the initial letter is given. The child may copy his story and shares it with his classmates. Sometimes the story is placed with others in a bound volume. Children frequently offer stories without a title, probably because a title or name inhibits their ease of writing. The teacher or other children may suggest a title when the child shares his unnamed story with them.

Here is an early effort of an above-average boy in the first grade: [1]

The Dome Bird

(*as written by Richard, Grade 1*)

One day dome bird thote
two + two was twente. One day
men buill schools up. and it
was time for dome bird to come
to school. One day the
teacher put up some arethmatik.
then dome bird sat down to
rite. The dom bird saw two +
two on the board. He put
twente on the paper. the
teacher saw dome Bird
arethmatick so she put an X
on the paper so the dome
bird saw the X so dom bird
Learnd how much two + two
was.

The Dumb Bird

(*as read by Richard*)

One day dumb bird thought
two plus two was twenty. One
day some men built schools and
it was time for dumb bird to
come to school. One day the
teacher put up some arithmetic. Then dumb bird sat down
to write. The dumb bird saw
two plus two on the board. He
put twenty on the paper. The
teacher saw dumb bird's arithmetic, so she put an X on the
paper. The dumb bird saw the
X, so dumb bird learned how
much two plus two was.

As soon as print script has been mastered, the children follow the pattern established by the teacher and write their own story.

---

[1] South Bay Public Schools, *Our Writing*, 1964. (San Diego County, Calif., published annually.)

These will show a great range of interest and expression. But each is important to the writer.

One will laboriously write "The House" with many smudges and add his name. Another will cover pages as he writes a story like this:

Robert   Jan. 22, 1958
wonts there was a 1 and a half year old girl.
her name was tiny because she was so little.
One day she saw a dog. she wanted to bathe
him because he was so dirty. she asked her
mother but she said no get that dirty thing out
of here. but tiny brahgt a tub in the yard. then
she brahgt some waters and put in it. she bathed
him. she got wet and dirty. but the dog was not
dirty any more. he went away and he did not
come back again because he did not like water.
                    the end.

The only capital letters Robert knew were those in his name—but that did not stop him. He probably asked for help on *brahgt* and having spelled it wrong once was loyal to his first spelling when the word was repeated. Most revealing of all is a little note in one corner of the page: "I love to make storys."

As children learn to read the pattern of the controlled vocabulary, it is reflected in the material they write. Jon wrote this one:

> Jane and Billy play
> Run Billy
> Billy jumps.

The picture was much more original. Two children were shown with a jumping rope tied to a tree, Billy was jumping while Jane held the rope.

The pattern of teacher-made charts soon appears in the writing of children.

Peggy produced this story:

> This is Ann and Linda.
> They are looking at the kittens.
> The kittens are in the basket.
> The basket is yellow and red.
> The kittens are cute.

But in the same school another first-grade class was writing these stories:

This is in the Dineohsire's Days. A sea manstre is going to land and eat. a trtaile is under his tail. in those days the were no people.
                    JEFFREY

This is the sivl war wen the Americans fot the inglish. The Americans wun the wor becas the American's they did not giv up.

by BOBBY

It is obvious that two different philosophies are at work here. In one there has been an emphasis on form, in the second upon ideas. The natural question to ask is when should these children be expected to spell and write correctly? Teachers who permit the second type of writing say that late in the second grade or sometimes the third grade the children seek correct form. These new standards are the result of wide reading and the gradual mastery of writing mechanics. It is true that unless the principal and parents understand the purposes of the teacher there will be criticism. But it should be recognized that children are not going to attempt words like *monster* or *turtle* if they face criticism with respect to spelling and writing.

News reports of the day are popular:

Donald brought in a
record for Mrs. Cummins.

A car hit a teacher's
parked automobile
It even hit a house
It almost poured rain too.

by LINDA

Today was a happy
day. Today Miss Bovee [student teacher] came. She will stay until school closes.

BELINDA

Holidays receive special notice.

April 7, 1960   Sylvia C.
Easter Day

On Easter Day we had an egg hunt. I found more eggs than my brother. One egg was under the abalone shell. I found an egg in both vases. I had fun on Easter. Most of the eggs were in the living room. But some were in the dining room. The eggs were all different colors. They are very pretty. I helped dye the eggs. I had fun on Easter.

Before this story was written certain words were written on the board as the result of a discussion of words needed. Among these were: *dye, Easter, colors.* The words *different* and *dining* were corrected before

the story was posted. In this class all children wrote on the same topic.

A favorite writing experience at the beginning of second grade is to write "What I Want to Be" stories. These can be reproduced in a little book for parents' night. If the children use a ditto pencil or write on ditto masters, this also provides an example of the child's writing. These are typical examples:

A Jet Pilot

I want to be a Jet pilot. You have to learn many things before you can be a Jet pilot. You must know how to fly your plane are you might crash. If the plane runs out of gas I will parachute out

by BILLY

A Fire Man

I want to be a fire man and put out fires and help people out of fires. I want to be a good fire man I want to slide down the poles. I want to help people to be good and not cause fires

by RICHY

A School Teacher

I want to be a school teacher and teach children how to spell and do numbers. I want to teach them how to tell time and many other things I want children who do good work and not spend their time talking

by DIANE

But second-grade children advance rapidly. By the end of the year some will write this well. The literary pattern now follows that of favorite books.

Flicka the Filly

Dick's father was at the Johnson's farm getting a colt. Dick was going to train it. When his father came home Dick ran to the truck. The colt was beautiful. It was pure white with a black mane and tail and right on its forehead was a gold star. "What will you name her, son?" asked his father.

"I'll call her Flicka," said Dick.

The next day Dick got up early. He ate his breakfast and went to the stable.

"Come on, Flicka," said Dick. "I'm going to

train you." Flicka went with Dick to the pasture.

"First you must learn to obey your master," said Dick. Dick walked away and said "Stay."

Flicka did as he said. Flicka obeyed him with the other tricks, too. And they had lots of fun for the rest of their lives.

by JAYNE

After hearing several of the "Just So" stories by Rudyard Kipling, one of the boys wrote this original story:

The Story of the Elephant That Had No Trunk

Once upon a time there lived an elephant. This elephant was very sad because he had no trunk. The way this elephant lost his trunk was.

He was walking along just minding his own business, when out of the blue came a rhinoceros. This rhinoceros was the biggest, fattest, rhinoceros you have ever seen. And the elephant crouched down of fright. The rhinoceros stepped on the trunk and off it came. That's the way the elephant lost his trunk.

by DONALD

A teacher may plan a lesson in written composition in a six-step sequence. First, the child is either motivated to write or helped to recognize that he has something to express in writing. Second, the vocabulary needed to express the writer's ideas is made available. Third, forms already taught are recalled, because we want the child to practice correct habits. Fourth, time is provided for the writing experience. Fifth, the written material is shared. Sixth, improvements are made in the composition appropriate to the writer's purposes.

This six-step procedure cannot always be completed in one language period. A letter might be started in the language class and completed during the spelling or social studies time. A story or poem might be started on one day, completed on a second day, if needed, revised on a third. The amount of writing will depend on the interest and purpose of those involved. Writing should never become "busy work" or a time-filling activity. A limited amount of writing that has a purpose and is carefully guided to prevent the repetition of error will produce the most satisfying results.

The following classroom procedures have been suggested by teachers for each of these six steps:

1. Motivation

Preprimer Stories. Children are encouraged to make their own preprimers. These may be a compilation of the stories of several students or the work of one. Topics may concern Cowboys, Our Town, My Family, Our Pets, Our School.

Diary or Daily News. At first the children will dictate a report to the teacher on "what we did today." Later they will write their own. This may be a rotating activity. One group may be sharing orally for the day or week, another working on a project, and a third keeping the diary. "Our Friday News" is an excellent way to summarize the work of the week for parents and the principal.

Wishes, Fears, Troubles. Feelings stimulate a great deal of creative thought. Expression of such feelings helps the teacher understand the child as well as helping the child to get problems out in the open. Making pictures, then talking or writing about these topics, illustrate this suggestion.

"If I could have my wish"
"I do not like _____"
"Things that scare me"
"If I could be something else I would be a _____ _____"

Reports. Most adult writing is done to tell what happened, what a person learned, or what a person did. Simple encyclopedias make it possible for children to share interesting information through written reports. Some even call these "term papers," with sources appropriately indicated.

Seasons, Holidays, and Nature. The environment is a natural stimulation for writing. Windy days, storms, rain are things to tell about. A "Halloween," "Thanksgiving," or "February Hero" book, made of a compilation of writing, is a rewarding project. In the second grade and beyond children can print directly on ditto masters so that a book for each child can be assembled.

Titles. All that some children need to start the flow of ideas and the desire to write is a title.

Witches Brew	The Old House
My Pet	Vacation Fun
Adventures of a	My Toys
Penny	Dear Santa
Chimpanaut Tells	When I Was Sick
All	Danger
My Old School	Fire! Fire!

First Lines. Getting started is difficult for many. These first lines reproduced on writing paper will often help a straggler:

1. Dear Santa, Please _____.
2. My name is _____. I live at _____.
3. Once there was a monkey _____.
4. I am _____. I have _____. I can _____.

"If" Stories. Suggested plots:

1. If you were a circus pony, what adventures might you have?
2. If you were a lost dog, what might happen to you?
3. If you were a calf that liked to run away, what might happen to you?
4. If you were a dog that saw a turtle in the road, what might happen?
5. If you could go anywhere in the world, where would you go?
6. If you had ten dollars to spend for Christmas, what would you buy?

Tell a Story About These Facts:

1. I am a crow named Chicago. Tell the story of how I hid some silver and what happened to it.
   Suggested words: thief, chased, claws, dogs, barked, fireman, ladder, afraid, tired.
2. I am a fireman named Jim. One day there was a big fire. Tell what happened.
3. I am a monkey named Bimbo. I love to tease my master. Tell how this got me into trouble.

4. I am a baby brother. I got lost one day. Tell what happened to me.

Post Office. Establish a mail box for each child. At any time any child may write a letter to any other child in the class. The teacher may write a letter as well. Letters may be mailed only at noon and picked up only in the morning before school. To maintain standards it must be understood that no letter will be put in the receiver's box unless it is correctly written. The Postmaster and his staff examine all mail to see whether it is "mailable."

Outer Space Stories. Discuss the following: Today we are going to write a space story. Should we take a trip to Venus or stop at the moon? Will it be a dream, or an original story, or a news account in the "Venus Morning News"? Maybe it will be a colony of Pilgrims on the Moon or the diary of one who stayed at home. Perhaps the trip was not planned at all but the result of an accident.

Picture Stimulators. Picture stimulators are among the best means of motivating a child to write. A picture of a clown cut from a magazine is glued to an idea card. Below it are some stimulating questions: Have you been to the circus? Why is the clown so happy? On the back are words the child might wish to use as he writes a story. Appropriate words might be *clown, circus, tent, laughing, trick, joke, music.* These pictures are equally good as stimulators for oral stories prior to writing.

A Writer's Corner. A technique used by many teachers to stimulate writing is a writer's corner in the classroom. The corner consists of a table and chairs placed below a bulletin board. Questions, pictures, and ideas for word usage can be attractively displayed on the bulletin board for motivation. These are changed frequently. Writing paper, pencils, a dictionary, and needed lists of words are kept on the table. Folders of pictures with words describing the picture are placed on the table. Large sheets of paper with a mimeographed picture in the corner have been successfully used by some teachers to obtain a variety of stories about one picture.

The materials on the writer's table must be introduced to the children so that they know how to use them correctly. The pictures should be used by the class as a regular writing activity before the materials are placed on the writer's table. This does not mean that every new game or picture placed on the writer's table must be introduced to the group first. It does mean that any different type of material that the teacher places on this table should be explained so that the child knows exactly how to use it.

Periodically some recognition should be given to children who are using the writer's desk. Putting up "The Story of the Week," which can be selected by the teacher or the class, or making a booklet of the best stories are two ways to help stimulate more creative work. Material written may be put in a box and later read aloud by the teacher. The children guess who is the author in the manner of a television quiz program.

One device for the writer's table is a three-fold stand made of cardboard. Each fold is about 9 × 11. The center fold has a stimulating picture that is slipped behind a sheet of acetate. On the right is a group of words appropriate to the picture also in an acetate envelope. On the left are reminders to the writer. The teacher can change the pictures and vocabulary as she wishes. The reminders might be "Every story has a title." "All sentences begin with capitals." "All names start with capitals."

There might be envelopes for letters, a calendar, a usable dictionary, a telephone book (for addresses), extra pencils, special paper (stationery), erasers, and other items to make writing attractive.

The writer's desk can be used by children when they have finished other assigned work. It is desirable to have only one child using the desk at a time. However, if the teacher wishes, children may take certain materials to their desks.

In developing language material for this individual activity, teachers should remember that "above-average" or "gifted" children are more likely to use them at first, and teachers should plan activities that will be challenging to them.

2. Vocabulary Development

When children write they sometimes wish to use words from their listening vocabulary. One child may ask, "What do you call the signs in the newspaper that tell what people have to sell?" He is seeking the word *advertisement*. The same is true of such words as *alfalfa* (what do cows eat?) or *infinity* (space). At such times the teacher provides the word desired.

In other situations the teacher anticipates that the writing and spelling of certain words will be needed and provides convenient references. Interesting words in stories read should be noticed so that they will be available to future authors. Simple picture dictionaries of the names of things may be consulted or created.

Word Cards. Because seasonal words will be needed every year, a packet of cards for Halloween, Thanksgiving, and Christmas can be constructed by older children or the teacher. At the appropriate time these words are spread along the chalkboard to help writers. Pictures on each card, such as a picture of a pumpkin beside the word, will help those still having reading problems.

Word Lists. A folder for each child which contains the words most often used will prevent errors as well as make writing easier for the child. This is a combination of a spelling and reading list:

The Words We Use Most Often

These are the words we use most often.
We use them when we write.
We use them when we read.

We can use this as a dictionary.
We can check the spelling of words here.

Check yourself to see how many you know.
Learn the ones you do not know.
Learn to say them very quickly.

a	don't	nice	then
about	door	night	there
after	down	no	these
again	each	not	they
all	eat	now	thing
along	enough	of	things
also	ever	off	think
always	every	old	this
am	father	on	thought
an	few	once	three
and	find	one	through
another	fire	only	time
any	first	or	to
are	five	other	today
around	for	our	told
as	found	out	too
asked	four	over	took
at	friend	people	town
away	from	place	tree
back	fun	play	two
be	gave	pretty	until
beautiful	get	put	up
because	getting	ran	us
bed	girl	read	use
been	girls	ready	used
before	give	right	very
best	go	room	want
better	going	said	wanted
big	good	saw	was
book	great	say	water
boy	had	school	way
boys	happy	see	we
brother	hard	she	week
but	has	should	well
by	have	side	went
called	he	small	were
came	heard	snow	what
can	help	so	when
car	her	some	where
children	here	something	which
Christmas	may	soon	while
city	me	started	white
cold	men	stay	who
come	money	still	winter
comes	more	summer	with
coming	morning	sure	work
could	most	take	would
country	mother	teacher	write
days	much	tell	year
dear	my	than	years
did	name	that	you
didn't	never	the	your
do	new	their	
dog	next	them	

Other Words That Will Help Us

ask	fall	own	stop
ate	far	please	ten
black	fast	pull	thank
blue	fly	red	those
both	full	ride	together
bring	funny	right	try
brown	goes	round	under
buy	green	run	upon
call	grow	seven	walk
carry	hat	shall	warm
clean	hold	show	wash
cut	hurt	sing	why
does	its	sit	wish
done	jump	six	yellow
draw	myself	sleep	yes
drink	open	start	

A word book or a card file of frequently used words are handy references for words that are used in certain situations.[2] These are usually created by the teacher after discussion with the children. Contents might include some of the following:

Days of the Week

Sunday	Thursday
Monday	Friday
Tuesday	Saturday
Wednesday	

Months of the Year

January	July
February	August
March	September
April	October
May	November
June	December

Sounds That Animals Make

quack	bow wow
mew	oink oink
cluck	whinny
moo	neigh
coo	

_____

[2] Based upon seminar papers of Catherine Came, Eugene M. Fowler, and Horace McGee, San Diego State College, San Diego, Calif.

Kinds of Weather

foggy	rainy
cloudy	windy
sunny	hot
clear	cold

Places We Go on Trips

beach	zoo
mountains	harbor
museum	country
desert	farm

Special Words for:

tastes	feelings
color	action
smells	sights

Social Studies Unit Words

Words will vary according to unit.

Training the Five Senses.   Play games that emphasize sensory response. Have a child do an act while the others listen. Then tell how it sounded. Such actions as tap on the desk, tap on the window, drop a book, drum with two pencils, open a window, and so on, are appropriate.

Next imagine that you are a bird that could fly anywhere. Tell what you hear and have the class guess where the bird is.

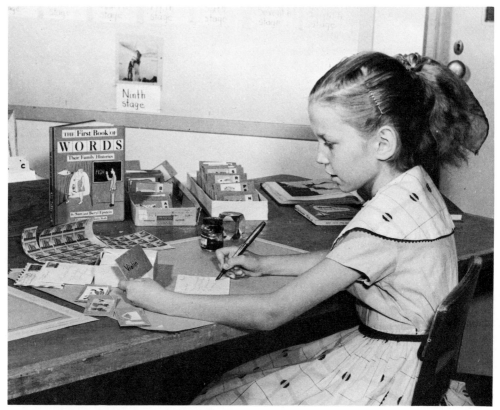

A "writer's desk" with spelling aids and real stamps provide a motivation for correspondence to sick classmates, schools in other states, or relatives. (*Courtesy of the San Diego County Schools.*)

Close your eyes and picture something you saw at home this morning or on the way to school. See if your words will help others see the same thing. The teacher or a student may ask questions until the complete image is visualized.

Match the beginning and ending of sentences such as these:

The door bell	tiptoed softly
The clock	screamed
Mother	hummed
The whistle	clanged
The fire alarm	whimpered
The baby	blew

3. Standards

Standards are designed to assist expression of ideas, not interfere with them. Yet we do not value a language anarchy. Se-

curity built on a knowledge of proper form will aid any writer.

Reminder Charts. Prior to writing, attention is called to certain skills previously used. These can be reviewed rapidly, then posted as a reminder while writing.

Capital Letters

Names start with capital letters.

Sally, Dick, Paul

Sentences start with capital letters.

See the cat.
Where are you going?

Because all writing involves handwriting skills, the quality practiced is important. Prior to a writing lesson, a five-minute review of the formation of certain letters is

A laboratory period to examine sentence structure, proofreading techniques, or other specific items can clarify information and provide an opportunity to determine instructional needs. (*Courtesy of the San Diego City Schools.*)

valuable. This may involve chalkboard demonstrations by the pupils, an examination of small handwriting reference cards at each student's writing place, or a review of the letter forms usually posted over the blackboard. Second-grade children should know all the letter forms. Primary children should be helped with letters as needed, especially the capital letter forms.

A major use of standards is to direct proofreading of material. Children should not be expected to proofread for all errors, but they should check for certain specifics. The following would be appropriate:

Did I capitalize the words in my title?
Did I keep a margin?
Did I use my best writing?
Did I put only one line through words I wanted to change? (Prevents erasing or scribbling over a word.)

4. Laboratory Writing Exercises

Such activities as the writer's table are individual devices which free the child from classroom pressures. At other times the guidance of the teacher is desirable as certain skills and understandings are practiced.

Group Composition. Working on composition as a group helps to establish security among members of the class, gives the teacher an opportunity to prevent errors in spelling and usage, and builds good human relationships. Some children need this experience before they are able to organize their thoughts and express themselves independently. Subjects for group composition can develop from a common experience or the social studies. The children contribute ideas which the teacher writes on the chalkboard. Later those who wish may copy the product. Letters to a sick classmate, notes home about a program, or letters to another class are examples of group composition.

Staggered Writing Assignment. Although writing will frequently be done by the entire class, a variation is to have only one group write. This makes it possible for the teacher to give more personal help, evaluate with greater care—because there are fewer papers—and provide for the individual differences in a group. There is a competitive element in writing as well as reading. Those operating at approximately the same levels profit most by group instruction.

Classroom Helpers. At times it will give recognition to a few and help others to appoint one student in each group who may give help with spelling, punctuation, or other problems. Upper-grade children may be given recognition by permitting them to be "human dictionaries" in a lower grade during a writing period.

Prevention of Error Practice. Practicing an error tends to fix it as a habit. With experience teachers learn to anticipate problems that the class or individuals will have. To prevent spelling errors and to encourage the use of vocabulary, word cards with illustrations of meaning might be made for the seasons. Halloween words that children want to use would include *gate, witch, ghost, haunted, screamed.* These words might be reviewed, then placed on the chalkboard. A child who wants to use a word has a clue to identify with the picture. After selecting the word he wants, he takes it to his desk, copies it, then returns it to the chalkboard. Review of handwriting and punctuation standards may be carried out before the writing period. The children should be given time to proofread, with questions to guide them. The teacher should never ask a child to do something he knows is beyond the ability of the child. Because some write a dramatic sketch does not mean that all should. It might be well to have some writing as a partner or group activity either at the planning level or at presentation time.

5. Sharing the Written Compositions

Use the sharing time at the beginning of the day to read some of the compositions.

Post compositions on the bulletin board. Make a booklet such as "Our Halloween Stories."

Some authorities strongly recommend that the teacher or a parent type stories written by children correcting the major errors. This enhances the child's confidence that he can write and has something to say. There is much testimony that with confidence thus established the children improve with respect to error and expression.

Collect the written efforts in a folder, which is sent home after the parent conference.

Publish in a school newspaper compositions that have special merit.

Exchange compositions with another class at the same level or a different one (appropriate at the end of a year).

6. Improving Composition Skills

The teacher finds something to praise in each composition. "I like the way you used (a word)" "The ending is good."

But errors are noted as revealing instructional needs of children. The teacher then composes a story that reflects these errors or with the permission of a child uses one of the papers submitted. The problem is presented to the class as "How can we make this interesting paper better?"

The story is written on the board:

Spooky

Spooky was a ghost. He was a friendly ghost. He could be everything. But he could not float. He could not moan. He was a funny ghost. He was a happy ghost too.

After the story is read aloud, the class discusses the sentences and the possibility of joining some of them to make the story sound more interesting and flow more easily.

The class may practice on a written drill of this type (the term *transform* might be used if the students are familiar with the new grammar):

Making Our Sentences Sound More Interesting

Make one sentence from these two short sentences:

1. Spooky was a ghost. He was a friendly ghost.

2. I have a ball. It is a red ball.

3. John has a pencil. It is green.

4. Mary is my friend. She is my best friend.

5. Jane threw the ball. She threw it to me.

6. This is my wagon. It is big.

7. I have a doll. She is pretty.

8. They have the blocks. There are six.

9. I like your story. It is a good story.

10. It is on the table. The table is large.

The children then look over their previous stories and change sentences. Other drills of the following nature may be used:

Make a sentence by drawing a line from a group of words in List *A* to a group of words in List *B*. Be sure they belong together.

A	*B*
1. The dog	me his book.
2. The little boy	see the game.
3. John gave	ate some ice cream.
4. We went to	ran after the cat.
5. I like	to read

Write the words you need to finish each sentence. Choose them from the group of words below.

the red ball	ice cream and cake
We have	splashing down
I wish	three blocks to school
She went	four new dresses

1. I like _____.
2. _____ three new girls now.
3. Every day I walk _____.
4. _____ I had three dollars.
5. The rail came _____.
6. Mary has _____.
7. _____ to the skating party.
8. We are going to have _____.

Paragraph Drill

Copy these sentences so they tell a story. When you decide which sentence to use first, be sure to indent the sentence. These sentences should make a one-paragraph story.

She ate their porridge and sat in their chairs.
They lived in the woods.
Once there were three bears.
A little girl came to their house.

For Discussion

1. Why is it better to recognize a situation a child will want to write about than to use a device to motivate him to write? Indicate such a situation.

2. What causes some children to be so literal-minded that they seem to have a limited imagination?

3. Some say that there is a creative element in all writing. For some children, writing their name is creative. Do you agree with this? How would you encourage other writing?

4. One of the objectives of the primary grades is to help the child distinguish fact from fantasy. Does creative writing contribute to this?

5. If possible, compare some of your own writing efforts while in grade school with material being written by children today.

How May Creative Writing Be Fostered in the Intermediate Grades?

It takes more than a permissive classroom climate and a teacher interested in children to produce worthy written work in the intermediate classroom. First of all, writing takes time. If a teacher attempts to suggest a topic and have the child write something in a single language period, it means incomplete and hurriedly done papers. Creative writing is a questionable homework assignment. There is a suggestion of coercion in homework that will limit the creative expression of some children. Although a child may willingly rework a piece of writing at home, the first draft should be completed under the teacher's supervision. There are a few self-motivated children who like to write, just as others like to study music or play ball. No restrictions should be placed on such children.

An attractive display can motivate additional writing of stories. (*Courtesy of the Burbank Public Schools.*)

A three-day sequence provides adequate time for most writing endeavors. The first period should be used for the stimulation of ideas, discussion of various words and skills needed to develop a topic, and the experimental first drafts of the material. The second period should be a true writing laboratory with each child writing and receiving help as needed. The third day should be used to correct errors, reorganize material, and write the final copy if the child wishes to revise the material. Some projects will take longer. This means that during the year less written composition may be done, but what is done will have purpose and merit.

The teaching sequence is that of motivation, skill development, refinement, and use. Motivation involves any experience that starts a flow of ideas. The discussion helps the student determine the thought he wishes to develop in his writing. Skill development involves planned vocabulary materials, reviews of punctuation, writing and spelling skills, and help with organization of ideas.

Refinement involves making corrections, proofreading, and writing to improve content, form, usage, spelling, and handwriting. Use is the recognition given the final product as it is read to the class, reproduced in a newspaper, placed on a bulletin board, or shared in a way appropriate to the content.

Just as storytelling pictures are used in the primary grades, so they may be used in the intermediate. Those with great human interest, such as the illustrations of Norman Rockwell, are especially good. But pictures expressing beauty, mood, and action are equally motivating. The class may select their own picture from the group presented by the teacher, or all write about the same one. Because children sometimes are impressed by the ideas of other children and thus limit their creativity, it is a challenge to be original and see a story in a picture that no one else imagines. The class discusses two or three before making a choice to use as the basis for a story. The characters are discussed. The children are asked to imagine what is happening now, what happened previously, and what is likely to happen next. Words are selected that describe the action, beauty, or feeling. Possible titles are suggested and first lines written. During a second period the stories are written. Later, children may select pictures from magazines for the writing table or for additional stories.

After the imagination of children has been aroused it sometimes takes only a title to start them thinking of a story. Such titles as these may be put in a box on the writer's table to help some get started:

The Midnight Visitor
The Falling Star
The Hidden Valley
Lost in a Storm
An Animal Friend
A Secret
My Ambition
Flying at Night
Faster Than Sound

In a similar way, first-sentence starters help a writer get on his way:

"She's gone! Now I am going to find her diary," muttered John to himself as he crept up the stairs noiselessly.

John stood stock still. His legs refused to go. The sweat broke out on his forehead.

Bill walked to the window to let in a little air. As he began to raise it, something outside caught his eye. He stood with his mouth open. There on the lawn below the window was the strangest thing he had ever seen.

At first the noise was very faint and seemed far away. It was an odd noise, one that the boys didn't recognize. As it moved closer they went out to see what it might be.

Mary knew that if her mother found out, she wouldn't be able to sit for days, but she was determined to carry out her plan in spite of this.

The children were playing on the beach when they found the strange footprints in the sand. Their curiosity got the best of them and they decided to follow them along the shore.

"Quick, come here," called Tom, "I want to show you what I've found!" As the others ran to join him, they stopped short, staring in surprise.

When father came home that evening he was whistling happily. The children knew what that meant. He had another of his wonderful surprises.

There was a strange silence about the forest that night. It had an air of waiting for something to happen.

These may be put on cards and placed in an "idea box" to help those who seek ideas.

Some children need only a word to start a series of thoughts that lead to writing:

ghost
fog
gravy
my worst scare
nightmare
rolling waves
little old lady
a bright idea
late again
mud
some luck
pride
rolling along
long journey
longest day of my life
face like a lion
time to think

The object of writing does not need to be a story. Frequently the purpose is to help children write with vividness and insight. The actual plotting of a story, with beginning, characterization, episodes, climax, and ending, may be too complex for many in the elementary school. It does not matter whether the material is a story, report, autobiography, dramatic play, or sketch. It does matter that the child is learning to express ideas in writing effectively.

Painting word pictures will interest students, yet not demand the time that story writing involves. Ask the children what pictures the word makes them see. Then have them write a word picture. These are examples:

snow   Snow, soft and cold and white, drifted lazily through the air, rested fluffily upon the boughs of the evergreen trees, and in time covered the earth with quiet beauty.

waves   Waves rolled endlessly toward the shore, crashing thunderously against the gray rocks and sending countless sprays of foam skyward.

airplanes   Airplanes roared down the runways, then effortlessly left the ground and soared majestically into the sky, soon becoming mere specks in the distance.

Objects will start a child's imagination working. One teacher brought in a bag of old shoes—a football shoe, a tennis slipper, a satin pump, and so on, and presented such questions as "Who wore this shoe?" "Where has it been?" "Why was it thrown away?" The class was motivated, and writing of a highly imaginative nature resulted.

Variations on old themes will help some get started. What happened to Goldilocks on the next day? What did the three bears do at Christmas? What type of queen was Cinderella? Social studies may motivate historical writing in the form of a news account of such events as Columbus' discovery of the New World or the discovery of gold in California. "Hansel & Gretel go back to school" by George Creegan, published in *Plays* (October 1966), will remind students of such possibilities.

A "story formula" will challenge some. A good story has five parts: a beginning, a problem, a high point or climax, a following action or solution, and a satisfactory ending. This chart may be used to check the formula:

1. Does your story have a good beginning? Tell the four "W's": Who, When, Where, and What's the problem?
2. Did you make the reader aware of the problem?
3. Does your story reach a high point or climax?
4. Is there an adequate explanation of how the problem was solved?
5. Do all the parts fit together at the end in a way that satisfies the reader?

Five sentence stories may outline the plot of a story:

1. Mother and I were sitting in the kitchen after dinner one quiet evening.
2. Suddenly we heard a scratching noise at the back door.
3. Mother screamed and jumped up on a chair as a gray mouse darted across the floor.
4. I stood there and laughed at the funny sight, while Mother recovered from terror.
5. I imagine the mouse was more frightened than Mother was.

Charts of this nature may be used as guides:

How Stories Begin

1. With conversation to set the stage for action.
2. With the end of the story, then going back to the beginning.
3. With the middle of the story, then to the actual beginning.
4. A characterization of the chief character or characters.
5. A summary paragraph to tell the point of the story.
6. With description.

7. With the time, place, or circumstance.
8. With a question.

Describing Our Characters

1. Simple statement of fact: Bob is lazy.
2. By describing how Bob does things.
3. By telling an episode to prove that Bob is lazy.
4. By telling how little of his work is done.
5. By comparing him with others when lazy.
6. By using synonyms of the word.
7. By reporting what others say.
8. By telling what he is not.
9. By repeating his own characterization of himself.

Self-characterization is easier than describing another. A "Who Am I?" paper that may be read by the teacher while the class identifies the writer may be the beginning of character study.

A recent text provides this help (see next page) in guiding children as they describe a character.[3]

Strange to say, some of the major interests of children do not lend themselves to creative writing. Baseball and other sports writing apparently calls for greater language power than that possessed by children. The same is true of food. Although this is a major interest, children find little inspiration for imaginative writing about the subject.

A major effort in teaching creative writing is directed toward developing the vocabulary necessary to present the desired thought. As the teacher reads aloud to the children, time is taken to note effective use of language. Sometimes this is done in association with a library book, at other times with examples of children's writing. Approval of vivid ways of saying things sharpens awareness of words and reveals new areas for exploration.

---

[3] Andrew Schiller and others, *Language and How We Use It* (Glenview, Ill.: Scott, Foresman Co., 1969), p. 153.

Create a Character

When an author writes a story, he creates the characters out of his imagination. You can do that, too. Look at the figure to the left. Can you imagine what sort of person it might be?

Is it a picture of a man or a woman or a boy or a girl? Is it a big person or a little person? What are the things this person likes most? What kind of person is he? What is his name?

Suppose you decided it was a little boy who liked to play baseball, and always wore his uniform and his red baseball cap. His favorite food was hamburgers. He was an absent-minded boy who forgot the things he was supposed to do. His name was Sam.

Try to write a story about Sam. Here is the story that John wrote.

One day, Sam got up early to play baseball. His mother told him she was going to have hamburgers for his lunch. Sam was happy. He played baseball all morning. He was so busy playing baseball, he forgot to go home at lunchtime for his hamburgers!

To the left there is another figure. Ask yourself what kind of person it might be. Make up your own character for this figure, draw his picture, and write a story that shows what kind of person he is.

EMPHASIS
Like the preceding lesson, this one has to do with character description. But now pupils provide the details that help make fictional personalities seem real.

EXPLANATION
Begin this lesson with a discussion of various personalities—real and fictional—whom all the children probably know. For example, have pupils think about what characteristics make these individuals distinct personalities: Crow Boy, Mickey Mantle, Bob Hope, Pippi Longstocking, Charlie Brown.

Point out that an author gives distinctive qualities to characters so readers will feel they know them as well as they know friends and neighbors.

Then have youngsters read and discuss page 153. During discussion, have children consider what they might tell about a person to bring him alive for readers. A description might include details about the character's interests, likes and dislikes, habits, speech, clothing, physical appearance, and anything that makes him a little different from most other people.

After pupils have followed the lesson's final suggestion, invite them to show their drawings and to read their descriptions aloud. Encourage the class to comment on details in the descriptions that made the characters lifelike. Select several drawings and descriptions for a bulletin-board display.

EXTENSION
At a later date, divide the class into three groups to write a composite story. Let the first group introduce a character with distinctive personality traits. The second group may then develop the plot by presenting a problem. The third group will solve the problem and provide a story ending. Point out that the problem should be one which this type of character would be likely to encounter and that the solution, if it is one that he works out, should also be in keeping with his character.

Using new words, imagining an experience, or recalling an event brings delight to the writer as well as to those with whom the composition is shared. (*Courtesy of the San Diego County Schools.*)

Some children, by virtue of personality, home, or early school training, are alert to the details of the world in which they live; others need help in the development of all five senses. These children must be encouraged to find pleasure in observation and in the discussion of what they see.

It is easy to start an enthusiastic discussion concerning the flavor of certain foods. It's fun, too, to put into words the taste of cod-liver oil, an uncured olive, or a mouthful of the Pacific Ocean. Children soon discover that following one's nose may be an interesting experience leading to the earthy smell of recently turned sod, the tang of the sea, the fragrance of clean linen just off the line, the musty odor of old newspapers stored in the garage.

Vocabulary is increased and power of expression heightened when pupils are helped to see the importance of contrasting words and ideas. They will enjoy trying it, too.

quietness of the forest
        vs. *clang of the city streets*
smooth as the snow-covered lawn
vs. *rough and jagged as the ice on the pond*

Children are easily helped to understand that whole sentences can be built to reflect contrasting ideas that will best express their own feelings:

> The forest was dim. Billy thought of the meadow near his home where a sparkling brook with little minnows rushed down mossy rocks in warm sunshine.

Children enjoy the euphony of a sentence or line in which the same first letter or sound in a group of words is repeated a number of times. Alliteration can become stilted when it is used as a mechanical exercise. With older children it should be encouraged not as a game, but to enhance the meaning of words.

soft slumbering summer
lonely leaf
nodding noon
whispering wind
weird white world

Young children use similes naturally and easily. Although they may not label them as such, older children use metaphors in the same manner. Comparison is a natural method of description for young and old alike. Children enjoy completing these phrases:

as soft as
as loud as
as happy as
as sad as
as stern as
as drowsy as
as bright as
as cold as

as hot as
as muffled as
as slippery as
as long as
as short as
as pointed as

They become conscious of the use of similes in writing about things that "looked like" or were "as gentle as." One class found that the wind today "was as gentle as":

a lamb
my mother's voice
God's voice
a soft, furry cloud
a rose opening
when night falls

Tactile perception can be used to enrich children's writing. Various objects can be passed among the children and their reactions written on the board. One teacher passed a bowl of ice cubes. In seeking to express their reaction, the children sought and found many words to describe what they had touched. Ice is

cold
slippery
smooth
hard
sharp
shivery

The teacher can use a small figure or figurine, holding it up and asking the class to look at it closely, then putting the figurine behind something. The teacher now asks the class to describe what was seen. The teacher can pretend she has never seen the object, so that she can be very curious about the responses, encouraging accurate, descriptive analysis. After the first attempt, the class tries again, looks at the object once more, develops vocabulary to explain, and goes through the entire process. The same thing can be tried with a second object—all responses being verbal. On the third try, using a new object, the class can try writing a description.

After preliminary work on developing "word pictures," the teacher can put three sentences on the board, such as:

An airplane went up.
It flew.
It came down.

The class can be encouraged to develop a more interesting and exciting picture of the situation. Action words and descriptive words can be included orally. As a real picture begins to form, children can appreciate the power of such words as *soared, skimmed, floated,* and so on.

As a written work experience, children can take another set of three sentences and see how well they can paint another word picture:

The wind blew.
The windows shook.
The storm came.

Ask the children what pictures a word makes them see. Then let them write a word picture.

Rain

Rain splashed upon the earth, forming puddles on the ground, pelting against the windows, and dripping endlessly from the eaves of the buildings.

Waves

Waves rolled shoreward in long unbroken lines, each crest forming for an instant a magic crown of transparent green before toppling over into a churning mass of yellow-white foam.

Children are amused by their first encounter with metaphors. Their practical minds create laugh-provoking pictures when they read such statements as "His eyes dropped," "She turned green with envy," "He put his foot in his mouth," "The doctor was tied up," "Someone spilled the beans." Cartoons can be made to accompany metaphors.

Teach shades of meaning by mounting pictures of increasing size on deepening shades of colored paper. Blow "word bubbles" to get synonyms. Start each row with a word, such as *went, pretty, small,* or *old.* Let children blow their bubbles larger by giving synonyms for each word.

While use of a thesaurus is beyond the ability of most children, it does help to make a "classroom thesaurus" of words to use instead of *said, funny, beautiful,* and other overused words. The study of words separated from the situation where children would use them is an isolated and usually ineffective learning situation. Meaningful exercises of this nature, however, are helpful after the need for adequate vocabulary is felt by a writer.[4]

To the Pupil:

Life would be pretty dull if we ate the same foods at every meal, or played the same game every day. Life would be equally dull if we said and heard the same words all the time. We need to know enough words so that we don't wear out the same old, tired ones. We can give words a rest by using synonyms. Synonyms are words which have almost the same meaning, like "little," "small," and "tiny."

1. Do you know a word to use in place of "big"? _____

2. Do you know another word which is a synonym for "big"? _____

3. Use your dictionary to help you find three more synonyms for "big."

_____   _____   _____

[4] San Diego City Schools, *Oral and Written Language* (1956), with special acknowledgment to Elizabeth Stocker.

4. In the exercise below, *circle* the three words that have meanings somewhat alike. Choose the best word to *fill the space* in the sentences. Use your dictionary to help you.

space	distance	New York is a long _____
expanse	praise	from here.
place	install	

deposit	plan	I will _____ my money in the bank.
crack	split	There was a _____ in the plaster.
break	build	

5. You can find synonyms for these words in the box below. *Write* the correct synonym on the line beside each word. *Check* by using your dictionary.

pair _____   doze _____

jammed _____   funny _____

coast _____   pretty _____

coarse _____   strange _____

nap	lovely	amusing	odd
crowded	shore	couple	rough

To the Pupil:

One day during sharing period Terence told the class this story about his trip to the circus:

"The girl did stunts. Everything she did, the clown tried to do, too. The girl was graceful, but the clown—well, the clown wasn't graceful."

Terence needed a word to tell the opposite meaning of "graceful." He could have used "awkward" or "clumsy," but he just couldn't think of these words. Words which are opposite in meaning to other words are called *antonyms*. To speak and write better we need to know many antonyms.

Circle the word that means the opposite, or almost the opposite, of the first word in each line:

leave	play	sleep	stay
attempt	attach	try	wish
powerful	different	homeless	weak
great	small	large	buff
scarce	plentiful	first	thin
most	least	soft	sweet
expensive	late	next	cheap
damp	clean	strong	dry
good	right	bad	ready
give	grow	take	go

To the Pupil:

Think of the word "apple." Does this word do something to you? Now think of "the juicy, red apple." These added words which tell about the apple make us think about the delicious taste of this fruit. When we describe or tell about something we can make it much more interesting by using words which make our listeners or readers see, hear, touch, taste or smell.

Write a word in the blank in front of each word below which will help to describe that word.

     1. the _____ car (see)

     2. the _____ motor (sound)

     3. the _____ flowers (smell)

     4. the _____ pie (taste)

     5. the _____ satin cloth (touch)

Use these describing words to write in the sentences below:

     howling   rough   sour   pungent   glittering

     1. The _____ floor scratched his feet.

     2. The sky was sprinkled with _____ stars.

     3. Pine needles have a _____ odor.

     4. The _____ dog kept some people awake.

     5. She had a _____ pickle in her lunch box.

To the Pupil:

When we write or speak we paint word pictures in the minds of readers and listeners. These word pictures can be simple black-and-white drawings or they can be wide-screen, 3-D, technicolor, action movies. Compare these two sentences:

     1. The fire engine stopped in front of the burning house.
     2. Siren screaming and tires screeching, the bright red fire engine braked to a halt in front of the blazing building.

Which sentence painted a better word picture for you? Now see if you can rewrite the following sentences. Make them paint better pictures.

1. John was doing tricks on his bicycle.

_____

_____

2. Susan was playing with her dolls.

_____

_____

3. Bob hit a home run.

_____

_____

4. The girl was wearing a red dress.

_____

_____

5. The horse jumped over the fence.

_____

_____

Proofreading and rewriting are aspects of the refinement of ideas. The fact that the first effort to write is a rough draft of ideas or an experiment with ideas needs to be established as early as the fourth grade. Because rewriting a long selection can be a burden at this level, the short episode, the humorous incident, the descriptive paragraph, or the news item should be the writing objective.

Standards for proofreading should be established one at a time. Many children need freedom to write without the threat of proofreading or editing all their efforts. The goals of the learner and the teacher will determine the extent to which material should be examined. These will reflect the language skills being taught at the grade level. The following items would be appropriate for the fifth grade:

Proofreading My Story

1. Is my paper headed correctly?
2. Did I skip a line after my heading?
3. Did I capitalize the important words in the title?
4. Did I skip a line before I began to write my story?
5. Did I indent for each paragraph?
6. Do I have a margin?
7. Is each word spelled correctly?
8. Is each sentence complete? Did I omit words?

9. Have I a period or question mark after each sentence?
10. Did I include the important points in my story? Did I tell my story in sequence?

A class may be organized so that each writer has an editing partner. This partner then edits the paper. This report is submitted with the original and rewritten paper.

Proofreading

1. Did this person indent?
2. Did this person watch his margin?
3. Has he checked his spelling?
4. Did he use capitals when they were needed?
5. Is his paper neat?
6. Does this person know when to end a sentence and begin a new one?
7. Has this person used too many "ands"?
8. Do you feel this person checked his paper when it was finished?

I checked _____ paper.

My name is _____

Lessons in proofreading should be included in the language period. Exercises of this nature emphasize the skills of proofreading.

Proofread the following story:

1. Does each sentence start with a capital

letter? (There should be twelve sentences.)

2. Are all the words correctly spelled? (There are five misspelled words.)
3. Do all the sentences tell about the topic? (There is one that does not belong.)
4. Are the paragraphs indented?

Once upon a time there lived a boy named Timothy he lived with his mother and father. Once when his father was outside getting water the Indians came along and burned the house. Only Timothy was alive and then he ran to the mountains and stayed there for five days. Timothy and his famly came from Ohio.
On the fifth day he saw a nest on a rockey cliffth. In the nest he saw a baby eagle. The mother eagle had been shot with an arrow. He took the baby eagle for a pet. Timothy and the eagle grew up in the forrest. They ate together and slept together. They had no famly but they were not alone.

Displays of work "Before Proofreading" and "After Proofreading" will emphasize the improvement possible. A committee of proofreaders can serve the class. Three students are assigned the task of proofreading stories placed in a box at the reading table. When their work is completed, the work is placed in a "rewrite" box. Some children who are less imaginative than others are good proofreaders. Of course, the more able students are most helpful at this task. After a visit to a newspaper, the role of editor can be dramatized in this way.

Classroom recognition can be given to children's writing in several ways. One school makes a scrapbook of "Our Very best Writing." When the class feels that something is worthy for this collection, the material is added. At the end of the year this is presented to the principal. Scrapbooks made in former years are available on certain occasions.

Children enjoy reading something written by an older brother or sister. Upper-grade children are impressed with material they wrote while in a lower grade. Eventually it may be possible for a child to read material written by one of his parents when the parent was in the fifth grade. The teacher must plan so that the best product of each individual is included and so that no one is left out. During the year a child might substitute a new selection for one previously selected.

Bulletin boards of children's writing provide recognition and encouragement. Some schools have strict rules about the display of imperfect papers. In light of the objectives of creative writing, it seems that a paper with a few errors checked is still worthy of display. Few children are going to find pleasure in rewriting an entire paper just to have it placed on the bulletin board.

Publication in a school paper or magazine is the ultimate recognition for many. Creative writing is not news writing and as such must have a special place in any publication. Many school systems now publish an annual magazine of creative writing. When a selection is considered worthy it is sent to an editing committee. This committee acknowledges the selection with a letter of recognition explaining that the work will be considered, but that not all material submitted will be used. The letter is adequate recognition for many children. If a child's material is selected for the magazine, he receives three copies of the publication and another letter. The existence of such a publication influences many teachers to attempt projects involving creative writing who ordinarily would be more secure stressing drill on the mechanics of language.

Perhaps the most important idea that those who work with children in the area of creative or imaginative writing have found to be true is one of the utmost simplicity. You cannot teach children to write creatively—you can only help them express the original ideas within them. Behind the story, poem, or letter—behind the clear, concise sentence or the stumbling search for words—is the child and all that he can become. Creative writing is one more way to understand him.

As young writers develop confidence a greater awareness of good composition qualities will improve their written expression.[5]

In the intermediate grades many children make definite advancement in the following areas of good composition:

---

[5] *English Language Arts in Wisconsin.* Robert Pooley, Project Director, Madison, Dept. of Public Instruction, 1968.

- Unity: staying with the subject
- Continuity: developing topic statements by addition and illustration
- Form: sense of order; organization
- Sentence structure: the levels of subordination
- Diction: choosing fresh, colorful, precise words
- Tone: developing individuality of style

The following sentences exemplify progress in unity, sentence structure, and diction.

Unity. The following beginning and closing sentences of compositions indicate "staying with the subject":

Grade Four

When the sun comes up, all is still on the lake

It's very still on the lake when no one's up but me.

I was sitting on the porch watching TV when all of a sudden the TV went out.

From then on the TV was OK.

Grade Six

To have a vacation without any accidents this summer, we should be careful in everything we do. Remember, most accidents can be prevented.

By being careful and using common sense, you will have a very safe summer.

Sentence Structure. The following sentences exemplify logical subordination:

Grade Four

When I look at Brownstone Falls in Mellen, Wisconsin, I think of purple rocks and water falling down them.

When Ranger VI went to the moon he did not bring back pictures because he met space men and they took his camera.

Grade Six

Summer would be a lot more fun if people would obey summer safety rules.

He replied, "I feel that the American people have a wrong impression of my country of Peru, for my country is a contrast of old and new, of gaiety and sorrow."

Diction. The following sentences contain fresh, colorful words:

Grade Four

It was very quiet on the marsh, no fish leaping, no birds singing.

[The wind] makes the flowers nod their heads and twist around and rise off the ground.

Grade Six

Cars are speedy now, whizzing by at one hundred miles an hour.

Whispers come from a motor purring softly.

As a boy I could look down the terraced hillside, to the green valley snuggled between the mountains; or I could look upward to the lofty peaks, their diamond snow shimmering in the blinding sun.

Children use figurative speech as early as fourth grade. For instance:

[Mars] looked like a big beach ball in the air.

A rhinocerous is big and bold. He has horns like sharp fat long tacks.

Practical writing is done in any situation in which there is need for it. In comparison with creative writing, practical writing is more utilitarian, realistic, or intellectual, and needs the discipline of correct mechanics to be acceptable. Correct form seems intrinsically a function of realistic writing because other people are practically concerned. This is the type of writing in which the author works more as a reproducer of known facts, conditions, or ideas presented in his own words. Here the emphasis may be placed upon the mechanics of writing, spelling, penmanship, neatness, punctuation, and similar external items without injury to the child's creative expression.

When a child writes creatively, he expresses in one way or another his feelings or his intellectual reactions to an experience—something he has seen, heard, or otherwise come in contact with through his senses. This expression of personal reactions constitutes the quality of originality because no one other than the writer can produce it. It is his own contribution. This type of writing is that of artistic self-expression. It is personal, individual, imaginative, and highly perishable. To keep it alive there must be complete freedom to experiment and complete assurance of a respectful reception of the product regardless of its nature.

Though in a sense the two aspects of writing develop separately and serve different purposes, the child gradually carries over what he has learned of techniques in practical writing and applies it where it suits his purpose in personal writing. The emphasis is first and last on saying something that is worth saying, and saying it effectively. *A balance between the two types must be maintained, and to give all writing the same treatment is to suppress or inhibit the creative spirit of children.* Lois Lenski stresses the importance of the treatment of creative writing.[6]

It is such a simple thing to help children enter the creative life, to help them to think clearly and to communicate their ideas to others through the spoken or written word. Provide the opportunity—let the child talk and let him write, enjoying both. Share his enthusiasms. All children can and should learn the free and easy use of words. Creative expression should never be confused with the teaching of the techniques of writing. These are two distinct procedures.

It should always be remembered that creation is a flowing of ideas. Given a stimulus, ideas come pouring from the mind like water from a fountain. It is all too easy to stop this creative flow. Rules for punctuation, spelling, grammar, and handwriting will stop it. Emphasis on rules is sure to stifle creative thinking.

There are some who would not be as positive with respect to rules as Miss Lenski. Confidence in the craftsmanship of writing and expression also releases creativity. Great writers and artists have also been expert craftsmen. Certainly no great painter has emerged by ignoring the disciplines of his craft. By mastering these disciplines he is able to project his own personal qualities more effectively. Our objective is to use the child's desire to create to make disciplined craftsmanship acceptable.

Alvina Burrows emphasizes that evalua-

tion of practical writing serves a different purpose than evaluation of personal writing.[7]

One of the acknowledged tasks of the elementary school years is to further the pupil's self-concept. Few experiences in school can so effectively destroy a positive self-image as the teaching of composition. Excessive correction has thwarted the pencils of many a beginner. In other cases, no correction at all has been offered for fear of cramping self-expression. When to correct and when not to correct children's writing has been a dilemma for many teachers.

Solutions arrived at in both England and America reveal surprising agreement. Correction is applied to children's practical writings—letters, reports, records, and other forms of factual prose in which the written paper itself is seen by an audience.[8] A British study reaching essentially the same conclusion calls these businesslike forms "recording writing." [9]

Pride in achieving correct form is developed in these more objective examples. On the other hand, imaginative expression is for enjoyment. Story and verse are to be read aloud to one's class, either by the author or by the teacher, and need not be corrected or rewritten. After being enjoyed by an audience, they are filed privately; their physical form is relatively unimportant. They have already served their purpose in oral communication. Here again the oral basis for learning to write operates with real efficiency. Only when stories or verse are to be made public in a class newspaper or school publication must they be edited and rewritten. When they are made public they must be put into good form, as an obligation to others as well as a mark of self-respect.

Correction of any writing is best done orally by teacher and pupil in an editing conference, taking turns reading aloud. Thus they apply the oral–auditory facility estab-

[6] Lois Lenski, "Helping Children to Create," *Childhood Education,* 26 (November 1949), pp. 101–105.

[7] Alvina Trent Burrows, "Children's Language," *National Elementary School Principal* (1965), p. 16.

[8] Alvina T. Burrows, Doris C. Jackson, and Dorothy O. Saunders, *They All Want to Write* (New York: Holt, 1964).

[9] A. B. Clegg, *The Excitement of Writing* (London: Chatto and Windus, 1964).

lished long before the newer learnings of writing and reading.

When writing is an opportunity to reveal one's own feelings and imagination without fear of criticism and with the assurance of respectful listeners, the pupil's picture of himself is enhanced. Not being on the defensive, he can appreciate the good writing of others, both peers and professionals. He can enjoy what is worthy in his teacher's eyes because he too is worthy as a writer. Both his listening audience and those who see his corrected public writing fortify his pleasure and his pride in writing and in himself.

For Discussion

1. Do you consider that children can be as creative in such tasks as letter writing as in imaginative writing?

2. To what extent is it true that the skills of language are the skills of conformity?

3. Alvina Burrows reports, in the *N.E.A. Bulletin*, No. 18, "Certain procedures have not stood up to the testing of research. Among these are encouraging children to plan stories before they write, checking the mechanics as they write, experimenting with words for the sake of using 'colorful' or 'different' ones, studying vocabulary lists, writing for school newspapers, and requiring self-evaluation of writing." Why do you think some of these have proved unsuccessful?

4. Some years ago it was popular to have "picture study" in the language arts. Small reproductions of great paintings were made available for each child. Why do you think the same idea might work as a stimulation of creative expression?

5. Few children will ever become authors or even reporters. Should a greater effort be made in the area of practical writing than in the area of creative writing?

How May the Writing of Poetry Be Fostered?

A teacher is an artist at releasing the creativity in others. Truly creative writing cannot be taught; it can only be released and guided. If we see our task as releasing and guiding poetic expression, certain conditions must be established. First, there must be a climate in which creative effort is fostered. This can be done by pointing out that certain expressions used by children are imaginative and contain poetic ideas. One day a child mentioned that the sun seemed to be playing peek-a-boo as it hid behind a cloud, then shone again. A comment that this would make a good poem may be enough to get the individual to write. A quiet place to write, away from the group, is another aspect of climate. Then when such expressions emerge the teacher might ask, "Would you like to go to the writing table and write a poem now while the idea is fresh?" A part of the climate in a room is represented by things valued. The fact that the teacher uses a poem as a central theme for a bulletin board, reads poems to the class with personal enjoyment, or sends a notice home in verse form makes poetry have significance. Second, the teacher provides stimulations that motivate the writer to get started. Sometimes these dramatize a feeling. One student teacher played a recording of a choir singing "The Battle Hymn of the Republic," then asked, "How would you express your thoughts if asked what the United States means to you?" One verse written under these conditions won a national award. Holidays act as punctuation marks in the humdrum repetition of living. Someone has said that one trouble with life was that it was "so doggone daily." When we make some days have special feeling in them it provides all of us with a bit of variety. Halloween, Thanksgiving, Valentine's Day, Mother's Day, and birthdays have emotional associations that stimulate writing.

In addition to a classroom climate that enhances poetry appreciation and personal motivation, the teacher releases creative talents by providing specific writing aids. This includes help with the mechanics of writing and spelling, the development of a vocabulary that expresses the right shade of meaning, and the understanding of poetic form. Before the children write Halloween poetry the class might discuss possible words to use. These would include *ghost, witch, haunting, creeping, scare, afraid*. With older children a rhyming dictionary is a great help. Occasionally after a poem has been enjoyed by the group, take time to look at it as one craftsman admires the work of another. The poem "Trees" can be studied in this way without diminishing its beauty. Notice the rhyme pattern. Then discuss the use of words. Why is "lovely" better than "pretty" in the second line? What image did the writer create by using the words "a nest of robins in her hair" and "lifts her leafy arms to pray"? Ask the group to think of similar images such as "finger chimneys pointing toward the sky" or "little cars pouting in the parking lot."

A combination of words and ideas must be brought together in order to create a poem. Some children are more talented with respect to words and ideas than others, but all children should be able to achieve this combination to a degree. The greater the command a child has over words and the more original or varied his ideas, the better will be the quality of the poetry he can create.

The temptation, then, would be to set up a series of lessons designed to build vocabulary and extend ideas. Before doing so it is well to consider the influence of patterns on creativity. Suppose we set up a series of exercises like this:

1. See the cat
   It wears a _____.
2. I have a bill
   It is from the _____.
3. This boy is tall
   He must be _____.
4. This girl is late
   She must be _____.

It would appear that the child *completed* a rhyme, but did he *create* one? At best he learned a small element of the poet's craft concerning words that rhyme.

Another type of exercise provides an idea in the form of a picture, usually of a nursery rhyme. One might be of "Jack and Jill," another of "Jack Be Nimble" or "Mistress Mary." Here again the emphasis is not on creativity, but on the pleasure of repeating familiar rhyme forms. Still another exercise provides lists of words that rhyme:

day	nice
hay	spice
old	mice
told	ice
ball	sail
tall	mail
wall	pail
all	whale
kitten	tree
mitten	see
bitten	free
written	bee

A suggested verse is given:

I threw a ball
High over the wall
And a boy named Jack
Threw it right back.

Although this is patterned, there is the possibility for a bit of original thinking and the satisfaction of completing a verse. Certainly the rhyme words influenced the idea. Instead of starting with a feeling or something to say, the child was assigned the task of manipulating the words of others. The results have little more emotional appeal than the original list of rhyming words.

Creativity from a child's point of view might be thought of as a personal interpretation of experience. The child might ask "What do certain sounds or sights mean to me? How do I feel when I see or do something? What words can I use that will help others re-create my feelings?"

One group of first-grade children was asked to think of favorite sounds. The following responses were typical:

The sound of nice music.
The sound of the recess bell.

But there were others more personal and possibly more creative:

The sounds my mother makes in the kitchen getting supper ready.
The sound of the slamming of the car door when my daddy comes home from work.

One of the charming books for and by children is a book of definitions of young children. The title is one of the definitions:

A Hole Is to Dig.[10] The definition of a principal is an appealing one: "A principal is to pull out splinters."

A third-grade class was fascinated by this book and decided to make some definitions of their own. "A desk is to clean up." "A penny is to lose." They were delighted when the comic strip "Peanuts" came up with: "Happiness is an A in spelling."

These definitions have the novelty of being functional rather than descriptive. They have an unexpected quality that lends charm to the language. They are probably not poetry, but poetic expression often has this element in it.

From the beginning it would be well to share with children poetry both with and without rhyme patterns. Help them discover the beauty or fun of an idea or word picture in a verse as well as the song of rhyme. "Fog" by Carl Sandburg is a good illustration of a poem without rhyme.

I do not want this to sound too complex to a beginning teacher. The caution with regard to patterns and their influence on creativity is only that there are some who would be more harsh in their criticism of this type of procedure. If you can proceed in no other way, then my suggestion is to use the devices you wish. I shall never forget a boy in a rural school I visited as a supervisor who finally completed this verse:

I know a boy whose name is Jack
His horse went away and never came back
So now he rides to school on the bus
And is no better than the rest of us.

I praised his effort and in good school teacher manner asked him to write it over in his best handwriting. The next week I had forgotten, but not Jack. There was the verse ready for me and another verse about "going to town and getting a coat that was brown." This continued throughout the year. Never did Jack produce a poem of the type teachers send in to be published. But what he did produce made life more interesting and satisfying for him. I suspect that one reason teachers get discouraged about writing poetry in the classroom is that most of the products

---

[10] Ruth Krause, *A Hole Is to Dig* (New York: Harper, 1952).

equal Jack's. As we consider the technique of writing poetry, it might be well to think how some of these suggestions might have helped a boy like Jack.

A type of pattern which is free from emphasis in rhyme would be of this nature:

Spring Music

Spring is a singing time,
Birds sing in the trees,

. . . .

. . . .

And I sing too.

The Feel of Things

I like the feel of things,
The softness of pussy willows,
The smoothness of velvet.

. . . . .

. . . . .

I like the feel of things.

Children sense the meter of poetry and eventually will want to write with this in mind. The teacher might put a line on the board and have the class count the beats one would hear if each syllable had equal emphasis.

The man in the moon looked down

— — — — — — —

Then the class experiments with lines like the following and decides which sounds best:

Upon the sleeping little town.
Upon the laughing happy clown.
To see the children gay and brown
To see that snow had fallen over hill and town.

Then they take some words they know and note how these words have similar points of emphasis:

altogether	player
manufacture	remember
tangerine	suggestion
doorkeeper	happiness
pleasant	

This can be changed with the usual markings for accented and unaccented syllables in poetry:

altogether becomes __ __ __′ __
remember becomes __ __′ __

Then note that when some poetry is written some words appear as unaccented syllables. If you say the words *ta* for unaccented and *tum* for the accented syllable you can note the meter of a poem.

Then the little Hiawatha (or tum ta tum ta tum
   ta tum ta)
Said unto the old Nakomis
All the hills are edged with valleys

Writing words for songs emphasizes meter. One student-teacher interested a group of below-average sixth-grade children in writing by using Calypso music. After explaining that the singer made up his song as he went along, the class tried to write "songs." These were the results:

I got a donkey he's a big and fat,
He sits on a pillow and the pillow goes flat.
My donkey, he's a good for nothing beast
Cause he takes all my food for his Sunday feast.
                                                    MAXINE

One class listened to a recorded reading of translations of famous Japanese Haiku.

The ideas of suggestion, emphasized in the last line, and imagery were captured by the children who wrote these lines at the Hunter School in Fairbanks, Alaska.

The boy turned to me
And he smiled with a cute grin.
I did the same thing.

Big Indian Chief
You are brave but very dumb.
Let people rule too!

I hate dogs a lot.
They bark when someone walks by,
Especially me.

I left Alaska, but on the way
I saw purple mountains
And turned back.

A cry is heard. All is still
A pack of wolves
Has made its kill. . . Silence.

The morning sun
Chasing night shadows
Across the awakening world.

The pattern of a haiku poem consists of three lines, the first having five syllables, the second line seven, and the third line five.

Since the syllable in English differs from the Japanese it is not always possible to follow this pattern.

Cinquains have much of the same effect in English. The first line has five words and each succeeding line one less:

The white waves bite at
the sandy ocean shore
like a hungry
child eating
cookies.

or starting with only four words, one gets this result:

The empty house stands
among dead grass
lonely and
still

A purpose for each line will add dimension to a cinquain:

First line—one word giving the title.
Second line—two words describing the title.
Third line—three words expressing an action.
Fourth line—four words expressing a feeling.
Fifth line—another word for the title.

Poetic thought does not depend upon rhyme. These two selections appeared in the *Albuquerque Public Schools Journal* of March 1970.

I have a tree
With a bee
I love the tree
My friend does too.
                    DEMMY VIRGIL, First Grade, Chapparal

I went to the waterfalls cold and sly,
I waded myself past knee high.
I went to the waterfalls cold and sly,
And I waded through streams of pretty foam.

By then I was tired,
Climbing up paths,
Climbing log bridges,
Sliding down sand,
Venturing through groves,

Watching stick boats
Go through one hole
And come out another.

But by and by we went away,
Away from the falls
And all of the play.
                    KRISTINA HOLM, Fourth Grade, Osuna

A Room Full of Scary Thoughts

It's a stormy night,
All the lights in the house are out
My room is very dark, and suddenly,
I'm alone!

Tall plants and furniture form figures
against the shadow of the blinds.

The rain falling sounds like a million
fingers tapping on my window—as if they want
*   me to let them in.*

Lights from cars flash through my blinds onto
the wall, and, as the cars move, flashing of the
*   lights*
moves from wall to wall as small ghosts.

And I quickly sit my head up and then
sit it back down.

Then suddenly, the storm dies down and the
sound of cars splashing water in the streets
*   seems so close, but it's really quite far.*

And I sit up in my bed, turn on the light and
realize that I'm in a room full of scary thoughts.
                    ANNA BAIN, Fifth Grade, Inez

The Clown

Enter the chief clown:
Shouting the age-old line,
"Is everybody happy?"
It used to be that
The audience would answer,
*   "Yes!"*
But now many reply
with a violent,
*   "No!"*
Soon there won't
be any clowns left.
                    KEN STAHL, Ninth Grade, Jefferson

Rather than have children start with such a complex task as writing verses about how they feel or things they saw, some teachers prefer to start with group composition.

A second-grade teacher once asked her children to think of quiet things. As each child made a suggestion she wrote it on the chalkboard. This was the result: [11]

As quiet as snow falling
As quiet as butter melting
As quiet as a cloud in the sky
As quiet as a kitten
As soap bubbles
A tree growing
Santa Claus coming
As quiet as you and I

The children knew that they had created a mood because of the hush in the room. Such experiences can be a step toward individual effort.

A method of writing that will give everyone a sense of participation is the word-stimulus method. The teacher asks the pupils to get ready for a surprise. First assure the children that this is not a test and that the papers will be ungraded.

"I am going to tell you a word," the teacher continues, "and you are to write the picture that comes to your mind. You may tell what you see, hear, feel or imagine. Just tell me the picture that you see in your imagination. Spell as well as you can, we will get the exact spelling later." Then she gives a word like rain, sunshine, baby, wind, spring, or night.

After the children have finished writing, the papers are collected. Now these individual efforts are assembled into a group poem. This is called a mosaic poem, or cumulative composition, because, like a mosaic painting, it is made from many parts. First the closely related ideas are grouped. One stanza might contain those about gentle rain, another about violent storms, another about the blessings of rain. These are put together with some rearrangement of word order but with no effort to rhyme. Then the class usually has to add several lines at the bottom that create a conclusion.

The following account by Samuel Gilburt, Principal of The William J. Morrison Junior High School, Brooklyn, New York, gives this

---

[11] Based on an experience of Eileen Birch, Campus Laboratory School, San Diego State College, San Diego, Calif.

interesting account of group poetry with older children: [12]

When I use the *cooperative technique* in the classroom, I devote the first lesson to the playing of records. I select songs with strong rhythmic undertones such as *"Surrey with the Fringe on Top"* from *Oklahoma!;* Burl Ives' *"Rock Candy Mountain";* an American folk dance, "Golden Slippers." I encourage the pupils to tap out the rhythm with fingers or to clap. It is rough on the teacher's nervous system sometimes, but I have an aim. It does relax the class. They "let go" inwardly and become much more receptive.

I follow up with Vachel Lindsay's "Congo," Masefield's "Sea Fever," and Kipling's "Boots." These are records supplied by the National Council of Teachers of English with readings superbly done by Norman Corwin. As "Boots" is played, I ask for volunteers to march up and down the aisles in rhythm to the poem. The dullest pupil in the class eventually is aroused to a sensitivity to rhythm and thus grasps the simplest aspect of poetry. Now he is ready to feel and enjoy rhythm, and I suggest he try marching.

I follow up with recordings of Tennyson's "Break, Break, Break," Browning's "Boot and Saddle," and Lanier's "Song of the Chattahoochee."

In ensuing lessons, I read in my best orotund manner: "Casey at the Bat," "The Charge of the Light Brigade," or Poe's "The Bells." "The Barrel-Organ" by Noyes and Psalms XXIV and XLVI are rendered by the class chorally. Poetry was meant to be read aloud and heard.

We talk about rhythm in nature—the seasons, night and day. The pupils tell me about rhythm in "boogie-woogie" and "bebop." They bring in their own records and favorite poems. Edgar Guest gets a square deal in my room.

I explain that poetry is far from "sissy stuff." John Masefield was a tough sailor. Joyce Kilmer and Rupert Brook were topnotch soldiers. Sandburg was a truck-driver. We chat about crowbars and steel spikes and we study "Prayers of Steel." I play Corwin's reading of "Fog" and "Lost," and the class reads with him, softly and lingeringly, absorbing the mood and sound pictures.

We play and sing "Trees," "Road to Mandalay," "Drink to Me Only with Thine Eyes."

[12] S. G. Gilburt, "Cooperative Poetry—A Creative Project," *Language Arts News* (Fall 1957).

The class understands by now that songs are poems put to music. We even discuss popular songs and decide whether the lyrics are good or bad. The pupils gradually develop yardsticks of judgment. They select any one poem they enjoyed most for memory purposes.

Throughout, I emphasize the fun, the enjoyment, the movement and the zest of poetry. The feeling for poetry is caught—not taught. The rhythmic exercises, the choral reading, the musical aspects all make for an emotional climate of relaxed interest. These emotional tones, frequently repeated, are associated with poetry and should be retained by the pupil.

By now, the class is eating out of my hand and I come to cooperative writing.

I have had functioning all along in connection with an integrated unit on descriptive writing, a smell committee, a sound committee, a taste committee, etc., who had been compiling actual advertisements from magazines that best reflected these senses in writing. I read Morley's "Smells" or "Swift Things Are Beautiful" by Elizabeth Coatsworth and then invite each pupil to write but *one similar line* on the subject of "Noises." In a few minutes I call on the pupils to read their lines. The class either accepts the line as good, or suggests improvements such as a more picturesque word or phrase. As each pupil's line is accepted, the pupil goes up to the board and proudly writes his line.

A volunteer is alerted to write a brief introduction, another to write a concluding stanza while the class is still working on the body of the class poem. The group composition that follows was turned out in one forty-five-minute period, with a supervisor observing the lesson. We were caught a little short by the bell, hence the weak ending which was not polished up, marring an otherwise interesting piece of work by an average eighth-grade class.

Noises We Like

Most people hate noises,
But a few like them indeed,
Howling, screaming, clicking,
Crying, laughing, walking
These noises some people need.
These be noises one class likes!
The crack of the bat on the first day of spring,
The click of the camera shutter,
The scratch of a pen when writing to a friend,
My dog's bark when he comes to meet me,
The breaking of Rockaway waves at the beach,
The ticking of a clock old and dear,

The beating of drums at a parade,
The tap-tapping of a long wanted typewriter,
The backfiring of a car and the shot of a gun,
The clatter of hoof-beats in the city's streets,
The hoot of a train whistle coming round the
*   bend,*
The crunching of a dollar and the jingling of a
*   coin,*
The light pitter-pat of the rain against the pane,
The chitter-chatter of people in the street,
The gurgle of a baby in the cradle,
The chirp of the sparrows around a crust of
*   bread,*
The thump of my heart at report card time,
Roller skates whizzing along pavement streets,
The sound of electricity when I comb my hair,
The crashing and slashing of lightning to earth,
The hiss of a radiator on a cold winter day,
The crackling of an autumn bonfire,
The moo of cows grazing in the field,
The words of a baby who has just begun to talk,
The dancing ivory under the fingers of a
*   "boogie" player.*
Hundreds of other noises
Can be acclaimed
But hundreds of others
Cannot possibly be named.

Meanings experienced through poetry call for personal and individual responses. The deep feeling that one person senses in a sentence may be missed by another. We do not seek to have children write a verse in order to please the teacher, to get a good grade, or to participate in a program. Our purpose is to help children discover in poetry some inner satisfaction that is an intimate personal experience. In one fifth-grade room in which a creative climate had been established, a student went to the writer's table and after about fifteen minutes produced the following poem: [13]

A Question to God

When did the first tree start to grow?
When did the first breeze sing so low?
When did the first bird spread his wings?
When was the start of everything?

When did the first little humming bird hum?
When did the first little creek start to run?

When did the first snow start to fall?
When did the first little cricket call?

When did the first star light the night?
When did the first flower come into sight?
When did the first sunset glow?
When did the first little thing grow?

Oh God, when was the first faintest sound?
When was the beautiful earth made round?
Even though we may never know,
I thank you God, for things made so.
SUSAN TUCKER

The children in the class recognized that this was a superior poem. Some might have stopped writing because they felt unequal to creating material of this quality, but instead of establishing the poem as a standard, the child was praised and honored—much as we praise outstanding musical or athletic talent.

Deserved praise is an important aspect of encouraging children to write. Expect them to present a tremendous range of quality but encourage each child as he creates at his appropriate level.

An equally important aspect is time to write. Providing a quiet time during the course of the week when children may choose to write or read will reward the teacher with worthy contributions. Occasionally this time has to be scheduled, but often it will have to be taken from some other activity. Sometimes the weather is a deciding factor. During a winter snow when the flakes are sinking slowly to earth or just after a spring rain when every object appears clean-washed would be excellent occasions for such work. The teacher might say, "Let's have a quiet period now. You may read or write. We will tune in on thirty minutes of silence."

Children like to write poetry in areas that have emotional appeal. Here are some examples:

1. Gripes and Protests

To the Boy That Sits in Front of Me
You think that you are funny
You think that you're the best

---

[13] Reported by Margaret Brydegaard, Fifth Grade Supervisor, Campus Laboratory School, San Diego State College, San Diego, Calif.

You think that you're a honey
While you're really just a pest.

In arithmetic you're terrible
In reading you're a dunce
And when you talk the teacher must
Remind you more than once!
        MERRY LEE TASH, GRADE 5

Hobbies

They tell me that a hobby
Is to help us make the day
To seem a little shorter
And to pass the time away.

But our teachers seem to think
That we have nothing else to do
But to get one of these hobbies
And then write about it too.

They load us up with homework
And then they go and say,
"Children, you need a hobby
To pass the time away."

"Get yourself a hobby"
That's what the teacher said,
Dear teacher, we need hobbies
Like we need holes in the head.

So when we turn in papers
That don't quite meet perfection—
Don't be angry when we say,
"We are building our collection."
        MERRY LEE TASH, GRADE 7

2. Personal Experiences

After School

I'm staying after school again.
This is an awful mess;
I might as well get down to work
'Til I can leave I guess.
Let's see, arithmetic's all done,
And so is reading work,
(Just think ME staying after school!
I sure feel like a jerk.)
I could improve my writing,
Oh no, I'd just hate that,
If I could just get out of here
I'd gladly eat my hat,
I guess it's just what I deserve
For acting like a fool,
But you won't catch me here again
Staying after school!
        SILAS, GRADE 6

Cookies

Measure
  Sift
    Beat
Cut
  Cook
    Eat.
        VERNON, FIRST GRADE (DICTATED)

3. Wonders

Grass

Green and soft and sweet,
Grass is glistening

Lying on warm grass
I feel relaxed and lazy

With an ant's small size
Grass is probably a kind of jungle.
        JANE, AGE 10

4. "If I Were" Poems or Flights of Imagination

If I were a star on the top of the tree,
On Christmas night, here's what I'd see:

Angels and candles, tinsel and balls,
Bright lights and bells and Santa Claus;
Popcorn and long red cranberry strings,
Chains of paper—both red and green.

And if I look closely—I'll take my chances—
I see tiny packages tied to the branches.

Around the tree, all over the floor
Are lots of packages—and there's more—
A train, a bike, a doll, a bat,
A DOG? A puppy—imagine that!!

5. Special Days

Dear Mom

Long years ago, someone decided
That the second Sunday in the month of May,
Should be a day for the women
Who have taught and guided
Their children. Yes, a Mother's Day!
In return for years of dedication
And love and devotion that has never abated;
One day set apart for the mom's of the nation
To show them that they are appreciated.

The gift we give you is modest indeed,
But with this gift is planted the seed
Of a prayer of hope for this family
To spend the next year in harmony.

For all of us know that there is no other
To take the place of you, our mother.
MERRY LEE TASH, GRADE 8

There are others: wishes, surprises, questions, poems "to my doll or dog." But there is one more that should receive special consideration. Sometimes we forget that each child must discover anew the wonders of our world. It is a stimulating experience to watch a group of city boys and girls discovering the beauties of the outdoors in a summer camp. I watched a camp director lead a group that rediscovered the place where the Indians long ago had obtained the clay they used in pottery making. Then as the group rested he asked them to be still and notice what was happening around them. Imaginations were filled with Indians, of course, but these boys and girls looked at the trees, the brook, the clay bank, the birds and squirrels in a new way. Then the leaders asked them how they might share this experience with others. Some sketched the scene, others wrote descriptive letters, but many wrote poems.

The following situation reveals a similar experience of a boy rediscovering the familiar:

Have You Ever Sat on the Shore of a Harbor?

Have you ever sat on the shore of a harbor
And watched the seagulls play?
It's really very interesting
More fun than studying, I'd say.

Have you ever sat on the shore of a harbor
And watched the freighters sway,
Then listened to their whistles
And watched them sail away?
Have you ever sat on the shore of a harbor
And listened to a fog-horn blow,
And wondered where the fog came from
And when and where it will go?

Have you ever watched the sun go down
And have you seen the waves roll in,
Then have you ever wondered,
"When did this all begin?"
BROOKE, GRADE 7

If we accept as our responsibility the releasing of the talents and abilities of the students, there are some teaching practices which should be considered. One does not put a grade on a poem created by a child. Even an evaluative remark such as "Very Good" is not appropriate. It would be much more helpful to the writer to receive guidance and encouragement in other ways. A comment such as "What a novel idea. I never would have thought of that!" or "I can *feel* the snow" indicates the response that a creative talent needs. But young talent will welcome help as well, "instead of *flat* what do you think of the word *level?*" or, "try *inviting* in place of *nice.*" Such comments must be given as suggestions. If the writer accepts them because he feels he must, it can destroy the joy of being creative.

Praise is powerful if it causes continuous growth. Point out the strength of a creative effort. At first teachers are so pleased to get any completed work that a low level of expectancy can be established by excessive praise. The expressions "Your first line is especially good," or "The words *lonely lullaby* create a good sound and feeling" give praise to the points of best quality.

Two major faults of children's poetry call for special attention. A child may start with a good idea, then come to a dull thump of an ending just to get something that rhymes.

As I looked up at the sky
I saw some planes go flying by
And as I walked home to rest
There came a plane from the west.

After children have achieved some security in the writing of verse it is well to discuss this problem. Encourage them to write non-rhyming poetry until they have discovered how to use many of the aids available such as rhyming dictionaries and a thesaurus.

The second fault is that of writing parodies on familiar verse. It is fun to write parodies when this is the purpose of writing, but the following is questionable as creative poetry. Call it a parody. Then help the child use his idea in a more original form.

I think that I shall never see
An airplane tiny as a bee

A plane that may in summer fly
Into a piece of apple pie.

Closely related to this problem is that of the child who hands in something not his own. Little children sometimes get the idea that the task is to write any poem, rather than one of their own creation. Some misguided older person helps them and they show up with "Roses are red, violets are blue," etc. When this happens, remember there is no moral issue involved. The child wanted to please. You might say, "That is a cute verse but it has been written before. I think you can write one that no one has ever heard." Or the teacher might suggest, "Maybe instead of writing a poem you could draw a picture or cartoon of your idea." And the teacher might ask herself if she has made poetry writing a bit too important for the present time if children feel pressured to do this type of thing to gain approbation.

Nearly all children and many adults write rhymes and doggerel that have few poetic qualities. As they listen to great poetry read and grow in appreciation, their writing will reflect the appreciation they have developed. Consumers of poetry are needed as well as writers. Crude efforts produced by experimentation with rhyme may increase a person's awareness of the skill of other poets.

Releasing poetic expression for some who have little inherent talent should not become a challenging burden to the teacher. The object is to release the talent in those so endowed so that all may be enriched by sharing their contributions. Our task is done if we help all to develop this talent to some degree and those gifted in this area to achieve expression in quality that is worthy of them.

For Discussion

1. Assume that you have been selected to judge some children's poetry for a contest sponsored by a local radio station. What basic criteria would you establish to guide your judgment?

2. Collect five poems to enhance a child's concept of seeing or hearing things.

3. Collect five poems that primary children might respond to with rhythm or movement.

4. Poetry might enhance a theme such as a season, rain, the joy of living, protest. Find two or more themes that might be used for poetic expression.

How May Literature Be Used to Influence Written Composition?

In recent years there has been a return to an old practice of using examples from literature to encourage writing by students. At one time students imitated the sentences of Sir Walter Scott or Charles Dickens. Such exercises do influence students who identify with authors and who wish to acquire the disciplines of authorship. Like a knowledge of grammar, the knowledge of plot structure or technique of description and characterization can be useful to some young writers.

We do not know if children grow in ability more from writing a fable than from "writing a story." We do not know if an awareness of story line helps the young writer any more than his intuitive imitation of favorite story patterns. Teachers who are trained in the discipline of English and who believe that simple elements of the discipline should be taught to children frequently gain good results with a planned formal series of lessons on specific writing techniques. Other teachers equally well trained gain impressive results through programs which encourage the child to write creatively without starting with analysis of specific forms. In order to contrast the practice it is necessary to consider the extremes.

Dr. Eldonna L. Everts suggests this procedure with respect to a fable.[14]

May Hill Arbuthnot equates writing an original fable to a mathematical procedure. She suggests selecting some animal character and a moral such as, "Pride goeth before a fall." If a rabbit is chosen, he cannot be a well-rounded

---

[14] Alexander Frazier, *New Directions in Elementary English* (Champaign, Ill.: National Council of Teachers of English, 1967), pp. 216–17.

individual with only one weakness; rather, he must be all weakness—and in this case the weakness is *pride*. So the mathematical equation becomes: Proud Rabbit + X (single episode) = Pride goeth before a fall. The writer must solve for X by finding an episode to explain the moral.

Teachers who wish to experiment with fables in their classrooms will find these seven steps for presentation and writing of fables helpful:

1. Read many fables scattered throughout several months.
2. Review the easier fables and those liked by the children. Write the lesson or moral on the chalk board.
3. List other lessons on the chalk board which could appear in a fable.
4. Select one lesson from either group of morals and write a fable together in class.
5. Let pupils select a lesson or moral from these on the board or suggest a new moral and tell how a story or fable could present the idea.
6. Let pupils work in groups or committees and write fables with one of the group acting as secretary or scribe. Go over the fables together in class.
7. Let pupils write their own fables after selecting a moral.

These steps should not be compressed into a tight time pattern but should be extended over a period of time since learning to write fables requires both experience with that type of literature and the development of the intellectual discipline to stay within the form.

The fable which follows illustrates the first type of fable plot pattern. The characters are flat and impersonal, and no one regrets the fate of the lazy chicken. Like most simple fables, this composition by a fourth grade pupil is brief, involving a single incident, and the ending is expected and justifiable. The originality found in other types of writing is not often found in a fable because the form is restricting and the content is prescribed by the moral.

Once there was a chicken who, even though chickens get up early, this chicken did not. She liked to sleep late in the morning. But her friends who got up early, got the best food. And one day the farmer who owned this chicken was discouraged with this chicken. "She never gets up early, or lays good eggs, or eats good food," said the farmer very discouraged. So the next Sunday that little chicken was on the farmer's plate.

Moral: Laziness does not pay off.

The second fable was also written by a fourth grade boy after a number of fables had been studied in class. Note that the young writer has developed a clear, concise plot and has concluded with a moral.

The Woodsman and the Hawk

There was once a woodsman who lived alone in a little hut.

One day he was out in front of his hut when all of a sudden he heard two things at once, a hawk screaming and gunfire. He looked around. All of a sudden he happened to hear some flapping of wings. He looked down. There beside him was a panting hawk. The hawk said breathlessly, "Please kind sir, could you help me; a couple of dogs and a hunter are chasing me. Do you have a place to hide me?" "Why of course I do. Go into the hut and eat as much meat from my dog's bowl as you want. But come out when I tell you." In a few minutes the hunter and his two dogs came by the hut. The hunter asked, "Have you seen a hawk in the sky or on the ground around here?" "No, I haven't," he said, but as the woodsman said these words he winked his eye and pointed towards the hut. Anyhow the hunter did not see these signs, and so went on. When the hunter was out of sight the woodsman told the hawk to come out. The hawk went on its way without saying a word. The woodsman asked, "Why do you go without thanking me for what I have done?" The hawk turned around and said, "I saw what you did as you said those words." Adding to that, he said, "The tongue can be as sly as the hand."

One text, *Composition Through Literature,* approaches the teaching of all written work as well as the study of grammar through literature. Following a selection from *Tales of the Arabian Nights* by Charlotte Dixon the text provides this discussion: [15]

Exaggeration in Stories

How exaggerated was the account of the trip? You have heard stories exaggerated to the point of ridicule. Too much enlargement becomes ridiculous. But certain types are enjoyable.

---

[15] H. T. Fillmer and others, *Composition Through Literature,* Book C (about grades 5–6) (New York: American Book, 1967), pp. 74–76.

Exercise A

The quoted statements or word groups came from the story. Would you accept them as facts or as exaggerations? Explain your answer.

1. The egg "had a circumference of about fifty feet."
2. "I found myself in a hollow surrounded by huge mountains."
3. Its foot "was as thick as a tree-trunk."
4. The snakes "could easily have swallowed an elephant."

Exercise B

Tell in your own words the difference between creating an imaginative story and exaggerating a story in its retelling.

Exercise C

From what you can recall, tell with what each of the following was compared:

1. the bird's shadow
2. the large egg
3. the shining stones
4. the length of trees

Steps in Your Story

Even in very imaginative stories, the events must be kept in order. If you have to retrace your steps, the reader becomes confused and his interest lags.

Exercise A

The following events of the story you have just read are not in sequence. Put them in step-by-step order.

The ship landed on a deserted island.
His escape from the island was effected by tying himself to the foot of a huge bird.
Sindbad grew restless in Baghdad and decided to set out on a second journey.
He hid in a cave where he remained all night, too frightened to sleep.
Sindbad decided to picnic on the island and do some investigating of the land.
The bird dropped him in a valley of snakes.
Then he discovered a means of escape from the valley.
He fell asleep and on wakening, found the ship had pulled out without him.
Finally, he arrived back in Baghdad.
He found and collected many diamonds in the valley.

Exercise B

The translator of the story made a number of comparisons, such as "feet as thick as tree-trunks," "snakes as long as trees," and the globe "felt like soft silk." The following comparisons are worn out. Use your imagination and write a fresh comparison for each one.

1. dead as a doornail
2. sick as a dog
3. pretty as a picture
4. clear as a bell
5. smart as a whip
6. cool as a cucumber

Exercise C

In the story you found the expression "out of the frying pan into the fire." You know its meaning: jump from one troublesome situation into an even worse one. Write a sentence in which you express each of the following in a straight-forward way:

1. get down to brass tacks
2. chip off the old block
3. snake in the grass
4. calm before the storm
5. hit the nail on the head

Writing Your Story

It's time to put your imagination to work in a story.

First, select a title and when you write it, be sure to capitalize the first, last, and all important words.

Second, decide how you will reach the place you wish to visit—by train, plane, ship, or any way you like.

Third, decide how many events your story will cover. Plan one paragraph for each event.

Fourth, conclude your story with an account of your return trip.

The Writing Assignment

Write your story with as much imagination as possible. Remember to keep the events in order, each one leading into the next. Bring the story to a climax with your return trip. Use some exaggeration if you like, but keep it within limits. If you cannot think at the moment of a place you would like to visit, consider one of the following suggestions:

A Journey to Shangrila
A Journey to the Bottom of the Sea
A Journey to the Land of Elephants

A Journey to Hobbitland
A Journey to the Moon
A Journey to the North Pole

A recent fourth-grade textbook uses this approach from literature to write a descriptive paragraph: [16]

Variations in Prose

Now that you have read how three poets expressed their feelings about fall, see how four different authors write about the same theme in prose. Each author sets a mood for the changing of the seasons from summer to fall.

The first description of autumn comes from *Farmer Boy* by Laura Ingalls Wilder.

> Now the harvest moon shone round and yellow over the fields at night, and there was a frosty chill in the air. All the corn was cut and stood in tall shocks. The moon cast their black shadows on the ground where the pumpkins lay naked above their withered leaves.
>
> In the beech grove all the yellow leaves had fallen. They lay thick on the ground beneath the slim trunks and delicate bare limbs of the beeches. The beechnuts had fallen after the leaves and lay on top of them. Father and Royal lifted the matted leaves carefully on their pitchforks and put them, nuts and all, into the wagon. And Alice and Almanzo ran up and down in the wagon, trampling down the rustling leaves to make room for more.
>
> When the wagon was full, Royal drove away with Father to the barns, but Almanzo and Alice stayed to play till the wagon came back.
>
> A chill wind was blowing and the sunlight was hazy. Squirrels frisked about, storing away nuts for the winter. High in the sky the wild ducks were honking, hurrying south. It was a wonderful day for playing wild Indian, all among the trees.
>
> LAURA INGALLS WILDER

In *My Side of the Mountain,* Jean George expresses her view of the changing seasons.

> September blazed a trail into the mountains. First she burned the grasses. The grasses seeded and were harvested by the mice and the winds.
>
> Then she sent the squirrels and chip-

munks running boldly through the forest, collecting and hiding nuts.

> Then she gathered the birds together in flocks, and the mountaintop was full of songs and twitterings and flashing wings. The birds were ready to move to the south.
>
> JEAN GEORGE

How have Jean George and Laura Ingalls Wilder differed in their descriptions of squirrels gathering nuts and birds flying south? Which is more appealing to you? Why?

Notice how Majorie Kinnan Rawlings pays particular attention to the changing weather in her description of fall from *The Yearling.*

> The first heavy frost came at the end of November. The leaves of the big hickory at the north end of the clearing turned as yellow as butter. The sweet gums were yellow and red and the blackjack thicket across the road from the house flamed with a red as bright as a campfire. The grapevines were golden and the sumac was like oak embers. The October blooming of dog-fennel and sea-myrtle had turned to a feathery fluff. The days came in, cool and crisp, warmed to a pleasant slowness, and chilled again. The Baxters sat in the evening in the front room before the first hearth-fire.
>
> MARJORIE KINNAN RAWLINGS

Pay close attention to the way that Virginia Sorensen describes the colors of the trees in this selection from *Miracles on Maple Hill.*

> You would think Maple Mountain was on fire.
>
> In every direction the trees were red and yellow. When the sun struck them suddenly, flying through windy clouds, the brightness was almost more than Marley could bear. The redness seemed to come from inside each tree in a wonderful way; it was the red she saw through her hand when she held it against the sun. The yellowness glistened like golden hair, and the wind shook it, and bits of gold spun down upon the grass.
>
> What a lovely world! Every morning on Maple Hill, Marley woke in the very middle of a scarlet and golden miracle.
>
> VIRGINIA SORENSEN

Read the descriptions again to look for techniques the authors have used to present their observations about fall.

1. Which senses do the four writers appeal to?
2. What are some of the sensory words and phrases you especially like?

---

[16] Muriel Crosby and others, *The World of Language,* Book 4 (Chicago: Fullett, 1970), pp. 275–77.

3. Take your senses to an imaginary spring picnic or a summer barbecue. Use pantomime to show what you see, hear, smell, taste, and touch.

4. How does fall come to the city? Think of images that will re-create the sights, sounds, tastes, smells, and feel of a city autumn. Build these images into a descriptive paragraph.

Literature is evidence of the success that some individuals have achieved through written composition. As a child identifies with the authors of fine books the knowledge of technique used will influence his reading and writing. It is possible for an overemphasis upon literary form and analysis to be a block to effective writing and reading. Instead of communicating with the thought of the material the student might become so involved with analyzing how the task is done that what is being said becomes secondary. With this caution in mind many teachers will find that children's interest in great writing can motivate their desire to grow in written communication.

For Discussion

1. Is there some value in having a child paraphrasing great writing as one might memorize a favorite poem?

2. Why do some teachers feel that enrichment requires children in the elementary school to do something that was formerly taught in high school?

3. The national poetry day is October 15. Plan a school assembly program for this occasion.

4. A "Junior Author's Tea" sponsored by a school is an annual event in El Cajon, Calif. At such a tea should only the "books" written by those especially talented be displayed? Should awards be made? How would you plan such an event?

How Are Children Taught to Make Reports and Keep Records?

Informal reporting of information and observation, and discussion of this information in small or large groups play major roles in the activities of children. Later these oral expressions may be put into written form. Young children have a need for some written records as they plan together. As the experiences of children grow in complexity, more detailed plans must be made, and children will have further needs for records and reports.

Until such time as children attain sufficient skill in handwriting, the teacher records the information for the group. Later she transfers this information to charts or booklets. Children may then read the written record when they need to review the steps in specific processes, or simply for the pleasure of reliving the experience.[17]

Making Butter

We put cream in a jar. We shook it a long time. Little yellow lumps of butter came to the top.

We poured the buttermilk out and drank it. We washed the butter and tasted it. It needed salt. We added salt. We put it in a mold.

We ate butter on crackers. It was delicious!

There are numerous occasions when children are helped to make simple records. They record:

The growth of a plant
The date
The daily weather
The daily temperature
The changing appearance of the polliwogs
The days the fish are fed
Monthly height and weight
The number of children present each day

Children enjoy watching the teacher record interesting daily events.

News
Today is Monday.
It is a sunny day.
We are going on a walk.
We will look for wild flowers.
Billy brought a horned toad for us to see.

[17] San Bernardino County Schools: *Arts and Skills of Communication for Democracy's Children,* San Bernardino, Calif., 1954, is the source of many examples given here.

One group of children carefully recorded the number of days it took for the eggs of the praying mantis to hatch. They recorded:

> Ralph found a green bug.
> It looks like a grasshopper, but it is not a grasshopper.
> It is a praying mantis.

Later, they recorded:

> Our praying mantis laid some eggs.
> It laid them on December 20, 1952.
> Then it died.
> We are counting the days until the eggs hatch.

After listening to a story, seeing a film or filmstrip, taking a trip, or talking with a resource person, children may wish to record information. As they list the information in the order of occurrence, they gain an understanding of sequence.

After they had seen a filmstrip about the truck farmer, one group recorded:

> Jobs of a Truck Farmer
>
> The truck farmer plows the soil.
> He plants the seeds.
> He irrigates the plants.
> He sprays the plants.
> He harvests the crops.
> He sells the produce to a wholesale market.

Children often record individual and group plans for ready reference. The teacher guides the discussion and helps children decide which suggestions will be most helpful. Later, she places these plans on charts for future reference:

> How We Clean Up
> How We Use Our Tools
> How We Go on a Trip
> How We Share Together
> How We Work Together

Children are helped to organize their thinking by listing questions, recording tentative solutions, testing solutions, and arriving at conclusions. Many of these problems arise in the social studies and related science activities. Problems such as the following may develop after dramatic play:

We Need to Find Out

> How the gasoline station gets its gasoline
> How the groceries get to the store
> How people get money from the bank
> What do trucks bring to the community

After a group of children had taken a trip to the wholesale bakery, they set up the problem:

> What makes bread dough rise?

As children suggested answers to the problem, the teacher recorded their ideas.

JOHN: Because of the warm sun shining on the dough.

SUSAN: Because of the way the baker beats the dough.

SAM: Because of the things that are mixed in the dough.

JEAN: Because of the kind of pan the baker uses for the dough.

This list of suggested answers was held tentative by the group until they could arrive at valid conclusions. The group performed a simple experiment which helped to dismiss the incorrect assumptions and to identify the valid conclusion. They dictated the following story, telling how their final conclusions were reached:

What Makes Bread Dough Rise?

We wanted to find out what makes bread dough rise.

We took two bowls. We mixed flour and water in one bowl.

We mixed flour, water, and yeast in another bowl.

We took turns beating and stirring the dough in each bowl.

Some of us beat fast and hard. Some of us beat slowly.

We poured the dough from each bowl into two bowls.

The bowls were the same shape and size.

We put the bowls in the sunshine on a table by the window.

Then we went out to recess.

When we came back to the room, we looked at the dough.

We saw that the dough in one bowl was spilling over the edge.

The dough in the other bowl was just as we had left it.

Now we know why bread dough rises. Why? Because there is yeast in the dough!

Girls and boys often wish to record the experiences they have shared or special information they have gained from study trips, special classroom activities, films, filmstrips, or visits of resource people. As children discuss the events which they will include in their story, the teacher guides the group in determining proper sequence, in selecting contributions which best describe the situation, and in choosing words and phrases which are colorful and descriptive.

A group of six-year-olds had carefully watched two caterpillars as each became a chrysalis and later emerged as a "mourning cloak" or purplish-brown butterfly. The teacher put captions near the jar, changing them at appropriate intervals. She recorded the children's observations as they watched this sequence of events. Later the children discussed all that had taken place from the first day the caterpillars were brought to their room until the beautiful butterflies emerged. The teacher recorded the following story as the group recalled the experience. She helped the children recall the events in sequential order by referring to the changing captions and to the comments the children had made during the past weeks. Later, the group delighted in hearing their story read back to them.

Our Caterpillars

There were two caterpillars eating geraniums when we found them. They were soft and black, and had real pretty spots on them.

We put the caterpillars and some geraniums into a big jar. We gave them fresh leaves to eat.

One day one made a house. He sort of knitted with his head. He shook it up and down, and up and down. Then he went sideways and up and down. We thought he would get dizzy and fall, but he didn't. Pretty soon he had a brownish, grayish colored house without any door and windows.

The other one made a house too, but he made it when we were not looking. Both houses hung down from the geranium.

After a long time, one moth came out. He sat real still and looked at the jar and every-thing. After recess he was wiggling his wings. The next day he flew in the jar. By the next afternoon the other moth came out.

They were just alike. Maybe they will be a mother and daddy. They visited together. They were pretty black velvet with pretty yellow trimming on the wings. The spots made the trimming maybe. Anyway it's the same color.

We brought them flowers and leaves. They might lay some eggs and then we'd have lots of moths. We are going to keep them a long time to see. They seem to be happy.

The moths didn't live so very long, but we will still keep them.

Shorter stories may be recorded on the chalkboard and later placed on charts.

As children gain in the ability to write down factual experiences, they begin recording their own stories. To the extent that they project their own personalities into their writing, their stories become more than simply stated facts and a recording of information. These stories become creative as they take on the unique character that is distinct to the child who is the writer. As in all other forms of independently written expression, girls and boys are given all the help they need to set down their thoughts with ease.

Jo Ann wrote:

Our Trip

We went to the trucking terminal today. We saw the big trailers and tractors. I got to see the fifth wheel and the dolly wheels. That's what I wanted to see most of all.

Willis wrote:

The Post Office

The post office is a busy place. There are many workers there. I watched how the mail is sorted and how the letters are canceled.

One man showed us how the mail is put into the boxes. He showed us how the rest of the mail is put into bundles for the mail man.

Taking care of all the mail is a big job.

Nikkie wrote:

Willie's Hamster

Willie brought his little hamster to school. His name is Brownie. His eyes are bright and shiny. When he sleeps, he looks like a little ball of fur. He is brown and white and he wiggles all the time. Willie feeds the hamster two times a day. He feeds it oatmeal and lettuce. The little hamster is asleep now. Shhhh.

The development of reporting and recording clearly, accurately, and interestingly expands as children have many and varied experiences in many and varied activities. Girls and boys are helped to gain in the skills of reporting and recording as they are given opportunity to

1. Express themselves orally in many different situations.
2. Dictate and record information which is of real need and value.
3. Set down their own needs and stories independently when they have gained adequate skill and ability in writing.

Children are fascinated with facts. The popularity of information books and children's encyclopedias equals that of story books. This is a report Debra wrote toward the last months of second grade:

Comets

Comets are the closest thing to nothing that could be something. Comets are made up of: gas, dust, little molecules of dirt and maybe some sparkes. The closer the comet is to the sun the longer its tail is. The farther away the comet is from the sun the shorter its tail is. Comets tails are formed like this: the comet has a very short tail. Then it get longer, longer, and longer untill it's very long. One Comet comes back every 75 year's. It's called Halley's Comet because he was the man who discovered it. He discovered Comets in 1810 many year's ago.

In the fourth grade, Sammy placed a picture of the Rosetta Stone on the bulletin board next to his report, which started:

For many, many years scholars tried to find out what the old Egyptian hieroglyphics meant. Until 1799 there was absolutely no way of telling what the Egyptians had recorded. In that year the Rosetta Stone was found that contained the same message in three languages. Hieroglyphics were used in one of these. The known languages were used to interpret the meaning of the ancient Egyptian writing.

Reporting is a natural outgrowth of a child's interest in his environment. When the material is pertinent, well organized, and interestingly presented, the report serves to enrich the on-going experiences of children.

Through this medium children project themselves, their understandings of their world, and their feelings about people, animals, things, or situations. They achieve status with their peers while increasing their own knowledge as well as that of the group.

Maturation and experience are factors which have a cause-and-effect relationship to all communication. Writing a report requires more mature thinking than many of the other written language activities. Because of the difficulties involved, most teachers feel that the written report should not receive much stress until the later elementary years. The background for the organizational thinking required for making written reports, however, is laid during the earlier years in the giving of many oral reports and the occasional writing of group reports.

The writing of a report often serves as a challenge to the exceptional child or to the girl or boy who has some special interest or hobby. Children painstakingly engage in independent research on topics that pique their curiosity. The research and reporting meet individual needs and at the same time add to the fund of knowledge of the entire group.

The following report was made by a sixth-grade boy whose hobby was collecting rocks:

Mr. Fields has over four hundred specimens in his mineral collection. Almost two hundred of these are geodes. What fun and adventure he has making his collection. He said that finding a geode is like receiving a surprise package. You cannot tell from the wrappings what wonderful treasures are inside. When Mr. Fields discovered his first geode, he would have passed it by had a fellow collector not pointed it out to him. It was somewhat round but irregular and no different in color from the rocks and earth around it.

Have you ever seen a geode after it is cut in two? It is filled with six-sided crystals which are called quartz. How these rose and lavendar crystals sparkle! I hope I can find a geode to put in my rock collection.

Facts and imagination can combine to create reports like this:

I Was There with Lewis and Clark

I am a flea. I live in Lewis' hat. It all started out in 1803 when Lewis stopped to pet a dog and I jumped on Lewis' leg.

I did not like it there, so I went to higher flesh; that is, his head or hat. Before I knew it, I was boarding a keelboat. From then on I had many adventures. One day we met a grizzly bear. I was going to jump on him, but the men started shooting at him. I then changed my mind. Another time we were going to see the Sioux Indians. Lewis was all dressed up and his boots were shining. All of a sudden the boat hit something and the boat rolled over. I was almost drowned and Lewis was all wet. I never wished I would go to the dogs so badly in my life. But I was saved.

Later on we came to the Mandan Indians. They were much friendlier than the Sioux. More important, we met a French trapper. Lewis found out he could interpret for them, so they took him along. He had an Indian wife name Sacagawea. He was whipping her one night; when I found out, I leaped over to that trapper and bit him so hard I almost set him in orbit. Another time when our boat turned over, Sacagawea saved some very important papers. One time we saw the Rocky Mountains. Then we came to Sacagawea's people who gave us food and ponies. Soon we came to the Pacific Ocean. I was the first American flea to see the Pacific Ocean. Soon we left for home.

Written by Me, the Little Flea.

DONALD, GRADE 5

Children in the middle grades are "joiners." Organized activity clubs give girls and boys a feeling of belongingness and help them to find their places in the social environment. There are many clubs of this type. Some of the most common are 4-H, Brownies, Cub Scouts, Boy Scouts, Blue Birds, and Campfire Girls. Some clubs are formed around interest and service areas, such as: Science, Reading, Dramatics, Photography, Recreation, and Safety and the Junior Red Cross.

Most of these clubs have secretaries. Although children enjoy being chosen secretary, they have difficulty learning to keep detailed minutes. Girls and boys are generally so interested in the club activities that they feel little need for more than simple records of the happenings.

Mary showed considerable skill as she recorded the following minutes of the sixth-grade Science Club:

The Science Club met in Room 5 Tuesday afternoon at 2:30. Bill called the meeting to order. I read the minutes. Tom showed us the planetarium he made. He helped us find the Big Dipper and Venus. Mary's mother sent cup cakes.

But Mary is not the only one who needs this practice. After the first meeting the entire group should participate in the writing of the minutes under the teacher's leadership. "How do we start a report of a meeting?" the teacher asks. "Yes, we name the club, the place, and the time." After writing these on the board the teacher continues, "Who called the meeting to order? What happened first? And what happened next?" Finally the teacher tells them of the form used by club secretaries. "Respectfully submitted" is not needed at the close of minutes. The secretary's signature is adequate. After they are approved the minutes are an official record.

Simple mimeographed or dittoed newspapers provide an incentive for written reports. Here is a typical page from a monthly paper.[18]

My Letter Brought Results

After I wrote a letter to the Chula Vista Telephone Co., Mrs. O'Neill got my letter and called my teacher about it, then Wednesday, Mrs. Wallace told the class that my letter had brought results and that we would see a film on telephone service and would have a field trip to see the inside of a telephone building. Telephones mean a lot to us, don't you think so too?

BILLY RINEHART

Mr. Halsema's Girls Won

The girls in Mrs. Wallace's room had a baseball game with Mr. Halsema's girls, Friday,

---

[18] Selections from the "Emory Epitaph," publbished by Emory School, South Bay School District, San Diego, Calif.

May 2nd. Linda Baker and Carolyn Ferguson were the captains of the two teams. It was a great game. The baseball was flying all over the field. Mr. Halsema's girls won 7 to 6.

LINDA BAKER

Feeling About Moving to a New School

It is quite interesting, going to different schools, because some schools have more unusual things than others. Some have bigger and better playgrounds for children to play on. Some have bigger and more colorful rooms and other interesting things. When you first go to a new school, you will probably be afraid, but when you check into school the children will start playing with you, and the second day at school, you will know a lot of kids, and you won't be afraid anymore.

JUDITH HAWKINS

Book Review

BIG RED, the dog Danny had always wanted is the name of this book. But first, he must teach the Irish Setter the ways of the woods. Together, they roamed the wilderness meeting nature on her own hard terms. When the outlaw bear injures his father, the boy and his dog must hunt him down. How do they do it? Read the book!

GEORGEANNA MULLIGAN

Play Day

On Friday, April 25, we went on a trip to Imperial Beach School. All the sixth grades in the district met there for Play Day.

We all met in the auditorium where we sang songs of North and South America. Then we went out on the black top for square dancing.

Locating information is an essential research skill. (*Courtesy of the Burbank Public Schools.*)

The square dances we danced were: Pop Goes the Weasel, Patty Cake Polka, and Parles Vouz. After lunch, we divided up into groups for games, dashes and relays. We came back to school in the afternoon tired but happy. Everyone had a good time.

BUTCH RURCHES

Our Playground Setup

Our playground setup is the only one of its kind in the South Bay Union School District, and is the best one that Emory has had yet. Each class is assigned certain games to play each week. This saves the time of assigning games each day, and also certain areas won't be overcrowded.

With this new plan, everyone will get a chance to play all the games. By the end of the year, you may learn to like a game you never cared for before. It will save a lot of arguments and confusion.

SHERRY HUDMAN

We'd Like You to Meet

Mr. Hanavan, our principal, likes his job. He taught at Pineville Junior High School in Missouri for eight years. He taught in Imperial Beach sixth grade for two years, and taught one year at Fort Growder.

He has a daughter, Connie, ten years old. She is in the fifth grade. He was born in Pineville, Mo. April 5, 1922.

Mr. Hanavan has been at Emory for two years. His favorite foods are baked ham, mashed potatoes, angel food cake, and chocolate milk.

He served in the army during World War 2 and in the Korean War. He is one of our favorite people.

LINDA BAKER and DIANE WILBUR

The teacher should develop, with the class, standards for checking the form and neatness of a written report. This checking method is often called proofreading, editing, or correcting. The standards might be as follows:

Standards for Editing a Report

1. Write the title of the report in the center of the line. Leave a space between the top of the paper and the title. Skip a line after the title.

2. Begin the first word of the title with a capital letter. Capitalize each important word of the title. Do not capitalize *a, an, at, as, the, of, to, in, from, with,* etc., because they are not considered important words.
3. Have good margins at the top, bottom, left, and right.
4. Use clear writing.
5. Use correct spelling and punctuation.
6. Have "sentence-sense." Do not use incomplete, run-on, or choppy sentences.
7. Indent all paragraphs.
8. Sign your name at the bottom of the last page.

The teacher and the class might develop an editing code using those signs familiar to the newspaper office, as well as other signs which might prove helpful. The signs should be charted as follows:

Editing Signs

sp = spelling
c = capital letter
inc = incomplete sentence
ℓ = take out
∩ = transpose, or turn about
lc = small letter (lower case letter)
⊃ = join sentences
mb = margins too big
ms = margins too small
‖ = margins not straight
p = punctuation wrong or omitted
wr = making writing clear
ind = indent paragraph
om = something should be omitted
? = material not clear
= space should be left

One of the most valuable activities in association with a school newspaper is the development of a "style sheet," which summarizes the major rules of punctuation, capitalization, and spelling. The local newspaper will usually give a school a copy of the style sheet which guides their writers.

Longer reports employ two areas of skills which involve gathering information and organizing the material. Textbooks provide adequate guidance with respect to note taking and simple outlining. Neither of these skills should be taught in isolation. It is the report that provides the purpose for taking notes. Planning the report provides the outline. These skills should first be studied in association with oral reports. This permits greater concentrated attention on the problems of gathering and organizing information.

The following standards are suggested with respect to note taking:

1. Read the material through before taking notes.
2. Complete one reference before you read another.
3. Use key words, phrases, or sentences to recall ideas.
4. Record the source of ideas.

With regard to organization, list the big ideas that are to be presented then add the details under each idea. Children find the creation of an outline prior to writing the report very difficult to make but they can outline the report after it has been written. This outlining can be a part of the editing before a report is rewritten. Social studies materials lend themselves to the study of outlining. Normally this is not a skill to be stressed before junior high school.

This pattern for an outline is an established language procedure:

Simple Outline

```
                        Title
    I.
        A.
        B.
        C.
    II.
        A.
        B.
        C.
```

Through discussion the children should be made aware of the following:

1. The main topics have Roman numerals. A period is placed after each numeral.
2. The supporting topics (subtopics) are designated by capital letters. A period is placed after each capital letter.

3. The written report contains as many paragraphs as there are main topics.
4. Each subtopic represents at least one sentence within the paragraph.
5. Each main topic and supporting topic begins with a capital letter.
6. There are no periods at the ends of the main topic or supporting topics unless it is a sentence outline.
7. In the simple outline, Roman numerals are kept in a straight column.
8. In the simple outline, capital letters are kept in a straight column.
9. If a topic is two lines long, the second line begins directly under the first word of the topic.
10. All the topics of an outline are written in the same form. That is, they are written *all in the short form* or *all in complete sentences.*

Children should be given many experiences, such as the following:

1. Making a group outline for a report.
2. Making a group outline for a current event.
3. Outlining, as a class, a short article in their readers.
4. Making individual outlines.

Reports are motivated by these activities:

1. Write a riddle about an insect, bird, or animal.
2. Write one-paragraph reports on famous people.
3. Write an imaginary news report of a historic event, or write the news that must have appeared when the historic event took place.
4. Make believe that you are an animal or a famous person. Write a description of yourself.
5. Visit a museum and report on an object observed.
6. Make comparisons of things we have with those in other parts of the world.
7. Summarize a topic in the encyclopedia in a few sentences.
8. A favorite newspaper feature is "Ask Andy." Put a question on the board and let the children write the answers as if they were Andy. Make certain

first that adequate reference books are available.

Questions like:

How far is it to the sun?
What is the brightest star?
How fast does sound travel?
What causes a sonic boom?

9. Provide background comments for a current news story. How large is the Congo? How do people make a living there?
10. Make a travel folder for a city, state, park, or country.
11. Write an autobiography. Parts might be My Birthplace, My Parents, My First School, My Pets and Hobbies, My Ambitions. A baby picture on the cover makes these an appealing Parents' Night attraction. Primary children can make a notebook "About My Family and Me."
12. Write a biography. This would involve interviewing a parent, grandparent, or classmate. In addition to place of birth and school experience, items of the following nature might be included: Special likes and dislikes, travel, honors, most important event in his life.
13. Make a class record or folder. This is especially appropriate if the sixth grade is the highest grade in a building. Parts might be History of Our School, Where Our Teachers Were Educated, Our Ambitions, Our Class Will, Twenty Years from Now, Who's Who in the Sixth Grade.
14. The very slow child in the upper grades will find satisfaction in preparing material for young children. Make an alphabet book for the first grade, a farm book for the second, or an animal book for the third grade. These would contain pictures and written explanations. Simple cookbooks and travel records based upon a road map are within their level of achievement.
15. Surveys of favorite books, opinions about grammar, simplified spelling,

or a school problem, such as social dancing in the sixth grade, are stimulating and involve a great deal of language learning as the material is gathered, organized, and written into a report.

For Discussion

1. How can a teacher discourage research reports that are little more than copied from an encyclopedia?
2. What values would an "in-depth" report have in which each student wrote a book on a country, a holiday, a state, a city. What problems do you foresee in such a project?
3. To what extent should all bulletin boards be student projects?
4. Is the school in an adequate community to train reporters to write news accounts?

How Should Punctuation Be Taught?

Man has been speaking for well over 700,000 years. Man has been practicing alphabetic writing only for about 3,450 years. Man has punctuated, in the modern sense, for less than 250 years. He has still not mastered an ideal punctuation. In the system as it stands, the distribution of the marks is as follows:

1. For *linking,* use:

   ; semicolon
   : colon
   — linking dash
   - linking hyphen

2. For *separating,* use:

   . period
   ? question mark
   ! exclamation point
   , separating comma

3. For *enclosing,* use:

   , . . . , paired commas
   — . . . — paired dashes
   (. . .) paired parentheses
   [. . .] paired brackets
   " . . ." paired quotation marks

PEANUTS ®   **By Charles M. Schulz**

(Courtesy of United Features Syndicate.)

4. For *indicating omissions*, use:

' apostrophe
. omission period in abbreviations
  (or dot)
— omission dash
. . . triple periods (or dots)
. . . . quadruple periods (or dots)

Have you ever wondered how the punctuation marks came to be? Maybe you have noticed that in pages of Chinese writing there is no punctuation. As recently as 1945 there were no such marks used in the Korean language. However, when they decided to write horizontally rather than vertically the need for such marks was recognized.

The ancient Greeks and Romans frequently wrote without separating the words, let alone separating sentences. It was the orators who made the first separations in order to emphasize the thoughts they were expressing. Originally punctuation was built upon a single series of pauses. The comma was for a one-unit pause, the semicolon for a two-unit pause, a colon for a three-unit pause, and a period for a four-unit pause. The question mark was a sign to raise the voice at the end of the word. The exclamation point was a little dagger similar to that used to fasten important notices to buildings.

One of the first printers, a Venetian named Aldus Manutius, explained the system in this way.[19]

Let us proceed, as it were by steps, from the lowest of the points to the highest.
The least degree of separation is indicated by the comma.
The same mark, if it is used along with a single point, as this is (;) is found in passages in which the words are not opposed in meaning, but the sense depends upon the words in such a way, that, if you use the comma, it is too little; if the double point too much. I was thinking to give an example: but, I felt the point had come out plainly enough, in the immediate preceding sentence.

The doubling of the point is next to be considered: the effect of this doubling is, that the mark thus formed takes rank between the point used in conjunction with the comma, and the point standing alone.

There remains the single point, with which the sentence is closed and completed. It is not difficult to understand, for one cannot fail to notice with what word a sentence ends, although when it is short and another short one follows, I myself use the double point more freely than the single, as for instance: Make ready a lodging for me: for I shall arrive tomorrow: and so again: I give you no orders concerning my affairs: you yourself will decide what is to be done.

It was this type of punctuation that was used in the King James Edition of the Bible. The Bible was designed for oral reading and was so punctuated. The original Shakespeare folios were punctuated in this manner, although the modern editions follow conventional punctuation.

An experiment by E. L. Thorndike illustrates the personal nature of punctuation. Hamlet's soliloquy was punctuated twenty-three different ways by fifty-seven graduate students; the first twenty-four words of The Lord's Prayer were punctuated thirty-two different ways. The study also indicated that after a week the same individuals would punctuate these selections differently.[20]

---

[19] Quoted in Rudolph Flesch, *How to Make Sense* (New York: Harper, 1954), pp. 114–15.

[20] E. L. Thorndike, "Punctuation," *Teacher's College Record* (May 1948), p. 533.

In the primary grades the child first learns about the period. Three uses of the period are taught:

1. At the end of a sentence: *The books are here.*
2. After an abbreviation in titles of persons and things: *Dr. Jones.*
3. After initials in proper names: *H. A. Brown.*

The teacher stresses the period in the first reading the child does and in the first sentence written on the board. "This little dot is called a period," she explains. "It tells us to stop because this is the end of a statement." The other uses are taught as an aspect of spelling.

Two uses of the question mark are taught:

1. At the end of a direct question: *Is this your ball?*
2. After a direct question but within the sentence: *"Will you be ready?" the man asked.*

The first can be understood and used by beginners in the first grade. The second should not be presented until late in the third grade. This form is less difficult: *He asked, "Will you be ready?"*

Lord Dunsany once complained that there were so many comma rules that printers could write one of his sentences like this: "Moreover, Jones, who, as, indeed, you, probably, know, is, of course, Welsh, is, perhaps, coming, too, but, unfortunately, alone." In some handbooks one can still find hundreds of rules for the comma. Fortunately for the teacher, eleven seem to be enough to meet the needs of elementary school children.

Four of these eleven rules are those that concern the writing of a letter.

1. To separate the parts of the date and the day of the year: *June 5, 1964.*
2. To set off the name of a city from a state: *Greeley, Colorado.*
3. After a salutation in a letter: *Dear Jim,*
4. After close of a letter: *Your friend,*

Additional comma rules taught in the elementary grades include:

5. To set off short direct quotations: *"We are ready," called the boys.*
6. After clauses of introduction: *While they were eating, the bell rang.*
7. Between parts of a compound sentence joined by a short conjunction: *Mr. Smith took Paul, and Jim went in Mrs. Anderson's car.*
8. Before and after appositives: *The principal, Mr. Nardelli, talked to the parents.*
9. Before and after parenthetical expressions: *You told your mother, I suppose, about your report card.*
10. Before and after a nonrestrictive clause: *That boy, who has the dog, is in the fifth grade.*
11. To separate the words in the series: *John, Paul, and Jack are cousins.* (Immediately we run into the problem of the comma before *and*. It seems more exact to use one in that position to prevent a reader from combining Paul and Jack.)

The colon is quite simple to teach, because there are only four ways it is used:

1. After the greeting in a business letter: *Dear Sir:*
2. Before a long series: *Mother bought: oranges, lemons, bread, jam, and cake.*
3. To separate the hour from the minutes: *2:30 A.M.*
4. To denote examples: *A proper name should be capitalized: Mary.*

The apostrophe receives a great deal of attention in spelling. It is used:

1. With the letter *s* to show possession: *Mary's coat, boys' coats.*
2. To show where letters have been omitted: *don't* (do not), *o'er* (over).
3. To show the omission of number from a date: *Class of '64.*
4. To show the plural of figures and letters: *A's, 2's.*

Quotation marks are a special problem for schoolchildren. Few adults ever write quotation marks unless they are professional writers. The reader is the best textbook for these marks. After a story has been read, go back and have children take the parts of the story characters. Then while the narrator reads all material not in quotations, the characters read their proper lines. Then examine how the material was punctuated so that each person knew what to read. If the class is engaged in story writing, examples of all the varieties of use should be illustrated on the blackboard as a reference. These are two basic understandings that all children need to learn:

1. The unbroken quotation with the descriptive element preceding the quotation: *He cried, "Get a new man on first base!"*
2. The reverse of the above: *"Get a new man on first!" he cried.*

In order to use a semicolon properly it is necessary to understand conjunctions. Conjunctions may join either words or groups of words. When a conjunction is preceded by a comma (as when joining two clauses) a semicolon may be used instead of the comma and conjunction.

Mary was happy, but Joe was sad, may be written: *Mary was happy; Joe was sad.* Clauses joined by a semicolon must be related and independent, however, the situation must be related in that it affects both Mary and Joe. One may write: *The sea is beautful at sunset; the water reflects the brilliant glow of the sky.* But not: *The sea is beautiful at sunset; the cry of the seagulls makes me homesick.*

Textbooks contain other rules for the semicolon. It confuses children to present this work as a compromise between a comma and a period.

The hyphen is usually considered an orthographic feature rather than a punctuation mark. It is a growing practice to avoid the hyphen except where a word is divided at the end of a line. Many words formerly hyphenated are now either "solid" (i.e., one word, like *flannelboard*), or two words, like *decision making.* Webster's *Third New International* is a safe guide to follow in hyphenating. Children in the elementary school are not encouraged to use the dash, because they overuse it. Parentheses seldom appear in children's writing.

Interesting exercises in punctuation can be made by taking material from readers and reproducing them without any punctuation. The child is told how many sentences there are. These can be made self-correcting by putting the title of the book and page number at the bottom of the exercise.

Six Sentences, 10 Capital Letters, 5 Commas, 4 Quotation Marks

she reached into a big box and pulled out a santa claus suit and held it up it was bright red with real fur trimmings billy could see that there was a cap and a set of whiskers and even boots to go with it

isn't that lovely she said to billy the minute i saw it i thought of you im sure it will fit just perfectly she held it up to him

Because some of the punctuation rules are applied primarily in letters, writing a group letter and then copying it from the board is a good way to introduce the comma rules involved. Practice with letter headings is equally good.

Provide the missing capitals and punctuation:

1.
        astor hotel
        new york n y
        may 3 1966

dear teacher

2.
        607 adams st
        madison wis
        june 6 1964

dear mother

3.
        gunnison colo
        dec 5 1960

dear santa claus

Charts and bulletin boards which act as constant reminders are valuable in the classroom. The making of these charts (see next page) should involve the children.

A bulletin board such as this acts as a reminder:

Watch Your Commas

        713 Olde St.
        Austin, Texas
        Sept. 19, 1961

Dear Frank,

        Your friend,
        Bill

Capitalize these words:

1. The beginning of a sentence.
2. Names of months and holidays.
3. Names of particular streets and schools.
4. First word and important words of a title.
5. Names of people, pets, and initials of people.
6. Names of countries, cities, rivers, and mountains.
7. First word in greeting and closing of a letter.
8. References to God.

We saw a show

January, Halloween

Biona Ave., Hamilton School

My Visit to the Farm

Helen, Spot, A. J. Boyd

Mexico, Mt. Hood, Columbia River

Gentlemen, Yours very truly

Lord, Savior

One teacher makes punctuation marks come alive through dramatization. A question mark with a face and legs, a comma with a smiling face and wearing a hat, and a chubby little period are placed on a bulletin board, each with a caption telling one thing they do. These characters—Chubby Little Period, Jolly Question Mark, Mr. and Mrs. Comma, and Tall Exclamation Point—are introduced via the bulletin board. Each figure with its rule and title is shown. Other rules of punctuation are added as introduced.

This is the way the teacher describes their use:

I have the little people made up into plywood puppets. They are kept on hand in the schoolroom at all times. We use them to point up discussion of punctuation in many ways—in language class, social studies, written work, spelling. For example: in oral reading, we talk about "Chubby Little Period being at the end of a sentence to tell us that we stop here for a short time before going on." "Mr. Comma helps us by telling us this is the place to pause when we are reading a sentence."

I use this lesson in teaching how to begin and end sentences. In this lesson I also introduce the good English habit. "Use a question mark (Jolly Question Mark) after each sentence that asks a question."

Using the wooden "Chubby Little Period," I say,

Chubby Little Period
Runs and sits,
The end of the sentence
Is always his place.

A sentence is written on the board. Using the puppet, I then demonstrate the period's place.

Upper-grade children enjoy a television quiz program in which each punctuation mark appears and is questioned concerning its activities or in which there is a "What's My Line?" or "To Tell the Truth" format, with the punctuation marks appearing as guests. The master of ceremonies starts by saying, "Our guest does four things [or ten if it's the comma]. We must name all of them to identify him completely."

Older students enjoy trick sentences like the following:

Bill, when Henry had had *had,* had had *had had; had had* had had the teacher's approval. [Omit italics and punctuation when writing this sentence on the chalkboard.]

The fight over the boys came home.

This is the story of walter who has not heard the story through it walter gained lasting fame a beautiful girl and a glorious name he also gained one autumn day on the grassy field in gridiron play the team was losing the clock moved fast any play might be the last of the game injured walter then called his own signal explaining men ill take the blame if we dont score he ran a full ninety yards or more

Another procedure is deliberately to displace punctuation in a passage and thus illustrate how the meaning becomes lost. The same passage can be reproduced several times with varying degrees of distortion. The pupil sees how difficult it is to get meaning from a passage so treated. In the exercise below the first copy completely obscures the meaning, the second copy is frustrating but not impossible, and the third is reproduced correctly.

Billy listened, carefully as the teacher. Explained how punctuation helps. The reader commas periods exclamation marks and question marks? All help a reader get meaning. From the printed page. Billy wondered what would happen. If the printer got the punctuation marks mixed. UP it was hard for him to imagine. What this would do to a story.

Billy listened carefully as the teacher explained. How punctuation helps the reader. Commas periods, exclamation marks and question marks all help. A reader get meaning from the printed page. Billy wondered. What would happen if the printer got the punctuation marks mixed up. It was hard for him to imagine what this would do. To a story.

Billy listened carefully as the teacher explained how punctuation helps the reader. Commas, periods, exclamation marks, and question marks all help a reader get meaning from the printed page. Billy wondered what would happen if the printer got the punctuation marks mixed up. It was hard for him to imagine what this would do to a story.

To emphasize that punctuation marks reflect the pauses and emphasis of speech, reproduce a page from a book such as *Island of the Blue Dolphins, Charlotte's Web,* or a story in the reading textbook without punctuation marks. As the teacher reads the story with appropriate stress, pause, and juncture the students put in the appropriate punctuations. When they check their marks with the original text, the point can be made that punctuation at times is a personal interpretation and that the student and author may disagree and both be correct. In a discussion as to why the author punctuated as he did, rules may be reviewed or clarified.

Students enjoy making up punctuation marks to represent voice signals for which we have no written signals. Tell them that one writer has invented a new punctuation mark to use after such utterances as *How could that be so,* which is actually a question yet requires no answer. This combination exclamation mark and question mark is called an *interbang.*

Ask students to invent punctuation marks to indicate the tone of voice in which a statement is spoken: a low tone of voice, a sad tone of voice, a sarcastic tone of voice, and so on. Then have them use their new punctuation marks in sentences.

For Discussion

1. To what extent is punctuation a personal matter?

2. The newspapers frequently carry stories about errors caused by punctuation. At one time a tariff law was passed to admit fruit trees free of duty. A comma between fruit and trees cost the government a great deal of revenue before it was corrected. Do you know of other examples?

3. Why is it possible for two people to punctuate a paper in different ways and both be correct?

4. Do the following three rules cover most situations?
   a. A comma may be used to prevent a possible misreading.
   b. A nonessential part of a sentence should be set off with one comma if it comes first or last in the sentence and with two commas if it comes anywhere else.
   c. When two or more words or groups of words are similar in form or function, they should be separated by commas.

A textbook for fifth grade suggests this form of evaluation of the children's understanding of punctuation.[21]

1. To see if the students understand the purpose of punctuation ask them (a) why we call punctuation marks *signals;* (b) which punctuation marks stand for voice signals; (c) which punctuation marks do not stand for spoken signals; and (d) why those marks that do not stand for spoken signals are also necessary.

2. To see if the students know how to use the comma, have them insert commas in the sentences below. Have them explain the use of each comma they insert.
   a. The knight mounted his black steed(,) passed through the gate(,) rode across the drawbridge(,) and sped to Lady Ann's castle.

---

[21] *New Directions in English* (New York: Harper, 1968), pp. 68–70.

b. The dragon arrived on August 21(,) 1100 A.D.(,) at 10 Moat Drive(,) Rhine Valley(,) Germany.

c. Although the knight's horse was fleet of foot(,) Lady Ann could not be saved.

d. Yes(,) the knight was sad.

e. Dragon(,) that was a very rude thing for you to do.

3. To see if the students know when to use exclamation points rather than periods or question marks, have them add end punctuation to the sentences below. Have them explain their punctuation.

a. The king demanded to know if the smith could make a new golden goblet in three short hours(.)

b. Is this rush necessary(?)

c. It is indeed(!) You wouldn't look nice at all without a head(. or !)

d. Stop scribbling on the walls(!)

4. To see if the students can differentiate between direct and indirect quotations, have them add quotation marks wherever necessary in the sentences below. Have them explain their punctuation.

a. Lady Ann requested that the dragon put her down.

b. (")Never!(") roared the fire-breathing snorter. (")You shall not go free!(")

c. Martha said, (")I think this story should end now.(")

d. The knight said that he, too, was tired of the chase.

5. To see if the students know when to use colons, have them add colons, where necessary, to the sentences below.

a. Trees have many enemies(:) fire, disease, parasites, and drought.

b. I saw three people at the party(:) Jane, Dale, and Nancy.

c. The space station was launched at 4(:)32 A.M.

6. To see if the students know when to use hyphens in numbers, have them write the numerals below in words, hyphenating where necessary.

a. 98   <u>(ninety-eight)</u>

b. 665   <u>(six hundred sixty-five)</u>

c. 3,479   <u>(three thousand four hundred seventy-nine)</u>

d. 8:55   <u>(eight fifty-five)</u>

7. To see if the students know when and how to use the apostrophe, have them insert apostrophes where needed in the sentences below, and then contract words when possible, placing an apostrophe in the correct place.

a. I can(')t come to the play.

b. He(')s not home.

c. She does not (doesn't) understand how the accident dashed that boy(')s hopes.

d. All the schools(') teams entered the contest.

e. He has not (hasn't) put the dragon to bed.

f. We are (we're) seeing your mother tonight.

1. Add commas, wherever they are needed in the sentences below.

a. Alfred, George, Bob, and Don climbed into the capsule.

b. The launching was to take place on March 31, 1999, from pad sixty-three, Podunk, West Petunia.

c. Marty, I can't stand the noise of the rockets.

d. Besides, it's too hot near the site.

e. Although I would like to see the lift-off, I don't think I'll go out there.

2. Put the correct punctuation mark at the end of each of these sentences:

a. Dry ice is cold, solidified carbon dioxide.

b. Watch out! It will give you a frostbite. *or* !

c. Can't I make it melt?

d. Hey! Where did it go?

3. Some of the sentences below need additional punctuation. Add the punctuation that is missing.

a. Sonya asked Bob if he wanted to go on a bike hike.

b. "I think," said Karen, "that this show could be improved."

c. "It's horrible!" Ken shouted. "How can you stand to look at it?"

4. Decide what type of punctuation is missing in these sentences. Add the needed marks.

a. He got up at 5:15 and collected his gear: rod, bait, rope, tent, and knapsack.

b. Some dinosaurs were small and graceful: the ornitholestes was a dainty dinosaur.

5. Write the following numerals in words.

a. 32   <u>thirty-two</u>

b. 787   <u>seven hundred eighty-seven</u>

c. 4,999   <u>four thousand nine hundred ninety-nine</u>

d. 8:45   <u>eight forty-five</u>

6. In the sentences below, run together any words you can, and insert apostrophes for any letters you leave out.

a. He is in the bank.   <u>he's</u>

b. We had made an appointment.   <u>we'd</u>

c. You are late. <u>you're</u>

d. Do not take those flowers yet. <u>don't</u>

7. Explain the difference in meaning between the words with apostrophes in each pair below.

   a. the flutist's notes <u>notes belonging to one flutist or played by him</u>

   b. the flutists' notes <u>notes played by more than one flutist</u>

   c. the clipper ship's sails <u>sails belonging to one clipper ship</u>

   d. the clipper ships' sails <u>sails belonging to more than one clipper ship</u>

8. Punctuate the paragraph below.

   T

   the small plane pitched about in **. P**
   the storm perry had to decide on one of **:**
   two plans land and wait for the storm **,**
   to end or ride out the storm while **. A**
   heading toward home although he
   had flown over the canyon dozens of **,** **,**
   times before he couldnt recall having **.**
   seen a single flat strip suitable for landing
   N **,**
   nevertheless he decided to dip under the
   clouds and look more closely at the can- **,** **. "** **,"**
   yons ridges X67 calling T-1 he said
   . "C **,** **." H**
   into the radio come in please he
   heard static splutters squeaks and then **,** **,** **,**
   . D !W
   silence dead what would happen to him **?**
   now

How Should Letter Writing Be Taught in the Elementary Grades?

In each classroom beyond those of the first grade there should be a chart or other ready reference illustrating the form of letters appropriate for the grade. Some teachers put a permanent form on the blackboard with crayons. This shows the lines for date, salutation, body of the letter, and closing.

Every language textbook provides adequate examples of various letter forms.

In the primary grades the children start by dictating the letter to the teacher, who writes on the blackboard. Afterward, each child copies the completed note to mother or the janitor. As soon as the basic pattern is mastered children are encouraged to write individual messages. These may be to classmates who are ill, to relatives, to the principal, to the janitor, or to a speaker who visited the class.

The satisfaction of expressing ideas in an accepted social manner seems to be sufficient motivation for most children. But this satisfaction soon ends if the letters are not read and there is no response. Because the post office is usually studied in the second grade, letter writing within the class will interest the children. The letters are carefully written, envelopes prepared, and the letters mailed and delivered as a part of the classroom project. With a little cooperation this can be extended to the second grade in another room or a neighboring school.

As the children advance, letter writing is best motivated by real purposes. Pen pals in other states and countries can be located through the *Christian Science Monitor* in Boston, Mass.; the Junior Red Cross in Washington, D.C.; The International Friendship League, 40 Mt. Vernon Street, Boston, Mass.; and the Parker Pen Company in Janesville, Wis. Sources of free and inexpensive materials are listed in "The Wonderful World for Children" by Peter Cardoza, published by Bantam Books. This inexpensive book will be found wherever paperback books are sold. Some of the major corporations, such as General Foods, Westinghouse Electric, Union Pacific Railroad, and Goodrich Rubber Company, have materials designed for classroom use that will be sent to children who write for them. The highway departments of many state governments will send illustrated highway maps. The National Audubon Society, 1130 Fifth Avenue, New York, N.Y. 10028 and the National Wild Life Federation, 232 Carrol Street, N.W., Washington 12, D.C, have interesting material for children concerned with conservation.

A post office in a rural school provides an incentive for letter writing. There are so many real purposes for letter writing that such a laboratory exercise should be extended as soon as mail services are understood. (*Courtesy of the San Diego County Schools.*)

It should be noted that there are some letters that should not be written. The children's magazines contain many offers to send stamps on approval. Some companies offer free stamps as an incentive. The child who receives such stamps may not understand that he will be expected to pay for them. Another type is the advertisement that offers a bicycle for solving a puzzle. This will involve the child in selling seeds, candy, or other items with a compromise award, such as a box camera.

A second type of letter requiring careful consideration is that written to prominent people. Writing a letter of appreciation to the author of a book is one thing. Writing such a letter to gain information for a book report is another. The author John Steinbeck appealed to high school English teachers to stop assigning such letters. He was getting from seventy-five to 100 on some days. Congressmen have the help and mailing privileges that do not make this a great burden. Few community leaders are in such a comfortable position.

When the need to write a letter has been established, use the lessons in the textbook that deal with the proper form. Some classes make a "Letter Form Handbook." This is a folder that illustrates the blank form of a letter and contains examples of letters which the children have made or brought from home. If the children come from homes where examples of good letters are available, an excellent bulletin board can be made exhibiting these letters. A collection of letters with special offers, which seems to be a modern merchandising practice, might be studied with respect to form and context.

Letters written to express appreciation for a favor or to express interest in a child who is absent provide opportunities for class discussion of the context of such letters. The teacher might start the discussion with the question, "What are some of the things you would talk about if you could go to the hospital to visit Joe?" "Let me list the ideas on the board."

1. Tell about things that have happened at school.
   a. The bicycle test.
   b. The map we finished.
   c. The new bulletin board.
2. Tell something about ourselves.
   a. John has a baby brother.
   b. Mary went to visit Disneyland.
   c. Jane lost her glasses.
3. Say something about Joe.
   a. Tell him we miss him.
   b. Tell him we hope he gets well soon.
   c. Tell him to have fun at the hospital.

Then discuss the questions, "Should all of us write these ideas in the same order?" "Should all of us write about the bicycle test?"

After the letters are written let the children judge the quality of their own letters. None need to be rewritten but some may wish to do so. All should be mailed. Those who wish may read their letters to the group. The following ideas might be used in the evaluation:

1. Does the letter sound like talking?
2. Would you like to receive the letter yourself?
3. Does it tell what the reader would want to know?

The pen pal letter to a stranger is an incentive for descriptive writing. The fact that a child in Alaska has never seen the writer, his home, community, or school provides a good reason for writing about the familiar. Unfortunately, doing this as a classroom assignment detracts from the natural rewards of the activity. After the first letter it is wise to permit the activity to continue as a personal choice. Praise those who do continue writing, let them read the letters received to the class, have displays of letters and items received. Although intermediate-grade children are interested in foreign lands, the children in non-English-speaking countries who wish to write are usually in the upper grades. It thus seems wise to postpone this type of pen pal until children are in junior high school.

Usually a letter to an adult is much more difficult to write than a letter to another child. This seems especially true of "duty letters." "Thank you" notes or expressions of appreciation require specific patterns of language that apparently seem unnatural to some children. Examples of such letters or notes might be used as the beginning of a discussion.

Which of these letters would you like to receive?

1616 Madison
Albany, N.Y.
Jan. 6, 1962

Dear Grandmother,

Christmas is so full of surprises. I never expected to have a pair of mittens made by my own grandmother. The colors are just right for my coat. It must have taken you a long time to make them. I'll think of you whenever I wear them.

We gave a Christmas play at school. I was an angel. Daddy says they must have made a mistake to give me a part like that. He is always teasing.

With love,
Donna

Newburgh, Ind.
Jan. 6, 1962

Dear Grandmother,

Thanks for the mittens. I got a sled, a coat, a book, a necktie, a knife, and lots of other things.

I was in a play at school.

Respectfully yours,
Dan

An incentive for letter writing is provided when a child has his own stationery. This should be lined. Parents might be encouraged to buy such material as birthday presents for children. The Cub Scouts and Brownies have such stationery for their members. If the teacher gives a gift as a birthday present, it is wise to have a local printer create the type of writing paper the children need. Children might make their own "crests" in art.

Tests of the following type provide a check of the understanding of letter form.

Correct ten errors in this business letter form:

4854 adams
chicago illinois
july 4 1962

Sears Co
1616 Grove St
Denver, Colo.
dear sir,

A chart illustrating the terms used in letter writing should be mimeographed and given to each intermediate child. An example of a friendly letter is shown with these parts identified: heading, salutation, body, complimentary close, and signature. A business letter should have these parts identified: inside address, salutation, body, complimentary close, and signature.

A challenging task for able students would be to make a list of salutations and complimentary closings. How would one greet the Queen of England, the Archbishop of a church, a senator, a delegate to the United Nations, or a firm of lawers?

The following standards may be placed on a chart and used to evaluate letters.

1. Did I tell something interesting? Was I thinking of the receiver and not of myself?
2. Do I have five parts to my letter?
   A heading.
   A greeting.
   A message.
   A closing.
   A name.
3. Did I write neatly so that the person who receives my letter can read it easily?
4. Did I indent the first word of each paragraph?
5. Did I leave a straight margin on each part of my letter?

Closing and Name

Name _____

Begin the first word in the closing with a capital letter. Copy over the following closings correctly.

your friend, _____

sincerely yours, _____

with love, _____

Write the closing you would use if you wrote a letter to your mother.

_____

Write the closing you would use if you wrote a letter to a friend.

_____

Write the closing you would use if you didn't know the person very well.

_____

Put a comma after the closing. Write the following closings correctly.

Your friend _____

Sincerely yours _____

With love _____

Begin each part of your name with a capital letter. Write the following names correctly.

mary smith _____

jane johns _____

sue jones _____

jack hall _____

For Discussion

1. In addition to reports and letter writing there are other functional language situations when a child needs to write. When would a child need to write a description, an advertisement, a notice, an invitation, a biography, a joke?

2. Do you think writing postal cards should be a part of the letter writing program in school?

3. It is said that women write better letters than men. Is there any factor in our culture that might cause such a difference?

4. Because schools have publications for creative writing, do you feel that outstanding reports, letters, and other such material should receive similar recognition? How might this be done?

Suggestions for Projects

1. Mauree Applegate suggests an I-W-S Formula to start some children in creative writing. This means: *I*deas, *W*ords, and *S*timulators. Use this formula to devise materials that might be used in the classroom.

2. Problems stimulate the able child. Create some folders that present a series of problems and the suggested means whereby the answers may be found to use with such students.

3. Make an anthology of poetry written by children.

4. Evaluate ten films or filmstrips that might be used to stimulate imaginative writing. "The Hunter in the Forest" is suggested in many school courses of study.

5. Evaluate a specific suggestion with respect to creative writing. Such suggestions as the following may be used: Have children write the story of a comic-book episode, write a summary of a television show, encourage children to experiment with flannelboard characters or puppets as they develop a story or play before writing.

6. Investigate the procedures used with respect to publication of a collection of creative writing. How are the materials selected, who pays for the publication, how is the material distributed?

7. Investigate the way composition is taught in England. The Ministry of Education Pamphlet No. 26, "Language," published by Her Majesty's Stationery Office in London, is an interesting source of such information.

8. Make a study of worthy free materials that may be secured through letters written by children. Use the following sources as a guide:

Where to Get Free and Inexpensive Materials, by David L. Byrn, and others. San Francisco, Calif., Fearon Publishers (2263 Union St., San Francisco).

Elementary Teachers Guide to Free Curriculum Materials, by Educators' Progress Service. Randolph, Wisconsin. Annual.

Free and Inexpensive Learning Materials. 9th edition. Nashville, Tenn.: Peabody College for Teachers, 1960.

So You Want to Start a Picture File.

Sources of Free and Inexpensive Pictures for the Classroom.

Sources of Free Travel Posters and Geographic Aids.

All the above by Bruce Miller and available from him, c/o Box 369, Riverside, Calif.

Sources of Free and Inexpensive Educational Materials. Chicago: Field Enterprises, 1958. (Merchandise Mart Plaza, Chicago 58, Ill.)

Bibliography

Books

Arnstein, Flora. *Poetry in the Elementary Classroom.* New York: Appleton-Century-Crofts, 1962.

Burrows, Alvina Trent, Doris Jackson, and Dorothy O. Saunders. *They All Want to Write,* 3rd ed. New York: Holt, Rinehart and Winston, Inc., 1964.

Holbrook, David. *The Secret Places.* London: University Paperbacks, Methuen, 1964.

Joseph, Stephen M. *The Me Nobody Knows.* New York: Avon Books, 1969.

Kahl, Harbert. *36 Children.* New York: Signet Books, 1968.

Lewis, Richard. *Miracles*. New York: Simon & Schuster, Inc., 1969.

Meams, Hugh. *Creative Power—The Education of Youth in the Creative Arts*. New York: Dover Publications, Inc., 1958.

Petty, Walter T., and Mary E. Bowen. *Slithery Snakes and Other Aids to Children's Writing*. New York: Meredith Publishing Co., 1967.

Torrance, Paul E. *Guiding Creative Talent*. Englewood Cliffs, N.J.: Prentice-Hall, Inc., 1962.

Wilt, Miriam. *Creativity in the Elementary School*. New York: Appleton-Century-Crofts, 1959.

ABC's, Alameda County Schools Dept. (224 West Winton Avenue, Haywood, Calif. 94544), 1968.

McCord, David. "Excerpts from 'Write Me Another Verse,' " *Horn Book* (August 1970), pp. 364–69.

Northwestern University Curriculum Center in English. *Project English: A Teacher's Experience with Composition*. Evanston, Ill.: Northwestern University, 1965.

Redkey, Nancy. "Free Writing for Fluency," *Elementary School Journal* (May 1964), pp. 430–33.

Torrance, Paul E. "Creative Thinking of Children," *Journal of Teacher Education* (December 1962), pp. 448–60.

Articles

Burrows, Alvina T. *Teaching Composition—What Research Says to the Teacher*, No. 18. National Education Association, 1969.

Carlson, Ruth Kearney. "The Sunset Is a Pretty Pink Dove—Children's Voices in Poetry," *Elementary English* (October 1969), pp. 748–57.

English Curriculum Study Center. *Project English: Written Composition—A Guide for Teachers in Elementary Schools*, Bulletin No. 101965. Athens, Ga.: University of Georgia, 1964.

Hofsteller, Arthur N., Lorena A. Anderson, and Ruth Frame. *Cooperative Evaluation of Proficiency in English and Creative Writing*, Kanawha County Schools, Charleston, West Virginia, 1962.

Joy, Joan. *Nonsensical Nuances of the*

Sources of Children's Writing

Applegate, Mauree. *When Teacher Says to Write a Poem* and *When Teacher Says to Write a Story*. New York: Harper & Row, 1968.

Koch, Kenneth. *Wishes, Lies and Dreams*. New York: Chelsea House, 1971. (Paperback: Random House, 1971.)

Kids (a magazine written for and by children). Write to Box 30, Cambridge, Mass. 02139), for sample copy.

Right On (a magazine by youth in East Harlem, New York City). East Harlem Youth Service, 2037 Third Avenue, New York, N.Y. Send 50¢.

Teachers and Writers Collaborative Newsletters. Pratt Center for Community Improvement, 244 Vanderbilt Avenue, Brooklyn, N.Y. 11205. $3 for four issues.

seven

spelling

Soliloquy on Phonics and Spelling

This year—I firmly made a vow—
I'm going to learn to spell.
I've studied phonics very hard.
Results will surely tell. . . .

"I thought I heard a distant cough
But when I listened, it shut ough."
Oh, dear, I think my spelling's awf.
I guess I meant i heard a coff.

"To bake a pizza—take some dough
And let it rise, but very slough."
That doesn't look just right, I noe.
I guess on that I stubbed my tow.

"My father says down in the slough
The very largest soybeans grough."
Perhaps he means "The obvious cloo
To better crops, is soil that's nue."

"Cheap meat is often very tough.
We seldom like to eat the stough."
I'm all confused—this spelling's ruff.
I guess I've studied long enuph.

ISABEL SMYTHE

A Boy at Sault Ste. Marie

A boy at Sault Ste. Marie
Said, "Spelling is all Greek to me,
    Till they learn to spell 'Soo'
    Without any 'u,'
Or an 'a' or an 'I' or a 't.' "

ANONYMOUS

A Small Boy When Asked to Spell "Yacht"

A small boy when asked to spell "yacht,"
Most saucily said, "I will nacht."
    So his teacher in wrath,
    Took a section of lath,
And warmed him up well on the spacht.

ANONYMOUS

361

What Is the Place of Spelling in the Language Arts Program?

The task of the teacher is to guide the student's growth in the ability to spell the language. It has been assumed by many that if the teacher supervised the student's use of a spelling book or workbook, this objective would be realized. Sometimes this has resulted in efforts to master the content of the book, much as if it were a geography text, rather than to develop individual spelling skills. Many young teachers are so influenced by their own memories of spelling classes that their efforts are directed toward the motivation of the mastery of twenty words each week regardless of the usefulness of these words to the student.

Some of the major skills needed to spell are

- An understanding of the relationships of phonemes (sounds of the language) with the graphemes (letters) used to represent them in writing. This means that the relationship between the beginning sound of *put* and the letter *p* are understood or that the sound of the group of letters at the end of *seeing* is represented by *ing*.
- An understanding of the historical reason for such a spelling as *know*, which shows the Scandinavian source of the word and contains a letter no longer sounded. According to one linguist *kn* is the phoneme.
- An understanding of sound variations represented by vowels and such consonants as *g* in *garage*.
- An understanding of consonant–vowel patterns as used in English spelling.

Because spelling, like reading, is seldom done for the purpose of creating nonsense words, there are skills related to understanding the meaning of words. These include understanding word roots and the changes produced by prefixes and suffixes, knowing how to use a dictionary, and seeking to conform to widely accepted standards of correctness which facilitate communication.

A person who wants to spell a word starts with a concept, or idea of a thing which he wishes to express in writing, such as *pain* or *cake*. The idea must be associated with its speech symbol, or word. After the word is selected, the speller thinks of the separate sounds in that word (or words). These sounds are identified with the letters of the alphabet which represent them. The next step requires the speller to reproduce those letters in the sequence that will spell the word in an approved form, so that the letters *c-a-k-e*, rather than *k-a-k, c-a-k,* or *k-a-k-e* are used, normally in their written form.

After one has mastered the spelling of a word, parts of this sequence are performed without conscious effort. If you learned to use the typewriter, you will recall how you progressed from a conscious effort involved in striking each letter to an automatic "cluster" of whole words and phrases. Similarly, the fluent writer expresses abstract ideas or involved concepts without having to grope for words letter by letter, and without resorting to the dictionary or thesaurus, except when an unusual word or its spelling eludes him.

It may help to clarify the steps in the spelling process to note that they are the opposite of the steps in the oral reading process. In reading, one starts by seeing the printed word. If the reader is not completely familiar with the word, the letters are examined. These are associated with the sounds they represent in the oral *vocabulary* of the reader. This oral word is next connected with the meaning which it represents in the *experience* of the reader.

The process used to read and spell differs with individuals. The present analysis may not be descriptive of what *you* do. Some will use sound association much less than others, substituting visual associations. "Seeing" the word for spelling involves a problem that is not present in "seeing" the word for reading. In spelling, the word form must be supplemented by a clear impression of different letter elements in correct sequence. This impression requires not only a longer period of time to see the word for spelling than reading, but also better visual memory and discrimination.

A serious spelling problem is posed by

the phonetic inconsistencies in the way our language is written. Ernest Horn analyzed the word *circumference* by syllables and by letter in order to determine the possibilities for spelling the word by sound. He discovered 288 possible combinations when the word is broken by syllables and 396.9 million possible combinations when each letter is analyzed. In summarizing this study, Horn states: [1]

It is no wonder that a few months after a word has been temporarily learned in a spelling lesson, and subsequently used only occasionally in writing, the child is sometimes confused by the conflicting elements which his pronunciation of the word may call out of his past experience. With so little of the rational character to guide him the wonder is that the child fixes as easily as he does upon the one arbitrary combination which constitutes the correct spelling.

This point can be illustrated in its most extreme form by spelling *potato* as "gh-ough-pt-eigh-bt-eau" by using these sounds: *gh* in *hiccough*, *ough* in *though*, *pt* in *ptomaine*, *eigh* in *weigh*, *bt* in *debt*, *eau* in *beau*.

Everyone knows the uncertainty of the English graphic form *ough* in such words as *though, through, plough, cough, hiccough, rough*. Only slightly less troublesome to the learner are such ambiguities as, *doll–roll, home–come, sword–word, few–sew, break–squeak, paid–plaid*.

When the child meets the letter *a* in a word, it may have one of these sounds: *all, allow, nation, want; e* is different in *legend, legal; i* in *fin* and *final; o* in *pot, post, come; u* in *cub, cubic; y* in *cyst* and *tyrant*. The combinations of vowels are still more perplexing: *ea* has such variations as *clean, bread, hearth; ei* in *receive*, in addition to being a variety for *ie* in *siege*, has a different sound in *neigh* and *weight* and still another in *height*. The *o* combinations give forms like *blood–bloom, cow–crow, shout–should, shoulder—tough, though–rough, couple–court, cough–enough, plough–rough*. Final *e* is generally mute and is supposed to affect the preceding vowel as in *van, vane; rob, robe;* but in *change* and *sleeve* it has no effect and there is a series—*come, dove, love, some, have*—in which the vowel is shortened rather than lengthened.

In our writing of the language, the letter *a* has forty-seven different sound associates. There are 300 different combinations which express the seventeen vowel sounds.

The short *i* sound is especially difficult. It is spelled at least fifteen ways in common words and only in a little more than half the time with the letter *i* alone. Examples are *i* (*bit*), *e, y* (*pretty*), *ie* (*mischief*), *ui* (*build*), *ey* (*money*), *a* (*character*), *ay* (*Monday*), *us* (*busy*), *ee* (*been*), *ei* (*foreign*), *ia* (*marriage*), *o* (*women*), and *ea* (*forehead*). There are other spellings in less common words. In these words one would expect the long vowel sound: *furnace, mountain, favorite, minute,* and *coffee*.

Another sound, the schwa (ə), is found in half of the multisyllabic words in the 10,000 commonest words. It is spelled thirty ways with almost any vowel or vowel digraph: *about, taken, pencil, lemon, circus, teacher, picture, dollar, nation*. Although the use of the schwa may simplify the pronunciation of the unstressed syllables, the implication for spelling is quite different.

Good auditory perception and careful listening habits are a part of spelling study procedure. If children use common pronunciation as a guide for spelling, they face many difficulties. If the pronunciation of a word is somewhat blurred in reading, the sound is still near enough to carry the meaning. In spelling, the word must be exact. Any word with a schwa calls for careful visual discrimination in order to learn the pattern used to spell the sound.

Silent letters are especially perplexing in spelling. If one includes letters not pronounced in digraphs, as in *please* or *boat*, and double letters where only one is pronounced, nearly all letters of the alphabet are silent in some words. In reading we can call them ghosts or use them to identify words that may be confused with others, but in spelling, all these silent letters must be remembered. There is no phonetic clue to their presence in a word.

---

[1] Ernest Horn, "Phonics and Spelling," *Journal of Education* (May 1954). See also E. Betts, "Phonics: Practical Considerations Based on Research," *Elementary English* (October 1956).

But it is wrong to conclude that no phonetic aids exist in the spelling of the language. An analysis of the 3,381 monosyllables in our language and the separate syllables of 2,396 polysyllables in words from the Jones spelling list shows that the English language is 86.9 per cent phonetic. James T. Moore reports that our system of writing is basically alphabetic and that for almost every sound there is a highly regular spelling. He states: [2]

Eighty per cent of all the speech sounds contained in words used by elementary school children were spelled regularly. Single consonants are represented by regular spellings about 90 per cent of the time.

The vowel sounds cause the most spelling difficulty but even here the short a is spelled with an a about 99 per cent of the time as is the short i at the beginning of a word. Short e is spelled with an e about 89 per cent of the time, short o with an o 92 per cent, and short u with the letter u 72 per cent of the time.

The long vowel sounds cause much more trouble in spelling than short vowel sounds. All the long vowels may be written in a variety of ways.

Other studies have indicated that some of the frequently used words of our language do have phonetic consistency.[3] Of the first thousand words on the Rinsland spelling list we find the sound a is spelled as follows, the figures in parentheses representing percentages:

a = *able*(57)	ei = *reindeer*(3)
ay = *lay*(23)	ea = *break*(3)
ai = *laid*(13)	ey = *they*(1)

The sounds of the consonants are more consistent:

b = *bad*(100)	f = *phone*(10.5)
p = *pin*(100)	d = *dog*(99.5)
j = *age*(58.4)	r = *run*(100)
j = *jump*(31.5)	k = *came*(60)
f = *fun*(85.3)	k = *keys*(15.9)

s = *sit*(67.3)	l = *lit*(89.7)
s = *city*(25.1)	l = *ball*(10.3)
m = *me*(100)	n = *no*(99.8)
t = *time*(99.8)	v = *vine*(99.4)
z = *his*(75.5)	z = *zero*(17.4)

The letters that seem so consistent, such as *b*, present spelling problems in words where it is silent as in *bomb, debt, doubt,* or *subtle.* The letter *d* is silent in *handkerchief, handsome,* and *Wednesday,* and in *solder* it has a *j* sound. *P* is silent in *raspberry, receipt, cupboard, corps,* and words like *psalm, pneumonia,* and *psychology.*

An analysis made by Sister Roberta Wolfe of spelling errors in a fifth grade indicated that 36.3 per cent were phonetic mistakes.[4] Vowel substitution formed 8.1 per cent—*sence* for *since, togather* for *together, eny* for *any, lissen* for *lesson.* Vowel omissions form 6 per cent—*busness* for *business.* Doubling or nondoubling caused 5 per cent—*currant* for *current, refuell* for *refuel.* Consonant substitution, endings, and diphthongs caused the remaining errors—*pance* for *pants, feels* for *fields.* Vowel and consonant insertions were not grouped with phonetic errors but are related—*pagun* for *pagan, leater* for *later, stolden* for *stolen, finely* for *finally.*

Phonetic errors seem to indicate a need for emphasis on visual and auditory imagery, but it is apparent that there are elements of unreasonableness in the way our language is spelled.

It would only confuse the child more if this problem were presented to him as he started to learn to spell, but as teachers, we need to understand the phonetic complexity of the task we seek to have mastered.

Spelling is a field in which there is little systematic relationship between growth and the amount of time spent in teaching. It appears probable that growth in ability to spell is related to extensive reading, maturational factors, and the specific needs for oral or written communication. A successively larger number of children spell a given word correctly in each grade. However, the prog-

---

[2] Paul R. Hanna and James T. Moore, Jr., "Spelling—From Spoken Word to Written Symbol," *Elementary School Journal* (February 1953). (Republished as a pamphlet by Houghton Mifflin Company, Boston.)

[3] Unpublished study by R. Madden, San Diego State College, San Diego, Calif.

[4] Sr. Roberta Wolfe, "A Study of Spelling Errors," *Elementary School Journal* (April 1952).

New words from social studies texts or the news are added to the bulletin board as a challenge to good spellers. The notebooks contain an alphabetical list of new vocabulary added by the children. (*Courtesy of the San Diego City Schools.*)

ress does not appear to be closely related to the presence or absence of the word in the formal curriculum. In one study a spurt caused by using a sixth-grade book in the fifth grade was followed by a decline to normal rate. Apparently substantial gains made in special drives, as in spelling contests, prove ephemeral. Perhaps the results are to be expected because of the significance of total maturation in individual spelling abili-

ties when all children have adequate opportunity for learning.

A teacher can build a good spelling program that is consistent with modern psychology and can gain additional time in the curriculum with the following program:

1. Be aware of the words used frequently in everyday speech as revealed by a word list, and make occasional checks

to see if these are being mastered. The *Iowa Spelling Scale* would serve as a guide in judging the appropriateness of specific words for the children in a class.

2. Have the children keep a notebook of words they misspell and once a week have a lesson pertaining to these words. A class list may serve as well.

3. Have planned worksheets available for use by those who are not able to make letter–sound association; divide words into syllables, identify base words, use abbreviations, apply generalizations, etc. These should be ungraded and are appropriate to some children's needs in each of the intermediate grades.

4. Base spelling grades on spelling proficiency as evidenced in written work. (Papers retained in the writing portfolio of each student are a good source of material.)

For such a program to be practical, more individual planning and work are required than most teachers can give to this one subject of the many in the curriculum. Modern textbooks reflect the careful thinking and planning of many individuals. Used as a means for teaching spelling rather than the end of spelling instruction, these textbooks will serve the teacher well. The teacher should feel free to change the words in the assignment to meet the needs of her students. The fact that grade placement of words follows no absolute rules should encourage her to select the lessons in any sequence that seems wise. Above all, she must remember that the average textbook presents the minimum needs of children. Only the teacher can meet the spelling needs represented by each child's desire to express his ideas in words that are uniquely his own.

In light of this, one writer makes an interesting proposal:

Perhaps schools and teachers need to take a new view of spelling. If the demand for absolute perfection in spelling at all stages in all written expression were abandoned in favor of a developmental approach—that is, movement *toward* correct spelling—then children would eventually become more effective spellers. Spell-

ing should facilitate communication of written thought, not limit it. Rather than being limited to writing with words they can spell correctly, children should be encouraged to use their language in as rich a form as possible. They will tend to learn to spell the words they use.[5]

For Discussion

1. How may an awareness of the spelling process used by an individual help the teacher in giving remedial help?

2. What major difficulties does a primary child face when spelling a word that an older individual does not know?

3. What words cause you to have unpleasant feelings as a result of spelling difficulties or other associations?

4. Why would a child write *great* rather than *enormous* if too much emphasis were placed upon correct spelling in creative writing?

What Words Should a Child Study in the Spelling Period?

There are over 600,000 words in a modern dictionary. Textbook writers must determine how many of these should be included in a spelling program. Their decisions have been guided by two significant pieces of research. One, made by Ernest Horn of the University of Iowa, examined correspondence of business firms to learn what words were most frequently used by adults.[6] The second was a nationwide study of children's written material directed by H. D. Rinsland of the University of Oklahoma.[7]

In addition to these research efforts, other scholars have examined the words most frequently misspelled at each grade level, words that are of frequent usage in both adult and

---

[5] E. Brooks Smith, Kenneth Goodman, Robert Meredith, *Language and Thinking in the Elementary School* (New York: Holt, 1970), p. 241.

[6] Ernest Horn, *The Basic Writing Vocabulary* (Iowa City: University of Iowa, 1927).

[7] H. D. Rinsland, *A Basic Writing Vocabulary of Elementary School Children* (New York: Macmillan, 1945).

children's word lists, words common to reading lists, and words that contain special difficulties.

When a group of authors starts to write a spelling textbook, the authors consult all these studies and make a list of their own that reflects their personal philosophy as to what should be done with respect to spelling instruction. Those who feel that success motivates students will usually have a rather short list. Those who stress phonics may include words that are not used very often yet provide phonetics practice. Those who feel that children learn to spell many common words outside of school will emphasize the words in the language that cause misspelling. Usually they include about 4,000 words. A survey of twenty-four of the most popular spelling textbook series revealed that there were just short of 10,000 different words to be found in all these texts.[8]

All studies reveal the interesting fact that a few words of our language are used over and over again. Over one-half of our writing consists of a repetition of the following 100 words:

a	down	I
all	eat	I'm
am	for	in
and	girl	is
are	go	it
at	going	just
baby	good	know
ball	got	like
be	had	little
big	has	look
boy	have	made
but	he	make
can	her	man
Christmas	here	me
come	him	mother
did	his	my
do	home	name
dog	house	not
doll	how	now

of	she	tree
on	so	two
one	some	up
our	take	want
out	that	was
over	the	we
play	then	went
pretty	them	what
put	there	when
red	they	will
run	this	with
said	time	would
saw	to	you
school	too	your
see		

Horn noted that after the first 1,000 words the addition of the next 1,000 added a very small percentage of the words used by writers.

TABLE 7–1

FREQUENCY OF WORD USAGE IN THE AGES OF THE WORD COUNT DERIVED FROM THE HORN BASIC WRITING VOCABULARY *

Different Words	Percentage of Total Word Count
100	58.83
500	82.05
1,000	89.61
1,500	93.24
2,000	95.38
2,500	96.76
3,000	97.66
3,500	98.30
4,000	98.73

* Reprinted by permission of E. Horn from the Twenty-third Yearbook of the National Society for the Study of Education.

A person who learns 2,800 words knows 97 per cent of the words in common use. If he learns the 1,200 words next in frequency he increases his writing vocabulary only 1.1 per cent or up to 98.3 of all the words he will write, which are found among the frequently used words of our language.

Henry D. Rinsland discovered similar facts, as illustrated in Table 7–2.

[8] E. A. Betts, *Spelling Vocabulary Study: Grade Placement of Words in Seventeen Spellers* (New York: American, 1940), p. 143; *Grade Placement of Words in Eight Recent Spellers* (New York: American, 1949).

Table 7–2
Frequency of Word Usage in the
Rinsland Vocabulary *

(e.g., 10 words comprise about 25 per cent of
all children's word usage.)

Different Words	Percentage of Total Word Count
25	36
50	40
100	60
200	71
300	76
500	82
1,000	89
1,500	93
2,000	95

* Reprinted by permission of Henry D. Rinsland and The Macmillan Company from *A Basic Vocabulary of Elementary School Children,* copyright 1945 by The Macmillan Company, New York.

Gertrude Hildreth explains,[9]

The richness of the English language results in infrequency of use for the majority of words. Beyond the short list of words learned in the elementary school years is a tremendous store of thousands of words from which people may wish to select. There are relatively few words used as frequently as *girl* or *get,* but a word such as *gigantic* can be matched by 5,000 other words that are used with about equal frequency in English writing. Ten thousand words is a conservative estimate of a person's life writing needs. It is practically certain what 2,500 of these words will be, but not the remaining 7,500. Some persons will use two or three times ten thousand words in a lifetime of writing.

Some recent research disagrees fundamentally with the principles of functional frequency in the grade placement of words. A Stanford University team studied the sound–letter correspondence or relationships of over 17,000 of the most frequently used words. They sought to find the per cent of these words one could spell correctly on the basis of knowledge of certain phonetic generalizations. They discovered in their re-

search that knowing the phonological structure of written language would allow one to spell correctly 85 per cent of the words one needed. These researchers have given "Some Suggestions for the Study." [10]

The selection of a vocabulary for a modern spelling curriculum should not be primarily a casual compilation of words considered important in children's writing or a basal list drawn from adult usage. True, children must learn to spell the words they need to write, and there must be a selection of words which are appropriate representations of the particular phoneme–grapheme correspondences being taught in a lesson. However, to select a list of "important" words first is to elevate the word list to a position of more importance than it deserves. Instead one should begin with a linguistic analysis of American English, select those correspondences to present for study, and then prepare a group of study words that illustrate the principle, generalization, or correspondences being taught. While it is interesting and useful to know which words most children are likely to write in a given grade, such a list should not limit a child's spelling vocabulary. Spelling is not only a process of mastering the orthography of the spoken vocabulary a child possesses at a certain age; it is at the same time an exercise of continuously expanding both his speaking and writing vocabularies.

By using the resources of linguistic analysis, one can enlarge and deepen the scope of the spelling programs. Children can be expected to be able to spell, in the elementary grades, a vocabulary of from 6,000 to 12,000 or more words, depending upon the size of usable oral vocabularies. By building into the child the analytic power that comes from a knowledge of the structure of the American–English orthography, there will be almost no limit to the eventual size of his spelling vocabulary—except the size of his aural–oral vocabulary itself.

Many spelling programs of the past were based upon such a linguistic approach. The problems of such an approach are illustrated in the study. A computer was "taught" the generalizations regarding the phoneme-grapheme relationship in the syllables of 17,000 words. With this knowledge 49% of the words were spelled correctly and an additional 36% with only one

---

[9] G. Hildreth, *Teaching Spelling* (New York: Holt, 1955), p. 141.

[10] Paul Hanna and others, *Phoneme-Grapheme Correspondence as Cues to Spelling Improvement* (Washington, D.C.: U.S. Department of Health, Education and Welfare, 1966).

error. One cannot question the value of a speller's understanding the association of phoneme and grapheme. Undoubtedly many learn these generalizations by studying the functional word lists of Horn and Rinsland. The fact that the computer misspelled almost half of the words indicates that there are aspects of our spelling that must be specifically taught with respect to individual words. Words such as *acre, buoy, chain, cough, depot, iron, one, colonel, beaux, massacre, myrrh, victual, reservoir* could not be programmed for the computer. . . .

In the previous discussion it appears that the purpose for learning to spell a word is related to the real-life experience the user has with it. If the purpose of studying a word in spelling is due to the child's need to use the word, the mastering of the word would be immediately functional. If the purpose for the study of a word is to learn more of the nature of the language as a code of sound and symbols the words strengthen the child's understanding of the structure of the language. It is that understanding or generalization that becomes functional.

Dr. Horn summarized the reasons for specific instruction about individual words, without disputing the value of understanding the alphabetic nature of our language.*

1. More than one-third of the words in a standard reference work on the pronunciation of American English showed more than one accepted pronunciation.
2. Most sounds can be spelled in many ways, one spelling not being sufficient to call it the most "regular" spelling.
3. Over one-half of the words in a conventional dictionary of American English contain silent letters, and about one-sixth contain double letters when only one letter is actually sounded.
4. Most letters spell many sounds, especially the vowels.
5. Unstressed syllables are especially difficult to spell.

What is implied by the research is that spelling can probably best be taught strictly from a word list with a pretest for each week's words before the children begin studying. This pretest, with immediate correction by the child, should be followed by review of the study method as

needed and by application of the study method to the words that were missed on the pretest. A retest on Wednesday of the words missed and a retest on Friday could comprise the entire spelling program.

Such an approach was piloted in the Glenview, Illinois Schools in 1964, using experimental and control groups with a pre- and post-test design.* Results indicated that children in the experimental program scored as well on the test of studied words as did children in the control group who used a commercial program, and that children in the experimental program scored significantly better on unstudied words, despite the fact that the control group supposedly was building spelling power. The experimental group was studying twice as many words per week as the control group but was devoting only three days a week to spelling, as compared with the five days a week given to spelling in the commercial program.

What happened in the two periods each week that were stolen from the traditional spelling program? This probably is the crucial point in the entire program. Those two periods were devoted to additional experiences in written language: writing, revising, and the teaching of proofreading skills. Teachers reported a great increase in interest in spelling correctly.

What with the crowded school day, children were able to do at least twice as much in the way of written language as they had done in the past because of the two added periods. Such an approach puts spelling into proper perspective. There is no point in learning to spell orally, and there is no point in learning to spell words that one is not going to use in his writing.

In order to develop a current word list, the Glenview Schools, in 1966, engaged in a frequency count involving over a third of a million running words from children's creative writing in grades two through six. That word list is being used as part of the spelling program described above. Teachers, during the school year 1966–1967, kept a tally of words missed by children so that an estimate of the difficulty of each word could be established. The word lists are now balanced in terms of difficulty as well as frequency.

Equal in importance to the problem of *what* words should be taught is the question of *when* a word should be taught. This problem might be emphasized by asking yourself, "At what grade level should the word *school* or *elephant* be taught?" Textbook authors have been guided by the answers to these two questions: "When do children want to use this word? How difficult is it to spell?"

It is a complex task to decide about the difficulty of a word. If we were to take a single word, such as *elephant,* and give it to ten children in each grade in school, we would learn that some children in each grade would spell it correctly and that others would misspell the word. If the following figures indicated those who spelled it correctly in each grade, we would have the beginning of a scale to measure how difficult the word is.

Grade	Number Spelling Word Correctly
2	2
3	4
4	7
5	9
6	9
7	10
8	10

On the basis of both need and possible errror, it would seem that these students needed help on the word during the third and fourth grades. It may be that the word is too difficult for the second and would challenge no one in a seventh-grade class.

The first spelling scale was made in 1913. The most recent scale is the Iowa Spelling Scale by Harry A. Greene.[11]

The extent of the Iowa Spelling Scale indicates the amazing scope of modern research. Approximately 230,000 pupils in almost 8,800 classrooms in 645 different school systems were involved. Because each pupil

[11] Harry A. Greene, *The New Iowa Spelling Scale* (Iowa City: University of Iowa, 1955).

undertook to spell 100 words, a total of over 23 million spellings comprise the data for this scale. With respect to the words *elephant* and *school* the scale provides the following information:

	PER CENT OF CLASS SPELLING WORD CORRECTLY	
Grade	elephant	school
2	0	32
3	5	68
4	24	86
5	55	92
6	57	97
7	74	99
8	82	99

It is obvious from the above table that *school* is a much easier word than *elephant*. However, we still do not know how interested the child in your room is in using the word *elephant*. As a teacher you need a copy of this scale on your desk at all times to give you information about other words that grow out of classroom writing.

Although the Iowa Spelling Scale provides better information than we have had in the past concerning word difficulty, there will remain uncertainties about the grade placement of individual words. When we recognize that the linguistic maturity of each child differs, it is apparent that a formal graded list will be unrelated to the needs of certain children in a classroom.

The first lesson in a spelling textbook may be as difficult as the last. Thus if there are units designed for Halloween or Christmas, it is good judgment to skip to those units at the appropriate time. Similarly, the words in a fourth-grade speller may actually be more difficult for a specific child than those in a fifth-grade lesson. Individual needs cannot be met in spelling, as they often are in reading, by having a sixth-grade child use a fourth-grade book. Each spelling list must be examined and individual needs met by adjustment to the words to be studied.

The Stanford Study suggests this ordering of linguistic information.[12]

First grade is not too early to expect children to make initial examination of the code by which they carry on intercommunication. The average child enters first grade with an understanding and speaking vocabulary of from 5,000 to 10,000 words. But a literate person needs also to communicate by writing. Just as the child learns to speak by first making those sounds easiest to enunciate, so his first writing efforts should be based on those graphemes that most regularly represent the phonemes of his language. The first grade spelling program ought, therefore, to start with a presentation of the beginning and ending consonant sounds, and the "short" vowel sounds, both regularly exemplified in appropriate monosyllabic words in his oral vocabulary. He should also be taught to form carefully the upper and lower case alphabetical letters that represent the phonemes he is learning to identify in words.

As the child develops, more challenging correspondences may be introduced: (1) single sounds spelled with two different letters, (2) consonant beginning and ending clusters, and (3) other correspondences of increasing complexity.

The second grade spelling program ought to lead the pupil to the discovery of rules and generalizations which help explain both consistencies and peculiarities of phoneme–grapheme behavior as illustrated in various spellings of "long" vowel sounds, formation of plurals and third person singular, irregular spellings of "short" vowel sounds, and the beginning concept of syllabication. Further, the second grade pupil should be introduced to the importance of alphabetical order and its value in relation to dictionary usage.

The spelling program in subsequent grades should continue to expand the pupil's knowledge of the orthography of his language and be concerned with increasing emphasis upon examination of factors that influence the correct choice of graphemic representation in increasingly complicated words. Both phonological and morphological bases for mastery of phoneme–grapheme correspondences will be-

come part of his program of study as he becomes more sophisticated in his analysis of the relationships between spoken and written American English.

For Discussion

1. Why do classroom teachers frequently favor a workbook in spelling? What advantages and what disadvantages exist in such a program?

2. Why is a word easy for one child and difficult for another in the same grade?

3. What words do you think will be in the adult needs of children now in school which are not included in the studies listed, such as *computer* and *transistor?*

4. How can you explain the frequent misspellings of such words as *going, Christmas, knew,* and *hear?*

5. Because the basic list of 100 words appears over and over again in the writing of children, why do they need to be isolated for spelling instruction?

6. Think of the number of words you spell correctly that were never in a spelling lesson. How did you learn to spell them?

7. What are some words that would be used in the vocabulary of children in your locality that are not frequently used nationally?

8. Would it be necessary to put all the words in a spelling lesson that children want to use in a special report?

9. Demonstrate that the words in the last lesson of the speller you use are more difficult than those in the first?

A Laboratory in Spelling for Teachers

Psychology confirms two ideas that teachers use to guide their activities. One is to start with the needs and goals of the learner and the other is to make learning an active process. It will help you as you plan for classroom work to experience some of the activities suggested in this chapter for children.

Start with this exercise in proofreading:

---

[12] Paul Hanna and others, *Phoneme-Grapheme Correspondence as Cues to Spelling Improvement* (Washington, D.C.: U.S. Department of Health, Education and Welfare, 1966), p.129.

Your job is to decide, without hesitation or confusion, which is which. If a word is correct, check the space next to it; if it is incorrect, rewrite it correctly.

1. irridescent _____
2. inimitible _____
3. putrify _____
4. superintendant _____
5. tyranny _____
6. ecstacy _____
7. indispensable _____
8. dependant _____
9. descendant _____
10. vilify _____
11. proceed _____
12. sacreligious _____
13. inoculate _____
14. embarrassed _____
15. anoint _____
16. occassional _____
17. perseverance _____
18. achieve _____
19. drunkeness _____
20. dissapoint _____
21. supercede _____
22. ukelele _____
23. coolly _____
24. irresistable _____
25. disappate _____
26. occurence _____
27. seperate _____
28. seize _____
29. alright _____
30. definately _____
31. neice _____
32. wierd _____
33. liquefy _____
34. recieve _____

KEY: 1. iridescent, 2. inimitable, 3. putrefy, 4. superintendent, 5. √, 6. ecstasy, 7, √, 8. dependent, 9. √, 10. √, 11. √, 12. sacrilegious, 13. √, 14. √, 15. √, 16. occasional, 17. √, 18. √, 19. drunkenness, 20. disappoint, 21. supersede, 22. ukulele, 23. √, 24. irresistible, 25. dissipate, 26. occurrence, 27. separate, 28. √, 29. all right, 30. definitely, 31. niece, 32. weird, 33. √, 34. receive.

Following are twenty spelling demons, each spelled two ways. Decide which is the correct form. Consider yourself fair or above average if you get half of them right, but that is not the real purpose of the exercise. Hold a laboratory to diagnose the reasons errors were not identified.

1. (a) alright, (b) all right
2. (a) supersede, (b) supercede
3. (a) embarassed, (b) embarrassed
4. (a) drunkeness, (b) drunkenness
5. (a) irresistible, (b) irresistable
6. (a) occurrance, (b) occurrence
7. (a) ecstasy, (b) ecstasy
8. (a) anoint, (b) annoint
9. (a) occassion, (b) occasion
10. (a) disappoint, (b) dissapoint
11. (a) analize, (b) analyze
12. (a) tyranny, (b) tyrrany
13. (a) inoculate, (b) inocculate
14. (a) cooly, (b) coolly
15. (a) indispensable, (b) indispensible
16. (a) superintendent, (b) superintendant
17. (a) battalion, (b) batallion
18. (a) perseverance, (b) perseverence
19. (a) iridescent, (b) irridescent
20. (a) reccomend, (b) recommend

KEY: 1-b, 2-a, 3-b, 4-b, 5-a, 6-b, 7-a, 8-a, 9-b, 10-a, 11-b, 12-a, 13-a, 14-b, 15-a, 16-a, 17-a, 18-a, 19-a, 20-b.

Have someone dictate the words that follow while you write them. Do not read further at this time.

athletics	bachelor	rheumatism
analyze	buoyance	resistance
apostrophe	ecstasy	persistence
liquid	liquefy	anoint
		siege

Now compare what you wrote with the spelling above. In the group were there common misspellings? What explanation might be given for the erroneous spelling? How did those who spelled each word correctly remember the standard sequence of letters? Did anyone follow a rule to spell correctly? How may your individual errors be analyzed in a manner that will cause you to avoid repeating the error?

One of the simplest spelling games is Endless Chain. A third grade might start with three-letter words. The first child spells *cat*. The next child must then start with a three-letter word starting with the last letter of the previous word, which in this case is *t*, so he might spell *ten*. The next child's word must then start with *n*, such as *not*. When a child cannot think of a word or misspells the one he selects, the chain is broken. Sometimes each child writes the words being spelled orally in order to get a visual image. A college class might start with five-letter words. For variety the words may be adjectives (any number of letters) or names of places (thus involving capital letters). Very soon the students want to use their dictionaries. It adds to the game to let each child have one so that he can find a five-letter word starting with *o*, or whatever letter happens to be the last one in the word previously spelled. See how many words you can make into a chain in two minutes. You might start, for example, with *stand—draft—teach.* . . .

A review of alphabetical order might be given in the fourth grade by having the following message put on the chalkboard:

Can you break the code?

Bmm tuvefout bsf jowjufe up b usftvsf ivou gsjebz jo uif hznobtjvn

Clue: Write the alphabet in sequence and note position of the letters in the message.

How Should Spelling Be Taught?

We have noted the efforts that have been made to find *what* words should be taught, and *when* they should be taught. The problem of *how* words should be taught has been of equal concern. In 1897 J. M. Rice [13] suspected that the methods of spelling instruction were not very efficient. He conducted experiments which convinced many schools that they were spending too much time on the direct teaching of spelling. (To this day we have not been able to decide whether it is best to teach spelling in association with other school work or to have a specific period each day.) The amount of time spent in the spelling period has been reduced to about seventy-five minutes a week

---

[13] J. M. Rice, "The Futility of the Spelling Grind," *Forum* 23 (1897), pp. 169–72.

and the child who already knows the words is permitted to do something of greater value than learning to spell more words.

Ernest Horn demonstrated the efficiency of the test–study plan of organizing a week's work. In this plan the students take a pretest of the weekly assignment the first day. This separates the words they know how to spell from those that need drill. Exercises and other activities to encourage writing of the words that were misspelled are used during the week; a final test of all the words is given at the end of the week. A chart of progress is kept by each student, words missed are added to the next week's lesson, and review lessons are given at intervals to assure a respelling of words studied.

A variation of the above is used under the *study–test* plans. In this program fewer words are given each day but these words are known to be difficult for most of the class. There are daily tests as well as one at the end of the week on all words. The following plans for spelling instruction are typical of many school programs.

Plan A

First Day

1. Introduce the words in the new lesson in a meaningful way.
2. Discuss meanings of words.
3. Use words in sentences.
4. Note which words are phonetic.
5. Note likenesses to words previously learned.
6. Note any unusual spellings.
7. Form visual images and sequence of letters in each word.
8. Write the words.

Second Day

1. Use the words in a worksheet.
2. Do the exercises in the spelling book.
3. Write sentences using the words.
4. Write a story suggested by the words.

Third Day

1. Test and check words with the children.

Fourth Day

1. Study the words missed on the test and words from individual card files.
2. Give additional words to children who have mastered the list by the third day. (This may be done earlier in the week.)
3. Teach additional words by making derivatives.
4. Work with individuals and small groups with special needs.

Fifth Day

1. Give the final test. It is advisable for each child to have a booklet in which to write the words.
2. Check the tests with each child.
3. Test children on additional words learned.

Plan B

In some cases, teachers may wish to (1) present the lesson on Monday, (2) test on Tuesday, giving additional words to children who need no further study on the regular lesson, (3) study the words and use them on Wednesday and Thursday, and (4) give the final test on Friday.

Plan C

Still another plan might be used with some groups. They might be given a pretest on Monday and then plan the following days according to the results of the test.

Tests can be made more interesting and valuable by variety in method. In addition to writing the words of the lesson, certain abilities may be tested. Among them are

1. Circle or underline vowels in certain words.
2. Mark long or short vowels in certain words.
3. Select the words of more than one syllable.
4. Divide words into syllables and mark accents.
5. Write abbreviations of words.
6. Alphabetize the words.
7. Change all singular words to plurals.
8. Show contraction or possession.
9. Introduce words similar to those in the word list to apply generalizations.

Although students sometimes may profit from grading each other's tests, this task is best done by teachers. Students should understand the standard for scoring a test. A word is marked wrong if the letters are not in correct order, or if a capital letter is omitted in a word always capitalized, or if either the apostrophe, period, or hyphen is omitted.

After the papers have been returned to the pupils, a short discussion of the common errors is valuable. Review the steps used in individual study by asking:

1. Did you pronounce and *hear* the word correctly?
2. Did you try to spell by sound when the sound does not agree with the letters?
3. Did you forget the letters in one part of the word?

Each misspelled word should be written correctly in the pupil's individual review list or workbook. Teachers should praise pupils who initiate their own review work. This is one of the habits of the good speller. He is concerned over his misspelling and makes an effort to correct it.

The learner and the teacher should recognize the fact that testing in spelling is done to guide learning. Errors should help the student to direct his study efforts. After the children have rewritten each misspelled word in the review list correctly, the class and teacher should analyze words to diagnose the nature of error. Common types of error are

1. Omission: *the* for *they.*
2. Carelessness: *surily* for *surely.*
3. Phonetic spelling: *Wensday* for *Wednesday.*
4. Repeating or adding a letter: *theeth* for *teeth.*
5. Transposition: *esaily* for *easily.*
6. Ignorance of the word: *parell* for *parallel.*
7. Failure to hear or perceive words correctly: *bureau* for *mural.*

As a teacher examines errors made by children she should analyze possible causes:

Error	*Cause*
acurate for *accurate*	faulty observation
docter for *doctor*	group pronunciation or faulty teacher pronunciation (Break into syllables and point out difficult spots.)
laffun for *laughing*	inaccurate auditory and visual perception
horse for *hoarse*	inaccurate visual perception
athalete for *athlete*	pronunciation error
ate for *eight*	incorrect meaning association
bying for *buying*	incorrect root word association
non for *none* *opn* for *open* *Wensday* for *Wednesday*	too dependent on phonics (Children must be helped early in spelling to note orthographic irregularities of our language.)
beyoutey for *beauty* *exampull* for *example*	overemphasized pronunciation (Words should be spoken naturally.)
cents for *sense* *except* for *accept*	incorrect meaning association (Such words should be taught in pairs.)
askt for *asked* *berrys* for *berries* *largist* for *largest*	unfamiliarity with common word endings (These should be taught as they apply to many common words.)
dissturb for *disturb* *preevent* for *prevent* *bysect* for *bisect*	unfamiliarity with common prefixes
acke for *ache* *bucher* for *butcher* *juge* for *judge*	Failure to note silent letters that appear in some words (Help children to form correct mental images.)
bill for *bell* *brin* for *brain* *alog* for *along*	lack of phonics or faulty writing habits
allright for *all right* *goodnight* for *good night* *airlines* for *air lines*	unfamiliarity with expressions that must be written as two words (Specific teaching is required.)

An analysis of the errors made by a class will reveal a wide variety of spelling of a single word. Usually one point of major difficulty can be located as indicated on page 376. The word *almost* was spelled twenty-six different ways. The most frequent misspelling was a doubling of the *l*. Study exercises are planned to place emphasis upon such parts of words without identifying them as "hard spots." It is apparent that other spots caused spelling trouble as well.

Some persistent spelling errors demand specific attention. *To, too,* and *two* are often confused. The error is usually of the following type:

I am to tired to play.

Seldom is the error:

Word	No. of Misspellings					No. of Ways	Common Type	No. of Occurrences					Specific Errors	No. of Occurrences				
	III	IV	V	VI	Total			III	IV	V	VI	Total		III	IV	V	VI	Total
almost	21	23	28	15	87	26	almost	6	14	19	8	47	ll for l	13	17	20	10	60
													n for m	4	4	6	4	18
already		46	45	25	116	44	allready		13	11	8	32	ll for l		28	19	12	59
													y omitted		11	12	7	30
													e for ea		10	8	4	22
													a for ea		8	3	1	12
family		45	53	31	129	66	famly		10	7	7	24	i omitted		15	21	15	51
													ey for y		6	13	3	22
													n for m		8	10	4	22
													l misplaced		7	9	3	19
first	45	36	27	16	124	35	frist	12	4	18	9	43	ri for ir	14	8	19	9	50
lock	69	38	10	6	123	33	loke	17	14	2	1	34	e added	24	15	3	1	43
													c omitted	21	14	3	1	39
													a for o	10	3	2	1	16
makes	55	33	25	16	129	32	maks	24	15	8	3	50	e omitted	45	21	11	3	80
passed	52	48	58	47	205	22	past	28	44	38	34	144	t for sed	34	44	39	35	152
													st for ss	5	3	18	4	30
vacation		58	51	37	146	86	vaction		9	20	23	52	2nd a omitted		30	26	30	86
													c omitted		10	6	1	17
													ca omitted		6	6	4	16
													k for c		10	2	0	12
while	33	25	22	23	103	54	wile	9	9	5	9	32	h omitted	24	17	12	19	72
													ll for le	6	2	2	6	16

Source: G. C. Kyte, "Errors in Commonly Misspelled Words in the Intermediate Grades," *Phi Delta Kappan* (May 1958), pp. 367–71.

The game is two easy.
To more days until Christmas.

Have the children make charts of this type:

Too = more than enough:
The window is too high.
Too = also: *Jack went too.*

Use *to* like this: *I rode to town.*
I went to see the game.

---

two = 2 (1 + 1): *We found two pennies.*

Note that each is a different part of speech. *Too* is an adverb, *to* a preposition, and *two* an adjective.

The drill found in the exercise above will provide meaningful contrast. Divide the class into teams and choose captains. The captain will give each pupil on his team one of the words listed below. The pupil writes a sentence on a slip of paper, using the word he has been given with *to, two,* or *too.* Take the word *loudly* for Team 1. The pupil may write, "We sang too loudly." Then he writes "Team 1" and his name on his slip and gives it to his captain. The captain tells him whether or not it is correct. Look carefully

for capitals, periods, and correct spelling.

Each team may now choose a pupil to write his sentence on the board. Is each sentence correct? If so, the team scores a point. Then a second pupil is chosen from each team. When any pupil makes an error, his team fails to score. The team that scores the highest wins the game.

When the teams have a perfect score, the teacher may dictate sentences to both teams that involve greater difficulty, such as the following:

1. You have far too many apples to go in that basket.
2. I have two pencils too many.
3. I came to school too late to see the exhibit.
4. Were you too late to go with Tom to town?

Another frequent error is confusion between *its* and *it's*. Make the charts below to help students see the difference.

Have the children write exercises similar to these and write on the chalkboard a story for class practice.

What Is It?

On a sheet of paper write the numbers 1 to 23. Then write *its* or *it's* after each of your numbers, following the numbered blanks in the stories on the next page.

The Teaching of Spelling

Team 1	Team 2	Team 3	Team 4	Team 5
loudly	cold	hot	exciting	sneeze
quietly	run	help	wrestle	whistle
stoves	town	movies	camp	swim
marbles	dogs	puppies	the circus	sing
young	heavy	automobiles	carrots	thin
jump	bad	fast	school	books
dark	the beach	slippery	icy	warm

It's is a contraction meaning "it is."

Examples: *It's a new desk. It's too sweet.*

Its is a passive, like *his* or *your:*

The motor hummed its tune.

A Red Breast

___1___ breast is red. ___2___ song is "Cheer up!" ___3___ home is a nest of grass and twigs. What is it? ___4___ a robin.

Man's Best Friend

___5___ called man's best friend. ___6___ eyes are kind. ___7___ tail wags when ___8___ friendly and happy. ___9___ teeth are sharp, but ___10___ heart is all gold. What is it? ___11___ a dog.

Fenders Easily Bent

It has four wheels. ___12___ motor hums. ___13___ tires screech. ___14___ steering wheel is round and smooth. ___15___ fenders are easily bent or battered. What is it? ___16___ an automobile.

Good for Bones and Teeth

___17___ something to drink. ___18___ color is creamy white. ___19___ good for bones and teeth. Butter is made from ___20___ fat. ___21___ best when ___22___ cold. What is it? ___23___ milk.

A useful extension of this idea is for each pupil to write a story like those above in which the word *its* appears much more frequently than the word *it's*. When a pupil writes his own sentences or stories to illustrate a principle of usage, he is relating a part of his experience, however superficial, to the pursuit of correctness.

Capital letters are a cause of spelling confusion. Have the children note the words that are capitalized in their social studies books, then make a chart of this nature:

A Capital Letters Chart for Me

Do Capitalize

1. The first word of each sentence:
   This afternoon we went to the game.
2. The names of months of the year, days of the week, and holidays:
   February   Wednesday
   Halloween   New Year's Day
3. The names of particular streets, schools, and buildings:
   Adams Avenue   Central School
   Fifth Street   State Office Building
4. The first word and all important words in the titles of books, movies, stories, magazines, and poems.
   Skid
   Charlotte's Web
   My Visit to the City
   The Star Spangled Banner
5. The names of people and pets, the titles and initials of people, the word *I:*
   Miss Helen N. Leech
   My dog, Sport
   Arthur, Jane, and I
6. The names of countries, states, cities, mountains, and rivers:
   New York City, New York
   Cincinnati, Ohio
   Rocky Mountains
   Colorado River
7. The first word in the greeting or closing of a letter.
   Dear Jack,
   Gentlemen:
   Sincerely yours,
   Yours very truly,
8. Words referring to the deity.
   God   Holy Ghost
   Lord   Savior
   Jehova   He

Do Not Capitalize

1. The names of seasons:
   spring
   summer
   winter
   autumn
2. The names of games, birds, trees, flowers, vegetables, fruits, and animals:
   baseball   carrots
   oak   apples
   robin   chickens
   rose   maple

Have the children write the answer to such questions as the following:

Where do you live?
What is your father's name?
What school do you attend?
What countries would you like to visit this summer?
When is your birthday?
What is your favorite subject in school?
How would you address a letter to your principal?
What is the title of your favorite book?

Mimeograph an exercise and have the children change the small letters to capitals.

my cousin lives in denver. her name is emma low. she attends jefferson school. each wednesday they have a class in spanish, last year she went east for her vacation. she heard the president in rhode island. her favorite book is the little house in the woods.

The children who find the above too difficult might be helped by omitting the small letter. (This also avoids showing an error.)

___y cousin lives in ___enver.

Have the children copy this letter, putting in correct capital letters.

115 south hill street
san diego, california
september 6, 1971

dear jim,
our boy scout troop just made an overnight trip to palomar mountain. it was fun since i slept in my own sleeping bag. please write and tell me how the evanston little league made out.

your friend,
jack

A mnemonic device is one that aids the memory. Such devices are highly personal; although they may help some children, they may be merely an additional burden to others, because in order to remember one thing the individual must remember the association among several things.

Below are a few association ideas that may help some children who are having specific spelling difficulties:

all right	*All right* is like *all wrong.*
cemetery	Watch the *e*'s in *cemetery.*
principal	The *principal* is a prince of a *pal.*
separate	There is a *rat* in *separate.*
balloon	A *balloon* is like a *ball.*
familiar	There is a *liar* in familiar.
parallel	*All* railroad tracks are par*all*el.
almost	*Almost always* spelled with one *l.*
capitol	There is a d*o*me on the capit*o*l.
bachelor	The *bachelor* does not like *tea.* (Common error is batchelor.)
yardstick	A *yardstick* is in one piece.

A mnemonic association that works for one person does not always work for another. The associations you think up for yourself are better than the proclaimed masterpieces of others. The more startling an association is, the better it will be remembered.

```
        l
        e
        t
        t                   stationary
stationery                      t
hear        You have to use your ear
                for this one.
independent  We made quite a dent in
                England in 1776.
gram mar    Anyone can spell the first
                half. Copy the second
                part from the first, in
                reverse order.
```

The hardest spelling rule concerns when to double a final consonant and when not to. Note how a single consonant favors a long sound and how a double consonant favors a short sound. Examples will make it clear:

hated	(hatted)	bated	(batted)
mated	(matted)	dined	(dinned)
fated	(fatted)	planed	(planned)
rated	(ratted)	writing	(written)

An association between related words will clarify some spellings. One can remember the *a* in *grammar* by relating it to *grammatical.* One can remember the *a* in *ecstasy* by relating it to *ecstatic*. These blanks can be filled properly by noticing the vowel in the associated words.

dem__cratic	democracy
pres__dent	preside
prec__dent	precede
comp__rable	comparison
comp__sition	composer
hist__ry	historical
janit__r	janitorial
manag__r	managerial
maj__r	majority
ill__strate	illustrative
ind__stry	industrial
imm__grate	migrate
ab__lition	abolish
comp__tent	compete
si__n	signal
bom__	bombard
cond__mn	condemnation
mal__gn	malignant
sof__en	soft
mus__le	muscular

For Discussion

1. Classroom management of testing procedures needs to be planned. How would you distribute workbooks and collect them? Should children check their own papers or exchange them? How do you handle individual words in a test? (Each child will have different errors.)

2. Should one have a "100 per cent" club for those who always achieve 100? Should some who are perfect in an early test be excused from the final? Should a student who is assigned only five words and gets them correct receive the same grade as one who is assigned ten and spells them correctly?

3. Should some students become spelling tutors to help the less able? What would such a student learn from the experience?

4. Why is the term *remedial* inappropriate with respect to teaching a developmental skill?

5. The following examples of phonetic differences in the way we spell might be used to help parents understand the spelling

problem. What other use might be made of such information?

What common word could you get by pronouncing the letters *ssworps*?

Sure. Ss as in *mission*, *wo* as in *two*, and *rps* as in *corps*. What common word could you get by pronouncing the letters *psolocchousc*?

Circus. Ps as in *psychology*, *olo* as in *colonel*, *cch* as in *Bacchus*, *ou* as in *famous*, and *sc* as in *science*.

"*Sugar* is the only English word beginning with *su* sounded as *shoo*."

"Are you sure?"

What common word could you get by pronouncing the letters *ghoti*?

Fish. Gh as in *rough*, *o* as in *women*, and *ti* as in *fiction*. What word has five consecutive vowels?

Queueing.

What word has five *e*'s and no other vowels?

Effervescence.

Pronounce *Pothzwabyuckeling*.

There's nothing to pronounce! Every letter is silent: the *p* as in *pneumonia*, *o* as in *leopard*, *t* as·in *ballet*, *h* as in *catarrh*, *z* as in *rendezvous*, *w* as in *wrong*, *a* as in *dead*, *b* as in *dumb*, *y* as in *today*, *u* as in *four*, *c* as in *czar*, *k* as in *knock*, *e* as in *blue*, *l* as in *would*, *i* as in *cruise*, *n* as in *condemned*, and *g* as in *gnu*.

How Should Spelling Be Taught in the Primary Grades?

In the primary grades the child's individual development in relation to the school objectives strongly influences his spelling needs. It must be remembered that the child is attempting to master the physical skill of writing and that the major teaching objective during these years is to establish sound reading habits.

The peculiar phonetic nature of our language has created a teaching dilemma. We want the child to establish some competence in the use of sounding so that he can learn how to pronounce new words. Reading programs have been designed to help the child do this by means of a carefully selected group of words on which he can practice. As long as the spelling and reading involve the same vocabulary there is a limited amount of conflict. But the reading vocabulary in primary readers is more like the vocabulary of the normal three-year-old. The six-year-old child of today has a relatively large vocabulary. When he writes, it is normal for him to use the words in his oral language, some of which contain the spelling irregularities peculiar to the English language. Any demand for conformity to accepted spelling places a serious limitation on the child's willingness to write his ideas. For this reason we accept the application of phonetic spelling to a primary child's writing. The primary child writes to express his ideas. He uses the letters that will make the proper word sound. The teacher who has been trained to expect it will not be confused when she sees *elephant* spelled *lefant* or *once* spelled *wants*. The acceptance by the teacher of such unconventional spelling seems to give the child confidence in writing.

If the teacher wishes to introduce a spelling period late in the first grade, the words should be related to reading words and should be phonetically simple. Thus spelling can be a successful experience and the child begins to think of himself as a *good* speller.

The close association of the skills of handwriting, reading, listening, and spelling at the primary level creates a number of factors that must be considered carefully. Nearly all that is done to achieve what is called reading readiness leads also to spelling readiness. When the child notes sounds, makes his first phonetic associations, practices at the easel to coordinate hand and eye, or works with clay to develop small hand muscles, his growth in these areas will influence his subsequent development in spelling.

Spelling starts when the child first seeks to produce a written word in order to tell something. First-grade children do this as they label, do reading exercises, write at the chalkboard, or compose group charts.

Many schools do not have specific spelling books or a formal spelling period in the first three grades; instead, the work is directed by means of reading workbooks and writing instruction. When a textbook is used the following procedure is effective:

1. *Introduce the word* (recognition and meaning):
   Teacher writes the word on the board.
   Children point to it in their books.
   Children find it in the story.
   Children use the word orally in meaningful sentences.
2. *Identify letters* (visual and auditory imagery):
   "What letters are needed to write the word?"
   "Have we a new letter in this word?" If so, the teacher shows on the board how to write the new letter.
   Children practice the letter. (Teacher observes and helps where help is needed.)
   (*Again*) "What letters are needed to write the word?"
   "Betty [Joe, all the girls, all the boys, row two, row five, etc.], say the letters needed, fingers pointed to the word and eyes taking a picture of it."
   "Who can tell the letters [spell the word] without looking at the book?"
3. *Write the word* (visual and motor imagery):
   Teacher writes the word on the board, calling attention to the details of letter formation. (Uses ruled lines to set example for height of letters.)
   Teacher writes the word again, and a third time if necessary to strengthen visual imagery and the know-how of writing the word. Children write the word once. (*Compare.*)
   Repeat until the word has been written four or five times, not more.
   Teacher in the meantime observes and helps where necessary.
4. Same procedure for the next word.
5. *Recall:*
   Children spell orally new words learned during a particular study lesson.
   Children recall and spell orally words learned the day before.
   If time permits, children may take a

written trial test on words learned thus far (in a given week).

At the primary level the following drill procedures are suggested:

Teacher flashes a spelling card (written). Child identifies the word and spells it, or all children write the word. In the latter case, children check written words and write those misspelled in a notebook for further study.

"I am thinking of a word that rhymes with *cat* but begins with *h*." Child identifies the word *hat* and spells it orally or all the children write the word.

"I am thinking of a word that tells [means] the kind of weather it is when you need to bundle up to keep warm." (Cold.)

"I am thinking of the base [root] word in *farmed*."

"I am thinking of a word that means the opposite of *high*." (Low.)

List a number of words on the board. Children put heads on desks while the teacher erases one word from the list. Then a child recalls the word and spells it. Repeat until the entire list is erased. Everyone can participate in the game if all children *write* the words as they are erased.

The following are examples of specific spelling lessons:

Grade 2

Objective

To develop the ability to attach inflected and derived forms of known words in which the final *e* is dropped before an ending.

Procedure

1. Write the word *ride* on the board and have it pronounced. Erase the final *e* and add *ing*. Call attention to the dropping of the *e*. Have *riding* pronounced.
2. "What is the root word of *riding?*" Write *ride* opposite *riding*. "How many vowel letters do you see in *ride*? What vowel sound do you hear? Does dropping the silent *e* and adding *ing* change

the sound of the root word? Can you hear *ride* in riding?"
3. Write *talking* on the board. Ask pupils to tell what ending they see and to what root word *ing* was added. Write the root word.
4. Repeat with *coming*.
5. Use the same procedure with *nice—nicer; bake—baker; fine—finer*.
6. Lead the children to formulate the generalization that when a word ends in final *e*, the *e* is usually dropped before adding an ending.

Seatwork

Write the root words after each word:

finest _____
making _____
talking _____
slower _____
liked _____
finer _____
colder _____
moving _____
faster _____
baker _____
longer _____
riding _____
fired _____

LESSON PLAN—STRUCTURAL ANALYSIS

Grade 2

Objective

To develop ability to recognize variants formed by adding *es* to root words.

Procedure

1. Write the following: "I found a mother fox. She had two baby foxes." Have the sentences read; then point to the first and ask, "How many does the next one tell about? What letters are added to *fox* to make it mean more than one?"
2. Write the following: "Johnny rolled the potato across the floor. Johnny

rolled the potatoes across the floor."
Have the sentences read silently and
ask, "Which sentence means that
Johnny rolled more than one potato
across the floor?"

3. Write the following: I wish I had some
cake. Jane wishes she had some cake."
Point to *wishes* and ask, "What ending
is added to *wish* to make *wishes*? Does
es make *wishes* mean more than one?"
Explain that we say, "I wish" but we
say, "Jane wishes" or "he wishes." Read
the sentences using the word in the incorrect way: "I wishes" and "Jane
wish."

Grade 2

Objectives

To promote ability to recognize inflected
forms by adding *er* and *est*.
To express ideas in comparative terms.

Procedure

1. Write the word *short* and have it pronounced.
2. Add *er* to make it *shorter*. What word
is this?
3. Erase *er* and add *est*. Now what word
is this?
4. Repeat with *long*. (*longer, longest*)
5. Draw three lines and write these sentences and fill in the blanks:

   first   The _____ line is the longest
   of all.

   second The _____ line is shorter
   than the second.

   third   The _____ line is the shortest of all.

6. Write the following words on the board,
have each pronounced, and have pupils
use them in sentences: *cool, cooler,
coolest; hot, hotter, hottest; big, bigger,
biggest; deep, deeper, deepest.*

Seatwork

1. Write these sentence on the board and
have the children copy the sentences
and all the comparative endings.

I am big_____ than you are.
It is hot_____ today.
He is the nice_____ boy I know.
She is much nice_____.
The wind is getting cold_____.
He is the fast_____ boy on our team.

2. Write *-er* endings and *-est* endings for
  fast   *big*   *cold*   *hot*
  nice   *deep*   *slow*

LESSON PLAN (Spelling)

Grade 2

Objective

To teach the children how to spell words
through observing, listening, and writing.

Materials

Spelling story (on board).
Pencils (in desks).
Paper. (Distribute before children come
into the room.)
The story: *Our News*
  There are thirty-six at *school* today.
  We will *read* a new book.
  We have a *new* turtle.

Method

Have the children:

1. Put name on paper and fold into four
columns.
2. Look at the story and be able to read
it.
3. Read the story, one sentence at a time.
4. Frame the words.
5. Put a box on the board with letters
in it.

Ask the children:

6. "What spelling word do we have that
has all of these letters?"
7. "What letter goes first?" (school)
8. "Can you use it in a sentence?"
(child's name)

9. "What can you tell me about the word?" (silent *h;* double vowel)
10. "Let's close our eyes and think of the word. Think of the silent *h,* double vowel, size. Spell it to yourself."
11. "Look at the board to see if you spelled it right."
12. "Close your eyes and spell the word for me." (child's name)
13. "Write the word in your first column. Write it in the second."
14. "Let's spell the word once."
15. "Who can read this word for the class?" (Point to *read.*)
16. "Can you use it in a sentence?"
17. "Let's look at the word carefully. What can you tell me about it?"
18. "Let's close our eyes and think of the word. Think of the two vowels, silent *a,* three short letters, and one tall letter. Spell it to yourself. _____. Can you spell it?"
19. "Let's look at the word and spell it once again."
20. "Write it on your paper."
21. "Write it in the second column."
22. "Write it in the third column by memory."

For Discussion

1. Evaluate the influence upon primary spelling of the forty-four symbols taught in the Initial Teaching Alphabet (I.T.A.). Does it actually teach misspelling?
2. What is gained by combining primary handwriting and spelling instruction?

How Are Generalizations Formed in Spelling?

In psychology the word *generalization* describes the process of discovery in a learner as he notices identical elements in different situations. If one teaches generalizations made by others, these become the traditional spelling rules. Good spelling teachers plan situations in which the identical elements needed for a generalization may be discovered by the learner. For example:

TEACHER: Quick is an interesting word. The *qu* sounds like *k.* What other words do you know that start like *quick? (These words are listed on the board.)* Do you notice anything about these words? Yes, they start with *q.* Let's look in our dictionary and notice the words that start with *q.* What do you notice about spelling words that start with *q?* Yes, usually *q* is followed by *u. (An exception is Iraq.)*

Follow these suggestions:

1. Before considering a generalization be certain that enough words are known to the child to form it.
2. Help the child to notice why there are exceptions, such as attempting to pronounce the plural of *dress* only by adding an *s* rather than *es.*
3. Consider only one generalization at a time. The following generalizations are usually taught:
   a. Forming plural of nouns by adding *s* to the singular.
   b. Forming plurals by adding *es* to words ending in *s, x, sh, ch.*
   c. Forming plurals by changing *y* to *i* and adding *es.*
   d. Forming plurals by changing the singular forms.
   e. Using an apostrophe in a contraction.
   f. Using a period after abbreviations.
   g. Forming singular possessives by adding *'s.*

   Dropping final *e* when adding a suffix beginning with a vowel.

   Keeping the final *e* when adding a suffix beginning with a consonant.

The following two lessons will illustrate the development of generalizations with children:

Type of Lesson: Simple Generalization.[14]
Generalization: "Many new words are developed from root words by simply adding -*s,* -*ed,* or -*ing* to a root word, without any other change."

_____
[14] Grosse Point Public Schools, *Thinking About Spelling* (Grosse Point, Mich.: 1948).

Individualized instruction is usually an essential aspect of spelling instruction. (*Courtesy of the Burbank Public Schools.*)

Aims

1. To show that by adding -*s*, -*ed*, and -*ing* to many words one can spell three or four more words after learning to spell the root word only.
2. To extend gradually the concept of generalization so that pupils can use it as an aid in discovering correct spellings.

Materials

The words were chosen from word lists for grades 2 and 3.

play	rain	help	spell
want	garden	burn	clean
need	open	paint	pull

This list was chosen for the simple meanings at the grade 3 level and because they are base words to which the suffixes -*s*, -*ed*, and -*ing* can be added to make new words without any other change. Thus, if the child learns to spell *play*, he should be able to generalize and spell *plays*, *played*, and *playing*.

Procedure for the Week

Monday

1. Present root words somewhat as follows: "Here are the new words to be learned this week. Some of them you

already know because you had them in the second grade. Who can point out one that we know?"

2. Have a child point out one and spell it. Continue somewhat as follows: "This week we have chosen some words that we already know how to spell because we are going to learn to use a spelling trick that will save us time and work. We will take the word *play*. Let us call this a root word. *Root word* means the simplest form of a word. In talking, writing, and spelling, we use many forms of a root word by adding one or more letters to it to make new words that we need. Let us see what happens to *play* when we add an *s*. What word does this make?"

3. Use both in sentences and demonstrate on the board. "Barbara and Bill play with the dog." "Barbara plays with the dog," etc.

4. Have pupils demonstrate with other words in list, until you are sure they understand. Have pupil tell what he does as he changes word at the board. Have pupil spell new word without looking at the board.

5. Use remainder of the period for supervised study period. *Pronounce, use,* and *study* each word.

Allow the best spellers to spell the root words and make a new word from each by adding *s*. Their work can be checked individually.

Tuesday—Review

1. Have the root words written on the board. Give ample opportunity for recall of the new spelling trick. Select several pupils to go to the board and change a word by adding *s*, spelling it as they do so.

2. Point out again that we only had to add one letter to make a whole new word, which we could spell without studying.

3. Suggest that there is another trick by which one can add another ending and get another word. (Perhaps some child will be able to show this step.)

4. One of these endings is *-ing* with the sound, *ing*. Using *play*, add *ing* to show that the new word now becomes *playing*. Example: "Bobby is *playing* with James."

5. Call for a volunteer at the board to change *help* to *helping*.

6. Go through the whole list, showing by pupil demonstration how each word may be changed and used.

7. In the same manner add *-ed* and get *played*, *rain* and get *rained*, etc.

8. Have all pupils make a chart as follows. Pronounce several of the words. Have pupils spell the other forms.

Base Word	New Words Formed		
	+ -s	+ -ing	+ -ed
1. play	play*s*	play*ing*	play*ed*
2. rain	rain*s*	etc.	etc.

9. Announce that there will be a test on Wednesday. Suggest that maybe only the root word will be given and they will be asked to build three new words from it.

10. How many new words should we be able to spell by Friday (count) (36 new words) (48 words counting root words)?

Wednesday

The trial test may be a game. Explain that different forms of the words will be given, such as play*ed*, jump*ing*, help*s*, etc. Each pupil must spell the word correctly and then write the root word following the form pronounced. Give children time to correct the mistakes and rewrite the words (NOTE: Do not give words that end in *k* for examples of the *-ed* ending. The pronunciation is not clear enough. It sounds like *t*. Example: *bark, barked*. Explain this later to the pupils.)

Thursday

1. Reproduce chart on board.
2. Give only the root word. Have indi-

vidual children fill in the spaces under careful guidance. (Choose those who had errors on Wednesday.)

3. Have pupils spell orally all four forms.
4. To show a working knowledge, give about three new base words, such as *look, fill, hunt,* and have the children discover the derived forms from them.
5. Select only words to which the generalization will apply.
6. Caution the children that there are some words which have other changes before *-s, -ed,* or *-ing* are added. To explain an instance in which other changes in words are necessary, select the word *grow.* Try the generalization. Show pupils that they do not say *grow—ed,* but use *gr—w.* See if some child can supply the *e.* Such exercises develop *thought spelling.*

Friday—Final Test

1. At this time, as many of the derived words as desired may be used.
2. After the derived word is pronounced, the group could be asked to give orally, then write the root words beside the other as an aid to spelling.
3. Check papers. Make note of pupils who do not understand the process. Repeat this type of lesson soon for these pupils.

Individual needs may be met in these ways:

1. Pupils who are able to learn more words could be allowed to take their readers, find words with these endings, and write the root word, followed by other derived words. These should be checked individually.
2. A few extra words from the grade 2 or 3 list could be given, such as *add, hunt, wheel, seat.*
3. Those pupils who did not learn the trick should be given copies of the chart and several of the easy words to work on the following week for extra practice.

After a generalization is discovered it is important that a maintenance program be planned to use this knowledge.

1. Every subsequent list of words should be studied for new words, derivatives of which are formed by adding *-s, -ed,* and *-ing.*
2. A number of words in the third-grade list are formed with other generalizations, which will be learned later. The teacher should explain this to the pupils as they discover them.
3. One group of words which may confuse them—such as *know, hear, grow, bring, buy, fall, find*—may be used to show how new words are formed by adding *-s* and *-ing,* but a different word is used to form the past, such as *knew, heard,* and so on, instead of simply adding *-ed.*
4. Extending the pupils' experiences to include the spelling of derived forms as they learn the base words will prepare them to write more fluently and with fewer errors in written English situations. Individual discovery of spellings creates an interest in the various forms of words they use and causes pupils to scrutinize more carefully the arrangement of letters in all words. The feeling of success in achievement (learning the spellings of forty-eight new words in a week) has a tonic effect on attitude toward learning to spell.
5. This generalization is a valuable one at this level for there are many words to which it applies.

Other words that can be used for this generalization are the following:

Second-Grade List

ask	look
call	last
end	show
milk	snow

Third-Grade List

add	land	park
count	learn	part
fill	light	pick
jump	nest	pull

The following lesson might be taught in

grade 4 and above to establish the silent *e* generalization.

General Aims

1. To provide children with adequate methods of word study, so that they may gradually solve their spelling difficulties individually.
2. To increase child's written vocabulary.
3. To stimulate pride in correct spelling in all written situations.

Specific Aims

1. To introduce the use of the generalization: "Many words ending in silent *e* drop the *e* before adding *-ing* or *-ed*."
2. To extend gradually the use of the silent *e* generalization to include the use of other common suffixes, such as *-er, -est, -able,* beginning with a vowel.
3. To emphasize the fact that in adding suffixes, such as *-ly, -ful, -ness, -less,* beginning with a consonant, do not drop the final *e*.
4. To develop the concept of learning to spell by the use of insight' or transfer of training as well as automatic memory.
5. To emphasize the economy of time and effort in becoming a good speller when insight is used.

Materials

The following word list was selected from the word list for grades 3 and 4:

skate	hope
dance	bake
close	chase
share	divide
vote	smoke
move	love
place	trade
line	

Approach

A very easy group of words ending in silent *e* was chosen from the third- and fourth-grade list so as to present as few spelling difficulties as possible in mastering the root words. Attention here should be focused on what happens to the root word ending in silent *e* when the endings *-ing* and *-ed* are added to make new words. When this is clearly understood, the fun of discovering new words and their spellings by adding these endings to other silent *e* words should follow.

Procedure for the Week

Monday

1. Teach or review meaning of *root word, syllable, vowel, consonant, silent letter, derived.* Illustrate and ask for examples to make sure pupils understand.
2. Begin the lesson in the following way: "Most of you already know how to spell some of these words, for several of them you learned in the third grade. The others are easy. Let us look carefully at these words. What final letters do you see in all of them? Yes, it is *e*. [Bring out the fact that it is silent by having words pronounced.] This week we are going to learn how to spell twenty-four or more new words without studying them. To do this, we will use a spelling trick on these root words. Before we are ready to learn the trick we must be sure we can spell the root words. Remember, they all end in a silent *e*."
3. Study ease words. Make sure pupils can spell them.

Tuesday

1. "Yesterday we noticed some things that were alike in all these root words. What are they?" (Each ends in *e*. Final *e* is silent.)
2. "You often learn to use new words by adding new endings to root words. (Illustrate with *skate-s*.) Each ending changes the meaning and the spelling of the word. Let us see what happens when we add the ending *-ing* to *skate*.

This is the trick." Write *skate* on the chalkboard. Erase *e,* adding *-ing.* "What new word does this make? What happened to the final *e* when we added *-ing?*"

3. Write *skate* on the board and say, "Let us see what happens when we add the ending *-ed.*" (Erase *e* and add *-ed,* calling attention to return of the *e* when we add *-ed.*) Illustrate on board the need for dropping final *e,* to avoid skat*eed.*

4. Repeat same procedures with *dance, close, share.*

5. Let pupils make new words with *vote, move, place,* by adding *-ing* and *-ed.* Carry on with pupils at chalkboard and in seats. Bring out the fact that the trick works for all words in the list.

6. Let pupils try phrasing the generalization for all of these words. A simple wording is this: "Most words ending in silent *e* drop the *e* before adding *-ing* or *-ed.*" Write this on the chalkboard and leave for further reference.

7. Let several pupils come to the board to illustrate by stating the rule and spelling the word formed.

8. Address class somewhat as follows: "This week's spelling words should not be difficult. When you learn the base words you can easily spell the derived words by following the rule. How many words will we have in our final test?" (Three times the number of root words.)

Wednesday

1. Turn to the list of base words on the chalkboard. Have one child pronounce all the words. Review the application and statement of the generalization.

2. Pass out duplicated sheets (see sample) and say: "Complete this chart by adding *-ing* and *-ed* to the words you learned Monday. The new words are called derived words. The first one is done for you. Perhaps you will need to read the generalization before you start to work."

3. Call attention to the increase in pleasure

and the decrease in work that comes from spelling by transfer.

4. Check work of poor spellers as they proceed.

Thursday

1. Pass out duplicated sheets again. Explain to children that you will pronounce the root words or their derivatives and they are to put them in the correct spaces. See that the children are following directions.

2. Be sure that the children think of the generalization as a way to increase their ability to spell without study.

Friday

1. Test on generalization: "dropping the final *e.*" Have pupils prepare three columns on their papers.

2. Mastery test: spell root word and both derivatives for each as pronounced.

3. To give practice in recognizing word variants by identifying the base word, the following lesson might be used: Write the following words on the chalkboard. Have pupils copy in a single line on paper. Then opposite these words write the word from which the derived word was formed. (Example: *glancing—glance.*)

faced	saving	smoking
sneezing	poked	graded
taking	prancing	stating
chased	loving	becoming
noticing	taken	blamed

4. Children may show that other derived words can be made by adding other suffixes such as *-er* or *-est,* or *-able* to *love, notice, move,* etc. Continue to show how many new words they can spell by using this generalization.

5. In order to avoid the development of incorrect ideas concerning the addition of *-ed* to all base words when we wish to make them tell what happened yesterday rather than today, it is advisable to call attention to other ways of changing a root word. We say *lost* not *losed,*

took not *taked, drove* not *drived,* etc. These changes should be noted, not as exceptions to our present generalization ("Most words ending in silent *e* drop the *e* before adding *-ing* or *-ed*"), but rather as unusual changes in root words in order to change the meaning of the word.

6. There are a few exceptions which may well be noted. We do not drop the silent *e* in such words as *see, free, agree,* when we add *-ing,* although we do so when we add *-ed* in order to avoid *freeed.*

Lessons of the following type should follow in order to reinforce the learning.

1. Extension of the use of generalization—for words ending in silent *e* to include *all* common suffixes.

   a. Use small groups of words ending in silent *e* to which common endings or suffixes, such as *-er, -able,* or *-est,* can be added. (Note that *-ed, -ing, -er, -est, -en,* and *-able* all begin with vowels.)

   love lov*ed* lov*ing* lov*er* lov*able*
   use us*ed* us*ing* us*er* us*able*

   Pupils should be encouraged to note other words ending in final *e* which they use often in their writing to add to spelling lists.

   b. Use groups of words to show that final *e* is *not dropped* when adding common endings such as *-s, -ly, -ness, -ful, -less,* and *-ment.* (Note that these suffixes begin with consonants.) Use only the forms of words which pupils understand readily and can use in meaningful sentences. The following words are appropriate.

   voice voice*s* voice*less*
   care care*s* care*less* care*ful*
   love love*s* love*ly*
   bare bare*ness* bare*ly*
   brave brave*s* brave*ly*

   case case*s* case*ment*
   sore sore*s* sore*ness*

   Have pupils suggest others that they use.

   c. Formulate a statement of the generalization for suffixes beginning with a consonant.

2. Maintaining and developing skill in the use of the generalization as a spelling aid.

   a. Pupils should be exposed to many new situations with root words in which they are asked to discover spellings of derived words. They should say orally the derived form for a given use of a base word, try to spell it by substituting other letters or adding syllables, then write it. "Checking guesses" is an important step in this procedure. This play with words combines ear, eye, and thought spelling so that pupils have several types of associations to aid in recall. Games based on such procedures can be devised. Saving of effort and time and having fun with words should be stressed.

   b. When selecting words for spelling lists in grades 3, 4, 5, and 6, make sure that representative root words or their derivatives are used each week so that the new word list can be analyzed for the purpose of detecting words with which pupils have learned to deal through generalization, i.e., include a *-y* word; one ending in silent *e;* others to which *-s, -ed,* or *ing* can be added without change; and so on.

   c. Group root words included in grade list ending in silent *e* to which pupils are to add common endings beginning with vowel or consonant through using generalization, such as nic*er,* nic*est,* nic*ely;* care*ful,* car*ing,* care*less,* car*ed;* clos*er,* clos*est,* clos*ely,* clos*eness.*
   Make hectograph chart as follows:

Base Word	Derived Words								
	-ing	-ed	-er	-est	-s	-able	-less	-ful	-ness	-ly

d. Other words in the list for grade 4 that can be used for the application of this rule should be noted.

e. Note important exceptions, such as *tie, die, lie, tying, dying, lying.* (Final *e* preceded by *i* is dropped and the *i* changed to *y.*) Teach these individually, because they are common words often used. See if children can think of others.

f. *Emphasize* the value of using generalizations by having pupils select certain derivatives or root words formed from words in list which they agree to add to list *without study.* Provide opportunity each week for pupils to practice use of generalization with these unlearned words. A limited number of such words should be pronounced and spelled in the *final* test each week.

g. A correlated lesson with reading will extend the use and understanding of this generalization dealing with the spelling of one-syllable words. Change the emphasis of the reading aid, "Words of one syllable containing two vowels, one of which is a final *e*, the first vowel is usually given long sound."

Apply it as an aid in spelling one-syllable words when they are pronounced. Take such a word as *safe* —ear spelling would stop at *saf*, but applying the reading rule for final *e* spelling would help the children to remember to add the silent *e*— *safe*, also *side, shake, cave,* and so on.

In the middle and upper grades a number of generalizations may be drawn inductively from experience with words. Examples of such generalizations suggested as important are the following: [15]

1. Plurals of most nouns are formed by adding *s* to the singular: *cat, cats,* etc.
2. When the noun ends in *s, x, sh,* and *ch,* the

plural generally is formed by adding *es: buses, foxes, bushes, churches.*

3. A noun ending in *y* preceded by a consonant forms its plural by changing the *y* to *i* and adding -*es: body, bodies.* Words ending in *y* preceded by a vowel do not change *y* to *i: boy, boys.*

4. Plurals of a few nouns are made by changing their form: *woman, women; mouse, mice; scarf, scarves.*

5. An apostrophe is used to show the omission of a letter or letters in a contraction: *aren't, we'll.*

6. An abbreviation is always followed by a period: *Mon., Feb.,* etc.

7. The possessive of a singular noun is formed by adding an apostrophe and *s: father, father's.*

8. The possessive of a plural noun ending in *s* is formed by adding an apostrophe: *girls, girls'.*

9. A word that ends in silent *e* usually keeps the *e* when a suffix beginning with a consonant is added: *nine, ninety; care, careful.*

10. A word that ends in silent *e* usually drops the *e* when a suffix beginning with a vowel is added: *breeze, breezing; live, living; move, movable.*

11. A one-syllable word that ends in one consonant following a short vowel usually doubles the consonant before a suffix that begins with a vowel: *fat, fattest; big, bigger, biggest.*

12. A word of more than one syllable that ends in one consonant following one short vowel usually doubles the final consonant before a suffix beginning with a vowel provided the accent is on the last syllable: *commit, committed, committing; forget, forgetting.*

13. A word ending in *y* and following a consonant usually changes the *y* to *i* before a suffix is added unless the suffix begins with *i: cry, crying.* A word that ends in a *y* and following a vowel usually keeps the *y* when a suffix is added: *buy, buys, buying.*

14. The letter *q* is usually followed by *u* in a word.

15. The letter *i* is usually used before *e* except after *c*, or when sounded like an *a* as in *neighbor* and *weight.* Exceptions: *neither, either.*

16. Proper nouns and adjectives formed from proper nouns should always begin with capital letters: *America, American.*

Other phonic generalizations that apply two thirds of the time or more are

1. If the only vowel letter is at the end

---

[15] Board of Education of the City of New York, "Teaching Spelling" (Curriculum Bulletin, Series No. 6, 1953–54).

Reading exercises frequently concern spelling skills. Spelling instruction and practice occur in all areas of the curriculum. The spelling period is a laboratory for practice and study of specific aspects of spelling. (*Courtesy of the Burbank Public Schools.*)

of a word, the letter usually stands for the long sound (*he, she, me*).

2. The *r* gives the preceding vowel a sound that is neither long nor short (*horn, more, worn*).

3. When a vowel is in the middle of a one-syllable word, the vowel is short (*rest, grass, glad*).

4. The first vowel is usually long and the second is usually silent in the digraphs *ai, ea,* and *oa* (*nail, bead, boat*).

5. Words having double *e* usually have the long *e* sound (*seem, tree, week*).

6. In *ay* the *y* is silent and gives *a* its long sound (*play, say, day*).

7. When the letter *i* is followed by the letters *gh,* the *i* usually stands for its long sound and the *gh* is silent (*high, fight, might*).

8. When *y* is the final letter in a word, it usually has a vowel sound (*dry, my, fly*).

9. When there are two vowels, one of which is final *e,* the first vowel is long and the *e* is silent (*bone, home, write*).

10. When *c* and *h* are next to each other, they make only one sound, usually pronounced as in *church* (*catch, child, watch*).

11. When *c* is followed by *e* or *i,* the sound of *s* is likely to be heard (*cent, city, circle*).

12. When the letter *c* is followed by *o* or *a* the sound of *k* is likely to be heard (*camp, came, call, come*).

13. When *ght* is seen in a word, *gh* is silent (*fight, though, might*).
14. When a word begins with *kn*, the *k* is silent (*knew, know, knife*).
15. When a word begins with *wr*, the *w* is silent (*write, wrote, writing*).
16. When two of the same consonants are side by side, only one is heard (*happy, called, guess*).
17. When a word ends in *ck*, it has the same last sound as in *look* (*black, brick, sick*).

Many old rules must be evaluated carefully not only as to their accuracy but also as to the child's ability to use the rule in practice. It was once taught that when two vowels are found together in a word, as in *each*, the second is silent but helps the first to "say its own name" or have the long vowel sound. If you check the words in spellers, you will find more exceptions to this rule than applications of it.

It is not true that one can spell correctly by "spelling the word the way it sounds." In fact thiss staytment iz enuff to mayk won shreak. However, some phonetic generalizations should be mastered in the intermediate grades. The polysyllabic words in the Rinsland list contain 23,000 syllables. Of these, fifty are key syllables spelled consistently the same way. The fifty are listed on the page following.

(*Courtesy of United Features Syndicate.*)

Initial Syllable	Medial Syllable	Final Syllable
re ceive	an i mals	go ing
in to	Jan u ar y	start ed
a round	sev er al	mat ter
de cided	dec o rated	on ly
con tains	af ter noon	hous es
ex cept	el e phant	va ca tion
un til	pe ri od	ver y
com mon	reg u lar	pret ty
dis covered	In di an	re al
en joy	won der ful	ta ble
an other	car ni val	af ter
o pen	gym na si um	base ment
e ven	ar ti cle	sto ry
pro gram	ear li est	long est
ac ci dent	o ver alls	sev en

The syllable which occurs most frequently is *ing,* which is found in 881 words. Thus a child who has learned to spell the *ing* syllable in one word will know it in 880 more. A test might be given asking that only the first syllable heard be spelled, as the words in the first column are pronounced, the second syllable as the next column is heard, and so on.

A test of the following type might be given to intermediate-grade children to discover those who already are able to apply some phonetic knowledge to spelling.

To the students: I am going to pronounce some words that do not have a meaning. You are to spell these words as they sound to you.

băb	lib	tad	chad	theet
dod	mif	ving	clace	twit
fim	nam	wed	cray	spug
gog	paber	yim	flest	squat
huf	rading	zet	gloil	quam
jil	sim	blash	plold	over
			brays	shork

When the regular spelling test is given check the ability to transfer phonetic knowledge in this manner:

Word in Spelling Lesson	Pronounce This Word and Use in a Sentence
stop	stopping
blow	black
shrill	drill
nation	vacation

There are some learners who do not form generalizations with ease and thus need special help in spelling. If you have a poor speller who is an able student capable of doing better work and who *wants* to spell correctly, suggest that the following steps be followed in learning to spell a word: [16]

Step 1. Look at the word very carefully and say it over to yourself. If you are not sure of the pronunciation, ask the teacher to say it for you, or look it up in the dictionary yourself.

Step 2. See if the word can be written just the way you say it. Mark any part of the word that cannot be written the way you say it.

Step 3. Shut your eyes and see if you can get a picture of the word in your mind. If you cannot get a clear picture of the word, you can remember the parts that are written the way you say them by pronouncing the word over to yourself or feeling your hand make the movements of writing the word. If you are learning the word *separate,* all you need to do is to say the word to yourself very carefully and then write what you say. If there are any parts of the word that you cannot write the way you say them, you will probably have to remember them by saying something you can write. Say the letters, if necessary, for these syllables of the word, but not for the rest of the word.

Step 4. When you are sure of every part of the word, shut your book or cover the word and write it, saying each syllable to yourself as you write it.

Step 5. If you cannot write the word correctly after you have looked at it and said it, ask the teacher to write it for you in crayon on a strip of paper. Trace the word with your fingers. Say each part of the word as you trace it. Trace the word carefully as many times as you need to until you can write it correctly. Say each part of the word to yourself as you write it. After you have learned words in this way for a while you will find you can learn them as easily as the other children do without tracing them. (Some teachers have the child trace the word in sand or on fine sandpaper in order to achieve a greater touch impression.)

Step 6. If the word is difficult, turn the paper over and write it again. Never copy the word directly from the book or from the one

---

[16] From *Remedial Techniques in Basic School Subjects,* by Grace M. Fernald. Copyright 1943, McGraw-Hill Book Company, Inc. Used by permission.

you have just written, but always write it from your memory of it.

Step 7. Later in the day, try writing the word from memory. If you are not sure of it, look it up again before you try to write it.

Step 8. Make your own dictionary. Make a little book with the letters of the alphabet fastened to the margin so that it is easy to see them. Write any new words you learn, or any words that seem especially difficult for you, in this book. Get this book out often and look these words over, writing again, from time to time, those that seem difficult. When you write these words by yourself, do just as you did when you learned them the first time. Say them, looking at them while you say them, and then write them without looking at the word in your book.

For Discussion

1. Recall a student who was bright in other school work but was unable to spell. Was attitude a part of the problem? What other explanations might be given?

2. What pressures cause children to cheat in a test?

3. Why are students unmotivated by continuous failure?

4. Are there some words you habitually misspell? What remedial action would you suggest?

5. Make a tabulation of errors from one final test of a class. Detect common needs suggested by the errors?

6. Why is it more difficult to change the habit of misspelling than to teach the correct spelling of a new word?

7. Recall an association you have used to help remember the spelling of a word. These are called mnemonic devices. Sometimes the more absurd they are, the easier they are remembered. For example, one could say *dessert* has *ss,* whereas *desert* has only one *s,* because one would rather have more of it. Or remember the stationery you write on has *er,* just like *letter.* Make a collection of these devices used in your class.

8. For some groups such simple generalizations as saying that adding *s* makes more than one or that each syllable has a vowel are quite an achievement. Tell how you would teach one of these.

9. What spelling rules help you spell a word? How do you use them?

10. Do you think it might be possible to omit a spelling period in some classes? Give reasons for your answer.

11. Are there words in your listening or reading vocabulary that are not in your speaking and writing vocabulary? Which vocabulary is largest?

What Dictionary Skills Do Children Need?

Children need to appreciate the tremendous effort that has gone into the production of the dictionary they use. Let them discuss what it must be like to live in a country that does not have a dictionary for reference. There are many such countries.

Yet the idea of a dictionary is not new. The Assyrians prepared a dictionary of their language nearly 2,600 years ago. Other people, notably the Greeks and Romans, prepared dictionaries, but these included only the rare and difficult words to be found in their language. With the coming of the Renaissance, during the fourteenth and fifteenth centuries, a great deal of attention was turned to the early literature of the Greeks and Romans. This brought about the preparation of lexicons and glossaries containing the translated meanings of foreign words.

It was not until about the middle of the eighteenth century that any attempt was made to catalogue the common words in the English language. The most complete work was done by Samuel Johnson, who brought out his famous dictionary in 1755. Johnson spent nearly eight years in getting his book ready and did make an effort to include the most accepted spelling and definition for each word that he used.

The first American dictionary of 70,000 words came from the pen of Noah Webster in 1806. The Merriam Brothers brought out their dictionary in 1864 with 114,000 words. The Second Edition (1934) contained over 600,000 entries. The last revision of the Second Edition contained a little more than 750,000 words, of which over 100,000 were new entries. In 1962 the radically new Third Edition appeared, causing considerable controversy among scholars because of its inclusion of many words and expressions previously considered to be substandard or slang. The Third Edition contains 100,000 "new" words, but the total number of entries is less than that of the Second Edition. The fact that many words are dropped explains the lack of a great increase in the number of entries.

The last twenty years have brought a newcomer to the dictionary field, the dictionary designed for elementary classroom use. Up until now each classroom, regardless of the age of the pupils, usually had a large Webster's Unabridged Dictionary on a stand or shelf for use by the entire class. A few of the more enterprising pupils might have small dictionaries of their own, but these were rather drab, uninviting books with diminutive type, few illustrations, perplexing definitions, and a selection of words ill suited to the pupils' needs. The newer dictionaries have hundreds of illustrations of plants, animals, and objects, with their scale indicated by a numerical fraction. The point-size of the type has been increased, the format made more attractive, the definitions clarified, and illustrative sentences added. All words are carefully appraised before inclusion in an effort to eliminate rare, obsolete, or obsolescent words. A good modern dictionary is one of the most valuable books the pupil can have. It is as essential as any textbook.

Picture dictionaries have been developed for use in the primary grades. The picture-word association does help some children as they look up words for spelling. Picture dictionaries are subject to two serious limitations: they seldom provide new meanings, and the vocabulary is usually unrelated to other words the child is learning in his reading.

In all classroom work with the dictionary, the words to be alphabetized, located, or discussed should be carefully chosen to contribute some real purpose in the pupils' writing or reading. The children, as well as the teacher, should recognize the need or use.

Some fourth-graders will be more ready to begin with more advanced work than will some sixth-graders. The teacher should determine each child's ability and then work with small groups having common needs. She should vary and repeat practice at intervals until the children achieve mastery of a given skill. Besides a list of words, the dictionaries for schools frequently contain other information: the story of language, flags of nations, foreign words, biographies, geographical names, pronunciation, syllabication, and even instructions on how to use the dictionary.

Steps in teaching the use of the dictionary are discussed here in an approximate sequence of difficulty, but teachers may vary the order of presentation and omit or add material to meet the needs of their classes.

The first dictionary skill to be taught is the location of a word. Some children may not know the alphabet sequence because it has not been used frequently prior to this time. Check to be sure that the children know the sequence of letters in the alphabet, and then practice until they can find words in the dictionary by their first letters. To avoid the necessity of having some children recite the alphabet before they can locate a word, discuss the relative placement of letters. Have the children discover that when the dictionary is opened in the center we find the words that start with *l* and *m*. If it is opened at the first quarter we find the words with *d* and *e,* and the third quarter we find the *r* and *s* words. Discuss how this will help them to locate a word more rapidly than if they just start at *a* and go through the alphabet.

Next, have the children suggest a word near the place the initial letter would be found without thumbing through the pages. Then have one pupil open the dictionary at random while the other members of the group guess the initial letter of words on that page.

To teach pupils how to arrange words in alphabetical order have them alphabetize brief lists in which no two words begin with the same letter. When this has been mastered, alphabetize by second letters (*sat* before *seven*); by third letters (*share* before *sheep*); and so on. For additional practice, ask children who finish work early to arrange the books in the classroom library alphabetically according to titles, write an index page for a class book, make a card catalogue for a collection of pictures, or find in a telephone directory the telephone numbers of absentees.

The second skill to be learned is the use of guide words. After discussing the advantages of being able to find a word quickly, show the group that at the top of each page in the dictionary there are two words. The one at the left is the same as the first word on the page. The one at the right is the same as the last word on the page. These are called guide words. For practice give a page number. Have the children turn to that page and read the guide words.

Then write on the board a word that the group wishes to find. Above this, write the guide words on the page at which you happen to open the dictionary. Have the group decide whether you must look nearer the front or nearer the back of the book. Continue the process in this manner until you find the right page and word. To check understanding write a word on the board. Have the pupils find the word without opening their dictionaries more than three times, (1) at the right beginning letter, (2) in the neighborhood of the word, and (3) at the exact page. This type of work should be repeated many times under supervision and then independently.

Chalkboard drills may be used to develop skill in the use of guide words. Start by writing on the board a pair of guide words taken from the dictionary. Below them write a group of four words. Two should be words that are listed in the dictionary between the given guide words, and the other two should not. Have the children select and check the words that belong on the page of the dictionary. For example:

kent	khaki	*kindred*
	kennel	
	kine	
	kidnap	

This kind of work should be repeated on successive days. At first it should be done under teacher guidance at the board. Later the children may do it independently at their own desks. Individual children may create exercises of this nature for the class to do.

The following game is helpful as a review: Divide the group into two teams. Write a word on the board. Ask children to find the word and hold up their hands when they have found it. First child to find the word scores one point for his team. First team to finish scores one point. (Check by page number.) The game should be limited by using a certain number of words (e.g., ten), or by playing for a certain number of minutes.

Another exercise is built on word meanings. The teacher prepares a list of words that the children will need to know, locates each word in the dictionary, and notes the guide words for each word. When the game begins the teacher writes a pair of guide words on the board and gives a brief definition of the word that the group is to find. The pupils find the page and scan it for the right word. For example:

Guide words: springboard and *spurt*
Definition: a short run at full speed
Answer: sprint

The third major area of dictionary skills is that associated with the definitions. Whenever a word is found in reading or social studies which cannot be defined from context, use the dictionary. Many words have only vague meanings. Use the dictionary for more exact meaning. Explain the difference in meaning between the following words: *climate* and *weather; less* and *fewer; hotel* and *restaurant.*

Some words get so overworked that we call them tired words. The dictionary can suggest other words to use for *said* or *grand.*

Considerable thought is required in selecting the right meaning from several meanings given in the dictionary. For a few children it will be a discovery that words have more than one meaning. Introduce this work with the word *run.* Have the group think of several meanings before looking it up in the dictionary, or use a sentence from some child's story. For example: "The initial expense was about thirty dollars." Have the children find *initial* in the dictionary.

Discuss the meanings given, and choose the one most applicable. The children may be asked to select the best meaning for a word in a given sentence and then to write another sentence in which the same word has a different meaning. Choose a word having several meanings, such as *pack*. Write at least two sentences to illustrate each meaning. After placing the sentences on the chalkboard ask the children to define the meaning of the word. This could be followed by having pupils select a common word, such as *safe, strike, husband,* or *signal,* and discover how many different meanings for it they can find and illustrate.

Interesting lessons can be planned to show how the illustrations in the dictionary clarify meaning. The arithmetic in the ratio should be studied so that the phrase *one-sixth actual size* has meaning. An interesting discussion can be planned around the topic, "Which words can be illustrated and which cannot?"

An understanding of prefixes and suffixes is another aid to word meaning. When the children understand that *trans-* means "across" or "over" in *transportation, transfer, translate,* and *transcontinental,* they have a meaning clue to other words with this prefix. They can discover that the dictionary gives the meanings of many prefixes.

A discovery or inductive lesson is easy using the dictionary. Have the students read a series of definitions of words starting with another prefix *sub-,* then decide what meaning the prefix gives to the words.

One of the basic clues to meaning is the ability to identify the root word. Start by supplying a root word and have pupils list other members of the same family: *kind* (*kindly, kindness, unkind, kindliness*). Discuss the fact that these words are similar in meaning as well as in appearance. Children need help in learning how the dictionary deals with word families. The root word is listed at the margin in heavy type and other members of the family are not listed marginally but are explained under the root word. In spelling and reading, root words should be identified and sometimes checked with the dictionary. This is important when the word is to be divided into syllables. Even though we divide the word as we pronounce

it, the basic root is seldom divided in writing. Some children will enjoy knowing about a few common Greek and Latin roots which will help them guess word meanings. These were used by a fifth grade:

Latin

annus (year)	annual perennial anniversary
aqua (water)	aqueduct aquaplane aquarium
audio (listen or hear)	auditorium audible audition
avis (bird)	aviary aviation aviator
ducere (to lead)	conduct educate aqueduct
via (way)	viaduct trivial deviate

Greek

aster (star)	aster astronomy asterisk
cycle (ring or circus)	bicycle motorcycle cyclone
graphein (to write)	autograph telegraph graph
logos (word)	catalogue dialogue astrology
metron (measure)	meter thermometer speedometer
phone (sound)	phonics telephone phonograph

The most frequent use of a dictionary is to locate the correct spelling of a word. This is not easy when it is a word that the child cannot spell. Take as an example a word that a child has asked you to spell for him, such as *usable*. The group will be sure of the first two letters. Have them look up the word as far as they are sure and then glance down the page until they find the word. Even after looking up a word it is possible to make a mistake. Before copying the spelling from the dictionary the definition must be read in order to prevent such errors as the use of *complement* for *compliment*.

Sometimes a word is located through the trial-and-error method. Words with difficult beginnings, such as *cistern,* when not located under *s* must be sought under other letters having the same sound. It takes real detective work to track down some words, such as *light*.

Other spelling help in the dictionary concerns abbreviations, the use of capitals, and plural forms, but children must be shown how to locate each of these items.

Another area of dictionary skills concerns pronunciation. The first step involves dividing words into syllables. These rules are usually taught in third-grade reading. This is a good time for children to discover that the dictionary can act as a check on their syllabication. A few listening lessons in which children tell how many syllables they hear when words are pronounced will reveal the fact that the number of vowels we hear in a word tells us how many syllables there are in it. While dividing words into syllables, notice that we pronounce some syllables with more force or accent than others. Then show how the dictionary indicates this stress with the accent mark. Children will be interested in words where a change in accent may indicate a change in meaning, as in "Use the movie machine to *pro ject'* the picture," or "He found that building the dam was a difficult *proj' ect*."

Some dictionaries indicate a secondary as well as a primary accent, as in *mul' ti pli ca' tion*. To check understanding of accent, give the children sentences containing blanks and a choice of the same word syllabized and accented in two different ways. The pupils decide which form to use in the blank and then write a sentence of their own using the other form. For example: "The chairman will (*pre' sent* or *pre-sent'*) the speaker.

Another skill involves the use of diacritical marks as an aid to pronunciation. The pronunciation key at the bottom of each page (or on the end papers of the book) is a basic reference. Although this key may differ according to the dictionary, its use remains the same. If the children can read the key words there is no great need to be able to identify all the markings. The sound association can be made between the key pronunciation word and the one in the dictionary.

Instruction needs to be given which involves marking long and short vowels and then discovering that vowels have other sounds as well as the long and short. Illustrate how these are indicated in the key words on each page in the dictionary.

Have available such assignments as the following as spare-time work for superior students.

Underline words which have the same vowel sound.

ă as in *at*	rattle, sale, athlete, clasp, gas
ā as in *age*	pale, name, display, radio, pat
â as in *care*	square, maple, fair, compare, dare
ä as in *art*	harvest, tame, star, depart, arm
ȧ as in *ask*	grass, vast, grant, brave

Teach the children to use the phonetic respelling given in the dictionary as an aid to pronunciation. Have the group make a list of words in which:

ph or *gk* sound like *f* (*elephant, tough*)
ch or *ck* sound like hard *c* (*chorus, tack*)
d, dg, or soft *g* sound like *j* (*soldier, ridge, ages*)
c sounds like *s* (*cent*)
c sounds like *k* (*act*)
c, x, s sound like *sh* (*ocean, anxious, sugar*)
l, w, k, b are silent (*calf, wrong, comb*)

Teach the children that for some words there is more than one accepted pronunciation and that the preferred one is given first.

Although the dictionary is usually not introduced for the student's use until fourth grade, there are several good practices which will familiarize the students with dictionary procedure prior to the fourth year of school.

In grades 2 and 3 children should be encouraged to keep their own file of words they have learned in reading. A brightly painted shoe box makes an excellent file of this sort. Each divider cut from cardboard should be labeled with a letter of the alphabet in both small letters and capitals. Children write the words they want to keep on file on cards or construction paper, or they can find words in magazines to cut out and paste on the cards. Then the words are filed behind the proper letter of the alphabet.

Another device is to make picture dictionaries either for individual or class use. Children choose a big scrapbook, label the pages with each letter of the alphabet, and write the words on the scrapbook pages, complete with accompanying pictures.

After the dictionary is introduced in either the third or fourth grades, the following exercises may be used to facilitate its use.

1. A dictionary is placed on the first desk of each row. The teacher writes any ten words on the board. At a given signal, the first pupil in each row looks up the first word. When he finds it, he jots down the page number and passes the dictionary to the person behind him, who does the same for the second word, and so on. The first row finished is the winner. If a mistake is made in a page number, the second row finished is the winner.
2. The same game is played with definitions or pronunciations.
3. The same game may be played with names of mythological characters.
4. Each student brings to class a sentence containing a difficult word. A dictionary is placed on each student's desk and the class is divided into two teams. A pupil reads his sentences and states the word he wants defined. The opposing team is given approximately half a minute to look up the word in the

dictionary. At a signal from the teacher, dictionaries are closed and the one who presented the sentence calls a pupil from the opposing team to define the word. If the pupil misses he is eliminated and another is called. The game is continued until all of one team has been eliminated.

Worksheets like the following are sometimes used to practice dictionary skills:

Dictionary Activities

These are individual activities. Each individual has a dictionary, paper, pencil. Questions for the contest have been put on the board and covered with a map or newspaper.

What letter or letters have been omitted?

pro___dure	picni___ing
dorm___tory	place___able
vac___um	cartil___age
super___ede	indel___ble
reform___tory	privil___ge

Give the plurals of

alumnus	stratum
bandit	court-martial
basis	bacillus
index	teaspoon

Write in alphabetical order:

Denver	St. Louis
Milwaukee	Chicago
Nashville	San Francisco
New York	St. Paul
New Orleans	Los Angeles
Miami	Seattle

Give the comparative and superlative degrees of *silly, polite, tidy, wet, sad, old.*

Prefix

The children find the meaning of the following prefixes; then write a word that uses it. Example: Prefix *re* means "again," "back," or "down" (*retreat, return, relate*).

Use these prefixes: *re, in, sub, ex, inter,*

Use of the dictionary is an essential aspect of spelling instruction. (*Courtesy of the Burbank Public Schools.*)

intra, de, con, pre, dis, ante, bi, contra, extra, post, trans. dia, hemi, semi, demi, poly, peri, syn, mis, pro, over, be, un, mal, ultra, super, medi, tri.

Words of All Nations

The following English words have been adapted or borrowed from other languages. Look up the word and list the country from which it comes:

ski	canoe
coffee	circus
kimono	sky
sonata	radio
garage	dachshund
kindergarten	piano
tobacco	menu

sauerkraut
waltz
rodeo

fiesta
ranch
cafeteria
assembly

Where Are They Found?

After each word in the following, write on the blank line the place where each is found; that is, in the air, on the land, or in water.

1. sturgeon _____
2. tripod _____
3. amoeba _____
4. dromedary _____
5. Octopus _____
6. linnet _____
7. prawn _____

8. eglantine _____
9. oracle _____
10. obelisk _____

Who Uses What?

In this group a word is given, such as *plane*. Opposite the word is listed the worker or profession, such as *lawyer, carpenter, taxi driver*. You are to underline the one who uses the tool or item named. In the example it is the *carpenter* who uses the *plane* in his work.

1. splice	aviator, tea taster, sailor
2. snaffle	cavalryman, marine, auctioneer
3. palette	miner, artist, telephone operator
4. girder	knight, builder, gardener
5. font	minister, librarian, horticulturist
6. harpsichord	undertaker, druggist, musician
7. calk	blacksmith, painter, author
8. awl	cobbler, grocer, sculptor
9. pestle	chef, jeweler, druggist
10. creel	schoolboy, fisherman, mail carrier

Alphabetizing

Correct the arrangement of the words in each line into alphabetical order by writing a 1 before the word that should be first, a 2 before the word that should be second, and so on. The first line is done correctly:

1. bewitch	2. boiler
offend	tan
suspect	scrape
peanut	penny
hog	hold
under	understand
custom	cart
please	plea
summer	sum
reach	suit

3. custom	4. wag
you	wall
real	task
piano	plot
home	hook
understood	underneath
cult	cartridge
pedal	pleasure
sit	simmer
tank	wander

Synonyms

A synonym is a word that has the same meaning as another word. Write a synonym for each of the following:

craven	aspect
lucid	wrath
irksome	adept
fickle	soothe
robust	rebuke

Abbreviations

Write down the meanings of the following abbreviations:
bbls., A.D., bldg., no., cong., gal., Rev., St., P.M., doz., ans., Capt., inc., Gen., Hon., Gov., P.O., M.D., R.F.D., B.C., supt., Y.M.C.A., mfg., wk., R.R., P.S., etc., i.e., A.M., vs., O.K., Pvt., D.D., Fem., adv., Apr., dept., vol., S.W., Ry., pp., U.S.N., S.S., viz., riv., nat., I.O.U.

Syllabication

Words divided at the ends of lines in printing, typing, and handwriting should be divided between syllables. Copy from your dictionary the following words, showing their proper division into syllables. Spell them correctly and omit the diacritical marks.

nicety	miraculous
geranium	phraseology
locomotive	European
suburban	statistics
democracy	burglar
originate	armistice
comparable	dirigible
finale	lamentable

heroine   despicable
seizure   syllable

Identification Exercises

Tell whether the following are bird, fish, or tree: tanager, barnacle, almond, vulture, cardinal, flicker, anchovy, gannet, yew, warbler, vireo, sumac, auk, toucan, acacia, tarpon, avocado, sucker, bittern, rock, cinnamon, sycamore, sole, chestnut, ebony, starling.

Tell whether the following are flower, animal, or vegetable: anemone, gherkin, hyena, syringa, kohlrabi, yak, gibbon, jasmine, mammoth, gentian, okra, lemur, rhubarb, poinsetta, puma, sloth, arbutus.

Tell who uses the following: trowel, platinum, rifle, scissors, snaffle, accordion, kilt, adz, splice, anvil, kayak, davits, lute, calumet, palette, mosque, girder, auger, font, percolator, brig, puck, discus, strop, calk, doily, epaulet, hoop, canister, creel, scepter, awl, lasso, mangle, metronome, easel.

Tell where the following are found: sturgeon, autogiro, bison, tripod, cobra, weevil, amoeba, dromedary, chalet, brougham, veranda, dolphin, constellation, corral, caisson, cheetah, squid, sloop, mollusk, phoebe, ketch, manatee, osprey, obelisk, ferret, coot, ermine, merganser, scrole, elevator, eglantine, phaeton, grebe.

Matching

From the endings in the right-hand column pick out the one that goes with each of the beginnings in the left-hand column, and write it in the blank space:

acci____ize   veri____dent
sever____fy   trans____et
special____ance   wheth____ty
tick____pose   para____er
uni____dox

Homonyms

In our language we have a number of words that are pronounced alike but that have different meanings. The words *to,* *too, two* are homonyms. Try to find a homonym for each of the following and write it on the line after the word given:

bear_____   days_____
pair_____   there_____
him_____   whole_____
way_____   tacked_____
ewe_____   right_____
feet_____   meet_____
here_____   blue_____
peace_____   our_____
ate_____   rain_____
ball_____   sun_____
be_____   rode_____
air_____   sea_____
sew_____   cent_____
deer_____   would_____
won_____   steak_____

Word Analysis

Use a dictionary to do these exercises. Write the words in the blanks provided. Find a word beginning with the indicated prefix and having the indicated meaning.

Prefix	Definition	Word
ab-	to take a person away by force	_____
ab-	to go away hurriedly and secretly	_____
ab-	to free a person from debt or a duty	_____
ad-	to stick fast	_____
ad-	to be next to	_____
ad-	to warn	_____
ad-	to move forward	_____
ad-	to give notice of something	_____
anti-	to be against society	_____
anti-	a remedy that prevents poison from taking effect	_____

The following exercise is done in the same manner as the one preceding.

Prefix	Definition	Word
com-	to fight with someone	_____
com-	to speak of something with approval	_____

com-	to find fault with something	_____
com-	to mix with	_____
de-	to keep from entering	_____
de-	to grow less in size	_____
de-	to protect from danger	_____
dis-	to not be honest	_____
post-	afternoon	_____

For Discussion

1. Compare the definition of a word in an elementary dictionary with a collegiate edition. Why is at least one collegiate dictionary needed in an intermediate classroom?

2. Evaluate the teaching lessons found at the beginning of the primary dictionaries published by Scott, Foresman and Company.

3. Compare the glossary in an intermediate science or social studies text with a dictionary.

How May Spelling Games Be Used to Motivate Learning Spelling?

Games provide extra motivation for some of the drill that children need to master spelling. Although it is unlikely that spelling will ever have the fascination of baseball for some children or of golf for some adults, interest in words and their spelling can be heightened by using a game, such as the spelling bee of our frontier traditions, involving spelling.[17]

Games call for considerable planning to be successful. In introducing the game, first give the name, then have some children "walk through" each step as you describe it. After that, have a trial run to be certain that everyone understands. Establish a few rules during the practice period. Choosing partners or teams can create considerable social tension. This can be avoided by using

---

[17] Unless otherwise noted this material is adapted from Paul S. Anderson, *Resource Materials for Teachers of Spelling* (Minneapolis, Minn.: Burgess, 1958.)

row against row or counting and having "odds" versus "evens." Because girls as a group are usually superior in spelling, a "boys-against-girls" contest is unfair, and it may brand the ability to spell as a feminine skill.

The timing of a game is important. Just before recess is usually a good time, because it avoids the necessity of a difficult transition from an exciting game to an uninspiring page in a history book. Do not make a game last too long unless it is a special privilege. Ten to fifteen minutes should be the maximum. To be of value the game should provide drill on needed words or skills.

College students using these games will find this list of words that were missed by the finalist in the National Spelling Bee a challenge.

Famous Last Words

The following list consists of thirty of the words on which national championships have been won or lost since the National Spelling Bee began in 1925. Can you spell them?

brethren	pronunciation
abrogate	acquiesced
plebeian	albumen
luxuriance	therapy
intelligible	promiscuous
knack	deteriorating
foulard	fracas
asceticism	flaccid
gladiolus	semaphore
sacrilegious	propitiatory
interning	chrysanthemum
onerous	dulcimer
canonical	stupefied
sanitarium	oligarchy
abbacy	psychiatry

A Fateful Fifty

The fate of fifty contestants in National Spelling Bee championship finals in recent years was determined by the following fifty words. On each of them a boy or girl finalist missed, and a championship chance was lost. See if you know them.

pallor

catalyst

jocose

fission

scintillate

wainscot

consensus

meretricious

agglomeration

manumit

bier

elision

quandry

medallion

peripatetic

exacerbate

effeminate

requiem

guttural

vilify

glacial

imitator

impostor

mattock

emendation

efflorescence

minatory

rue

urbane

aggression

insouciant

assonance

berbaceous

pomegranate

peroration

febrile

aplomb

cuisine

aeriferous

coruscation

saponaceous

disputatious

archetype

yawl

foment

ennoble

obloquy

homiletic

shellacked

indissoluble

Games for Primary Grades

1. Puzzle Elements.

a. I am in *see, sing,* and *say.* What sound am I?

b. I am in *took,* but I am not in *look.* I am ___.

c. *Baby, book, ball.* The *b* is at the
   _____.

2. Making New Words by Changing a Vowel.

bat	fur
bet	far
bit	ham
but	hum
cat	him
cot	pen
cut	pan
bug	pin
big	pot
beg	pat
for	pit

3. Writing Alliterative Senter

Bob bought big blue balloc

This might be a team affair with working together to produce th Older children like to make ...sing slogans:

Buy Billie's Best Boston Beans;
Can Charlie's Canaries Comfort Charlie's Comrades?

4. Treasure Box.

Words are written on separate slips of paper which are then folded and put into a box called the treasure box. Each child in turn draws out a slip which he hands to the teacher without opening. The teacher pronounces the word and the child attempts to spell it. Any misspelled words are handed back to the children who had difficulty with them. The object is for the pupil to end the game with no slips of paper. Those who do have slips learn to spell the words that are on them. Two children can thus provide extra practice for each other as they play this game in the quiet corner.

5. Turn Up Letters.

The players are seated at a table. Before them on the table face down are a number of alphabet cards. The players decide on some object for the game—animals, birds, cities, flowers, and so on. Then each player in turn picks up a card and exhibits the letter.

The first child to write a word beginning with that letter, belonging to the category decided upon and spelled correctly, gets the card. The player to the right of the first one who writes the word may challenge the spelling. If it is incorrect, the challenger gets the card.

When all the cards have been turned up, the player having the most cards wins. Letters which appear infrequently at the beginning of a word, such as *j, u, x, y,* and *z,* should be omitted.

6. Alphabet Jumble.

Two sets of the alphabet are placed in a long chalk tray. Two children compete to see which one can be first to arrange one set in correct alphabetical order.

7. Find It. Words are listed on the chalkboard. The teacher or a student gives the definition of the word and the children in turn spell the word defined.

8. Hear It. The words are listed on the board. The leader says, "I am thinking of a word that starts with the same sound as one hears at the beginning of _____," or "one that rhymes with _____." The children write the words indicated and gain a point for their own score for each correct selection.

9. Guess and Spell. "It" selects an object that is in plain sight in the room. The other children start guessing the first letter of that object. When the first letter is guessed, they start working on the second, then the third, until the word is spelled. The correct letters may be put on the chalkboard as they are spelled by the one who is "it." When any student thinks that he may be able to spell the total word after the first few letters have been guessed, he may challenge the leader and complete the word. He then becomes "it."

10. Novelty Spelling. Instead of calling words from a spelling list, the teacher asks questions such as, "Spell a word that rhymes with *joint*." "Spell a word containing *ph* which sounds life *f*." "Spell a word that means _____." Have members of the class in turn read their lists. The variety adds interest and influences vocabulary.

11. Chalkboard Spelling. Primary children feel it is a privilege to write on the chalkboard. Reserve a place at the board where a child may go during his free time just as he might go to the library corner. Put a different exercise on the board for each child, such as:

> What children in our room have names that start with B?
> What do you want for Christmas?
> What do you like to eat?
> Where would you like to visit?
> How many words do you know that start with *wh?*

12. Use the Word. The words of the spelling lesson are placed on the board and left during the day. Each time one of the words is used in a child's writing during the day counts one point for his side. This can be row-against-row competition. The word does not count unless the one who writes the word reports it for the count.

13. Pear Tree. How many pear (pair) trees can you develop with your class? Synonyms and antonyms? But how about such pears (pairs) as *horse, colt; cow, calf?* Or *hands, gloves; feet, shoes?* Or *swimming, swimmer; archer, archery?* Divide your class into committees to develop these trees. Each committee draws a large tree and puts pairs of words on yellow or light green pears. Add leaves for effect.

Spelling Games for Upper Grades

1. Dictionary Games. One child opens the dictionary at random, saying, "I have opened the dictionary to an *sp-* page." Each child then writes as many words starting with *sp-* as he can. Two teams may compete, each child in turn adding a word. To prevent careless or poor writing, each team may have a "recorder" who writes the words suggested by the team. Have three to five on a team. The winning team may be challenged by another team.

2. Memory Game. Several picture cards, each portraying a single object, are shown to pupils (or it might be the objects themselves). The pictures or objects are then concealed and the children are asked to write the names of all the objects they remember. To vary this game, expose a list of words and then have pupils write as many as they can recall. It is more difficult if the words must be written in alphabetical order. For some children a test of listening is valuable. Start by having them listen to three words, then write them. Keep increasing the number of words.

3. Baseball. One form uses word cards and is especially good for practice on words frequently misspelled. Each card contains a word, a value such as one base hit, home run, and so on, and the name of the position who is to catch the ball if it is misspelled. The cards would look like this:

all right 2-base hit 3rd baseman	separate home run pitcher	February 3-base hit right field

Sometimes children take positions in the classroom as if it were a baseball diamond. It is equally interesting to use a chalkboard diagram with players remaining at their seats while the team captain indicates their movement on the diagram.

In another form, four diamonds are drawn on the chalkboard. The first member of the team at bat goes to the first diamond. The first word is given by the pitcher. The pitcher may be the teacher or a member of the opposing team. The child at the board writes the word. Those at their seats write the word for practice. If the word is spelled successfully by the batter he moves to the second diamond (first base) and a new player goes to the first diamond. Again the teacher pronounces a word to be spelled. Both players at the board write the word. If both spell the word correctly each player moves to another diamond and a third player goes to the first diamond. If either player misspells the word, he is out. Thus it is possible for two or more players to be put out by one word. When a player advances through all four diamonds a score is made for the team he represents.

4. The Maiden and the Dragon. At one chalkboard area a "maiden" is drawn, tied to a rock by five ropes. On the other side a dragon is drawn facing five waves. (Flannelboard figures make this easier.) One group represents the maiden, the other the dragon. The game proceeds in the manner of a traditional spelldown. Each time a member of the team of the maiden misspells a word, one of the waves is erased. The waves are protecting the maiden from the dragon. Each time a member of the dragon team misspells a word, one of the ropes is erased. When the five waves are gone the dragon

will be released to devour the maiden. But if the five ropes are cut the maiden is freed and the dragon dies. Suspense develops although no player leaves the game.

5. Roots and Branches. This game is intended to develop awareness of parts of words. Make four cards for each of several root words; for example: *march, marched, marching, marcher; fear, feared, fearing, fearful;* and so on.

Make enough copies of each set of words for four "books." Shuffle the cards and deal six cards at a time to each player. Players sort their cards as in playing "Authors." If a player holds four cards of words from the same root, he can make a "book." Each player in turn may call for a card by naming the card he holds and may continue to call as long as other players hold wanted cards. When there are no more available cards of the kind he calls, he discards, and the next player takes his turn. The objective is to get as many books as possible. Care should be taken in preparing the cards for this game not to introduce different elements too fast for retarded readers; for example: doubling the final consonant of a root, or changing the sound, as *lose* and *lost.*

6. Word Addition. To facilitate the use of word endings and prefixes, words are listed on the board. Each child uses that list of words to see how many new words can be made by adding beginnings and endings. Plural forms and *-ing, -er, -est, -ed, -r, pre-,* and *im-* may be used. Words that may be used are *run, occupy, view, prove, write, large, build, hear, stand, call, part, play.*

7. Ghost. One child starts with a letter that is also a word, as *I* or *a.* The next child adds another letter to make still another word, as *in.* The next child might spell *tin,* the next *into.* The letters may be rearranged, but each previous letter must be included and just one new letter added. The child who cannot make a new word in this way is a "ghost," the object of the game being to avoid becoming one. This is a good game for a large number of players.

8. Spelling Jingles. When the children come across a new word, they can help establish its spelling in their minds by writing jingles using the word in rhyme. The children enjoy composing the jingles and, at the same time, learn to spell the new word and other similar words. When the word *night* was learned, for example, the following was written:

When it is night
We need a light.

9. What's My Word? Each child has a different word. One stands in front of the group. Each student in turn may ask one question, then spell the word he thinks is the word of the one in front. The questions may concern the meaning, the beginning sound, a rhyming word, or the word root. The student who identifies the word takes the leader's position.

10. Travel. Ticket salesmen are appointed for various points, such as "Airplane ride to New York," "Bus ride to Los Angeles," and so on. Each has a group of words. Students in turn apply for tickets and are given them after spelling all the words on the salesmen's list. A variation might be a county fair or a circus, with the ticket admitting the speller to special events.

11. Smoked Bacon. Make two or more sets of cardboard letters with the letters of *smoked bacon.* Teams face each other with each child holding one letter. The teacher calls out a word which can be spelled by these letters. The first team to get in correct positions gets a point. These letters form at least 100 words.

This can be a chalkboard game. Write *smoked bacon* on the board. Let each team write a word in turn. The winner is the one who writes the longest list of words in a certain time limit. As a flannelboard game, this may be a group or individual activity.

12. New Spelldown. The fifteen to sixteen words of the week's lessons are put on the board. Each child is assigned one word, which becomes his "name." (Two or more may have the same word.) The leader goes to the front of the room and calls on one of the students. This child faces the rear of the room (because the words are still on the chalkboard) and is asked to spell the leader's word. If he is incorrect, he sits down; if correct, he asks the leader to spell his word. The class, looking at the words on the chalkboard, acts as judges. When the leader misses, the challenger takes his place.

13. Fourth-Grade Scramble. Take any week's lesson and scramble the letters in each word. The teacher scrambles the letters of a word on the board and the children write the word correctly on their papers. If each letter of the word is on a separate card, they may be placed on the chalk rail. One child unscrambles the word, writes it on the chalkboard, and uses it in a sentence. The class watching this may write the words as each one is unscrambled. A true scramble avoids placing the letters in a horizontal sequence but writes all over the board. Letter cards may be so scrambled on a flannelboard.

14. You Can't Catch Me. As the teacher gives the first word, each child writes it on his paper. Then the papers are passed in a predetermined order (to the left, for example). The child receiving the paper checks the last word and writes the word correctly if necessary. Then the teacher gives the second word and the papers are passed. Every paper should be perfect if all errors are caught. While this may not always happen, those words needing review will have received attention in a different way.

1. Spelldowns. Traditional spelldowns involve one team which competes with another. If a child misspells a word and the person whose turn it is to spell on the opposite team spells it correctly, that child is "spelled down" and takes his seat. He can be saved if the opponents misspell the word and the next person on his team spells it successfully. A good P.T.A. feature is to have a group of girls spell against their fathers. Ordinarily, "boys-versus-girls" is not a fair contest, but sometimes Boy Scouts will challenge Girl Scouts, or a fifth-grade team will challenge a sixth-grade team. (The National Education Association has a clever little play available which uses a spelldown dramatically. Write for "Command Performance," by Tom Erhard.) Rather than using oral spelling alone it adds to the educational value to have the words written neatly on the chalkboard by the contestants.

2. *Checkers* is a spelldown in which the student who spells a word correctly "jumps" two persons in the direction of the end of the line. When he reaches the end, he goes to his seat. The advantage of such procedure is that those who need practice remain, whereas those who know the words have time for independent work. This may be called a spellup and the students may move from the end of the line to the top when they drop from the line.

3. *Spellups* are the same as the traditional spelling bee with one exception—instead of the teams lining up, each team member remains seated until he misses a word; then he stands. When a player misses a word, the person standing is given a chance to spell the word correctly. If he succeeds, he sits down. Remember this is a game. If errors are embarrassing to any individual, it would be wise to avoid such direct comparison.

For Discussion

1. Why is it better to use one or two instructional games at a single grade level?
2. How can a teacher give recognition to the successful students without discouraging those less competent?
3. Should games be used at a time when parents or a supervisor are visiting a classroom?

How May the Spelling Program Be Enriched to Challenge the Able Students?

In every intermediate classroom there are children who do not respond to formal spelling instruction or who are far beyond the spelling level of the class. The suggestions that follow may be used in light of the teacher's knowledge of the children's needs.

These may be assigned by the teacher or self-assigned by the student as is appropriate to the situation. The child who gets 100 per cent in the week's assignment in spelling instruction or who is far beyond the class might profit by doing one of these activities. The child who never succeeds with the words in a spelling assignment may find motivation for proper spelling through an interesting writing experience. Correct spelling is a refinement of writing, and a writing approach to spelling makes sense to many students.

- Write a news report of an event in the school or classroom.
- Find other meanings for words in the spelling list and write a sentence illustrating the meaning.
- Write a paragraph about a secret wish, or a wish you make but do not really want, such as being a baby again, or a dog.
- Write a story of the first Thanksgiving (or any holiday) you remember.
- How did people first learn to use fire, the wheel, or glass? Make up a story answer or find the material in a reference book.
- Take an old story or fable and make it modern, such as "Christmas with The Three Bears."
- What was the bravest thing your father or mother ever did?
- Make up a story of a dog hero (or any pet).
- Write a description of a bird or flower.
- Make a list of first-aid suggestions that should be in every automobile.
- Look up in an encyclopedia and report how long these animals usually live: dog, horse, bear, elephant.
- Write a description of someone in the room; let the class guess who it is.
- Try to write twenty compound words.
- How many words can you list that end with -le (-age or any other common ending)?

- Report on a radio and TV programs that you think your class would enjoy.
- Make up a Paul Bunyan story.
- Make a list of words that have *tele-* in them (or any other base Latin or Greek form).
- Cut out a newspaper story and do one of the following: Underline each adjective (or noun, adverb, etc.). Underline each compound word. Underline the topic sentence. Make an outline of the story.
- Correct the English used in a comic strip or book.
- Discover different ways in which the same meaning is expressed in different parts of the English-speaking world; for example, in England: *lift* for *elevator; cinema* for *movie; petrol* for *gasoline; sweets* for *dessert* or *candy;* in Canada: *spool of cotton* for *spool of thread; tap* for *faucet; window blind* for *window shade;* in Australia: *sundowner* for *hobo.*
- Report on the origin of some of the words we use.
- Collect and discuss words that have come to us from other peoples. For example:

African	zebra, chimpanzee
American	
Indian	hominy, persimmon, squaw
Arabian	admiral, alfalfa, magazine
Australian	kangaroo, boomerang
Chinese	silk, pongee, tea, ketchup
Dutch	skipper, sleigh, waffle, boss
French	cafe, bouquet, aileron, dinner
German	hamburger, waltz, kindergarten
Greek	theater, botany
Hebrew	amen, hemp, shekel
Hindu	calico, jungle, chintz, dungaree
Hungarian	goulash, tokay
Irish	brogue, colleen, bog
Malay-	
Polynesian	gingham, bantam, tattoo

Persian	scarlet, caravan, lilac, seersucker
Portuguese	veranda, marmalade, yam
Scandinavian	ski, squall, smelt, keg
Scotch	clan, reel (dance)
Slavonic	sable, polka, robot
Spanish	barbecue, bronco
Turkish	tulip, coffee, fez
Welsh	flannel, crag

- Collect and discuss words that have been derived from place names. For example:

Italics	Italy
cashmere	Cashmere (Kashmir, India)
morocco (leather)	Morocco
calico	Calcutta
milliner	Milan

- Discuss new words invented to meet new needs; for example: *airplane* (1870); *vitamin* (1930); and *jeep* and *radar,* in the last few years. Explore the new section of the dictionary.
- Find out how the days of the week and the months of the year got their names.
- Discuss and list the origin and meaning of the names of members of the class. (Example: John = Hebrew *Yohanan,* "God Is Gracious.") The following references will be helpful:

Ernst, Margaret. *Words.* New York: Alfred A. Knopf, Inc., 1954.

Funk, Charles E. *Heavens to Betsy.* New York: Harper & Row, Publishers, 1955.

Funk, Charles E. *Thereby Hangs a Tale.* New York: Harper & Row, Publishers, 1950.

Garrison, W. B. *Why You Say It.* Nashville: Abingdon, 1955.

Laird, Helen & Carlton. *Tree of Language.* Cleveland: The World Publishing Company, 1957.

- List slang expressions heard by the class and using the following criteria discuss the survival possibilities of each expression. Is there no other word that expresses exactly this meaning? Does this expression have a definite, single meaning? Slang that is vague in meaning and that is overused as filler in conversation soon dies. Does it have originality, spontaneity, or genuine humor?

- Discuss and list occasions for which slang is appropriate and those for which it is inappropriate.

Original writing may be used for spelling reviews. A story is written using as many review spelling words as the child wishes. The third-graders average about fifteen words. After the story is written with the spelling words underlined, the teacher makes duplicate copies of it. Blanks are put in to replace the spelling words. The child who wrote the story then gets to read it to the class. The class fills in the blanks as he reads. The writer of the story also enjoys checking the papers.

NAME _____

Barbara's Story

At school we made a house of _____. We asked _____ Leaverton to come to our _____ to see it. We asked her to please come _____ _____. We will make some _____ _____ for the house. We used a _____ _____ to make them. You _____ look at everything we have made. Our _____ is about homes. We _____ it every day. Most of the children have a good _____ studying about homes. Sometimes we _____ the names of the houses. We have to write the names of the houses or _____ we will not get a _____ of 100. We asked _____ Leaverton to ask _____ Leaverton if he would come too.

For Discussion

1. How does it help the able student to act as a clinician for those who need spelling help?

2. An enrichment project reported by two teachers in Castro Valley, California, is reported in an article titled "Dictionopolis" [*Elementary English* (April 1964), pp. 351–61]. Norman Juster's *The Phantom Tollbooth* was the inspiration. Students should report on both the article and book.

Suggestions for Projects

1. Evaluate or create a series of spelling games designed to accomplish specific purposes with a group of children.

2. Report on the simplified spelling movement in the United States.

3. Compare three different spelling textbook series with respect to similarities and differences.

4. Analyze the spelling errors made by a specific class. Are there patterns of errors or common needs revealed?

5. Write a talk to give at the P.T.A. explaining the school's spelling program to parents.

6. If children study spelling words that are based on those that are quite certain to appear in their writing, why shouldn't these words be taught in the writing association and less frequently used words be taught in the spelling lessons?

Bibliography

Books

Hall, Robert A. *Sound and Spelling in English*. Philadelphia: Chilton Co., 1964.

Hanna, Paul R., Jean S. Hanna, Richard E. Hodges, and Edwin H. Rudorf, Jr. *Phoneme-Grapheme Correspondences as Cues to Spelling Improvement*. Washington, D.C.: U.S. Department of Health, Education and Welfare, Office of Education, 1966.

Tiedt, Sydney W., and Iris M. Tiedt. *Exploring Words*. San Jose, Calif.: Contemporary Press, 1964.

Articles

Blake, Howard E., and Robert Emans. "Some Spelling Facts," *Elementary English* (February 1970), pp. 241–49.

Graham, Richard T., and E. Hugh Rudorf. "Dialect and Spelling," *Elementary English* (March 1970), pp. 363–75.

Key, Mary Ritchie. "The English Spelling System and the Initial Teaching Alphabet," *Elementary School Journal* (March 1969), pp. 313–26.

Research Study

Groff, Patrick. "The Syllable: Its Nature and Pedagogical Usefulness." Northwest Regional Educational Laboratory, 500 Lindsay Building, 710 S.W. Second Ave., Portland, Oregon 87204.

eight

grammar, old and new

What Grammar Should Be Taught in the Elementary School?

Since 1935 the National Council of Teachers of English has urged teachers to use the following criteria to determine what is good English:

1. Correct usage must find its authority in the living language of today.
2. It must recognize dialect and geographical variations.
3. It must judge the appropriateness of the expression to the purpose intended.
4. It must recognize social levels of speech.
5. It must take into account the historical development of the language.

Much confusion has resulted in practice from the acceptance of arbitrary standards of English grammar and usage. In the list of basic principles it is apparent that the authoritarian viewpoint of what is correct is not acceptable. Good English, then, is

that form of speech which is appropriate to the purpose of the speaker, true to the language as it is, and comfortable to speaker and listener. It is the product of custom, neither cramped by rule nor freed from all restraint; it is never fixed, but changes with the organic life of the language.[1]

One interpretation of this definition for teachers would indicate that in American

---

[1] National Council of Teachers of English, *An Experience Curriculum in English* (New York: Appleton, 1935).

speech from Maine to California, six levels of language use may be recognized.[2] They are "(1) the illiterate level, (2) the homely level, (3) the informal standard level, (4) the formal standard level, (5) the literary level, and (6) the technical level." These are neither distinct nor mutually exclusive. Nor are they entirely arranged in ascending order beyond level (3). The elementary teacher is interested in obtaining more proficiency at the informal standard level and in moving individuals up from the "illiterate" to the "homely" level.

The standard for good English, so far as elementary school is concerned, is the informal standard level. Because many pupils do not use English of this level naturally, the teacher's job is really to help them acquire a new dialect. Their basic dialect has been acquired at an early age, practically entirely by ear. The task of remedial education, or changing these basic patterns, must proceed slowly by listening to and using the higher level of speech. Unless the school program has been effective in altering the level of the student's real or basic speech, little progress has been made, no matter how glibly he may repeat rules of usage.

In some homes the informal standard level would not be accepted as good English. These parents, as well as some who would impose their own definitions of "pure" English, will not agree that the informal standard level should be the goal of the schools.

Others feel that there are actually only two levels: standard English and substandard English, with slang as a kind of no man's land between the two. The basic point concerning levels of language is that the situation frequently determines what is the correct or best form. Language at a baseball game is quite different from that in a college lecture, yet both are acceptable in their respective milieus. This means that our task or aim is not to have all children

speak the "King's English," but to help them express themselves clearly and effectively in the classroom and in their daily language situations.

The grammar needed for adequate expression is our next concern. The term *grammar* causes some confusion because it has many meanings. Some think of grammar as the parts of speech, syntax, sentence structure, and paragraph organization. Others prefer to think of grammar as the way our language is used. Some authorities suggest that the term *grammar* be applied only to the study of language structure, that the matters of correctness be called usage, and that matters of form in expression be called conventions.

William Martin, the author and editor of *The Sounds of Language* readers, comments,[3]

When I was a child growing up in Kansas, I used to say,

We put the dishes in the zinc.
Let's wrench the clothes.
I just et.
Give me some more marshmarlows.

and many other family expressions that we learned from the environment of our early childhood. It wasn't until I started to school that I learned that certain other people didn't use these same expressions. Their expressions sounded strange to me; my expressions sounded strange to them. The pity is that in those days we did not have a real appreciation for the in-group language of different families and regions. Consequently, children were made to feel uncomfortable and often were ridiculed if they did not speak the so-called "standard" English.

The traditional standard of language behavior was then and still is the rightness or wrongness of an expression as measured by classical grammatical analysis. Think of the unrewarding classroom practices we have developed in our adherence to such a standard. Ugly red slashes through a child's written work and unkind expressions such as, "Nice people don't talk that way," are not useful ways to in-

---

[2] Robert C. Pooley, "The Levels of Language," *Educational Method,* 16 (March 1937), 290; "What Is Correct English?" *National Education Journal,* December 1960, pp. 12–19.

[3] Published by Holt, Rinehart & Winston, 1967. Program Eleven, Bill Martin, *Language Arts Teachers Manual,* Bay Region Instructional Television for Education, Redwood City, Calif., 1967.

vite a young child to experiment with and develop a love for language, especially if the people he grew up with do talk "that way." . . .

To ask a child to take on new ways of saying things is virtually to ask him "to jump out of his skin." Jumping out of one's skin can be fun provided there are sensitive people around who understand the risk involved.

When a child feels comfortable and at home saying *Ah's Henry,* it can be risky for him to attempt to say, *I am Henry.* His words may even come out, *I am is are Henry.* At times like this, a child needs pervasive understanding and acceptance. When his own ears tell him that this pattern of words is strange and new and not quite his, he needs our patient support all the more.

Any division of language into distinct levels is arbitrary, but three general levels can be identified for purposes of discussion. They are:

1. The *in-group language* of the home.
2. The *public language* of the society.
3. *Life-lifting language* encountered in many ways but especially in literary communications. . . .

To further complicate the problem for children, the school traditionally has failed to appreciate idiosyncratic in-group language as successful language. The criticism is so clearly communicated to the children early in their school careers, that they soon learn it is better for them not to talk at all.

How much better for a child to bring his language into the classroom with him instead of checking it at the door! How much better that he encounter a teacher who helps him appreciate whatever language skill he possesses in order that he can enjoy his linguistic embarking on the quest for more and more skill with language.

"Let me interrupt," you might say. "Give me something specific. What exactly do I do when a child comes into my classroom talking in ways that sound wrong to me?"

Let's think back to Henry, who says, *Ah's Henry.* How would you react to that?

YOU: Well, I'd probably say, "Say it again, Henry. Tell me who you are."

HENRY: Ah's Henry.

YOU: (*appreciatively*) It's interesting that you say, "Ah's Henry." I say it differently. Would you like to hear me say it?

HENRY: Uh-huh.

YOU: I say, "I am Henry." Can you say that?

HENRY: Uh-huh.

YOU: Let's hear you say, "I am Henry."

HENRY: Ah's Henry.

YOU: (*appreciatively*) Try again, Henry. Say, "I am Henry."

HENRY: (*tries again without success.*)

YOU: Well, you keep trying, Henry, and I'll keep helping you, and soon you'll be able to tell me in two different ways who you are. You'll be able to say it your old way, "Ah's Henry," and you'll be able to say it a new way, "I am Henry."

HENRY: (*grinning*) Yez, Miz Sheppard, I is gonna try.

YOU: Do you know why you want to learn to say it two ways, Henry?

HENRY: Uh-huh.

YOU: People have different ways for saying the same thing, Henry. You say, "Ah's Henry." Some people say, "I am Henry." You say, "Let's git goin'." Some people say, "It's time to start." Nobody's right and nobody's wrong. Our language just makes it possible to say things in more than one way. When you learn to say things in more than one way, more and more people can understand you. When you are with a group of people who like the sound of "Ah's Henry," that's what you say. When you are with a group of people who like the sound of "I am Henry," then that's what you say. You are the person who chooses. You can rely on your own judgment as to which expression is most suitable. Do you understand me, Henry?

HENRY: Uh-huh.

Although Henry may not be able to verbalize what you say, he does in truth understand the spirit of what you are saying, and he intuitively knows that he is not threatened by your concern for his language.

As you observed in Henry, you inherited not only him but also his home-rooted linguistic world when he entered your classroom. Today, when society is extremely mobile, every teacher is likely to encounter a few children with linguistic problems rooted not only in the home but also in the geographical regions from which they came. The child moving from a rural area into a city, for example, is often headed for linguistic problems. This contributes to a basic conflict in education that we have never comfortably resolved. The conflict stems from our lack of awareness that classroom–textbook–public language is a second realm of language quite different from the in-group language of many children.

This is not to suggest that there is anything wrong with public language. It is essential that every child learn to speak and read and write the public language. Otherwise, as George Bernard Shaw observed, he will be *condemned to the gutter by every syllable he shall utter. . . .*

Once I worked with a group of fifth-graders and thought they understood the noun. A few days later I asked them for the definitions we had discussed. A Spanish boy waved his hand with enthusiasm, so I called on him. "Teacher," said Manuel, "a noun is a person who plays and sings." After recovering, I discovered that my "person, place, or thing" definition meant little more to the others than it did to Manuel. Because of experiences similar to this, Robert C. Pooley, in his book *Teaching English Grammar,* takes a strong stand.[4]

It is my point of view that the foundations of spoken and written English are best laid up to and including the sixth grade without formal instruction in the terminology of grammar—that means learning the parts of speech —or in the practice of identifying and naming the various parts and functions of the sentence. This statement is based upon considerable research and background which will be summarized under the following divisions:

1. The first consideration is the question of time. Time that is used in teaching children the names of parts of speech and the identification and classification of parts of the sentence is time taken away from the practice of the skills of writing and speaking English.

2. All the evidence of research studies shows that formal grammar has very slight influence on the usage habits of children. Children learn their language by listening to their parents and by the conversation they have with other children in the home and on the playground. By the time a kindergartener reaches school, his patterns of speech are pretty well set up by his experience and have become very largely unconscious. If he has heard excellent English in his home, he speaks excellent English. If he has heard good English with some minor defects, these minor defects will show up in his speech. The child is not responsible in the sense that he is doing anything wrong. He is simply reflecting the background which he brings to school. To change such habits requires more than just knowledge.

3. All the evidence available shows that formal grammar has little or no effect upon the skills of composition in the elementary grades. Many studies have been carried out to determine the relationship between structural grammar and the writing skills of children. As early as 1923 William Asher conducted such an inquiry into the writing abilities of children in the upper elementary grades and derived this conclusion: "We may, therefore, be justified in the conclusion that time spent upon formal grammar in the elementary school is wasted so far as a majority of students are concerned." Other studies working on this same problem have yielded the same conclusions.

4. Various studies which have been conducted over the years indicate that grammatical terminology, when not particularly connected with a skill regularly used by the child, is easily confused and forgotten. To avoid teaching these terms does not mean that the child is unable to learn them. The question is how much effort is required and how valuable is the effort at this point. There is no evidence to show that excellent writing and speaking result, at least through grade six, from teaching the terms of formal grammar. In fact, the reverse seems to be true, that where a great deal of grammar is taught at the expense of practice in writing and speaking, the children make very poor gains in their English expression. It is wasteful of student and teacher time to attempt the mastery of grammatical terms at least until the beginning of the seventh year.

Despite the truths contained in the preceding statement teachers will find in textbooks and courses of study a great emphasis upon the concepts of either the old or new grammar.

Thus we face a true dilemma. We are required to teach what some authorities feel is of questionable merit. The reaction of teachers has been to place more emphasis on the use of language in the intermediate grades and to seek more meaningful ways to teach the required grammar of the courses of study.

---

[4] Robert C. Pooley, *Teaching English Grammar* (New York: Appleton-Century-Crofts, 1957), pp. 126–28.

For Discussion

1. Why would you disapprove of a minister or college teacher who used the language of the golf course in the pulpit or classroom?

2. Why do you approve of the school accepting the informal standard level?

3. Which writers of our time would you accept as authorities on the use of language?

4. Why do you agree with Pooley that the emphasis should be on writing and speaking experience rather than on analysis in the elementary school?

How Can We Teach Traditional Grammar?

As teachers, we need to know what linguistic scholars are doing when they develop the grammar for language. Words in a language are grouped in terms of some similarity. In Navaho, words are classed as words naming round objects, words naming granular objects, and so on. (The word for *news* is found in the round-object class.) The traditional parts of speech in English are form classes based upon notional definitions or semantic (meaning) terms.

In English we conjugate our verbs for tense. To name an action is to place it in time as past, present, or future. In the language of the Wintu, verbs are conjugated for validity rather than time. In naming an action the Wintu must describe his grounds for believing in the action. Thus the event *Harry chops wood* can be conjugated for direct visual evidence; hearsay evidence, if he has been told this; or predictable evidence, if it is something done regularly. There are other validity modes in the language but it is obvious that the verb system forces a different set of observations than those concerned with time.

In Japanese the concept of honor is a part of the form class. The user must consider such questions as whether the person is older, of higher social rank, or male. Each element demands a different form. Many languages stress gender more than English

does. Such objects as chairs, tables, books, are masculine or feminine, with appropriate articles, modified endings, and verb forms to correspond.

With respect to English, there seems to be a merging of many concepts of traditional and new grammar. The distinctions made to identify the new grammar can be understood only by teachers who understand traditional grammar.

In the past, grammars usually began with the definition of a sentence; Curme's is a good one: "A sentence is an expression of a thought or feeling by means of a word or words used in such form and manner as to convey the meaning intended." [5] Kinds of sentences then follow, with distinctions based on the meaning we see in them: exclamatory, declarative, and interrogative (or command, statement, and question). This kind of grammar classifies the sentences it encounters by grasping their intention and meaning. Then it turns to a discussion of the parts and their internal arrangements.

Our traditional grammar begins in meaning and ends in function. Consider the sentence *Paul gave Jane the book.* It is a statement because it asserts. But next we shift the ground. *Paul* is the subject of the sentence because it expresses the doer of the action expressed by the verb; *gave* is the simple predicate because it expresses the action the actor did; *Jane* is the indirect object because it is the receiver of the action specified in subject and predicate; and *book* is the direct object because it is the thing acted upon. We identify the parts functionally only by knowing first what the sentence means.

Traditional grammars go on to describe a wealth of syntactic detail. They make a distinction between phrases and clauses—with the latter containing subjects and predicates and the former not containing them—and they observe how these fit into the simple sentence or connect to it as modifiers, compounds, or dependencies of various sorts. All these parts and their functions are named, and we end with a very detailed account of the kinds of constructions in English sen-

---

[5] George O. Curme, *Syntax* (Boston: D. C. Heath, 1931), p. 1.

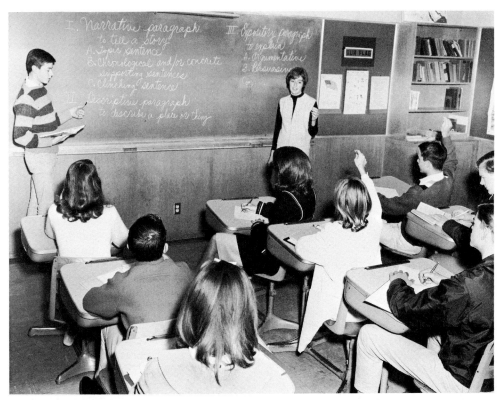

An understanding of the sentence and paragraph are essential if students are to mature as writers of English. (*Courtesy of the Burbank Public Schools.*)

tences and how they function, usually elaborately illustrated with real examples.

A second line of development in traditional grammars is the examination of the *parts of speech*. These classifications are based on meaning, function, or both. And some classifications, like the pronoun, may also be based partly on form.

The main fact is that meaning is the basis for defining the two most important of the traditional parts of speech, the noun and the verb. A noun, for example, is defined in traditional grammars as the "name of a person, place, or thing," or as a "word used as the name of a thing, quality, or action." We can identify and classify nouns, then, only by knowing their referents, the concepts or things for which they stand. In these traditional, notional grammars the noun as a part of speech is defined notionally.

Traditional grammars usually identify

eight parts of speech: noun, verb, adjective, adverb, preposition, conjunction, pronoun, and interjection. The *nouns*, sometimes called substantives, are name words. They can be further subdivided into proper and common nouns. Proper nouns are the names of particular people, places, events, organizations, and so on, which English usually distinguishes formally only by capitalization in writing. All other nouns, usually not capitalized, are common nouns.

Other groupings of nouns are also notional: categories such as collective nouns and abstract nouns are defined in traditional grammars on the basis of their meaning or on the basis of logic. For example, *committee,* a collective noun, is described as being either singular or plural, depending on whether it is thought of as a unit or a collection of individuals. This is a notional distinction. Traditional grammars lean rather heavily on the written language, as the distinction between common and proper nouns shows.

Once the traditional grammar has identified nouns by their meanings, it turns almost at once to examine the function of nouns; it becomes clear that words we have classed as nouns serve regularly as subjects, objects of various kinds, and predicate complements. And then we discover some of these same nouns used apparently as adjectives, as in "The coconut cake was made of fresh coconut."

In traditional grammars, an adjective is a "word that modifies a noun or a pronoun." Curme's definition of an adjective continues, "i.e., a word that is used with a noun or pronoun to describe or point out the living being or lifeless thing designated by the noun or pronoun: a *little* boy, *that* boy, *this* boy, a *little* house." [6] This is a functional definition. Further classes are both notional and functional. Adjectives are either descriptive or limiting: "*little* boy" is descriptive; "*this* boy" is limiting. This is a notional distinction. Adjectives are also either attributive (placed before or in immediate contact with the noun) or predicative (following a verb like *be*).

The *pronoun* definition in a traditional grammar usually goes something like the following: a pronoun is "a word that may be used instead of a noun or noun phrase (personal, relative, demonstrative, indefinite, and reflexive pronouns), or as an adjective (adjective pronoun), or to introduce a question (interrogative pronoun). In each of these categories our identification depends ultimately on our identification of nouns. It is notional first, and then functional.

But this raises an interesting point: how do we tell nouns from pronouns if functionally they do the same work? The answer is "partly from meaning, partly from form." Pronouns take most of their meaning (except for the grammatical matter of case) from the nouns they replace. They have no other referents, as can be seen from the definitions of the various pronouns in this

dictionary. But their forms are distinctive, because they are a small, finite list of words. The personal pronouns, for example, show many distinctive formal characteristics: case (*I, my, mine,* and *me*), number (*I* and *we*), person (*I, you,* and *he*), and gender (*he, she,* and *it*). But the personal pronouns are a finite list, and we are not likely to add new ones as readily, or at least as speedily, as we add other words to the vocabulary. Pronominal changes occur of course, but only very slowly. (Note how long it is taking to lose completely the *thou, thy, thine, thee,* and *ye* forms, which have been disappearing for hundreds of years.) Form, function, and meaning all are used as bases for identifying and classifying pronouns.

The definition of the *verb* in traditional grammars is also notional, perhaps with an overtone of functionalism. Curme said, "The verb is that part of speech that predicates, assists in predications, asks a question, or expresses a command: 'The wind *blows*.' 'He *is* blind.' '*Did* he *do* it?' '*Hurry!*' " [7] This is a notional definition. Verbs are further classed as transitive or intransitive (verbs that require or do not require an object), linking or auxiliary. These are functional classifications.

The other parts of speech—adverb, preposition, conjunction, and interjection—are similar mixtures of notional functional distinctions. The chief virtue of these traditional grammars when they are well done is that they are so fully detailed. The terminology developed for classrooms has been a hindrance to later grammars in some ways, but ultimately it has served as a useful standard: no modern grammar can be said to be accurate, however high its apparent efficiency, if it cannot account for all the varieties of construction so fully delineated in the best traditional grammars. The traditional terminology is still useful.

Let us look at each part of speech and find ways of teaching the concept. Then we will consider how that knowledge might be used to improve sentences composed by a student.

Rather than waiting until grade 4 or grade

[6] George D. Curme, *Parts of Speech and Accidence* (Boston: D. C. Heath, 1931), p. 42.

[7] Ibid., p. 63.

5 to mention nouns, it is sensible to start in the primary grades, when children label things. *Doors, windows, desks* are naming words or nouns. So are *John, Joe,* and *Susan.* The same would be true of verbs. Words like *jump, run, play* are action words or verbs and should be so classified from the first grade on.

With fourth- or fifth-grade children, teachers may start with a picture and have the children list the people they see in the picture, then the places, then the things. In the discussion it is brought out that they *named* these items. There are other things we name, such as ideas like democracy and feelings like happiness. Words that name something are classed as nouns. The same thing can be done by having each child write two sentences about persons, places, things, ideas, and feelings. After the sentences are written the child is asked to underline words that name something. Check by having the children find the nouns in the sentences of a textbook or by having them write nouns that they think of when you say *home* or *vacation.* Once the idea is taught it should never be permitted to fade from the memories of children. In the spelling list, ask children to use the appropriate words as nouns. In reading ask them to identify nouns. Make a bulletin board on which children add a noun a day.

Most courses of study suggest that singular versus plural forms and possessives be taught in grade 5 and that compound nouns and concrete versus abstract distinctions be added in grade 6. Some teachers feel that this is an arbitrary spread of the concept. Certainly possessives and plural forms will be used by the children long before these grades are reached. One teacher had fifth-grade children keep notebooks titled "All About Nouns and Verbs." The children brought together all basic information on these two parts of speech during a period of six weeks. Interest did not lag, nor was the material forgotten, because the books were constantly used for reference.

A way to introduce verbs is to put a group of simple sentences on the board and erase the verb. Then discuss what part of the sentence was removed. Develop the idea that these are the words that tell the action.

Paul *drove* a black car.
He *went* to see his cousin.
The cousin *lives* in Yuma.
He *stopped* in Denver.

Then provide some sentences in which the student adds an action word.

Mary _____ a new dress.
My dog _____ the cat.
Mice _____ cats.
Mice _____ cheese.
Cats _____ mice.
Jack _____ baseball.

Still stressing the action concept, look at sentences in the readers to "spot verbs." Being "verb detectives" has some appeal. A trick to teach children is that if they can put *I, you,* or *he* before a word and the two words make a sentence, then the second word is a verb. One can say "I eat," "you draw," "he plays," because the second words are verbs. But you cannot say "I piano," "he desks," or "you newspaper," because the second words are not verbs. This "trick" does assume that the child has a sense of what a sentence is. A variation is to have the children be hunters who put words in noun, verb, and adjective cages.

Very soon the students find sentences that contain only the *to be* verbs. The definition terminology "verbs of being" rarely makes sense to children. It is best to identify these words as a group. The teacher might say,

There is a group of verbs that are a part of the verb *to be.* I have made a list of them on the board: *am, is, are, was, were, have been, shall be, will be.* Let us make each one into a sentence.

I am in the fifth grade.
He is my teacher.
We are here.
I was sad.
You were happy.

Then discuss the fact that although the words do not show action, they do indicate existing. Students might keep a chart of these nonaction verbs (there are not many) and simply memorize them as one would certain sight words in reading. These verbs are used with action verbs as helpers.

Helping verbs are used to show time:

Paul is cracking a nut. (*present*)
Paul will crack a nut. (*future*)
Paul has been cracking nuts.
                    (*past and present*)
Paul cracked a nut. (*past*)

These words are used as helping verbs:

am	do	might
are	does	must
be	had	shall
been	has	should
can	have	was
could	is	were
did	may	will

In a question the helping verb is frequently separated from the main verb:

Where *are* you *going?*
Did you *find* it?

No and *not* sometimes separate the verb from its helping verb.

I *have* not *found* it.

A game called Employment Agency provides oral practice in use of helping verbs. It may be played by several children. All except three children are given a verb card, such as:

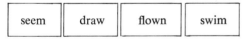

| seem | draw | flown | swim |

The children holding these verb cards are the "Employers." The three other children (the Employees) hold the card with a helping verb, such as:

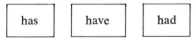

| has | have | had |

Each employer in turn holds his word card in front of the group and says, "Do I need help? Does anyone want a job?" If the word on his card needs a helping word, one of the three helpers who raises his hand may be chosen to stand beside him. The teacher chooses another child to use the word in a sentence.

Exercises like the following stress verb identification:

- Replace "tired," often used verbs with words that are more vivid, such as *trudged* for *walked, consumed* for *ate,* and so on.

- Cut pictures from magazines that illustrate action verbs and post in a bulletin or use to illustrate a "verb collection."
- Combine two words, a noun and a verb, to form a sentence: *Boys walk. Turkeys strut. Babies cry. Stars twinkled. Dogs barked.*
- Keep a record of one morning's activity. Note the use of verbs.

At 9:00 school ⸻
The teacher ⸻
I ⸻
Then the class ⸻
At recess we ⸻
After recess I ⸻
One boy ⸻
One girl ⸻
At noon I ⸻

Children should find adjectives as easy to understand as nouns. Whenever a word describes a noun, as *red* dress, or whenever a word points out, as *that* grade, it modifies the noun and is an adjective. Adjectives answer the questions: What color? What kind? What size? How many? Which one? After explaining this, have a class think through the following exercise:

Which question does each underlined adjective answer:

The <u>old</u> house was dark.
We sat on <u>three</u> benches.
The <u>back</u> door is open.
I need a <u>wet</u> cloth.
Do you see <u>those</u> girls?

Have an "adjective search" of a page in a reader. See who can find the largest number.

Make lists of adjectives that answer each of the questions that adjectives answer.

Have the children spell only the adjectives in the week's spelling list.

Make a collection of advertisements that use adjectives to make the product attractive.

Put a picture on the bulletin board. Let each child add one adjective that might be used in telling about the picture.

There is little reason for considering the articles *a, an,* and *the* as separate parts of speech. Mauree Applegate suggests that they be given some personality by calling them *towing words.* This suggestion is appropriate because articles always appear before a noun. The idea also helps children remember that when the word *towed* starts with a vowel, *a* will not do the towing job—only *an* and *the* want that type of work.[8]

The concept of modification is an important one in understanding the sentence. Ask the children to picture in their minds what they see when they read, "The girl ran down the street." Discuss the age each visualized the girl and the kind of street that was in their mental pictures. Then ask the children to read this sentence: "The little girl ran down the shady street." Again discuss the mental picture in their minds and note that their ideas are more alike or that the number of meanings have been limited by the use of little and shady. Modification means just that, to limit the meaning. One way of making our meaning more exact is to use modifiers.

Experiment with substitution exercises like the following to see how these words limit the meaning:

The (big) (happy) (dirty) (handsome) boy went to the (haunted) (new) (enchanted) (girl's) house.

As understanding of modification develops, more involved material can be used. It will interest some classes to attempt to construct a sentence that will be so clear that everyone will have exactly the same mental picture:

The dog ran.
The dog ran down the muddy street.
The little yellow dog ran down the muddy street.
The little yellow dog ran down the muddy street barking.
The little yellow dog ran down the muddy street barking at the newspaper boy.

The traditional diagram form is a good visual aid for adjectives. List a noun on the board and then place a modifier suggested by a child under it. In a series this represents the limiting aspect of modification.

_____
[8] Mauree Applegate, *Easy in English* (New York: Harper, 1960).

Then point out that in our speech and writing we sometimes use two or more adjectives modifications:

Adverbs have three functions: to modify verbs (run *swiftly*), to modify adjectives (*strangely* silent), or to modify another adverb ("The bell rang unusually long."). Adverbs usually answer the questions *how, when,* or *where:*

How words: slowly, well, neatly, fast.
When words: early, often, once, then.
Where words: inside, up, here, away.

To clarify the use of adverbs, have the children identify *how, when,* and *where* words in sentences like the following:

I ran up.
The baby cried loudly.
I ran inside.
I will eat now.
He came early.
He came here.
The cake is light blue.
The boy secretly tasted it.
He very noisily smacked his lips.
The cake was very good.

A few adverbs seem to stand alone because the verb modified is understood rather than spoken: *yes, no, probably, surely, truly, perhaps, indeed, please.*

Some adjectives and adverbs have the same form. The following words can be used either as an adverb or adjective. Challenge the students to construct two sentences for each word and to label which has the adjective and which the adverb.

best	close
better	deep
bright	direct
cheap	early
clean	fair

far	pretty
fast	quick
full	right
hand	shop
high	short
ill	slow
just	soft
late	straight
long	well
low	wide
near	wrong

Examples would be

This is the best cake. (Adjective)
Of the three she writes the best. (Adverb)
He ran fast to catch the plane. (Adverb)
The jet is a fast plane. (Adjective)

Conjunctions as connectors in such expressions as "Paul *and* Bill," "We will go to the show *but* you must stay home" cause few identification problems. Neither do exclamations such as "Oh!" "Ouch!" "Hello!" Charts can be made of such words and their function illustrated.

Prepositions are more difficult. One child told me that a preposition could be used to describe anything a squirrel could do to a hollow log. A diagram might illustrate such words as *over, under, by, into, in, above, beside, around.* The idea does help define prepositions as directional words. The term is a combination of *pre-*, meaning "in front of" or "before," and *-position*, meaning "place." A preposition is a word that is placed before another word. It is placed before a noun to show relationship between the noun and some other word in the sentence. This relationship can be illustrated in the following expressions:

The hat on the chair.
The dog under the tree.
The cat in the tree.
The boy by the car.
The trailer behind the car.

Make a master list of prepositions:

about	behind
above	below
according	beneath
across	beside
after	between

in	by way of
in front of	during
in regard to	except
in spite of	for
into	from
throughout	like
to	of
toward	on
under	on top of
until	out of
against	over
along	through
among	up
around	up to
at	upon
because of	with
before	within
beyond	without
by	

After the children have looked for prepositions in a story they should note that a preposition always takes an object.

Some prepositions have meanings that need to be clarified. In oral language the following are frequently confused:

1. *Among* and *between.*
   a. *Among* applies to *more than two* persons or things: "The baseball equipment was divided *among* all the boys."
   b. *Between* applies to *only two* persons or things: "Mother placed the flowers *between* the books and the basket."
2. *At* and *to.*
   a. *At* means already in place: "The boy is *at* school."
   b. *To* means going toward a person, place or thing: "The boy is going *to* school."
3. *In* and *into.*
   a. *In* means inside or within: "Mary is *in* the pool."
   b. *Into* means to move from the outside to the inside: "Mary is going to dive *into* the pool."
4. *From* and *than.*
   a. *From* is a preposition and shows position in time and space.
   b. *Than* is a conjunction (a joining word) and not a preposition. It usu-

ally joins two parts of a sentence: "I would rather go *than* stay at home."

 c. Read these sentences carefully:

  "This book is different *from* the other books in the room." (correct)

  "This book is different *than* the other books in the room." (incorrect)

5. *Of* and *from.*

 a. The prepositions *of* and *from* are never used with the adverb *off* such as:

  "The men jumped *off* the boat." (correct)

  "The men jumped *off of* the boat." (incorrect)

  "The men jumped *off* the log." (correct)

  "The men jumped *from off* the log." (incorrect)

Posters, charts, and bulletin boards dramatizing these confused meanings (only one group at a time) might be made by intermediate-grade students for a "pure language" week or program.

One part of speech remains to be described—the pronoun. The term *pronoun* means "for a noun." Children can see this when the teacher substitutes pronouns in sentences of this nature: *Mary lost her lamb.*

Boy Blue went to sleep. The spider sat beside Miss Muffet. Such sentences become: *She lost her lamb. He went to sleep. It sat beside her.*

When children learn about forming possessives in the third or fourth grade, lessons should be planned on the possessive forms of pronouns. This can be associated with the pronoun definition. *The boy's coat* becomes *his coat, the girl's dog* becomes *her dog,* and *the fifth-grade team* becomes *our team.* Contrast the two forms of pronouns:

Pronoun	Possessive Pronoun
I	my
he	his
she	her
we	our
you	your
it	its

The pronoun *it* presents a special difficulty. The possessive of *it* is *its.* There is confusion because of the contraction of *it is,* which is *it's.* Because *man* in the plural becomes *men's* by the addition of an apostrophe and an *s,* the logical association is to do the same for *it.* Point out to the children that *its* is like *his.*

The major problem concerning pronouns is the form taken when a pronoun is the object of a verb or preposition. Illustrate the form again with sentences:

Mary hit John.	Mary hit him.
John lost the book.	John lost it.
Mary knew John and Jane.	Mary knew them.
Jane liked Mary.	Jane liked her.
Bring the paper to the teacher.	Bring the paper to her; bring it to her.

Again, contrast the forms in a chart:

Subject Pronouns	Possessive Pronouns	Object Pronouns
I	my	me
he	his	him
she	her	her
we	our	us
you	your (s)	you
they	their (s)	them

But there is a group of words sometimes used as pronouns that are indefinite in that they do not stand for a definite name of something. Among them are *another, anyone, anybody, each, either, everybody, all, everyone, neither, no one, nobody, everything, some one, none, other, somebody, several, both.*

Notice their use in such sentences as the following:

Give me another.
Anyone can do this.
Each must give something.
No one is here.
Nobody can do this.
Everything is ready.
One must drive slowly.
Somebody lost it.
Both have finished.
Some like candy.

Some pronouns correct or relate parts of sentences:

	Connecting Pronoun
I have a little dog. He has fleas.	
I have a little dog who has fleas.	who
I saw the people. Their house burned down.	
I saw the people whose house burned down.	whose
The dog ran away. He was mine.	
The dog that ran away was mine.	that

Other pronouns are those used in questions such as *who, what,* and *which,* and the *self* pronouns which are used for emphasis.

As each part of speech is taught, some useful way to employ that knowledge in speaking and writing needs to be established. This will involve the use of the parts in sentences. Basic to such understanding are the terms *subject, object,* and *predicate.*

Primary children can locate the subject of a sentence. "What are they talking about?" or "Who is the subject of this sentence?" are natural questions in any reading instruction.

Even compound subjects such as *"John and Joe* bought a dog" are understandable to young children. The one new difficulty added is that of selecting a plural form of the verb. If the oral language patterns are correct this presents little difficulty. When there is difficulty, it is usually restricted to one or two children rather than to an entire class. One teacher reported that there were few errors made with this construction until after a lesson had been taught stressing the agreement in number of the verb with the compound subject. In other words, the children were unaware of the problem until it was taught to them. Then it resulted in a concern that produced errors. It might be well to assess the class needs before teaching such a lesson. A simple test having the children supply the correct word will reveal what the teacher needs to know. Use sentences like the following:

Mary and Jane _____ Girl Scouts.
Mother and father _____ there.
Where _____ Jane and Jack?

The direct object of the verb is that which receives the action: *John hit Mary.* In this sentence, Mary was *hit* and is therefore the object of the verb. Some children are confused if the teacher says *Mary* is the "object of the sentence." This terminology is too much like "the meaning or purpose of the sentence." At this point, audiovisual devices help the children see these words as parts of a sentence. The labeling of words in simple sentences will help establish the concepts. Some use the S-V-O as symbols of the pattern of sentences like the one following:

The arrow hit the target.

S   V   O

Putting the words on separate pieces of cardboard and reassembling the sentences on the chalk rail or flannelboard helps to dramatize this construction. Pass a different word to each child. One list will be those of nouns, the other will be of verbs. The teacher asks, "Who has a noun that will be the subject of a sentence?" "Who has a verb that will show what the subject did?" Then, "Who has a word that received the action?" Use the following nouns: *John, Mary, mother, father, the dog, the cat, the teacher, a bird, an apple, candy.* Use the following verbs: *bought, chased, ate, taught, fed, sold.* Objects have a way of getting quite complex, because other parts of speech may have an object, but this type of beginning exercise will help establish the concept.

The term *predicate* is an awkward one. It is used to describe the part of the sentence that tells about the subject. As such it includes more than the verb of most sentences. Yet in writing, the problem is usually the verb alone. The verb fails to agree with the subject in number, or the verb is in the wrong tense (time) when related to other sentences in the writing. It is easier for children to understand the verb of the sentence and its operation without including other aspects of the predicate.

At one time a knowledge of the parts of speech was used widely to diagram a sentence. Research has shown that children in the fourth grade can be taught to diagram, but that this knowledge has little influence on their writing. In the junior high school and beyond, some students profit from their ability to diagram.

As a teacher in the intermediate grades, you will find simple diagrams a help in explaining certain sentences and sentence parts. Do not hesitate to use this visual aid as an aspect of your explanation. But do not expect children to diagram any but simple sentences and a few modification positions.

In the discussion of adjectives and adverbs the relationships of these words are indicated in diagrams. Children find this sentence pattern helpful. At first each major part of the sentence, such as the subject, should be studied separately.

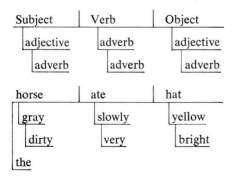

Prepositional phrases are like branches on a tree. A diagram will help the child to identify the related nature of such a group of words. Here is a simple sentence: *The house burned.* Here is a simple sentence with a prepositional phrase used as an adjective: *The house by the old mill burned.* The diagram of the phrase looks like this:

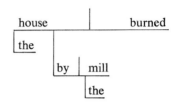

At the beginning the entire phrase could be written on a slanted line under *house* but the form illustrated above is actually easier to write.

The concept of the compounds can be illustrated through diagrams. Here is a simple sentence with a simple subject: *Mary ate an apple.* It would be shown this way:

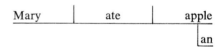

Here is a simple sentence with a compound subject: *Mary and Jack ate the apples.* It would be shown like this:

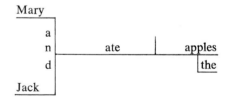

Here is a simple sentence with a compound verb: *The truck rattled and squeaked.* It would be shown like this:

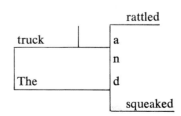

Positive	Comparative	Superlative
tall	taller	tallest (common form)
beautiful	more beautiful	most beautiful (easier to say with long adjectives)
good	better	best (irregular form)
bad	worse	worst (irregular form)
little	less	least (irregular form)
perfect	more nearly perfect	most nearly perfect (for natural superlatives)

This is a compound sentence made up of two related but independent clauses. With children we would point out that each part is a sentence by itself: *The cowboy walked and the lady rode his horse.*

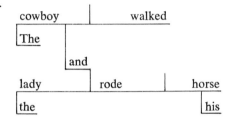

Another use of the knowledge of the parts of speech would be to clarify some common usage errors.

1. *To—too—two.* These three homonyms are confused because of sound. The error is a spelling problem. Each has a different meaning and represents a different part of speech. *To* is a preposition, *too* is an adverb, and *two* is an adjective.

Send the bill to me.
It is too late.
I want two dollars. (Note that *twin* also has the *w* in it as a way to remember the meaning and spelling.)

2. *Good—well. Good* is an adjective. "This is a *good* cake." *Well* is an adjective only when referring to health: "I am *well*."

Otherwise it is an adverb: "He plays *well*."

3. *Real—really—very. Real* is an adjective meaning "genuine": "This is *real* gold." *Really* is an adverb meaning "actually": "Is he *really* [actually] going?" *Very* is usually an adverb meaning "exceedingly": "I am *very* happy."

Both *really* and *very* may be used in the same sentence but the meaning differs.

In the comparison of adjectives typical errors are *most best, beautifulest, more sweeter, more dead.* Children should know the terms used and the standard forms of comparative adjectives.

The idea that comparison is made between two and superlative between more than two is easy to illustrate and prevents many errors.

Because adverbs are also compared there is sometimes confusion of the two forms. *Easier* is the comparative of the adjective *easy.* The sentence "I can lift the table _____ than you," calls for an adverb. The adverb is *easily* and the comparative would be *more easily* rather than *easier.*

There is a group of language errors related to verb tense (time) that concern us as teachers in the language arts.

There are over 8,000 verbs in the English language. Most of these are "regular" verbs; that is, they form the past tense and past participle by adding *-ed* to the present tense:

Present Tense (today)	Past Tense (yesterday)	Past Participle (*with* I have)
walk	walked	walked
talk	talked	talked
cook	cooked	cooked

But there are enough irregular verbs to cause trouble. Those learning English as a foreign language find this one of the most difficult problems encountered. Fortunately, few children will find all of these a problem. Some are used infrequently whereas others are so common as to be simple patterns which the child masters in his speech before starting to school. Frequent errors are indicated in parentheses.

Present Tense	Past Tense	Past Participle (with *have, has, had*)
beat	beat	beaten
begin	began	begun (never used alone)
blow	blew (never *blowed*)	blown
break	broke (not with *have* or *has*)	broken
bring	brought	brought (no word *brang* or *brung*)
burst	burst	burst (no verb *bust, busted,* or *bursted*)
come	came (never with *have* or *has done*)	come
do	did	done (along with *have, has*)
draw	drew (not *drawed*)	drawn
drink	drank	drunk
eat	ate (*et* only in Britain)	eaten
flee	fled	fled
flow	flowed	flowed
fly	flew	flown (nothing to do with *flow*)
go	went (always alone)	gone
grow	grew (not *growed*)	grown
hang	hung	hung
hang	hanged	hanged (used only with reference to executions)
ring	rang (always alone)	rung
swim	swam (always alone)	swum
swing	swung	swung (not *swang*)
write	wrote (always alone)	written
cast	cast	cast (not *casted*)
broadcast	broadcast	broadcast
throw	threw	thrown (not *throwed* or *thrun*)
fall	fell (always alone)	fallen
freeze	froze (always alone)	frozen
run	ran	run
see	saw (always alone)	seen (with *have* or *has*)
sing	sang	sung
speak	spoke	spoken
steal	stole (always alone)	stolen

In English, a verb must agree with its subject in person and number. Thus when the noun or pronoun is changed to show person or number, the verb must also be changed. It will be best to explain this rule with respect to one difficulty at a time. By person we refer to the speaker, those spoken to, and those spoken of.

I play the piano. (first person speaking)

We sing in school. (first person plural speaking)

You sing well. (second person spoken to)

John plays the piano. (third person spoken of)

These flowers match her dress. (third person spoken of)

By number, we are thinking of the persons or things considered as being one or more than one. These errors will illustrate the problem:

The boys was happy.
for
The boys were happy.

We was happy.
for
We were happy.

Most indefinite pronouns are singular: *either, neither, each, another, much, one.* All compounds of *one, body,* and *thing,* such as *anyone* or *nobody,* are also singular. The pronouns *both, few, many,* and *several* are plural. The words *all, any, more, most,* and *such* may be either singular or plural, depending on the noun they represent. When these rules are not understood we find errors like these:

Each of the boys are to try.
Neither of the dogs are hungry.
Nobody who was there are here.

Another problem illustrated above is that the subject and verb are separated. Few would say, "Nobody are here." One help is to suggest enclosing such phrases in parentheses to check the agreement of subject and verb:

Nobody (who was there) is here.
A set (of the tools) is very useful.
One (of the girls) is going home.

Sometimes agreement depends on the idea of the writer. One may write, "Bread and butter are expensive"; in this instance the writer would be thinking of two ideas. Compound subjects are usually two ideas but they may be one. The same is true of collective nouns, such as *tribe, team, class, club.*

It is difficult for an adult to realize how abstract language becomes when we look at language as a thing apart from the meanings communicated. A teacher needs to place himself in the learner's position in order to understand how complex this can be. Imagine that you are a child again. You have learned to name many of the things you can hear and see. You know the meaning of *apple, orange,* and *banana.* In kindergarten

or first grade you learned that all of these can be fruit. In time you have learned other generalized meanings for such words as *people, animals, games, toys,* and *house.*

At first all these words were learned orally. The sound was the symbol for the thing. Then in reading you learned the printed word which was a symbol for the sound. The printed word is actually a double symbol. It represents both the sound and the meaning. From 8 to 12 per cent of the children in school have difficulty understanding this double symbolism and thus are remedial or slow readers. When such a child is asked to use another level of abstraction and classify words as nouns, verbs, or other parts of speech, he usually fails. Rather than classification of the sentence parts, these children need opportunities to use the written language with an emphasis upon the ideas expressed. But there are some aspects of sentence structure that can be understood by most of the children in the intermediate grades and that can be applied to improve their written communication.

For Discussion

1. Someone has said we have been teaching language in the same way a coach might teach swimming, by having each person memorize the names of bones and muscles of the body. Is this a fair analogy?

2. The parts of speech were developed by a monk 800 years ago as he analyzed the Latin of Cicero. Would it be possible to classify our words in other ways?

What Is the New Grammar?

(This section is designed to inform teachers about the new grammar as well as to suggest methods of teaching it.)

Language has a lexical meaning carried by the words and a grammatical or structural meaning carried by the system. The isolated words *girls, cat,* and *wanted* carry notional meanings which one finds in the dictionary. These words also contain grammatical meaning: *plural, singular, past tense.* When combined in a sentence the structure reveals a further grammatical meaning:

actor, action, goal. The word order determines who is acting. *The girls wanted a cat.* It is the system of the language which constitutes the new grammar. *Morphology,* or word form, and *syntax* are the point of emphasis in the new grammar.

If one examines a nonsense sentence, it becomes apparent how these signals operate. Read the following aloud: "The lunky garts sickled the slinest glurbs yetly." Only two words are recognized, yet a grammatical meaning is evident. The intonation of the voice indicates that the words form a sentence. The article *the* identifies *garts* as a noun that can be made plural. *Lunky* is marked as an adjective by the suffix as well as by its position between an article and a noun. *Slinest* is similarly located and identified as an adjective by the superlative degree inflection *est. Sickled* is read as a verb because of the *-ed* past-tense ending, by the *le,* and by its position between two nouns. *Yetly* is an adverb because it has the *-ly* adverbial suffix and comes at the end of a sentence, where an adverb often appears. The sentence pattern is the dominant subject—verb—object.

Consider the following taken from Nell Stevenson: [9]

Here are some sentences, along with a few suggestions on identifying each non-word. They are suggestions only. You and your youngsters will be able to make up many fascinating nonsense words of your own. You'll have fun doing it, too.

You may write on the *grosin.*
(*Grosin* is a noun, object of the preposition, identified by the determiner *the,* singular because of use and form.)

These *blettabs* taste good.
(*Blettabs* is a noun, subject of the sentence, plural because of the ending and the determiner *these.*)

Please give me some *drusels.*
(*Drusels* is a plural noun, used as a direct object, identified by the word *some.*)

Run along and find *Tocrod.*
(*Tocrod* will be identified as a proper noun

because of the capital letter; also identified as a noun because of its use as direct object.)

Show me how to make *gnibes.*
(*Gnibes* is plural, could be a noun, object of *to make;* could be used to point up fact that *g* is often silent before *n.* The singular is probably *gnibe,* pronounced with a long *i* because of the vowel-consonant-silent *e* rule in phonetics.)

She *blickened* the window and looked out.
(*Blickened* is a verb showing action, *recognized* by the *ed* clue; shows *ck* combination at end of first syllable.)

The *glimsy* chicken was eating grain.
(*Glimsy* is an adjective because it qualifies the noun *chicken;* could be compared by adding *er* and *est,* after changing *y* to *i,* becoming *glimsier* and *glimsiest.*)

He waded in the *siming.*
(*Siming* is a singular noun, identified by the determiner *the;* object of preposition *in.* Could be a noun of quantity.)

The starting point of the new grammar is with the oral language.[10]

There are approximately forty-four to forty-six distinctive sounds in English, which are conventionally represented with the twenty-six letters of the alphabet in different combinations. For example, the /f/ sound may be represented in English orthography by *f,* by *ph,* by *gh,* by *ff.* To avoid this problem linguists have devised a set of symbols to represent the various sound units of speech. Each of these units—the smallest unit of meaningful sound—is known as a phoneme, from a Greek word meaning "sound." The sounds of /p/ in *pin, spin,* and *sip* are not actually the same sound, but they are so close to one another that we can in English accept them as equivalents. Thus these three sounds of /p/ are one sound unit—one phoneme. In English there are twenty-four consonant phonemes. Most of the symbols for the phoneme in English are the familiar consonant letters. Other symbols are needed for some sounds, however. Note that not all conventional alphabet letters are used. The phonemic alphabet contains these consonants:

---

[9] Nell Stevenson, "My Word! What Words Are These?" *Grade Teacher* (October 1967), p. 92.

[10] Much of the material is based upon service bulletins issued to teachers in the Denver, Colorado, Public Schools.

	First Sound in	Middle Consonant Sound in	Final sound in
/b/	bath	rubber	rib
/c/ *	charge	inches	winch
/d/	dog	widow	planned
/f/	fill	siphon	cough
/g/	gap	ragged	hug
/h/	horn	behind	——
/j/ *	joy	enjoin	ridge
/k/	kill	anchor	attack
/l/	like	taller	chill
/m/	man	summer	ham
/n/	nap	dinner	thin
/p/	pin	supper	trap
/r/	roll	rearing †	here †
/s/	sight	tassel	purpose
/t/	tail	bitter	pinched
/v/	veil	prevent	alive
/w/	win	reweave	——
/y/	yell	beyond	——
/z/	zip	design	churches
/θ/	think	ether	cloth
/ð/	that	neither	bathe
/š/	should	reassure	flash
/ž/	Zhivago	azure	rouge
/n/	English	stinger	sing

* /c/ and /j/ are sometimes written with a wedge ( ) to represent the sounds illustrated.

† Dialectal differences, particularly in New England and in the South, will account for slightly different sounds in these words.

Linguists speak of *nine pure vowels* in English. They are

/i/ This sound, previously known as short *i*, is the vowel sound heard in the word *bit*.

/e/ This vowel, formerly called short *e*, represents the sound heard in the word *bet*.

/ae/ This symbol, which combines the letter *a* and *e*, stands for the sound formerly known as short *a*. Phonemically, the word *bat* is *baet*.

/I/ This symbol is known as barred *i*. The sound it represents is heard in words like *can* and *just* when they are being spoken rapidly and without conscious attention to enunciation, as in *I can go* and *wait just a*

second. It also occurs for some speakers as the weak vowel in the *-es* and *-ed* endings of words like *lunches* and *waited*.

/ə/ This symbol, the schwa, represents the "uh" sound characteristic of many vowels in unstressed syllables. It is the vowel sound heard in *but*.

/a/ The vowel sound heard in words like *father, lock, talk, hot, bomb,* and *calm* is represented by this symbol.

/u/ The letter *u* stands for the vowel sound heard in words like *good, look, put, full,* and *should*.

/o/ For practical purposes, this symbol is not needed because the "pure" sound it represents is heard only rarely. Words like *go* and *so* are transcribed phonemically as /gow/ and /sow/ simply because most speakers use the diphthong /ow/.

/ɔ/ This symbol (a reverse *e*) is called the open *o*. It represents the vowel sound heard in words like *caught* and *water,* particularly when the mouth is rounded and the sound comes from deep in the throat. Phonemically, *caught* is written /kɔt/. Many speakers use the /a/ phoneme in these examples.

In addition there are at least seven diphthongs (vowel plus semivowel) common to most dialects, and other diphthongs peculiar to specific dialects.

There are twelve additional phonemes known as *suprasegmental* because they may extend over several segmental phonemes. These phonemes are *pitch, stress,* and *juncture.* They are phonemic because they affect the sound units in any given stream of speech.

Linguists identify four pitch levels in English speech. Although the theoretical number of levels is large, ranging from bass to soprano for any given speaker, the practical use of any language contains only a few pitch levels. English has four. Simply stated, pitch is the way our voices rise and fall as we speak.

Ordinarily, most speakers use pitch level 2 for normal, matter-of-fact speech. (Level 1 is low and 4 is high.) In typical declarative sentences, the voice drops to level 1 at the end of the sentence; in most interrogative sentences (questions), the voice rises to level 3 at the end of the sentence. Pitch level 4 is used, as a rule, only in times of great excitement or alarm.

Is there any difference in meaning in these two sentences?

> Are you going tonight?
>   night?
> Are you going to

Note that the pitch level is a structure signal which conveys meaning and extends over several segmental phonemes. In the first sentence the speaker is in doubt about whether the listener plans to attend; in the second, the speaker assumes the listener *will* attend, but he wants to know which night the listener will go.

Similarly, in declarative sentences, the distinction between one pitch level and another indicates a certain meaning:

> ```
>                swim
> We're going        ming.
> We're       swim
>      going        ming.
> ```

In the first example, the statement seems to be a matter-of-fact declaration; in the second, with the first word on pitch level 3, there is a tone of, "We can go but you can't. Ha, ha, ha!"

Note that pitch levels contain no meaning in and of themselves; they indicate certain meanings only by contrast between one pitch level and another.

Closely related to pitch levels is the concept of stress. In English we use *loudness* or *stress* to make a word or syllable more prominent than others near it in the stream of speech. Stress, or accent, is seldom shown in writing but is always present in speaking.

> We met the English TEAchers.
> We met the ENGlish teachers.

In the first example, with the stress on the first syllable of *teachers,* we are not sure what subject matter these people teach, but we do know they are from England. In the second example, with the stress on ENGlish, we are fairly confident that these teachers conduct classes in the English language.

Linguists identify four degrees of stress:

Primary (loudest) /ˊ/
Secondary /˄/
Tertiary /ˎ/
Weakest /ˇ/ (or no mark at all)

The way in which many speakers pronounce the word *coordination* exemplifies all four degrees of stress: còôrdĭnatĭŏn.

Some speakers, however, might give only weak stress to the first syllable (*co-*) and therefore have only three degrees of stress exemplified.

Stress patterns often indicate differing meanings, particularly with phrases and compound words. For example, the eye of a bull is written as *bull's eye,* whereas a *bull's-eye* is the center of a target. Sometimes, too, the stress pattern of a word indicates its meaning and use (part of speech):

content—/kəntent/ (adj.)
content—/kantent/ (noun)

subject—/sibkelt/ (noun)
subject—/səbjekt/ (verb)

Juncture is thought of simply as a pause, either within a sentence or at the end of the sentence. Linguists have determined that juncture is a complex combination of features which most speakers learned as habits very early in life.

Of the four types of juncture, three are usually *terminal;* that is, they occur at the end of a sentence. The first of these, falling juncture, is often found at the end of statements and sometimes with questions, especially those questions which begin with *who* or *where.* Consider these sentences:

Who was that at the window?
There are four types of juncture.
A down-pointing arrow shows falling
   juncture.

Notice that, as you pronounce these sentences, your pitch rises to level 3 on the next-to-last syllable and falls to level 1 on the last. Then you pause before reading the next sentence. Notice also that you lengthen the *vowel sound* in the next-to-last syllable and that your voice intensity fades on the last syllable. The combination of these three phenomena—fall in pitch level, lengthening of vowel sound, and voice fading—forms the complex falling juncture.

Rising juncture, the second type, usually occurs with questions. Almost all questions not beginning with *who* or *where* (and some that do) show rising juncture. Like falling juncture, the pitch level is closely related; in these sentences, pitch usually rises from level 2 to 3. Again, the accented syllable is lengthened slightly and the intensity of the voice fades somewhat on the last syllable.

a. Is rising juncture indicated by a rising
   arrow?
b. Will you spend Thanksgiving at home
   or at the convention?

Note that, in sentence b, there is an example of rising juncture at the end of a phrase within the sentence. Such juncture is common in sentences which contain appositives, series, or some kind of choice (sentence b).

Level juncture, the third type, is characteristic of a few speakers who do not customarily drop their voices to pitch level 1 on the last syllable. In addition to keeping the pitch at the normal level (2), these speakers lengthen the vowel sound in the next-to-last syllable, let their voice intensity fade on the last syllable, and leave a considerable pause at the end of the word. Examples of level juncture can often be seen more readily *within* sentences at points we customarily mark with the dash or the colon in writing. Note these sentences:

Anyway, he has one good trait . . .
   brevity.
Few teachers appeared . . . they have
   so many meetings.

In addition, if you read aloud the first half dozen words in each of the preceding two paragraphs, you would use level juncture at the points indicated by ellipses.

Perhaps the most complicated, and least common, example of juncture is the *plus juncture,* which always occurs within a sentence. It involves a pair of words or phrases which might be confused in speech if we failed to use the plus juncture appropriately. Say these groups of words aloud:

a. the night rates   b. a gray day paper
   the nitrates   a grade A paper

Note in example a, the /ay/ diphthong is held slightly longer in the word *night* than it is in *nitrates.* In addition, the tongue position for /t/ is held a bit longer and the voice picks up intensity on the /ey/ round in *rates.* These characteristics, including what seems to be a slight pause between *night* and *rates,* are called plus junctures because the phonemic transcription uses a plus sign:

/nayt + reyts/ and /naytreyts/

A classic example of the use of plus juncture is found in the use of the three words *light, house,* and *keeper.* Try pronouncing these words together to mean (1) a person who does only light chores in maintaining a house, (2) a person who works at a lighthouse, and (3) a housekeeper who doesn't weigh much.

A morpheme is the smallest meaningful unit in a language. Sometimes the meaning is lexical, as in *cat;* sometimes it is grammatical as the *s* in *cats* or the *ing* in *parting; est* in *biggest.*

Some linguists use the morphology above to define the parts of speech. Nouns are words which can be inflected for the plural and possessive. Verbs are words which can be inflected for the past tense. Adjectives are words which can be inflected for the comparative and superlative.

Others use function or position in the sentence as the basis for classification. Nouns are words which can fit in the position of the subject and objects in a sentence such as *"John* gave *Mary* the *book,"* or in positions after prepositions in patterns such as "in the *night.*" Adjectives are words that fit patterns such as "John was _____," or "the _____ boy."

These positional classifications of parts of speech line up two kinds of words: (1) large numbers of nouns, verbs, adjectives, and adverbs and (2) limited numbers of function words. The main meaning of most of these functional words is grammatical.

Some texts contrast these two groups on the basis of changing form. Nouns, verbs, adjectives, and adverbs are called form-class words because they can change form by adding parts or changing spelling to show difference in number, time, comparison, and the like. Those that do not change form are called structure words.

The pronouns have some features of both classes and are considered a subgroup of the nouns, a separate group, or junction words.

Auxiliaries are words such as *may, shall, be,* and *have* that combine in various ways with verbs. *Do,* for example, lives a separate life both as verb and as auxiliary; some list it also as a special question-asking word: "*Did* he *do* it?" In speech *have* and *has* distinguish the full verb from the function word in the present tense: *I have two books* /haev/, and *I have to go home* /haef/.

These function words signal verb or predication, and when we use them, they, rather than the verb itself, take the inflections for number and tense which make for agreement of subject and verb and for logical sequence of tenses.

Prepositions are a finite list of function words which signal a special structure of modification: "the man in the street." These structures always have noun (or nominal) objects, and they can fit as units anywhere that nominals, adjectivals, or adverbials can fit.

Determiners are a longer but still finite list of words which mark constructions headed by nouns or nominals. *The, a, an, this, that,* and so on, are determiners: "*these* boys," "*the* big house."

Conjunctions are a short list of function words which relate words or larger structures to each other. There are two parts to the list: one, fairly small, is composed of words such as *and* and *but,* which are used to join words or constructions in parallel: "John *and* I came *and* sat here and there early *and* often, *and* we liked the atmosphere." The other, larger part contains conjunctions which relate subordinate or dependent structures, mainly those with verbs in them, to the main part of the sentence. "*Since* he came, we've been busy." "I like her *because* she's happy."

Pronouns are often not classed in descriptive grammars as function words but as a special group of nominals. Because they have limited and mainly grammatical meanings, however, and because they comprise short, finite lists of forms, they can fit the broad definition of function words. They can also be broken up into lists which classify largely under other function-word and part-of-speech classes.

Interrogatives are a finite list of function words used as the first element in questions, especially with *be* and the function word *do:* "When is he coming?" "*Who* does he think he is?" Obviously some of these overlap with pronouns.

Intensives are a group of function words which fit before adjectives or adjectivals in modification patterns. *Very* in "It's a *very* large order" and "He felt *very* sick" is the most common word of the class.

Various modern grammars add function word classes for a handful of words almost empty of other than grammatical meaning. *Not,* for example, and its contracted form *n't,* mean *negative. There,* as in "There *there* is a place" (the first *there* is an adverb, the second the function word) means a transposed sentence pattern wherein the subject follows the verb.

Some linguists use the following code to diagram sentences:

1. Nouns   Class 1 words
2. Verbs   Class 2 words
3. Adjectives   Class 3 words
4. Adverbs   Class 4 words

A linking verb becomes 2L. Class 1 words show they stand for the same referent by adding a, b, c, and so on, to the numerals.

In sentence patterns the numbers of the class form represent the words

   1   2
Birds sing.
   1a   2   1b
Robins like worms.
   1a   2L   3
Robins are beautiful.
   1a   2   1b   1b
Robins consider worms candy.

The other parts of speech have been identified by these letters:

D—Determiners.
V—(for *very*) Intensifiers.
A—Auxiliaries.
P—Prepositions (P-groups are prepositional phrases).
C—Conjunctives.
T—(for *therefore*) Sentence connectors.
S—Subindicators which form dependent classes. Subclass Group 1 are words that pattern like *when, because,* and *although.* Subclass Group 2 are words that pattern like *who* and *which.*
Q—Are words which signal a question.

Thus the sentence formula may be used to help students write sentences.

   1   2
Boy play
   1a   2   1b
Boys play baseball.

   1   2   C   2   P   2   1b
Boys bat and run to win the game.

Make a sentence using this sentence formula:

1a	2	1b	3	1c	S

	1b	2	1a	D	1a

The generative–transformationalist grammarian is another aspect of the new grammar. This school of linguistic thought maintains that a satisfactory grammar of English should explain how a native speaker of English understands what is meant by a sentence even though he has never heard that particular sentence before. In other words, how does the mind sort out various sounds and arrange them into meaningful statements? The generative grammarians build on the work, especially in phonology, of the structuralists, but they go further and attempt to establish rules for generating any possible sentence in English, whether or not it has ever been spoken. *Phrase-structure* rules explain how various phrases in English develop and *transformational* rules describe the several arrangements and rearrangements of these phrases which take place in the development of more complex sentences. We might say that *phrase-structure* rules tell us how to generate sentences and *transforms* tell us how to change or generate new sentences.

Let us see how a simple sentence can be generated and transformed. Begin by writing *S,* which stands for *kernel sentence.* This first step tells us that we are going to generate sentences from a pattern which will follow. The next step will be to indicate that S → NP (noun phrase) + VP (verb phrase) where "→" indicates *"rewrite as."* We now have the model for the sentence which we are going to generate. The next step will be to rewrite NP by choosing a word like *John, boys, dog.* The commas here indicate that one may choose only one word from the list. The fourth step will be to choose one word from a second list which contains such words as *sang, is tall, steals,* in order to rewrite VP. We have now generated a sentence such as "John is tall" or "Boys sang." We might show this sentence in a diagrammatic way as follows:

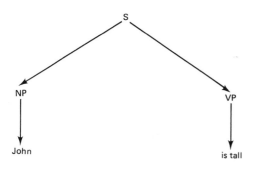

If we wanted to add determiners (D) or modifiers, our diagram might look like the following:

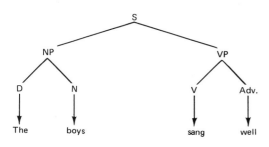

Seven kernel sentence patterns are widely recognized.[11] The NP (noun part or phrase) is not differentiated for the different patterns, but the VP (verb part or phrase) is rewritten differently for each pattern. Thus the differences in the VP (the predicate) distinguish the patterns. In the first four patterns each verb phrase contains a different kind of verb, which determines the pattern for the rest of the sentence. In the last three patterns the verb phrase is formed with *be,* which is put in a class by itself because it has more forms

---

[11] A great deal of the following discussion is based upon "English Language Arts in Wisconsin" published by the Department of Public Instruction, Madison, Wisconsin, 1968. Frequently the quotations are direct. In order to facilitate reading, specific examples are not identified since this presentation represents a reorganization of that material.

than other verbs and differs from them in various other respects. (In fact, many grammarians do not classify *be* as a verb at all.)

The table on the next page, adapted from Owen Thomas's *transformational Grammar and the Teacher of English,*[12] set up the grammatical rules for the seven kernel sentence patterns in four positions, or slots. The first two slots must be filled in all patterns, and the third slot is all but the first pattern. The fourth position is optional in all patterns. The NP appears in column 1; the verb, with its classification, including *be,* in column 2; the complement (whatever is needed to complete the verb including *be*) in column 3; and an optional adverbial element in column 4.

Vi stands for *verb intransitive; Vt* for *verb transitive; Vb* for the verbs *become* or *remain; Vs* for the verb *seem* and for other verbs of the senses (*appear, feel, sound, taste,* and so on); the repetition of NP_1 in a pattern means that the two NP's refer to the same thing; NP_2 means that the second noun phrase has a different referent from the first NP; *adv-p* stands for *adverbial of place.* Column 4 will be filled later.

Kernel sentence patterns can be represented by trees, as illustrated at the bottom of the following page.

Students might write original sentences following each pattern. For patterns 1 and 2 a list of verbs might be provided at the beginning both to ensure success and to stimulate the choice of reasonably interesting nouns. For pattern 1 such verbs as *continue, grow, roar, prattle,* and *whine* might be used. For pattern 2 verbs that are invariably transitive will be selected, such as *discover, deliver, destroy, twist, provide.* If transitive verbs are used, the second NP is bound to have a different referent from the first. Then the students might work with some verbs that can function in either pattern 1 or pattern 2: *blaze, mumble, drag, survive.* (This is the time for students to become familiar with the labels *Vt, Vi,* and *Vt and Vi* in their textbooks.) Though kernel sentences do

---

[12] Owen Thomas, *Transformational Grammar and the Teacher of English* (New York: Holt, Rinehart and Winston, 1965).

NP (Subject) →	VP (Predicate) →		
1 (det +) N	*2* Verb or be	*3* A Structure That Completes the Verb—Complement	*4* (Adverbial)— Optional
Pattern 1 NP Boys	Vi compete.		
Pattern 2 NP₁ Some boys	Vt enjoy	NP₂ (direct object) sports.	
Pattern 3 NP₁ The boys The boys	Vb (become, re- main) became remained	⎰ NP₁ ⎱ ⎱ Adj. ⎰ friends. (NP₁) competitive. (Adj.)	
Pattern 4 NP The boys	Vs (seem, etc.) seem	Adj. energetic.	
Pattern 5 NP The boys	be (is, are, was, were) are	Adj. reliable.	
Pattern 6 NP₁ The boys	be were	NP₁ classmates.	
Pattern 7 NP The boys The boys	be are were	adv-p (word or phrase) here. in Chicago.	

have limitations, students often construct amusing and unusual illustrations. They may even be interested in writing a sequence of kernels, such as, "The fire crackled. The bacon sizzled. The coffee steamed. The campers ate breakfast." Pattern 2 offers an opportunity to show that NP's in kernel sentences are structured the same wherever they occur and that word order can signal meaning: "The dog chased the cat. The cat chased the dog."

A classroom example of teaching patterns 1 and 2 is found in the Wisconsin Course of Study:

A seventh-grade class had agreed that it would be interesting to test their sentence sense by trying to distinguish English sentences from groups of words that do not form grammatical English sentences. The opening discussion centered around the idea that while great variety occurs, there are a few recurring patterns which underlie nearly all sentences. Out of this, the idea of two main parts of a sentence evolved, and from there the discussion moved to the term "kernel" sentence.

The teacher placed these sentences on the board. He asked the class how the sentences

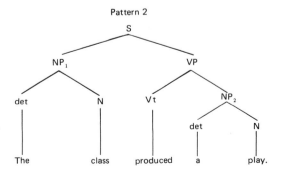

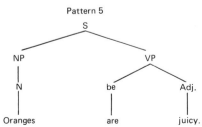

were alike. Without difficulty, the two main parts of the kernel sentence pattern 1 (NP + Vi) were recognized; the noun phrase functions as subject, the verb phrase as predicate.

NP	Vi
Helen	cried.
Clarence	smiled.
Canaries	sing.
Crowds	strolled.
Horses	galloped.

It was discovered that only certain verbs fit into this pattern. These verbs are called intransitive (Vi). To explain this pattern, the following rewrite rule was used:

$$S \rightarrow NP + Vi.$$

Students were asked to fill the subject "slot" in each of the following:

_____ stumbled
_____ sank
_____ trembled
_____ roared
_____ growled

After which they filled the predicate slot in this list:

Cars _____
The bus _____
Accidents _____
The boy _____
Students _____

Then the teacher asked the students to write five original kernel sentences illustrating the $S \rightarrow NP + Vi$ pattern. (Note: This exercise should show the students the limitations of sentences which contain only the bare essentials.)

Next, the students were asked to form pattern 1 sentences with words from the following list. They were instructed not to use a word more than once, and they were informed that words which do not fit in either slot are neither nouns nor verbs. (This list was extracted from *New Dimensions in English*, Allen, Newsome.)

continue	returned	geese
flocked	when	frontiers
experiments	crisis	adventurers
congressmen	gently	Pilgrims

within	voted	survive
sailed	ships	hears

Example: $\dfrac{NP}{geese} + \dfrac{Vi}{flocked}$

To show that some verbs need complements the teacher reminded the students they had learned that sentences have two parts: the subject and the predicate. The teacher wrote the following structures on the board and asked the class whether the structures were sentences:

Jim sold
Sandy sent
Dogs like
Bees make

After they concluded that something is needed to complete the verb, the class supplied words that did this. They were then able to see that pattern 2 has three parts, and that the third part must be a noun phrase because it is constructed like the noun phrase preceding the verb.

The verb in pattern 2 is a transitive verb, and the noun phrase that completes it functions as the direct object. To explain this pattern we can use the rewrite rules: $S \rightarrow NP_1 + Vt + NP_2$. The second NP is labeled NP_2 because the first NP and the second NP have different referents.

The teacher wanted to see if the class had grasped this concept, so they completed these patterns orally:

The artist examined _____.
_____ commanded the army.
The batter hit _____.
The hostess _____ her company.
The secretary wrote _____.
A cat chased _____.
Dr. Smith prescribed _____.
_____ brought in the mail.
Lincoln freed _____.
The customer drank _____.

To see the progress of each individual, the teacher had the class complete similar sentences of their own.

When the teacher was satisfied that the students could add direct objects, he presented these sentences to the class to help them see that some verbs can be used in both patterns:

The fire blazed.
Daniel Boone blazed a trail.
The child mumbled a reply.
David mumbled.

Then the class was asked these questions: "What pattern does each sentence follow?" "What do you notice about these verbs?" "What might we conclude about some verbs like *mumble* and *blaze?*"

These sentences were used by the teacher to determine whether the class was ready to go on. The students were asked to give the grammatical formula for each pattern:

Connie celebrated her birthday.
The expedition returned.
His ancestors survived.
The Indians defeated Custer.
The colonists gained their independence.

Pattern 3 is based upon the meaning of the words *became* and *remain*. In some elementary textbooks these verbs and those in the remaining patterns are called *linking* verbs. In the exercises found in fifth-grade textbooks such as those used later in this chapter the third part of such sentences is called a *completer* and includes nouns, adjectives, and adverbs.

Pattern 4 provides the test frame for teaching the adjective:

The _____ seems (very) _____.

Any word that can fill the slot after the linking verb *seem* is an adjective. Moreover, the adjective can be preceded by the intensifier *very*. Oral work is effective in establishing the pattern and concept of adjectives. As students supply words for the blanks, such sentences as these will result: "The day seems very cold"; "The building seems very old"; "The girl seems very silly." Some students will undoubtedly suggest that the adjectives can be inserted before the noun in the first blank, and, of course, they can. But adjectives do not appear before nouns in kernel sentences. Prenominal adjectives will be introduced through the relative-clause transformation. An adjective in the predicate is

not a modifier of the NP subject. It is part of the verb phrase, not of the noun phrase, and has only one function—that of complement of the verb.

This test frame eliminates nouns from the adjective class, for we do not say, "The walk seems very stone," or, "The road seems very sand," even though we do speak of *a stone walk* and *a sand road*. The term used for nouns in this structure is *noun adjunct*. The adjective forms of these words do, however, fit the frame: "The walk seems very stony"; "The road seems very sandy."

The difference in meaning between the verbs of the senses (Pattern 4) and *be* (Pattern 5) is also interesting: "The bridge *looks* unsafe"; "The bridge *is* unsafe"; "The teacher *seems* unfair." The dangers of the irresponsible use of *be* provide an elementary lesson in semantics.

Such an oral activity as the following might be used to help establish the pattern and the concept of adjectives. One student selects an NP and a Vs: "The team seems _____"; "The floor feels _____"; and so on. One student after another supplies an appropriate adjective: "The floor feels gritty"; "The floor feels cold"; "The floor feels damp, clammy, sticky." The game continues until someone repeats an adjective already named. Then this student selects a new NP and, if possible, a new Vs, and the game starts again.

A rewriting of NP could be introduced at this point:

NP → personal pronoun
personal pronoun → *he, she, it, they* (*I, you, we*)

Students can now substitute personal pronouns for noun phrase subjects and for noun phrase direct objects (NP₂): "Jim went," "He went," "Jack saw Wendy," "He saw her." At this point the personal pronouns *I, we, you* can also be introduced into kernel sentences. If students are asked to try to discover the ways in which personal pronouns differ from nouns, they will observe that these pronouns have a distinctive form that is used as the direct object and that the plurals in most instances are really different words. They can also see that personal pronouns do not always refer to persons. Now the students are ready to induce the concept of grammatical person distinguishing the speaker, the person spoken to, and the person or thing spoken about.

Substituting a pronoun for the second noun in sentences where the two nouns have the same referent will provide an introduction to the reflexive pronouns:

Tom likes Tom. ———→ Tom likes
                          himself.

These boys admire   These boys ad-
these boys.   ———→ mire themselves.

(Obviously the use of him and them would destroy the meaning of these sentences.) Then other sentences can be constructed using the reflexive: "I entertain myself," "They invited themselves," "She hurt herself," and so on.

Though these sentences are formed with transitive verbs, students will observe that the reflexive pronouns do refer to the same thing as the subject, in contrast to NP_2, which normally follows a transitive verb.

After students have had practice in using all patterns, they are ready to add optional adverbials in column 4 (p. 437) to expand the verb phrase. The term adverbial is used to cover both single words (adverbs) and groups of words (prepositional phrases and noun phrases). There are principally three kinds of adverbials:

Adverbials of place (adv-p)
    Adverbs: here, there, everywhere, outside, upstairs, and so on.
    Prepositional phrases: at school, in the cafeteria, near the lake, and so on.
Adverbials of time (adv-t)
    Adverbs: now, then, sometime, soon, always, and so on.
    Prepositional phrases: in the summer, at noon, before dinner, after sundown.
    Noun phrases: last week, Monday, all winter, every day. (He came last week; He saw the play Monday; He visited us all winter; He reads the paper every day.)
Adverbials of manner (adv-m)
    Adverbs: reluctantly, energetically, enthusiastically, fast, hard.
    Prepositional phrases: with reluctance, with energy, with enthusiasm.

Students will observe that many adverbs of manner end in the suffix -ly and that a choice can often be made between an adverb and a prepositional phrase.

Numerous illustrations make the structure of a prepositional phrase evident as preposition + NP. Lists of prepositions that can be used to introduce phrases which expand the entire verb phrase are helpful. Prepositions having the greatest frequency should be included: in, to, for, at, or, from, with, by. Of will be omitted at this time because it will produce a modifier of a noun phrase within the verb phrase: "I saw the end of the play."

Oral practice in using prepositional phrases is one of the best ways of familiarizing students with structure. One possible activity is to have one student give directions for reaching a particular place while another student at the chalkboard (and possibly the other students at their seats) lists the prepositional phrases: "Go down Cedar Street to the first stop sign; then turn left on Main Street and drive about four blocks through town to the Court House. Turn right on Highway 66. . . ."

Because adverbials are the most movable structures in a sentence, it is interesting to discover what effects can be produced by placing them in different positions. For example,

The storm ended suddenly at noon.
The storm suddenly ended at noon.
Suddenly the storm ended at noon.
At noon the storm suddenly ended.

Some students might even be interested in trying to figure out what positions the various kinds of adverbials can occupy in a sentence. Such transpositions are actually transformations, for the adverbial occupies the final position in a kernel. A recent fifth-grade text points out the following: [13]

. . . a Standard Sentence (ones used in most formal speech and writing) has two parts: the Noun Part (NP), which usually contains a noun (N); and the Verb Part (VP), which

---

[13] Development Group. New Directions in English 5 (New York: Harper, 1955), pp. 63–67.

always contains a verb (V). By comparing sentence patterns, it can be illustrated that what makes one pattern different from another is the nature of the Verb Part. These three patterns can be summarized as follows:

Pattern 1: Noun Part + Verb
The spaceman / slept.

Pattern 2: Noun Part + Verb + Direct Object (DO)
The spacemen / brought *a helmet.*

Pattern 3: Noun Part + Linking Verb (LV) + Completer (C)

a. Noun Part + Linking Verb + Noun Completer (C$_N$)
The spaceman / is *my father.*

b. Noun Part + Linking Verb + Adjective Completer (C$_{ADJ}$)
The spaceman / seemed *exhausted.*

c. Noun Part + Linking Verb + Adverb Completer (C$_{ADV}$)
The spaceman / is *out of town.*

Instead of using the terms *intransitive* and *transitive* to distinguish Pattern 1 verbs from Pattern 2 verbs, it is shown that Pattern 1 verbs can stand alone, but Pattern 2 verbs cannot. Whereas Pattern 1 verbs are usually followed by words telling *how, where,* or *when* (adverbials), Pattern 2 verbs usually must be followed by words telling *who* or *what* (nominals). A sentence like "The boys chased" leaves a question in our minds because the verb *chased* implies that *something* was chased. Thus we might analyze Pattern 2 as follows:

N$_1$	V	N$_2$
The boys	chased	the girls.

The noun in the Verb Part of Pattern 2 is traditionally called the *direct object.*

To distinguish Pattern 3 verbs from Pattern 1 and Pattern 2 verbs, the chapter calls them *linking verbs.* Many new grammars no longer consider the word *be,* or any of its forms, as a verb. Like Pattern 2 verbs, linking verbs cannot stand alone. They need to be completed by nominals, adjectivals, or adverbials. A sentence like "The women were" puzzles us because *were* implies additional words.

The words that complete linking verbs are called *completers.* Completers in the Verb Part of Pattern 3 directly refer to the Noun Part of the sentence. The distinctions between patterns become clear to the students as they analyze, sort, and write sentences.

To clarify the patterns, the following suggestions are made:

1. To see if students can detect differences in sentence patterns, ask them which sentence in each set (*a, b,* and *c*) is different from the others in its set, and *why* it is different.

    a. (1) Tom threw the coconut down from the treetop.
    (2) It broke open.
    (3) It hit Bess on the head.
    (4) She scolded Tom.
    (2) is different. *Broke* is the only verb here that can stand alone.

    b. (1) Sam patted his dog on its head.
    (2) George walked around the block.
    (3) Nina cried.
    (4) The bridge collapsed.
    (1) is different. *Patted* is the only verb here that cannot stand alone. It takes a direct object.

    c. (1) Dan crossed off this day on his calendar.
    (2) His team lost the game again.
    (3) They even lost the football!
    (4) He was really upset.
    (4) is different. *Was* is the only verb here that needs a completer—the only one that does not need a direct object.

2. To see if students can recognize examples of the three basic patterns, have them head each of three columns with the sentences they chose in answer to each set in exercise 1. Then have them sort the sentences below according to the models at the tops of the columns.

    a. Henry laughed.
    b. Sam caught the fast ball.
    c. The drooby smiled ridiculously.
    d. Lana is Don's cousin.
    e. Rena enjoys whale steak.
    f. The peaches were rotten.
    g. Sue needs more friends.
    h. Janice was downtown.
    i. The kitten purred softly.

It broke open.	Sam patted his dog on its head.	He was really upset.
Henry laughed.	Sam caught the fast ball.	Lana is Don's cousin.
The drooby smiled ridiculously.	Rena enjoys whale steak.	The peaches were rotten.
The kitty purred softly.	Sue needs more friends.	Janice was downtown.

3. To help students identify Pattern 1 sentences, no matter how long those sentences are, have them find the NP and verb in each of the following sentences. Then let them test the ability of the verb to stand alone, by saying aloud only the NP and verb, and deleting all word and phrase modifiers.

   a. The dragon growled fiercely at his attackers.
   b. The men in the zebra suits escaped over the prison wall.
   c. The rusty old door creaked on its hinges.
   d. The whole surface of the lake froze solid.

4. To help students identify Pattern 2 sentences, have them locate both the verb and its direct object in each of the following sentences. Then have them test the verb by saying aloud the NP and verb, as they just did in Exercise 3, without including the object. Finally, ask them what question the direct object answers in each instance.

   a. The astronauts chased the shooting star.
      Object answers question: *What* did the astronauts chase?
   b. Jeff carried the poor lame dog away from the scene of the accident.
      Object answers question: *Whom* or *what* did Jeff carry?
   c. Grendel frightened the superstitious people.
      Object answers the question: *Whom* did Grendel frighten?

5. To see if students can recognize linking verbs, have them open their readers or their science or social studies texts and tell you what the linking verbs are on any given page. They can test these verbs by reading aloud the NP and verb of each sentence, without modifiers, and then finding the completer.

6. Another way to reinforce the idea of LV + C is to give students a list of incomplete sentences, like those below, and have them (a) complete the sentences; (b) tell you what types of words they used in each case—noun, adjective, or adverb.

   a. This space ship seems _____.
   b. That green-faced boy looks _____.
   c. The forest became _____.
   d. Letitia had been _____.
   e. His stew tasted _____.

   f. Denise's pet hamster felt _____.
   g. Laura has been _____.
   h. Beowulf is _____.
   i. Mr. Grimes was _____.

7. To see if students understand what an indirect object is, ask them what the indirect object is in each sentence below, and what question the indirect object answers.

   a. Jim made his little brother a paper airplane.
      For whom did Jim make a paper airplane?
   b. Jerry handed Ned the canteen.
      To whom did Jerry hand the canteen?
   c. Douglas tossed Sam Ginny's pocketbook.
      To whom did Douglas toss Ginny's pocketbook?

8. To see if students can determine the sentence patterns of questions, have them convert the questions below into statements and identify the pattern of each one.

   a. Did Jim yell at you?
      Jim did yell (or yelled) at you. Pattern 1.
   b. Is it true?
      It is true. Pattern 3.
   c. Has Dorothy brought Toto?
      Dorothy has brought Toto. Pattern 1.

How May a Knowledge of the Kernel Sentence Be Established?

Four kinds of words or groups of words function as subject in a kernel sentence:

1. Determiner + common noun. → (*The boy* milked the cow.)
2. Proper noun. (*Mr. White* is a violinist.)
3. Personal pronoun. (*They* walked to school.)
4. Indefinite pronoun. (*Everyone* seemed friendly.)

Each of these kinds of subject is called a noun phrase, even though it may be a single word. A noun phrase is the name for a structure, but not for a word class. Noun and personal pronoun are examples of names of word classes. A noun phrase such as *he*, which is a member of the personal pronoun word class, can take the place of another noun phrase:

The boy milked the cow. →
                He milked the cow.

The arrow is the rewrite symbol, showing in this case that the first sentence is rewritten with a different noun phrase as subject. Notice that the pronoun does not take the place of the noun *boy,* but of the complete noun phrase *The boy.*

In a kernel sentence, the first word of the predicate is usually a verb or a form of the word *be—am, is, are, was,* or *were.* The word *be* and its forms do not behave the way verbs do, so *be* is not called a verb, but is considered a class by itself.

One way in which *be* differs from a verb is the way it functions in the predicate. Every predicate of a kernel sentence must contain either *be* or a verb. If it contains a form of *be,* something else must follow *be:*

	Followed by
He is a soldier.	a noun phrase (*a soldier*)
She was pretty.	an adjective (*pretty*)
They are in the boat.	an adverbial of place (*in the boat*)

But if the predicate contains a verb, the verb may or may not be followed by something else:

	Followed by
They surrendered.	nothing
They wanted some water.	a noun phrase (*some water*)
They looked sick.	an adjective (*sick*)

Verbs may also be followed by other words, such as adverbials of manner, place, time, frequency. This difference between *be* and verbs is one reason *be* is considered a class by itself.

One of the ways in which generative transformational grammar makes the study of English more rational and understandable is in its treatment of tense.

In studying a language, scholars determine the number of tenses by finding how many inflectional changes in verbs there are that indicate time. Modern Italian has five tenses shown by inflectional changes in verbs. Spanish is similar to Italian in that it, too, is a highly inflected language. In Spanish, for instance, *com-ere* ("shall eat") is

the future tense of the verb *comer* ("to eat"), and *com-i* ("ate") is the past tense.

But English has no future tense—that is, there is no inflectional change in the verb to show future. We can indicate future time in many ways, of course; by saying *they will eat, they are about to eat, they eat tomorrow morning.* But notice that there is no inflectional change in the English verb *eat* for future as there was in the Spanish verb *comer.* In English we have to show most time differences by using other words with the verb: *may, shall, be, have,* and so on. Only one change in time is shown by inflectional change in English verbs, that between present and past—*eat, ate; walk, walked.*

The reason English has been said to have six tenses is that Latin has six tenses—six inflectional forms of verbs to indicate time differences. To make English appear to work the way Latin works, it was necessary to superimpose the six Latin tenses on structures in English other than the underlying verb. In giving us a Latin grammar for our English language, grammarians had to use phrasal combinations like *may go* and *will eat* to indicate the tense.

In generative transformational grammar, then, there are only two tenses: present and the tense shown by an inflectional change in the verb—past. In a kernel sentence the tense, present or past, is always shown by the first word of the predicate:

They want some food.	(present)
They wanted some food.	(past)
They may want some food.	(present)
They might want some food.	(past)
They have wanted some food.	(present)
They had wanted some food.	(past)

An important concept to establish is that every verb phrase forming a predicate must contain tense—either present or past. It is essential to show that tense and time are not identical: tense is contained within language; time is something in the outside world. Though tense and time are related, they are not identical. For example, we say, "San Diego *plays* Los Angeles Friday" (present tense, but future time signaled by *Friday*) and, "Susan sings well" (presumably Susan

Root Word *(no inflection)* Modal + root word	Past Tense {-ed} *morpheme* *(no auxiliary)*	Past Participle {-en} *morpheme* have + {-en}	Present Participle {-ing} *morpheme* be + {ing}
will travel	traveled	have traveled	are traveling
may go	went	has gone	is going
could sing	sang	had sung	was singing

sang well yesterday, sings well today, and will continue to sing well tomorrow). If we want to denote present time we have to say, "Susan is singing."

Once the tense requirement in a predicate is grasped, students have an effective tool for detecting certain kinds of fragments. "The boy running down the street" is not a sentence, because it lacks tense.

Exercises of the following type are suggested for leading students to discover which word carries the tense when one or more auxiliaries precedes a verb:

If the word *yesterday* were added to the sentence "The wind is blowing," would any of the words in the sentence need to be changed?

If the word *today* were added to the sentence "The ducks had landed," would any of the words in the sentence need to be changed?

If the phrase *last Saturday* were added to the sentence "The students will have been dancing," would any of the words in the sentence need to be changed?

This type of exercise will reveal the auxiliary (or the first auxiliary if there is more than one) to be the word which shows tense. When no auxiliary is used, the verb carries the tense.

A logical follow-up to the preceding exercise would be to have the class work on fragmentary statements. For example, why wouldn't "The trainer whipping the lion," "The quarterback passing the ball," and "Jerry driving the car" be sentences? Hopefully, the students will see that these groups of words lack tense and can be made into sentences by adding tense in the form of an auxiliary.

An exercise from a recent textbook for grade 5 will help verb and pronoun forms: [14]

Using Grammar to Solve a Mystery

What you have learned about grammar will help you solve the mystery in this story. You are to supply a word for each numbered blank. The clues to the words are on each page. When you have done all the detective work, you will find out why the story is called "Some Ghost!"

Some Ghost!

The day before Halloween Pete and Tony were walking home from school. It   1   a dark and gloomy afternoon.

"Do you believe in   2   ?"   3   Pete.

"Of course not," Tony   4   . "But Ted Smith does. He told   5   that he   6   a real ghost last Halloween."

"Where?" asked Pete.

"Right over there behind that clump of   7   ," Tony said.

Suddenly Pete turned around and   8   to walk back toward the school.

Clues

1. past tense of *be*
2. plural of *ghost*
3. past tense of *ask*
4. past tense of *reply*
5. a form of the pronoun *I*
6. past tense of *see*
7. plural of *tree*
8. past tense of *start*

[14] Andrew Schiller and others, *Language and How to Use it,* Book 5 (Chicago: Scott, Foresman, 1964), pp. 232–34.

"I just   9   something," 10   explained. "I   11   some books at school. I'd better go get   12   ."

"I'll go with you," said Tony. "You'll need   13   to help carry   14   books."

Just then the   15   16   a spooky noise. It   17   to be coming from behind the clump of trees. Something dressed in white   18   out. It   19   over to the boys.

"A ghost!"   20   Pete. And he froze in   21   tracks.

Tony   22   to run. But he stumbled and   23   down.

"Oh boy!"   24   the ghost. "You two   25   easy to scare. Even Ted Smith wasn't that scared last Halloween."

"You're no ghost," Tony   26   . "You're just Billy Stewart dressed up in a couple of old white   27   ."

Then Pete   28   the sheets off Billy and   29   at   30   .

"It's not Haloween until tomorrow. Why are you pretending to be a ghost today?" Tony   31   .

"   32   have to practice, don't   33   ?" Billy   34   . "How do you think I got to be such a good ghost? Don't tell anyone that you saw me and spoil   35   fun."

"Don't worry," said Tony. "I never tell ghost   36   . Your secret   37   safe with   38   ."

"You don't have to worry about either one of   39   ," Pete   40   . "We don't believe in ghosts."

Clues

9. past tense of *remember*
10. pronoun referring to Pete
11. past tense of *leave*
12. a form of the pronoun *they*
13. a form of the pronoun *I*
14. a possessive form of the pronoun *you*
15. plural of *boy*
16. past tense of *hear*
17. past tense of *seem*
18. past tense of *dart*
19. past tense of *come*
20. past tense of *yell*
21. possessive form of the pronoun *he*
22. part tense of *begin*
23. past tense of *fall*
24. past tense of *shout*
25. present tense of *be*
26. past tense of *hoot*
27. plural of *sheet*
28. past tense of *grab*
29. past tense of *glare*
30. a form of the pronoun *he*
31. past tense of *ask*
32. pronoun Billy used to refer to himself
33. same as 32
34. past tense of *say*
35. a possessive form of the pronoun *I*
36. plural of *story*
37. present tense of *be*
38. a form of the pronoun *I*
39. a form of the pronoun *we*
40. past tense of *odd*

How May a Knowledge of the New Grammar Be Extended for Able Students?

Generative transformational grammar puts morphemes together in "strings" to show the structure of sentences. In the strings of morphemes that follow, the morphemes of tense (present or past) apply to what follows them.

In the following morpheme string, the morpheme pres. (present) applies to the verb *seem:*

the + girl + pres. + seem + hungry

The student sees that the subject is the singular noun phrase *the girl,* the first word of

the predicate is the present tense form of the verb *seem* that goes with a singular subject, and the last word is *hungry*. So he translates the morpheme string into this sentence:

The girl seems hungry.

Notice the emphasis on the agreement of subject and verb and the highlighting of sentence structure which exercises of this kind provide.

In the following morpheme string the tense is past, the first word of the predicate is *be,* and the subject is plural:

the + boy + plural + past + be + late

Here the student must choose the past tense form of *be* that goes with a plural subject, *the boys.* He translates the morpheme string into the following sentence:

The boys were late.

The strings of morphemes can be made more and more complex, of course, as the student grows in his capacity to deal with structural interrelationships. This morpheme string contains a *be + ing:*

they + pres. + be + swim + ing
+ in + the + pond

The noun phrase *they* is the subject; the present tense form of *be* that goes with *they* is *are;* when *ing* is added to *swim,* the word *swimming* results. So the morpheme string yields this sentence:

They are swimming in the pond.

The following string contains a have + part.

the + woman + plural + past + have
+ part. + be + busy

Woman + plural is *women,* so the subject is *the women;* the past tense of *have* is *had;* the participle form of *be* is *been.* So the morpheme string yields this sentence:

The women had been busy.

Most of the sentences we say and write are much more complicated in structure than the "noun phrase + verb phrase" kernel.

The purpose of generative transformational grammar is to teach students how to generate well-formed grammatical sentences which express their ideas effectively. The thorough, careful background in the structure and grammar of the kernel sentence is merely a foundation for the part of the program to come. Kernel sentences are to be put together in what are called *transformations* to create new, more complex sentences.

The possessive transformation is very simple, and therefore can be introduced early in a generative transformational grammar program. This transformation changes one of two kernel sentences to a noun phrase showing possession, and then inserts this noun phrase into the other kernel sentence:

The dog has a collar. → the dog's collar
I found the collar.
I found the dog's collar.

The third sentence expresses all the meaning of the first two sentences.

As the students gain more experience and greater insight, they can start to generate sentences of greater complexity. The relative-clause transformation, like the possessive transformation, may be used to combine two kernel sentences into a single more complex sentence which expresses all the meaning of the original two sentences.

The first sentence, which is to be converted into a relative clause, is called the insert sentence.

insert
sentence: The dog begged for its dinner.
relative
clause: that begged for its
                      dinner.

The matrix sentence is the second sentence —the one into which the relative clause is to be inserted.

matrix sentence: The dog refused its
   breakfast.

The relative clause is inserted into the matrix sentence:

            that begged for its dinner
The dog   refused its breakfast.

The resulting sentence, which contains all the meaning of the two original sentences, is called a transform:

transform: The dog that begged for its
   dinner refused its breakfast.

There are, of course, many different kinds of transformations to be experienced as the student progresses in generative transformational grammar.

Experience in generating well-formed sentences will give the student mastery over the mechanisms by which sentences are generated, making it possible for him to create sentences of increasing complexity. Improvement in composition should result.

Furthermore, the new English will improve reading comprehension by making the student aware of the kernel sentences which underlie the complex matter he encounters in prose and poetry.

After students have worked on kernel sentences for some time, they will not be satisfied until they can expand the sentences. Unfortunately, this usually means one thing only—longer sentences which students tend to join together with *and*'s. One way to assist students in writing more mature sentences is to call attention to open points in kernel sentences, places where they can insert single words or groups of words. Students can locate these points before and after each noun and before and after each verb. For example,

Kernel	*NP*		*VP (Vi)*	
Pattern I	The 1 2 boy 3		4 ran 5	
	1. little		4. frequently	
	2. freckle-faced		5. down the alley	
	3. in our block			

Kernel	*NP₁*	*Vt*	*NP₂*
Pattern II	The 1 hunter 2	3 received 4	a reward 5
	1. fearless	3. gratefully	5. for his
	2. who killed	4. from the	service to
	the Alas-	Sports-	the com-
	kan brown	man's	munity
	bear	Club	

Kernel	*NP₁*	*Vb*	*Adj.*
Pattern III	The child	1 became	2 happy 3
		1. sometimes	2. very
			3. in the
			morning

The sentence-expansion principle may be used in any sentence pattern.

This procedure may result in sentences so overloaded with words, phrases, and clauses that they resemble linked sausages. This, then, is the time for evaluation and discarding. More honest, less artificial sentences may result if students write descriptive sentences based on their own immediate observations: a bookshelf, a clock, a tree, a view through a doorway, an animal at a given moment.

Example:
   The cat stared.
   The light brown Siamese cat sitting erect on the sofa stared across the room haughtily.

Any sentence that is not a kernel is a transform, derived by transformation rules from the string of grammatical elements underlying one or more kernel sentences.

Single-Base Transformations

Among the single-base transformations are those which produce questions, negatives, imperatives, sentences beginning with the expletive *there,* the indirect object, and passives. The rules need not be specified for all transformations. Students can often figure out from the results what has happened.

The Yes/No Question Transformation.   The way *yes/no* questions are formed is revealed when the following statements are changed into questions that can be answered by *yes* or *no*. It should be kept in mind that the transformation would work in the same way for all sentences constructed on the same pattern, though for convenience the effect of the transformation upon specific sentences is being illustrated. Double arrows designate transformations, in contrast to the single arrows used for rewrite rules:

Jane will sing $==>$ Will Jane sing
America.   America?
Someone is at $==>$ Is someone at the
the door.   door?
Fred owns an $==>$ Does Fred own an
alligator.   alligator?

The Negative Transformation. The parallel between the *yes/no* question transformation and the negative transformation is easy to establish:

Jane will sing $==>$ Jane will not
America.   (won't) sing
                     America.
Kenneth has $==>$ Kenneth has not
gone.   (hasn't) gone.

Double-Base Transformations

Double-base transformations lend the greatest variety and flexibility to sentences, for they make it possible to embed one sentence in another, usually in reduced form, and to combine sentences with reduction of elements. Space permits us to consider only two but others are present in most school curriculums.

The Relative-Clause Transformation. The relative-clause transformation has high utility, for from it are derived nearly all structures that expand NP's. And certainly the ability to create nominals of varied and condensed structures is one mark of the mature writer.

The first step in teaching the relative clause is to present sentences containing relative clauses. By extracting the kernel, students can isolate the relative clause:

The speaker who gave the address was interesting.
I enjoyed the story (that, which) you told.

The transformation is simple. Study the following illustrations:

Base: The speaker $(+ S)$ was in-
            teresting.
Insert: The speaker gave the ad-
            dress.
Transform: The speaker (The speaker
            gave the address) was in-
            interesting $==>$ The
            speaker who gave the ad-
            dress was interesting.

Base: I enjoyed the joke $(+S)$.
Insert: You told the joke.
Transform: I enjoyed the joke (You told
            the joke) $==>$ I en-
            joyed the joke (you told
            which) $==>$ I enjoyed
            the joke which you told.

Base: This is the bus $(+S)$.
Insert: I came on the bus.
Transform: This is the bus (I came on
            the bus) $==>$ This is
            the bus (I came on that)
            $==>$ This is the bus
            that I came on.

In the last illustration, if the relative pronoun *which* had been chosen instead of *that,* the transform would have read "This is the bus which I came on." Then it would have been possible to perform another transformation and move the preposition to a position before the relative pronoun: "This is the bus on which I came." However, "This is the bus that I came on" is a correct English sentence, for sentences do frequently end in a preposition.

The Subordinate-Clause Transformation. Any sentence can be reduced to a subordinate clause by putting a subordinator in front of it:

sub $+ S$ $==>$ subordinate clause

He did the   if he did the work
work $==>$ because he did the
                     work
             before he did the work

Subordinate clauses are one means of expanding verb phrases. If students are given a list of subordinators, they can transform sentences into subordinate clauses and embed these clauses in the verb phrases of base sentences:

Base: He stayed at home.
Insert: He had a cold.
Transform: He stayed at home because he had a cold.

A list of some of the most commonly used subordinators follows:

> since (denoting time)
> as (denoting time or manner)
> as if
> as though, as soon as

We can do this . . . *until* someone objects.
                     unless someone objects.
                     whenever someone objects.
                     wherever someone objects.

Though the work in transformational grammar is directed toward the construction of more sophisticated sentences, it can also be utilized in helping students eliminate ambiguous and ungrammatical sentences. An ambiguous sentence has two possible meanings:

When the dog saw the skunk it stood still.
Kernels: The dog saw the skunk.
        The dog stood still.   (or)
        The skunk stood still.

An ungrammatical sentence results when a writer loses his way in following the rewrite rules or the transformation rules. The dangling modifier provides a good example:

Looking out the window, a sparrow was pecking in the gravel.

This sentence derives from a faulty relative-clause transformation. If a writer goes back to the kernels, he will see what is wrong:

Base: A sparrow was pecking in the gravel.
Insert: A sparrow was looking out the window.
Transform: A sparrow, which was looking out the window, was pecking in the gravel.
= = > A sparrow, looking out the window, was pecking in the gravel.
= = > Looking out the window, a sparrow was pecking in the gravel.

If the writer wants to use the participial phrase, he will have to start all over with a different subject, such as *I*.

Excellent opportunities for integrating grammar and proofreading should occur. With emphasis on the inductive approach students form the habit of self-sufficiency. Suppose that during the study of kernel sentence patterns, the students are creating their own sentences and testing them against the seven kernel sentence patterns recognized in this curriculum; if they are then asked to write a paragraph, will not the same testing occur?

Whenever a student has written an unusually good sentence, the teacher should take time to point it out, commend the writer, and invite the student and other students in the class to study the sentence to see why it is good. This relates grammar to writing so that students see that there is purpose and sense in grammar.

For Discussion

Check your understanding of the new grammar by completing this test taken from questions in fifth-grade language textbooks.

1. Read the following then answer the questions below: "Gloopy is a borp. Blit is a lot. Gloopy klums with Blit. Gloopy and Blit flomed."

    a. List four words above that are probably nouns.
    b. List three words above that are probably verbs.

2. Write two sentences that are examples of each pattern below.

    a. S = NP + VP
    b. S = NP + VP + O
    c. S = NP + VP + Adj.
    d. S = NV − beN
    e. S = NVN

3. Expand the NP of each sentence below by substituting a noun with a modifier for the pronoun given.

    a. She wore a kimono.
    b. It exploded.
    c. He is very talented.
    d. They are shipbuilders.

4. Divide each sentence below into NP and VP then circle the main verb in each sentence.

    a. The gigantic hulk of a man screamed like a baby lost in the woods.
    b. One goose among the gaggle of geese that had gone astray cruelly nipped the beak of the goose who was honking at all the people they passed.
    c. The doorman who stands in front of that new hotel looks quite handsome in his bright red uniform and cap.

5. Using only pronouns, main verbs, objects, and completions, rewrite the sentences in exercise 4 so that sentence (a) contains only two words, (b) only four, and (c) only three.

6. Expand the following sentence until you have made the image as exact as possible: *The dog ran.*

What kind of dog?   When?
Where?   Why?
How?

7. a. Circle the number of the sentence that is different from all the others.
    (1) Jack slammed the door on his finger.
    (2) He yelled loudly.
    (3) He kicked the chair in anger.
  b. What makes the sentence you marked different from the other? <u>The verb *yelled* is the only one here that can stand alone.</u>
  c. Which pattern does that sentence follow?
    Pattern 1.

8. a. Circle the number of the sentence that is different from all the others.
    (1) Nancy is the class president this year.
    (2) She is very happy about it.
    (3) She rapped the gavel on the desk.

    (4) That was a call for order.
  b. What makes the sentence you marked different from the others? <u>It is the only sentence with a direct object following the verb.</u>
  c. Which pattern does that sentence follow?
    Pattern 2.

9. a. Circle the number of the sentence that is different from all the others.
    (1) The magician was tricky.
    (2) The ghost walked in.
    (3) They trembled before him.
    (4) They ran away.
  b. What makes the sentence you marked different from the others? <u>It is the only sentence here that has a linking verb and a completer.</u>
  c. Which pattern does that sentence follow?
    Pattern 3.

10. Sort the twelve sentences listed in questions 8, 9, 10, and 11, above, by writing them in one of these columns:

Pattern 1	Pattern 2	Pattern 3
He yelled loudly.	Jack slammed the door on his finger.	Nancy is the class president this year.
The ghost walked in.	He kicked the chair in anger.	She is very happy about it.
They trembled before him.	He pushed his brother.	That was a call for order.
They ran away.	She rapped the gavel on the desk.	The magician was tricky.

11. Write the following sentences on the chart provided, placing each object, direct and indirect, in the section where it belongs. *Example:* Gene gave him a truck.

    a. We sent the president a telegram.
    b. Lola wrote me a letter.
    c. Nan asked her a question.

NP	VP		
N	V	O	
		IO	DO
Example: Gene	gave	him	a truck
a. We	sent	the president	a telegram
b. Lola	wrote	me	a letter
c. Nan	asked	her	a question

12. Transform each of the following questions into statements. After each statement, write its sentence pattern number.

Example: Is the book interesting?

The book is interesting. Pattern 3.

    a. Did the horses sleep?

      The horses did sleep (*or* slept). Pattern 1.

    b. Do Sis and Jim give presents?

      Sis and Jim give presents. Pattern 2.

    c. Are the Martians at home?

      The Martians are at home. Pattern 3.

    d. Did the dogs bark?

      The dogs did bark (*or* barked). Pattern 1.

    e. Do sailors sail boats?

      Sailors sail boats. Pattern 2.

13. Transform each of the following statements into two different questions, using the words that are given in parentheses following each statement.

Example: The team played a double-header on Saturday. (who, when)

Who played a double-header on Saturday?

When did the team play a double-header?

    a. Gladys does exercises so that she can stay healthy. (why, what)

      Why does Gladys do exercises?

      What does Gladys do to stay healthy?

    b. The lazy cat sleeps in the warmest spot he can find. (where, who)

      Where does the lazy cat sleep?

      Who sleeps in the warmest spot he can find?

    c. There were gale-force winds along the coast all last week. (when, where)

When were there gale-force winds along the coast?

Where were there gale-force winds all last week?

How Is Sentence Sense Taught in the Elementary School?

Throughout the elementary school the emphasis in teaching sentence structure is on how to express ideas and how to ensure being correctly understood. The language conventions that are taught as being correct help to clarify a child's language and ensure understanding.

As the child uses the language, his experiences build a foundation for the type of analysis that leads to definition. A definition of *sentence* as "a group of words that present a complete thought" is meaningless unless it grows out of experience.

At the beginning of the kindergarten year it might be wise to introduce the children to the school plant and its physical facilities along with its personnel. Perhaps a good beginning is a trip to the principal's office, where the children can learn how to address him and the office staff. The children learn the custodian's name and how to speak to him. As they progress through the building, learning place names and staff, they will add to their knowledge of language as a tool of sound.

The resourceful teacher will be alert to use verbal patterns of social convention and patterning in language for meaningful play. At the tables, the play can center around passing items from one child to another: "Please pass the salt," "Thank you," "You're welcome." Making introductions, answering the door, answering the telephone, and asking for help are other examples of social situations in which language patterns can be practiced.

When "The Three Billy Goats Gruff," "The Gingerbread Boy," or a similar story is read, the teacher asks, "How did the Little Billy Goat Gruff sound as he walked over the bridge?" "What did the Troll ask him?"

"And how did the Little Billy Goat Gruff answer?" After the informal review of the characters and the bridge, the children dramatize the story. The question and answer process gives the children practice in repeating key sentences from a story and in working with sentence patterns.

The question and answer activity also helps the child develop a sensitivity to language and a sense of sentence pattern. The teacher will initiate the questioning, and as the pattern is learned, it can continue with a pupil as questioner:

"What is your *name?*"
"My *name* is _____."
"Where do you *live?*"
"I *live* on _____."
"How *old* are you?"
"I am _____ years *old.*"
"Is your *sweater red?*"
"My *sweater* is/isn't *red.*"
"Do you *like* to *run?*"
"Yes, I *like* to *run.*"

Many varieties of sentences, of course, may be chosen; the teacher can strive to elicit from the students those utterances that will repeat in the reply the words used in the question. These sentence patterns may be practiced without pupil consciousness of the process.

Children are introduced to the punctuation of a sentence long before they are expected to use punctuation themselves. As a teacher writes a dictated group story on the board, for example, she might point out: "You have given us such a good sentence that I am going to include it in our story. You see, I start the sentence with a capital letter and I put a period at the end. The period tells us to stop before we read the next sentence."

Later a child is helped to gain a sentence sense by the teacher's reading his story with him. It is pointed out that he has told two things about his dog; hence the teacher writes two sentences on the chalkboard. Periods and capitals are added.

Still later, children's sentences may be written on the chalkboard or projected on a screen for examination: "Did I tell something?" "Did I begin with a capital letter?"

"Did I end with the correct punctuation mark?"

Number work offers an opportunity for the direct teaching of the question mark. Children learn that a problem has two parts, a telling part and an asking part. When they write their own problems they ask themselves: "Did I put a period after the telling part, and a question mark after the asking part?"

In order to help children understand sentences, one first-grade teacher held up a picture showing a little girl in a green dress and red shoes, sitting on a chair, looking at a book, and eating a big red apple. She seems to be interested and happy.[15]

TEACHER: Would you like to have me tell you a story about this picture?
CLASS: Yes.
TEACHER: Red shoes, a chair, a big red apple, a little girl, a picture book. Does that sound like a good story, boys and girls?
CLASS: (*A chorus of no's.*)
TEACHER: Did it make sense?
CLASS: No.
TEACHER: Why not?
BOBBY: You just said a lot of words.
TEACHER: Yes, I did. Wasn't that a story?
ANITA: No, you should tell what she is doing.
TEACHER: That's right. I should make a statement that says something. You do it, Anita. What would you say for your story?
ANITA: A girl is reading a book and she is eating an apple.
TEACHER: That is a good statement. You really told us something about the little girl. And what was she doing? Could we say something else?
MARCIA: We could call her Jane and say, "Jane is reading a book."
TEACHER: Yes, that is a good statement.
SAMMY: Jane is wearing a green dress.
DICK: She has red shoes, too.
TEACHER: Good work. Let's *all* make up a story about this picture. I will write it on the board. Each statement will say something about the picture.

The following is the composite story.

---

[15] Minneapolis Public Schools, *Communication Curriculum Guide,* 1953.

Jane is looking at a picture book.
She is eating an apple.
She wears a green dress.
She has pretty red shoes.
Jane is happy.

TEACHER: Here is a picture for each of you. Tomorrow each one may tell a story about his picture.

Using linguistics blocks is a delightful way for children to discuss the movable and immovable parts of a sentence.

The blocks are about 1½ × 1½ inches in size. One block has all words of one class. The following are examples only:

Nouns

dog	boy
cat	girl
baby	ball

Verbs

is	helps
jumps	has
runs	likes

Determiners

a	a
an	an
the	the

Names

Mother	Dick
Father	Spot
Jane	Puff

Adjectives

big	pretty
little	red
good	happy

Linguistics blocks may be purchased from Scott, Foresman and Company or they can be home made. The basic materials needed are blocks of wood about 1½ × 1½ inches in size. The words are typewritten (or use your own manuscript) clearly on paper and glued onto the blocks. Brushing the blocks with shellac or librarian's fixative makes them more durable.

One class had been working with words in the reading program and had a basic sight vocabulary. Each child was given five blocks (one of each class) and placed them on his desk. "What do you see on these blocks?" the teacher asked. Of course the children noticed the words. The teacher then suggested, "Let's roll our blocks to find out what we can make them say for us."

After practice on the first day the blocks were rolled to see how quickly sentences could be made. This moved along well, so blocks using other words of the same classes were substituted. Prepositions were added after several days. The teacher did not use the names *noun, verb, adjective, determiner,* and *preposition.* If the occasion had called for it, she might have given names to the blocks (*noun block, verb block,* and so on) or have colored each block differently, but it was not necessary.

Scrambled sentences are fun and develop the idea that language has structure:

ran cat the (The cat ran.)
walked Ann slowly (Ann walked slowly.)
store John went the to (John went to the store.)

Working with transformations can be done orally as early as grade 2. For example,

John went on his bicycle.
John went downtown.
} John went downtown on his bicycle.

Sentence recognition is reviewed by a third grade in the following manner.

TEACHER: Today we are going to write a story about our snails. How might we build our story?

CHILDREN: We'll have to have some sentences about our snails.

TEACHER: Do you know what a sentence is?

CHILD: A sentence is a bunch of words.

TEACHER: I'll write a group of words on the board and you decide if it looks like a sentence. (*Writes.*)

CHILD: No. It doesn't make sense.

TEACHER: Then a sentence is a group of words that tells something.

CHILD: It needs a capital and a period, too.

TEACHER: That's right. That's the way we separate sentences one from the others. As we write our story about our snails, let's check our sentences and ask ourselves: Does it tell something? Does it begin with a capital? Does it end with a stop sign?

The children might experiment with re-arranging words in sentences to discover the different meanings that are possible:

Mary and Bob helped Mother to write a letter.
Mother helped Mary and Bob to write a letter.
Mary and Bob helped write a letter to Mother.
Mary helped Bob write a letter to Mother.
Mother helped Bob write a letter to Mary.

Changing the word order of the sentence, but retaining the same meaning is another helpful technique:

I got a new suit yesterday.
Yesterday I got a new suit.

The two-part nature of the sentence can be explored using simple sentences:

The _____ runs.   The boys _____.
_____ sings.   Birds _____.
The _____ roar.   Children _____.

Children can think of interesting beginnings to sentences using such words as *while, after, since, because,* and *when:*

While we are in school our fathers are working.
After breakfast we get ready for school.
Since astronauts can walk in space maybe we will someday.
Because we walked too near the edge we fell into the lagoon.
When school is out the boys go to Cub Scouts.

Investigate the generation of sentences, to make language more interesting. This is developed in much more detail at the intermediate level, but can begin at this level:

The girls jumped.
The girls jumped rope.
The girls jumped over sticks.
The girls jumped high.
The man walked.
The man walked with a cane.
The man walked briskly.
The man walked downtown.

Children can share examples of interesting and less interesting sentences, either those they locate in books or some they compose:

The brook babbled and rippled through the meadow.
The brook went through the meadow.

In the fourth grade children discover facts about sentences through inductive reason. The teacher began this lesson by saying, "Today we are going to build sentences from words. We must have words before we can have sentences. Do words alone make sentences? Let's take the words *cake, mother,* and *bakes:* 'Cake mother bakes.' Is this a sentence, Mark?"

"No."

"Why do you say it's not a sentence?"

"Well, the words aren't right. They don't mean anything. If you changed them around, though, they could make a sentence. You could say, 'Mother bakes a cake,' and then you'd have a sentence. The way it is it doesn't make sense."

"You're right, Mark, if the words aren't in the right order they don't seem to mean much, do they? Could we say that the arrangement of words makes a difference in a sentence?" (The class will probably agree.)

"How about this group of words?" The teacher wrote on the board *The gluny trown dickled a luby.* "Is it a sentence? Does it make sense? Linda, what do you think?"

Linda thought that it didn't make sense, but it seemed to make more sense than the first one. When the teacher asked her if she could tell why it seemed to make more sense she floundered a bit but managed to say that there were words that sounded "sort of" familiar. Asked to tell what words sounded familiar she managed to say, "It starts with *the* and lots of sentences start with *the,* and there's an *A* in it. I recognize that. Lots of words end in *-ed,* but I never heard *dickled* before."

"Linda, do you think if you thought of some other words that ended in the same letters as the nonsense words, you could make sense out of that group of words? Would you like to try?"

Linda went to the chalkboard and wrote the following: *The funny clown tickled a baby.* The class was delighted and could easily see that by putting in certain "signal" words they might be able to make a nonsense sentence themselves. (The teacher cautioned the pupils first to get a group of words in their minds that did make sense, and *then* to substitute the nonsense words in their place. This is not as easy as it seems.)

The children each made up two nonsense sentences of their own, kept track of the "real" words they had used, and then gave their sentences to a "neighbor" who tried to figure them out. After the neighbor had replaced the words with words of his own choice he passed the sentence back to its originator, who was quite surprised to discover that often (in fact almost always) the words his neighbor had chosen to replace the nonsense words were different from the original words. This brought out two points for discussion: first, that "pattern," or word order, is very important to sentence structure; and second, that within a "pattern" there are many variations—many words that can perform equally well within a particular open point or "slot" of a sentence.

There are many ways in which this lesson could be followed up. One way would be to put several sentences on the board and have the class replace certain words (nouns, verbs, adjectives, and adverbs) with nonsense words. This will lead to the discovery that certain words, such as *the, a, this*, etc., must be very important to sentences, because when these small but very important words are omitted or replaced, the sentence loses its sense. Developing this observation slowly and carefully is important because it not only reinforces the concept of the importance of word order or position, but also reinforces the idea of word structure. In other words, certain words, patterned in a certain way, must be present in a particular place within a structure, and surrounded by particular kinds of "signal" words, before a group of words can be called a sentence.

In another lesson the teacher opened the class with these words: "We know that our words change in different ways. We also know that when we change a word in any way we usually change the way it operates in a sentence. Let's look at one way certain

words change and see if we can discover something about the word itself, the words around it, and how it works."

The teacher put the following words on the chalkboard for the class to experiment with:

boy	noise	porch
girl	house	dress
barn	horse	church
wrap		

During the discussion which followed, the pupils discovered that the words all have just one syllable. Each also consists of one morpheme. (The teacher explained what is meant by a *morpheme*.) The next point was to illustrate that these words could all be made to mean "more than one."

Turning to the words again, the teacher invited various pupils to give him the necessary letter or letters to make the words mean more than one (in other words, to form a plural). The pupils added the following letters:

boy(s)	noise(s)	porch(es)
girl(s)	house(s)	dress(es)
barn(s)	horse(s)	church(es)
wrap(s)		

Now the pupils were asked to look closely at the words again. "What do you see in each word now?" the teacher asked. The pupils responded that they now saw an additional letter or letters in each word. "How many morphemes do you think we have in each word, then?" continued the teacher. The pupils concluded that there were now two morphemes in each word, because an additional letter or letters had been added to the first word, with each addition making one morpheme.

"What is the new sound heard in *boys, girls*, and *barns?*" The pupils answered that it was the *z* sound. "Do you hear the same sound in *cats* and *wraps?*" The pupils answered that here they heard the *s* sound. "What about the words *noises, houses, horses, porches, dresses*, and *churches?* Do they sound just a little different?" The pupils decided that here they heard the *iz* sound.

The discussion then turned to what had happened to the meanings of the words with the addition of another morpheme to the first morpheme. The pupils were led to the discovery that by adding *s* or *es* to the words they had become plural. Many examples of each sound class were then presented orally to cement the idea.

Then the pupils wrote each word in a simple, short sentence, containing a simple subject and a predicate. The purpose of this was to allow them to make the discovery that all these words fit into the sentence position reserved for nouns. The pupils were invited to use further examples, to see if it was safe to make the generalization that words which form plurals are the kind of words we call nouns.

After the teacher had looked over these papers he distributed them to the children for inclusion in their notebooks. About a week later he used the papers again as a base for showing agreement of subject and verb by having the pupils write the same sentence, first using the singular noun and then using the plural noun.

Class participation in building sentences is often a valuable preliminary to the improvement of individual sentences. In the exercise that follows, the class chooses one of several sentences and builds it up in seven steps.

"Here are some short sentences—choose one of them. Let's see how many things we can make it say:

A pencil broke.
A bell rang.
A door opened.
A fire burned.
A leaf fluttered.

"We'll make our sentence do these things":

Step 1. Tell *where*.
    A fire burned on the beach.
Step 2. Now put the *where* words first.
    On the beach a fire burned.
Step 3. Tell *when*.
    On the beach a fire burned one May evening.
Step 4. Put the *when* words first.
    One May evening a fire burned on the beach.
Step 5. Use a color word.

One May evening a red fire burned on the beach.
Step 6. Use a sound word.
    One May evening a red fire roared on the beach.
Step 7. What did it say?
    The fire said, "I'm so hot this evening. Do you suppose I have a fever?"

As a follow-up, each individual would have some sentences of his own to work. Kernel sentences might be dictated, or they could be written on slips of paper, placed in a box, and then drawn out by the pupils.

The class is introduced to kinds of sentences in grade 5.

TEACHER: Your written stories and your reports are improving, but there is still something you can do to make them read more smoothly. You remember that in our spelling lessons the stories we have been reading have longer sentences. We call some of them compound sentences, and some complex sentences. Your ordinary sentences we call simple sentences. Harold, I often hear you using compound sentences. Can you explain what they are?

HAROLD: They're longer.

TEACHER: (*Writing on the chalkboard*) Yes, but they are more than that. Look at these two simple sentences:

Beverly came home last night.
It was getting dark when she arrived.

Who can put them together in one sentence?

JUDY: Beverly came home last night just as it was getting dark.

HAROLD: A compound sentence is two sentences combined.

TEACHER: That's right, only that may also be true of a complex sentence. It all depends on *how* they are put together. Judy's sentence is a complex sentence because she used *just as* to join them, and made the second part of the sentence dependent —as we say—on the first: it merely tells *when* it was she returned; it doesn't add another thought which is just as important as the first. But we won't worry about the difference between complex and compound yet—not until you get used to the idea of combining very short sentences into one longer sentence. Let's try that first. Then we'll look at the various kinds of joining words which make the difference between a complex sentence and a compound sentence.

The terms *subject* and *predicate* were introduced by one fifth-grade teacher in this manner: A pupil was appointed to write on the blackboard what it was he saw the teacher do before the class. He wrote, "She went to the window. She sat on a chair. She picked up a book."

TEACHER: (*pointing to the statements on the chalkboard*) What are these?

PUPIL 1: Statements.

PUPIL 2: Things the teacher did.

PUPIL 3: They are sentences.

TEACHER: That's right. They are all three, but for our purposes this morning, we'll call them sentences. (*Drawing a vertical line between subject and predicate.*) Notice that each sentence is made up of two parts. What does this much of the sentence (*pointing*) seem to tell you?

PUPIL 1: Who did it.

TEACHER: That's right, and this? (*Pointing*)

PUPILS: What she did.

TEACHER: Does anyone know the names of each part? (*as pupils hesitate*) If not, I'll tell you. We call the person who does something the *subject;* we refer to what it was the person did, the *predicate.* In these sentences, *I* was the subject. Not all sentences are as simple as this. Let's make them a bit more difficult. This time each of you will be the subject and do something, but instead of just doing it, try to do it in a particular way. How many different ways might I have walked to the window, for example?

PUPIL 1: Slowly.

PUPIL 2: In a hurry.

PUPIL 3: Straight.

TEACHER: Let's do something more exciting than what I did and act it out so that we can see not only what was done but how it was done. As each person acts out his sentence, the rest of us will write down what we see. Later we will compare our sentences and name the parts which we recognize.

The best sentences describing what happened were put on the board and discussed. Adjectives, adverbs, and phrase and clause modifiers appeared in the sentences and were identified and named.

There are many variations of this method: pupils may be asked to include in their dramatizations a gesture or posture that can be referred to by a phrase or clause: *in a haughty manner,* for example, or *as if she were dazed.* To increase interest, groups might compete with each other in acting out and recording complete sentences.

Pictures from magazine covers may be used as the basis for sentence study: What does the picture tell you? *A small boy is pulling a red wagon along the sidewalk. Two girls are jumping rope.* Unless warned, pupils may leave out the verb and say, "A small boy pulling a red wagon." In such a case, class discussion may center around the incompleteness of the thought, the importance of the verb, or even the various forms, such as *pulling,* which can be made out of a verb.

Children enjoy building sentences. Start with a verb of action, such as *break, eat, sew, sing, touch.* Have the children take turns using the word in a statement. When objects are added the sentence can frequently be acted out.

Some children are challenged by the idea of sentence kits. The idea is based on model car kits which children assemble. Use sentences from the textbooks read in that grade.

Basic sentence:	People	burned	fires
Spare parts:	at the doors	of caves	to keep animals
	some	primitive	away

Basic sentence:		houses	were	
Spare parts:	first probably real	houses	lake	

Words might be put on cards with flannel backing so that these parts could be used for class demonstrations.

Combining short sentences is excellent practice. Upper grades might take an "Easy to Read" book from the library and summarize the material in longer sentences.

Needs Improvement	*Improved*
We went to the zoo.	When we went to the zoo we
We saw the monkey.	saw a monkey that ate a ba-
We gave him a banana.	nana we gave him.

There are many ways of expanding sentences. Bill Martin presents an effective technique.[16]

"Hello, boys and girls and teachers." Now there is a sentence worth expanding! Notice how the boys and girls and teachers come alive with the addition of these carefully selected words and patterns.

As children learn this technique, *expanding sentences,* they gain much flexibility in their use of language in reading and writing and speaking. Expanding a sentence is exactly what the term connotes. Any simple sentence can be expanded by adding phrases, clauses, or describing words.

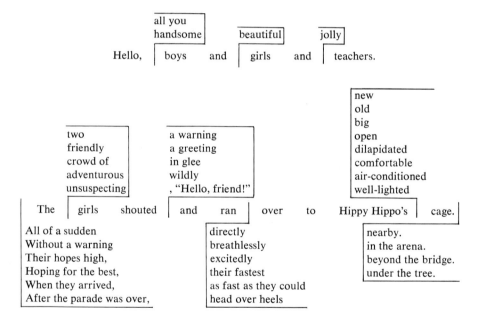

An expanded sentence can be more dramatic, "paint more pictures," or produce a more interesting array of sounds, but it is not necessarily a better sentence. Children need to read their expanded sentences aloud, comparing them with the original sentence to decide which sentence sound is more pleasing to the ear.

In the process of expanding sentences children become keenly aware of the placement and function of phrases, clauses, and individual words within a sentence. And as they read their selected sentences aloud, they overtly are making judgments about the kinds of sentences they do and do not like, thus taking another step in development of and appreciation for a personal style in writing and speaking.

---

[16] Bill Martin, *Language Arts Teachers Manual,* Bay Region Instructional Television for Education (Redwood City, Calif., 1967), pp. 63–66.

Reducing sentences can be introduced in the intermediate grades by using long sentences in the textbooks. This is an understanding essential to discovering the basic kernel parts of the new grammar. Bill Martin explains,[17]

Most sentences can be trimmed of a word or two, or perhaps of a phrase or clause. This linguistic trimming is known as *reducing sentences.* The danger in attempting to eliminate unnecessary words and phrases and clauses from a sentence is that one is apt to alter or destroy the sentence meaning or to tamper with the author's style of writing. Consider this opening sentence from "Mool, the Mole," with its obvious repetition:

Something in the earth
is digging upward,
digging upward,
moving and lifting,
lifting and pushing,
pressing outward,
pressing upward and downward.

One can see at a glance that there are several words in this sentence that do not add to the sentence meaning. "Do they intensify the meaning?" we must always ask ourselves about repetition, and if they do, would the sentence be robbed of some of its impact if they were eliminated?

We must also ask ourselves whether or not the author is attempting to create a unique style by his use of repetition. One way to answer these questions is to trim away the repeated words and phrases and then listen to the sentence sound in its reduced form.

Something in the earth
is digging upward,
moving, lifting,
pushing,
pressing outward,
upward and downward.

Now our sentence will look something like this if we write it in its chunks of meaning.

Something in the earth
is digging upward,
moving, lifting, pushing,
pressing outward,
upward and downward.

---

[17] Ibid. pp. 74–76.

How does the sentence sound to you and the children now? Do you have a clearer picture to carry to the next sentence now that this first sentence has made its point more quickly? Or do you find yourself missing certain dimensions that were in the first sentence—perhaps even ad-libbing a few repetitions in the new sentence we have created?

Don't be dismayed if you don't come up with quick answers to these questions. Any skilled writer will tell you that it can take nights of listening and revising and listening before coming up with just the right sentence sound. And don't be dismayed if you and the children come up with differing preferences or even with differently reduced sentences. Linguistic experiences of a lifetime enter into this kind of decision making. There are no right answers. The important thing is—the children are beginning to know what they do and don't like in a spoken or written sentence, and by your reading aloud with later analysis of sentences, they are beginning to broaden the base on which they make these linguistic selections.

In the intermediate grades, the pupils will have discovered the techniques of changing word order in English sentences. The following lesson is designed to make children aware of how the order of words changes to make questions and exclamations. The teacher might begin by asking, "When your mother makes a dress for you, Janice, what does she do after she has the material?"

"She puts the pattern on the cloth so she can cut it out."

"That's right, and does she use the same pattern for each dress she makes? No, of course she doesn't. You wouldn't have any fun out of getting a new dress if each dress were cut from the same pattern. We wouldn't have any fun with our language, either, if everything we said came from the same pattern and was said in the same way.

"When we are speaking and we ask a question, how do we know that we are asking something and not telling something?" Here the teacher drew from the pupils that questions rise at the end so that we distinguish them by intonation. Then the class was asked, "When we write a question, how do we know it is a question?" Here some child is bound to say, "Because it ends with a question mark." To this the teacher might reply, "That's right, it ends with a question mark. But is there any other way that we know it is a question, I wonder? Let's find out." Moving to the chalkboard, the teacher wrote the following sentences:

You study your science.	(Did you study your science?)
You wash your hands.	(Did you wash your hands?)
You will be waiting at nine.	(Will you be waiting at nine?)
You are able to open the window.	(Can you open the window?)
You are polite.	(Are you polite?)

Calling on the pupils at random, the teacher had each statement made into a question. Making no comment, he then wrote the following questions on the board:

Can Prince do tricks?	(Prince can do tricks.)
Should I call on Mary?	(I should call on Mary.)
Did Eric play the piano?	(Eric played the piano.)
Has Bob memorized his part?	(Bob has memorized his part.)
Is this paper finished?	(This paper is finished.)

After the teacher had called on various pupils to change the sentences back into questions, the pupils could see that they made a new pattern when they wrote questions. When the teacher asked the pupils how the sentence had changed, they responded that something had been added to it, that some words had been changed around, and that the endings of certain words had been changed. Together the pupils and teacher observed that while many sentences had hardly been changed at all, in a few cases, the pattern had changed considerably.

The teacher thought that it might be fun to introduce another new idea, so he said to Jim, "Are you hungry?" Jim answered, "Yes." Turning to Donna the teacher said, "Is your sister coming to get you after school?" Donna answered, "No." Next the teacher said to Kathy, "Were you at the show last night?" Kathy answered, "No." Again, without comment, the teacher turned to Janet and said, "What is your oldest brother's name?" Janet answered, "His name is Lenny." Turning to Scott, the teacher asked, "What does Leroy have on his desk?" Scott replied, "Leroy has his math book on his desk." Then the teacher said to Karen, "Which two girls were the captains for the Phys. Ed. activities?" Karen answered, "Cheryl and Ann were the captains." As the exchange progressed, the teacher had been placing the questions and answers on the board, and now he asked the pupils to look closely at them to see if they could discover anything interesting about them. This took some time, and required some "leading" from the teacher, but before too long one of the pupils made the discovery that when one of the forms of be began a question, the answer could be a simple "yes" or "no." Having made this discovery it was not long before the class further discovered that questions beginning with words like *who, what, when, why,* and *how* cannot be answered "yes" or "no."

The students will probably not be satisfied with just the "discovery." If they want to know "why," it is time to introduce sentence patterns.

Bill Martin suggests this technique to teach transformation.[18]

Transforming sentences is a linguistic activity involving structure. It is the act of using the exact structure of a sentence as the basis for

---

[18] Ibid., pp. 49–54.

creating a semantically new sentence through vocabulary substitution. When children replace words in a sentence with words of their own choosing, they learn much about the way language works and they tend to claim the sentence pattern for their own personal use. Let's use this sentence from the poem "Someone" by Walter de la Mare,

Someone came knocking at my wee, small door.

As you can see, there are *naming* words, *action* words, *describing* words, and *function* words in this sentence. It is not necessary for the children to assign categorical names to these various words. They probably don't know the names, but the important thing is that they understand the function of each word. This they know intuitively, if not consciously. Such intuitive knowledge becomes conscious as they substitute words of their own choosing in each word slot to create a totally new sentence meaning built on the identical structure of the original sentence. Your first step in helping children learn to transform this sentence is to copy the model sentence on the chalkboard, leaving space between each word. By the time you have finished working with the children, you will have a diagram that looks something like this, with the original sentence widely spaced and the children's word substitutions listed below the appropriate word.

Someone	came	knocking	at	my	wee,	small	door.
Something	began	creeping	up	the	dark,	narrow	stair!
Somebody	was	walking	down	his	dim,	unlighted	alley.
Milly	is	jumping	through	her	old,	screen	door.
What	started	sliding	over	my	long,	skinny	neck?
	likes						fence.

Then your conversation goes something like this: "Children, suppose we didn't want to use the word *Someone* to begin this sentence. What other words could we use?" Undoubtedly, they will suggest *She, We, They, I, Something,* and perhaps a proper name or two. Since nouns and pronouns can perform the same function within a sentence, the children will readily discover that nouns and pronouns are often interchangeable in a given word slot. In some sentences, they will also discover that gerunds and nouns are often interchangeable, as in this structure:

Jimmy liked playing best of all.
Jimmy liked girls best of all.

Occasionally, they will discover that adverbs and adjectives can be interchanged:

Hill City is a quiet little town.
Hill City is a very little town.

But gerunds cannot be substituted for nouns nor adverbs for adjectives when they perform different functions in the sentence. How more practically can we teach children that words cannot be arbitrarily classified until we see how they function in a sentence?

For example, if a child wants to insert the word *suddenly* in lieu of *knocking* in the model sentence, it will be worthwhile to help him see that while he is creating a semantically correct sentence, he has changed the structure of the model sentence by substituting a word that serves a different function.

After you have listed the children's vocabulary substitutions under the word *Someone,* you follow this same procedure for the next word in the sentence. If the children do not quickly suggest substitutions for the word *came,* you can help them by indicating the function of the word in the way you frame your supportive question: "Children, suppose you didn't want to say, 'Someone *came* knocking,' what else could you say he did?" This will bring forth such substitutions as *began, started, stopped, liked,* etc. In a similar manner, you move through the sentence, inviting vocabulary substitutions for each word, keeping the word in its structural context. When substitutions have been suggested for all words, then the fun begins! Invite the children to consider the diagram of vocabulary substitutions for the whole array of sentences that are now available to them. At first, the children will probably read a set of substituted words straight across the columns to create a new sentence, but soon they will discover that they can select from any of the words in the vertical column. Their far-ranging choices will produce serious and silly sentences offered by the framework, each of which is structurally correct.

Milly is sliding up the dim, narrow stair!
What began creeping down my old, skinny
neck?
Somebody likes knocking down the wee,
rickety fence.

From time to time in these transforming activities, you yourself may suggest a vocabulary
substitution such as *skeleton, ghost, ferocious,
monotonous, upending,* etc., knowing that one
strong, colorful word will result in a flurry of
additional substitutions that will greatly expand
the possibilities for sentence mood and semantic
inferences. When children become deeply involved in transforming activities like this, there
never will be time enough for each of them to
read aloud all of their self-selected sentences.
This offers an opportunity for them to write
their newly created sentences to read aloud to
one another.

At some time you may wish to discuss some
of the word groupings or punctuation marks.

1. Isn't it interesting what a difference the
   question mark or exclamation point makes
   in the meaning of a given sentence?
2. Isn't it interesting that only the *ing* form
   of the action words can be substituted for
   the word *knocking?* (If the children experiment, they will see that the present
   form, the *ed* form, or any other form of
   the verb simply will not work in this
   structure.)
3. Aren't the describing words interesting?
   Isn't it fascinating that in our language they
   nearly always precede the described word?
   *Someone came knocking at my door small
   wee* just wouldn't sound right.
4. And how about the words that pattern like
   his, her, my? Isn't it interesting that they
   can represent an unlimited number of
   people?
5. And what about the words *at, down,
   through?* Whenever a person encounters
   one of these words in his reading, he can
   make certain predictions about the kind
   of language that will follow.

It is these excursions into language that help
children verbalize their own intuitive hunches
about the workings of language and that help
them claim new insights.

You can also suggest to the children that
they keep in their language notebooks a list of
model sentences that especially appeal to them
for later transforming in their personal writ-

ing. Awarenesses of this kind are a sound linguistic base for both reading and writing.

Bibliography

Books

Lamb, Pose. *Linguistics in Proper Perspective.* Columbus, Ohio: Charles E. Merrill,
1967.

Liebert, Burt. *Linguistics and the New English Teacher.* New York: The Macmillan
Company, 1971.

Newsome, Verna L. *Structural Grammar in
the Classroom.* Oshkosh, Wis.: Wisconsin
Council of Teachers of English, 1962.

Postman, Neil, and Charles Weingartner.
Linguistics: A Revolution in Teaching.
New York: Dell Publishing Co., 1967.

Wardhauth, Ronald. *Reading—A Linguistic
Perspective.* New York: Harcourt Brace
Jovanovich, Inc., 1969.

Articles

Aston, K. O. "Grammar—The Proteus of
the English Curriculum," *Illinois Association of Teachers of English,* Vol. 55, Ur-
bana, Ill. (November 1967).

Ellis, Dorothy. "Grammar for Composition
—A Pupil Built Handbook," *Journal of
Education,* Boston University School of
Education, Vol. 147 (December 1964),
pp. 20–54.

English Development Center. *Seventh Grade
Curriculum,* Project English, Western Re-
serve University, Euclid Central Junior
High School, Cleveland, Ohio, 1963.

Eyman, John P. *Comparison of Materials
and Methods of English Instruction,* Arlington Heights Public Schools, Arlington
Heights, Texas, 1967.

Lowenbraun, Sheila, and James Q. Affleck.
"The Ability of Deaf Children to Use
Syntactic Cues in Immediate Recall of
Speechread Material," *Exceptional Chil-
dren* (July 1970), pp. 735–41.

Postman, Neil. "Not to Bury Grammar but
to Reapprove It," *Holt's Dialogue* (Fall
1965), pp. 8–15.

nine

evaluating and interpreting the language arts program

How Are Standards Established and Used in the Language Arts?

The term *standard* is used in three different ways in evaluation. One of its meanings is synonymous with *goal*. The children and teacher establish standards one by one that the children use to guide their work. In this sense the standard of achievement is determined by the individual child's stage of development and the personal effort he is able to exert. A second use of standard is as an *average* or *norm*. A series of tests or experiences establish what most fifth-grade children are doing with respect to a skill, such as the spelling of the word *constitution*. According to the *Iowa Spelling Scale* only ten children out of 100 in the fifth grade spell this word correctly. Thus a child in the fifth grade who does spell the word is above the standard. The third use of the term is in association with a predetermined level of achievement or expectancy. Teachers or parents decide that we must have higher standards of achievement in the sixth grade. To do this any child who fails to do certain tasks is not promoted to sixth grade. Or a college will decide that only the "upper half" of those graduating from a high school class may seek admission to the institution.

Standards reflect the school's philosophy and purpose. Some countries feel that the schools should act as a filter and eliminate all but the very able. The concept of an educational elite has been a strong influence on all education. Some countries give national examinations at every level and permit only a percentage of those taking it to ad-

Standards for Proofreading

Are my name and date written neatly?
Do I have good margins?
Is my title properly placed
Did I remember when to use capital letters?
Did I remember correct punctuation
Is my spelling correct?
Do I have a complete idea in each sentence?

Our Word Box

Standards once established must be continuously practiced. The charts provide a guide for those developing proofreading skills. (*Courtesy of the San Diego City Schools.*)

vance to the next grade, class, or form. Other countries feel that education should be made available to all the people at all levels. In order to do this, teachers adjust to the needs of the students rather than being guided by predetermined achievement standards.

Standards also reflect the acceptance or rejection of the teaching of modern psychology. Most teachers accept a concept of individual differences that is based on different levels of intelligence as measured by the IQ, cultural experiences of the learner, and the learner's interest. In some countries even an IQ test is rejected. There are parents who have never accepted the concept in the same way that teachers have. Although it is recognized that people are different, there is an assumption of lack of effort on the part of either the students or teachers which produces variable results in education.

The area of work also influences the stand-

ards. Music teachers must be very tolerant of the untalented who pass through their classrooms. To require a predetermined performance standard would eliminate many pupils from further study, so teachers must accept the fact that music for some students will be an avocation rather than a career. Nearly all teachers have at times determined to improve standards on the playground or in the auditorium. These standards have little relationship to the goals of the children or the average kind of behavior of children. Within a subject area such as handwriting, we do not expect everyone to write identically, but we do have a minimum standard of legibility.

The elementary teacher has a double task with respect to standards. The young child needs help to understand what the standard means. Then he must be taught to use that standard to guide his work. In the classroom one standard is developed at a time and practice is designed to give some meaning to the standard. During the sharing time the teacher may discuss the problem of being a good listener. After discussing why we listen (to learn, to be courteous) the teacher asks them to think of things a listener should do to help the speaker. The teacher accepts one of the suggestions, such as, "Look at the speaker." "That is a good suggestion, Bill," the teacher remarks. "Let me write that for us so we will remember." Then the teacher writes as the first standard for the group under the title "Good Listeners Do These Things."

At the end of the period, after praising those who shared, the teacher asks, "Were we good listeners?" "Why were we good listeners?" The children will thus be reminded of the standards. In time other standards will be added. Some might be: Ask questions at the end. (Do not interrupt.) Laugh *with* the speaker (not *at* him). Sit quietly.

In addition to providing criteria for evaluation, charts of standards remind the student of the factors to consider in preparing an assignment. The following charts developed by teachers and students at the San Diego State College Campus Laboratory School meet both these needs:

Announcements Can Be Interesting

1. Speak clearly.
2. Speak in a friendly manner.
3. Tell what is going to take place.
4. Tell when and where it will be.
5. Speak briefly.

Ask These Questions About Your Letters

1. Does the letter sound as though you were talking with your friend?
2. Does it tell the things your friend would like to know about?
3. Does it make your friend feel that the letter was especially for him?
4. Does the letter express your opinion about a topic?
5. Is it interesting to read?

Telephone Standards

1. Speak pleasantly, slowly, and distinctly. If people cannot hear you, do not shout. Shouting does not help.
2. Keep your lips an inch or two from the mouthpiece. If you hold the mouthpiece too close, your voice will be muffled or blurred.
3. Hold the receiver lightly against your ear.
4. After the number has been given, keep the receiver at your ear until the person you are calling answers. If you hear a buzzing or clicking sound, it means that the line is busy.
5. Keep the conversation moving and to the point. Do not prolong it.
6. Use correct language.
7. Avoid slang.
8. If the message is for someone who is not at home, write it down.
9. Call someone to the telephone by going to him. Do not yell from one room to the other.

Respecting the Rights of Others When Jokes Are Being Told

1. A good joke never makes fun of another person.
2. A good joke never hurts anyone's feelings.
3. Race, religion, and nationality should never be the subject of a joke.
4. A good joke never makes anyone feel unhappy, uncomfortable, or ashamed.

Language textbooks develop standards that children need to have recalled. Some of the publishers provide bulletin board material which reviews the the standards developed in the lessons.

The teacher may evaluate each child in terms of the proposed goals stated in a curriculum guide. Note the questions with respect to goals in literature.

1. Does the child have an interest in and an appreciation of good literature?
   a. Does he bring books from home to share with his friends?
   b. Does he respond to a variety of moods?
   c. Does he ask the teacher to reread a story?
   d. Are his interests and tastes broadening as evidenced by the books he selects?
2. Is the child getting to know himself and others?
   a. Does he understand and interpret the characters?

b. Is he growing in his ability to state his own beliefs?

c. Is he willing to change his beliefs if they are proved inaccurate?

d. Does he test his ideas and beliefs?

3. Is the child developing sensitivity to a greater degree?

a. Is the child's hearing of sounds becoming more acute?

b. Does he respond to rhythm?

c. Is he aware of mood and feeling?

4. Is the child broadening his understanding of cultures—other cultures as well as his own?

a. Does he have an understanding of his own culture?

b. Does he have a broadening appreciation of the contributions made by people of other lands?

5. Is the child finding beauty, adventure, and the great out-of-doors?

a. Is he developing a greater appreciation of beauty?

b. Does he read adventure stories to get vicarious experiences?

c. Are the wonders of the out-of-doors becoming an ever-widening experience?

6. Is the child developing increasing awareness of form, including plot, setting, characterization, mood, and theme?

a. Can the child give the main ideas of a story in sequence?

b. Does he understand the setting?

c. Does he understand the characters?

d. Is he able to sense mood or tone?

e. Does he understand the author's intention or message?

7. Is the child growing toward the ultimate goal of complete experience?

a. Is he a regular reader?

b. Is he maturing in a permanent love for literature?

c. Does he have a reverence for all living things?

d. Does he create and preserve rather than destroy?

The teacher's day-by-day observation of these standards is of greater importance than formal testing. Expectancies in terms of the students' individual goals can best be judged by the teacher and learner. Evaluation establishes new standards and new goals for each child.

Although standards guide children in evaluating the classroom work, they are misused if the emphasis is always upon error or failure.

It is difficult to set standards for creative work or assignments in which a student chooses his own subject and form of writing. Such standards almost always must be individual and must be set up in terms of the kinds of jobs different students are attempting. Considerable reading of good literature, with attention to how effects are achieved, will give some students an idea of what makes a good poem, essay, story, or play. Upper-grade students can also profitably consider standards like these as they write:

1. Did I choose a topic that I knew or could imagine something about?

2. Did I really do what I set out to do—tell how I felt about some experience, describe something that appealed to me, tell a story in an entertaining way with a rich choice of expressions?

3. Did I end my composition when the job was done, instead of writing just to fill up space?

4. Did I use verbs that will help a reader see what I saw, feel what I experienced?

5. Did I remember that in re-creating an experience for other people I could appeal to all five of their senses instead of just the sense of sight?

6. Did I remember that it is often more effective to let a reader draw his own conclusions on the basis of specific things I say rather than to *tell* him how he should feel or how I felt about something? For example, was it necessary for me to say, "This was a very thrilling adventure"?

7. Did I use comparisons that were really my own rather than old ones I had heard over and over again?

8. If I used conversation did I use quotation marks, commas, periods, and

capital letters correctly? Did I indicate change in speakers by paragraphing?

9. Can I give a reason for every mark of punctuation I have used?
10. As I read my paper aloud, did I observe any places in which additional punctuation will help make my meaning clear?

Few teachers would want to use a list of standards as long as the foregoing. They are simply suggestions for the kinds of items a class and teacher might use as basis for the evaluation of certain kinds of imaginative writing.

It will be understood that standards that are set for any kind of writing should be cumulative so that common spelling words, usage, grammar, punctuation, capitalization, mechanics, and form taught in one assignment are reviewed and made part of the expected achievements in the next piece of writing.

For Discussion

1. Are standards established in a textbook as effective as those developed by a class? Why?

2. Are most materials written in a classroom directed toward the teacher as the audience? What other individuals or situations might be used?

3. Some experiments in psychology indicate that people try harder when they know they will be evaluated or a score is being kept. Does this justify grading all classroom assignments?

4. Another term used for standards is expectancies. Are there differences in the meaning of these terms as used in elementary education?

5. What are the advantages and disadvantages in system-wide use of a scale or way of grading papers?

6. Does the following statement from Bell contradict what has been said about standards? [1]

Whether I like the idea or not, there is one hard fact that sticks out whenever I come to consider this business of standards. It is that, in the long run, the standard which I require doesn't matter, because a child will soon be carried beyond my direct influence. What matters is the standard by which the child himself will judge his own words and thoughts, and those of others. . . . He is going to acquire his standards by the light of a growing experience. They will come to him subtly and unseen, and they can't be given to him or forced upon him.

How Should Composition Work Be Evaluated?

Certain principles about the correcting and marking of students' work have been recognized by experienced teachers and authorities in the field of English.[2] Some of these are as follows:

1. The teacher who strives only to have students increase their skill is generally wasting her time until she interests them in wanting to write, in having a purpose for writing, and in writing with honesty and responsibility. Until this period is reached, there is little real value in marking papers.

2. In reading any composition, a teacher will want to look first for the answers to the following questions: What prompted the student to write the paper? What limitations did he have? What does the paper really say? What are its strengths and weaknesses?

3. Oral and written criticisms should encourage students and suggest further effort in writing. Any comment made by the teacher, even though it is critical, should indicate respect for what the student has written.

4. A student who truly understands that adherence to the conventions of language is a courtesy to the reader and an aid in conveying the meaning intended by the writer will be more inclined to write correctly than will a

[1] Vicars Bell, *On Learning the English Tongue* (London: Faber, 1953), p. 25.

[2] Denver Public Schools, *Course of Study for the Language Arts, K-12* (1955), pp. 383–86.

student who thinks of spelling, grammar, and so forth as something aside from "thought."

5. If a teacher places undue emphasis on form, he or she is penalizing the bold, original, aggressive thinker whose ideas sometimes get ahead of his command of written language. Teacher and class should have a common understanding of the relative "weight" to be assigned content and form.

6. Marginal symbols are useful in showing a student where his writing is weak. Teachers recognize, however, that certain kinds of weaknesses (particularly in structure of sentences) cannot be easily explained by any symbol but must be discussed orally with the student or elaborated on in a written comment.

7. Teachers in the upper grades need not *make* a correction for a student. Rather they might indicate the point of error or weakness and let the student, with whatever help he needs, work out the correction himself. It is equally important to mark strong points in a student's paper.

8. Teachers will always want to be cautious in suggesting that students "vary sentence patterns," "subordinate" a particular idea, and the like. The relationship of ideas shown in complex sentences by the use of modifying phrases is a highly individual matter. What the writer means to say will determine his sentence structure, as far as subordination is concerned. If the meaning in a given sentence or paragraph is not clear, the student, not the teacher, must decide how sentence structure should be changed to clarify the *student's* ideas. Often this can best be worked out in an individual discussion.

9. The extremely poor speller frequently has some psychological or emotional disturbance. Ignoring his spelling until some diagnostic and corrective work can be done is sometimes the best course of action.

10. Older students should expect to revise and rewrite, or copy, their work. Because revision is important, they must be given time to think about it, time to do it, and help when they need it. However, if a student can correct a minor error or two without completely recopying a paper, he should certainly be allowed to do so.

11. All teachers know that "it is poor teaching to demand what the teacher knows *cannot* be done." Criticism and suggestions for revision, therefore, must be in terms of an individual's capacities.

12. Highly general suggestions for revision are fruitless. To say to a student, "Make this more interesting (or entertaining, or effective)," will probably result in baffling rather than helping the student.

The busy teacher (a term that describes all teachers) is always seeking ways to make the task of reading and grading papers a little less laborious. The following suggestions have been used with profit.

The more time a teacher spends teaching composition, the less time will be spent correcting errors or marking mistakes in students' papers. Teachers know that the purpose of correcting papers is to help students improve their writing, not to catch them in mistakes. If a teacher tries to anticipate the mistakes students might make in a given situation and spends considerable time "pre-teaching" the items, students' writing will be better and, as a result, the burden of grading is less heavy.

Students should have a chance to do much of their writing in class under the guidance of the teacher. Such classes are true laboratory situations. As students write, a teacher can go from desk to desk offering help where it is needed, assisting students in organizing their ideas, calling their attention to obvious errors, sending them to dictionaries and textbooks for help, and making comments on the strengths and weaknesses of the papers under production. If the teacher discovers a common weakness in the papers, a direct attack on the problem should be made in a class session. Writing done under close supervision is almost "graded" and "corrected" before it is finally submitted.

Students should be held responsible for correction of obvious errors. To ensure their meeting this responsibility, a teacher can supervise proofreading sessions before final drafts of papers are written, and again before papers are turned in. A checklist of items or criteria will help to guide students' proofreading. For example, one item on every checklist would be adherence to whatever manuscript form has been established as standard for a class or school; another would be avoidance of careless omissions or repetitions of words. During part of a proofreading period, students should be told to whisper their words aloud to themselves so that they may hear how it sounds.

Before papers are turned in, have students exchange papers for additional proofreading. The teacher can again circulate in the classroom and act as an arbiter if criticisms are not accepted wholeheartedly or if a difference of opinion cannot be settled by reference to a dictionary or textbook. Occasionally, have the class divide into small groups. Let each student read his paper to this group, ask for suggestions, and make revisions that the group advises. Again the teacher will act as arbiter or final court of appeal in debatable cases.

As a variation of these procedures teachers can occasionally distribute students' papers to the class and have each student write a comment about the paper he reads. The comments are best if they are specifically directed to some major point. For example, if students have written letters to a sick friend, the comment might read: "I would (or would not) like to receive this letter because. . . ." The paper and the comment could then be given to the original writer, who would revise his work if necessary.

If a teacher makes a chart of errors that are common to a given set of papers, teaches and reteaches the items in question, and notes with the class the disappearance of these errors in subsequent papers, many students will gradually learn to avoid the mistakes in question.

Students need time in class to consult reference materials, complete certain proj-

ects, or read and work with other students. During some periods devoted to these activities, teachers can have individual conferences with certain students, go over written work, point out strengths and weaknesses, and return the paper to the student immediately for revision. Occasionally, it is possible to call together two or three students whose written work shows somewhat comparable characteristics and correct their papers together. No teacher can or should do all the necessary paper work in class, but working directly with students to improve their written work is certainly a valid and useful teaching procedure.

Teachers can save time and decrease the burden of grading papers if they do not try to mark every error on every paper. Gross errors, errors in items specifically pretaught, and errors in items that have been emphasized repeatedly should be marked. Other errors can be ignored. What constitutes a "gross error" will be determined by the grade level, the attainment and ability of the class, and the course of study. Conscientious teachers may feel that permitting students to commit errors without correction will be detrimental to the students' work. But common sense suggests that helping students eliminate a few gross errors at a time is a sensible procedure. Able students whose work is superior to that of the average should, of course, be given every chance to improve to the limit of their abilities. Such students can be working on complicated problems of subordination and transition while the bulk of the class is still wrestling with specific forms of verbs.

There is no valid reason for having every student write at exactly the same time. Assigning papers irregularly will help relieve the burden of having a large number of papers that should be marked and returned within a brief period. Although no real saving of time results from this procedure, it relieves the press of work and teachers can find short periods of time more easily than they can find many consecutive hours in which to grade papers.

On most occasions students should decide how long their compositions should be. But if teachers emphasize the virtues of brevity and conciseness, if they help students select subjects that can be limited easily, and if they encourage frequent writing of very short papers instead of less frequent submission of long, involved compositions, the problems of grading seem a bit less formidable. Mature students must at times have a chance to prepare and submit long reports or lengthy themes of one kind or another, but if such long compositions are prepared under fairly close supervision and observation, much of the grading can be done as the job is in progress.

Although it may be understood that the first writing is to be only a rough draft that will be refined through editing or proofreading, some children may resent rewriting the entire paper. Unless there is real motivation for this rewriting, it can appear to be "busy work," especially when only a few major corrections are made by the teacher. Making only a few corrections seems to imply that all of the uncorrected writing or spelling is above criticism and completely acceptable— which, of course, is not necessarily true. Teachers in grades 3 to 5 should use judgment in requiring material to be rewritten. If the child realizes that rewriting will help him, it should be done. But there is little justification for a complete second draft merely as a matter of policy.

Probably no one system of marking is materially better than another. Most schools find it desirable to establish a reasonably standard procedure so that students (and teachers) can become familiar with the marking procedures used. For young children, evaluative statements by the teacher, such as, "This is an improvement," "You are writing more interesting stories," "Your *n*'s still look like *r*'s," "You have written better stories than this one," or, "Your spelling is improving," are more informative, and in some cases more remedial, than merely marking the paper "A," "B," "C," or 90, 70, 65, and so on.

An occasional faculty or departmental meeting devoted to the subject of grading can be helpful. In such meetings teachers discuss procedures they follow, ask for help on special problems, try to work out a composition scale, examine standardized scales,

work as a group in grading a few sample papers, and the like.

Sometimes instead of assigning a grade and marking specific errors, a teacher might simply indicate the number and type of errors, as "10 misspelled words," "3 omissions of necessary capitals," or "1 example of incorrect end punctuation." The students must then take responsibility for finding and correcting mistakes and returning the paper.

Some teachers like to use a three-track system of grading. One grade is assigned for content; the second, for appearance (neatness, handwriting, observance of manuscript form, and the like); the third, for techniques and mechanics (grammar, usage, punctuation). The CAT mark, then, covers content, appearance, and techniques. Other teachers like to use two grades, one for general content and one for form. Some teachers believe that a single grade comes closest to expressing the dual importance of "ship and cargo." It is important in any school that teachers agree on some general principle regarding the relative values to be assigned form and content, so that a student's progression from one class to another means no great change in the way in which his progress is evaluated.

Oral and written comments made by a teacher will be in terms of both form and content. Such comments are meant to point the way to improvement, encourage further writing, and help the student understand his grades. Students who have been conditioned to regard the number of "red marks" as the real criteria of strength and weakness in a paper sometimes find it hard to see that a paper which may be mechanically correct is still an inadequate job if the content is weak. A written or oral explanation is due such a student if he is expected to produce better work next time. Such constructive criticism as challenging unfounded statements, querying the use of foggy words or syntax, pointing up illogical reasoning, or praising a discriminating choice of words, keen observation, and use of fresh comparisons can be communicated in teacher-written comment.

There are indications that students think that proofreading by the teacher is of greater help than having another child do it or attempting to do this themselves. Instead of "correcting" a paper, it might be well for the teacher to look upon this work as "editing" to assist the writer, similar in kind to the professional copy-editing of manuscripts done before publication.

Teachers who type the stories written by the children often observe that a remarkable growth in expression begins to take place as a result. In typing their stories, the teacher corrects basic errors. This form of editing is especially important if the material is to be used for reading instruction. Improvement takes place largely because the child wants it. First, typing his stories gives him confidence in his ability to write. Then he discovers that the typing makes it easier for him to read his own stories as well as stories written by other children. As the stories are assembled in stapled folders or ring binders, he develops pride of authorship. Eventually, as an "author," he seeks correct spelling, better writing, and more effective expression.

The purpose of all evaluation should be to foster learning. A teacher in England reminds us of this when he says: [3]

It is necessary to remind myself now of the basic truth that all education and all learning must partake of the nature of growth. We should all of us repudiate the suggestion that our teaching methods are based upon the injunction, "be like me—now." We should all of us with our hearts reaffirm that our motto is: "Be like yourself—now and always."

In the teaching of English, it is even more important to act upon this principle than it is in the teaching of any other subject. For we must always regard language as a means whereby the child may honestly, sincerely, and unaffectedly express his own opinions, his own feelings, and—thereby—his own inviolate and unique nature, so far as he has discovered it at a particular moment of time.

I am prepared (and so are hundreds of other teachers who feel as I do) to show, at any time, work written by some of my own nine- and ten-year-olds, which is neat, accurate, correctly spelled, and grammatically well constructed.

And I am equally prepared to show without blush or apology, written work which is untidy, misspelled, badly punctuated, and generally "illiterate."

But in order to satisfy me, there must be one quality apparent in the work of each group. It must be fun to read it. It must have a contact, direct, simple and friendly, between writer and reader.

Marie Hughes' studies have highlighted the importance of language in all aspects of teaching.[4] That used to evaluate children's work has an effect upon their attitude toward study. The off-hand statement of mild praise does not have the educational effect of a thoughtful comment about a child's work that includes an assessment of strengths and weaknesses to be improved in terms of a problem to be faced. Instead of, "That's nice, Jimmy," the teacher should comment, "I like your ideas here but they seem repetitive. Can you think of some way of saying this so that all your sentences don't start in the same way?" Any comment that influences the self-image of an individual or that would discourage the use of alternatives should be avoided.

With mature students who are ready to assume responsibility for correcting their own errors the following three-step procedure may be accepted as a challenge by the learners: (1) Ask the students to leave a 1-inch margin on the left hand side of their paper. Divide the margin into three or four columns. The first will be Sp. (spelling); the second P. (punctuation); the third Str. (structure); the fourth V (vocabulary). (2) The teacher or reader underlines the error and puts a check in the appropriate column. (3) The child makes the corrections.

An evaluation form used by teachers who participate as judges in the successful Saturday morning writing clinics in San Bernardino, California, suggests a number of uses to the classroom teacher, regardless of level.[5]

Key Questions
for Each Manuscript

1. What is (was) the author's purpose?
2. To what reader(s) is it addressed? The in-

---

[3] Bell, op. cit., pp. 20–21.

[4] Marie Hughes, "What Teachers Do and the Way They Do It," *N.E.A. Journal* (September 1964), p. 13.

[5] Mimeographed handout. San Bernardino, California Public Schools, 1969.

tended readership should be clearly identified even if it is as large and as nearly universal as the *Reader's Digest* audience or has the universal appeal of *Gulliver's Travels*.

3. To what extent does it succeed in achieving the author's purpose?

4. How does it compare with something of similar intent that has been published?

Specific Aspects of the Whole and Its Parts

1. Is the opening appropriate and otherwise effective?

2. Is the organizaiton effective logically? Psychologically? Otherwise?

3. Are the paragraphs effective in terms of unity, impact, variety in pattern and length? Are the transitions adequate?

4. Are the sentences well constructed, with variety in pattern, length, and emphasis? Are they coherent? Which one(s) should be made more compact, more definite, more emphatic, or clearer?

5. Is the diction well suited to the purpose in every instance? What words or phrases should be reconsidered in terms of sharpness, sound, length, connotations, or appropriateness in terms of the cultural "wave length" of the intended reader?

6. Is the ending well suited to the author's purpose?

Suggestions as to Policy

1. Neither the virtues nor the faults of a paper should be overstressed, and the criticism should be vigorously related to the author's intentions.

2. Critics should avoid getting involved in controversial content except as it involves the probable effect on the intended reader(s).

3. The most serious defects in writing are likely to be the result of unclear, inadequate, unresourceful *thinking*. It is a good idea to isolate this problem from the methodological problems of craftsmanship and mechanics and focus on it, if only because craftsmanship is at best but a means to an end.

4. It would be a good idea to have some excellent examples of the kind of writing you are to criticize ready to use in illustrating the points you made.

5. It is important to consider that the effect of the whole is more important than the virtues or the faults in component parts. Originality often vindicates itself by the unexpectedness

and unconventionality of its approach or its disregard for certain of the standard virtues. A critic can at times be too doctrinaire, too analytical, or too much obsessed by the lesser virtues and thus insured against proper respect for originality.

For Discussion

1. The following essay is a composite of many errors made by children as well as the zest for expression. What would you need to know to evaluate it properly? How would you evaluate it in terms of the following criteria?

    a. The story is written by a fourth-grade girl.

    b. The story is written by a sixth-grade boy.

    c. The story is written by a migrant worker in junior high school.

My Most Exciting Experience

One sumer my father said I cud go to my unkles farm ranch in mew mexico so I went. At first it seemed awful dull cuz nothing happened but one morning my uncle said I could go with Bill and Pete to brand cattle at dry gulch which was meny miles from the ranch house acrost the dessert. We took lots of lunch and a big canten of water and left early in the morning on horseback. We got the cattle branded allright but it was gettin dark when we started home and jus as we was leavin dry gulch we herd some awful screamin and Bill sed it was cyotes. Bill road on one side of me and Pete of the other. It was too dark to see anything but tinie lights comin tord us and Bill and Pete both shot at the lights. They shot two cyotes and the rest ran away. Boy was I scared!

How Are Standardized Tests Used in the Language Arts?

Those who make tests seek to establish validity in measurement. The validity of a test means the extent to which it accurately measures what it is designed to test. Some areas of the curriculum allow for such a wide range of personal response that it is difficult

The greatest motivation for learning is an awareness of personal growth. A comparison of handwriting and composition at different times during the year is far more effective than grades alone. (*Courtesy of the San Diego City Schools.*)

to find a test which will measure those areas and still be easily scored by a machine or other device. Art appreciation, oil painting, cooking, and enjoyment of poetry are some of the skills or talents for which it is difficult to construct quick-scoring written tests.

There are aspects of the language arts that standardized achievement tests do not measure. Appreciation of literature, creative writing, ability to construct an expressive sentence, oral reading and interpretation, response to poetry, ability to organize a re-

port, ability to organize an interesting talk, and ability to participate in a conversation or discussion are among those not measured in standardized tests.

Sometimes a principal will report that his school is doing well in language arts. When questioned he will refer to the scores made on an achievement test. It is well for all teachers and parents to know exactly what these tests measure.

The spelling score is often based upon the ability of a child to check the correct spelling from a choice of three or four in items like this:

elefant (4)

An elefunt (5) is big.

elephant (6)

Check One
(4) (5) (6) (Not given)

Although for many children the ability to detect correct spelling is closely related to the ability to spell, some children can correctly proofread this type of spelling test and yet misspell the word. In the process of standardization, these children are lost in the vast number used to establish the norms.

The language section usually provides a choice between two items such as these:
Denver Colorado

Denver, Colorado

Uncle Jim $^{said}_{said}$, "We can eat here."

I've $^{did}_{done}$ my lesson.

Tell Bill and $^{I}_{me}$ where it is.

These act as measurements of a child's knowledge of punctuation and correct-usage items. Again it measures an understanding of usage rather than an opportunity to use the knowledge.

One teacher happened to have a set of creative stories to be evaluated at the same time the test was being graded. Although many children did not use quotation marks in their stories, approximately half did. There were three who had not put the comma after *said*. Investigation revealed that all of them had checked the correct item in the test.

In situations where teachers are judged by children's responses on standardized tests, it is common practice to have the class work on drill sheets closely related to the usage items tested. If a teacher stresses such work with the upper third of a normal group, they will score so high that the entire class average will be over the expected norm. This result may satisfy some uninformed adminis-

trators, but the teacher knows that the test is not a measurement of the children's ability to use language in original speech or writing.

Investigation will reveal that items in many achievement tests are not those taught in the textbooks used by the children tested. Of seventy questions measuring language skills in one test, thirty-seven items were not presented in the fourth-grade language book used in one school, thirty-two were not in the fifth-grade book, and twenty-one were not in the sixth-grade book. Twenty-one tested items were not included in the textbooks for the fourth, fifth, or sixth grades. The results could mean that a child who had a perfect mastery of all items taught in the books of these grades would still fail in 30 per cent of the items on the test.

If the fifth-grade child answered correctly only the items taught in his textbook, his grade placement on the test would have been below the third grade. To make this point still more vivid, another test which contained items more clearly related to those in the text in use would have measured this knowledge as being in the second month of the eighth grade.

Reading-achievement tests are more apt to measure the skills that have been taught than language tests. Tests of vocabulary and paragraph meaning, together with reading to predict outcomes, understand directions, interpret attitudes, reorganize sentence meaning, note details, use the index, or get information from charts, are among the items usually included. In addition to comparative achievement in relation to established norms, these tests reveal specific strengths and weaknesses that guide the teacher.

But even the best reading tests must be examined critically if they are to be used correctly. Some sections contain only two choices, so that there is a strong element of chance present. In some sections, failing to answer one or two questions can make a year's difference with respect to the score. Teachers normally dislike grading standardized tests, but it is only by comparing what they know about a certain child and what he did on each test item that the full value of these teaching instruments is realized.

Interpretation of test results must include a number of factors. In some schools the children in the primary grades frequently test below national reading norms when they are at the norm in grade 4 and above the national norm in grades 5 and 6. This is due in part to a shorter primary school day than that in other areas and to a different curriculum emphasis during the first two years of school. It is the total growth pattern that needs to be observed. Factors such as part-time school sessions, mobility of population, and environmental differences would enter into any interpretation of results.

A positive function that standardized tests serve is that of diagnosis of need. Most manuals for tests indicate action to take if the score in any area is low. It is quite possible that some language skills have not been adequately emphasized as the curriculum has become crowded with science and social studies content.

A grade score of 5.0 on a reading test indicates that the child is reading at the average for beginning fifth grade. If the child's mental age and IQ indicate that he is capable of working at a 6.1 level, this score would be cause for concern because it indicates that his reading achievement is below his ability level. In the same way, the child with a 3.0 ability level who is in the fourth grade and reading at a 3.0 achievement level is working at an expected achievement level.

In the early grades there is a rapid increase in the difficulty of material. Thus a child who is reading at a grade level of 1.5 would find second-grade material difficult, but a child in the sixth grade with a 4.5 reading achievement would have less difficulty because there is not as great an increase in reading complexity at that level.

It seems only fair to inform children concerning the use of a test. Tensions and anxieties concerning promotion or grades can make standardized testing a mental-health hazard. If possible, an individual conference should be held after the test to show where errors were made, to learn the child's explanation of strange interpretations of material, and especially to establish goals in terms of the child's needs. "Here is a section that caused trouble," the teacher will indicate. "Let's see what you need to study." And then teacher and child will determine the next step.

A standardized scale helps a new teacher define the expected achievement of a child. To construct a handwriting or composition scale, hundreds of writing samples are judged until a typical one is found for each age or grade level. By careful comparison the teacher can use these selected samples to judge the achievement of her pupils. Composition scales may be based on a single basic quality, as in the samples that follow. The first example is considered good; the second is an example of a child's work that needs greater direction. Individual schools and classes can construct such scales as a learning exercise with profit to the participants.

A Chart Showing Growth in Ability to Organize Thought [6]

Grade 2

The Clean-Up Campaign

The children in Hancock School are working to keep Saint Paul a clean city. We started it by cleaning up our school block. We are cleaning up our yards, too.

Clean Up

We are cleaning up this block.
We are trying to have a clean city.
Our school children are taking turns cleaning up our block.

Qualities to Be Noted

1. The title refers accurately to the subject being written about.
2. The first sentence states clearly *what* the composition is about.
3. The order of sentences is good: *from* the general *to* the particular.

Contrasting Points to Be Observed

1. The title is not clear.
2. The first sentence should come second.
3. Sentences one and three overlap.

---

[6] Minneapolis Public Schools, *Communication, A Guide to Speaking and Writing*, 1953, pp. 106–107.

Grade 3

A Safe Vacation

We are all going to have a vacation soon. But we must not take a vacation from safety.

Safe things in a home:
    Not to play with matches.
    Not to handle lights if you have water on your hands.
Safety things outdoors:
    Not to play in the streets.
    Not to leaf your toys out after dark.
    Be careful when you are going barefooted not to walk on glass.
    Be careful not to be hit by a swing.

These are good safety rules. Be careful this summer and make it a good one.

Vacation Safety

Be careful on your bickl on the street. Cross at the corner. Do not go betwy parked cars. Look out where you run so you won't hit people. Cars stop at stop sins so you can cross when the sin ses red. Stay away from moving swings so you won't get hit.

Qualities to Be Noted

1. The opening sentences make a point. The closing sentences clinch it.
2. The illustrations are accurately grouped under the headings.
3. The illustrations aptly support the point made.

Contrasting Points to Be Observed

1. There is no general introductory statement tying the illustrations together.
2. The composition begins and ends abruptly.
3. The fourth sentence is out of place in the sequence.

Grade 4

A Story About Norway

Norway is a beautiful country. It has big blue mountains, with streams running through them and it is really pretty.

They're greatest sport is skiing. They have the greatest skiers in Norway.

The fiords are so beautiful that thousands of tourists from other countries visit them in summer. They come in ships that sail along the coast inside the skerry guard and make side trips into the fiords.

The Mountains of Norway

It was a beautiful day on the mountains. The little mountain streams were dancing gayly, and looked beautiful in the bright sun. Now if we went down the mountain we might see herds of cattle grazing. But still down farther you would see the winding fiords, they too look beautiful in the sun. When it rains the fiords are often visited by fishermen. Ships are often seen going in and out of the fiords. Someday I hope to go on a ship in and out of the fiords.

Qualities to Be Noted

1. Three points are neatly made, each in a separate paragraph.

Contrasting Points to Be Observed

1. There is a shift in point of view after the fourth sentence and again after the sixth —from *it* to *we* to *you* to *I*.

Grade 5

What We Believe About Brotherhood

We should not ignore people whose religion is different than ours. They are American people just like we are. Everyone is equal.

Sometimes you will see a group of children playing and having fun. Only it isn't fun for one little girl. She is from a foreign country. She can't talk too well so the children ignore her. It is just like saying, "We can't play with you because you are from a different place than we are."

We should be friends with everyone and not ignore them because they are from a different country or go to a different church, or are of a different race.

Brotherhood

We had some very nice friends in Chicago and we hated to leave them. They were of different nationality and religion, too.

My mother said it would be nice if everybody was of the same religion and nationality. I think so too, but then, like in the olden days, there would be fights, wars and quarrels about the different beliefs. Then the different religions and nations would start all over again. It would be best to stick to the religion and nationality each person believes in. It doesn't make any difference what nationality or race a person is.

Every week should be Brotherhood Week.

Qualities to Be Noted

1. Opening paragraph introduces topic. Closing paragraph clinches point.
2. Second paragraph contains specific illustration. Illustration makes its point.
3. Paragraphing is accurate.
4. Development lives up to the promise of the title.

Contrasting Points to Be Observed

1. Title broad and general. Compare with "What We Believe About Brotherhood."
2. Opening paragraph does not consider the reader, *begins* but does not *introduce.*
3. Relationship between paragraphs 1 and 2 is not clear.
4. Paragraph 2 is jumbled and contradictory.
5. Last sentence not justified by what has gone before.

Grade 6

The World Is Growing Smaller

Although it still maintains its regular size, the world is growing smaller. This all started when the raft (which later became the hollowed-out log or makeshift boat) was invented by the caveman. The world got smaller then, because people could go from place to place faster. The world got smaller yet, when beasts were tamed to transport people. As time went on these things were improved on, and finally the airplane and car were invented. All of these helped greatly in shrinking the world. Science is still experimenting, and soon, who knows, if there may be a time when a person can have breakfast in New York, dinner in Paris, supper in London, and be home in time to read the evening paper. The world has grown smaller from the caveman's raft to the jet plane and is continually shrinking from view of yesterday's hardships.

The World Is Growing Smaller

The world is growing smaller because scientists are inventing fast planes and ships that can go around the world in a few days. The world has changed. Its not a large world anymore but a small world. Transportation has changed from slow transportation to fast transportation and transportation is getting faster all the time. The world is growing smaller and smaller every day. The world is like a midget caught between modern transportation.

Qualities to Be Noted

1. Each succeeding sentence grows out of the preceding; thus the idea of the paragraph grows. It does not, as in composition above, stand still.
2. While the composition might be better divided into two paragraphs—the second one beginning "Science is still experimenting"—the development from sentence to sentence is consistent.

Contrasting Points to Be Noted

1. The thought of this paragraph does not advance. Each succeeding sentence merely repeats what was said before.
2. The final sentence is obscure.

Such a scale should be discussed with students. With some classes a self-developed scale would be a valuable learning activity.

For Discussion

1. Why are parents apt to accept the results of a standardized test yet reject work samples that indicate immaturity or lack of effort?
2. What would be gained and what might be lost if all schools used a composition scale to evaluate creative writing?
3. Why is it important to know the number of students tested to establish a norm in a test? Why is it important to know the locations of the schools used in establishing the norms of a test?
4. How frequently should standardized tests be used? What is the best time of year to give them?

In the language arts statistical validity and reliability are difficult to achieve. In order to get a normal distribution those who construct tests must add such factors as time. Whether speed should be a factor in mental tests has been questioned. Items of exceptional difficulty are sometimes used, such as the spelling of *parentheses* so that answering a single question on some tests can mean a difference of two or three months in the achievement norm. Test exposure is a serious problem. One college student reported that in seeking employment he had been given the same mental test so often he could make a perfect score. More serious is that teachers do not participate in test evaluation to the extent that they are involved in selecting other education equipment. This is because it is feared that teachers then will devote too much time to test items and thus influence the test results.

Because the language of numbers represents an exactness, test results have a finality that satisfy many. The state of California has a state-wide testing program. Recently the papers reported a noted improvement in reading achievement. A careful reading of the article revealed that the new results were based upon a new test that did not stress generalization skills to the extent that the one used previously had. In other words, a different yardstick simply measured in a different way, but this was concealed in the numerical grade-level-reporting system used.

To secure a comprehensive listing and evaluation of standardized tests on the markets, the reader is advised to consult the most recent edition of the *Mental Measurements Yearbook,* edited by Oscar K. Buros and published by the Gryphon Press; 220 Montgomery Street; Highland Park, N.J. 08904, or *Tests in Print* (latest edition) by the same editor and publisher.

Dr. John Bordie of the University of Texas has recently examined the standardized tests available in the Language Arts. He states,[7]

A final point to be noted: since curricula change and students change, the older a test, the more satisfactory a local group will appear when measured against national norms; obviously if one wants to demonstrate that a new methodology has solved a particular problem, one should use an older test rather than the newest test to appear. Such new tests tend to measure areas not previously considered in the methodology while the older tests measure those items which the methodologies have had sufficient experience and practice in solving and teaching.

---

[7] John G. Bordie, "Language Tests and Linguistically Different Learners: The Sad State of the Art," *Elementary English* (October 1970), pp. 824–26.

In other words statistical norms gathered in various cities ignore the variant goals that different curricula seek.

Our needs in the area of tests include six concerns: (1) we must be able to measure an individual's competence in language (whether he speaks a nonstandard dialect or another language), as contrasted with his competence in standard English; (2) we need a convenient checksheet so that teachers and school administrators can determine what standard of language is used in school or in the community; (3) we must have an acceptable definition of standard English which allows for the richness of some of the dialects spoken in the United States; (4) we need tests which distinguish between language proficiency and degree of socialization; (5) we need to know what it is that is required for satisfactory performance in the school curriculum in language other than that performance solely based on written language; and (6) we need a definition of language which takes into account all the abilities used in human communication. We are still an inordinate distance from a satisfactory definition, let alone a detailed specification of skills.

For Discussion

1. In the book *Pygmalion in the Classroom* by Robert Rosenthal published by Holt, 1968, a study was reported that indicated that teachers' attitudes influenced the results teachers produced. When told that children were of low ability, they garnered poor results. When told that the same children were able, the teachers garnered good results. Have you ever noticed such an effect of mind-set in your learning experience?

2. Devise a test for one part of this book. Give it to your class. Determine the norm. Now decide if high scores indicate who will be good teachers.

3. In *The Reading Teacher,* January 1971, there is an article, "The Orangoutang Score," which points out that an ape, through pure chance, would get 25 per cent of the questions correct on some stand-

ardized tests. This would place his reading achievement as high as 5.6 (fifth grade) on some tests. To what extent is this a valid criticism of standardized measurement?

How Should the Language Arts Program Be Interpreted to Parents?

Because some teachers look upon the non-school hours in the life of a child as being educationally insignificant, it is well to remind ourselves that the use of language by a child is greater during those hours than during the school day. For this reason and others, it is especially important that parents understand the program in language arts and share in it with their children.

The report card is a report to parents. As such it should communicate information that parents want to know. If they desire a competitive rating that tells them how John performs in relation to others in the class,

it must be given to them. If they want to know how John compares with other boys of similar ability, this comparison must be indicated.

On the other hand, there are additional facts that teachers want parents to know about their children and the school program. The schools are a public concern and the teacher's responsibility is not only to the children but also to those who support the schools. When we do a good job of classroom teaching we assume that it will be recognized by the public. But recognition is rather unlikely if the public has no idea of why we use such things as print script, verse choirs, and vast numbers of library books.

To prepare a report on the individual child, the teacher needs a folder of work samples. Children can help by assuming the responsibility for putting samples of writing, creative work, and classroom tests in these folders. In addition to the child's work samples, classroom charts giving informa-

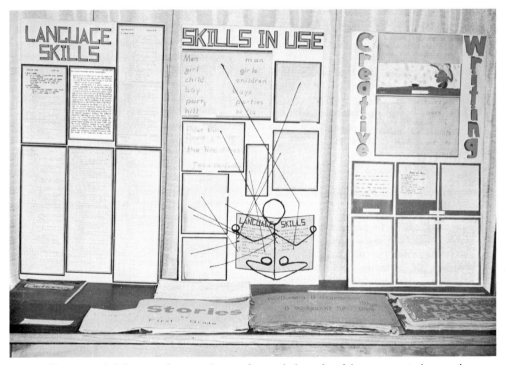

Parents and fellow teachers need to understand the role of language arts in association with the total school curriculum. A display of this nature for parents will reassure the most doubtful that the teachers know what they are doing. (*Courtesy of the San Diego County Schools.*)

tion on books read, spell test scores, and other achievement records should be kept as supporting evidence for evaluation activities. Consider the following report by Glogan and Fessel: [8]

Written Language

Comments can be made regarding the child's ability in terms of:

1. Participating in original or creative writing.
2. Writing a variety of letters (e.g., friendly letters, invitations, announcements, business letters).
3. Addressing envelopes and folding letters correctly.
4. Thinking clearly and expressing himself effectively.
5. Participating in writing poetry, plays.
6. Building an understanding of functional grammar.
7. Increasing ability to outline, take notes, and summarize.
8. Increasing ability to make book reports or review activities.
9. Increasing ability to write captions for pictures, label articles, and file materials.
10. Increasing ability in the skills of evaluation of work of other pupils.
11. Increasing ability to express his ideas clearly and interestingly (not from source).
12. Increasing ability to use correct forms (e.g., capitalization, punctuation, and grammar) (not from source).

Oral Language and Speech

Comments can be made regarding the child's ability in terms of:

1. Increasing ability to participate in group conversations and discussions.
2. Increasing ability to perform underlying processes of gathering, organizing, and presenting ideas for speaking situations.
3. Increasing ability to participate in the evaluation and interpretation of materials presented by the teacher or other pupils.
4. Developing effective articulation and enunciation, easy use of voice.

5. Increasing capability to speak before an audience.
6. Developing confidence in speaking before a group (not from source).
7. Expressing ideas clearly and interestingly (not from source).
8. Listening intelligently while others speak (not from source).

Spelling

Comments can be made regarding the child's ability in terms of:

1. Increasing ability of the child to proofread all written work.
2. Using a few simple rules which apply to a large number of words.
3. Increasing ability to use syllabication as an aid to spelling.
4. Increasing ability to utilize dictionary skills.
5. Reviewing words previously learned.
6. Learning words that are within the reading ability of the child.
7. Maintaining an individual spelling list and lists of currently used words from content areas.
8. Illustrating word meanings and compiling picture dictionaries.
9. Articulating and pronouncing all words.
10. Correcting handwriting difficulties that handicap spelling.
11. Increasing ability to recognize correct and incorrect spelling.
12. Increasing ability to spell words needed for his writing.
13. Developing the habit of consulting the dictionary or some other source to verify spelling.
14. Learning spelling words easily, remembering spelling words, applying spelling words (not from source).

Handwriting

Comments can be made regarding the child's ability in terms of:

1. Developing proficiency in the fundamentals of form in handwriting.
2. Developing legibility in his daily writing.
3. Developing speed in handwriting.
4. Effectively applying the techniques of good handwriting in other school subjects.
5. Increasing development of form, legibility, uniformity of slant, spacing, alignment, quality of line, speed.

[8] Lillian Glogan and Murray Fessel, *The Nongraded Primary School* (West Nyack, N.Y.: Parker Publishing Company, 1967), pp. 266–67.

6. Using good writing position for the sake of comfort and effective performance.
7. Writing with right (left) hand according to his natural tendency.
8. Participating in group discussions of common class errors.
9. Having begun the transition to cursive writing, not being ready at present for the transition to cursive writing (not from source).

Teachers are also urged to keep anecdotal records of incidents in the child's school day. This is a burden for a busy teacher, but important because this evidence is needed. Brief notes written in the plan book are a quick means of jotting down short reminders, such as, "John's uncle is in Japan," "Mary seems to resent any mention of her mother," "Billy went out of his way to help the new boy." A crisis in the classroom calls for a more detailed comment. "Mary deliberately spilled paint on Jane's picture. She denied this and accused Jack of the offense. Finally she admitted the offense and agreed that she should not be permitted to paint for the rest of this week." Children seldom disclose such events at home, yet they may be part of the material you will wish to share in a parent conference.

The report card, however, is a very limited means of interpreting the school program. Some teachers enclose a bulletin with each report. One calls her's "Kindergarten Confidential." In it are descriptions of expected behavior of this age group as revealed by studies of child growth. School events and policies may be explained. In October parents are informed that the children may come to school in costume for a Halloween celebration. It is also suggested that masks are a safety hazard and should be avoided. At Christmas time an explanation of why gifts are (or are not) exchanged at school is included. A list of songs the children have learned, finger plays to teach at home, and examples of seasonal verse all add to the general attractiveness of the material.

First-grade teachers who want the parents to help children with print script should send home a copy of the alphabet with directions showing how each letter is made. At another time it may be appropriate to explain why the basic reader is not sent home. Simple progress reports contain news the children bring home in their own handwriting. "Everyone in the class now knows twenty-five words." "Everyone in the first grade can write the figures to 10." A parent might be told how to evaluate the early art efforts of a child. Warnings should be given about belittling early efforts or making gratuitous suggestions. Many parents feel that children should be urged to "do better," not realizing that such urging takes all joy out of sharing something with them. Acceptance, recognition, and praise are the rewards sought by a child when he shows his school work. A child should not be constantly reprimanded for his mistakes or errors. Certainly the parents cannot expect him to bring home only perfect papers. Rather than send a paper or two home each day, it is more effective to keep them for a week, then staple together the workbook pages, art, and writing efforts and send them home on Fridays. Beginning teachers should be warned about sending home good work that they wish to use in an exhibit or other purpose. Too many parents will give it due attention and then throw it out with the daily papers.

Upper-grade teachers will find that a school or district-wide pamphlet on "What We Are Doing in Spelling," "When You Buy a Book for Your Child," "Our Reading Program" will meet a common need and be more efficient than a teacher's individual efforts. Many systems now publish parents' handbooks which are distributed at a parent–teacher conference. Those in Denver, Colo., Cincinnati, Ohio; Des Moines, Iowa; Contra Costa County, Calif.; and Arlington, Va., are outstanding. The material need not be expensive to be effective. However, some of the mimeographed materials sent from schools leave a poor impression of a group as supposedly well trained as teachers in language and art. The form is important, but what is said is more important.

An after-school meeting with parents or a demonstration of teaching is an effective way to communicate for some teachers. There are other teachers who do an outstanding job when alone with children but are nervous or ill at ease when adults are present. At all times it is good to remember that modern parents are usually high school or college graduates, are informed about many aspects of education through magazines and study groups, and expect a professional presentation of the school program and the problems being considered. It is not unreasonable for them to expect the teacher to know why she does certain things. Here is a letter that one second-grade teacher sent to parents:

Dear Parents,

Several have asked about the misspelling of children in the written work they bring home. You have probably noticed that the errors are usually phonetic in nature, such as *wants* for *once* or *pepl* for *people*.

During the primary grades the major task of the children is to learn to read. The phonics taught is to help them sound out words in their books. It is natural then to use this skill when they write a word. Since their oral vocabulary is much larger than their reading vocabulary, they write many words that have not been studied in reading.

It helps them think of the ideas that they wish to write if we accept this phonetic spelling. Some would hesitate to write at all if they were to be criticized for not spelling all the words correctly.

We do have a spelling period and some of the words that have been misspelled will be studied. You will find it interesting to keep a collection of the papers your child brings home. There will be a gradual decrease in phonetically misspelled words as he conforms to the conventional forms which he is learning. In the meantime, he is expressing his ideas with ease and confidence. We want him to try to use words like *enormous* and *television* instead of substituting *big* and *T.V.* merely because these are easier to spell.

Please read what the child wants to say. Comment about his ideas and share his joys as a creative writer. Do not comment on the spelling of single words.

You might like to visit our spelling class. It is held each day at 2:15.

Respectfully,

Some aspects of the language arts program require the active participation of parents. A child with a speech defect needs to practice at home. Lessons for the parent to use should be created by the school. A child who makes a usage error is reflecting an error heard at home. Send a game home that emphasizes the correct form, and suggest that the family practice it with the child so that the source of the trouble can be corrected. Spelling can be studied at home. A workbook soon becomes tattered and torn after it has been sent home. A better practice is to have the child make a copy of a few words from the list to study at home. This list can be given some importance if he writes it on colored paper or has each word on small individual cards which can be manipulated like flash cards.

Suggestions for enrichment activities might be sent to parents who want to be given a larger role in the formal teaching of their children. These activities might involve the use of encyclopedias, selection and discussion of library books, and application of some of the inexpensive workbook materials available in variety stores. Because children like to read aloud to their parents, some teacher-approved books should be available to read at home. These might be supplementary books, stories taken from discarded material and rebound as little books, or especially prepared story sheets that reinforce the vocabulary of the basic program. Worthwhile books to study with respect to parents are *Everybody's Business —Our Children,* by Mauree Applegate (Harper); *Helping Parents Understand Their Child's School,* by Grace Langdon and Irving W. Stout (Prentice-Hall); and *Enjoy Your Children,* by Margo Gerke (Abingdon).

Any involvement of the child's home may involve the parents. Bringing a news item for sharing, a picture of an ice cream cone for the bulletin board, used coffee cans or milk cartons for science experiments may involve complex discussions at home. One parent was disturbed because a child was asked to bring her *favorite* toy. The decision kept the child awake all night. Another parent found that coffee was emptied into a platter because the can was needed at school and that her best hat was missing because it was needed for a character in a play (not played by her own child, who was in charge of costumes).

Homework involves the entire family. The following guidelines will help a teacher plan successfully:

Characteristics of Good Homework Assignments [9]

1. Homework should be carefully planned, with pupils motivated to complete the assignments: assignments that are definite, interesting, meaningful, and geared to individual abilities.
2. The teacher should take some responsibility for helping the child to form efficient habits. How to study and learn is, unfortunately, not taught very well, if at all in most schools. Too many children waste too much of their study time because they have never learned how best to use it.
3. Most homework should be of an informal nature, supplementing formal preparation in the class and following the bent of the child: reading good fiction, poetry, history, popular magazines and newspapers, watching good TV programs, seeing excellent movies, etc.
4. The homework assignments should be made only after children understand the process and have had enough practice in class to do homework on the subject unaided.
5. Most homework assignments should be personalized, geared as far as possible to meet individual needs, and should be within the pupil's range of skill. This means that there should be very little or no regularly assigned drill-type homework for the entire class. Exercises that can be done mechanically encourage copying, while an assignment that calls for initiative and individual creative effort rules out copying and challenges the pupil to work effectively.
6. Most homework assignments should be of a type which can be better done away from school. This includes collecting information, sharing ideas with parents, and situations in which children are involved in something like creative writing or preparing reports.

[9] Laurence Rosebush, *Non-Grading—A Curriculum for Continuous Progress in Learning* (New York: Parker, 1970), Appendix.

It is unfair to beginning teachers, however, to imply by the foregoing that all parents are equally interested in the education of their children. There are certain areas where the parents never visit the school, ignore report cards, do not participate in P.T.A. activities, and in extreme cases, even express disapproval of the entire curriculum. There are, unfortunately, some parents who do not want the responsibility of raising their own children. This rejection often takes peculiar forms. Some parents seem to transfer their own shortcomings and sense of guilt to the schools and teachers. From their point of view it is the fault of the teacher and the school that Joe and Mary are "problem children." Such criticism of our educational effort is, of course, most unfair.

In these situations remember that the child is not responsible for his parents. Give him the security, help, and recognition that he may need so desperately. Sometimes teachers must be substitute parents.

For Discussion

1. Should parents be asked to send money to school to buy the "Weekly Reader" for children? To buy library books?
2. Why would it be difficult for some parents to note the difficulties their own child was having as they observed a reading lesson?
3. Modern homework is considered to be an enrichment of the child's experiences rather than a catching-up on competitive assignments. Give examples of this type of homework in a language area.
4. What would be your reply if a parent wanted you to spend an extra half-hour after school working with his child?
5. What would be your reply if a parent wanted to have a birthday party for a child in your classroom at school during school time?
6. How can such days as Christmas, Mother's Day, Father's Day, Education Week, be used to interpret the school program to parents?

How Do Behavioral Objectives Assist Evaluation?

In order to evaluate achievement both the learner and teacher need to know what was to be done. Long-term educational purposes usually are stated in broad, flexible terms, such as "to develop the creative potential of each child" or "to establish a lasting appreciation of poetry." One evaluates achievement of such objectives by general evidence of growth, such as the voluntary reading or writing of poetry, a willingness to write stories or letters, and personal testimony of students. To many, such evaluation is not measurement but simply personal judgment and perhaps wishful thinking.

The term *behavioral objective* refers to a specific way of acting or achievement that both learner and teacher can see. Instead of stating an objective as "to appreciate literature" or "to enjoy recreational reading" one finds "classifies a story as a fable" or "determines the climax of a story."

Examples of such objectives would be the following:

> Given a paragraph containing verbs, the student will indicate the adverbs and state what questions they answer.
> Given orally an unfamiliar word, the student will find the word in a dictionary, note its spelling, and copy the word correctly.[10]
> Given a poem for choral reading, each student participates actively in the reading and contributes suggestions concerning a way to improve the reading of a particular line.[11]

When writing such objectives three things must be kept in mind:

1. What it is the student will be able to do.
2. Under what conditions the student will perform.

3. To what extent the student will be expected to perform.

Do these statements meet all three conditions?

> The student will be able to write, in print script, the small letters of the alphabet, *a* to *z*.
> Given a statement to proofread, the student will correct the spelling of six words.

In what way are these more effective?

> Each student will write the small letters of the alphabet, *a* to *z,* as described as average on the city handwriting scale.
> Given a statement containing six spelling errors the student will correct all errors.

Well-written instructional objectives suggest how their accomplishment can be measured. An objective such as, "The students should know the alphabet" might better be written, "Shown the letters of the alphabet in random order, the student is able to say the name of each letter with 100% accuracy."

A careful consideration of objectives influences the nature of the assignment, the materials needed, the class procedure, and the diagnosis of next steps for each learner.

Many aspects of the language arts which are of paramount importance do not lend themselves to such specific classroom activities. One might ask, "Isn't the person who is comprehending something doing something? Isn't intellectual, emotional, or creative performance an acceptable kind of student performance?" [12] It should be recognized that limiting classroom activities to specific measurable behavior with language would place an emphasis of teaching effort on the mechanical, classification aspects of language rather than on personal expression of or response to the ideas being shared. It must be noted as well that even the most specific behavior is subject to interpretation by a good teacher who would not evaluate handwriting or punctuation without con-

---

[10] U.C.L.A. Graduate School of Education, Center for the Study of Evaluation, *Instructional Objectives Exchange Language Arts,* 4–6 (1970).

[11] J. W. Hook, The Tri-University BOE Project: *A Progress Report on Writing Behavioral Objectives for English* by John Maxwell and Anthony Toratl, N.C.T.E. (1970), p. 83.

[12] James MacDonald and Bernice J. Wolfson, "A Case Against Behavior Objectives," *The Elementary School Journal* (December 1970), pp. 119–26.

sidering the development and purpose of the student who is performing. But it is possible that even such an emotional response as appreciation of poetry can be better taught by thinking of some of the specific behaviors involved. When the student compares three poems about trees and is aware of the difference in the presentation of three writers, his appreciation of them may grow as he only listens to the teacher read each one or says them with others in a verse choir.

Note how effectively the objectives have been achieved in the following lessons: [13]

Distinguishing Between Verbs and Nouns by Use of "Let's" Frames

A. Generalization
  1. Words that name something are nouns.
  2. Words that fit the frame "Let's _____" are verbs.
B. Purpose—Pupils should be able to
  1. Identify words on cards as nouns or verbs.
  2. Tell how they knew each was a noun or a verb.
  3. Check their own answer.
  4. Identify nouns or verbs in sentences read to them.
  5. Name some nouns and verbs of their own.
  6. Make the generalizations.
C. Introduction
  1. Distribute word cards, some of which contain a noun and some a verb.
  2. Show pupils the "noun box" and "verb box" which will be used to check their answers. In the "noun box" are objects to go with the noun card. In the "verb box" is a card with "Let's," which fits each verb card like a puzzle piece. (See Materials.)

D. Developmental Activities
  1. Each pupil will identify the word on his card as a noun or verb, tell how he knew this, and check his answer in the appropriate box.
  2. Place sentences on the board. The pupils will identify the nouns and verbs in each. Make a little game out of this by keeping a score.
     a. I sing a song.
     b. We throw a ball.
     c. They dig in the sandbox.
     d. You chase the dog.
     e. I ride in a train.
     f. I eat an apple.
     g. They walk to the store.
     h. I talk to the baby.
     i. We play with a doll.
     j. You run up the street.
     Ask the pupils to name some nouns they know; some verbs.
E. Conclusion
  1. Ask: What kinds of words did we work with today? How did we recognize nouns? How did we recognize verbs?
F. Materials
  1. Word Cards: some nouns, some verbs; and one with "Let's" which fits each verb card like a puzzle

  | Let's }{ sing |

  2. Noun and verb boxes
  3. Objects for each noun.

Identification of Nouns by Use of the Noun Frame

A. Generalization
  A noun is a word which fits in the frame. "(The) _____ is here." "(The) _____ are here."
B. Purpose—Pupils should be able to
  1. Identify determiners and nouns in a sentence and test these nouns in the substitution frames.
  2. Identify nouns in sentences with no determiners by using the substitution frames.
  3. State the generalization (above).
  4. Select singular and plural nouns to

insert in the noun substitution frames.

C. Introduction

   1. Place a cardboard picture frame before the class with three pictures along side (one too large, one too small, one which fits). Ask the pupils which picture fits the frame.

   2. Tell the pupils that today they are going to learn about a new kind of frame.

D. Developmental Activities

   1. Show a chart on which are printed the following sentences, which will serve as substitution frames for nouns:

The _____ is here. The _____ are here. Ask the pupils to supply words which would fit in the blanks to complete the sentence. Write the words supplied in a list below each frame. Let the pupils read each list and think of how all the words are alike. (Apply known clues to identify them as nouns: nouns are words that name things; determiners point to nouns.)

   2. Have the following sentences with determiners printed on a chart. Ask the pupils to identify the nouns and test them in the substitution frame.

     a. A snake crawled along the wall.

     b. His sister saw the game.

     c. The boys put some stones on the table.

     d. Her coat was torn.

     e. My mother baked some buns.

   3. Follow the same procedure as in Activity 2, using nouns without determiners. Have the nouns identified using substitution frames.

     a. Girls like funny games.

     b. Tadpoles wiggled all around.

     c. Big clouds rolled by.

     d. They cooked fish for supper.

     e. Leaves blew into piles.

   4. Pass out cards on which nouns are printed; some plural, some singular. Have the pupils identify the words as nouns by using the substitution frame. Place the words under the frame where they fit. When all

nouns are placed, ask the pupils to decide which kind of nouns is under the first sentence (singular), and what kind is under the second sentence (plural).

   5. Distribute printed cards containing words that are not nouns. The pupils will discover that these do not fit the substitution frames.

E. Conclusion

   1. Ask: "Do you remember earlier in our lesson we talked about picture frames? What did we do with the pictures?" (Found one to fit.) Point to substitution frame. Ask: "Could we say our sentences are a kind of frame? What did we find would fit in these frames? (words) What kinds of words fit our frames? (nouns) Can someone tell us how we use these frames to help us with our nouns?" (Generalization: If a word fits in one of the frames it is a noun.)

   2. Distribute a duplicated exercise. Read the directions and have the class do one example together. As the pupils work on the exercise give individual help as needed.

F. Materials

The following reproduced exercise.

Match the nouns to the right frame.
The _____ is here. The _____ are here.

cats	dog
girl	books
trees	

Use the noun frame to find the words that are nouns. Draw a line around the nouns.

ants	was
this	lamp
dish	shoes

"Correct" Usage—Don't and Doesn't— Grade Four

A. Objectives—Children should be able to

   1. Use the verb substitution frames to find forms of *do.*

   2. Form contractions of *do* and *does not.*

   3. Reach the generalization that

doesn't is used with the pronouns *he, she,* or *it.*

4. Apply the generalization.

B. Introduction

1. Read the following series of sentences from the board, and ask pupils if any verbs or auxiliaries do not "sound right":
   a. I don't like lemon pudding.
   b. Tom said that he don't like chocolate.
   c. You don't have my pen, do you?
   d. We don't have much homework.
   e. They don't have any.

2. Discuss the usage in each sentence. If some pupils are aware of the non-standard form in sentence b, ask why they think it doesn't "sound right."

3. Tell the children that they might call upon some of their knowledge of grammar to help them be sure of usage.

C. Grammatical Application

1. Elicit from pupils and list on the board the forms of the verb *do,* using verb substitution frames.
   Let's *do* (that).
   Now he *does* (that).
   He is *doing* (that).
   Yesterday he *did* (that).

2. Write *do does did* on the board. List subject pronouns and any forms of *do* that can follow. Then write the negative contraction.

I do	I don't	I did	I didn't
You do	You don't	You did	You didn't
He does	He doesn't	He did	He didn't
She does	She doesn't	She did	She didn't
It does	It doesn't	It did	It didn't
We do	We don't	We did	We didn't
They do	They don't	They did	They didn't

3. List the pronouns that precede the forms of *do.*

do-don't	does-doesn't	did-didn't
I	He	I
You	She	You
We	It	He
They	I	She
		It
		We
		They

4. Write on the board:
   a. That girl don't want to play.
   b. This girl don't have a pencil.
   c. That dress don't look becoming on you.
   d. John don't have a bike.
   Underline the noun phrase and rewrite the sentence, using a pronoun to replace the noun phrase. (He don't want to play, etc.)
   Refer to this list of pronouns that occur with the forms of *do.* Notice that *don't* does not occur with *he, she* or *it.*
   Correct the above sentences. Say fully the contractions, e.g., That boy don't (do not) want to play. He don't (do not) want to play. That boy doesn't (does not) want to play. He doesn't (does not) want to play. Which of these forms is the *-s* form of *do: do does doing did?*

D. Generalization
   Ask: Which form of the verb occurs with the pronouns *he, she,* and *it* and the noun or noun groups these pronouns can replace? Which negative contraction occurs with *he, she, it?*

E. Application

1. Ask pupils to listen to the following sentences read aloud:
   a. I don't want to go.
   b. You don't take your time.
   c. He doesn't like movies.
   d. She doesn't like skating.
   e. It doesn't look like rain today.
   f. We don't need any rain.
   g. You don't have to do it.
   h. They don't want to play softball.

2. Read a second series of sentences to the children, and ask them to react by a show of hands to any in which *don't* or *doesn't* is misused.
   a. I don't have a new dress yet.
   b. She don't have one either.
   c. They don't suit me.
   d. He doesn't like any of them.
   e. You don't need one.
   f. It don't matter if you don't go.

g. We don't care.
3. Have pupils correct sentences b.
and f. above. Then provide additional usage practice by asking
them to repeat each sentence.
4. Encourage the pupils to make up
their own sentences, using correctly
don't and *doesn't*.

Consider also the following: [14]

Introduction to Plot—How Plot Is
Influenced by Theme

I. *Differentiated Behavioral Objectives:*
A. *Cognitive Domain*
1. *Comprehension and Applica-*
tion:
The learner describes the
theme in a story by telling the
over-all meaning of the story
in a sentence.
2. *Analysis, Synthesis, and Eval-*
uation:
The learner tells how the
theme of a story influences its
plot, style and *mood.*
B. *Affective Domain*
1. *Receiving, Responding and*
Valuing:
The learner perceives, accepts
or rejects a story theme in
terms of moral values and
human relationships.
2. *Organization:*
The learner recognizes and iso-
lates paradoxes, irony, human
strengths and weaknesses in
story themes.
3. *Characterization by Values or*
Value Complex:
The learner describes instances
in which the story action causes
him to experience the same
feelings and emotions as those
of the characters. The learner

tells how his own set of ethics
and philosophy of life has been
influenced by identifying with
story characters and situations.
II. *Motivation and Discussion*
Put the following sentences on the
board or on a chart:
"Crime does not pay."
"It is no sin to be poor."
Ask, "What kind of thoughts do these
sentences represent? What kind of
story has a lesson or a moral? Does
every story have a lesson or a moral?
Does every story have a message, or
a general purpose? How is a *moral*
different from just the message in a
story?"
Read the following sentences to the
children. (If written on a chart, they
can be referred to often.)
1. Courage, patience and faith can
overcome the most insurmount-
able of obstacles.
2. Patriotism is a virtue more honor-
able than self-preservation. "It is
better to be a dead hero than a live
coward."
3. Good things come inevitably to
those who are generous, thoughtful
and kind.
4. Poverty is not unbearable when
the characters are courageous and
resourceful.
"Do you think each of these sentences
could be considered a moral? Why or
why not?" "Could any of these sentences be used to describe the purpose
or meaning of a story?" "There is a
literary term which tells the total
meaning of a story. Who knows this
term?" (Theme)

> *Note to teacher:* The *theme* of a
> story can be described simply as
> its *total meaning.* The theme, or
> purpose of a story, usually repre-
> sents a lesson or an observation
> by the author about life. Without
> a *theme,* a story would not have
> much significance, and probably
> wouldn't be much of a story.

[14] B. J. Deming and J. L. Klein, *Literature*
for Gifted Pupils in Grades 4, 5, and 6, State
Department of Education, Sacramento, California (1969), pp. 21–24.

III. *Extending the Concept of Theme:*
  A. "Just a few traditional themes were included earlier in this lesson—dozens of others could be listed, each with a moral, or a lesson, or merely an observation of life. Most traditional themes fit into patterns which are *familiar* to the reader personally, even if he disagrees with the inherent implications of the themes. Many good stories deliberately violate these traditional themes, however, sometimes even depict a morally bad theme." (For example, in *Huckleberry Finn* the main character was an habitual truant, he smoked, and was generally a sort of nineteenth century juvenile delinquent. In fact, he was a lawbreaker in terms of helping Jim, an escaped slave, to avoid capture.)
  B. Ask the children to tell of stories or episodes in stories where the theme represents an idea which is not generally acceptable as *morally good*. If children need guidance, the following situations may be used to stimulate further discussion:
    —A rich person may be generous only because of personal vanity.
    —Crime sometimes *does* pay.
    —In some situations, a person's feeling of hopelessness and futility is quite accurate.
    —An act of bravery may turn out to be foolish and unnecessary.
  C. As the children discuss story characters who are involved in "morally bad" themes, have them explain *why* they think the theme was bad. Invite a variety of opinions. A healthy discussion of this type should lead to a certain amount of disagreement, and hopefully, some critical analysis of human values, morals, and characteristics. Children can begin to relate these ideas to real life values.
  D. Pass back the children's original stories. After each child has re-read his own story, give the following assignment:
    1. Write one sentence which tells the *"theme"* of your own story.
    2. Write the *kind* of theme you think your story has. (Such as *morally good* or morally *bad*, teaches a lesson, or is it just an observation of life, etc.)
  E. After discussion of their own story themes and how their plots are influenced by their themes, permit rewriting based on newly formulated criteria. Then have all stories collected for future reference.

What Has Research Contributed to the Teaching of the Language Arts?

Although everyone agrees that the teaching of the language arts is important, the funds available for research have been meager indeed. Most of the research has been financed by individual teachers as they sought to earn advanced college degrees. As a result there are few studies of great magnitude (the Iowa Spelling Scale is a recent exception) or of long duration (the San Diego County Reading Study represents another exception). From 1940 to 1950 research in the language arts remained at a standstill because of the war. At the present time there are a number of studies in process but it will be some years before the work of the classroom teacher will be influenced by it.

Much of the existing research is subject to valid criticism. Frequently one sees the statement that, according to research, phonics should be taught in kindergarten or that teaching proofreading fails to improve composition. When one reads the studies quoted, one often finds that the "research" was done with a small group of children by a teacher determined to "prove" a theory without realizing that the particular situation is not typical of most classrooms. Much of this research sounds more like testimonials for a patent medicine. Other studies have been subject to so many controls that only a single item of difference may be studied. Teachers usually reject these results as something obtained under unrealistic teaching conditions.

The greatest limitation to most research in child education is that we cannot risk complete failure. In a laboratory many failures are expected before a formula is perfected. As soon as teachers feel that all is not well they either abandon the study or modify procedures. I once asked three teachers to ignore the spelling textbooks and to teach spelling only in association with writing. All expressed fear that the children would not do as well on a standardized test as the nonexperimental classes. It was inevitable that in order to protect their own reputations as teachers they would use word lists and drills that were not related to the writing done by the children.

A related problem is the Hawthorne effect, so named because of a study of incentive motivation in the Hawthorne plant of the Western Electric Company, located in a Chicago suburb. No matter what was done in the experiment, some improvement was noted. Finally it was decided that the fact that the workers knew an experiment was going on was in itself the motivation, rather than any specific thing done. A change in textbooks often produces the same result in a school program. A year after the change to a new speller it can usually be shown that an improvement has taken place. In a few years the novelty has worn away, the teachers have reduced some of the procedures to routines, and the test results may indicate that spelling achievement is unsatisfactory. A change to any other program, even to the one discarded four years ago, will again produce an apparent improvement.

Hubert C. Armstrong indicates other limitations to educational research: [15]

---

[15] Hubert C. Armstrong, "The Place of Values in American Education," *California Journal of Elementary Education* (February 1955), pp. 141–44.

Research may involve some of the most common interpretations of statistics. We may take average class size, average cost per pupil, average cost per square foot, and yet these averages are no more an indication of what should be than is the average number of colds per child, or the average number of accidents, or the average number of ulcers per elementary school principal.

A conspicuous example of error is the manner in which we interpret test scores. We measure a group of children of the same age, take the average score and call it a norm. We then refer to the norm as a sort of a standard. We then make two errors in interpretation. The first of these errors is that we interpret a score which is higher or lower than the mean as if it should not be higher or lower. We speak of "retardation" in reading, of being "ahead" in arithmetic. We speak as though the mean were the point that separated the normal from the abnormal. We do not expect all children to be the same height or weight, yet we talk as if we expected all children to be precisely alike in their school work.

The other error we make is in presuming that an average which is based on all sorts of school systems will necessarily give us a desirable standard applicable to any one school, grade, or group, including the group on which the test was standardized. We have added elephants and rabbits, and we turn out to have an average what—cow? If we were actuaries and were interested only in prediction, we might use the average as the best measure of what would happen next, provided conditions were not changed. We are not actuaries. It is change, improvement, betterment that we are most concerned with. We are engaged in encouraging a process of growth, in producing greater (or different) learning than the average. We, like the physician, are really interested in an ideal that is entirely different from a central tendency in any sense of that term. The present method of establishing norms of tests is outmoded. Two new types of criteria should take the place of a single "standard."

One of these types is based on criteria from each child himself. We now have available in the field of language—reading, spelling, writing, speech—a means of deriving scores on an *intra*-individual difference basis. Let me illustrate. If a child's hearing vocabulary is known to be 12,000 words and he can read about 6,000, we know that it is only the form of the word, not its meaning, that has to be learned. We might reasonably expect him to learn in visual form as many words as he already knows in auditory form. Similar approaches are possible in other fields.

Another type of criterion may be employed. That criterion will be essentially a means of stating the conditions and circumstances under which any level of achievement was made. We would state what may be expected of children who are healthy, who have had ample opportunities to read books, whose teachers have been well trained, whose attendance has been regular and at the same school, who have not been subjected to undue emotional stresses or to nervous disorders, and who are within, say, ten points of a stated level of intelligence. We might then have many types of norms based on stated conditions.

We educators have been seduced into this error of misinterpreting measures of central tendency by confusing a major distinction between the physical sciences and the social disciplines. The physical scientist is interested in nature—the nature of nature. He observes and reports and generalizes concerning what nature is like and how it behaves. He never quarrels with the way things are. He is elegantly terse in his reporting. He may write an equation as the shortest way of stating some aspect of nature. He isn't concerned about how nature *ought* to be. He is glad enough to find out about what natural "reality" actually is. The scientist is forever seeking the shortest possible answers to questions as to *how* nature works.

We in education and other realms of social science began by borrowing methods from the physical sciences. We tried to proceed as the physicist does, that is, to observe, record, relate, generalize, predict, and if possible to control. We, too, observed and took averages. But we were observing not the behavior of matter in the sense that H_2O always means water, or that py equals mk; but we were observing man who is subject to modification.

The educator aims to induce changes in a given direction, to produce results of a given kind, to approach more closely what we want and value. If we ignore change toward values we can easily confuse the way social conditions are with the way we think they ought to be. But we should be clear on these three points. First, it is perfectly legitimate to state in statistical terms the central tendency of data when we are describing that characteristic of a *group*—an existing state of affairs. Second, we cannot necessarily judge an individual deviation from a group average as though that deviation were undesirable. Third, when we are attempting to state standards, ideals, values, or criteria which indicate how we want things to be, we cannot take recourse to a description of things as they are.

Sometimes we attempt to evaluate by comparing the present with the past. We seem to have two contradictory views. One is to glorify the past. We might speak of this as the nostalgic view. When translated in terms of its root meaning, this may be called the "homesick" view. For those who would like to read a bit of comparative research, I recommend the book, now out of print, but found in many libraries, *Then and Now in Education—1845–1923,* by Otis W. Caldwell and Stuart A. Courtis, describing in abundant detail the first survey in education in this country which was conducted by Horace Mann in Boston in 1845.

Another way of comparing the present with the past is to take the view that progress has been made. This might be dubbed the "look-how-far-we've-come" point of view. There is an implication that change is generally in the direction of the better. This is a tricky method to deal with, for we can easily fall into what Lewis Mumford calls "improved means to unimproved ends," or, in more common parlance "a short cut to a doubtful destination." Either of these methods of comparing the present with the past inevitably leads to the problem of knowing whether any change has been in the right direction; that is, in the direction of what we value.

We sometimes take stock of the present by recourse to a legalistic basis. We often explain or justify present practice by quoting rules, regulations, laws, or even the state or federal constitution. This type of explanation is satisfactory if we have only consistency, or the avoidance of penalties in mind, but it does not indicate to us whether or not a given procedure is a good one, for laws and even constitutions can be changed. We must then ask ourselves if a law or a constitutional provision is good, or if it should be changed.

A related way of judging ourselves and our practices is in terms of habit, custom, and tradition. This is the most pleasant way by far, for there is something about the old, the usual, and the habitual that seems almost as right and true as nature itself. But we are reminded of an instance in which we visited a college professor. She cautioned us about a projecting prong on her desk, pointing out that she had torn her own clothes on it a number of times. It was suggested that perhaps the desk drawer was

A teacher instructs but also sets standards of dress, courtesy, and values for those in her classroom. (*Courtesy of the Burbank Public Schools.*)

in backwards. "Oh, no," she said, "it has always been that way ever since it was moved in here several years ago." But on examination we found that changing it end for end was all that was necessary. Apropos of custom, it was Friar Roger Bacon who in the thirteenth century stated four stumbling blocks to truth: (1) the influence of fragile or unworthy authority, (2) custom, (3) the imperfection of undisciplined senses, (4) and the concealment of ignorance by the ostentation of seeming wisdom.

It is a step forward when educators question so much that has passed as research. The mistakes that have been made will be corrected. Today funds are available in amounts seldom granted in the past; universities and colleges concerned with the training of teachers are providing time and equipment for research, and more school systems are developing research projects.

Action research is used by many schools to improve the curriculum. This research is a cooperative effort of a group of teachers who work together to solve specific problems. Records are carefully kept and the results discovered are used to improve practice. Projects may involve such educational problems as these: planning a series of assembly programs to celebrate important holidays, creating drill sheets to use with certain reading textbooks using phonic games, developing a reading record card, or determining a way to teach a child how to transfer from print script to cursive writing.

Action research makes no attempt to proclaim the results of a single study as universal truths. Because it is a shared experience, action research is the basis of theory or opinion on analogous situations, just as conferences among bankers and lawyers help clarify certain aspects of their respective financial and legal activities.

Action research is not as objective, controlled, or well structured in advance as research of the traditional type. The need for carefully controlled research has not decreased. It is quite possible for action-research projects to lead to problems that must be studied by directed techniques.

Action research involves teachers in programs that lead to desired changes, reveals sources of information that might not have been discovered, and satisfies the need to take corrective measures.

For Discussion

1. Under what circumstances may a school research problem risk failure?

2. Make a list of the outstanding authorities in such areas of the language arts as spelling, reading, and handwriting. How would such a list compare in length to a list of authorities in another field that is familiar to you, such as physics?

3. Compare the amount of money available for educational research with that for agriculture, medicine, and business.

4. Report on one of the research studies in A. Montgomery Johnston and Paul C. Burns, *Research in Elementary School Curriculum* (Boston: Allyn & Bacon, 1970).

Your Future as a Teacher

The last topic in this book should look to the future and anticipate some of the changes that are needed. This might include more individualized learning, a wider range of educational materials—including films, textbooks, and so on—the means to account more carefully to those who pay for the educational efforts we make, the use of teacher assistants in the classroom, the year-round school program, and the many innovations being tried to understand and reach the cultural differences in modern society. In all that is new there are seeds of the old that need to be understood and built upon.

But the real future is what each beginning teacher brings to the profession. Rather than dwell upon the exceptional, let us look at what will happen to you as you spend your first years in the classroom as a teacher. Indeed you will determine the future of the language arts program as you guide the language growth of children.

Beginning teachers frequently ask, "What does the person evaluating teaching look for when visiting the class?" Seven basic areas are observed by supervisors.

Area 1: Preparation and Planning. Proper preparation of class material and method of presentation is essential for most effective teaching. Some teachers willingly spend hours planning their day's work, whereas others, it must be admitted, prepare little or not at all. Plan books should be kept and checked. Lack of preparation is usually quite obvious to the evaluator in the classroom.

Area 2: Recognition of and Provision for Individual Differences. Recognition of individual differences is almost an instinct of good teachers. Teachers who do not group their pupils according to ability are easily recognized—as are the ones who spare no pains to get to know each of their pupils individually.

Area 3: Motivation. It has been said that two things are essential for pupils' academic success in school: intelligence and motivation, with motivation being the more important of the two. Some teachers surge far ahead of the others in this area and become sources of inspiration to their pupils. The best motivation results when pupils and teacher have similar purposes.

Area 4: Command of Subject Matter. It is obvious that if teachers are to teach, they must know what they are talking about. The teacher's command of language and her ability to put the subject matter across also enter the picture here.

Area 5: Teaching Techniques. Teaching techniques are too numerous to mention, but include such tactics as using a positive rather than negative approach, varying the teaching methods, and using visual aids.

Area 6: Classroom Control. Teachers employ different strategies in controlling behavior in the classroom, some clinging to the despotic approach, others leading their classes with the magic wands of interest, cooperation, fair play, and mutual respect.

Unfortunately, a few are never really in control and their school lives become a desperate effort to "hold the line." These indications, of course, can all be perceived and evaluated by a skilled observer.

Area 7: Classroom Atmosphere. Area 7 has to do with the mechanical features of the classroom, such as heat and light, neatness, use of bulletin boards, class projects, color combinations, interest centers, displays of children's work, and the way the students work.

The skilled supervisor needs only a few minutes in a room to note that the program is proceeding in a well-planned and a purposeful fashion. It takes even less time to notice that this is not happening. Long periods of observation and counseling are required to diagnose the causes of trouble and to find a solution. The personality of the teacher, the individual abilities of the children, and the expected results all must be examined in the same way a doctor diagnoses an illness. There are seldom quick solutions or "magic words" that will solve the problems. This type of experience is the process whereby an unsuccessful teacher can improve. It is not especially pleasant to paraphrase Burns: if we could see ourselves as others see us, we probably wouldn't like it.

A beginning teacher's relationship with a supervisor should be based on the premise that the supervisor is genuinely concerned about the children's education. This means that he or she stands ready to give you whatever assistance you require.

It should also be recognized that supervisors are people with human strengths and frailties. Individual differences are as pronounced among adults as they are among children. Some supervisors will appear to be imposing their own methods in seeking to advise you. These methods may not work for you, but at least consider such suggestions with an open mind. Others who are less direct will perhaps outline a philosophical or theoretical approach. Still others may tend to suggest or recommend certain materials. In any case, few supervisors expect every teacher to use a stereotyped formula instead of analyzing each case on its individual merits.

The beginner is always permitted a few mistakes. When you recognize your shortcomings and seek to improve, you will usually be met more than half way. If you cannot see the mistake, or attempt to ignore it, there will be difficult times ahead for you and for your superiors.

As experienced professional people, supervisors can give you considerable assistance in working with the individual child or small group. Their knowledge of materials naturally exceeds that of the new teacher, and they expect to be asked about such matters as third-grade books on Mexico or sources of space pictures. Sometimes new teachers will hesitate to ask these questions for fear that their weaknesses will be criticized. Actually, such questions are evidence of professional concern.

One of the wisest practices a new teacher can follow is to locate an older teacher who is working at the same level. Ask this person if he or she will grant you a few minutes' discussion time after school each day. There is much significant information on the community, school policies, and teaching practices that is not written down which you can gather through this kind of relationship. In turn, share some of the newer materials or techniques that you have picked up in your training. When possible, visit with other new teachers. Nothing brings people together like common difficulties, and your morale will receive a boost when you learn that your troubles are not unique.

The new teacher needs to make special plans for the first weeks of school. Security for both the teacher and the children may be provided during the first day by the familiar. Discuss ways of having the children salute the flag, talk about summer experiences, sing favorite songs, talk about favorite books and show some of the work that was done last year.

Parents and visitors should be told that they will be invited back at another time, with an added explanation that during the first few days of school some children are disturbed by too many visitors.

Help the children learn to know each

other. Provide games that have to do with learning names. Make a rough map and have children point out where they live. During the first week the children can make a class directory. The children help the teacher decide what should be put into the directory. It may contain facts like these:

Betty Jones   Second Grade
4116 Walnut Street
Telephone Wa 7-1268
I have a dog at home.

Each child during the routine of getting acquainted tells something about himself, his name, where he lives, and so on. This information is recorded by the teacher on separate sheets. A child may want to bring a picture of himself and paste on his page. It sustains interest to add to each page the new things children have to tell about themselves. The teacher should have a page too.

It is wise to give little children simple work to take home. Older children should have a specific thing to do at home.

Supplies are sometimes a problem during the first days of a term. A collection of old magazines can be used in many ways. Pictures can be cut out and mounted, words and sounds can be underlined, cartoons might be collected and put on the bulletin board. Among the teacher's resources should be several good books to read aloud. With only one, the teacher always faces the possibility that the children listened to the book last year.

Time spent during the first week establishing social habits and classroom procedures will make both teaching and learning more effective throughout the year.

From the beginning it should be realized that children expect the teacher to be a leader and an arbiter of classroom behavior. Classroom control cannot be divorced from learning. When children are successfully motivated by an important goal, there are few discipline problems.

Emergencies, both major and minor, need to be anticipated. The school will take care of illness, fire drills, and civil defense procedures. The teacher must anticipate such minor catastrophes as spilled ink or paint, broken pencil points, missing lunches or lunch money, emergency phone calls during class sessions, an irate parent's visit, broken projector or torn film, and the many embarrassing moments of childhood that later become anecdotes.

Good discipline is not magic, but merely the application of common sense and past experience. A few simple, direct, and inflexible rules are essential to classroom control. These ten ideas may help you:

1. *Begin right.* Make a good impression. Get the children to feel from the outset that school is going to be a happy place with a friendly but efficient captain at the helm.
2. *Avoid conditions that lead to disorder.* Plan well, have materials ready, be composed, calm, dignified; have variety and surprises in your program; provide enough mental stimulus for even the cleverest children.
3. *Don't let minor incidents go uncorrected.* "Good" children tend to imitate the conduct of "bad" children so that minor incidents become major. Slowness in stopping work, a rough-and-tumble fracas in getting ready for the playground, disobedience in slight matters—such habits may be easily checked at first but soon become established forms of schoolroom behavior. If you allow the children to practice disorder, they will soon become expert at it.
4. *Be tactful.* Tact is a lubricant. It has been called the "art of getting your own ends by the other fellow's means." Children are real persons. Tact is even more effective in dealing with them than it is dealing with adults.
5. *Be good-natured.* A good-tempered teacher with a sense of humor and a smile can eliminate friction far better than a stern or sarcastic one. Regard all offenses as against the group and not against you personally. Avoid the high-pitched, raspy voice, the authoritative manner, the habitual frown.

6. *Be just.* No quality has a worse effect on children than injustice. They are much keener at reading the minds of adults than adults are at reading the minds of children, and will remember for years the teacher who tore up the paper because the name was written in the wrong place, or who refused to adjudicate a quarrel impartially because of favoritism.

7. *Be persistent.* Peg away at important matters without allowing exceptions until the desired form of conduct is habitual.

8. *Be consistent.* Don't be severe one day and lenient the next. To allow late hours or an outside worry to affect professional conduct is a sign of immaturity, weakness, or lack of poise. Those who show self-control only when they are not under stress are really demonstrating complacency.

9. *Have decision.* "I don't know what I shall do with you if you don't behave yourself" is an oft-heard plaint of distracted mothers. Teachers sometimes feel that way too, but it does no good to let the children know it. *Quiet decision often saves a precarious situation.*

10. *Avoid conflicts.* Do not try to "fight it out" with a child. Tense situations bring hysteria and emotional disturbance. A child simply can't yield when so involved. If a conflict arises between yourself and a child, give him some mental relief. One of the simplest ways to solve a situation is by giving him an either-or choice. Not "you must and shall" but "this must happen or." For example: "Either pick up your clay or I shall ask the class helpers to do it, and you must not have clay again until we so decide." The clay is picked up, all feel that justice has been done, and the emotionally upset child has, instead of a searing experience to recall, a feeling of dissatisfaction at the unreasonableness of his own behavior which will help him to make a better adjustment to the next situation.

Teaching in the elementary school is an art. Techniques and materials can be shared, but the human relationships of the teaching–learning process cannot be learned through words alone. In recent years, printed outline pictures have been designed for "do-it-yourself" painters, using key numbering to indicate which areas are to be painted a certain color. If one follows the directions one can produce a tolerable facsimile of the original painting, but at best it is a mere copy of another's creative expression and planning. Maybe the exercise will teach the rudiments of brush techniques of color combination, as well as the laws of balance and harmony. One's first efforts at original painting will perhaps betray uncertainties of line and form, but the result, however labored, is a creation rather than an imitation. With talent, training, and determination, the amateur painter may in time produce a genuine work of art. In teaching, some start with great talent and seem to know not only how to work with children but also how to use suggestions for the best results. Others start with nothing more than interest and must master the skills supplied by talent. But the rewards are worth the effort. Few professions offer the satisfactions that a teacher knows as children develop the communication skills that will help them face with confidence their responsibilities as adults.

The longer you teach, the more you will realize that it is difficult to separate the art of teaching from the science of education. Some teachers are able to gain amazing results with the simple resources of their environment; others, surrounded by texts, films, typewriters, and the latest audiovisual devices, only reduce those who would learn to boredom.

We look at life through our attitudes. If yours is one that each child has a worthy contribution to make and that your task is one of helping him achieve the maximum that his stage of growth and capacity will permit, you will have made a major step in the direction of teaching success. It will also cause you continually to seek improved ways of meeting the needs of children.

Any art that cannot be specified in detail cannot be transmitted by specific prescriptions alone. It can best be passed on by example from master to apprentice. Colleges educate some who are fine young teachers, others who are fine scholars, and still others who have enough credits to graduate. The difference seems to be the quality of craftsmanship displayed by those with whom the future teacher associates. One aspect of this association is supervision. Beginning teachers should seek employment in a district where there is adequate service to guide them through the beginning years of their professional apprenticeship. There are many great teachers who are unknown because only the parents and children know what they do and have no basis for comparison. Such teachers may be unaware of their own excellence or conversely of their incompetence. There are many who could be much better teachers if guided by a professional person. If you choose to "spend" your life teaching, give it the best of your talent. This can best be revealed by association with other teachers equally dedicated to continuous improvement of their craft. It is on the wings of words that children claim their identity with their culture. There is no more rewarding role for an elementary teacher than sharing such growth.

BUILDING WITH CHILDREN A BETTER TOMORROW

The teacher asked of the child,
"What would you have of me?"
And the child replied,
"Because you are you, only you know some of
the things
I would have of you.
But because I am I,
I do know some of what
I would have of you."

The teacher asked again,
"What would you have of me?"
And the child replied,
"I would have of you what
You are and what you know.
I would have you speaking and silent,
Sure and unsure, seeking for surety,
Vibrant and pensive.
I would have you talking and letting me tell,

Going my way with my wonderings and enthu-
siasms,
And going your way that I may know new
curiosities,
I would have you leading step by step
Yet letting me step things off in my own
fashion."
"Teach me," said the child,
"With simplicity and imagination—
Simply that the paraphernalia and the gadgets
Do not get between us;
Imaginatively that I may sense and catch your
enthusiasm,
And the quickening thrill of never having been
this way before.
Too, I would have you watching over me, yet
not too watchful,
Caring for me, yet not too carefully,
Holding me to you, yet not with bindings,
So when the day comes, as it must,
that we, each, go our separate ways,
I can go free.
Let me take you with me not because
I must, but because I would have it so.
Let me take you with me because
you have become, in me,
Not just today—
Tomorrow!"

LELAND B. JACOBS

Suggestions for Projects

1. Write to the Children's Bureau in the U.S. Office of Education, Health and Welfare in Washington, D.C., for the latest copy of "Research Relating to Children." Report on recent studies in the language arts.

2. Examine a copy of the STEP Essay Test published by Educational Testing Service, Princeton, N.J. Use it as a basis for evaluating a set of children's compositions. Report your conclusions.

3. Create a handwriting scale from samples collected in the class you now teach.

4. Survey recent magazine articles with reference to proofreading and editing skills. What suggestions are made to facilitate this practice in elementary classrooms?

5. Examine samples of report cards used in a number of school districts. Note how they differ with respect to reporting achievement in the language arts.

6. Ask teachers for samples of tests they have made and used in the intermediate

grades. What similarities and differences exist with respect to emphasis and method?

7. Create a spelling and reading test to be used early in the year to diagnose the needs of children you will teach.

8. Write to the publishers for samples of testing programs that are keyed to textbooks you will use. What would be the strengths and weaknesses of such texts?

9. The Center for Programmed Instruction; 365 West End Avenue; New York, N.Y., publishes information concerning current work relating to teaching machines. Evaluate this material with respect to its use in a language arts class.

Bibliography

Books

Dinkmeyer, Don, and Rudolf Dreikurs. *Encouraging Children to Learn.* Englewood Cliffs, N.J.: Prentice-Hall, Inc., 1963.

Gronlund, Norman. Measurement and Evaluation in Teaching, 2nd ed. New York: The Macmillan Company, 1971.

Lindgren, Henry Clay. *Educational Psychology in the Classroom.* New York: John Wiley & Sons, Inc., 1968.

Morse, William C., and G. Max Wingo. *Psychology and Teaching.* Chicago: Scott, Foresman and Company, 1969.

Nelsen, Clarence H. *Measurement and Evaluation in the Classroom.* New York: The Macmillan Company, 1970.

Articles and Pamphlets

Burns, Paul C. "Corrective and Remedial Aspects of Elementary School Language Arts," *Elementary English* (December 1969), pp. 1008–1015.

Early, Margaret J. "What Do They Want to Learn?" *English Journal* (November 1955), pp. 459–63.

Greene, Harry. "Direct vs. Formal Methods in Elementary English," *Elementary English* (May 1947), pp. 273–86.

Keene, Katherine. "Students Like Corrections," *English Journal* (April 1956), pp. 212–15.

Leonard, Roger T. "What Can Be Measured?" *The Reading Teacher* (March 1962), pp. 326–37.

McHugh, Walter J. *Pupil Specialty Guide Book,* Castro Valley School District, Castro Valley, Calif., 1964.

Research Division. *Ability Grouping—Research Summary* 1968–S3. Washington, D.C.: National Education Association, 1968.

Research Division. *Marking and Reporting Pupil Progress—Research Summary* 1970–S1. Washington, D.C.: National Education Association, 1970.

Shane, Harold G. *Improving Language Arts Instruction Through Research.* A.S.C.D., N.E.A., 1201 16th Street N.W., Washington, D.C., 1963.

Shane, H. G., J. Walden, and R. Green. *Interpreting Language Arts Research for the Teacher.* A.S.C.D., N.E.A., Washington, D.C., 1971.

Shapiro, Bernard O., and Phyllis P. Shapiro. "Testing in the Schools: A Response to John Holt," *Elementary School Journal* (January 1970), pp. 202–205.

Singer, Harry. "Research That Should Have Made a Difference," *Elementary English* (January 1970), pp. 27–34.

Steinberg, Erwin R. *Needed Research in the Teaching of English,* Conference Proceedings at Carnegie Institute of Technology, May 5–7, 1962.

Whipp, Leslie. "The Child as Language Teacher," *Elementary English* (April 1969), pp. 466–70.

Zahorik, John A. "Pupil's Perception of Teachers' Verbal Feedback," *Elementary School Journal* (November 1970), pp. 105–14.

Every child, every person can delight in learning. Every educator can share in that delight. The methods are available. The needs for reform are clear. The chief obstacles are simply inertia and low expectations. Actually, a new education is already here, thrusting up in spite of every barrier built against it. Why not help it happen?

George B. Leonard, "The Future Now," *Look,* October 5, 1968

glossary[1]

Antonyms, Synonyms, Homonyms

Antonyms, synonyms, homonyms
Are not as difficult as they sound,
And they do give a wonderful choice
Of words to pass around:

Antonyms oppose each other:
Good and bad—sister and brother.
Synonyms *mean* almost *the same:*
Glad and joyful—amusement, game.

Homonyms *agree in sound*
As knew *and* gnu,
But differ as widely in meaning
As too *and* two.

MARY O'NEILL in "Words Words Words"

absorption unit A unit of reading material which contains words already presented in previous units; materials containing no "new" reading words sometimes called plateau units.

adjective* A word like *happy, hungry, friendly, new.* Adjectives may occur in predicates after *be* and after verbs like *seem,* as well as before nouns. Adjectives describe things.

adverbial of manner* A word or group of words that can be replaced by *how* in questions: "John worked carelessly." "How did John work?" Adverbs of manner are made mostly by adding the suffix *-ly* to adjectives: *careless/carelessly, soft/softly.* An adverbial of manner may be not only a single-word adverbial like *carelessly,* but also a prepositional phrase like *with close attention.*

---

[1] Definitions that follow which are marked with an asterisk are those used by Paul Roberts in *The Robert English Series* published by Harcourt Brace Jovanovich and are used by permission of the publisher.

adverbial of place* A word or group of words that can be replaced by *where* in questions. Adverbials of place occur after *be* in the predicate or after certain verbs. Single-word adverbials of place—*outside, upstairs, there*—are called *adverbs.* Groups of words—*in the house, near a car*—are prepositional phrases.

adverbial of time* A word or group of words that can be replaced by *when* in questions: "The Mayor spoke yesterday." "When did the Mayor speak?" An adverbial of time may be one word, like *yesterday,* a prepositional phrase, like *in the afternoon,* or even a noun phrase, like *this evening.*

affix* Either a prefix or a suffix.

alexia Loss of ability to read; word blindness.

ambidextrous Skilled use of both hands.

analysis Taking apart or breaking down into smaller elements.

antonym A word having the opposite meaning of another word. Example: *good* and *bad* are antonyms.

aphasia Loss or impairment of the power to use or understand speech, caused by brain injury.

appositive* The function of the noun phrase residue which is the result of deletion from a relative clause. In the following sentence *a happy child,* which resulted by deletion from the relative clause *who was a happy child,* functions as an appositive: "Elsie, *a happy child,* recovered quickly from her disappointment."

article* The most important kind of determiner. There are two kinds of articles—definite and nondefinite. There is one definite article: the word *the.* There are three nondefinite articles: *a/an, some,* and *null.* Some nouns can ocur as noun phrases with no word before them: *pie is good.* We then say that they have the nondefinite article *null,* which

499

has the symbol Ø. Their nondefiniteness is marked by the absence of a word.

articulation Adjustment of the tongue, in relation to the palate, in the production of any speech sound; also, the act of uttering such sounds.

audiometer A device for testing hearing.

auditory discrimination Ability to discriminate between the levels or intensities of sounds, one speech sound from another.

basal-reader approach The development of basic reading abilities and skills by means of special textbooks; the development of initial reading skills and abilities by means of basal readers.

blend The fusion of two (or more) sounds in a word without loss of identity of either sound, as *bl.*

breve A short half circle placed over a vowel to indicate a "short" sound: *cŏt.*

closed syllable A syllable ending with a consonant. Example: *lit.*

complement* The function of a noun phrase used in the predicate after *be* or a verb of the *seem* type, like *a student* in "John is a student." A complement may also be an adjective or an adverbial of place.

complex vowel* Any vowel other than those of *pit, pet, pat, putt, pot.* The complex vowels are made and spelled in more complicated ways than the five simple vowels are.

compound phonogram A phonic element which does not make a word by itself. Examples: *sl, str, ing, ight, ay,* or *ou.*

configuration Pattern, general form, or shape of a word.

conjunction* The words *and, but, or* are conjunctions. They are used to join the combined structures in a compound sentence. *Correlative conjunctions* are related pairs of conjunctions: *not . . . but, either . . . or, neither . . . nor.*

connotation The significance that is suggested or implied in addition to the basic meaning of a word.

consonant trigraph A combnation of three successive consonants without vowels in between. Example: *tch* (in *watch*).

danging modifier* A grammatical error that may result when the subject of an insert sentence is not the same as the subject of the matrix sentence. For example, the *ing* verb phrase *seeing land* in the following sentence would have had to result from the

ungrammatical insert sentence "A shout saw land": "*Seeing land,* a shout was raised."

deductive Proceeding from general to the specific, as applying a rule in spelling.

demonstratives* The determiners *this, that, these, those.*

dentals Sounds articulated by pressing the tip of the tongue against the teeth. Examples: *d, t, th.*

determiner* An article, with the optional addition or substitution of other words, like demonstratives, numbers, quantities.

dextral (or **dextrad**) Innately right-handed.

diacritical marks Signs or small characters used to designate a particular sound value of a letter or letters.

dialect* a form of a language spoken in a particular geographical area or social group, different from other forms of the language in pronunciation, grammar, vocabulary, or idiom, but not different enough to be considered a separate language.

digraph Two letters representing one sound, such as *ea* or *ai.* There are consonant and vowel digraphs.

diphthong Two vowel sounds joined in one syllable to form one speech sound, as *oi* and *ow.*

dyslexia The inability to read understandingly, because of a central lesion. (The ability to read may be intact, but there is little or no understanding of what is read.)

euphony Pleasing sound; tendency to greater ease of pronunciation.

extrinsic Outward, external. For example, a gold star for classroom work is an extrinsic reward, whereas the learning acquired is the *intrinsic* reward.

eye–voice span The distance between the point being read (in oral reading) and the point at the right where the eyes are directed. In oral reading the eyes are usually ahead of the voice.

facet Literally, "a little face"; one of a set of small plane surfaces of a polished stone or diamond; by analogy, a sharply defined view or aspect of a subject. Reading, writing, and speaking are facets of the language area.

fixation pause. The length of time required for the eyes to fix on a given part of a line in reading.

framing words Isolating a group of words on a printed page by framing with the hands, i.e., placing one hand at each end of the group.

generative grammar* a model of how sentences are produced; loosely, transformational grammar.

grammar the study of the forms and structures of a language system.

grapheme a written symbol used to represent a single sound (phoneme).

heteronym A word spelled like another, but differing in sound and meaning. Examples: *lead* (a metal and a verb).

homonym A word having the same sound as another but differing in meaning and spelling. Examples: *fair* and *fare, bear* and *bare.*

homophone* One of two words pronounced alike but spelled differently and having different meanings: *meet/meat.*

juncture* A kind of break or pause in speaking, marked by a comma in the writing system. In the following sentence, this kind of break occurs after *John* and after *ahead:* "John, who was ahead, looked back at the other runners."

kernel sentence* A sentence to which no optional transformational rules have been applied. It is made up of two main parts—a noun phrase that functions as the subject, and a verb phrase that functions as the predicate.

kinesthetic Pertaining to or describing sensations arising from body movements.

labials Sounds articulated mainly by the lips. Examples: *wh, w, f, v, p, b,* and *m.*

legasthenia Inability to make adequate associations with the symbols of a printed page.

lexical meaning The "dictionary meanings" of affixes, or of the separate words in a sentence. For example, in *boys, boy* is the lexical meaning; *s* adds a grammatical meaning.

linguals Sounds formed with the aid of the tongue. Examples: *l, t, d.*

linguistics Technically, the study of the structures and systems of language; in a broader sense, the study of language in all its manifestations.

macron Short horizontal mark placed over a vowel to indicate its long sound.

matrix sentence* One of the underlying sentences in a double-base transformation into which a structure created by changing the other sentence is inserted to create a transform.

metaphor* Any comparison of something with something else. For example, "The grass was a sea rippled by wind."

Metronoscope A tachistoscopic device for the controlled time exposure of printed words and phrases for continuous reading (manufactured by the American Optical Company, Southbridge, Mass.).

modal* One of the words *may, can, will shall, must.* The first four of these have the past tense forms *might, could, would, should.*

monosyllabic word A word composed of only one syllable. Example: *bat.*

morpheme A language element (Greek *morphe,* form) that connects images or ideas; a language element showing relationships. Examples: affixes (i.e., prefixes and suffixes), prepositions, conjunctions, accentuation, etc.

myopia A condition of nearsightedness; inability to see clearly without minus lens correction.

nasals Sounds formed by using the tongue and palate to direct the sound into the nose.

noun phrase* The word or group of words used as subject of a simple sentence and in certain functions in the predicate. *Jerry, he, everybody, the boy* are all noun phrases.

onomatopoeic words Words formed by the imitation of natural sounds, such as *buzz.*

open syllable A syllable ending with a vowel. Example: *so.*

Ophthalmograph A device for photographing eye movements during reading (manufactured by American Optical Company, Southbridge, Mass.).

palatals Sounds formed between the tongue and palate. Examples: *k, g, y, q,* and *x.*

palindrome A word, phrase, or sentence that is the same whether read from the left or the right. Examples: *dad; madam.*

philology The study of language; philosophical study of language; linguistic science.

phoneme A group of variants of a speech sound, usually beginning with the same letter but sounded differently because of variations in stress, intonation, and so forth.

phonetic analysis The analysis of a word into its phonetic elements for pronunciation purposes; commonly used as a synonym for *phonics.*

phonology* The study of sounds.

phrase* A group of words used as a unit. The term is used also in the expressions *noun phrase* and *verb phrase,* which sometimes consist of single words.

pitch* The musical tone that is produced by the vibration of voiced sounds in speaking. An English sentence usually has three levels of pitch: *middle, high,* and *low.*

polysyllable A word composed of more than three syllables.

regressive eye movements Right-to-left return of one or both eyes during reading.

reversal tendency The tendency of immature children, or of children who have practiced immature habits, to reverse or confuse letters and word forms. See *strephosymbolia* below.

root An original word form from which words have been developed by addition of prefixes, suffixes, and inflectional endings.

sight word A word that is memorized or recognized as a whole.

simile* A particular kind of metaphor in which the comparison is made explicit by the use of *like* or *as.* For example, "The grass was like a sea rippled by wind."

sinistral (or **sinistrad**) Innately left-handed.

sonant A voiced sound. Examples: *b, v, w, d.*

stammering Inhibition of speech; involuntary stopping or blocking in speaking.

stanza* One of the parts of a poem.

strabismus Squint, a lack of parallelism of the optical axes; "cross-eyes."

strephosymbolia Literally, "twisted symbols"; a disorder of perception in which objects seem reversed as in a mirror; a special type of reading disabilty, inconsistent with a child's general intelligence, characterized by confuson between the letters *b* and *d, p* and *q,* or the reading of *saw* for *was, left* for *felt.* See *reversal tendency* above.

stress* The degree of loudness with which a syllable in a word or sentence is pronounced. There are four degrees of stress in English: first or principal (loudest), second (next loudest), third (next to softest), weak (softest).

stuttering Involuntary or spasmodic repetition of a sound or a syllable.

subordinate clause* A structure introduced by a subordinator and having a subject and predicate, but without being in itself a sentence. In the following sentence, *until he tried* is a subordinate clause: "Until he tried, Ed didn't know how easy it was." A semicolon or period is not used before a subordinate clause: "Bill ran, while John only trotted." To use a semicolon or a period instead of a comma here produces an error called a *fragment.*

subordinator* A word, like *because, if, unless,* *until, before, after, although, while, since,* which introduces a subordinate clause. In the following sentence, *after* functions as a subordinator: "*After* he had dressed, Joe went into the garden."

suffix One or more letters or syllables added to the ending of a word to change the meaning. For example: *farm + ing = farming.*

surd A voiceless sound. Examples: *p, f, wh, t.*

synonym A word that has the same or nearly the same meaning as another word.

synthesis A putting together; combination of modifying elements into inflected words; the opposite of *analysis.*

tachistoscope A device for exposing words, symbols, or other visual stimuli for one fifth of a second or less.

terminal sound A final sound; frequently referred to as the blend of a vowel with a final consonant, as *at* in *cat* or *ake* in *bake.*

transformation* The process by which kernel sentences are made into more complicated sentences (transforms). A *single-base* transformation affects only a single sentence. A *double-base* transformation involves changing the structure of one sentence and inserting it in another sentence.

VCe pattern* A system by which complex vowels are distinguished from simple ones by the letter *e* following a vowel (*V*) letter and a consonant (*C*) letter. Thus the vowel *pine* (/ī/) is distinguished from that of *pin* (/i/) by the *e* at the end of *pine.*

verb* A word like *sing, teach, think, feel, inspect.* Verbs usually express action of some sort. Some verbs, like *feel* and *know,* do not. In a kernel sentence, a verb is part of the predicate which says something about a subject. A *transitive verb* must be followed by an object. An *intransitive verb* does not take an object. Both kinds of verbs may be followed by certain other structures. Verbs of the *seem* type are neither transitive nor intransitive. Unlike other verbs, they may be followed by adjectives: *seem glad, look sad.*

word class* A classification of words like *noun, relative pronoun, preposition,* in which all the members are alike in some way. The four large word classes are *noun, verb, adjective,* and *adverb of manner.* Many words occur in more than one word class.

word phonogram A small word, usually learned as a sight word, which serves as a word element in longer words. For example, *at* and *an.*

index